Chronology Chart

	Historical Events	Happenings in Rock Music
1960	First use of satellite for TV transmission. Sit-ins to protest Woolworth store's refusal to serve African American students in Greensboro, NC. U.S. U-2 reconnaissance plane is shot down in Soviet Union.	Federal Bribery Act outlaws payola to DJs. Elvis Presley out of army. Gene Vincent is injured. "Twist" and other dance crazes are popularized. Beatles perform in Hamburg. Folk singers popular in coffee houses. *Bye Bye Birdie* first Broadway musical to feature rock music. Motown contracts Stevie Wonder. Eddie Cochran dies.
1961	Kennedy becomes president. "Bay of Pigs" intervention in Cuba. Amnesty International forms in U.K. Berlin Wall is built. Increase in U.S. military units in South Vietnam.	Surf rock popular on West Coast. Proto-soul music by Ray Charles, Sam Cooke, and Motown singers widely popular. Beatles popular at Cavern Club in Liverpool. Bob Dylan performs in NY. Chuck Berry is jailed. Stereo radio is authorized for FM stations.
1962	Cuban missile crisis. U.S. puts astronauts into orbit. First African American student is admitted to Univ. of Miss. after 3,000 troops stop riots. R. Carson's *Silent Spring* inspires environmental studies.	Blues revival bands form in U.K. and U.S. Beatles' first records hit U.K. charts. Bob Dylan releases his first album. Many folk singers change from traditional folk music to protest songs. Folk show "Hootenanny" on ABC TV.
1963	Supreme Court requires counsel for criminal defendants and outlaws use of illegally acquired evidence in courts. Civil Rights demonstrations in Birmingham, AL. M. L. King's "I have a dream . . ." speech in Washington, D.C. Kennedy is assassinated. Johnson becomes president.	Nationwide popularity of surf music and Spector's wall of sound. Girl groups popular. Dylan and Baez at Newport Folk Festival. Protest singers at "folk" coffeehouses. Proto-punk "Louie Louie" is released. British press report on "Beatlemania." First cassette tape recorders are sold.
1964	Escalation of fighting in Vietnam. Civil Rights Bill bans discrimination in voting, jobs, public accommodations, etc. U.S. Post Office assigns zip codes. M. L. King is awarded Nobel Peace Prize. Warren Commission concludes Lee Harvey Oswald's responsibility for Kennedy assassination.	Beginning of Beatlemania in U.S. and British Invasion. BMI rejects the Who demos. James Brown begins funk. Kinks popularize guitar distortion and Beatles use feedback. Moog synthesizer is developed. Alan Freed, Jim Reeves, and Sam Cooke die.
1965	First walk in space. Johnson orders more bombing of North Vietnam. Civil Rights march from Selma to Montgomery, AL. Voting Rights Act passes. 34 die in Watts riot in Los Angeles. Immigration national origins quota system is abolished.	Bob Dylan and the Byrds begin folk rock. Electric 12-string guitar popular folk-rock instrument. Term "soul" replaces "rhythm and blues." Jefferson Airplane and the Grateful Dead are featured at psychedelic dance halls in San Francisco. Ken Kessey's Acid Test concerts popular. Fuzztone distortion control and first transistor microphones are marketed.
1966	U.S.S.R. and U.S. land unmanned crafts on moon. U.S. forces fire into Cambodia and air-bomb Hanoi. Medicare coverage put into effect. Law against use of LSD passes.	Beach Boys release theme album *Pet Sounds.* Last public Beatles concert. Beatles' "Rain" first record to use reverse tape. Garage bands popularize proto-punk rebellion. Many radio and TV stations ban drug songs. Light shows are popularized in psychedelic night clubs. Jan Berry and Bob Dylan in serious accidents.
1967	Large antiwar demonstrations in Washington, D.C., New York, and San Francisco. Race riots in Cleveland, Newark, and Detroit. Marshall becomes first African American on U.S. Supreme Court. First human heart transplant operation (in Cape Town, South Africa). Three U.S. astronauts die aboard Apollo 1 craft still on launching pad. Abortions are legalized in Colorado. Microwave ovens are marketed for home use. First 911 emergency phone system is established in NY.	Human Be-In "happening" in San Francisco. FM radio allows for album-oriented rock programming. With release of Beatles' *Sgt. Pepper,* albums begin to take over the popularity of singles. Monaural records beginning to be phased out. Monterey International Pop Festival; the Who and Jimi Hendrix destroy equipment on stage. Proto-heavy metal by Hendrix and Cream. Brian Epstein and Otis Redding die.
1968	North Koreans seize *USS Pueblo* and crew. Vietnam peace talks begin. Martin Luther King and Robert Kennedy are assassinated. Large outdoor rock festivals popular. Riots at Democratic convention in Chicago. First African American woman is elected to Congress.	Reggae develops from ska in Jamaica. James Brown records "Say It Loud, I'm Black and I'm Proud." Electric Flag records jazz rock. Dylan, et al. begin country-rock style. "Bubblegum" music marketed for young and pre-teens. Moody Blues record with orchestra to begin art rock in U.K. Ralph Nader warns that loud rock music impairs hearing. Iron Butterfly popularizes heavy metal in U.S.
1969	Nixon becomes president. American lands on the moon. U.S. military to Cambodia. Vietnam peace talks expand. 250,000 march in Washington, D.C. to protest Vietnam War. My Lai massacre of civilians is reported. Manson family murders.	Woodstock and Altamont Festivals. Miles Davis records in fusion style. Elvis Presley, Chuck Berry, the Everly Brothers, Fats Domino, Little Richard, and Jerry Lee Lewis back touring after breaks. The Who performs *Tommy.* John Lennon/Yoko Ono "bed in" for peace. Jim Morrison is charged with lewd behavior in Miami. Brian Jones dies.

Rock Music Styles

A History

Third Edition

Katherine Charlton

Mt. San Antonio College
Walnut, California

Boston, Massachusetts Burr Ridge, Illinois Dubuque, Iowa
Madison, Wisconsin New York, New York San Francisco, California St. Louis, Missouri

To my husband and best friend,
Andrew Charlton,
who loves the blues.

McGraw-Hill

A Division of The ***McGraw-Hill*** *Companies*

ROCK MUSIC STYLES, A HISTORY, Third Edition

 This book is printed on recycled, acid-free paper containing 10% postconsumer waste.

6 7 8 9 QPD/QPD 04 03 02 01

ISBN 0–697–34055–4

Editorial director: *Phil Butcher*
Sponsoring editor: *Chris Freitag*
Project manager: *Peggy Selle*
Production supervisor: *Mary Jess*
Compositor: *A-R Editions, Inc.*
Typeface: *10/12 Times Roman*
Printer: *Quebecor Printing Dubuque, Inc.*

Cover design and manipulation by Ben Neff
Cover image *Jimi Hendrix* © Archive Photos

Library of Congress Catalog Card Number: 96–79450

http://www.mhcollege.com

Contents

7

Soul Music 71

8

The British Invasion 86

9

The Blues Revival 98

10

Garage Bands, Bubblegum, and Power Pop 112

11

Psychedelic Rock 118

12

Revivals of Country-Styled Rock 127

13

Jazz Rock and Fusion 138

14

Singer/Songwriters 147

15

Funk and Disco 156

16

Art Rock 164

17

Glitter and Glam 175

18

Hard Rock and Heavy Metal 182

19

Punk Rock and New Wave 204

20

Ska and Reggae 219

21

Hip Hop and Rap 229

22

Mainstream Rock of the Eighties and Nineties 238

23

Underground and Alternative Rock Styles 246

Preface

Rock Music Styles: A History is intended to be used as a text for a college-level course on the history of rock music. My primary concern has been to help students develop an understanding of both the musical and cultural roots of rock music and the ability to hear a direct relationship between those roots and the music currently popular. To that end, I have identified the various styles of music that influenced the development of rock and discussed the elements of those styles along with the rock music to which they relate. Careful and critical listening is necessary for one to hear and identify those basic elements of music and then understand how they help define characteristics of the individual styles. To listen critically does not mean that one must try to decide whether the music is pleasing or not, but rather to analyze exactly what one is hearing.

The listening guides to individual recordings in this book are intended to aid students in critical, or analytical, listening. Each guide begins with the tempo of the recording. To identify that basic beat in the recording all one has to do, in many cases, is look at the second hand on a clock while listening to it. We know that there are sixty seconds in a minute, so if the tempo is 120, the beats are the pulses in the music that are heard at the rate of two per second. Even if the tempo is 72, one can listen for pulses that are just a bit faster than the seconds to pick out the basic beat. Listening to the music is the most important part of this process, but many nonmusicians will need to force themselves to avoid the "tone bath" type of listening they might be used to and listen much more carefully.

After the tempo, the listening guides discuss the form of the recordings. Form in music is the overall structure of the music as defined by repetition and contrast. A song like "Hound Dog," for example, has lyrics in an AAB form. In other words, we hear one line of lyrics, "A" (the first letter of the alphabet is used for the first section of music), and then we hear that line repeated. Those two "A" lines are followed by new lyrics, so we identify those new lyrics by a new letter, "B." When we get into the music analysis we will be outlining when melodies repeat or are contrasted with new melodies. With either lyrics or melody, when we listen for form we listen for a musical element to repeat or for a new and contrasting element to be played or sung.

"Features" in the listening guides vary with the recordings and are my way of describing other musical elements or characteristics that are special in a particular recording and that help to define the general style of the music. This presentation does not allow for the type of detail that a musician who notates and analyzes music note by note or chord by chord uses, but that type of analysis is not the subject of this book. As I said earlier, what I have tried to do here is teach the interested student about the musical characteristics of many different types of music and help that student learn to listen critically so that he/she can make stylistic connections on his/her own.

Lyrics are very important in most rock music and, for that reason, each listening guide includes a simple explanation of the song's lyrics. In some light pop songs that explanation may say as much as do the lyrics themselves, but in most cases lyrics contain complexities that are open to many different interpretations that would go beyond the scope of this book. I hope that my representations of lyrics will be used as a point of departure for further thought and discussion about the meaning(s) conveyed in each song.

The availability of appropriate listening examples is a problem for many teachers of rock music history courses, and every effort has been made to concentrate detailed discussions in *Rock Music Styles: A History* on recordings that are fairly easy to obtain. The book's listening guides are intended to be used along with the recordings themselves. Whenever possible, I have selected recordings that are available in the Time-Life *Living the Blues, The Rock 'N' Roll Era, Solid Gold Soul, Classic Rock, AM Gold, Guitar Rock, Sounds of the Seventies,* and *Sounds of the Eighties* sets. For those teachers whose colleges may not be willing to purchase entire sets of recordings, individual cassettes or CDs can be ordered from the Time-Life Company (1–800–621–7026). For more recent examples, such as those in the chapters on Rap and on Underground and Alternative music, I used "best of" collections that represented several performers, thereby limiting the number of cassettes or CDs necessary to cover the chapters. I assume that teachers will add recordings from their own collections as they find appropriate.

Most rock listeners are well aware of the controversial aspects of some rock music, particularly its lyrics. In these cases, I have mentioned some of the issues, but avoided imposing personal judgments in the text. My goal is to be as objective as possible and provide the reader with an understanding of what the music means to the performer and his/her fans. Discussions about any possible negative impact the music or lyrics may have on some listeners can, and I expect will, take place in individual classrooms without any biased opinions from the textbook.

It may not be necessary to say this, but being a native Californian who has traveled all over Mexico and parts of Canada, I realize that my references to "America" for the United States of America may seem naive or even arrogant to people on the rest of the American continent. I am well aware of that potential problem and yet it is so very awkward to constantly write the full name of our country. Even "U.S.A." does not work in all cases and certainly not when the term to be used is "American." The United States of Mexico can be shortened to "Mexico" and the people there can be called "Mexicans" without assuming the name of the entire continent, but that not being the case for the U.S.A., I simply ask that my use of "America" be understood.

This book is dedicated to my husband, Andrew Charlton, for many reasons. I also owe much thanks for the hours of time and thoughtful advice given to me by my friend Robin Matthews of Golden West College, who owes the world a book of his own. Many improvements beyond the first edition have been made thanks to suggestions given to me by Peter Winkler, SUNY–Stony Brook, whose lectures I have often enjoyed at College Music Society conferences. In addition, I am grateful to my record collector and eternal rock-fan friend in Cleveland, Pat Phillips, who has introduced me to much wonderful music that I might otherwise have missed. The A.I.F.S. staff members at the University of London were a great help to me in organizing "rock tours" for my students during the semester (or "term" to the British) I taught there, and, while I cannot name everyone who helped me, I appreciate the support I received.

Rock historians whose advice was a great help to me include Paul Feehan, University of Miami–Coral Gables; John R. Harding, University of North Carolina–Charlotte; Ron Pen, University of Kentucky; Darhyl S. Ramsey, University of North Texas; Jim Albert, Eastern Washington University; Albert LeBlanc, Michigan State University; David H. Stuart, Iowa State University; Richard Weissman, University of Colorado–Denver; Robert Bozina, Santa Clara University; Carl Woideck, University of Oregon; Mark Forry, University of California at Santa Cruz; Stephen Young, University of Tennessee; and John Webb, University of Wisconsin at Whitewater. Others whose support was invaluable include Francie and Richard French, Susie and Doug Morrison, Ralph Spaulding, Andrew Markham, Ed Huddleston, Karen Speerstra, Raphael Kadushin, and Meredith M. Morgan, along with Julie Kennedy, Karen A. Pluemer, Karen Hostert, Deborah Daniel, Lorraine Zielinski, Rosemary Bradley, Chris Freitag, M. J. Kelly, Kris Queck, Shirley Lanners, Peggy Selle, and editors and staff members at McGraw Hill Higher Education. Of course, I must remember that it is my students who have asked questions requiring me to look at rock music from many different perspectives who are really the only reason this book exists. I thank them all, and hope for many more exchanges of ideas with more students in the future.

CHAPTER 1

American Popular Music Before Rock and Roll

Was there life before rock and roll? Died-in-the-wool rock fans might think not, or at least that whatever life there was was not worth living, but that, of course, was not the case for those who lived before the emergence of rock and roll. People have always entertained themselves and one another with songs, dances, and other types of music. Music that is simple and catchy enough to immediately appeal to large numbers of people is generally dubbed "popular," and a large body of popular music existed before rock and roll and alongside rock music through to the present time.

Much popular music today is rather complex and would be beyond the ability of an average person to perform. Before the existence of such twentieth century inventions as radio, television, and good-quality record, tape, or CD players, the only way most people could hear music was to perform it themselves, hire performers to play for them, or go to a public performance. Because of this, popular music of past times was often either relatively simple or composed to be part of large-scale public extravaganzas. In addition to its broad appeal, popular music is generally, although not necessarily always, **secular.** Through the years popular music has become very big business, and is usually produced primarily to generate financial gain for the writer, publisher, and performer.

The earliest popular songs in America were brought to the colonies by British and other European settlers. The business of producing, publishing, and selling music in America was aided by the passage of the first American National Copyright Act in 1790. **Copyright** protected the composer's credit and allowed him/her and the publisher to receive payment for the sale of published songs and maintain control of their distribution. With many people willing to pay for printed music, the popular music industry in the United States grew rapidly during the nineteenth century. It exploded in the twentieth century with the availability of phonograph recordings in the first decade of the century, radio beginning in the twenties, and television in the forties. Rock music developed into a large-scale industry of its own in the fifties, but that happened only after and because of the popular music that preceded it.

European Influences from Colonial Days through the Early Nineteenth Century

Many of the songs that were first published in the United States came from English or other European theatrical stage shows. English **ballad operas** such as John Gay's *The Beggar's Opera* (first performed in London in 1728) were staged in the American cities of New York and Williamsburg by an English theatrical troupe in the 1750s. Later performances by other troupes took place in large cities such as Philadelphia and Baltimore. Songs from

Gay's opera and other shows were published individually and entered the American popular song repertoire.

As was bound to happen eventually, songs by American-born composers began to appear in print. Many of the earliest American works were **psalms** and **hymns** composed to be used in church services. Francis Hopkinson (1737–1791), a delegate to the Continental Congress in 1776 and a signer of the Declaration of Independence, claimed to be the first American-born composer. Such credit was difficult or even impossible to prove, since many people may have written music that was not published, but he certainly was among the first. He wrote collections of songs to be sung with **harpsichord** or **forte piano** accompaniment, as well as a number of psalm tunes for use in religious services. Another important early American composer, William Billings (1746–1800), wrote over 340 psalm melodies, hymn tunes, and other compositions for four-voice chorus. In addition to his work for his church, Billings established a singing school in Boston in 1769. His school became a model for many later schools that helped to foster basic musical literacy in large numbers of otherwise untrained **amateur** musicians.

French operas had been produced in New Orleans as early as the late eighteenth century, but those large-scale "grand" performances in the French language had little appeal for American audiences in other cities. By the early nineteenth century, productions of Italian operas and some operas by Mozart written in the Italian style became popular outside New Orleans, but not in their original forms. The versions of Mozart's *Le nozze di Figaro* (*The Marriage of Figaro*) and *Don Giovanni,* and Rossini's *Il barbiere di Siviglia* (*The Barber of Seville*) and *La Cenerentola* (*Cinderella*) that became popular in London and in a number of American cities had been "Englished" by such composers as Sir Henry Rowley Bishop (1786–1855). To "English" the operas, Bishop not only translated the Italian into English, but also replaced **recitatives** with spoken dialogue and shortened many of the **arias** to make them popular with musically unsophisticated audiences. While music historians were uniformly horrified by these "mutilations" of the operatic art, the performances did add much to the body of American popular music and paved the way for the future large-scale popularity of American musicals.

In addition to songs from ballad operas and Englished versions of Italian operas, the development of American popular music was influenced by songs and dances from Ireland and Scotland. Influential Irish poets/composers/performers whose works were widely popular included Thomas Moore (1779–1852), whose poetry became lyrics for songs by Sir John Stevenson (1761–1833) and Samuel Lover (1779–1868). Lover came to America to perform his music and spent two years (1846–1848) touring from New York to New Orleans, Lake Superior, and then north into Canada. Texts by Scottish poet Robert Burns (1759–1796) such as "Auld Lang Syne" and "Comin' thro the Rye" were set to traditional Scottish melodies and published in the United States in and after 1787. Some of those songs have continued to be part of American traditions well into the late twentieth century, as any American who has sung "Auld Lang Syne" ("Should auld acquaintance be forgot . . .") at a New Year's Eve party can attest.

Minstrel Shows

African American styles of music eventually became an important part of American popular music, but not in any real sense until the twentieth century. Slavery and a general view of African Americans as inferior beings were still common among white Americans through most of the nineteenth century. Slavery was not completely abolished until the passage of the Thirteenth Amendment to the U.S. Constitution in 1865. (Note: The Emancipation Proclamation issued by President Abraham Lincoln in 1863 is sometimes given credit for freeing slaves, but because it proclaimed freedom for slaves in the South while the Civil War was still going on, it was not respected in the South and did not, therefore, really end slavery.) The very popular minstrel shows of the nineteenth century helped promulgate the common view of African American people as inferior, and for that reason are, from today's slightly more enlightened attitudes, an embarrassment in American history. They cannot be ignored, however, because they had a tremendous influence on the development of later types of entertainment.

Minstrelsy began with performances by English singer/actors such as Charles Dibdin (1745–1814), who played the comic black role of Mungo in the popular musical extravaganza *The Padlock* (1768). By the 1820s white American entertainers put burnt-cork makeup on their faces to play African American characters in their minstrel shows. George Washington Dixon (1808–1861) was the first American to become famous for his blackface performances. He played the two most popular images of African Americans, the "dandy" and the stupid and foolish Sambo. The "dandy" character (also commonly called "Zip Coon" or "Dandy Jim") portrayed an urban African American dressed in an ill-fitting blue coat, tails, and top hat, who looked ridiculous as he spoke with mispronounced and incorrectly used words. His look and talk indicated that he had gotten "above himself" and was trying to imitate his white "betters." Dixon also played the opposite type of character, the poor, stupid, and lazy "Black Sambo," who was superstitious and foolish. Another American, Thomas Dartmouth "Daddy" Rice (1808–1860), played the character that gave the name "Jim Crow" to the same type of shuffling clown image Dixon had played as Black Sambo. Rice eventually became known as the Father of American Minstrelsy.

The Virginia Minstrels: Dan Emmett (center, fiddle*), Dick Pelham (*tambourine*), Billy Whitlock (*banjo*), and Frank Brower (*bones*) from the title page of a song collection published in Boston in 1843.*

Reproduced by permission of Harvard Theatre Collection, The Houghton Library.

Minstrel shows included skits, dances, and crude jokes, all of which were calculated to ridicule African Americans by their use of exaggerated stereotypical images. The banjo, violin, tambourine, and bones (lengths of rib bones held between the fingers and shaken rhythmically) were the common instruments employed as accompaniment to songs and dances. The entertainers would sit in a semicircle on the stage with the main comic figures placed at each end. An interlocutor, who functioned as a master of ceremonies and straight man, introduced each act and would trade banter with the comics. Daniel Emmett (1815–1904), the composer of "Dixie" and a number of other popular songs of the day, was a white blackface violinist and entertainer in one such minstrel show, the Virginia Minstrels. Eventually some troupes began to downplay some of the blatant ridiculing of African Americans by including more genteel non-dialect songs by composers such as Stephen Foster in their shows.

After the Civil War and the abolishment of slavery, a number of African American minstrel troupes were organized, serving to display their talents as performers (although the African American performers still often wore burnt-cork face makeup). Their shows included songs, dances, and skits based on plantation life. Because their audiences were composed mainly of whites, they pandered, to a degree, to the white image of the African American, but without the extreme negative racial overtones that characterized the white blackface shows. The increasing popularity of minstrel shows allowed for more acceptance of African American performers by white audiences and helped to establish those entertainers and their types of music in the mainstream of American show business. The blackfaced white minstrel image was still popular in vaudeville shows of the early twentieth century. Al Jolson (1886–1950) wore black makeup and played a minstrel character in films, on radio, and on television, singing such hit songs as "My Mammy," "Swanee," and "Rockabye Your Baby with a Dixie Melody."

The Middle Nineteenth Century and the Civil War Era

The most popular American songwriter of the nineteenth century was Stephen Foster (1826–1864). He wrote the lyrics and music to over 200 songs. Many of his songs were nostalgic about the past or told about love and problems people experienced in their daily lives. He wrote some songs such as "Lou'siana Belle" and "Oh! Susanna" for blackfaced white minstrel troupes, but most of his music was intended for average Americans to play and sing for their own entertainment in their homes. "Jeanie with the Light Brown Hair," "Old Folks at Home," "Beautiful Dreamer," and many other songs soon came to represent American culture like no songs before them. Foster was at the end of his writing career when the Civil War began in 1861. He wrote several songs in support of the Northern cause, including "We've a Million in the Field" and "We Are Coming, Father Abraam, 300,000 More." Stephen Foster was the first American composer to sell enough music to give up other employment and make a living from his song royalties. He was also the first musician to be honored in the Hall of Fame for Great Americans.

The American Civil War (1861–1865) affected the lives of the people of both the North and the South, and many popular song texts were written for each side. Some, such as those by Stephen Foster, George Frederick

Stephen C. Foster, ca. 1859
National Portrait Gallery

Irving Berlin
Bettman Archive

Root (1820–1895), and Henry Clay Work (1832– 1884) were newly composed, but others were new texts sung to older popular melodies. The Confederate anthem "The Bonnie Blue Flag" was based on an old Irish tune originally called "The Irish Jaunting Car," and the very popular "When Johnny Comes Marching Home" was written to be sung to the traditional Scottish melody of "John Anderson My Jo." One of the most popular songs of the Confederate cause was "Dixie," written by Northerner Daniel Emmett for his minstrel shows.

Minstrel shows continued to be popular through the postwar era, and were often included as part of a new type of stage show called **vaudeville** that began just after the war. Vaudeville shows evolved directly out of the earlier British music hall shows and minstrel shows. They usually consisted of as many as fifteen different acts that included singing, dancing, comedy routines, and other types of entertainment. Until it was overtaken by radio and television during the twentieth century, vaudeville was the most popular type of live entertainment in the country, with, at one point, over 10,000 theaters nationwide. Entertainers of the recent past such as Jack Benny, George Burns, his wife Gracie Allen, and Fred Allen began their careers on the vaudeville stage.

Tin Pan Alley and Musical Theater

The term "Tin Pan Alley" referred to the thin, tinny tone quality of cheap upright pianos used in music publishers' offices on New York's West 28th Street. Songwriters used these pianos to play their songs for publishers in hopes of getting them printed, distributed, and sold. The name "Tin Pan Alley" eventually came to represent the style of the songs that were published in that area. Generally, the songs were sentimental ballads or songs that portrayed the "gay nineties" as being full of fun and escape from life's realities. Many of the songs were based on triple-meter **waltz** rhythms because of the popularity of that dance. Tin Pan Alley continued to be a very important source of American popular music well into the twentieth century, when the music helped to popularize other dances such as the Latin **tango** of the twenties, the **rumba** of the thirties, and the **samba** of the forties.

Not all American popular music originated in New York, however. The 1890's was also the time when **ragtime** piano and band music became popular along the Mississippi River. Ragtime was primarily, although not exclusively, an African American style. It was named for the "ragged" or **syncopated rhythms** played by the pianist's right hand, or the main melody played by the band. The ragged lines were generally accompanied by a steady alternation between a single note and a chord in the bass or lower band parts. Popular ragtime composers included Scott Joplin (1868–1917), James Scott (1886–1938), and Joseph Lamb (1887–1960). The spread of ragtime and other popular music was aided by the invention of new sound devices such as the player piano, the phonograph, and jukebox-type players.

Many of the greatest writers and entertainers of the Tin Pan Alley era were Jewish immigrants who had entered the United States after fleeing the anti-Semitism rampant in Germany, Austria, and Russia. One of the most important of the Jewish-American songwriters of this era was Irving Berlin (Israel Baline, 1888–1989). Berlin was born in Russia and moved to New York City with his family when he was only four years old. He began his singing career as a cantor in a synagogue and later was hired to be a singing waiter. He learned to play the piano by ear and became fascinated by ragtime rhythms. He adapted these rhythms to his own songwriting style and had his first big hit with "Alexander's Ragtime Band" in 1911. As an entertainer and songwriter, he moved on to vaudeville and finally to musical theater. "God Bless America," a song that some Americans have come to think of as a second national anthem, was written by Berlin just before America entered World War II. Of the musicals for which he composed scores, *Annie*

Get Your Gun, based on the career of Annie Oakley, was one of his most popular.

American musical theater was an important outgrowth of both vaudeville and the popular success of the British **operettas** *H.M.S. Pinafore* and *The Pirates of Penzance* by Gilbert and Sullivan. Musicals differed from the random acts put together for vaudeville shows in that musicals followed a unified plot and the songs and dances all related to that story line. The simplicity of the music and songs in musicals added to their popular success and made them different from operas composed in the classical tradition, but related to the lightness of operettas. With highly sophisticated musical works such as George Gershwin's (1898–1937) *Porgy and Bess* (1935), the line between musical and opera became unclear (at least to some) and has remained so into the late twentieth century with any number of works by Stephen Sondheim (born in 1930) or Andrew Lloyd Webber (born in 1948).

American musicals came to be called Broadway musicals because so many of them were first produced for performance in theaters on or around Broadway in New York. Most musicals were composed of two **acts** with an intermission between them. Melodies heard in the first act often returned in the second to provide a sense of unity for the audience. The earliest musicals were based on comic stories, but, by 1927, *Show Boat* proved that more serious plots could also attract popular success. As had been the case with many songwriters in the past, musicals were often composed by a pair of writers, one providing the lyrics and the other the music. Two of the greatest lyricists of the era were Lorenz Hart (1895–1943) and Oscar Hammerstein II (1895–1960). Some of the composers who worked with them in several combinations included Jerome Kern (1885–1945), Richard Rodgers (1902–1979), and Leonard Bernstein (1918–1990). Other writers such as Cole Porter (1893–1964) wrote both the words and the music for their works. Stephen Sondheim began his career as a lyricist for Bernstein's music in *West Side Story* (1957), but composed both the music and lyrics for *A Funny Thing Happened on the Way to the Forum* (1962). Sondheim collaborated with others on his later shows.

Swing Dance Bands

Beginning around 1934 and lasting through the end of World War II eleven years later, a couple's idea of a perfect night out would be one spent dancing to the music of a big band. Swing bands played jazz-related music and individual musicians were allowed to improvise solos in a jazz style, but the bands themselves were bigger than earlier jazz bands and improvisation time was limited. Most of the time the bands played music from written **arrangements** that were carefully planned for playing swing dance rhythms rather than the types of complex music of other jazz styles. Where earlier New Orleans jazz bands used one trumpet (or cornet), one clarinet, and one trombone as the principal solo instruments (called the **front line**), swing bands were much larger, comprised of numbers of trumpets, trombones, and saxophones in addition to the rhythm instruments. A typical **rhythm section** in the New Orleans bands was composed of banjo or guitar, string bass or tuba, and drums. The smoother style of swing dance music replaced the tuba with a string bass, the banjo with a guitar and/or piano.

Swing music not only increased the number of band instruments used, but also brought about new ways of playing them. The old bass lines played on tuba were usually single notes pumping back and forth between the first and third beats of a bar of four beats. Swing bassists created a much smoother effect by "walking" from note to note by playing a new note on every beat and occasionally between the beats to decorate the rhythmic flow. This bass style became known as **walking bass** and was later used in rhythm and blues and rock and roll. The new emphasis on the string bass freed pianists from having to stress bass lines so they were free to play rhythmic figurations in a style called **comping.** Comping meant that the left hand (or both hands) could play chords on or between selected beats and not play bass notes at all. Comping functioned to provide a rhythmic punctuation that complemented the rhythms the rest of the band was playing. Drummers, too, had to alter the way they played in order to fit into the swing style. With the swing bass player accentuating every beat, the drums only had to reinforce what the bass was playing. Drummers would often hit the bass drum on only the first and third of every four beats while lightly keeping the other beats and rhythmic pulses between them on the **high hat** cymbal or snare drum.

No one arranger, performer, or band leader in the early thirties can be pointed to as being the "inventor" of swing. There were a number of arrangers whose work, taken collectively, can be said to have led to, and finally realized, the new style. Some of the most important ones were Fletcher Henderson (1897–1952), Don Redman (1900–1964), Duke Ellington (1899–1975), and Benny Carter (born in 1907). They all played in various different bands and/or had swing bands of their own.

The most popular of the swing bands was led by trombonist Glenn Miller (1904–1944). Miller established his band's style by doing all of the arranging for the band in its early days, although he later brought in a number of others to write for the band. The Glenn Miller Band (sometimes called the Glenn Miller Orchestra) played at a number of large dance halls or casinos that broadcasted their performances nationally, allowing them to reach fans across the United States. Their records sold well and they were featured in the movies *Sun Valley Serenade* (1941) and *Orchestra Wives* (1942). To support the war

Glenn Miller and his orchestra
A/P Wide World Photos

effort and help raise the spirits of U.S. troops during World War II, Miller joined the U.S. Army Air Force and led his band to England to play for American soldiers. Even after his untimely death when his plane disappeared during a flight from London to Paris, his band continued to play in the style he had established and came to identify the swing era for a great many people.

Swing bands often backed male singers who sang in a style known as **crooning.** Crooning was different from earlier popular singing styles in that it was developed as a way of using a new invention, the microphone. Sound engineers were better able to control and amplify a soft and gentle voice than a loud, resonant one. The crooning style was one where men softened their natural voices into a smooth, gentle tone, sliding from one note to another to create the effect of warm sentimentality. Popular crooners of the swing era included Bing Crosby (1903–1977) and Perry Como (born in 1912). These crooners all had an influence on the pop rock singers of the fifties and early sixties known as "teen idols."

The Beginnings of Rock and Roll

Instrumental, vocal, and dance styles that were popular during the forties had a certain amount of influence on the development of rock music. It is important, however, to understand that rock music also had its roots in styles of music that had not yet gained the nationwide popularity of the Tin Pan Alley songs or the swing bands. For example, delta blues and rhythm and blues, which served as the basis of much early rock music, were mostly played and sold in African American neighborhoods and neither heard nor understood by the general American public. Similarly, some country music styles that influenced early rock music had their own particular regions of popularity and, therefore, rather limited numbers of fans. Racism and the forced segregation of African Americans was one of the reasons for this division of musical tastes.

In the forties and before, performing groups had generally been racially segregated, as were their audiences. White minstrel shows had no African American performers, and African American shows were performed exclusively by African American players. It was possible to integrate some jazz bands for radio shows and recording sessions because the performers could not be seen by the listeners. Technically, some of the bands were integrated. Puerto Rican valve trombonist Juan Tizol joined Duke Ellington's band in 1929, but the fact that he was not African American was not obvious enough to bother New York audiences. Other bands such as Benny Goodman's had all white members, but sometimes featured African American soloists in their shows. In Los Angeles, Johnny Otis was a white musician who worked with many African American performers on a regular basis. These examples, however, were exceptions. For the most part, segregation of races was the rule well into the fifties.

Racial barriers slowly eroded when white teenagers began to listen and dance to the rhythm and blues of such jump bands as Louis Jordan and his Tympany Five in the late forties. At first, many white radio-station and record-company owners resisted making music by African American performers widely available. But by 1951, the smooth rhythmic sounds of African American vocal groups like the Platters and the Moonglows were reaching white teens through radio programs hosted by maverick disc jockeys who refused to perpetuate racial exclusion, the most famous of whom was Cleveland's Alan Freed. The increased availability of radios, especially car radios during the early fifties and portable transistor radios several years later, was important in bringing both rhythm and blues and rock music to the teen audience. Bands and audiences were still segregated for the most part, but early rock music did help bridge some of the gap.

In 1954 the Supreme Court decided that equality could not exist when people remained separated by race. After deciding the case known as *Brown v. Board of Education,* the court demanded that public schools be integrated. It still took years before integration became more common, but gradually attitudes changed from the extreme racist attitudes of the past. The popularity of rock music that developed directly from both African American and white styles of music can be given a part of the credit for helping to relax racist attitudes. Of course, rock music did not replace other types of popular music when it finally came into being, and many other types of popular music still maintain a large following. For the purposes of this book, however, it is rock and roll and its development that will be discussed further.

Summary

America's earliest popular music was brought to the New World by British and other European settlers. Such popular music included songs from ballad operas, simplified versions of arias from Italian operas, and Irish and Scottish songs and dances. Eventually, American-born composers began to compose and publish their own music, providing popular songs that expressed more purely American interests and lifestyles. The earliest minstrel shows featured white performers playing mocking, stereotypical African American characters. Once slavery was abolished, black minstrel shows gave African Americans an opportunity to perform their own music for white audiences, leading to the development and widespread popularity of ragtime, jazz, and rock music—all of which were based primarily on African American musical traditions. Latin dances such as the tango, the rumba, and the samba also became important popular dance and musical styles during the first half of the twentieth century.

New York was an important center for several styles of popular music originating in Tin Pan Alley or Broadway musicals. Swing dance bands and the crooners who sang with these bands helped keep American optimism and spirit alive through World War II. Rock music developed out of a number of different styles of music that existed in the forties and became a style of its own in the early fifties. In many ways, the popularity of rock music among both black and white musicians and fans aided the movement toward racial integration and mutual respect of people of any ethnic background.

Terms to Remember

Acts
Amateur
Arias
Arrangement
Ballad opera
Comping
Copyright
Crooning
Forte piano
Front line
Harpsichord
High hat
Hymns
Operettas
Psalms
Ragtime
Recitatives
Rhythm section
Rumba
Samba
Secular
Syncopated rhythms
Tango
Vaudeville
Walking bass
Waltz

CHAPTER 2

The Blues Roots of Rock Music

The term "blues" has long been used to describe feelings of sadness and hopelessness. The music called the blues developed out of a very unhappy situation indeed—that of people taken forcibly from their homes and brought to a new world to live in slavery. Even long after they were released from servitude, African Americans were not accepted by the white society that had granted them their freedom. Despite that difficult fact, the blues was not always a sad music. It was often music used by African Americans to help them cope with the problems and frustrations they encountered in the harshness of their daily lives. The lyrics of many blues songs included an element of hope and the anticipation of better times. Some told stories, often including sexual references, sometimes euphemistically, sometimes blatantly, but in general they were an emotional outpouring by a people that had been relegated to existing on the fringes of a society that considered them social and genetic inferiors.

Musical Roots of the Blues

The very earliest roots of the blues lies not only in Africa but also in music from parts of Arabia, the Middle East, and even Spain during the Moorish occupation (eighth through the fifteenth centuries). Because that early music originated centuries before the advent of recorded sound and had not been notated, one can only listen to modern-day music from those parts of the world to hear similarities and assume intercultural exchanges among those peoples and Africans in the past. Musical devices, such as Arabic scale structures and melodic sequences, melodic and rhythmic patterns in Turkish ceremonial music, and the sense of rhythmic freedom used by Spanish **flamenco** singers, all share similarities with some types of African music and, ultimately, the blues.

To find the nearest direct predecessor of the blues, the ancestral music of African Americans must be examined. A potential problem in undertaking such a study is that Africa is a very large continent and the people who were brought to the New World as slaves came from many widely separated areas. Understanding this, the easiest single place to find pre-blues African musical traditions is Freetown, Sierra Leone. Freetown was given its name when it was established as a colony of Africans who were to be shipped to the New World as slaves, but were freed by an anti-slavery authority. It is interesting to note that although the people of Freetown represented nearly the same mixture of Africans as those who came to the New World, the blues as we know it did not develop in Freetown. The music there continued to be performed according to African traditions and ceremonies that were of and by the dominant culture of that part of the world. However, some of those musical practices clearly point the way to the blues.

Accompanied songs sung by **griots** from Sierra Leone share characteristics with early American blues songs. In Sierra Leone, as in many parts of Africa, griots have functioned for centuries as oral poets who tell the history of the people and their leaders. Before their society had a system of writing, griots maintained a social standing that was high and respectable, and the oral tradition continued on even after many Africans were able to write down their own history and poetry. Musical characteristics of griot songs include an expressive but somewhat rough vocal tone production, duple rhythm patterns, a vocal line that avoids following the rhythmic flow of the accompaniment, and an accompaniment without harmonic changes. Of those characteristics, the vocal tone and the duple rhythms are found in early American blues styles, but American blues singers tended to follow their accompaniment patterns more often than was common in the African tradition.

Although African griot songs heard today and the American blues have enough similarities to assume that they developed out of a similar source, American blues is not merely a transplanted version of the griot song. Part of the reason the blues had to be different from the griot song was that the blues functioned as a personal expression of an individual who suffered from a lack of human respectability, where the griot song was very central to the dominant social structure in Africa. African Americans had also been exposed to music from white European traditions, particularly the hymns sung in churches, and that music influenced their use of a three-chord harmonic progression and short verses that were equal to one another in length. From all of this one can see that the blues developed out of ancient musical traditions from many parts of the world, traditions that were synthesized by African Americans in the southern United States.

Country Blues

Because of their origins in rural areas of the United States, particularly the South, the earliest-known blues styles were called **country blues.** The composers and performers of country blues were, for the most part, people to whom the blues was an integral part of life. They usually accompanied themselves on battered guitars (if they were accompanied at all), and the texts they sang were often rough yet highly expressive.

The blues developed its form and style sometime in the late nineteenth or early twentieth century, but the earliest recordings were not made until the twenties. Exactly how the blues sounded at the beginning of the century can only be inferred from these later recordings. Even putting the performers in front of a microphone to record them must have affected the musical results to some degree.

Although much variation existed in the country blues styles that developed in various parts of the South, the style that had the most direct influence on the development of rock music came from the Mississippi Delta and was called **delta blues.** It was highly emotional and rough when compared to country blues styles from such places as the Carolinas, but its expressiveness and rhythmic vitality caused its popularity to spread. Delta blues musicians such as Robert Johnson, Charley Patton, and Son House accompanied their singing with guitars, strumming chords that they interspersed with melodic fills.

Delta blues guitarists would often break off the neck of a bottle, file down the rough edges, put it on the third or fourth finger of the hand controlling the fingerboard of the instrument (usually the left hand), and slide it from note to note on the upper strings of the guitar, leaving the other three fingers of that hand to play simple chords or bass lines. Breaking bottles soon became unnecessary as tubes (called **bottlenecks**) of glass or steel were made commercially available. Other guitarists, **Leadbelly** (Huddie Ledbetter, 1885–1949) for one, achieved a similar effect by sliding a knife along the guitar strings. Blues players like Big Joe Williams, who recorded for Vocalion as early as 1929, and Muddy Waters, who began to record for Aristocrat Records in 1945 (renamed Chess Records in 1948), were later musicians who retained the essence of delta blues bottleneck guitar style, while also updating it by using amplification and adding other instrumentalists.

Part of the general character of the blues was created by bending the pitches of notes to what were called **blue notes.** The exact origin of blue notes may never be known for certain, but they came either from **pentatonic** (five-tone) **scales** used in parts of West Africa, or perhaps even from Islamic influences on African music. In the blues as it was played by early blues artists, the commonly lowered blue notes were the third and seventh degrees of a major scale. In the key of C, for example, one of the blue notes was somewhere between E and E♭ and the other was between B and B♭. To perform these notes with the voice and on some musical instruments, and E or B could be bent down in pitch to produce the blue note. On many instruments, the piano for one, a note could not be bent to produce a blue tone, so the player simply lowered the tone a full half step. The following example shows the C scale with the blue notes a piano would play in parentheses:

Other scales, such as the pentatonic minor scale, were also often used in the blues, but even in these scales the lowered third and seventh degrees remain the common blue notes. In more advanced jazz styles such as **bebop,** the lowered fifth scale degree also became a blue note, but it was not often used as such in early blues.

While pianists were limited to either lowering the pitch of a blue note a full half step or by hitting two adjacent notes simultaneously to suggest the one in between, the pitch level of blue notes was much less exact on instruments that could bend notes. One reason for the popularity of playing the guitar with a bottleneck was that the bottleneck could be used to slide through the blue notes that fell between the frets (metal bars across the fingerboard behind which the strings were stopped). Another technique for playing blue notes on a guitar without a bottleneck was to play the fret just below a blue note and then push or pull the string, causing it to tighten and then loosen gradually, raising and lowering the pitch within the area of the blue note. This technique was called **string bending,** because the string being pushed or pulled would look "bent" compared to the other strings on the instrument.

Blues harp (harmonica) players used breath control to bend notes, but they needed to play blue notes so often that they would also use a harp tuned in a key different from the key of the song. Some harp players would choose a harp that was tuned one whole step lower than the key of the song, providing them with easy access to the lowered third and seventh scale degrees. Others played harps in a key a fifth below that of the song, giving them a scale with a lowered seventh. The use of an instrument in a key other than that of the song is called **cross-harp playing.**

The blues developed into a fairly consistent formal structure, influenced by European song forms, that was made up of repeated and contrasting lines of specific length. The form used in most blues could be outlined by the letters "AAB." In that outline, the first letter "A" referred to the first line of melody (four measures) and the first phrase of words. The second "A" represented a repetition of the same words and a melody that was exactly or nearly the same as the first. The letter "B" stood for a contrasting line of text (often rhyming with line "A") and a contrasting melody that functioned as a response to the words and melody of the "A" sections. In other words, blues lyrics usually had two lines of text, the first of which was repeated.

The rhythm of the blues form was organized into four-beat patterns, each of which was called a bar (or measure), and each section of the melody was made up of four bars. As the three phrases had four bars each, the complete structure for each AAB blues verse, chorus, or stanza (these terms are used interchangeably) had a total of twelve bars. For that reason, it was often referred to as the **twelve-bar blues.** Following is an example of a stanza of blues showing how the poetic (lyric) form was structured:

> *"I love my man when he treats me fine"* (The first A section)
>
> *"I love my man when he treats me fine"* (The second A section)
>
> *"I just wish he wouldn't drink so much wine"* (The B section)

A practice not always followed in blues-based rock music, but typical of traditional blues styles, involved the use of the West African practice of **call-and-response,** in which a leader would call out to a group, and that call was followed by a group response. The blues singer usually played the part of the caller by singing from the first beat of each section of melody through the first beat of the third bar, and the remainder of the four-bar section was filled by an instrumental response. The response could be played by one or more players on a variety of instruments, by the singer on the guitar or piano, or by the singer repeating one or more of the words at the end of each line of text. The following diagram shows the placement of the text, the instrumental or vocal fill (response to the singer's call), and the chord progression as it became standardized in the twelve-bar blues. In the key of C the **tonic chord** is C, the **subdominant chord** is F, and the **dominant chord** is G. All three are often **seventh chords.** (Early blues musicians often kept playing the G^7 chord through the first two bars of the B section instead of playing the F chord in the second bar.) Each repetition of the chord name represents a beat on which the chord would be played, and the vertical lines divide those beats into four-beat bars.

TWELVE-BAR BLUES FORM

A Lyric	Sung text__________Instrumental fill C C C C I C C C C I C C C C I C C C C I
A Lyric	Sung text__________Instrumental fill F F F F I F F F F I C C C C I C C C C I
B Lyric	Sung text__________Instrumental fill $G^7G^7G^7G^7$ I F F F F I C C C C I C C C C I

As was also true of most jazz styles, the beats were usually subdivided unevenly, creating a smooth flow of "long-short-long-short" in which each long note was twice the length of each short note, as shown by the following notation:

The uneven rhythm pattern was called a **shuffle beat**

when the bass was played on the beat and the chord was played on the last part of the beat. When performed slowly, the uneven **beat subdivisions** created a very relaxed feeling that was well suited to and became a characteristic of the blues. Even beat subdivisions are common in folk and country music.

One of the most influential country blues singer/guitarists who recorded during the thirties was **Robert Johnson** (1911–1938). Not much is known about his life, other than that he was poor, grew up on a plantation

Listening Guide

"Cross Road Blues"
as recorded by Robert Johnson (1936)

Tempo: The speed of the basic beat is approximately 88 beats per minute, but Johnson speeds up and slows down at will.

Form: Johnson plays slightly less than a four-bar introduction on the guitar using a bottleneck. (The introduction has been cut short, perhaps because the recording machine was turned on just after he had begun playing.)

After the introduction, the twelve-bar blues form is followed throughout. As was common in delta blues, the "B" section has two-bars of a dominant chord (the G^7 in the outline of the blues form) followed by two-bars of the tonic chord (the C chord in the outline).

Features: Johnson sings four stanzas of blues lyrics, providing his own responses on the guitar without any backup by other musicians.

The influence of polyrhythms can be heard in two ways:

1. Johnson's beat is usually subdivided into uneven parts, as is typical of the blues, but he occasionally breaks the pattern and uses sections of even beat subdivisions.
2. His singing often departs from the beat played by the guitar, following a different rhythm pattern, producing a polyrhythmic effect.

Lyrics: It is sometimes quite difficult to understand the words he is singing, but this was common in early blues because the rhythm and mood were often more important than the lyrics. In general, the song is the expression of a poor African American man standing at a road crossing trying to get a ride, but no one will stop for him. However, he is not bitter; instead, he has accepted the fact that the drivers do not know him and have not stopped for that reason. While waiting, he asks for mercy from God and then thinks about a friend of his named Willie Brown. As was often true of the blues, the song is not necessarily sad, although it is rather poignant that the singer is so easily accepting of the rejection he is experiencing.

Source: *Robert Johnson/The Complete Recordings*, Columbia 46222.

in Mississippi, and was reputedly either husband or lover to just about any woman who would have him. The lyrics of most of Johnson's songs expressed his insatiable desire for wine, women, and song. He recorded only twenty-nine songs, although when one includes alternate takes of some of those songs his recordings total forty-one. His recordings were done in makeshift studios in hotel rooms or office buildings, and the distribution of those recordings in his own time was extremely limited because large record companies simply were not interested in his kind of music. The recordings were reissued in later years, and consequently many blues-loving rock musicians have been influenced by them.

Johnson did not perform in formal situations for large groups, so relatively few people heard him in person. Those who did spread stories about the expressiveness of his music, and from those stories arose the Faustian myth that he had sold his soul in order to play so well. That myth was dramatized in the 1986 movie *Crossroads.*

Johnson's songs did follow the traditional AAB lyrical scheme and the chords of the basic blues progression as it was described earlier (with only two chords in the B section), but he was not confined by the rhythmic strictness observed by later blues musicians. He added extra beats to bars and extra bars to phrases seemingly at random, and sometimes even sang in a rhythmic pattern that differed from what he was playing on his guitar. The simultaneous use of more than one rhythm (**polyrhythm**) was known in some African musical traditions, and he may have been familiar with music based in such practices. The essentials of Johnson's musical style can best be discussed with reference to one of his recordings. At the top of this page is a listening guide for his "Cross Road Blues."

Two years after the recording of "Cross Road Blues" was made, Johnson's wild and free lifestyle was responsible for his death. Only twenty-seven years old, he was poisoned either by a woman with whom he had been involved or by the husband of such a woman. Johnson's songs have been recorded by many rock groups, including the Rolling Stones, who recorded "Love in Vain" and "Stop Breaking Down"; Cream, who recorded "Cross Road Blues" (although they called it "Crossroads"); and Fleetwood Mac, who recorded "Hellhound on My Trail."

Although most of the country blues singers who attracted the attention of record companies were men,

Memphis Minnie

Courtesy Sing Out *Magazine and* Yazoo *Records*

women also sang and played the blues, and some had fairly successful careers. One such musician was Lizzie "Kid" Douglas who recorded under the name **Memphis Minnie** (1897–1973). Minnie was born on a farm in the New Orleans suburb of Algiers. She ran away from her family when they moved to Walls, Mississippi, but the exact reason she left home is not known. At the tender age of eight she was living as a street musician in Memphis, Tennessee. Such a life was difficult for anyone, but it was particularly difficult for such a young girl. Minnie finally moved to Chicago where her career became better established, but before that her colorful life included playing in tent shows in the Ringling Brothers Circus and working the saloons and bars on Memphis' famous Beale Street. While in Chicago, she wrote songs, sang, and played the guitar on records made with her series of three guitarist/husbands, Joe McCoy, Casey Bill Weldon, and Ernest "Lil Son Joe" Lawlar. Illness caused her to stop performing in the late fifties, but she has been memorialized with a number of honors including Best Female Blues Singer in a Readers Poll conducted by the British magazine *Blues Unlimited.* Her recordings can be found on several labels including Columbia, Victor, Vocalion, OKeh, Decca, and JOB.

Despite the fact that Memphis Minnie spent much time in the urban center of Chicago, she retained the country blues style. Other country blues musicians in Chicago left the raw country sound behind, switching from acoustic to amplified guitars and playing with jazz musicians. The blues style that was associated with specific cities was called **urban blues.**

Urban Blues

Most urban blues was played by groups of instruments that included a rhythm section (bass, drums, guitar and/or piano) and solo instruments such as the saxophone or other wind instruments. The instrumental group, which at times was a full jazz band, accompanied the singer, played responses to the singer's lines, and also played instrumental choruses. A piano was loud

B. B. King in concert
Michael Ochs Archives/Venice, CA

enough to be used as a solo instrument, but an unamplified guitar did not project well enough (although some acoustic guitar solos were played on recordings). For that reason, the guitar was used primarily to strum rhythms until the invention of the electric guitar. Guitarist Floyd Smith and trombonist/guitarist Eddie Durham were pioneer electric guitarists who recorded solos in the thirties. Another jazz guitarist, Charlie Christian, further developed the innovations of Smith and Durham by playing melodic lines patterned after the solos of jazz horn players.

Urban blues guitarist Aaron Thibeaux Walker, nicknamed **T-Bone Walker** (1910–1975), was among the first musicians to use the electric guitar as a solo blues instrument. Born in Texas, Walker grew up playing country blues guitar in the style of Blind Lemon Jefferson, who was also from Texas. Jefferson played with the same casual approach to rhythm that delta singers like Robert Johnson had used, but his style differed in that the lines he played as fills between his vocal phrases were much longer and more complex than those of most delta guitarists. After years of playing both the blues and rhythm and blues, Walker grew away from his early rural roots and developed a flashy solo style in which he played highly embellished versions of the melody. He was a strong influence on both blues guitarist B. B. King and rock guitarist Chuck Berry.

B. B. King (born in 1925) came from Mississippi, the homeland of the delta blues. His very lyrical and expressive solo style was an important influence on many rock guitarists, including Eric Clapton, Jimmy Page, Jimi Hendrix, and Mike Bloomfield. King's initials, "B. B.," were derived from his nickname, "Blues Boy"; his real name was Riley B. King. An analysis of King's recording of "Three O'Clock Blues" (1951) showing the important elements of his playing, can be found on page 14.

It is helpful to compare the rhythmic informality of Robert Johnson to the formal regularity of the beat pattern and song structure of "Three O'Clock Blues" to hear the "urbanization" of the later style. Also, King's urban blues guitar style includes the playing of lines that are of equal importance to the lines he sings. Certainly no single recording could show all of B. B. King's abilities as either a guitarist or a singer. He has performed as featured soloist with jazz bands and groups of all sizes, as well as with large orchestral string sections playing arrangements of blues songs. He also performed with U2 in their 1988 movie *Rattle and Hum.* King's interest in playing melodic lines rather than chordal accompaniments was evident in that performance. Just before King went on stage with U2, he requested that "the Edge" take care of the chords. King's career continues on in the nineties with several new albums and even a performance on *Simpsons Sing the Blues* (1990). On the album *Blues Summit* (1993), King played a series of duets with John Lee Hooker, Lowell Fulson, and Robert Cray.

Although the urban blues was more complex than country blues, this style was not necessarily better. Rock musicians have taken advantage of both styles, drawing elements from the music of both the relatively untrained but tremendously expressive style of country blues artists and the musical sophistication of urban blues artists. Blues-based rock styles may differ greatly from each other, but this is proof that through the years the blues has remained a very adaptable and flexible music.

Listening Guide

"Three O'Clock Blues" as recorded by B. B. King (1951)

Tempo: The speed of the beat is slow (about 76 beats per minute), with four beats in each bar.

Form: Both the music and the text follow the classic twelve-bar blues form.

The recording starts with a four-bar guitar introduction, followed by four full choruses of the twelve-bar form, the third of which is instrumental with the guitar improvising on the harmonic progression.

Features: King sings and then plays guitar lines that function as a response to his vocal lines. (He plays the instrumental fills on the last seven beats of each section of the twelve-bar form.) The guitar lines imitate and expand on the vocal melody to which they respond and often use string bends to reach blue notes.

A chordal accompaniment is supplied by saxophones playing sustained (long held) notes. The drums are very soft (under-recorded?), with little or no accenting of the backbeat. A bit of urban sophistication in the arrangement is the occasional use of half-step slides into some of the main chords of the progression. Most of the time King slides down to the proper chord, but he reverses that and slides up to the tonic chord at the final cadence (ending).

Lyrics: The song is about a man who does not know where his woman friend is at three o'clock in the morning; he decides to go out and find his male friends instead of waiting around for her.

Source: *B. B. King Singin' the Blues/The Blues*, Flair Records/Virgin Records America 86296.

Chicago Blues

Other musicians whose recordings influenced the development of blues-style rock included John Lee Hooker, Muddy Waters, Elmore James, Sonny Boy Williamson No. 2, and Howlin' Wolf. All of these musicians were born in Mississippi and had originally played and sung in the delta blues style of Robert Johnson. But their work with other musicians in cities like Memphis, Detroit, and Chicago changed their music from rural and acoustic country blues to the amplified urban blues usually played by groups that included other instruments such as bass and drums.

Chess Recording Studios in Chicago must be given much credit for its recordings of the blues during the forties and fifties. The company was owned and run by two brothers, **Phil and Leonard Chess**, who had immigrated to the United States from Poland. Almost all of the blues artists discussed earlier were with the Chess label at one time or another, and while their styles were generally rural, country blues when they first came to Chicago, Chess gave them backup musicians and amplification that resulted in a more urban style. That combination of country blues and urban blues has often been called **Chicago blues.**

As one listens to music by the delta singers, one will notice that while many of their songs fit the twelve-bar form of the traditional blues described earlier, others avoided both the AAB lyrical structure and the prescribed chord progressions. Some songs had no more than a single chord throughout, but kept a general blues style by using other elements such as blue notes and uneven beat subdivisions. In other words, not every "blues-sounding" song played by a blues musician necessarily fit the formal structure of the twelve-bar blues. In order to aid the inexperienced listener's understanding of the basic differences between the sound of the twelve-bar structure (and some common variants) and the sound of the blues-style chant over a single chord, this section will conclude with some comments about the structure and other characteristics of a few representative songs by Chicago blues musicians, along with some information about their careers.

John Lee Hooker's (born in 1917) dramatic delta guitar style and deep, rich voice made him popular with many rock musicians. His twelve-bar blues song "Boom Boom" became a rock hit when recorded by a British group, the Animals, in 1965. Both recordings used a **break,** in which the instruments stopped playing during the vocal line and then responded by playing on the second, third, fourth, and first beats that followed. The break created an effective type of call-and-response that was used in other blues and blues-rock recordings as well. Other songs originally written and recorded by Hooker were also recorded by the Spencer Davis Group and by the later American blues revivalists Canned Heat and George Thorogood. Hooker was featured in the 1980 film *The Blues Brothers,* and he toured and recorded albums well into the eighties. On his album *The Healer* (1988) he was joined by Santana, Bonnie Raitt, Robert Cray, Canned Heat, Los Lobos, George Thorogood, and Charlie Musselwhite. Hooker has recorded several new albums, and collections of his old recordings have been released during the nineties. He stopped touring in 1995, but vowed to continue to sing and record for the rest of his life.

Although the origin of **Muddy Waters'** (1915–1983) stage name is not known for certain, popular legend has it that he was so called because he liked to "muddy" for fish (reach into water and catch fish with his hands) in a pond near his father's home in Rolling Fork, Mississippi. As a songwriter Muddy Waters used his real name, McKinley Morganfield. His style, which often included the whining sound of a bottleneck guitar, was rustic and was actually close to country blues in his early blues hits like "Rollin' Stone" (1948). That song was not a twelve-bar blues, but instead had only one chord played throughout, with the lyrics structured in eight-bar periods. Waters' bending of blue notes and relaxed flow of uneven beat subdivisions created a blues feel without the standard structure.

Although Muddy Waters began playing and singing in the rural delta blues style, his change to the electric guitar and the addition of a band that included Little Walter on blues harp, Jimmy Rodgers on guitar, and Waters' half-brother, Otis Spann, on piano shifted his sound from country blues to urban blues. It was for this latter style that he became best known. Waters never actually played rock and roll, but he often performed in rock concerts, including the Band's final concert in 1976 (subsequently made into the movie *The Last Waltz*) and a tour with Eric Clapton in 1979. Over the years Waters won many Grammy awards in the categories of "Best Ethnic" and "Best Traditional" recordings. He died in 1983 having spent over forty years performing and recording the blues.

Elmore James (1918–1963) claimed to have met and played with Robert Johnson who, James said, suggested that he try using a metal pipe to slide along the strings in much the same way that others were using a bottleneck. Like Muddy Waters, James eventually moved from Mississippi to Chicago to perform and record. Instead of just accompanying his singing with his own guitar as he had in the past, James took advantage of the availability of jazz musicians in Chicago and was among the first of the delta blues musicians to work regularly with groups including saxophone, piano, and drums. Through his work with those groups he gained a reputation as one of the early modernizers of the delta blues. While his groups gave his music a modern sound, his own guitar playing was an example of bottleneck country blues. Elmore James' recording of Robert Johnson's twelve-bar blues song "I Believe I'll Dust My Broom" exemplified that synthesis of urban and delta blues.

James' slide guitar style was copied by many rock guitarists, including British blues players Eric Clapton, Brian Jones (an original member of the Rolling Stones), and Jeremy Spencer (of the original Fleetwood Mac) and Americans Jimi Hendrix and Duane Allman. His lifestyle must have included Robert Johnson's fondness for women, because when James died of a heart attack in 1963 at age forty-five, six women claimed to have been married to him.

Blues harpist and singer **Sonny Boy Williamson No. 2** (Rice Miller, 1899–1965) was called "No. 2" because he actually stole the stage name of another blues singer, John Lee Williamson (Sonny Boy No. 1), in order to associate himself with Williamson's reputation before he gained one of his own. He toured Britain in 1963 and recorded live albums with the Yardbirds and the Animals. Because Williamson was willing to sit down and perform with the British groups at the very beginning of the blues revival, he had a great deal of influence in the development of their blues-styled playing. Dead of tuberculosis by 1965, he did not live to see how popular his rock musician disciples would make the blues among young people.

Chester Arthur Burnett originally called himself Big Foot Chester, but the wolf-like growls and howls that were part of his act earned him the name **Howlin' Wolf** (1910–1976). He played both the guitar and the harp, and claimed to have played with Robert Johnson, who influenced his guitar style, and with the original Sonny Boy Williamson, from whom he learned to play the harp. Burnett's aggressive, sometimes raunchy sound was not suited for the pop charts, but such recordings as "Little Red Rooster" (written by Willie Dixon) were often played by blues revivalists including the Rolling Stones. "Little Red Rooster" was a traditional twelve-bar blues, but many other recordings by Howlin' Wolf were not. "Smokestack Lightnin'," for example, was chanted over a single chord. His songs were also recorded by the British groups Cream, the Yardbirds, and Led Zeppelin, and in America by the Doors and the Electric Flag.

In 1972, Burnett (Howlin' Wolf took writer's credit under his real name) recorded the album *The London Sessions,* which included some of the rock musicians who had begun their careers playing his music—Eric Clapton, Steve Winwood, Bill Wyman, and Charlie Watts. After a long and successful career, Burnett died of kidney disease in 1976.

Willie Dixon (1915–1992) worked as a writer, producer, contractor, bass player, and occasional singer at the Chess Recording Studios in Chicago, but became better known as a blues songwriter than as a singer. He wrote many hits for others, including "You Shook Me" and "I Can't Quit You Baby," which have been recorded by many blues and blues-rock musicians. "You Shook Me" and another of his songs, "I'm Your Hoochie Coochie Man," represented a variant on the twelve-bar blues structure because both had an extra-long (eight-bar) first "A" section on each vocal chorus, followed by "A" and "B" sections of the usual four bars each, extending each full blues chorus to sixteen bars. "Little Red Rooster" and "I Can't Quit You Baby" followed the twelve-bar blues form. As a performer, Dixon played bass on many Chess recordings. He finally sang his own songs on recordings made during the seventies.

Classic Blues

Female singers were often the featured soloists in the jazz and blues bands found in the cities or on black

Willie Mae "Big Mama" Thornton
Michael Ochs Archives/Venice, CA

vaudeville tours, and their style of singing the blues (usually in strict twelve-bar form) was called **classic blues.** Two classic blues singers who served as inspiration for such later rock singers as Etta James, La Vern Baker, and Janis Joplin were Ma Rainey and Bessie Smith. **Ma Rainey** (born Gertrude Malissa Pridgett, 1886–1939) was sometimes called the Mother of the Blues because of her nickname, Ma (from Malissa), and also for her influence on singers who followed her. Rainey recorded with such jazz greats as Coleman Hawkins and Louis Armstrong, but much of her performing was done on tour with tent shows, in which she had to belt out over the sound of a band without the aid of amplification. Her style included gutsy moans, dramatic pauses, expressive bending of blue notes, and sliding from one melody note to the next. Rainey retired from touring in 1935 and succumbed to a heart attack four years later.

Bessie Smith (1894–1937) toured and performed with Ma Rainey—who was about ten years her senior—and was very much influenced by Rainey's singing style. Smith took Rainey's ideas about the bending of blue notes and the use of dramatic expression in her delivery beyond what Rainey herself had done, and eventually earned the title the Empress of the Blues. Smith was featured in the 1929 film *St. Louis Blues,* and throughout her career sang with such jazz pianists as Clarence Williams and Fletcher Henderson, swing bands led by Jack Teagarden and Benny Goodman, and, like Ma Rainey, with instrumental soloists Coleman Hawkins and Louis Armstrong. She was on a theater tour with a group called Broadway Rastus Review when she was in a car accident and died from her injuries.

The tradition of classic blues singers was continued by later rhythm and blues singers such as **Willie Mae "Big Mama" Thornton** (1926–1984). Like Ma Rainey and Bessie Smith before her, Thornton gained her first experiences as a performer by touring with a road show. She sang and danced with Sammy Green's Hot Harlem Revue in the forties, and in the early fifties she debuted at the Apollo Theater in New York as part of the Johnny Otis Rhythm and Blues Caravan. The song "Hound Dog," which was later a hit for Elvis Presley, was one of her biggest hits on the rhythm and blues charts in the fifties. Thornton was performing in several blues clubs in San Francisco when Janis Joplin moved there in the middle sixties, and Thornton's vocal style was a great influence on Joplin's own blues singing. One of Joplin's blues hits was the song "Ball and Chain," written and first recorded by Thornton. Both singers recorded and/or performed this song several times. The listening guides on page 17 are neither the first nor the last recordings either performer made, but are the most readily available and most representative of the style of each singer.

Listening Guide

	"Ball and Chain" as recorded by Willie Mae Thornton (January 1968)	***"Ball and Chain" as recorded by Janis Joplin (August 1968)***
Tempo:	The tempo is about 52 beats per minute, with four beats in each bar.	The tempo is about 56 beats per minute, with four beats in each bar.
Form:	The twelve-bar blues harmonic and lyrical form is followed throughout the recording.	The twelve-bar blues harmonic and lyrical form is followed throughout the recording.
	The recording begins with a four-bar instrumental introduction.	The recording begins with an instrumental chorus in twelve-bar blues form.
	The introduction is followed by four blues choruses with lyrics, the sound of which ends with a four-bar extension of a guitar solo.	The introductory chorus is followed by eight more choruses of the blues, the fifth of which is instrumental.
		The last chorus ends with an instrumental break with Joplin singing an out-of-tempo extension followed by a final chord from the instruments.
Features:	Uneven beat subdivisions are used throughout the recording.	Uneven beat subdivisions are used throughout the recording.
	The drummer keeps a strong backbeat.	The drummer keeps a strong backbeat.
	Thornton's vocal lines are responded to by fills played on electric guitar.	Joplin's vocal lines are not responded to by instrumental lines. The instruments simply maintain the accompaniment pattern to complete each four-bar phrase.
	The guitar solos are linear, in a style influenced by B. B. King.	The guitar solos use many repeated notes and riffs with much fuzztone and other distortion in a style influenced by Jimi Hendrix.
	An instrumental break allows Thornton to vocalize alone during the second bar and part of the third bar of her fourth chorus.	Many instrumental breaks are used throughout the recording. The dynamic level varies greatly from very loud and distorted use of instruments to a chorus where the guitars drop out and leave Joplin's vocals to be accompanied only by subdued bass and minimal use of the drums.
	The instruments used in the recording are guitar, tenor saxophone, piano, bass, and drums.	The instruments used in the recording are two guitars, bass, and drums.
Lyrics:	The singer cannot stop loving someone who has treated her badly. She feels that her love has her tied as if she were controlled by a ball and chain in prison.	The lyrics are based on those in Thornton's original version of the song. Joplin's minor changes do not alter the meaning of the song.

Source: Thornton's recording: *Big Mama Thornton—Ball N' Chain,* Arhoolie 305.

Joplin's recording: *Cheap Thrills,* Big Brother & the Holding Company, Columbia 9700. (The recording on *Janis Joplin's Greatest Hits* is somewhat different from the one used here.)

Bo Diddley
Michael Ochs Archives/Venice, CA

Rhythm and Blues

The blues might not have had as great an impact on the development of rock music of the fifties and sixties had it not been for the tremendous popularity of a related style, **rhythm and blues.** Called "race music" until the end of the forties, rhythm and blues was a type of rhythmic dance music in which every second and fourth beat of each four-beat bar was accented. Because it was more common in other styles of music to accent the first and third beats of each bar, that stress on the "off" beats was called a **backbeat.** The backbeat was used in the blues, but it became more obvious and important in rhythm and blues.

Whereas the blues developed as music reflective of the problems of African American life, rhythm and blues was a dance music that expressed the enjoyment of life. It originated in the African American ghettos of large cities and was played by organized, rehearsed groups that included a variety of instruments. These groups put on energetic stage shows in which saxophone players often swiveled their hips, lowered themselves to the floor (or into the audience), and rolled around on their backs while playing. Singers shouted out their often suggestive lyrics while maintaining a high level of physical activity. This excitement and energy, as well as the rhythm and backbeat of rhythm and blues, formed the very basis of much fifties rock and roll.

During the late thirties and through the forties, **Louis Jordan** (1908–1975) played alto saxophone and clarinet in various large jazz bands and finally formed his own band, Louis Jordan and His Tympany Five. His group often played big theaters like the Apollo in New York and the Regal in Chicago, and through these performances he gained a following as much for his sense of humor as for his musical ability. Jordan called his rhythmic style of playing the blues "shuffle boogie" or "jumpin' jive," and his group was often described as a "jump band." His music was so danceably rhythmic, his stage personality so engaging, and his songs so full of humor that his records were as popular with whites as they were with African Americans. Having heard and liked Jordan's jump band, white rock musicians such as Bill Haley imitated its shuffle beat in the early fifties. Newer tributes to Jordan's popular appeal include the rerecording of some of his songs on Joe Jackson's album *Jumpin' Jive* (1981) as well as the musical revue *Five Guys Named Moe* that opened in London in 1990 and then moved on to Broadway in New York.

Bo Diddley, born Ellas Bates in 1928, strummed his guitar in a constantly throbbing, rhythmic style that sounded almost as if he were playing drums. His name was legally changed to Ellas McDaniel by the adoptive parents who raised him, and he used that name as a songwriter. He studied the violin for a time before he decided to change to the guitar, an instrument that was more acceptable to the other kinds in his rough Chicago neighborhood. Many stories have been told about the source of his stage name, but he claimed that his friends gave it to him back when he was a boxer, because of his originality in coming up with new fighting tricks. It was quite possible that his friends chose Bo Diddley after the diddley-bow, a single-stringed instrument of African origin that was played by African Americans in the South.

Bo Diddley's strongly rhythmic style was rock-oriented, although it was considered rhythm and blues during the fifties. He was very influential on American rock musicians during the fifties, and was copied by British blues-revival rock groups of the sixties in their covers of his songs as well as in their own material. The Yardbirds did his "I'm a Man"; the Rolling Stones, his "Mona"; and the Animals, his "Bo Diddley." None of these three songs were in the blues form; in fact, both "Mona" and "Bo Diddley" were based on a single chord throughout. In both of these songs, Diddley used a bottleneck to slide up and down between the fifth and seventh frets on his guitar, giving the effect of more chord changes during breaks in the melody. "I'm a Man" used a modified form of an instrumental break that was also common in the blues. The harp and piano break (stop playing) during the vocals, but the drums and maracas continue throughout the song, repeating the characteristic rhythm known as the "Bo Diddley beat," which is notated in the next listening guide. Of course Bo Diddley was not the first musician to ever play this beat pattern, but it has taken his name because of the characteristic energy with which he strummed it and the fact that he popularized it.

The Bo Diddley beat has been used in many rock songs, including Buddy Holly's "Not Fade Away," Johnny

Listening Guide

"Bo Diddley"
as recorded by Bo Diddley (1955)

Tempo: The tempo is approximately 104 beats per minute, with four beats in each bar.

Form: The recording begins with four bars of instrumental introduction that establish the beat pattern that will repeat throughout the rest of the song.

The form is based on a series or chain of two-bar phrases, at least in the sections that have vocals. In those sections the first bar of the phrase is sung and the second repeats the instrumental pattern established in the introduction. The sections that begin with the vocal melody used just after the introduction vary in length; the first is seventeen bars, the second is twenty-four bars and the third is nineteen bars. There seems to be no set pattern to the number of bars the instrumental rhythm pattern is repeated.

Features: Even beat subdivisions are maintained by the maracas.

There is no stress on the backbeat other than the fact that the second and fourth beats are played as part of the basic Bo Diddley beat that is followed throughout the recording.

The Bo Diddley beat is notated as follows:

Along with this basic beat there are other beat patterns that, at times, create an almost polyrhythmic effect. Most of the variants make changes in the second beat of the four-beat pattern, maintaining the stress on beat one, the second half of beat three, and on beat four.

After the sections with vocals, the repetitions of instrumental bars are colored by rhythmic strums on the guitar stopped by a bottleneck on the seventh, the fifth, and then the seventh frets.

Lyrics: The lyrics make humorous and seemingly casual references to Bo Diddley's life and dealings with various people and situations.

Source: Time-Life Music, *The Rock 'N' Roll Era, 1954–1955;* and *Bo Diddley—His Greatest Sides, Volume 1,* Chess Records 9106.

Otis' "Willie and the Hand Jive," the Who's "Magic Bus," Bruce Springsteen's "She's the One," U2's "Desire," and the Pretenders' "Cuban Slide." In addition to covering Diddley's recordings, the Animals also recorded a tribute to him they called "The Story of Bo Diddley," in which they gave Diddley much of the credit for starting rock and roll. Bo Diddley himself was still performing, writing, and recording in the nineties, and the influence of his rhythmic, blues-based style was also apparent in the music of younger blues musicians including George Thorogood.

Blues- and Rhythm-and-Blues-Based Rock of the Fifties

T-Bone Walker, Louis Jordan, Bo Diddley, and Professor Longhair had hits on the rhythm and blues charts during the fifties, but few on the pop charts because recordings by African American musicians did not generally attain any great degree of popularity with the white pop music audiences of the time. Part of the reason was that the general white audience responded to a sound more closely related to white country or pop music, and part lay in the racist attitudes common among many whites during the fifties. Whatever the specific reasons, as the danceable rhythm and backbeat of rhythm and blues grew in popularity, many white musicians rerecorded songs originally performed by African American musicians. These versions were called **cover recordings,** or covers. When covers of blues songs were made by musicians with backgrounds in country or pop music, various changes occurred, creating a sound that was not exactly blues, rhythm and blues, country, or pop but rather a synthesis of all of them. This new style was soon named rock and roll, and some of these cover recordings became the biggest rock and pop hits of the time.

Along with the popularity of cover recordings, however, some African American musicians with backgrounds in the blues or rhythm and blues managed to break through the racial barrier and have hits of their own on the pop charts. Among them were Fats Domino, Lloyd Price, Chuck Berry, and Little Richard. In addition to being popular for the sound of their music, these artists also attracted audiences through the drive and enthusiasm of their performances and the appeal of their personalities on stage.

One of the most important rhythm and blues pianists to influence rock and roll was New Orleans' **Professor Longhair** (Henry Roeland Byrd, 1918–1980), whose rollicking boogie-woogie bass lines became essential elements in the rock styles of Fats Domino, Huey "Piano" Smith, Dr. John (Malcolm "Mac" Rebennack), and Allen Toussaint, to name only a few. **Boogie-woogie,** a spirited and rhythmic piano style developed by African Americans in the South during the twenties and copied by many white performers, eventually became basic to most rock piano styles from both blues and country roots. In boogie-woogie, the pianist's left hand played a fast, repeated note pattern with two notes played in the time of each single beat. Its effect was that of doubling the basic beat, creating a fast, motoristic, rhythmic drive. Some common boogie-woogie piano patterns are notated as follows:

These examples are notated in even note values, but they were also often played in a shuffle beat pattern. Over these left-hand bass patterns, the right hand often played short bits of melody (called **riffs** when repeated several times). Boogie-woogie most often employed the classic twelve-bar blues harmonic form. However, Professor Longhair also used pop song forms for some of his songs; his rhythm and blues hit from 1949, "Bald Head" is an example of this. In addition to his own successes and his influences on others, Longhair's music continues to be remembered in his hometown when his "Mardi Gras in New Orleans" is played every year as the famous Mardi Gras carnival's theme song.

Fats Domino (born in 1929) had recorded several hits on the rhythm and blues charts before his 1955 entry onto the pop charts with "Ain't That a Shame." Fats Domino's real name was Antoine Domino, the name "Fats" being given to him as a description of his girth. He was born in New Orleans, a center for jazz since before the turn of the century. In the mid-forties he met trumpet player and bandleader Dave Bartholomew, who became his producer and co-songwriter. Whether Domino was playing the slow, smooth rhythms of "Blueberry Hill," or the rollicking boogie-woogie style of "I'm Walkin'" (both 1956), his friendly, somewhat understated voice was backed by the honking saxophones in Bartholomew's backup band. Domino had a very long and successful career and was still performing in the eighties. Some basic musical characteristics of Fats Domino's style can be heard in his recording of "I'm Walkin'," for which a listening guide follows on page 21. For twenty-five years, Fats Domino enjoyed family life in his comfortable New Orleans home, only performing occasionally. He revived his recording career with the release of *Christmas Is a Special Day* in 1993.

Fats Domino was only one of many important rhythm-and-blues-influenced rock musicians who came from New Orleans during the fifties. Others included Roy Brown, the duo Shirley and Lee (Shirley Goodman and Leonard Lee), and Lloyd Price. **Roy Brown** (1925– 1981), a blues singer and writer, was more important for his influence on others than for his own hit recordings. His jump blues vocals were backed by

Fats Domino
Michael Ochs Archives/Venice, CA

Listening Guide

"I'm Walkin'" as recorded by Fats Domino (1956)

Tempo: The tempo is approximately 224 beats per minute, with four beats in each bar.

Form: A four-bar introduction alternates drum thumps on beats one and three with a hand-clapped backbeat.

The musical form is a standard **pop song form** (AABA) in which each A and B period is eight bars long. After a full AABA section with lyrics, an instrumental section follows the same AABA format, and this is followed by another AABA section with lyrics. The ending begins another repetition of the form, but fades out during the second A.

Features: Beat subdivisions are uneven, in a shuffle beat pattern.

The backbeat that was introduced by hand claps continues to be clapped, but is also supported by drums once the vocals begin.

Through each A period, the bass repeats a two-bar melodic pattern (in octaves with the guitar) that is notated as follows:

The instrumental section features a growl-toned tenor saxophone solo improvised around the melody of the vocal line.

Lyrics: The song is about a man who is walking, thinking about his loneliness without his girlfriend, and hoping she will return to him. In each B period of vocals, he reminds her that she is bound to run out of other men and will want to come back. In the first B he says that he will take her back, but in the second he warns her that he might not.

Source: Time-Life Music, *The Rock 'N' Roll Era, 1957;* and *Fats Domino's Greatest Hits*, MCA Records 6170.

his jazz-influenced band, the Mighty Men. In 1947 he wrote and recorded "Good Rocking Tonight," which was later covered by Wynonie "Blues" Harris, Elvis Presley, and even Robert Plant's group, the Honeydrippers (the Honeydrippers called it "Rockin' at Midnight"). Like Fats Domino, **Shirley and Lee** (Shirley Goodman, born in 1936, Leonard Lee, 1935–1976) worked with producer Dave Bartholomew. Many of their songs, like "Let the Good Times Roll" (1956) and "I Feel Good" (1957), were presented to fans as if they had been written about the duo's own relationship. **Lloyd Price** (born in 1934) was influenced as much by gospel as by rhythm and blues. His voice used the embellishments common in black gospel singing, and his recordings of "Stagger Lee" and "Personality" (both 1959) had a responding vocal group behind him. The shuffle rhythm used by jump blues bands before him was evident in "Personality."

Humor was not lacking in New Orleans rhythm-and-blues-style rock music. **Huey "Piano" Smith** (born in 1934) played with a rollicking boogie-woogie-based piano style on "Rockin' Pneumonia and the Boogie Woogie Flu" (1957), recorded with his regular vocal group, the Clowns. Smith and the Clowns acted out a lighthearted comedy routine as part of their stage show, and many of their recordings used a form of call-and-response in which various group members took turns singing lead. Another singer, **Ernie K-Doe** (Ernest Kador, Jr., born in 1936), made fun of one of the most common butts of humor in his hit, "Mother-in-Law" (1961). This and many other lighthearted dance songs from New Orleans in the early sixties were written and produced by **Allen Toussaint** (born in 1938), a keyboard player who worked in the studio with Fats Domino and Dave Bartholomew during the fifties and recorded his own debut album, *The Wild Sounds of New Orleans by Tousan,* in 1958. In the nineties, one might still be able to catch performances by Lloyd Price, Ernie K-Doe, or Allen Toussaint on a visit to New Orleans' clubs as they continue to perform the music they love.

An important and influential rock singer and pianist in the rhythm-and-blues-based rock style of the fifties was Richard Penniman. Born in Macon, Georgia, he began performing at a fairly young age and became known as **Little Richard** (born in 1935). Little Richard first learned to play the piano at his church, where he also sang gospel music and learned to use such gospel characteristics as vocal slides and embellishments (gospel vocal techniques will be discussed further in Chapter 4, The Gospel Roots of Rock Music). These influences remained with him and were used along with the shrieks and moans of his later jump-blues-influenced rock style.

Little Richard wrote (or co-wrote), played piano, and sang on his recordings, which included "Tutti-Frutti," "Long Tall Sally," and "Good Golly, Miss Molly." His piano playing usually had a boogie-woogie bass with chords pounded out above it, but it was the fast tempos and high energy level that made Little Richard's style stand out from that of other jump blues musicians. Sex was his favorite textual subject, and he teased his

Little Richard and his band during the fifties
Michael Ochs Archives/Venice, CA

audiences with his androgynous hairstyle and heavy facial makeup while singing songs with sometimes shockingly graphic or suggestive lyrics. He recorded "Good Golly, Miss Molly" in 1957, and in that year, at the height of his success, Little Richard quit rock and roll to become a preacher. He appeared in England in 1962 on the same bill as the Beatles, who covered some of his hits with Paul McCartney imitating his dramatic vocal style, and in 1964 he attempted a comeback in America. After that, he continued to do occasional rock shows, but devoted most of his time to religious work. An analysis of Little Richard's recording of "Long Tall Sally" can be found on page 23.

The use of **stop time** in the instrumental parts of "Long Tall Sally" gave the melody a rhythmic punch that has often been used in the blues, rhythm and blues, and blues-based rock music. As is clear in Little Richard's recording, stop time is different from the instrumental breaks in John Lee Hooker's "Boom Boom," discussed earlier (and in Chuck Berry's "School Day," the next listening example), because stop time is a break in which the instruments occasionally reenter with a short chord or note to punctuate the rhythm of the vocal line.

After years of vacillating between rock and religion, Little Richard returned to rock recording in 1986 with a new style he called "message music." The music to such "message" songs as "Great Gosh Almighty" (1986) still maintained the energy of Little Richard's fifties rock style, but he abandoned his androgynous image for that of a dancing preacher. This return to performing included television commercials and acting roles in several movies, including *Down and Out in Beverly Hills.*

In 1988 Little Richard gave tribute to Leadbelly (Huddie Ledbetter) by recording Leadbelly's "Rock Island Line" on the album *A Vision Shared—A Tribute to Woody Guthrie and Leadbelly.* From that, Little Richard went on to reach what may have been his youngest audience yet by donating to the Pediatric AIDS Foundation with his performance of "Itsy, Bitsy Spider" on Disney's *For Our Children* (1990) as well as the Disney album *Shake It All About* (1992). The National Academy of Recording Arts and Sciences honored him with a Lifetime Achievement Award in 1993.

Chuck Berry doing his "duckwalk"
Michael Ochs Archives/Venice, CA

Chuck Berry (born in 1926) was a guitarist and singer whose style was rooted in blues and rhythm and blues, but whose music was unquestionably rock and roll. He even defined rock's style and its essential backbeat in both his playing and his lyrics in the 1957 hit "Rock and Roll Music." Berry was born in St. Louis and started playing the guitar as a teenager. The greatest influences on his guitar style were T-Bone Walker and Muddy Waters (whom he met in Chicago in 1955), but his singing style clearly showed the influence of any of a number of white country and western singers. It was partly the fact that he derived his sound from both blues and country roots that made it neither of those, but instead their fusion—rock and roll.

Chuck Berry wrote most of his own material, and he both sang and played lead guitar on his recordings. His performances were electrifying, often including his famous "duckwalk" (in which he walked across the stage with his knees bent, moving his head forward and back). In his guitar solos, Berry would take a short riff and, with each repetition, dig into the notes more and more to increase the intensity of the sound, creating a rhythm with his melody that soon became a standard rock-guitar sound. He is sometimes referred to as the Father of Rock Guitar because of

Listening Guide

"Long Tall Sally"
as recorded by Little Richard (1956)

Tempo: The tempo is about 176 beats per minute, with four beats per bar.

Form: The musical form of the twelve-bar blues is followed, but, as was generally the case with blues recordings made by rock musicians, the text does not repeat the A section of the poetic form.

The recording has eight full choruses of the blues form.

Features: A shuffle beat rhythmic pattern is played by the piano.

The first, second, sixth, and seventh choruses begin with a four-bar instrumental device called stop-time. These are not complete breaks for the instruments; rather, the instruments play a single chord on the first beat of each of the first three bars, and then break for the rest of those bars and the entire fourth bar so the vocal line can be heard alone.

The third, fourth, and fifth choruses are strictly instrumental, with a tenor saxophonist playing an improvised solo employing a "growl" in his tone, effectively imitating Little Richard's rough vocal style.

The eighth chorus is sung and does not use the stop time instrumental beginning.

Lyrics: The lyrics hint at sexual activities, but in this case not so clearly as to horrify radio listeners. The intention was to excite teenagers who might want to guess who or what "Long Tall Sally" was, and what Uncle John was doing that he had to hide from Aunt Mary.

Source: Time-Life Music, *The Rock 'N' Roll Era, 1956;* Time-Life Music, *Solid Gold Soul, 1956;* and *Little Richard's Grooviest 17 Original Hits,* Specialty 2113.

Listening Guide

"School Day"
as recorded by Chuck Berry (1957)

Tempo: The tempo is about 148 beats per minute, with four beats per bar.

Form: The musical form of the twelve-bar blues is followed, but the text does not have the A-section repetition of the blues poetic form.

The recording has seven full choruses of the twelve-bar blues form, the fifth chorus being a guitar solo.

Features: The beats have uneven subdivisions. The drums and the guitar fills play with this shuffle beat.

The bass plays chord roots on the basic beats.

The backbeat is accented, but minimally.

The guitar fills often imitate the vocal line they follow.

With the exception of the fifth (which is instrumental), each chorus ends with a three-beat break in which the instruments stop and the voice sings words that introduce the next chorus. (The first chorus of the form actually begins with the word "school.")

The piano plays a subtle rhythmic background in a slower triplet pattern called a "hemiola" that is half the speed of the rhythm played by the guitar and drums. The effect of this is very interesting musically. It is most obvious behind the guitar solo in the fifth chorus.

Lyrics: The song is about the burden and drudgery of school, which teenagers can only endure knowing that once school lets out for the day they can enjoy their freedom by dancing to rock and roll music.

Source: Time-Life Music, *The Rock 'N' Roll Era, 1957,* and *Chuck Berry—The Great Twenty-Eight,* Chess 92500.

the great number of guitarists, including Buddy Holly, George Harrison, Keith Richards, and Carl Wilson, who have either copied his style or been greatly influenced by it. An analysis of one of his hit recordings follows on page 23.

Not all of Chuck Berry's hit recordings followed the classic blues form, but the blues practice of a vocal call followed by an instrumental response, as heard in "School Day," remained an important element of his style. His use of riffs in his solos was based on the way T-Bone Walker had employed riffs, and he even quoted Walker in some solos. Berry's energetic rhythms came, at least in part, out of Louis Jordan's jumpin' jive.

Berry's energetic music was overshadowed by the popularity of teen idols and girl groups of the late fifties and early sixties. In addition his career suffered when, late in 1959, he was charged with a violation of the Mann Act (transportation of an underaged woman across a state border for immoral purposes). He went through two trials, resulting in a prison term that lasted from early 1962 to early 1964. When he was released and was ready to record again, Berry was able to make a comeback. His mid-sixties style picked up right where his earlier recordings had left off—"No Particular Place to Go" (1964), for example, was strikingly similar to "School Day" (1957). Berry's influence on rock musicians was not forgotten, and some of them, including Eric Clapton and Keith Richards, joined him in the concert celebration of his sixtieth birthday in 1986 and the documentary film made at that concert, *Hail, Hail Rock 'n' Roll.* Tangles with the Internal Revenue Service and various other legal problems have plagued Berry in recent years, causing him to perform somewhat less than he had earlier. It still is possible to catch a chance to see him in a live performance from time to time.

Throughout the history of rock music there have been periodic revivals of the blues. In some cases those revivals have seen a return to the pure blues form and style of the Chicago-based guitarist/singers of the forties and fifties such as Muddy Waters, Elmore James, and Howlin' Wolf. In other instances they have been recreations of the fifties blues-rock style developed by Chuck Berry and Little Richard. Some of the revivals have led to the development of new styles of rock music. The sixties blues revival led Jimi Hendrix and others from the influence of the older blues artists to the beginnings of heavy metal, and led the Allman Brothers Band and others into the development of southern rock. The blues was again revived in the eighties by guitarist/singers Johnny and Edgar Winter, George Thorogood, Stevie Ray Vaughan, and Robert Cray.

Summary

The blues was performed by African Americans living in the rural areas of the southern United States around the beginning of the twentieth century. In its earliest form, country blues music was used to express the longings of people whose lives were generally very difficult. West African influences on the development of the blues included the use of polyrhythms and blue notes, and the practice of call-and-response between a leader and a group. European musical traditions such as a regular four-beat pattern in each bar, a repeating and contrasting AAB lyrical scheme, and a twelve-bar chord progression also became elements of the blues.

During the early years of the development of recording technology, blues musicians began moving to larger cities and working with organized jazz bands. The results were two very complex and sophisticated styles: classic blues, sung primarily by female blues singers backed by bands, and urban blues, in which instrumental styles developed to the point where the guitar moved beyond its earlier role as an accompaniment instrument to that of a solo instrument.

Rhythm and blues made use of blue notes and other musical characteristics of the blues, but did not usually follow the twelve-bar blues form. It was intended as lighthearted entertainment rather than as a reflection of the difficulties of day-to-day living. Often used as dance music, rhythm and blues shared a type of formalism with urban blues because it was usually performed by groups of musicians playing written or memorized arrangements, and yet the performances were wild and full of sexual innuendo. Both the blatant sexuality and the backbeat of rhythm and blues became basic characteristics of rock music.

Rock music of the fifties included several different styles, all of which were related in some way to the blues and/or rhythm and blues. Some early rock music had originally been blues or rhythm and blues, but became rock when covered by country musicians who sped up the tempos and added their solo styles to the rhythm and blues beat. Other rock music was played or sung by musicians with backgrounds in boogie-woogie or jump blues piano, and it made use of a variety of vocal practices and techniques that had their origins in Black gospel music. The amount of influence the blues had on any one particular rock song of the fifties depended on the background of its writer and performer, but no rock music existed that did not owe at least some debt to the blues.

Terms to Remember

Backbeat
Beat subdivisions (even and uneven)
Bebop
Blue notes
Blues harp
Boogie-woogie
Bottlenecks
Break
Call-and-response
Chicago blues
Classic blues
Country blues
Cover recordings
Cross-harp playing
Delta blues
Dominant chord
Flamenco
Griots
Pentatonic scales
Polyrhythm
Pop song form
Rhythm and blues
Riffs
Seventh chord
Shuffle beat
Stop time
String bending
Subdominant chord
Tonic chord
Twelve-bar blues
Urban blues

CHAPTER 3

The Country Roots of Rock Music

From the seventeenth through the nineteenth centuries, large numbers of settlers from the British Isles made their way to the mountainous regions of what is now the southern and southwestern United States, bringing with them many centuries of rich musical traditions that they maintained as cultural links with the Old World. Their dance music included simple rhythmic dances such as the jig, the reel, the polka, the waltz, and various types of round dances. Their vocal music included hymns and folk ballads as well as other types of songs. Much of their dance music was played by a fiddle, a folk term for the violin dating back to a medieval European bowed-string instrument, the *fidula* or *fidel.* The British settlers sang their songs either unaccompanied or backed with instruments such as the guitar, the plucked and strummed dulcimers, the piano, and later the harmonica. African Americans in the South developed the banjo out of an African instrument, the *banza,* and it was adopted by the white players of British-derived folk music around the time of the Civil War. By the end of the thirties, instruments such as the string bass, the steel guitar, and the autoharp had also come into common use in Southern folk music.

With the growing importance of radio and the developments in recording technology in the twenties, the folk music of the South came to be called "hillbilly" music as it was brought to the attention of the rest of the country. It was not long before radio stations were springing up across the country, bringing live music broadcasts into homes and gathering places. One of the most popular types of radio programs, the barn dance show, featured live performances of rural dance music for which people collected in barns or other large buildings to dance. *The WSM Barn Dance* (WSM were the radio station's call letters) was first broadcast in 1925, and its name was changed to the *Grand Ole Opry* as a playful commentary on the classical operatic program that preceded it.

Country Styles That Have Influenced Rock Music

Hillbilly music developed into several different musical styles. During the twenties, a style called **western swing** originated in Texas. Its origins lay in the music played by fiddle-and-guitar barn dance bands, which gradually adopted characteristics of African American blues and jazz. From the blues, western swing bands took some of their songs or instrumental works, borrowing the twelve-bar blues form and using blue notes in melodies. From jazz they took syncopated rhythms, instruments commonly used in jazz such as the saxophone, and improvisational practices in which individual musicians took turns playing solos. From both the blues and jazz, western swing bands borrowed the typical uneven beat subdivisions and the stress on the backbeat. Western swing was one of the few hillbilly styles that used drums, which were usually avoided in most country styles partly because of their association with African American music. In Texas, the king of western swing was fiddler Bob Wills (1905–1975), who led the Texas Playboys. Another fiddler, Spade Cooley (Donnell Clyde Cooley, 1910–1969), popularized the style in California. Both western swing and another blues-influenced country style called hillbilly boogie became important in the development of rock and roll through the music of Bill Haley.

During the forties, **hillbilly boogie** was the most rock-oriented of all proto-rock country styles because it used a combination of African American boogie-woogie rhythms and country music. It was imitated by Bill Haley in his early rock recordings, and it also influenced the development of rockabilly, particularly the piano style of Jerry Lee Lewis. Bands such as the Maddox Brothers and Rose (four brothers and their sister) not only used a boogie-woogie beat, but also used electric guitars on their recordings of "Rootie Tootie" (1946) and "Mama Says It's Naughty" (1949). Other hillbilly boogie performers of the forties included the Delmore Brothers and Clyde "Red" Foley.

Bluegrass was a style of hillbilly music that grew out of the music played by string bands (composed of fiddle and guitar and/or banjo) that performed at barn dances in the twenties. When standardized, the bluegrass groups featured four to seven musicians, including a rhythm section of guitar and string bass, and a combination of melody instruments including **five-string banjo** and any combination of fiddle, mandolin, **dobro** (unamplified steel guitar), and/or another guitar; they rarely used drums. Group vocals in which a high voice sang above the melody and other voices harmonized below were common in bluegrass. The melody instruments sometimes alternated solos with one another or with the vocals, but they would also improvise at the same time, resulting in a rather complex texture.

Bluegrass tempos were usually quite fast. Despite the fact that songs like "Blue Moon of Kentucky" by bluegrass star Bill Monroe (1911–1996) were recorded by rock musicians (Elvis Presley in 1954), the musical characteristics of bluegrass were not important in the development of the rock and roll of the fifties. However, its influence was very important in the music of many later folk-rock, country-rock, and southern-rock groups like the Byrds, the Eagles, and the Charlie Daniels Band.

A **honky-tonk** was a bar or saloon, often found outside the limits of "dry" towns (towns that prohibited alcoholic beverages). The honky-tonk atmosphere was one of boisterous, noisy camaraderie, and for that reason it was not the place for unamplified music like that played by bluegrass groups, or, for that matter, any groups with the slightest bit of subtlety in their style. The music in honky-tonks had to be loud (therefore amplified) and had to have a steady, danceable beat. Honky-tonk pianists played with a strong beat and rollicking boogie-woogie bass patterns. Honky-tonk song themes often stressed depression over a lost job or an untrue lover. Ernest Tubb (born in 1914 and also known as the Texas Troubadour), George Jones (born in 1931), and Hank Williams, Sr. (1923–1953) were all popular honky-tonk singers and writers. John Fogerty revived Hank Williams' honky-tonk style with his Blue Ridge Rangers' hit "Jambalaya (On the Bayou)" in 1973.

The use of amplified guitar, bass, and drums in honky-tonks influenced the development of the rockabilly styles of Elvis Presley, Eddie Cochran, and Gene Vincent during the mid-fifties, and Jerry Lee Lewis took his rockabilly piano style from the music of honky-tonk pianists.

Country music of the fifties existed in all of the styles just discussed, but descriptions are, of course, only of value in addition to (and not in place of) listening to examples of each style. What follows is an attempt to guide the listener's ear to those general elements of country music that influenced the rock and roll played by country musicians.

1. The beat is very steady and all musicians play exactly on that beat. Other styles of music have a steadiness to the beat, but musicians often play slightly "behind" it, thereby relaxing within that beat. Pure country style is based on a crisp, exact beat.
2. The beats are patterned with either four, two, or three beats per bar (four is standard in rock).
3. Four-beat patterns have even subdivisions. Even subdivisions have a "boom-chunk" feel, or to refer to music notation, an even eighth-note flow.
4. The harmonies are usually **triadic** (triads are simple three-note chords with no added sevenths).
5. Most of the music follows a repeating pattern of **eight-bar periods**, each composed of two **four-bar phrases**. The blues form is also often used.
6. The bass often plays the root of the chord on beat one and the fifth of the chord on beat three in a four-beat pattern, creating a regular alternation between those notes called **two-beat bass**.
7. Song lyrics often tell stories or are intended to express the singer's feelings about some person, event, or political issue, and they are meant to be heard over the accompaniment.
8. Vocals often have a nasal tone quality and are sung with either a deadpan style of delivery or with an intensity that gives the impression that the singer is on the verge of tears.
9. Hillbilly vocal duos often sing the melody below a high, slower-moving part. Vocal trios add another low part, and quartets another below that.

Hank Williams
Bettmann Archive

10. Except for the bass, which usually slaps down exactly on the beat, voices and instruments often slide from note to note. The steel guitar is played with a bar and pedals that can bend entire chords, not just single notes.

Any number of country recordings from the early fifties would serve as examples of most of the musical elements listed above, but one by the late, great **Hank Williams, Sr.** certainly deserves some attention. "I'll Never Get Out of This World Alive" was a number-one hit on the country charts in 1952. Williams was only twenty-eight years old when he recorded the song, but problems in his personal life and a dependency on painkillers and alcohol brought on his untimely death by heart attack only one year later.

Blues and Rhythm and Blues Played by Country Musicians

As rhythm and blues grew in popularity among white teenagers, country musicians began to cover blues and rhythm and blues recordings; likewise, blues or rhythm and blues musicians began to cover country recordings. As the styles were combined in various ways through the late forties and early fifties, rock and

Listening Guide

"I'll Never Get Out of This World Alive" as recorded by Hank Williams (1952)

Tempo: The tempo is approximately 118 beats per minute, with four beats per bar.

Form: Two fiddles play a two-bar introduction with three eighth-note **pickups.**

The musical form is that of a standard pop song form (AABA) in which each A and B period is eight bars long. The first full AABA section has vocals on each period, but the first two A sections in the next are instrumental followed by a B and another A with vocals. The recording ends with a two-bar extension.

Features: The beats are very steady, but a western swing feel is created by uneven beat subdivisions.

A string bass is played in a two-beat bass pattern alternating chordal notes on beats one and three of each four-beat bar.

Acoustic rhythm guitar accents the backbeats.

The steel guitar and a pair of fiddles alternate four-bar sections during the two instrumental A's. They often slide from one note to another.

Drums provide a very subtle support to the beat played by the other instruments.

The harmonies are simple and triadic with few additions of sevenths.

Williams' voice has a nasal tone quality and he occasionally ends words with hiccup-like slides away from the pitch, giving the impression that he is about to cry.

Lyrics: The singer gives many examples of how poor, depressed, and downhearted he is about his life. So many of the examples are, or are close to, impossible that a sense of humor emerges through the tears.

Source: *Hank Williams: Alone and Forsaken,* Mercury 697-124 057.

Cover Records

A cover record is a recording by anyone other than the songwriter, usually one that is recorded after the original recording, but it can be a first recording of a song that the writer has had someone else record. In the fifties the practice of white groups covering black blues or rhythm and blues records was very common, although race was not always a factor. Just about anyone who thought they could make a record that would sell covered whatever song they wanted, and sometimes more than one version of the same song would make the charts at the same or close to the same time. As long as the writer's credit on the cover record was given to the original writer, the writer could not prevent the cover from being made or have any control over changes that might be made in the music or lyrics. The writer did, and still does, however, receive the royalty income generated by the performances of the cover, so many writers benefitted from the fact that they wrote songs that became hits when performed by others.

Songwriters have the right to control the first recording of their songs. They can also have some controls over the use of their work if their publication contracts state that they maintain the right to approve of the use of their song in a movie or commercial. As will be seen in many examples of rock music, covers often change lyrics, completely change vocal or production styles, and even change the basic beat or meter of the song. Yet at other times, covers obviously imitate the production style of the original recording. Either way, the performers of the covers have the right to record or perform the song any way they choose.

Of course, attempts have been made to sue parties who made covers that the copyright owners did not like. In the early nineties, the Acuff-Rose Publishing Company sued 2 Live Crew over their parody cover of Roy Orbison's "Oh, Pretty Woman," which 2 Live Crew called "Bald-Headed Woman." Acuff-Rose claimed that the cover denigrated the value of Orbison's song. After several court cases and appeals, the Supreme Court decided in favor of 2 Live Crew because they had a right to parody the preexisting work. People who regularly parody the work of others often request permission first. They do this as a courtesy, as well as a protection against a potential lawsuit.

Songwriting credit can be sold, won as part of the settlement of a lawsuit, or given to someone by the writer. Songwriting credit and royalties may be shared with a publisher or record company depending on the terms of the contracts signed by the writer. A major change was made in the United States Copyright Law in 1978. Before that year, copyright remained in effect for twenty-eight years from the publication date and was renewable for another twenty-eight years. After January 1, 1978, copyright is in effect for the writer's life plus fifty years. The additional fifty years allowed the writer's heirs to collect royalty income generated by the song for that period of time. After the copyright has expired the song is in public domain, which means that anyone can use the song without any concern about paying a writer's royalty.

Note: This information applies to recordings. The writer's or publisher's written permission is needed to use someone else's melody in a written work one might like to publish.

roll was on its way to becoming a new and distinct style.

Bill Haley (1925–1981) was a country singer and guitarist from Michigan who played in western swing bands. A disc jockey during the late forties, he formed the Four Aces of Western Swing to play on his radio program. When the group broke up he formed another group, the Saddlemen, with which he recorded country songs. In 1951, Haley's group did a cover of "Rocket 88," a blues record by Jackie Brenston with Ike Turner's Kings of Rhythm. The record did not sell very well, but when he performed it, Haley could see how much white teens enjoyed the beat and vitality of the blues. He decided to drop his country image the next year, changing his group's name to the Comets (after Halley's comet), and record blues and rhythm and blues. Bill Haley and the Comets signed with Decca Records in 1954 and covered two blues songs, "(We're Gonna) Rock Around the Clock" (recorded by Sunny Dae in 1952) and Joe Turner's "Shake, Rattle and Roll."

Joe Turner (1911–1985) had been singing jazz since the late twenties, and had become an accomplished singer of slow, jazz-styled blues as well as the faster jump blues. As a jump blues singer he was often described as a "blues shouter" because of his rousing performances in which he made his voice match the honking sounds of the saxophones. As was common in jazz and blues, Turner's songs were often full of sexual references that white singers who wanted their music played on the radio in the fifties had to remove. A comparison of Joe Turner's and Bill Haley's versions of "Shake, Rattle and Roll" can be found on page 30. This comparison points out several of the differences between the blues and the early rock music based on the blues. Haley's version is faster than Turner's, it has fewer characteristics of jazz style, and the lyrics are toned down to be more acceptable to a broader audience that might have been offended by the sexual references in the original. Haley probably did not change the beginning of the verse about the "one-eyed cat" because he thought it was

Bill Haley and the Comets
Michael Ochs Archives/Venice, CA

subtle enough to get by the listeners who were easily offended and yet would please those who listened for sexual references.

Haley's recording of "(We're Gonna) Rock Around the Clock" also followed the twelve-bar blues form, used uneven beat subdivisions (except in the guitar solo), and had saxophones playing in riff patterns unlike the improvisations used by jazz musicians. The lyrics to the song used the word "rock" for dancing and partying, but young listeners certainly made the connection with the way blues singers used the word as slang for sexual intercourse. The recording was not as successful in 1954 as it was after being rereleased as the main-title music for the movie *Blackboard Jungle* (1955). Bill Haley was thirty years old, but because teen rebellion was the theme of the movie, he and his group were seen as reflective of that attitude.

Bill Haley and the Comets toured Britain in 1957, making them the first international rock stars. As popular as their combination of western swing, hillbilly boogie, and rhythm and blues was during the fifties, it did not prove to be as lasting and influential a rock style as the combination of honky-tonk, country music, and rhythm and blues called rockabilly.

Rockabilly

Sam Phillips (born in 1923), an Alabama farm boy, worked as a disc jockey while still in his teens. In 1944 he moved to Memphis and, at the age of twenty-one, started the Memphis Recording Service. Because he liked the blues, most of the artists he recorded were African American blues musicians from the South. He purchased recording equipment and built a studio, where he recorded Jackie Brenston's "Rocket 88" (1951, covered by Bill Haley in the same year) and performances by Howlin' Wolf, Rufus Thomas, and Junior Parker. Phillips' business was too small for him to be able to distribute large quantities of records all over the country, so many of his early recordings were sold to larger companies such as Chess Records in Chicago. By the end of 1951, Phillips formed the Sun Record Company in order to be able to release his recordings himself.

Phillips was aware of the growing interest white Americans had in the blues and rhythm and blues, but he was also aware of the fact that white Americans tended more often to buy recordings made by white artists. White teenagers wanted to hear references to sex in song lyrics, but record company executives and radio programmers were willing to do anything to keep them out. Sam Phillips knew that what he needed to sell hit records was a white performer who could capture the style and beat of the African American singers and, at the same time, adapt the song lyrics to white tastes. He found that singer in 1954 when the young **Elvis Presley** (1935–1977) came into his studio to record the songs "My Happiness" and "That's When Your Heartaches Begin" to give to his mother for her birthday.

Elvis Presley's recordings at Sun Records introduced **rockabilly** (rock+hillbilly) to American teenagers. The standard accompaniment used for Presley's recordings at Sun was simply an electric lead guitar, an acoustic rhythm guitar, string bass, and drums (although some early rockabilly recordings did not use drums and left the slapping of the bass notes to stress the beat). Presley's lead guitarist, Scotty Moore, played with

Listening Guide

	"Shake, Rattle and Roll" as recorded by Joe Turner (1954)	***"Shake, Rattle and Roll" as recorded by Bill Haley and the Comets (1954)***
Tempo:	The tempo is about 140 beats per minute, with four beats per bar.	The tempo is about 176 beats per minute, with four beats per bar.
Form:	Both the music and the text follow the classic twelve-bar blues form.	Both the music and the text follow the classic twelve-bar blues form.
	The recording has nine choruses of the blues.	The recording has seven choruses of the blues.
Features:	The rhythm section includes boogie-woogie-style piano, string bass playing on all four beats, and hand clapping and a snare drum accenting the backbeats.	The rhythm section includes piano and drums playing together in a shuffle beat pattern and the bass player snapping the strings of his instrument against the fingerboard (the **slapping bass** often used in country music). The backbeat is less obvious than in Turner's recording.
	The fills are played by saxophones playing repeated notes in some choruses and a riff pattern in others.	The fills are played by saxophone and guitar playing a riff pattern (different from the one used by Turner).
	The fifth chorus is instrumental, with a baritone saxophone playing a jazz-style improvised solo.	The fourth chorus is instrumental, with the saxophone and guitar playing the melody together in unison, with no improvisation.
	The recording ends with a saxophone line taken directly from the ending to Duke Ellington's recording of "Take the 'A' Train."	The recording ends with a two-bar **tag** (short ending tacked on after the last chorus).
Lyrics:	The lyrics include several sexual references: in the first verse, the singer and the woman to whom he sings are in bed together; in verse two he voices his appreciation at seeing the sun shine through her dress; in verse six he is looking at her and appreciating the fact that she is a woman.	The lyrics basically follow those of the original, but the references to a bed are removed and the lines about the singer's appreciation of the woman's sexuality have been changed to lines about her being cold (verse two) and her having stopped loving him and treated him wrong (verses five and six).

Source: Joe Turner's recording: Time-Life Music, *The Rock 'N' Roll Era, 1954–1955;* and *Atlantic Rhythm & Blues 1947–1974, Volume 2, 1952–1955,* Atlantic 14-81620.

Bill Haley's recording: *Vintage Music, Original Classic Oldies from the 1950's and 1960's, Volume 1,* MCA 31198 or MCA 1429.

the steady, even beat common in country music on some songs, but varied his style to include uneven picking patterns in others. A country sound was also suggested by Moore's sliding notes up the strings, giving the effect of the steel guitar, while Presley kept the rhythm on an acoustic guitar. Sun's bassist, Bill Black, slapped the strings against the fingerboard of his stand-up bass as he played, creating a sound that became typical of rockabilly. The bass usually played on beats one and three (two-beat bass), or on all four beats of a four-beat bar, while the drums played a rhythm-and-blues style shuffle rhythm and accented the backbeats of each bar. In addition to the way the instruments were played, Phillips used reverberation sound effects that exaggerated the music's throbbing pulse. Presley's Sun recordings, such as "Good Rockin' Tonight" and "Milkcow Blues Boogie," followed the traditional twelve-bar blues form, but the tempos of the songs were almost always faster than those used in blues or rhythm and blues. The faster tempo produced an energetic intensity that was an important characteristic of rockabilly.

Some of Presley's early recordings were taken from country sources and some from blues sources. One of his first singles had the Arthur "Big Boy" Crudup blues song "That's All Right" on side one and a rockabilly version of the country song "Blue Moon of Kentucky"

Elvis Presley in 1955 with bassist Bill Black
Michael Ochs Archives/Venice, CA

(by bluegrass writer and performer Bill Monroe) on side two. Having achieved some success locally, Presley was sent by Phillips to audition for the *Grand Ole Opry,* but he was not accepted. His style was too "black" for the *Opry* and too "white" for the rhythm and blues audiences. Despite these racial interpretations of Presley's style, his voice really had no direct precedents in either African American or white traditions. He had a wide, syrupy vibrato that suggested sensual warmth and yet he could suddenly shift into a falsetto that suggested bottled up tension and even a barely contained sort of wildness. It was this emotional intensity that made his voice perfect for the young white fans of the rhythm and blues beat. He was clean, good-looking in the rebel image of James Dean, and, although he often sang "cleaned up" lyrics to blues songs that were originally full of sexual suggestions, he put sex into his performances with suggestive poses and hip gyrations.

During 1955, Presley performed on radio programs, mainly in the South, and had his first chance at a television appearance on a local program. At that time he was considered primarily a country singer, and his success had been limited to the Tennessee area. He traveled to New York, but was turned down when he auditioned for Arthur Godfrey's program, "Talent Scouts." When Colonel Tom Parker took over as Presley's manager, he decided that Presley deserved to be with a company that was larger than Sun Records. After the release of "Mystery Train" (by Junior Parker, also of Sun Records) drew sufficient attention to show Presley's potential, the RCA company bought his contract. Under Parker's conscientious and aggressive management, Presley prospered at RCA. He was given better publicity, a more polished sound on his recordings, and he became a star within a year. For purist fans of the rockabilly sound, however, Presley's Sun recordings were superior to his RCA recordings.

Presley was not a songwriter, and at RCA many of his songs were written by pop writers and recorded with a clean, studio production that included doo-wop-style group vocals and Fats Domino-style piano accompaniment. Rockabilly instrumentation and style was sometimes used, on "Blue Suede Shoes" for example, but the white pop or pop-style doo-wop sound was more common. Presley's fans were not really concerned about the technical details of the recordings; it was his irresistible performance style that earned him the "King of Rock and Roll" reputation. In 1956, he captured the heart of many a teenage girl (and the resulting wrath of her parents) when he thrust his hips around while singing his hits "Heartbreak Hotel," "I Want You, I Need You, I Love You," "Don't Be Cruel," and "Hound Dog" on the Milton Berle, Steve Allen, and Ed Sullivan television shows and the Dorsey Brothers Stage Show.

Presley's style of that period included some use of the blues, but his recordings were molded to fit his image and to please his teenaged audience. One example of a blues song that became a hit for Presley was "Hound Dog," written by the songwriting team Leiber and Stoller for Willie Mae "Big Mama" Thornton, who first recorded it. A "hound dog" was African American slang for a man who cheated on his woman, but when Elvis sang the song, the title took on a very different meaning. In his version, he berated a woman by saying she was of no more use than a hound dog who was no good at catching rabbits—a complete shift from Thornton's recording, but suitable for Elvis' early tough-guy image. The comparison of the two recordings on page 32 outlines other changes made in Presley's recording, including an increase in the speed of the beat, and the replacement of blues instruments and blues-oriented instrumental improvisations with country-oriented ones. Thornton's recording was successful on the rhythm and blues charts, but did not come close to the #1 pop chart success of Presley's.

■ Willie Mae "Big Mama" Thornton's career was discussed in Chapter 2, The Blues Roots of Rock Music.

Presley became a movie star with the release of *Love Me Tender* in 1956, and each of his movies was followed by a string of hit songs. He had the world in his hands, but despite his semi-tough-guy image, he never forgot his home or his parents. With the large check he received when he left Sun Records, he bought them both Cadillacs. In 1957 he bought Graceland, the estate he

Listening Guide

	"Hound Dog" as recorded by Willie Mae "Big Mama" Thornton (1952)	**"Hound Dog" as recorded by Elvis Presley (1956)**
Tempo:	The tempo is about 140 beats per minute, with four beats per bar.	The tempo begins at about 176 beats per minute, but speeds up to about 184 during the first chorus. There are four beats per bar.
Form:	Both the music and the text follow the classic twelve-bar blues format.	Both the music and the text follow the classic twelve-bar blues format.
	The recording has eight choruses of the blues form. The fourth, fifth, and sixth are instrumental, with a guitar improvising solo lines and Thornton giving occasional vocal responses.	The recording has eight choruses of the blues form. The fourth and sixth are instrumental, with a guitar playing lead lines and a vocal group singing sustained-note chords in the background.
Features:	Thornton sings using a rough, classic-blues-style tone quality.	Presley sings in a polished urban blues style and tone quality.
	The rhythm section includes country-blues-style guitar rhythms, a bass playing a regular beat, and hand clapping with a drum stuck on the side (shell) for a very strong backbeat.	The rhythm section includes country-style guitar, a bass playing a riff pattern styled after the saxophone riffs in Bill Haley's version of "Shake, Rattle and Roll," and drums heavily accenting the backbeat.
	The fills are played by the guitar in a country blues style, with the player bending the strings to produce blue notes.	The fills are played by a country-style guitar and by backup singers sustaining chords.
Lyrics:	The lyrics are sung by a woman to a man who has cheated on her, and she responds by vowing to stop seeing him.	The lyrics are sung by a man to a woman whom he sees as being of no more value to him than a hound dog that cannot catch rabbits.

Source: Willie Mae "Big Mama" Thornton's recording: Time-Life Music, *The Rock 'N' Roll Era, Roots of Rock 1945–1956;* and *There's a Riot Goin' On: The Rock 'n' Roll Classics of Leiber and Stoller,* Rhino 70593.

Elvis Presley's recording: Time-Life Music, *The Rock 'N' Roll Era, Elvis Presley 1954–1961;* and *Elvis' Golden Records, Volume 1,* RCA 5196.

lived in and that enshrined him after his death. Because his mother never learned to drive, her pink Cadillac was parked at Graceland and remained there.

In 1957, Presley made two movies, *Loving You* and *Jailhouse Rock,* which featured the hit songs "Teddy Bear" and "Jailhouse Rock." The next year was not a good one for the new star. While he was shooting *King Creole,* his draft notice arrived. Only a short time after he left for basic training, his mother died before he was able to make it home in time to see her, an experience he called the worst loss of his life. Thanks to Colonel Parker, Presley's career survived his two-year absence. Parker took great care to keep Presley on the minds of his fans by judiciously releasing prerecorded songs such as "Hard Headed Woman" (from the movie *King Creole* in 1958) and "A Big Hunk O' Love" (1959) while Presley was in the service.

After his return to civilian life, Presley was more of a movie star than a concert performer. The soundtrack albums from his movies sold well and, beginning in 1968, he made a few concert tours and television films, as well as a number of Las Vegas appearances. He continued to release hit singles through the last year of his life, but his old, rough, rockabilly style was long gone. To lovers of country music, Presley had sold out to a pop style, but by the early sixties rockabilly had already lost its commercial appeal for most of the American audience. Presley's ability to change his style to fit current popular trends was part of the reason he was able to sustain his career through three decades. His image from the fifties was copied by, or was a great influence on, so many later performers that he had become a living legend, unable to go anywhere on earth without being recognized. He died in 1977, in many ways a victim of his legendary status.

Listening Guide

"Burning Love" as recorded by Elvis Presley (1972)

Tempo: The tempo is approximately 144 beats per minute, with four beats per bar.

Form: The form is based on eight-bar periods, each of which is made up of two four-bar phrases. After a four-bar introduction, the periods follow the pattern A A B A A B B A A B and end with repetitions of the final phrase and a fade out. The B sections all begin with the words "Your kisses" except for the third B, in which the B melody is played instrumentally.

Features: The instruments enter one at a time in the introduction in the following order: rhythm guitar, piano, bass, and drums.

Both even and uneven beat subdivisions are kept by the instruments, with the bass and guitar usually maintaining even subdivisions and the piano keeping unevenly subdivided beats. Presley's vocals are generally unevenly subdivided. A strong backbeat is kept in the drums.

The backup vocal group breaks into a black gospel style with two high male soloists during the ending repetitions of the final phrase.

Lyrics: The singer's love for his girl is so strong that he is burning up and can barely breathe.

Source: *Elvis Burning Love and Hits from His Movies, Volume 2,* Camden CAD 1-2595.

Elvis Presley in 1972
AP/Wide World Photos

Presley's voice was so versatile and he sang in so many styles that it would require a large portion of this book to include enough listening guides to cover his career. In an effort to at least recognize the length of his tremendous string of hits, the guide above discusses his last top ten hit, "Burning Love."

During the five years that followed the release of "Burning Love," Presley continued to record and tour, but his personal life was falling apart. His wife, Priscilla, divorced him and he spent most of his private time as a recluse on his Graceland estate. By the time he died he had spent over twenty years trying to avoid the anxious demands of his omnipresent fans. He paid large department stores to stay open in the middle of the night in order to shop with some sense of privacy. Similarly, he would rent whole movie theaters or other attractions to allow himself to enjoy them without the hounding fans. Exactly when he turned to the escape of drugs is not known, or at least not made public, but his dependence on a variety of barbiturates, tranquilizers, and amphetamines certainly contributed to his death at age forty-two.

Carl Perkins (born in 1932) grew up on a farm in Tennessee. He had been playing the guitar and singing at country dances when he first heard Presley's recordings on a local radio program. He had always liked the blues and rhythm and blues, and he decided to pattern his style after Presley's. Perkins traveled to Memphis, and auditioned and was signed by Sun Records in 1955. Though he did not have Elvis Presley's good looks, his sound was good and, unlike Presley, he also wrote songs and played lead guitar. His career was launched with a recording of his own composition, "Blue Suede Shoes," in 1956. Part of the reason Sam Phillips released Presley from his contract with Sun was that he felt he had another, possibly bigger star in Perkins. That bright-looking future was dimmed, however, by an automobile accident that injured Carl and claimed the lives of his brother, Jay, and his manager, David Stewart. The group had been on their way to "The Perry Como Show," where Perkins was to receive a gold record for his recording of "Blue Suede Shoes." That appearance might have led to many more successes, but Perkins was badly injured and it took him a long time to recover.

By the time he was ready to perform again, rockabilly was already being overshadowed by other styles. He did, however, continue as a country recording artist with much success. The Beatles paid him tribute by recording covers of several of his songs. During the sixties and seventies, Perkins performed with Johnny Cash and Bob Dylan, and in 1983, Paul McCartney featured him on his post-Wings album, *Tug of War.* A rockabilly revival band of the early eighties, the Stray Cats, took much of their style from Perkins. Perkins continues to write and record in the nineties, and his fans can enjoy being surrounded by memorabilia from his career at his restaurant, Suede, in Jackson, Tennessee.

Another rockabilly artist whose career in rock was short but influential was pianist/singer **Jerry Lee Lewis** (born in 1935). He grew up in Louisiana listening to both country and blues singers and playing the piano for anyone who would listen to him. After hearing Elvis Presley's recordings on the Sun label, he went to Memphis and was given a contract by Sun Records. Like Bill Haley and Elvis Presley before him, Lewis covered blues songs by African American musicians; his "Whole Lotta Shakin' Goin' On" (1957) had been recorded by Big Maybelle in 1955. The song was full of sexual references and, unlike Haley and Presley, Lewis chose not to sanitize the lyrics, although he did add to them.

Jerry Lee Lewis played his honky-tonk piano rock with a tremendous amount of energy. He threw his right hand all over the keyboard with **glissandos** (sliding runs) while his left hand smashed at the keys to maintain a rhythmically pumping bass line. He pushed the bench away and danced while he played, letting his backup band sustain the beat while he banged the piano keys with his feet and even jumped on top of the piano while singing. He deserved his nickname, "The Killer," for his treatment of both the piano and his audience.

Lewis knew he was a great performer, but he never dreamed that his fans would care about his private life. His career was ruined by an unofficial boycott of his records and performances when it became known that he had married his thirteen-year-old third cousin without having divorced his second wife. Though he remained at Sun Records to record country music, and continued to do live performances, Lewis could no longer draw the large crowds he once attracted. In later years he was remembered by British rock musicians Rory Gallagher, Alvin Lee, and Peter Frampton, who had him join them for an album called *The Session* (1973). During the late seventies and extending into the nineties Lewis played his old hits on various programs that paid tribute to his importance as an early rock performer, and he continues to tour. In 1995 he released a new album, *Young Blood.*

Roy Orbison (1936–1988) was another country singer who was attracted to Sun Records when he heard recordings by Elvis Presley. Sam Phillips signed him with the Sun label in 1956. Orbison considered himself primarily a ballad singer, but his most successful Sun release was the rockabilly-styled "Ooby Dooby" (1956). He eventually moved to Nashville and worked as a songwriter. Orbison had no problems surviving as a performer during the early sixties, when he dropped the rockabilly style and wrote and sang ballads, often about loneliness and problem relationships. Those recordings were released on the Monument label. He later recorded for Elektra and Virgin.

Orbison continued to perform his own ballads and traditional country songs, many of which were covered by others. After a quiet comeback in 1988 with a group named the Traveling Wilburys, whose members included Bob Dylan, George Harrison, Jeff Lynne, and Tom Petty, and a new solo album, *Mystery Girl,* Orbison died suddenly of a heart attack in December of that year.

Although the rockabilly sound was first synthesized in Elvis Presley's recordings of blues songs at Sun Records, the fusion of blues and country music was a natural happening for the time and it was soon copied by recording artists outside of Sam Phillips' studios. Rockabilly artist **Eddie Cochran** (1938–1960) had only a short career, but had a lasting influence on many of the rock stars who followed him. Originally from Oklahoma, he lived in Minnesota and California before settling in Nashville, where he co-wrote songs with his friend Jerry Capehart. He adopted the tough-guy image popularized by James Dean and Marlon Brando, and he was even given an acting role in *Untamed Youth* (1957).

Cochran's biggest recording success was "Summertime Blues" in 1958. Both that and his next hit, "C'mon Everybody" (1959), were the result of Cochran's experiments with **overdubbing,** in which he played and sang all the parts himself. Overdubbing was a new recording technique invented by Les Paul in the early fifties, and although it had been used before, Cochran was among the first rockabilly musicians to use it extensively. Overdubbing techniques soon became a common recording practice.

Cochran saw that the popularity of the rockabilly style was dying with the rise of teen idol pop stars in the late fifties. With his last hit, "Three Steps to Heaven," it appeared that he was going to change his style to include more of this new pop sound. The song was not rockabilly at all; rather, it featured a lightly strummed guitar keeping the rhythm, a doo-wop-style vocal group, and very little bass, drums, or backbeat. He never really got the chance to establish himself in his new style, however. He was killed in an automobile accident on his way to a London airport after a tour of England in 1960.

Buddy Holly with two of the three Crickets
© Beecher/Michael Ochs Archives/Venice, CA

Another rockabilly singer, **Gene Vincent** (Eugene Vincent Craddock, 1935–1971), was with Eddie Cochran on his last tour but survived the accident that killed Cochran. Vincent grew up in Virginia, where he had sung a type of religious country music called white gospel. After serving in the navy during the Korean War, he became interested in the rockabilly style of Elvis Presley and formed a group called the Blue Caps. They sent an audition tape to Capitol Record Company in Hollywood, which gave them a contract. Vincent's voice was similar enough to Presley's that Capitol saw him as good competition for Presley. In producing his records they used an echo effect to imitate the rockabilly recordings Sam Phillips made at Sun. "Be-Bop-A-Lula" (1956) was Gene Vincent and the Blue Caps' first recording, and it turned out to be the biggest hit of his career. Vincent's image was a bit rougher than Presley's, although both were styled very much in the James Dean tough-guy tradition. Because of a leg injury he had suffered while in the navy, Vincent could not perform the sexy hip movements that Presley did. Instead, he conveyed a feeling of sexual desperation through his breathy vocals. "Lotta Lovin' " was a hit for him in 1957, but by that time it was clear that rockabilly was beginning to lose popularity in the United States. Instead of trying to change to a pop style, Vincent moved to England, where he continued to perform as a rockabilly artist. In poor health, he returned to America in 1971, and died within a month.

Rockabilly-Influenced Rock

Charles Hardin Holley's last name was printed without the "e" early in his career, and he decided to let it stay that way. As **Buddy Holly** (1938–1959), he was another important innovator in rock music who first turned to rock after seeing a 1955 performance by Elvis Presley. Holly was from Lubbock, Texas, and learned to play the fiddle, guitar, banjo, and piano when he was a child. He formed various country and proto-rock groups and, in 1956, received a contract to record for Decca Records in Nashville under the name Three Tunes. Holly's Decca recordings were country songs and did not sell well, so he and his drummer, Jerry Allison, decided to go back to Texas, where they performed as a duo. Holly and Allison formed the Crickets, and went to New Mexico to record their first hit, "That'll Be the Day" (1957), produced by Norman Petty.

Although he credited Elvis Presley with introducing him to rock and roll, Buddy Holly was certainly no Elvis imitator. He wrote much of his own music, and his witty, personal, and emotional style appealed to male as well as female fans. His vocal style was light, characterized by his trademark hiccup on certain turns of phrase. Unlike that of leather-jacketed rockabilly stars such as Cochran or Vincent, Holly's image was not one of teen rebellion. He wore suits, ties, and horn-rimmed glasses that gave him the look of a clean-cut, respectable, and even a bit naive young man (an image Elvis Costello would later portray as neurotic).

The Crickets used the standard rockabilly instrumentation of two guitars (one for lead, and one for rhythm), bass, and drums, except that their guitars were electric (Holly's had a solid body), and Jerry Allison played a different and more important role than other rockabilly drummers had. Allison sometimes used subtle and interesting Latin rhythms, unusual for the rock music of the time. Apart from the fact that their bass player played a stand-up bass, not an electric bass guitar, the Crickets' instrumentation was the same as that used

Early Electric Guitars

Buddy Holly's Stratocaster guitar was one of several early solid-body guitars to be used in rock music. Solid-body guitars had a tone quality that was quite different from the types of acoustic guitars or electric acoustic guitars they replaced. Whether it is amplified or not, the body of an acoustic guitar is hollow with a soundhole to let the strings' vibrations bounce around inside of the body. This causes the body top (called a soundboard) to resonate, and then that resonated sound comes back out of the soundhole. Early jazz guitarists like Charlie Christian and T-Bone Walker played acoustic (hollow-bodied) guitars with two sound holes (called "f holes" because they were shaped like two small letter "f's" facing one another) and electric **pickups** attached to the soundboard. The Gibson model ES-150 is an example of such a guitar. Urban blues guitarists wanted more of a punch to their tone than the full hollow-bodied instruments allowed, so they opted for thinner, semi-solid-bodied guitars such as B. B. King's Gibson ES-335. King's love for his guitar is expressed by his having used it for years, affectionately calling it Lucille. Les Paul and others were concerned about the short sustaining power and occasional feedback with the amplifier of the semi-solid body and worked at improving their pickups to the point where the guitar body could be made of solid, high density wood. While Paul was still working on his model, Paul Bigsby came up with one that Merle Travis used in 1947, and Leo Fender created his Broadcaster (later called the Telecaster) in 1948. The Gibson company made the Les Paul model in 1952. The solid-body guitar Buddy Holly played, the Fender Stratocaster (first produced in 1954), was an improvement over Fender's earlier models and had a triple pickup. The Fender Telecaster, the Gibson Les Paul, and the Fender Stratocaster all became standard instruments for rock guitarists of the sixties including Eric Clapton, who used a Gibson Les Paul, and Jimi Hendrix, who used a Fender Stratocaster.

Listening Guide

"Peggy Sue"
as recorded by Buddy Holly (1957)

Tempo: The tempo is about 148 beats per minute, with four beats in each bar.

Form: The form is a modified twelve-bar blues. Few blue notes are used.

The four-bar instrumental introduction is followed by seven twelve-bar choruses and a four-bar final extension.

Features: The instrumentation is electric solid-body guitar, acoustic rhythm guitar, string bass, and drums.

On the verses that Holly sings, he strums the solid-body guitar with a pick, but the volume is quite low. The volume is higher on the instrumental fifth chorus, with Holly playing a solo in a strummed pattern with melodic fills, influenced by Chuck Berry's solo style. The strumming of the rhythm guitar is covered up by the amplification of Holly's guitar during his solo.

Throughout the recording the drums keep an energetic four-to-the-beat (sixteenth note) pattern on tom-toms with little or no backbeat.

Holly's characteristic vocal hiccup is most obvious on the fourth, sixth, and seventh choruses.

Lyrics: The song is about the singer's love for a girl named Peggy Sue. Holly originally wrote the song using the name Cindy Lou, but then renamed it for drummer Jerry Allison's girlfriend.

Source: Time-Life Music, *The Rock 'N' Roll Era, 1957;* and *Buddy Holly/The Crickets: 20 Golden Greats,* MCA 1484.

by many later rock groups, including the Beatles and the Rolling Stones, both of which covered Holly's songs.

Buddy Holly was one of the first rock guitarists to play a solid-body electric guitar. Bill Haley had played the hollow-body electric guitar commonly used in western swing bands, and the rockabilly singers had often played steel-strung acoustic guitars. The solid body of Holly's instrument gave it a more aggressive tone quality than guitars with an acoustic sound box. Within a short space of time the solid-body guitar became the standard guitar for rock music.

The listening guide for Buddy Holly's hit recording of "Peggy Sue" (1957) points out characteristics of both the blues and country music that have been molded together to create Holly's rock style. The Crickets' rhythm guitarist, Niki Sullivan, has said that he did not play on the recording of "Peggy Sue," so it is possible that Holly overdubbed the rhythm guitar part after the original recording session.

For two years, Buddy Holly and the Crickets recorded many other hit songs. Late in 1958, however,

Holly decided to make some changes in his career. He left the Crickets and their manager, Norman Petty, got married, moved to New York, and started to work on developing his writing skills, changing his style to fit the new pop trend. His last hit, "It Doesn't Matter Anymore" (1959), was written for him by the songwriting teen idol Paul Anka, whom he met in New York, and was produced with a pop-style orchestral string section instead of the Crickets' instrumentation.

Because Holly's finances were tied up in legal battles with Norman Petty and he needed money, he decided to go on the concert tour which turned out to be his last. On the tour, Holly was backed by a band that included one member of the Crickets, guitarist Tom Allsup, and bass player Waylon Jennings, who would later become a country music star. Other headline performers on the tour were the Big Bopper (J. P. Richardson), Ritchie Valens (Richard Valenzuela), and Dion (Dion DiMucci). The Bopper, Valens, and Holly all died in a plane crash on February 3, 1959, a date that has never been forgotten by many rock fans.

One of the few country-influenced rock groups to maintain popularity in the United States from the late fifties into the early sixties was **The Everly Brothers.** (Don Everly was born in 1937, and Phil Everly was born in 1939.) Phil and Don Everly's parents, Ike and Margaret Everly, were country musicians. They had a radio program on which Phil and Don performed as early as 1946, when they were only seven and nine years old. The closely harmonized tenor voices of the brothers were accompanied by their own rhythm guitars, electric lead guitarist Chet Atkins, pianist Floyd Cramer, bass, and drums. Their sound was different from the pure rockabilly sound recorded at Sun Records because it was smooth and full and lacked the slapping bass and some of the intensity of Sun rockabilly. The Everly Brothers' voices slid gradually up to high notes, capturing the sound of someone almost on the verge of tears. They signed with Cadence Records in 1957 and recorded many of their best-known songs, including "Bye Bye Love" (1957) and "All I Have to Do Is Dream" (1958). In 1960, they changed to the Warner Brothers label and recorded "Cathy's Clown," which turned out to be their biggest hit. They continued to record through the sixties, but sales did not match those of their earlier records. A breakup was inevitable after a fight on stage in 1973, and it took ten years before they gave a reunion concert. The Everly Brothers' distinctive vocal style influenced many singers who followed them. A fairly recent example can be heard in Extreme's 1990 song, "More Than Words." The brothers have not recorded any new material in the nineties, but the pair have continued to give occasional live performances.

The most popular form of country-influenced rock music of the early sixties was that of **crossover** or Nashville pop. It was not until the late sixties that non-pop country music was combined with rock to initiate the development of country rock, which became particularly popular in California, and southern rock, a vehicle through which the expression of southern pride reached an international audience.

Summary

The earliest styles of American country music were developed by people who came from the British Isles and settled primarily in the southern United States. Called hillbilly music until the early fifties, those styles included songs that told stories and dances accompanied by such instruments as the fiddle, the guitar, the dulcimer, the piano, the harmonica, and the mandolin. Eventually drums and saxophones from jazz and blues influenced some country styles, but many country performers at the time resisted association with music that was commonly played by African American musicians.

Musical elements typical of most country music styles included a very steady beat that was subdivided into two equal sections, simple triadic chords, four-bar phrases that formed repeating eight-bar periods, two-beat bass, the practice of sliding from one note to the next, and group vocals in which the second from the highest part carried the melody. Partly because the songs often told stories that developed as the song progressed, the vocals were never obscured by the instruments that accompanied them. The blues form was sometimes used in traditional country music, but usually the uneven beat subdivisions and blue notes commonly used by African American performers were not.

Various styles of country music have influenced rock music in a variety of ways at different times during the course of rock's development. Western swing and hillbilly boogie were the basis for early rock music played by Bill Haley. Another country style to use drums and amplified instruments, honky-tonk, was combined with the blues to create rockabilly. Bluegrass group vocals and the use of instruments common in bluegrass such as the banjo became important in the country-rock music popular during the late sixties.

Elvis Presley moved from rockabilly to pop music in 1956, and after rockabilly ceased to be popular in the United States, other versatile performers including Eddie Cochran, Buddy Holly, Roy Orbison, and the Everly Brothers changed their styles to fit the pop trend of the late fifties. Cochran and Holly both died before fully establishing their new sounds, and the Everly Brothers had little success after 1962, but Presley and Orbison remained popular long after the demise of rockabilly. Carl Perkins and Jerry Lee Lewis left rockabilly to continue their careers in country music. Gene Vincent did not want to change to either pop or country styles, and he left the United States to perform in England, where rockabilly was still popular. By the early sixties, only very pop-oriented country styles remained on the pop charts.

Terms to Remember

Bluegrass
Crossover
Dobro
Eight-bar period
Five-string banjo
Four-bar phrase
Glissando
Hillbilly boogie
Honky-tonk
Overdubbing
Pickups
Rockabilly
Slapping bass
Tag
Triadic harmonies
Two-beat bass
Western swing

CHAPTER 4

The Gospel Roots of Rock Music

Spirituals

Christians were directed to sing "Spiritual songs" in the New Testament of the Bible (Ephesians 5:19 and Colossians 3:16). Accordingly, the term **spiritual** was given to religious folk songs from both the white and the African American traditions from the middle-eighteenth century through the nineteenth century, but other terms such as "psalm" or "hymn" became more commonly used for songs by white composers while "spiritual" became associated with songs by African American composers. As was true of folk music in general, the original spirituals were not written down but were passed by memory from singer to singer. Exactly what the early spirituals sounded like can only be guessed from the descriptions written in slave owners' diaries or included in the earliest printed editions of the lyrics. According to *Slave Songs of the United States,* written by William Francis Allen, Charles Pickard Ware, and Lucy McKim Garrison in 1867, spirituals were not sung in the prearranged, multivoiced structures that whites called **"part singing,"** but yet the African American singers did not always sing the same melody at the same time either. Lead singers improvised, sliding from one note to another and singing "turns" around the melody notes. Other sources indicate that a similar style was used in African American work songs and field hollers. The use of leaders improvising while other singers stay in the background with the plain melody became common in Black gospel singing styles of the twentieth century.

Texts of spirituals varied from slow, melancholy **sorrow songs** such as "Nobody Knows the Trouble I've Seen" to fast and highly energetic **jubilees** such as "Didn't My Lord Deliver Daniel?" Both types of spirituals often contained coded messages that the singers did not want whites to understand. The messages were cleverly designed to sound on the surface as if they were being sung to celebrate the belief that Christianity would bring them to heaven, when they were really communicating the way to escape from slavery in the South to freedom in the North. Other lyrics like "We'll stand the storm" helped to encourage patience and endurance until the dream of freedom came true. The Fisk Jubilee Singers from Fisk University in Nashville, Tennessee, helped to popularize spirituals during the late nineteenth century through their performances in various parts of the United States and Europe. Modern choral groups from Fisk University and many other universities, colleges, community groups, and churches continue to perform and record spirituals in as close to the early tradition as possible, although most modern groups sing from modern arrangements and rely less on improvisation than did the earliest spiritual singers.

Gospel Music

Black gospel music developed from the same musical roots as spirituals and the blues. These roots included

Sam Cooke in 1964
AP/Wide World Photos

Listening Guide

"How Far Am I from Canaan?" as recorded by the Soul Stirrers with Sam Cooke (1952)

Tempo: The tempo is approximately 96 beats per minute, with four beats per bar for the first half of the recording, but then doubles to approximately 192 beats per minute for the second half. A doubling of the tempo is called **double time.**

Form: The slow beginning section of the recording is made up of four eight-bar phrases, each of which ends with words that lead into the phrase that follows. The fast section has four sixteen-bar phrases, the last of which functions as a **coda** in that it includes short, repeated sections from earlier parts of the song that help bring the song to a musically satisfying conclusion.

Features: Sam Cooke sings the lead melody throughout the recording, often adding **melismas** to embellish the melody.

The Soul Stirrers sometimes sustain chords to accompany Cooke's lead vocals and at other times they separate somewhat and sing portions of lyrics from the lead line. Even with their occasional breaks into separate lines, the Soul Stirrers never cover Cooke's lead or improvise melismas to the extent that Cooke does on his lines.

Only a drummer accompanies the singers. The drummer maintains a steady beat with thumps on the bass drum, and accents the backbeats with a high hat cymbal.

Uneven beat subdivisions are used throughout the recording.

Lyrics: Canaan is used generically to represent the promised land—in this case, heaven—where angels and saints sing and the singer has faith that he will meet his mother and his Savior there.

Source: *Sam Cooke with the Soul Stirrers,* Specialty 7009.

certain scale structures and the call-and-response tradition from parts of West Africa. European musical traditions contributed formal structure, harmonies, regular beat patterns, and use of such musical instruments as the guitar and piano. The blues and gospel music developed into different, but related, styles because the blues was the personal expression of an individual singer, whereas gospel was used to voice the shared religious beliefs of a group of worshippers.

The development of black gospel music came about as it did because of the manner in which African Americans were introduced to Christianity. African American slaves attended church with their white owners (or under the watchful eye of someone who represented the owners) because it was thought dangerous to allow large groups of slaves to meet together without the presence and dominance of whites. White churches had separate sections for African American congregations, but both groups sang the same hymns and came to share the same beliefs in the "good news" of the Gospels. Because churches were organized for white congregations, hymns were performed with white European traditions—a steady beat with even beat subdivisions and accents on the first and third beat of each four-beat pattern. Known as "white gospel," the music followed many of the same traditions as hillbilly music.

After the Civil War and the abolishment of slavery, African Americans built their own churches. While white gospel music continued to be sung in the white churches, African Americans developed their own style of religious music. Spirited by the new taste of freedom, they sang music that displayed the characteristics and energy of pre-Civil War camp meeting and jubilee spirituals, like "Swing Low, Sweet Chariot" and "In That Great Gettin' Up Morning." The African call-and-response tradition, as it was practiced in a church service, involved the preacher calling out a phrase from the

Bible, to which the congregation would respond with statements about their belief in its truth or with the next Biblical verse. Call-and-response was also employed during the singing of hymns, when the preacher or lead singer would sing verses and a group of singers would respond with the refrain of the hymn. By the thirties the term "gospel" began to be applied to sophisticated religious music by such composers as Thomas A. Dorsey and Lucie Campbell.

Probably first intended as an expression of enthusiasm for the religious subjects of the music, a number of highly stylized vocal devices or patterns were improvised by gospel singers and those improvisations became characteristic of the vocals in soul styles that followed gospel. One such device, sometimes called a "turn" (or melisma in its more elaborate form), was a type of embellishment that involved sliding around notes both above and below the melody note, thereby dramatically delaying that note, and then finally resolving to it. Another stylized vocal practice was the breaking of a single syllable of a word into several parts by punctuations or aspirations of breath. The effect was to build the intensity of the word.

As another result of the congregations' emotional involvement with religion, highly energetic and syncopated rhythms entered the performance of music in church services, along with dancing in the aisles, hand clapping, and shouting. It was not uncommon for preachers to become caught up in the fervor of these activities and faint during the service, something that became part of the stage act of many soul singers.

While the simple call of preachers followed by the congregational response continued to be part of church services, a more complex gospel style was being developed by established professional groups of well-rehearsed singers. Many of these vocal groups employed the harmonization and crisp rhythmic flow of the old hymns and adapted those to the energetic spirituals. Some of the groups recorded and toured professionally. **The Golden Gate Quartet** and **The Dixie Hummingbirds** were male groups that began singing in the late twenties and remained together into the eighties. At times these groups also sang secular music in a gospel style. The Dixie Hummingbirds, for example, sang the backup vocals on folk-rock singer Paul Simon's recording of "Loves Me Like a Rock," a gospel song the group rerecorded without Simon in 1973.

The **Soul Stirrers**, from Texas, recorded for the Library of Congress archives as early as 1936. They influenced many other gospel groups with their **falsetto** (higher than standard tenor range and generally somewhat breathy in tone quality) lead singing, use of polyrhythms, and textual improvisations. A rock singer and writer popular in the late fifties and early sixties, Sam Cooke (originally Cook), and the Memphis soul singer Johnny Taylor both did their first professional singing with the Soul Stirrers. The recording discussed in the listening guide on page 40 was made by the Soul Stirrers when eighteen-year-old Sam Cooke was their lead singer.

Female gospel groups became popular during the forties. Among the best known were **The Clara Ward Singers**, who gained such a following through their recordings and tours during the fifties that they left the church and concert hall circuit in 1961 to perform in Las Vegas. Although numerous gospel groups performed in secular settings, many popular gospel and, later, soul performers, were uneasy about taking gospel music out of the church and using it in nonreligious performances.

Although small groups of four or five singers remained popular, a full-choir style of gospel music based on a tradition began by Thomas A. Dorsey in the early thirties was popularized by pianist/arranger Edwin Hawkins in Oakland, California, during the sixties. Hawkins replaced the small vocal group with a large choir and accompanied it with a rock beat played by

The Edwin Hawkins Singers
Michael Ochs Archives/Venice, CA

Listening Guide

"Oh Happy Day" as recorded by the Edwin Hawkins Singers (1969)

Tempo: The tempo is approximately 112 beats per minute, with four beats per bar.

Form: The performance begins with a ten-bar introduction played by pianos and percussion.

The musical form is based on eight-bar phrases that are often extended by repetition of individual bars.

The first vocal section is fourteen bars long, with repetition of several lines of text and melody.

The entire fourteen-bar section repeats immediately after the first time it is performed, and repeats again several times later in the recording, with additional extensions toward the end.

Features: The beat subdivisions are even.

The rhythm section maintains the steady beat while the vocalists gradually speed up, often ending phrases one-half beat early. This pushing of the tempo produces an effect of enthusiasm and fervor.

Dorothy Morrison sings the lead and a large chorus sings responses. Her vocals use the stylized devices mentioned earlier; the chorus repeats her basic melody, but without her turns and inflections.

A contrasting section with new lyrics follows the repeat of the first section. The chorus is louder in this section, and a woman (possibly Morrison) sings above the chorus in a free and energetic style.

The new section is eight bars long, not having the repetitious extensions of the first vocal section.

The eight-bar section is repeated later in the recording, accompanied by hand clapping on the backbeat during one of the last repeats.

Lyrics: The lyrics keep repeating the joy felt by one who has been cleansed of sin.

Source: Time-Life Music, *Classic Rock, 1969: The Beat Goes On; Super Hits, Volume 3,* Hollywood HT-167; and *Jubilation! Great Gospel Performances, Volume 1, Black Gospel,* Rhino 70288.

keyboards, bass, and drums. His group, **The Edwin Hawkins Singers**, recorded gospel songs that became hits on the pop charts. In their recording of "Oh Happy Day," soloist Dorothy Morrison used the stylized vocal devices that had long been traditions in gospel singing, and because the large choir could not use those devices in their responses to her singing, her improvisations clearly stood out above their singing. Particularly on the words "oh" and "day," Morrison adds various melismas not sung by the choir in their repetitions of the same words. The recording also includes a high female voice improvising above the choir, a characteristic often copied in disco recordings by such singers as Donna Summer, and later included in songs by the Eurythmics. A listening guide for this recording is included on this page.

Hawkins' large-choir gospel style was copied by other groups as well, but the smaller groups in which each singer, or several of the singers, could have an opportunity to solo and improvise remained more common. Hawkins continues to play gospel music in the nineties, but the Edwin Hawkins Singers broke up after a series of personnel changes.

Doo-Wop

Secular music sung by gospel-oriented African American vocal groups was popular as early as the twenties. The term "doo-wop" came to be used to identify the vocal group sound, as the groups usually had a lead singer who was accompanied (or responded to) by other singers singing nonsense syllables or repeating a few words from the lead singer's line. The general label "doo-wop" referred to the nonsense syllables—"ahs" or "dum, dum, de-dums"—that the backup singers used. Two early African American pop vocal groups whose influences could be heard in the later doo-wop style were **The Mills Brothers**, who sang four-part harmony in a smooth, sophisticated style, and **The Ink Spots**, whose high-**tenor** lead singer often dropped out after a chorus to allow the **bass** singer to speak the lyrics, accompanied by the rest of the group humming chords.

In 1945, **The Ravens** took the mellow vocal style of the Mills Brothers and added the Ink Spots lead bass idea to bring to their New York audiences a musical combination of pop, gospel, and rhythm and blues. Even when the bass singer was not singing lead lines, he maintained a moving bass part that imitated the lines a string bass might play instead of merely singing the same rhythm pattern as the rest of the group, a technique the Mills Brothers pioneered. The Ravens worked with a pianist who played a constant triplet pattern behind the group's vocals; the basic rhythm was used in much doo-wop to follow. As doo-wop was essentially a vocal style, instruments were relegated to secondary roles as accompaniment. The Ravens began to record and tour nationally, and were eventually copied by many other vocal

Listening Guide

	"Crying in the Chapel" by Darrell Glenn (July 1953)	**"Crying in the Chapel" by the Orioles (August 1953)**
Tempo:	The tempo is about 80 beats per minute, with four beats per bar.	The tempo is about 69 beats per minute, with four beats per bar.
Form:	The song is made up of two repetitions of an AABA song form in which the A sections each have different lyrics, and the B section is the same both times (it tells of his search for peace).	The song is made up of one chorus of the AABA song form that uses Glenn's lyrics, but not in the same order as on the earlier recording.
	Each A section is eight bars long; the B section is unusual because it has three four-beat bars and one six-beat bar.	Each A section is eight bars long; the B section is the same length as in Glenn's recording.
Features:	Darrell Glenn sings solo, with no responding vocal group.	Sonny Til sings the lead, with the other Orioles singing "ahs" and a few words taken from the lyrics in response to his lead lines.
	Glenn uses **vibrato** (slight wavering of pitch) and dynamic changes for expressiveness, but rarely varies the basic melodic line.	Til varies the melody with many turns and other black gospel stylizations.
	Even beat subdivisions are maintained throughout the recording.	Uneven beat subdivisions are maintained throughout the recording.
	Instruments include country-style electric guitar playing fills, two-beat bass, and drums.	Instruments include trumpet, alto saxophone, Hammond organ, bass, and drums.
	The drums are soft and accent all four beats of each bar equally (no backbeat).	The drums keep a strong backbeat.
Lyrics:	The song is about the importance of religion in the singer's life	Slight lyrical changes do not change the song's meaning.

Source: Glenn's recording: *The Best of Gospel, Volume 1,* Richmond N5-2260.

The Orioles' recording: Time-Life Music, *The Rock 'N' Roll Era, Roots of Rock 1945–1956;* and *Sonny Til and the Orioles—Greatest Hits,* COL 5014.

groups, some of which also used bird names, such as the Crows, the Penguins, the Cardinals, and the Flamingos.

A group from Baltimore, Maryland took the name The Orioles from their state bird. **The Orioles** did not imitate the Ravens, because their sound depended more on the light lead tenor vocal style that the Ink Spots had used. The Orioles' recording of "Crying in the Chapel" (1953) was one of the first recordings by African American artists to be successful on the pop charts. Additionally, it was a cover of a country song by a white singer, Darrell Glenn (his father, Artie Glenn wrote the song), and was more popular than Glenn's version. (Actually, the Orioles' recording was the third cover released; others by June Valli and Rex Allen were made after Glenn's but before the Orioles'.) The styles were so different from each other that a comparison of the two by Glenn and the Orioles demonstrates the basic contrast between white and black gospel styles. White gospel music followed the steady beat and instrumental practices common in country music, while black gospel used a shuffle rhythm and backbeat, vocal improvisation, and a backup chorus. The two recordings are discussed in the listening guides above.

"Crying in the Chapel" was covered again by Elvis Presley in 1960, and his version was much closer to the style of the Orioles than to Glenn's. The Orioles broke up in 1954, but their Ink Spots-influenced sound was copied by many other groups.

Despite the Glenn/Orioles example, it was much more common for white groups to cover African American

Listening Guide

	"Sh-Boom" as recorded by The Chords (1954)	***"Sh-Boom" as recorded by The Crew-Cuts (1954)***
Tempo:	The tempo is about 134 beats per minute, with four beats in each bar.	The tempo is about 134 beats per minute, with four beats in each bar.
Form:	Most of the song is structured in eight-bar periods, each of which consists of two four-bar phrases. The only exceptions are the four-bar introduction and one four-bar extension sung in nonsense syllables after the first full eight-bar period of lyrics.	Most of the song is structured in the same eight-bar periods as in the Chords' version, except that the ninth period is shortened to only seven bars. The four-bar extension after the first verse of the Chords' version is not present in the Crew-Cuts' recording.
	The chords and melody of all periods except that sung by a solo bass singer are similar enough to be called A sections of a song form. The bass sings the contrasting B section, or **bridge,** of the song form.	The same A and B periods are used, except that the bridge is repeated to fit a standard AABA followed by another AABA format.
Features:	The vocal group is accompanied by a rhythm section consisting of a guitar, string bass, drums, and saxophone for instrumental solos.	The vocal group is accompanied by a full swing-style dance band including several saxophones, brass instruments, a rhythm section, and a kettledrum.
	Beat subdivisions are uneven.	Beat subdivisions are uneven.
	The recording begins with an introduction in which the vocal group sings **a cappella** (without instrumental accompaniment) for two bars and then is joined by the instruments for two more bars.	The recording begins with instruments accompanying a solo singer for a four-bar introduction.
	Most of the lyrics are sung by the vocal group, except for the bridge, which is sung by a solo bass singer (showing the Ink Spots' influence).	The introduction and first four eight-bar periods are sung by solo singers (not always the same one). The last seven periods are sung by the full group. None of the soloists is a bass.
	The sixth and seventh full eight-bar periods are instrumental, with a tenor saxophone improvising in a jazz style.	There is no instrumental section except for occasional fills between lines of text. During the fifth and sixth periods, the vocal group sings nonsense syllables and the band fills in behind them. After dramatic pauses at the end of each of those periods, the band returns with a strong beat and glissando on a kettledrum. (Its pitch is raised as it rings.)
Lyrics:	The song title represents the syllables sung by vocal groups, either behind a soloist or to fill time during breaks in the regular song lyrics. The song is about dreams of a future with someone to whom the singer has been attracted.	The lyrics are the same as those sung by the Chords, except that the nonsense syllables have been changed, with repetitions of "sh-boom" and "la la las."

Source: The Chords' recording: Time-Life Music, *The Rock 'N' Roll Era, 1954–1955,* and *Atlantic Rhythm & Blues 1947–1974, Volume 2, 1952–1955,* Atlantic 14-81620.

The Crew-Cuts' recording: *Partytime 50's,* PTY 9436.

material than the reverse. As with blues and rhythm and blues songs, many of the white covers had changes in lyrics, instrumentation, and production style that were supposed to make them more saleable to the white audience than the African American originals. One of the most famous examples of this was the song "Sh-Boom," which was written and first recorded in 1954 by **The Chords**, an African American vocal group, and covered by **The Crew-Cuts**, a white group from Canada. The Crew-Cuts did not make any substantive changes in the song's lyrics, but they did make other changes to take out African American musical characteristics and "whiten" their sound. Listening guides on page 44 compare the two recordings.

The chord progression of I–vi^7–ii^7–V^7 (C–Am^7–Dm^7–G^7, in the key of C) used in "Sh-Boom" was the harmonic basis of many songs in the doo-wop style. Some songs varied it slightly, but the regular use of this same basic chord progression at about the same rhythmic rate was the reason so many of the doo-wop songs sounded similar. It is commonly referred to as the **doo-wop progression.**

Another musical characteristic found in a large percentage of doo-wop is the constant pounding of repeated chords at the rate of three chords per beat with the bass line and the melody following that triplet pattern through their use of uneven beat subdivisions. An example of a simple form of a typical doo-wop accompaniment follows:

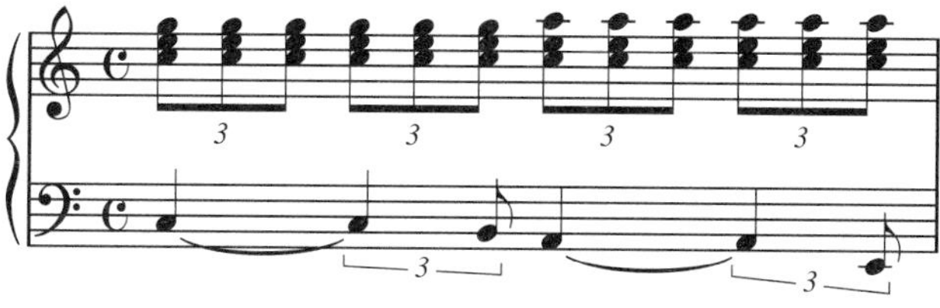

One doo-wop group whose music generally did not follow the stock doo-wop progression was **The Platters**. Their manager/arranger, Buck Ram, had studied jazz arranging and was able to incorporate more advanced harmonic ideas into their arrangements. The Platters also differed from many other doo-wop groups because they had a woman in their backup vocal group and used a strong rhythm section (with Ram on piano).

The Drifters were given their name because the members were known to drift from group to group; in fact, not a single member stayed with the group throughout its career. The Drifters added a Latin beat to some of their songs, an example of which could be heard in their

The Drifters
Bettmann Archive

recording of "Honey Love" (1954). The lead bass that the Ink Spots and the Ravens had introduced was copied by the Drifters in their recording of "White Christmas" (1954). The original Drifters broke up in 1958, but their manager retained the copyright on the group's name and renamed a group that had called themselves the Five Crowns (with Ben E. King singing lead) the Drifters. The old Drifters had recorded songs that made the rhythm and blues charts, but the new group broke through to the top of the pop charts with "There Goes My Baby." That record was not the first to use orchestral strings—Buddy Holly had done that with his last hit "It Doesn't Matter Any More"—but it was the first rhythm and blues record to use such a full, thick background, which became a trend toward the early sixties. The song was written and the recording produced by Atlantic Record Company's Leiber and Stoller, who had earlier written "Hound Dog" for Willie Mae Thornton. A listening guide to the recording that put the orchestral background into early sixties rock follows on page 46.

While most of the doo-wop groups sang songs with texts that were geared to an adult audience, **Frankie Lymon and the Teenagers** made the style popular with young teens and even pre-teens. Lead singer Frankie Lymon was only thirteen years old when they recorded "Why Do Fools Fall in Love?" (1956). That same year they were featured in the film *Rock, Rock, Rock,* singing "I'm Not a Juvenile Delinquent." Lymon later decided to

Listening Guide

"There Goes My Baby" as recorded by the Drifters (1959)

Tempo: The tempo is approximately 126 beats per minute, with four beats in each bar.

Form: The song is comprised of eight, eight-bar periods without clear contrasting sections of new melodies or new chord progressions.

A variant version of the doo-wop progression is followed in each period, with each of the four chords lasting for two bars and IV replacing the ii^7 ($I–I–vi^7–vi^7–IV–IV–V^7–V^7$).

The recording ends with the beginning of a new period, but then fades out.

Features: Even though a single melody and chord progression repeats throughout the recording, it does not sound repetitious because the vocals and background instruments vary from one period to another as follows:

1. Bass solo voice with backup vocal group, and no instruments until the strings swirl in during the final bar.
2. Ben E. King sings lead with instrumental accompaniment, but no backup vocals.
3. King continues to sing lead and the backup vocal group sings soft responses.
4. The backup vocal group takes the lead and King sings responses.
5. King again sings lead without backup vocals and the lower strings supply a dramatic accompaniment.
6. King continues with the strings and the backup vocalists return sustaining chords.
7. King sings lead and the swirling violins return to accompany him.
8. The full vocal group returns to back King on this final period.

The orchestral string group provides most of the instrumental accompaniment with kettledrums accenting beats.

No backbeat is accented.

Beat subdivisions are uneven throughout the recording.

Lyrics: The singer's lover, or "baby," has gone away brokenhearted and not said exactly why she left or whether or not she loves him. The singer wishes he could tell her of his love for her.

Source: Time-Life Music, *The Rock 'N' Roll Era, 1959.*

start a solo career, but without the doo-wop sound of his backup singers, he was not successful. After several years of heroin addiction, he died of an overdose in 1968 at the age of twenty-five.

Other doo-wop groups who had hits during the fifties included the Moonglows, the Coasters, the Five Satins, the Rays, the Clovers, Little Caesar and the Romans, and the Capris (in addition to the various "bird" groups mentioned earlier). Doo-wop groups named after cars became popular with the advent of the Cadillacs, the Impalas, the Fleetwoods, the Imperials, and the Edsels. The vocal styles of the Mills Brothers, the Ink Spots, the Ravens, and the Orioles were the main influences on all of the doo-wop groups. The general style was a fairly consistent, smoothly romantic, moderately slow, danceable sound in which the lead singers often used gospel singing devices including repeated breath punctuations on words needing emphasis and stylized embellishments at phrase endings.

The smooth, pop-oriented doo-wop style gave way to gutsier African American vocal styles from the late fifties through the early seventies. That music came to be called "soul." The term "soul" was first used for African American music in reference to gospel groups' ability to "stir peoples' souls." By the early sixties, however, it came to refer to secular music by and, for the most part, for African Americans, during a time of struggle for recognition in a white society. In general terms, soul music was not imitative of white styles, and it developed as an expression of African American pride.

Gospel and doo-wop are alive, well, and extremely popular in the nineties with such singers and groups as Amy Grant, Take 6, All 4 One, Boyz II Men, and many others.

Summary

Like the blues, black gospel music originated with influences from both African and European musical traditions. But unlike the blues, which tended to be a vehicle for personal expression, gospel was religious and was often sung by groups of people who used their music to share the beliefs that unified them. Early gospel songs were called spirituals, and they were usually sung by groups of believers in a highly energetic style that displayed the fervor of their religious commitment. As part of that display, gospel singers stylized their vocals with ornaments that were not part of the basic melodies, but were improvised by soloists and changed with each performance. Generally, choirs did not embellish the melodies they sang, resulting in an interesting variation between the style of the soloist and that of the responding group.

Professional gospel groups formed to record and tour as early as the twenties. Groups such as the Mills Brothers and the Ink Spots formed secular versions of professional gospel groups. By the forties, other groups who imitated them developed a style called doo-wop. Many doo-wop groups were popular during the fifties, and some added pop-style instrumental backgrounds and remained on the charts into the sixties. Gospel and doo-wop were revived by new singers and groups in the nineties.

Terms to Remember

A cappella
Bass (voice)
Bridge
Coda
Doo-wop progression
Double time
Falsetto
Jubilees
Melisma
Part singing
Sorrow songs
Spiritual
Tenor (voice)
Vibrato

CHAPTER 5

Pop-Styled Rock Music

In very general terms, most rock music could be considered popular music because it is intended to appeal to musically unsophisticated listeners who, for the most part, are not concerned with the intricacies and profundities of musical form, harmonic language, or lofty poetic imagery. Non-pop music, categorized as art or folk music, is created for rather specialized audiences. Art music requires a certain amount of listening skill, and a lot of folk music involves the understanding and appreciation of an ethnic or regional identity not easily shared by people outside that group. Pop music, on the other hand, is simple and fairly easy for a general audience to appreciate. The charm of pop music is that it involves catchy melodies, uncomplicated texts, and infectious rhythm patterns that can be enjoyed the first time it's heard.

It has not been the concern of pop music to raise levels of social consciousness or to make political statements. Rock music, however, from its very beginnings in rhythm and blues, gospel, and country musical styles, made social statements. Some of those statements were made by rebellious teens who yearned for an identity separate from that of their parents and other authority figures, and some called for more sexual freedom or affirmed an ethnic identity. Whatever message it carried, early rock music by performers like Chuck Berry, Little Richard, Elvis Presley, and Jerry Lee Lewis was not pop music in the normally accepted sense of the term.

By 1960, many of the strongest performers of the energetic rock music of the mid-fifties had stopped performing and therefore provided no competition for the new pop-rock style that emerged between 1957 and 1960. Carl Perkins had not reestablished his career after the 1956 car accident in which he was severely injured and both his brother and his manager were killed; Little Richard left the music scene to enter the ministry; Jerry Lee Lewis' music was banned because of public disapproval over his illegal marriage to his young cousin; Elvis Presley was serving in the army; Chuck Berry was on trial for a Mann Act violation (taking a woman across state lines for immoral purposes) and later went to prison; Buddy Holly, the Big Bopper, and Ritchie Valens all died in a plane crash in 1959; and Eddie Cochran was killed in the same automobile accident that badly injured Gene Vincent in 1960. It is impossible to say what might have happened had all of these performers lived or remained in the music business, but their absence certainly had some effect on the development of pop-rock music.

It must be noted that at least some of these performers had sensed that pop was an important wave of the future, because they had begun to change their styles to fit the pop trend before their careers broke off. Presley had signed with RCA and recorded more pop-styled music than rockabilly, and both Buddy Holly and Eddie Cochran had shifted to a pop style in their last-recorded songs, "It Doesn't Matter Anymore" (Holly in 1959) and

"Three Steps to Heaven" (Cochran in 1960). Rockabilly artists Gene Vincent and Ronnie Hawkins did not want to change to this new style and thus left the United States to perform in England and Canada, where rockabilly was still popular.

The Payola Scandal

Rock music had grown so popular so quickly that many people in the music business had economic interests to protect. The American Society of Composers, Authors, and Publishers (ASCAP), an organization formed in 1914 to collect royalties for its members, included few rock musicians. Most rock writers belonged to another royalty collection agency, Broadcast Music, Inc. (BMI). The two organizations had long been competitors. BMI was formed in 1940 by members of the National Association of Broadcasters who resisted ASCAP's licensing terms and fees for airplay as well as ASCAP's general monopoly on the business. With the growing popularity of rock music, ASCAP came to resent the competition from BMI and searched for ways to discredit the music BMI handled. An easy way to accomplish this was to report the common practice of using **payola** (payment to disc jockeys for airplay) in the promotion of rock music. Although payola was not specifically against the law at the time, it was considered a corruption of ethics in broadcasting, and ASCAP requested that it be examined by a Congressional committee in 1958. The investigation, known as the payola scandal, put many small record companies and some disc jockeys out of business, and also resulted in legislation that made the practice illegal. The companies and individuals who were ruined tended to be those who promoted music by African American performers, including disc jockey and promoter Alan Freed.

Teen Idol Pop

Some of the pop-styled music of the fifties, particularly that known as "teen idol" pop, grew out of the tradition of ballad crooners of the twenties through the forties, whose stars included Perry Como and Bing Crosby. In 1952, a teen dance show called "Bandstand" was first televised in Philadelphia. The show's host was a local disc jockey, Bob Horn, who was later replaced by **Dick Clark** (born in 1929) in 1956. By the following year the show had changed its name to "American Bandstand" and its audience expanded when it was syndicated and aired on sixty-seven TV stations nationwide. The show brought Philadelphia pop music and dance styles to teenagers all over the country.

"American Bandstand" did occasionally feature performances by rockabilly and rhythm and blues artists, but it more often spotlighted clean-cut, pop-styled white teen idols such as Pat Boone, Paul Anka, Frankie Avalon, Connie Francis, Fabian, Bobby Rydell, Brenda Lee, and Bobby Vee. The leather-jacketed outfits and rebellious messages of the rockabilly singers who copied the image of Marlon Brando in *The Wild One* had no place on the program. Although "American Bandstand" changed its dress code many times over the years, it always maintained a clean and conservative image. At a time when many leaders of the entertainment industry saw rock music as a threat to the moral base of American society, only shows like "American Bandstand," with its image of clean-cut kids having fun, were allowed to continue.

Dick Clark had financial interests in the records he promoted on his show and was investigated for payola practices, but was exonerated when his attorneys showed that he also promoted records in which he had no financial interest. Another reason Dick Clark's show was allowed to continue was because it was considered to be a positive influence on teens, whereas the music that Alan Freed played was considered a corrupting influence.

"American Bandstand" served to bring rock music, dancers, and performers to teenage fans, but was an afternoon program. Ed Sullivan, who had a very popular Sunday evening television variety program designed for family entertainment, realized that he would have to have rock performers on his show in order to attract the teenage part of the family audience. By 1965, in addition to the occasional rock performances on "The Ed Sullivan Show," ABC TV added a new prime-time rock show called "Shindig" and NBC TV added "Hullabaloo." In those pre-video and pre-MTV days, these programs served to bring live rock and roll performances into American homes to eager teenage fans.

Like many other white singers of the fifties, **Pat Boone** (born in 1934) recorded covers of blues or rhythm and blues songs, but he did not speed them up as most of the rockabilly singers had. Instead he made other changes to make them fit his own clean-cut, boy-next-door image. While Elvis Presley was tough and threatening to anyone who would dare to "step on his blue suede shoes," Pat Boone wore clean, white buck shoes, which became his trademark. Despite the different images the two singers projected, they both topped the charts with hits originally recorded by African American artists. On page 51 is a comparison between Pat Boone's hit recording (#12 on the pop charts) of "Tutti-Frutti" and the original version by Little Richard (#17 on the pop charts).

It is obvious throughout Pat Boone's recording that he is trying to imitate Little Richard's rhythmic singing style and vocal inflections, but without capturing Richard's growling tone quality and delivery. Jazz influences, in the ways the instruments are played in Richard's version, were not used in Boone's recording, with the exception of the tenor saxophone solo,

Pat Boone
UPI/Bettmann

which adds a jazz touch to what is otherwise a pop form of the blues. Many rock fans would argue, and rightfully so, that Boone was not a rock singer at all; and yet when one looks at the many different forms of music that were considered rock in the fifties, it is clear that Boone's version of "Tutti-Frutti" was well within the pop style favored by the white commercial audience, and it represented a direction in which rock continued to move for the rest of the decade and well into the sixties. Boone's version of "Tutti-Frutti" can be considered rock, then, but only because of its historical context. The same can be said for much of the pop-rock of the same period.

The movie and television industry supported the growth in popularity of the clean teen-idol image. Pat Boone played teenage roles in the movies *April Love* (1957) and *Journey to the Center of the Earth* (1959). After "American Bandstand" was telecast nationwide and introduced Philadelphia-based teen idols **Frankie Avalon** (Francis Avallone, born in 1940), **Fabian** (Fabian Forte, born in 1943), and **Bobby Rydell** (Bobby Ridarelli, born in 1942) to teenage rock fans, those singers were further popularized by such movies as *Beach Blanket Bingo,* starring Frankie Avalon and Annette Funicello (a former Mouseketeer on "The Mickey Mouse Club"), and many others. **Ricky Nelson** (1940–1985) was more important to rock music for his rockabilly recordings, but he did have a teen idol image that was introduced to fans through his appearances on his parents' television show, "The Adventures of Ozzie and Harriet."

Two of the most successful female singers of the teen idol era were **Connie Francis** (Concetta Franconero, born in 1938) and **Brenda Lee** (Brenda Mae Tarpley, born in 1944). Francis had a mature **contralto voice** and sang popular teen-theme songs as well as standards from the twenties and thirties. She also recorded Italian and Spanish ballads that became popular in Italy and Spain. In addition to having hit singles, she was featured in the teen movies *Where the Boys Are* (1960), *Follow the Boys* (1963), and *Looking for Love* (1964). Brenda Lee started her professional singing career when she was only seven years old, singing on both radio and television shows in her home city of Atlanta, Georgia. Her fifties style was rockabilly, but during the early sixties she changed to more pop-oriented ballads. In later years she became a country singer.

Most of the teen idol singers were successful more for their visual appeal and in-group identification than for their musical talents. Their natural, though untrained, voices captured the youthful enthusiasm that the style required. On television, in movies, and even in "live" performances they usually synchronized their lip movements to their recordings (known as **lip syncing**) instead of actually singing live. Rarely did any of the singers play musical instruments, other than some occasional simple chording on guitar, and they generally were not songwriters. **Paul Anka** (born in 1941) was the exception. He wrote many of his own hits, and his songs became hits for other artists as well, including "It Doesn't Matter Anymore," which was a hit for Buddy Holly in 1959, "My Way" (1959) for Frank Sinatra, and "She's a Lady" (1971) for Tom Jones. He also composed the theme music for Johnny Carson's "Tonight Show" and several movie soundtracks.

Teen idol song themes were as youthful and wholesome as the performers' images. The delicate balance between happiness and disappointment in puppy love romances and dreams about finding the perfect mate predominated. A few examples are Frankie Avalon's "Venus" (1959), Connie Francis' "Where the Boys Are" (1961), and Paul Anka's "Puppy Love" (1960). Other concerns of young teens were expressed through such songs as Bobby Rydell's "Swingin' School" (1960), but songs about love and temporarily broken hearts prevailed.

Because it featured teen dancers, "American Bandstand" started and/or spread the popularity of many dance crazes of the late fifties and early sixties. During the fifties, the Bop was danced to Gene Vincent's "Be-Bop-a-Lula" (1956) and "Dance to the Bop" (1958), as well as "At the Hop" (1957) by Danny and the Juniors. Dances that were basically variations on the Bop assumed animal names, like the Pony, the Chicken, and the Monkey. The Dog and the Alligator were also popular variations on the Bop, but were a bit suggestive and, therefore, not allowed on "American Bandstand."

Listening Guide

	"Tutti-Frutti" as recorded by Little Richard (1955)	**"Tutti-Frutti" as recorded by Pat Boone (1956)**
Tempo:	The tempo is about 172 beats per minute, with four beats per bar.	The tempo is roughly 176 beats per minute, slightly faster than Little Richard's recording.
Form:	Both the music and the text follow the classic twelve-bar blues form. The recording has eight choruses; the sixth chorus is instrumental, with a tenor saxophone playing the melody, imitating Little Richard's rough vocal inflections.	Both the music and the text follow the classic twelve-bar blues form. The recording has eight choruses; the sixth chorus is instrumental, with a tenor saxophone playing the melody, in an improvised bebop-jazz style.
	The last four-bar phrases of the second, fourth, and eighth choruses are vocal, with stop-time instrumental breaks.	The last four-bar phrases of the second, fourth, and eighth choruses are vocal, with stop-time instrumental breaks.
Features:	A two-bar introduction of nonsense syllables is sung by Little Richard, giving the listener a taste of his no-holds-barred vocal style, which was often punctuated by octave-leap "oohs."	The introduction imitates Little Richard's, but Boone's voice has a smoother, less rhythmic, more controlled and "polite-sounding" quality compared to Little Richard's.
	The rhythm section includes piano, presumably played by Little Richard, using even beat subdivisions to offset the uneven divisions of the basic beat, a jazz-style walking bass, and rhythmic punctuation by saxophones.	The rhythm section includes piano, which is most obvious during the instrumental chorus, and a backup vocal group sings "ahs." Beat subdivisions are uneven throughout.
	The drummer gives the backbeat a strong accent.	The backbeat is present, but less obvious than in Little Richard's recording.
Lyrics:	In verses two, four, and eight, Little Richard sings about rocking with Sue (rocking was slang for sexual activity). He also indicates that Daisy knows how to love him too, hinting that he may not be true to Sue.	In verses two, four, and eight, Boone has removed the sexual references. He avoids the reference to rocking, and instead of indicating that he has two girlfriends, he admits that Daisy is interesting to him, but that he remains true to Sue.

Source: Little Richard's recording: Time-Life Music, *The Rock 'N' Roll Era, 1954–1955;* and *Little Richard's Grooviest 17 Original Hits,* Specialty 2113.

Pat Boone's recording: *The Best of Pat Boone,* MCA 6020.

In 1960, a young performer from Philadelphia, Ernest Evans, covered a song called "The Twist," by blues singer Hank Ballard. In search of a stage name, Evans decided on **Chubby Checker** (born in 1941), a not-so-subtle variation on Fats Domino's name. The popularity of the Twist as a dance resulted in more than just a hit record for Checker; it started a craze that continued for the next few years, with more Twist recordings made by Checker and other performers, including the Isley Brothers and Sam Cooke. Other dances popularized by Chubby Checker's songs included the Pony, the Fly, and the Limbo.

When we consider the history of American popular music in the twentieth century, we must include Latin music. In general, Latin rhythms and other Latin musical characteristics have had a much stronger influence on jazz than on rock music, but there certainly have been instances of Latin rock hits. One such case was teen idol **Ritchie Valens'** (Richard Valenzuela, 1941–1959) hit based on a traditional Mexican dance song, "La Bamba" (1959). A listening guide can be found on page 52.

This recording of "La Bamba," as well as Los Lobos' cover version from the soundtrack of the film about Valens' life, *La Bamba* (1987), have remained popular on

Listening Guide

"La Bamba"
as recorded by Ritchie Valens (1958)

Tempo: The tempo is approximately 152 beats per minute, with four beats per bar.

Form: The recording begins with a four-bar introduction with pickups.

The song is structured around a two-bar chordal **ostinato** that repeats throughout. The ostinato is sometimes supported by a repeating bass line, but at other times the bass drops out and the chordal pattern is repeated without the bass.

The overall structure is comprised of four primary sections, the first, second, and fourth of which are each fourteen bars long (seven repetitions of the ostinato). The third section begins much like the others, but is extended by an instrumental section to total twenty-five bars.

Features: Even beat subdivisions are maintained throughout the recording.

The drums accent the backbeat.

A guitar solos during the instrumental section.

Rhythmic interest is added by a repeated rhythm pattern played by a stick hitting a hollow piece of wood.

Lyrics: Sung in Spanish, the song encourages people to get up and dance, and to dance with a bit of grace. The singer also claims that although he is not a sailor, he would be one, or even be a captain, for the girl to whom the song is directed.

Source: *The Best of Ritchie Valens,* Rhino 70178; *Best of "La Bamba,"* Rhino 70617; and *La Bamba and Other Original Hits,* 3C-101.

"oldies" radio stations, attesting to the lasting appeal of upbeat Mexican rhythms. However, it was only the "B" side of the original single release. The "A" side, which was the bigger hit in 1959, was the pop ballad "Donna."

The teen sound was not exclusive to "American Bandstand" or Hollywood movies. Dion DiMucci (born in 1939) grew up singing to friends in the Bronx, but started his career by appearing on "Teen Club" televised from Philadelphia. He liked the doo-wop sound of a solo singer backed by a group, and asked three friends from the Bronx to sing backup vocals for him. Because they all lived near Belmont Avenue, they took the name **Dion and the Belmonts**. The group went on the 1959 tour during which Buddy Holly, Ritchie Valens, and the Big Bopper were killed, and the stress from having narrowly escaped death himself (he had taken the bus) aggravated Dion's already serious drug problem. He and the Belmonts went their separate ways, and Dion continued his career recording under his name alone, but backed by the Del-Satins. After British groups invaded the American pop charts in 1964, he experimented with blues and country styles, but none of those efforts were commercially successful. In 1968 he resumed his career with an updated style, paying tribute to the slain leaders Abraham Lincoln, Martin Luther King, Jr., John F. Kennedy, and Robert F. Kennedy in his hit "Abraham, Martin and John." He continued to experiment with new songs, but was best received as a performer of his old hits.

Longer-lasting than most other pop groups of the time, **The Four Seasons** continued to have hits throughout the sixties. The focal point of the group's sound was the high falsetto (higher than tenor range) voice of their lead singer, Frankie Valli (Francis Casteluccio, born in 1937). Although they had been recording since they first performed together in 1956, the group's first real commercial success did not come until their recording of "Sherry" in 1962. After many other hits with the Four Seasons, Frankie Valli pursued a solo career, but did not sever his ties with the group until 1977. Valli is still performing with singers billed as the Four Seasons, but none of the original members of the Seasons are part of that group.

New York Pop

Because pop performers have seldom been songwriters, the burst of popularity of the style created a need for musicians who specialized in songwriting. Many pop-styled hits of the period between 1959 and 1963 were written and published in **The Brill Building**, located at 1619 Broadway in New York City, or across the street at the headquarters of Al Nevins and Don Kirshner's **Aldon Music Company**. Influences of gospel, doo-wop, and teen idol music were present in the music produced by these New York-based songwriters. Most of the writers worked in teams, the most famous of which were Howard Greenfield and Neil Sedaka, Barry Mann and Cynthia Weil, Doc Pomus and Mort Shuman, Gerry Goffin and Carole King, Jerry Leiber and Mike Stoller, and Jeff Barry and Ellie Greenwich. Sedaka, Mann, and King doubled as performers and sang on the recordings of some of their own hits. Writer/producer George "Shadow" Morton worked with Barry and Greenwich to create short story-line songs like "Remember (Walkin' in the Sand)" and "Leader of the Pack" (both sung by the Shangri-Las in 1964) that were unusual for pop music.

The Shirelles (clockwise from top): Micki Harris, Shirley Alston, Beverly Lee, and Doris Kenner
Michael Ochs Archives/Venice, CA

The pop sound of the early sixties gave women more of a chance to perform on the pop chart hits than had most blues- or country-related rock music of the fifties. Most of the time the women were singers, and although Bo Diddley had his half-sister, "The Duchess," play guitar in his band, it was unusual for a woman to be an instrumentalist. Many of the female singers were in all-female trios or quartets called girl groups. One girl group that placed twelve top ten hits on the pop charts between 1960 and 1963 and who actually did some songwriting—which was also unusual for pop singers of the era—was the Shirelles. The listening guide to their first number one hit, "Will You Love Me Tomorrow?," serves as a good example of the Brill Building pop sound. Carole King, who remains one of the most successful female songwriters in rock music, and her then husband, Gerry Goffin, wrote the song for the Shirelles.

The song "Will You Love Me Tomorrow?" cut right to the heart of one of the most common problems felt by young women faced by the sexual double standard of the era. Another important writer/producer at the Brill Building, Phil Spector, contributed much to the popularity of girl groups during the early sixties.

Phil Spector's "Wall of Sound" Productions

Many of the Brill Building writers were also competent producers, but few had production skills to compare with those of **Phil Spector** (born in 1940). Spector's productions had such a distinctive effect that his production style became known as the "wall of sound." The term "wall" was descriptive because he used so many instruments, and overdubbed and mixed them so thoroughly, the result was a massive fortification of instrumental colors and timbres behind the vocals. He did not like to record in stereo, because it separated some instruments from others. Spector's productions were generally very thick and full, but when he did allow an individual instrument to stand out from the rest, the effect was very colorful, as in the Spanish flamenco-style guitar fills in the Crystals' recording of "Uptown" (1962). He incorporated the natural sound of rain in the background of the Ronettes' recording of "Walking in the Rain" (1964). A standard rock drum set was not enough for Spector's sound. He liked classical music, particularly that of nineteenth-century German romantic composer Richard

Listening Guide

"Will You Love Me Tomorrow?" as recorded by the Shirelles (1960)

Tempo: The tempo is approximately 138 beats per minute, with four beats in each bar.

Form: After a four-bar introduction, the song has five sixteen-bar periods, each of which is made up of two eight-bar phrases. The overall form of those periods is A A B A A. Each A period ends with the question "Will you love me tomorrow?" The first phrase of the last A is instrumental. The ending fades during a final repetition of the title lyrics.

Features: Even beat subdivisions are maintained throughout the recording.

Shirley Alston's solo voice is backed by the rest of the Shirelles in a doo-wop style.

The backbeat is stressed through a drum rhythm with two eighth notes on each second beat and a single accent on each fourth beat through most of the recording.

An orchestral string section plays phrase-ending fills and the lead on the instrumental section.

Lyrics: A young woman is asking her date whether he really loves her for the future, or just for some fun this one evening.

Source: Time-Life Music, *The Rock 'N' Roll Era, 1961.*

Phil Spector with Ike and Tina Turner at the "River Deep—Mountain High" recording session

© Ray Avery/Michael Ochs Archives/ Venice, CA

Wagner, and imitated Wagner's coloristic use of percussion instruments such as chimes, castanets, triangles, timpani, and gongs by adding them to an already full sound. Spector's productions did not sound Wagnerian, but they had more orchestral fullness than earlier rock productions that had used only strings or brass sections. Spector considered his records symphonies for teens.

Spector worked both in New York and in Los Angeles. He started his own company, Philles (Phil + Les) with Lester Sill, who handled the business arrangements while Spector maintained control of the music. Late in 1962, Sill sold his interest in the company and Spector assumed complete control. With his own company, Spector often contracted singers, but kept ownership of their stage or group names for himself. Because he had the singers under contract and owned the rights to their stage names, Spector could use any combination of singers he wanted and call them the Crystals or Bob B. Soxx and the Bluejeans (two of the group names he owned). He presented Darlene Love (Darlene Wright) with an unnamed backup group whose personnel could change from record to record. The one group he kept as a regular trio was the Ronettes, whose lead singer, Ronnie (Veronica Bennett), he married in 1967.

Spector wanted to keep on top of current trends, so when the British invasion groups began to take over the American charts, he traveled to England and took part in some of the early recording sessions of the Rolling Stones and other British groups. Back in Los Angeles, he produced what he considered his finest work, Ike and Tina Turner's recording of "River Deep—Mountain High" (1966), but the rock audience's tastes had changed, and his heavily produced recordings were not selling as they had in the past. Spector's depression over the lack of success of his masterwork led to a life of isolation the new Mrs. Spector could not bear; their marriage ended in 1974.

A listening guide follows on page 55.

Phil Spector maintained his reputation for quality, hit-making productions, and was asked to sift through hours of tape made by the soon-to-disband Beatles, add backing filler, and produce their *Let It Be* album (recorded in 1969, released in 1970). Both George Harrison and John Lennon had him produce post-Beatles recordings for them, including Harrison's *All Things Must Pass* (1970) and *The Concert for Bangladesh* (1972), and Lennon's *Imagine* (1971). Spector attempted a comeback with productions for Cher and Dion in the mid-seventies, but he could not recapture his earlier successes. He produced the *End of the Century* album (1980) for the Ramones, giving it a style that made it strikingly different from any of the group's previous recordings. For Spector's wall of sound fans, the new sound represented a positive change for the Ramones, and the album sold well, but to most of the group's long-time fans it was a disaster. The future may see more revivals of earlier rock styles, but for the most part Phil Spector hit his peak of popularity during the pop-styled early sixties. The 1991 boxed set of Spector's work was entitled *Back to Mono* to emphasize the importance of monaural recording in his thick, wall of sound productions.

The Surf Sound

While pop-rock music from the East Coast was dominated by songs about puppy love and teen dances, West

Listening Guide

"River Deep—Mountain High" as recorded by Ike and Tina Turner (1966)

Tempo: The tempo is about 168 beats per minute, with four beats in each bar.

Form: The recording begins with a four-bar instrumental introduction that is repeated after the first B section and repeated again to end the recording.

The overall form is A B A B C B.

Each A section is made up of one eight-bar phrase, one six-bar phrase, and three four-bar phrases.

Each B section is made up of two eight-bar phrases, the second of which is a repetition of the melody of the first. The lyrics of each B section are the same as the first B and include the words in the song title, "River deep—mountain high."

The C section is introduced by the orchestra playing a two-bar riff pattern twice. The riff is kept at a low dynamic level and continues to repeat through the vocals. The vocal part of the C section is made up of two eight-bar phrases. The C section ends with the orchestra taking twelve bars to build to a very loud dynamic level.

Features: Even beat subdivisions are kept by the instruments, but Turner's vocals sometimes relax into uneven subdivisions.

The backbeat is subdued at the beginning of the recording, but gradually increases in volume as the recording progresses. It is most obvious in the finger snaps in the C section.

Both the chorus and the orchestra have been overdubbed several times, creating a very thick and full "wall of sound" out of which few instruments or backup singers can be heard individually.

Monaural recording is used to further mix the sound and avoid the separation stereo would have created.

The chorus generally sings "doo-doo-do-do" syllables or holds notes on an "ah," but varies that by supporting some of Turner's vocal phrases in the B sections.

The dynamic level of the orchestra, chorus, and Turner's vocals build in intensity and volume level after the C section and through the final B section.

Lyrics: The singer is expressing the depth and stability of her love to her loved one.

Source: *The Best of Ike & Tina Turner*, EMI 95846; and *Phil Spector: Back to Mono (1958–1969)*, AKO 7118.

Coast musicians developed their own danceable style known as surf rock. Surf rock was a type of pop music different from that of New York and Philadelphia because its vocals were not based on the old crooner vocal tradition, and surf bands played their own instruments instead of using large studio orchestras. In some ways, in fact, surf bands represented a return to the older rock music played on guitars, bass, and drums, but the surf band image and sound was so light and pop-oriented that it is still considered to be part of rock's more pop-oriented phase. Although vocals were an important element of the surf style, instrumental hits became more common in surf rock than in any style that preceded it. Saxophones and electric organs were often used, but the electric guitar was the most common lead instrument. The guitar style that became the foundation of much surf music was based on the styles of Duane Eddy, the Ventures, and Dick Dale.

Duane Eddy's (born in 1938) distinctive and influential guitar style (called "twangy guitar") was achieved by plucking the strings of the guitar very close to the **bridge,** where the strings are attached to the body of the instrument. The strings are their tightest at the bridge, and plucking them there results in a strong, nasal-sounding attack. Most of Eddy's recordings stressed the use of repetitious lead lines played on the guitar's bass strings, with the tremolo arm being used to bend the pitch. The pitch variation, called vibrato, and the studio- or amplifier-produced echo effects gave the guitar a sound that was constantly wavering. It may have been this wavering sound, reminiscent of the motion of water, that led the surf instrumental groups to incorporate it into their styles. Eddy's first hit, "Rebel-'Rouser" (1958), was very much influenced by the energy of gospel music; it used an instrumental form of call-and-response in which Eddy's lead guitar lines were answered by a saxophone. His second hit single, "Ramrod" (1958), was a blues, and "Forty Miles of Bad Road" (1959) had a standard pop-song form. By 1960, with his movie-theme hit "Because They're Young" (he also acted in the movie), Eddy had gone in the same pop-styled direction as other fifties rock musicians, and he included a large orchestral string section in his soundtrack recording. Eddy continued to do some

The Beach Boys (left to right): Al Jardine, Carl Wilson, Dennis Wilson, Brian Wilson, and Mike Love
Michael Ochs Archives/Venice, CA

recording into the eighties, including playing on "Peter Gunn" (1986) by Art of Noise.

From Tacoma, Washington, **The Ventures** were among the most important of the early instrumental groups to become associated with the surf image, although they did not actually adopt that image until after other surf groups had copied them. The group consisted of two guitarists, an electric bassist, and a drummer. Duane Eddy's twangy guitar sound was a clear influence on their style. The Ventures became one of the few surf groups to maintain their following through the sixties and beyond; they had several surf instrumental hits and also recorded a version of the theme music for the television program "Hawaii Five-O" (1969). With the help of a large following in Japan, the Ventures were still together and popular when the surf sound experienced a revival in the United States in the early eighties.

Dick Dale (Richard Anthony Monsour, born in 1937) was given the title "The King of Surf Guitar" because he originated an impressive guitar style copied by many surf instrumental groups of the early sixties. From Balboa, California, Dick Dale and the Del-Tones started out using the twangy guitar style of Duane Eddy and the Rebels in such recordings as "Let's Go Trippin' " (1961), which was a blues in form though not in style. In his version of the Greek melody "Misirlou" (1961), however, Dale developed a technique based on the tremolo playing used in Middle Eastern plucked-string instruments such as the bouzouki. **Tremolo,** in this case, refers to fast repetitions of a note. Like the Greek bouzouki players, Dale sustained notes by plucking a string up and down very fast with his guitar pick. While continuing that motion, he would slide the other hand up and down the fingerboard, achieving an impressive effect of speed. To that, Dale added Eddy's twangy style to create a sound often copied by other surf guitarists of the era. The Beach Boys were among the first groups to popularize Dale's style nationally when they recorded cover versions of his hits on their early albums. Dale joined other aging pop artists of the early sixties; Frankie Avalon and Annette Funicello, in the movie *Back to the Beach* (1987), and his 1961 hit "Misirlou" was featured on the soundtrack of *Pulp Fiction* (1994).

Other instrumental surf rock groups that followed the styles of Duane Eddy, the Ventures, and Dick Dale included the Marketts, the Chantays, and the Surfaris. Their hits (not to be referred to as "songs," since there was no singing in them) were often given titles from surfing terminology: the Chantays' "Pipeline" (1963) represented the coiled form of a wave, and even fans who were "sidewalk surfers" on skateboards knew what was meant by the Surfaris' "Wipe Out" (1963).

The Beach Boys were formed by three brothers, Brian (born in 1942), Carl (born in 1946), and Dennis Wilson (1944–1983), their cousin, Mike Love (born in 1941), and a neighbor, Alan Jardine (born in 1942), in Hawthorne, California. They first called themselves the Pendletones, a musical play on "Pendleton," a plaid flannel shirt-jacket popular among surfers. They then tried the name Carl and the Passions, but adopted Kenny and the Cadets for their first recording. No band member was named Kenny, but the name may have been chosen because the song they recorded was called "Barbie" (1961), at the time Barbie and Ken dolls were just becoming popular. The name the Beach Boys had been settled on by the time they recorded their first local hit, "Surfin'," in 1961. The Wilson brothers' father, Murry Wilson, managed them and, after the success of "Surfin'," got them a contract with Capitol Records.

From the beginning of their career, the Beach Boys were more than just a surf-rock group. Their guitarist, Carl Wilson, did use Duane Eddy's twangy guitar style

Listening Guide

	"Sweet Little Sixteen" as recorded by Chuck Berry (1958)	***"Surfin' U.S.A." as recorded by the Beach Boys (1963)***
Tempo:	The tempo is about 176 beats per minute, with four beats per bar.	The tempo is about 164 beats per minutes, with four beats per bar.
Form:	The recording begins with a two-bar guitar introduction that ends with vocal pickups leading into the first period of the form.	The recording begins with a two-bar guitar introduction (different from Berry's) that ends with vocal pickups that lead into the first period.
	After the introduction, the song is made up of a series of eight sixteen-bar periods, each of which is based on **antecedent and consequent phrases** that use the same chord progression, but have different melodic lines, the second of which sounds more conclusive than the first.	After the introduction, the song is made up of a series of five sixteen-bar periods, each of which is based on antecedent and consequent phrases that closely match those in Berry's recording.
	The first period begins on the word "Boston," and ends with "sweet little sixteen."	The first period begins on the word "ocean," and ends with "surfin' U.S.A."
Features:	Uneven beat subdivisions are used throughout the recording.	Even beat subdivisions are kept most of the way through the recording, but the backup vocals and the organ often relax into uneven subdivisions.
	The drums keep a strong backbeat.	The drums accent a strong backbeat, and the bass drum pounds out each bar's four beats.
	The instruments break for a voice solo in the second and seventh periods and the bars that lead into them.	The second and fourth periods have no breaks, but do change in that the backup vocals repeat a new phrase while the solo vocal line continues its own lyric line.
	After the guitar solo in the introduction, Berry's guitar maintains a riff pattern through most of the recording.	The rhythm pattern of Berry's riff is imitated through most of the recording.
	The fifth period is instrumental and features a boogie-woogie style piano solo that is decorated by long and elaborate glissandos.	The fifth period is mostly instrumental featuring an organ solo in the first (antecedent) phrase, and a guitar solo followed by voices in the second (consequent) phrase. The recording ends with four more repetitions of that final four-bar vocal line and then fades out.
Lyrics:	The song is about a sixteen-year-old girl's desire to talk her parents into letting her go out to "rock and roll."	The song is about surfing and surfers. The singer wishes that everyone in the country had an ocean and could have fun like the surfers in California.

Source: Berry's recording: Time-Life Music, *The Rock 'N' Roll Era, 1958.*

The Beach Boys' recording: Time-Life Music, *The Rock 'N' Roll Era, 1963.*

and the tremolo style of Dick Dale in many of the group's instrumental recordings, but he also imitated the riff-based sound of Chuck Berry. The group's main writer and producer, Brian Wilson, had been a fan of the jazz vocal group the Four Freshmen, and used their group vocal style and harmonies in many of the Beach Boys' hits. As Wilson learned more about studio production techniques, he came very close to the wall of sound fullness of Phil Spector's productions. Through more than twenty years of recording and performing, the Beach Boys' music developed so far beyond their original surf image that their surf-oriented name came to have meaning only for those who knew their earlier history.

One of their early hits, "Surfin' U.S.A." (1963), had the same melody, chord progression, and form as Chuck Berry's hit "Sweet Little Sixteen" (1958), and, although Wilson first claimed writer's credit, probably really believing he had written it, eventually the credit and royalty income was given to Berry. The listening guides on page 57 compare essential musical elements of the two recordings.

A fun way to compare these two recordings and clearly see how closely they match is to sing one of Berry's antecedent phrases and follow it with one of the Beach Boys' consequent phrases, and then try the reverse order. Most who do this will arrive at the conclusion that Berry did, indeed, deserve credit for "Surfin' U.S.A." Wilson may have attempted to keep part of the credit for his new lyrics, but one can only assume that the two writers agreed with the settlement that was reached.

By late 1963, Brian Wilson had developed into a fine songwriter, and he expanded the Beach Boys beyond beach themes to sing about other teenage interests, such as school spirit and fast cars. Wilson also aided in the writing and production of several popular car- and surf-theme songs for his friends, the vocal duo Jan and Dean.

By 1966, many changes had taken place in Brian Wilson's life. The result was a nervous breakdown that forced him to stop touring. His place onstage was taken at first by Glen Campbell and then by Bruce Johnston. Wilson kept writing, producing, and singing and playing on the group's recordings, however. Without the pressures of touring, he was able to focus his energies on songwriting. In 1966, he put together the Beach Boys' most important album, *Pet Sounds.* The album was not the group's greatest commercial success, but all its songs were connected thematically, and this influenced many rock albums that followed. Theme albums had existed in jazz and other non-classical music before with Mel Tormé's *California Suite; Perfume Suite; Black, Brown, and Beige;* and several others by Duke Ellington; and any number of soundtrack and musical-comedy recordings. Even Phil Spector's *A Christmas Gift to You* (1963) predates *Pet Sounds* as a theme album. But the standard rock albums of the time were simply collections of individual songs with no real connection to each other; it was *Pet Sounds* that sent rock albums in a new direction.

Pet Sounds was a different kind of theme album from its predecessors because the theme, which was not even hinted at in the title, emerged slowly as one song led to the next. In general, the theme was the expression of hopes, dreams, and anxiety about the present and future felt by a young person growing up. The hopes were expressed through the songs "Wouldn't It Be Nice," "Don't Talk (Put Your Head on My Shoulder)," and "I'm Waiting for the Day." Feelings of insecurity were evident in "I Know There's an Answer," "I Just Wasn't Made for These Times," "Caroline No," and "God Only Knows." Wilson's productions on *Pet Sounds* were thick, with many instrumental tracks layered one on top of another, not unlike the wall of sound productions of Phil Spector.

Pet Sounds could be credited for beginning the theme-album trend of the late sixties, but without a doubt, it was the Beatles' *Sgt. Pepper's Lonely Hearts Club Band,* recorded the following year, that stimulated other bands to produce theme albums. The Beatles gave subtle credit to the influence *Pet Sounds* had on their *Sgt. Pepper's* album when they put animal sounds and the sound of a galloping horse at the end of "Good Morning." Those sounds were imitative of the dog barking and the sound of a train rushing past the listener that Brian Wilson had added just after the end of the last song on *Pet Sounds,* "Caroline No."

The Beach Boys followed *Pet Sounds* with their best-selling single, "Good Vibrations" (1966). A Spector-influenced, complex production that included sound effects made by such nontraditional (for rock music) instruments as sleighbells, and an electronic instrument, the **theremin,** "Good Vibrations" represented a new artistic achievement for Wilson. On page 59 is a listening guide to the hit version of that recording.

Wilson had even greater artistic plans for the album *Smile,* on which he was collaborating with poet/musician/producer Van Dyke Parks, but the album was never finished. *Smiley Smile* (1967), which was released instead, contained only "Heroes and Villains" and a few other songs from the originally planned recording.

The Beach Boys' next effort, *Wild Honey* (1967), showed influences of the soul sound of the sixties, but beginning with this album the group was not able to match its earlier popularity. They continued to record, tour, and perform, but their most successful releases were compilations of old hits. Their biggest hit single of the seventies was "Rock and Roll Music" (1976), a cover of Chuck Berry's 1957 hit. Brian Wilson took years to recover from drug-related problems, and at the beginning of the eighties the Beach Boys attempted a comeback. Dennis Wilson, who had battled alcohol addiction for some time, drowned while diving in the cold ocean water of Marina del Rey, California, in December 1983. Although it was reported that he had been drinking, and the possibility

Listening Guide

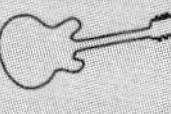

"Good Vibrations" as recorded by the Beach Boys (1966)

Tempo: The basic tempo of the recording is approximately 152 beats per minute, with four beats per bar, but the tempo slows to about 138 beats per minute at the end of the D section. The original tempo returns in the last section.

Form: The form is based on eight-bar phrases with an occasional four-bar extension.

Approximately the first half of the recording is made up of clear A B A B sections, each of which includes two eight-bar phrases. The "good vibrations" are sung about in the lyrics to each B section.

The rest of the recording has a less clear-cut formal structure. The C section begins with an eight-bar instrumental section, followed by a four-bar section with the voices holding an "ah" syllable and then singing an eight-bar vocal phrase.

The D section begins with sustained chords on the organ joined by a dampened maraca that establishes a slower tempo. The vocals return with a four-bar phrase played four-and-one-half times with the voices fading out during the third time through the phrase.

A vocal "ah" is followed by a pause after which the original tempo returns for an E section based, in part, on the second phrase of the B section, this time with a very gospel rhythmic feel, followed by eight more bars in which different singers respond to one another with various nonsense syllables. Two different melodies are sung at the same time during the nonsense syllables creating a **polyphonic texture.**

The recording ends with an instrumental version of the first melody in the B section and fades out in the fifth bar.

Features: Uneven beat subdivisions are maintained throughout the recording.

The instrumental background is very thickly produced with a lot of overdubbing to thicken the texture.

In the tradition of Phil Spector's "wall of sound," the recording is done in monaural to avoid the separation that stereo would have created.

The drummer is heard softly playing a drum set in the A sections, but the only percussion in the B sections is a tambourine on the backbeats.

An electronic instrument called a theremin is used during the B sections and at the end of the recording to create an oscillating sound that has an almost "ghost-like" effect.

Lyrics: The singer is singing about the "good vibrations" he feels when he thinks about his girlfriend.

Source: Time-Life Music, *The Rock 'N' Roll Era, The Beach Boys, 1962–1967;* Time-Life Music, *AM Gold, 1966;* Time-Life Music, *Classic Rock 1966;* and The Beach Boys, *Smiley Smile,* Capitol 93696.

of suicide had been raised, his death was officially ruled accidental. The Beach Boys continued without him and released the album *The Beach Boys* in 1985. It was not well received by the general rock audience. Brian Wilson received some attention for a self-titled solo album in 1988, but the group didn't have much success until their hit "Kokomo" (with which Brian Wilson did not have any involvement) was released later that same year on the soundtrack for the movie *Cocktail.*

Surf Revival

The early eighties was a time of many revivals of nearly forgotten rock styles, including the surf sound. The surf revival was centered in Southern California for much the same reason the sound had originated there: Surfing was a popular summer sport. While the group Jon and the Nightriders played in the early-sixties surf style, the Surf Punks in the late seventies combined a punk beat and electronic sounds, not used in the earlier surf music, with surf-style instrumentals. Other musicians, influenced by Jon and the Nightriders and the Surf Punks, put together groups such as the Malibooz, the Belair-Bandits, and the Wedge. They recreated the old surf sound through their covers of early-sixties hits and made new recordings based on the old style. The instrumentals played by these groups featured the old Duane Eddy and Dick Dale stylings, and their vocals copied the early Beach Boys' Four Freshmen-influenced style.

Summary

Pop music is light, direct, and uncomplicated. During the late fifties and early sixties, teen idol pop and dance styles from Philadelphia and New York became more popular than other rock styles, at least with teenagers. On the West Coast, a surf-rock style was played that differed from the East Coast pop style because the groups played their own instruments and did not depend on studio effects for their sound. However, it did not take long for the Beach Boys to leave surf music behind and create complex studio-produced records in the style of Phil Spector's wall of sound.

Critics tend to be very hard on pop performers and their music because pop music generally lacks the depth of personal commitment found in many other rock styles. Pop music is and always has been designed for an audience that does not look to music for expressions of deep emotion or thoughtful insights. That audience wants simple, uncomplicated enjoyment. Whether that pleasure comes from lighthearted love songs and youthful dreams, or from music that has little more to offer than a danceable beat, pop music is an important element of all cultures. It has never been a great art that expresses the values of its culture to future generations, but it has never claimed to be. It is called pop because it appeals to popular tastes on a fairly simple, uncomplicated level.

Terms to Remember

Antecedent and consequent phrases
Bridge (of a guitar)
Contralto voice
Lip syncing
Ostinato
Payola
Polyphonic texture
Theremin
Tremolo

CHAPTER 6

Folk and Folk-Rock Music

American folk music, like the folk music of most of the world, grew out of what was essentially an oral tradition—songs passed from one performer to another by rote. Unlike most art music, in which the composer plans and notates every interpretative nuance, the melodies, lyrics, and rhythms of folk songs were often changed as each new performer adapted a given song to his or her personality and performance style. Sometimes changes occurred as the result of a performer's faulty memory, but quite often changes were made intentionally so that old songs would speak to the concerns of new and different audiences. In other situations, particularly once written collections were published, traditional songs were performed very close to the way the singer had heard them done by another artist, but the folk singer or instrumentalist was not obliged to recreate an earlier performance exactly.

Folk music and performance traditions varied from one part of the United States to another, because the music was based on songs and dances people of different cultures brought with them from their homelands. Many of these settlers maintained their Old World songs and musical traditions as a connection with their cultural roots. Of particular importance to our discussion because of its influences on rock music of the sixties was the British-derived folk music from the Appalachian mountain region stretching from West Virginia to New York. The ballads, fiddle tunes, and dance melodies of that era can be traced directly back to comparable English, Scottish, and Irish music of Elizabethan times. Instruments used by American folk musicians, such as the fiddle, the acoustic guitar, the string bass, and the recorder, had been used in Scotland and Ireland hundreds of years earlier and were brought to the New World by settlers. Both the language of some of the songs and the types of chord progressions used to accompany them often reflected their sixteenth- and seventeenth-century origins.

Musicologists **Charles Seeger** (1886–1979), **John A. Lomax** (1872–1948), and **Alan Lomax** (born in 1915) researched, analyzed, notated, and recorded a large number of folk songs from the Appalachians. Seeger traced the often minute changes that had taken place through the passing of songs from one performer to another through the years, and published his findings in scholarly studies, one of which was *Versions and Variants of the Tunes of "Barbara Allen"* (1966). Seeger's work was used by his son, **Pete Seeger** (born in 1919), who sang and played guitar and banjo, performing many of the songs his father had researched as well as composing new songs. Both John A. and Alan Lomax recorded and collected folk music for the Archives of the Library of Congress and published collections of the songs they recorded, such as *Folk Song U.S.A.* (1947).

Most folk music was primarily vocal, and instruments were used to accompany singing, but instruments such as the fiddle and the recorder supplied lead fills much as the fiddle did in hillbilly music. Like traditional bluegrass country groups, folk singers avoided using electric instruments or drums, even after they were common in other kinds of music. In addition to using the British instrumentation, American folk groups borrowed instruments such as the five-string banjo from country traditions.

Early Folk Groups

Pete Seeger started **The Almanac Singers** in New York in 1941, and, just as the folk group **The Hutchinson Family Quartet** had done a hundred years earlier, the Almanac Singers took traditional folk melodies and performed them with new texts that stressed the social and political concerns of their time. The Hutchinson Family Quartet had sung about mid-nineteenth-century issues, such as the destructiveness of alcohol within the family, the need to abolish slavery, and women's right to vote. The Almanac Singers sang out for the development of strong labor unions, civil rights, and the need to end war. Most of the group's views were considered left-wing, which tended to limit their audience. They performed at political events such as American Federation of Labor meetings and were much appreciated and remembered by those who shared their political views. Two of their members, Pete Seeger and Woody Guthrie, established solo careers and performed with later folk groups.

In 1948, Pete Seeger, Lee Hays (also of the Almanac Singers), and two other singers formed **The Weavers**, whose harmonized group vocals were a new experience for many American audiences. The group quickly achieved national fame for their energetic and entertaining performances of folk songs such as "Goodnight Irene," "Kisses Sweeter Than Wine," and "On Top of Old Smokey." The Weavers also sang political songs, and their commitment to left-wing causes resulted in their losing some of their following in the early fifties, when members of the group were investigated by the House Un-American Activities Committee. The group temporarily broke up in 1953, unable to find any place to perform. Regrouped two years later, the Weavers continued to perform regularly for another ten years, with periodic reunion concerts afterwards.

Before joining the Almanac Singers, songwriter/singer/guitarist **Woody Guthrie** (1912–1967) had spent years traveling around the country singing on street corners. He sang about his concerns by putting new texts to traditional folk melodies as well as writing new folk-styled songs. Alan Lomax recognized Guthrie's effective expression of his times and recorded a collection of his songs for the Library of Congress. Guthrie served in the Merchant Marines during World War II, and he sang songs that supported the war cause, with "This machine kills fascists" painted on his guitar. By the early fifties, Guthrie was hospitalized with Huntington's chorea, a degenerative disease of the nervous system, and could no longer perform. Among his best-known compositions were "This Land Is Your Land" and "So Long, It's Been Good to Know You," both of which became classics in his own time.

Whereas the Almanac Singers, the Weavers, and their individual members were a politically oriented group of folk singers, other singers such as John Jacob Niles and Burl Ives were less so, and they performed traditional folk material for audiences as early as the twenties (thirties, in Ives' case) and for decades after that. They drew a lot of attention, particularly from college students, and by the late fifties and early sixties had inspired many groups to form and perform both traditional and newly written music in folk style. Some of those new groups—the Kingston Trio, Peter, Paul and Mary, Joan Baez, and others—recorded nationally popular singles, helping to establish a vocal sound favored over rock music among socially conscious college students and influencing folk-rock music of the middle to late sixties.

Bob Dylan

A young follower of Woody Guthrie, Robert Allen Zimmerman grew up in Minnesota. In high school he played with a rock group called the Golden Chords, but he dropped rock for folk music, accompanying himself with acoustic guitar and harmonica. He sang in coffeehouses while he was in college and began to use the pseudonym Bob Dylan. Many have said he chose the name because of his respect for the twentieth-century poet Dylan Thomas, but Dylan has denied this in some interviews. Regardless of the reason for the choice of name, eventually he legally changed his last name to Dylan. He moved to New York, where Guthrie was hospitalized, so that he could get to know the man behind the music and image he admired.

While in New York, Dylan performed in folk coffeehouses such as the Bitter End and Folk City in Greenwich Village, and began to develop a following for his elusive personality and expressive style. He soon attracted the attention of producer John Hammond, Sr., of Columbia Records, who gave him a recording contract. Hammond had earlier been responsible for bringing such important jazz artists as Billie Holiday, Count Basie, and Benny Goodman to Columbia Records, and later discovered and signed Aretha Franklin and Bruce Springsteen. Dylan's first album, *Bob Dylan* (1962), contained traditional folk material as well as two original songs that voiced some of his personal concerns—"Talkin' New York," about the beginning of his performing career in the big city, and "Song to Woody," a tribute to Woody Guthrie.

One of the traditional folk songs Dylan recorded was "House of the Rising Sun." As Guthrie had done in his own earlier recordings of songs written

Bob Dylan performing for 20,000 fans at Madison Square Garden, New York in 1974
UPI/Bettmann

from a woman's point of view, Dylan sang the song's traditional lyrics in which the "house" was a bordello and the singer a woman who ruined her life by running off with a drunkard and now had to support herself as a prostitute. Nothing androgynous was intended in a male folk singer's taking a female role; folk singers often chose to sing the traditional lyrics to a song no matter which sex was implied by the text. This practice was not part of the rock tradition, however, and when the British rock group the Animals recorded the song two years after Dylan, they changed the sex role by making the drunkard the singer's father rather than the singer's lover. The Animals' use of amplified guitar, electric keyboard, electric bass, and drums had a much more rock-oriented sound that Dylan's very rural folk style.

Dylan's second album, *The Freewheelin' Bob Dylan* (1963), gave him the protest-singer reputation that Woody Guthrie and others had established for themselves decades earlier. From that album, "Blowin' in the Wind," a hit when recorded by Peter, Paul and Mary, became a popular statement of support for both peace and racial equality. "Masters of War" and "A Hard Rain's A-Gonna Fall" contained strong antiwar statements.

Singer/guitarist Joan Baez aided Dylan's career by recording some of his songs and adding him to her tour in 1963. His fame was spreading fast among folk fans, but his national exposure would have been greatly aided by a television appearance. He was invited to appear on "The Ed Sullivan Show," but refused because he was not allowed to sing his song "Talkin' John Birch Paranoid Blues." Of course, he could have chosen other songs, but the statements he wanted to make were much more important to him than the fame afforded by television exposure. Dylan finished out the folk period of his career with two more albums, *The Times They Are A-Changin'* and *Another Side of Bob Dylan* (both 1964). The former contained protest songs that spoke out for civil rights and antiwar causes; the latter was less folk-oriented and expressed feelings about his personal life and relationships.

Dylan's music and much of his audience changed in 1965, when he shocked his folk-purist fans by walking on stage in front of the Paul Butterfield Blues Band, with their drums and electric instruments, at the Newport Folk Festival. Ever since the Animals had turned "House of the Rising Sun" into a rock hit, Dylan knew there was a potentially large audience for rock-style performances of folk songs. The album *Bringing It All Back Home* (1965) introduced Dylan's new rock-based sound, along with folk-styled material, and it was the rock-styled "Subterranean Homesick Blues" (1965) that became his first hit single. "Mr. Tambourine Man" was less popular when Dylan did it in his folk style on that album than when it was covered with rock instrumentation by the Byrds. The combination of folk and rock styles heard in Dylan's "Subterranean Homesick Blues" and the Byrds' recording of "Mr. Tambourine Man" was the beginning of an entirely new genre of rock music—folk rock.

Dylan continued in a rock-oriented style, touring with a former rockabilly band, the Hawks (they did not use that name while with Dylan). Despite his change of musical style, Dylan had not abandoned the folk tradition of using music to make social statements. Many of his songs contained rather obscure and cryptic messages that left room for interpretation by the listener, but a basic statement often emerged from his textual ambiguity. "Like a Rolling Stone" (1965), for example, generally described the transient value of wealth and material comfort. Exactly what caused the rich girl to whom he directed the song to lose her money and social standing could be any of several things, possibly heroin addiction or prostitution, but the point of the song was made no matter how the listener interpreted the details. Many fans may have liked Dylan's next big hit, "Rainy Day Women #12 & 35" (1966), because of its allusions to getting "stoned" on drugs, but the constant references to people being stoned (in a literal sense), people who were simply trying to live normal, unfettered lives, expressed his concerns about civil rights and the plight of African Americans in the United States.

After suffering severe injuries in a motorcycle accident, Dylan spent the rest of 1966 recovering and recording tapes at home with his backup band. Those tapes were eventually released on *The Basement Tapes* (1975), although a bootleg version of the album surfaced as early as 1969. With Dylan still recuperating, his backup band decided to record and tour on their own, calling themselves simply the Band.

■ The Band's career after leaving Dylan is discussed in Chapter 12, Revivals of Country-Styled Rock.

When Dylan began to record on his own again, he ignored the large-scale theme-album trend that had become popular among rock bands. Although he had been known to borrow ideas from others, Dylan was never one to latch onto popular musical trends. He even ignored the rock-oriented direction of his own hits and returned to the folkish simplicity of his earlier recordings, this time with country influences, in the albums *John Wesley Harding* (1968) and *Nashville Skyline* (1969). Again, Dylan was at the forefront of a new style; this time it was country rock.

For the next few years, Dylan worked with various country-rock musicians, including members of the Byrds and singer Doug Sahm (of the Sir Douglas Quintet). He contributed soundtrack music for, and acted in, the movie *Pat Garrett and Billy the Kid* (1973). "Knockin' on Heaven's Door," from that movie, was Dylan's biggest hit of the seventies. Dylan became a fundamentalist Christian in the late seventies, and albums like *Slow Train Coming* (1979), *Saved* (1980), and *Shot of Love* (1981) reflected his new-found religious position. His album *Infidels* (1983), while not actually questioning religious beliefs, employed more ambiguous language in referring to them.

The song "Union Sundown" from *Infidels* represented a return to social and political concerns, pointing out how American labor unions had been undermined by the widespread availability of cheap foreign goods that greedy, unfeeling people purchased to avoid paying the price of goods made by workers who received good wages and benefits. In a manner similar to that used in pro-union songs by the Almanac Singers during the forties, in which unions were portrayed as the solution to the needs of the working class, Dylan's song pointed out some of the negative effects of modern-day American materialism.

Dylan's continuing concern for social and political issues caused him to become involved in many fund-raising campaigns during the middle eighties, including the "We Are the World" recording and the Live Aid and Farm Aid concerts. Throughout his career, Dylan changed the course of the history of rock music more than once. His middle-sixties move from traditional folk music to folk rock sparked a new trend and then again a few years later, he stimulated the development of country rock. Official credit for those accomplishments and others was finally awarded him by the music industry when, in 1986, he was given the Founders Award by the American Society of Composers, Authors & Publishers (ASCAP). In 1988, Dylan was inducted into the Rock and Roll Hall of Fame.

As every "real" Dylan fan knows, bootleg recordings of everything from live concert performances to studio outtakes are very easy to come by and the desire to hear rare songs, as well as many different versions of popular ones, is irresistible. There is no hiding that fact, and Dylan and his record company have always been aware of it as are other performers whose work is often released in the same illegal way. Bootlegs are a problem for the performer, not only because he does not receive royalties from their sale, but because the performer and producer have no control over the quality of the recordings or the choices of material the recordings include. While other people in the industry try to ignore the problem and hope it will go away, Dylan made a straight and honest attack by releasing *Bob Dylan, The Bootleg*

The Byrds (left to right): David Crosby, Chris Hillman, Gene Clark, Michael Clarke, and Roger McGuinn

Michael Ochs Archives/Venice, CA

Listening Guide

	"Mr. Tambourine Man" by Bob Dylan (1965)	"Mr. Tambourine Man" by the Byrds (1965)
Tempo:	The tempo is about 168 beats per minute, with four beats per bar.	The tempo is about 122 beats per minute, with four beats per bar.
Form:	The recording begins with a four-bar instrumental introduction.	The recording begins with a four-bar instrumental introduction.
	There are ten different verses of varying length; the first two repeat several times, functioning as a refrain.	Only four of Dylan's verses are sung; the first two are repeated at the end.
Features:	The lead line is sung by Dylan alone.	The Byrds sing the refrain in close harmony; McGuinn sings the verses alone. The second voice is sometimes heard above the melody, in the style of country music.
	The instrumentation includes strummed acoustic guitar, electric guitar accents on beats one and three, and no bass or drums. A harmonica plays lead during instrumental sections.	The instrumentation includes twelve-string electric guitar, electric bass, tambourine, drums, and a thickly layered background.
	There is no accent on the backbeat.	A strong backbeat is played by both the drums and the tambourine.
	The recording lasts five minutes and thirty seconds.	The recording lasts two minutes and fourteen seconds.
Lyrics:	The song expresses the singer's loneliness and his desire to escape from his weary life by letting the sound of the tambourine erase his memories.	Most of the song's description of the singer's feelings about his life are not included.

Source: Bob Dylan's recording: *Bringing It All Back Home,* Columbia 9128; and *Bob Dylan's Greatest Hits,* Columbia 9463.

The Byrds' recording: Time-Life Music, *Classic Rock, 1965;* and *The Byrds Greatest Hits,* Columbia 09516.

Series, Volumes 1–3 (rare & unreleased) 1961–1991 in 1991. That collection not only included songs that had never been released legally before, but also included recordings that had never been available on bootlegs before, winning at least part of a music business vs. fan battle for Dylan himself. Dylan returned to his roots in traditional folk music for the albums *Good As I Been to You* (1992) and *World Gone Wrong* (1993). Both old and new fans welcomed him at Woodstock '94 and then on "MTV Unplugged" later the same year.

Folk-Rock Music

Bob Dylan's "Mr. Tambourine Man" was folk-styled music when he sang it, but it became folk rock when recorded by **The Byrds**. The Byrds were formed by musicians who had previously belonged to other folk groups. Their leader, singer/guitarist Roger (Jim) McGuinn, bought an electric twelve-string guitar in order to imitate the accompaniment style he had heard both the Beatles and the Searchers employ. The result was not simply a copy of the British sound, but instead became one of America's most effective responses to the British Invasion. "Mr. Tambourine Man" was the group's first recording, for which uncredited studio musicians were hired to record most of the instrumental parts; the track also featured McGuinn's distinctive twelve-string guitar and the rest of the members of the Byrds singing in close, folk-style harmony. A comparison of the folk recording by Dylan and the #1 pop chart hit recording by the Byrds can be found above.

The Byrds followed "Mr. Tambourine Man" with another Dylan song they turned into folk rock, "All I Really Want To Do" (1965), and a Pete Seeger composition,

"Turn! Turn! Turn!" (1965), the lyrics of which came from the Old Testament book of Ecclesiastes. Other groups, such as **The Turtles**, changed from earlier rock styles (they had been a surf band called the Nightriders, then the Cross Fires) to folk rock in 1965 because of the success of the Byrds. The Turtles copied the Byrds in recording Dylan songs and using heavy studio production on top of their folk-based style.

The Byrds' music moved further from folk music toward psychedelic rock with their recording of "Eight Miles High" (1966). The song, written by McGuinn and the Byrds' other guitarist/singer, David Crosby (David Van Cortland), had lyrics that were interpreted to refer to the effects of psychedelic drugs. Both writers denied it vehemently, explaining that the lyrics came from McGuinn's fear of air travel, but nevertheless it was banned by many radio stations. Frequent personnel changes plagued the Byrds during the late sixties, and they were joined by country guitarist/singer/songwriter Gram Parsons for the album *Sweetheart of the Rodeo* (1968), which influenced the development of country rock.

While most folk-rock music used Dylan-influenced vocals, folk-style strummed acoustic guitar, jangling tambourine rhythms, and occasional country stylings, as well as a rock beat, some groups were labeled folk rock more for their rustic dress and "do-your-own-thing" attitude than for their sound. One such example was the husband-and-wife team **Sonny and Cher** (Salvatore Bono, born in 1935; Cherilyn LaPier, born in 1946). Their recording of Bono's "I Got You Babe" (1965) included a tambourine shaking in a constant rhythmic pattern, but instead of folk-style instruments, an oboe was used to produce a sense of continuous motion. The two also attracted attention for their appearance. Sonny had long, straight hair and wore casual clothes and a fur vest. Cher started a teen fashion trend with her "poor boy" shirts and wildly colored bell-bottom pants; she also claimed not to own a dress or skirt, an image she gave up long before her later career as an actress. Sonny's image changed quite a bit after his divorce from Cher, and it changed even further when he became mayor of Palm Springs and later a Republican member of the U.S. House of Representatives.

While Sonny and Cher's folk-rock career rested on their image, most folk-rock groups were made up of folk musicians. The members of a folk and **jug band** from New York City called the Mugwumps (a term that meant political fence-sitters or politically uncommitted people) separated into two folk-rock groups, the Lovin' Spoonful and the Mamas and the Papas. The Mugwumps' lead guitarist/singer, Zal Yanovsky, started **The Lovin' Spoonful** with singer/guitarist/harmonica player John Sebastian, who had done some recording with the Mugwumps. The Lovin' Spoonful took their name from the title of a song by blues singer Mississippi John Hurt.

Sebastian, with occasional help from other band members, wrote lighthearted folk-rock songs such as "Do You Believe in Magic?" (1965). Although the Lovin' Spoonful was considered a folk-rock group during the mid-sixties, its music owed as much to jug-band country music and the blues as it did to folk. The most obvious example of the former was "Nashville Cats," with its steel-guitar lines, but many of their recordings used the high voice above the main melody that was common in bluegrass and other country music. The shuffle beat of "Do You Believe in Magic?" was typical of western swing.

Soon after Sebastian and Yanovsky left to form the Lovin' Spoonful, the Mugwumps broke up. The group's singers, Denny Doherty and Cass Elliot (Ellen Naomi Cohen), went their separate ways for a short time, but met again in California in 1965. Doherty had formed the New Journeymen with husband-and-wife duo John and Michelle Phillips. Elliot joined their group, and they changed the name to **The Mamas and the Papas**. John Phillips wrote most of their songs, praising California in "California Dreamin'" (1966), and tracing the group's history back to their Mugwump connection in "Creeque Alley" (1967). The Mamas and the Papas broke up in 1968, but John Phillips and Denny Doherty regrouped again under the same name with Phillips' daughter, actress Mackenzie Phillips, and Elaine "Spanky" McFarlane (from the folk-rock group Spanky and Our Gang). Mackenzie Phillips' sister, Chynna Phillips, recorded and performed pop-styled music with two daughters of Beach Boy Brian Wilson, Carnie Wilson and Wendy Wilson, in the early-nineties group, Wilson Phillips. Wilson Phillips broke up in 1993.

Paul Simon and Art Garfunkel became famous for their folk-rock music, but originally they sang songs that Simon wrote while they were in high school in Newark, New Jersey, during the mid-fifties. Using the names of the cartoon characters Tom and Jerry, they performed their first single (which copied the vocal-duo style of the Everly Brothers), "Hey, Schoolgirl" (1957), on "American Bandstand." After graduation, they lost touch with each other. Simon attempted to establish himself as a teen idol under the pseudonym Jerry Landis but later returned to folk music, performing in New York coffeehouses. His old partner rejoined him five years later to record a folk album, *Wednesday Morning, 3 A.M.* (1966), this time using their real names, **Simon and Garfunkel**. The album included traditional folk songs, songs by Bob Dylan, and some Simon originals, all recorded with only acoustic instruments to accompany their singing. Soon after the album's release, while Simon was traveling and performing on his own in Europe, the producer of the album, Tom Wilson (who also produced Dylan's *Bringing It All Back Home* album [1965]), took it upon himself to overdub electric guitars, bass, and drums on the album cut "The Sounds of Silence" and release it as a single. The single became a folk-rock hit before either Simon or Garfunkel even heard about the production changes. Having witnessed

Art Garfunkel (L) and Paul Simon (R) performing at Madison Square Garden in 1972
UPI/Bettmann

the success possible through the combination of folk and rock styles, Simon and Garfunkel reunited to record a folk-rock album using the new version of "The Sounds of Silence" as the title track.

After many folk-rock hits during the sixties and early seventies, Simon and Garfunkel stopped working as a duo and concentrated on solo careers, as both singers and actors, occasionally working together for special projects, such as the single "My Little Town" from Simon's *Still Crazy After All These Years* (1975), and an outdoor concert in New York at which the double album *The Concert in Central Park* (1982) was recorded. **Paul Simon** (born in 1942) continued to be influenced by music outside his own folk background. "Mother and Child Reunion" (1972), recorded in Jamaica, was influenced by regional Jamaican styles; a Black gospel group, the Dixie Hummingbirds, joined him on his recording "Loves Me Like a Rock" (1973); and "Late in the Evening" (1980) used Latin salsa rhythms.

For his *Graceland* album (1986), Simon traveled to Johannesburg, South Africa, to cut a record with musicians he had heard on recordings imported from there. Simon wrote the songs for the album, but captured a sense of internationalism by using musicians (and co-writers) from South Africa, Louisiana, and Los Angeles to record those songs. Simon's own performance was still very much connected to his past work in the American folk tradition, to which he added some country timbres with the Everly Brothers' vocals on "Graceland" and Linda Ronstadt's vocals on "Under African Skies." The a cappella group vocals by Ladysmith Black Mambazo in the introduction to "Diamonds on the Soles of Her Shoes," as well as other sections of songs in the Zulu language, were colorful South African additions to Simon's songs. Call-and-response vocals, so common in African music, were used effectively on "Homeless." In traveling to South Africa to record parts of *Graceland,* Simon broke the agreement made by many musicians not to go there until black South Africans were given political equality. He was greatly criticized by many for that action, although the album's statements for racial unity eventually led other anti-apartheidists to appreciate his efforts. The *Graceland* album and its title track won Grammy awards, but more important, the album introduced Ladysmith Black Mambazo to the rest of the world. Their own recordings were commercially successful in the U.S., and they won a Best Traditional Folk Recording Grammy of their own for "Shaka Zulu" (1988). This attention helped the anti-apartheid movement in South Africa tremendously. Continuing his involvement with "world music," Simon's next album, *The Rhythm of the Saints* (1990), included Brazilian and

Crosby, Stills, Nash and Young in concert (left to right): Neil Young, David Crosby, Graham Nash, and Stephen Stills

Michael Ochs Archives/Venice, CA

West African music as well as zydeco from Louisiana. In 1994 Simon changed his position in the studio from singer/guitarist to producer when he produced his wife Edie Brickell's (lead singer of Edie Brickell and New Bohemians) first solo album, *Picture Perfect Morning.*

Although most of the music by such folk-rock groups as the Lovin' Spoonful and the Mamas and the Papas consisted of light and simple love songs, Paul Simon's introspective songs introduced an additional depth to folk-rock music. Bob Dylan had followed the folk tradition of using music to raise social consciousness of political and social causes, but he was not alone in that endeavor. Several other folk and folk-rock singers expressed concerns over the same issues Dylan had—issues like the Vietnam War and the Civil Rights Movement. **Phil Ochs** (1940–1976) and **Tom Paxton** (Thomas Richard, born in 1937) were both singer/songwriters in the Woody Guthrie tradition who performed in New York coffeehouses. Ochs' songs such as "Talking Vietnam" (1964) and "Draft Dodger Rag" (1965), and Paxton's songs "A Thousand Years" and "Talking Vietnam Pot Luck Blues" (both 1968), put the two singers in great demand to perform at many antiwar demonstrations. Another writer, Philip **"P.F." Sloan**, composed "Eve of Destruction" (1965), which was recorded by ex-New Christy Minstrels singer **Barry McGuire** (born in 1937). The song questioned the ethics of war and racial inequities in a society that claimed to be based on biblical morality. Fifteen-year-old singer/songwriter **Janis Ian** (Janis Eddy Fink, born in 1951) made one of the era's most poignant statements about racism in "Society's Child (Baby I've Been Thinking)" (1967) in which she accused hypocritical parents and teachers of preaching equality while at the same time being intolerant of interracial relationships.

Whether the cause was war or racism, some marches and gatherings of protestors turned violent when police riot squads arrived. After a demonstration turned into a riot on Los Angeles' Sunset Strip, **The Buffalo Springfield**'s writer/singer Stephen Stills wrote what became an anthem of the protest movement, "For What It's Worth (Stop, Hey What's That Sound)" (1967). The group disbanded after a little over two years together, but many of their members continued to be important in both folk- and country-rock styles, writing and singing about the serious issues of the day. Stephen Stills formed Crosby, Stills and Nash; Neil Young had a solo career, but also worked with Crosby, Stills, Nash and Young as well as his own band, Crazy Horse; Richie Furay and Jim Messina formed the country-rock band Poco.

Crosby, Stills and Nash began singing together casually at a party at Mama Cass Elliot's home in Los Angeles in 1968. David Crosby had stopped working with the Byrds, Stephen Stills was freed by Buffalo Springfield's breakup, and Graham Nash had grown tired of working with the Hollies, who refused to record his "Marrakesh Express." He left them, and the song became the first of many hits by the trio Crosby, Stills and Nash. The pleasing vocal group arrangements gave their recordings a distinctive style. All its members were writers, providing the group with a wide range of original material. They had all had at least some experience in both folk and country music, and with the development of country rock during the late sixties, they incorporated some of its elements into their music.

Neil Young joined the group in 1969 and **Crosby, Stills, Nash and Young** performed at Woodstock. Although the group did not concentrate solely on protest

Listening Guide

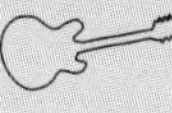

"Ohio" as recorded by Crosby, Stills, Nash and Young (1970)

Tempo: The tempo is about 80 beats per minute, with four beats in each bar.

Form: The eight-bar instrumental introduction begins with a solo guitar playing a repeated pattern used later in the recording. The drums join at the third bar and the bass and lead guitar enter at the fifth bar.

After the introduction, the song follows an ABCABCA form, in which the A verses are four bars long, the B choruses are eight bars long, and the C instrumental sections are partially based on chords from the A sections.

Features: Even beat subdivisions are maintained throughout. Near the end of the recording, the drummer builds the intensity by accenting four even subdivisions to each beat.

A rock backbeat is maintained by the drummer.

The bass plays on beats one, three, and four almost constantly through the recording.

The four singers are in unison during the first vocal section, then split into three-part harmony with a fourth part coupled at the octave (that is, the highest and the lowest voices sing the same melody an **octave** apart while the two other voices fill in chord tones between them).

Lyrics: The lyrics are about an antiwar demonstration at Kent State University in Ohio, at which four students were shot to death by the National Guard sent to the campus by the state's governor.

Source: *Crosby, Stills, Nash & Young So Far,* Atlantic 19119.

songs, they were affected by the violence that erupted during the antiwar movement. "Ohio" (1970) was Neil Young's lament over the shooting death of four students during a demonstration at Kent State University. The listening guide above discusses that recording.

Crosby, Stills, Nash and Young began to work on solo careers in the early seventies, but the members regrouped, sometimes in pairs or trios, to perform and/or record together in the years to follow.

Folk Rock in Britain

In the same year (1965) that Bob Dylan and the Byrds began combining folk and rock music, young folk musicians in the British Isles started doing much the same thing. It may have taken Dylan's influence to stimulate the idea, but Mike Heron fell into mixing the two styles quite naturally because he had previously played acoustic instruments in folk groups and electric guitar in rock groups. Together with Robin Williamson, who also played guitar and many other folk instruments, and rhythm guitarist Clive Palmer, Heron formed **The Incredible String Band**. From Glasgow, Scotland, they played in small folk clubs until their reputation soon reached England, where they were hired to give a concert at the Royal Albert Hall in London, sharing the bill with Americans Tom Paxton and Judy Collins. The Incredible String Band had been playing what was sometimes described as earthy rock-tinged music, but Heron and Williamson's interests in non-Western cultures and music from China, Arabia, and India caused them to add chahanai, oud, sitar, and other instruments from those countries to their folk-rock sound.

Throughout their career, which lasted into the seventies, other musicians came and went and their sound grew to include the fiddle, bass, and eventually, the drums. The Incredible String Band never achieved a great commercial following, but then they never really tried to. They wanted to play whatever they wanted whenever they wanted and, even after gaining a cult following in both Britain and the U.S., they often refused to play popular songs from their past in concert if those songs were not part of their current mood. In many ways they were the first "world music" group and the predecessors of the anti-commercial attitudes of the alternative bands of the late eighties and early nineties. Most certainly they established a full-rock movement in the British Isles.

A singer from the British Isles who did achieve commercial success in the U.S. was Scottish folk singer **Donovan** (Donovan Leitch, born in 1946). At the same Newport Folk Festival in 1965 where Dylan drew a negative reaction from folk fans with his blues- and rock-style performance with the Paul Butterfield Blues Band, Donovan won their favor with his soft voice and acoustic guitar accompanying his folk-style waltz "Catch the Wind" (1965). Donovan later followed Dylan's example and added rock instrumentation to his recordings. Also, following a trend that had been growing among youthful American antiwar activists, he festooned himself in a "flower power" image (named because many youths wore flowers as symbols of peace and alienation from "the establishment"). In later years, he moved to Ireland and toured occasionally, playing traditional folk music and recording folk songs geared for children. Donovan continued to do occasional tours, but little recording. In the early nineties, his career received a boost in England when a group from Manchester, Happy Mondays, gave tribute to the influence he had on them with their album *Pills 'n' Thrills and Bellyaches* (1990).

Like many young musicians in England during the sixties, **Richard Thompson** (born in 1949) listened to American musicians and started playing the guitar by imitating solos by Buddy Holly, jazz guitarist Django Reinhardt, and Scotty Moore (lead guitarist on many of Elvis Presley's recordings). Thompson's first professional work was with bassist Ashley Hutchings, who served as a band leader. Hutchings would find a job and then put together a band that could play whatever kind of music his clients wanted. They would play rock music one night and then switch to acoustic instruments and play as a jug band the next. **Fairport Convention** was formed when Thompson and Hutchings added another guitarist, a drummer, and one male and one female singer. On their first album, *Fairport Convention* (1968), the group played covers of American rock and folk-rock songs along with a few originals. The album was not very successful, forcing the group to change their diverse musical direction to one that concentrated on playing traditional music from the British Isles along with newly written songs in a contemporary setting. They gained a strong songwriter and singer when Sandy Denny replaced their previous female singer in 1968. Fairport Convention soon became leaders in the British folk-rock movement. One of their strongest albums was *Unhalfbricking* (1969) for which they added folk fiddle player Dave Swarbrick. As was true of most folk-rock music in the U.S., the album combined elements of Celtic traditional music with American Cajun influences and folk rock in the styles of the Byrds and Bob Dylan. From that album, "Si Tu Dois Partir" (a French translation of Bob Dylan's song "If You Gotta Go, Go Now") was a hit on the British pop charts.

Fairport Convention survived many changes of personnel including the loss of Sandy Denny (who formed Fotheringay), bassist/singer Ashley Hutchings (who formed Steeleye Span), and Richard Thompson (who formed a duo with his wife, Linda), and they eventually dropped the word "Convention" from their name. By the nineties, fiddler Dave Swarbrick had gained his own fans and recorded and toured as a soloist. Richard and Linda Thompson had split up their duo in the early eighties, and Richard Thompson continued his career as a soloist in the singer/songwriter tradition. The commercial success of his album *Rumor and Sigh* (1991) brought his twenty-five career to a long-deserved peak. He followed that with *Mirror Blue* in 1994.

Summary

Twentieth-century folk musicians were not the first to use music to express socially conscious themes. As far back as song lyrics have been written down or passed from one singer to another by rote, people have sung about things that concerned them and their cultures. Folk music has generally been the music of people who worked hard for a living and were concerned about the rights of their peers as well as of less fortunate people. The specific issues have changed through time, but in general terms, folk singers have always been people who sing for and about people.

Folk music was not written down, traditionally, and therefore it changed slightly as it was passed from one performer to another. Singers often updated lyrics to comment on contemporary issues. The Hutchinson Family Quartet sang about rights for women and black slaves during the mid-nineteenth century, and a hundred years later the Almanac Singers sang about the need for workers to unite and form unions. Throughout his career, Bob Dylan wrote and sang songs supporting civil rights, peace, and the causes of American workers. He reached a larger audience when he dropped his pure-folk music style, added a rock beat and instrumentation, and started folk rock.

Folk rock soon included a great diversity of musical influences and styles, but acoustic guitars were usually part of the sound. The image of folk-rock groups, at least during the sixties, was "down-home" and casual. While many of these groups wrote and sang lighthearted love songs, others used their music to make political and social statements.

Terms to Remember

Jug band

Octave

CHAPTER 7

Soul Music

The infectious beat of rhythm and blues and the exuberance of gospel combined to enhance one another in soul music. With the same impassioned performances gospel singers used in praise of God, soul singers conveyed their messages of human love and relationships. In fact, most of the singers who sang soul were also gospel singers. Their use of melismas added to the melody quick emotional changes ranging from sobbing to shouting and a falsetto vocal quality. These characteristics of black gospel singing also became important qualities in the soul vocal style. The smooth flow of uneven beat subdivisions, the stress on the backbeat, and the energetic horn or sax solos gave soul its gutsy richness. Soul styles varied from one part of the country to another, but all shared a dramatic emotional appeal.

The Musical Roots of Soul

The term "soul" did not really come into common usage to describe this style of music until the middle-to-late sixties, but the style was developing in the fifties through the work of such singers as Ray Charles, James Brown, Sam Cooke, and Jackie Wilson. Out of their influences came the many artists discovered and recorded by the Atlantic Record Co. in New York, Stax and Volt Records in Memphis, Chess and Vee Jay in Chicago, Motown in Detroit, and Philadelphia International in Philadelphia, to name only the biggest labels. To introduce ourselves to soul there is no better place to begin than with its genius, Ray Charles.

Glaucoma blinded **Ray Charles** Robinson (born in 1930) when he was only six years old. He had already been learning to play the piano, and music gave him a world where sight was not essential. In addition to keyboards he took up the trumpet, the saxophone, and the clarinet. He also learned to read and write music in braille and studied composition. Orphaned at age fifteen, he made his living by playing music. Dropping his last name to avoid confusion with the fighter "Sugar" Ray Robinson, Ray Charles moved from his home in Greenville, Florida, to Seattle, Washington, where he worked as a singer/pianist much influenced by Nat "King" Cole. Although Charles was one of the few soul singers who never actually performed gospel music in church, he incorporated gospel elements into his rhythm and blues style.

The use of call-and-response, common in gospel style, can be heard in Charles' blues song "What'd I Say" (1959). In its original release, a different version of the same song appeared on each side of the record. The more polished rhythm-and-blues-styled side was a hit, but the recording on side two, called "What'd I Say (Part Two)," featured a gospel-styled vocal group responding to Charles' lead vocals. Both recordings were reminiscent of the performance style of blues singer/pianist Clarence "Pine Top" Smith in the twenties. Charles even

Ray Charles and his orchestra with the Raelettes
Michael Ochs Archives/Venice, CA

paid tribute to Smith by quoting some of the lyrics of Smith's "Pine Top's Boogie Woogie" (1928). Charles started his "What'd I Say (Part Two)" with a tribute to another jazz singer, Cab Calloway, who often called out nonsense syllables to which his band (and the audience) responded in imitation. Charles plays an electric organ on both parts of the recording. The listening guide on page 73 compares the two parts of "What'd I Say."

Ray Charles had grown up listening to gospel music, and many of his hits—"Hallelujah, I Love Her So" (1956), for example—had clear gospel overtones in the music, though the songs themselves were quite secular. For some of his hit recordings he took more than just style from gospel. "I've Got a Woman" (1955) was derived from Alex Branford's gospel song, "I've Got a Savior"; and "This Little Light of Mine," recorded by the Clara Ward Singers, became "This Little Girl of Mine." Charles' gospel-style female backup vocal group, the Raelettes, provided responding vocal lines to his lead singing.

An essential part of the talent that sets Ray Charles apart from other soul artists is his ability to synthesize country, rhythm and blues, and jazz styles with gospel music. His band arrangements incorporated elements of country and blues music, and his piano playing owed much to gospel. The storyline texts common in country music were used in some of his songs. In 1962 he recorded two albums of country and country-style songs, *Modern Sounds in Country and Western Music (Vols. 1 and 2),* on which he covered songs by Hank Williams, Floyd Tillman, and Hank Snow. The single from Volume 1, "I Can't Stop Loving You," proved to be his biggest hit. In the mid-sixties, after a drug possession arrest, Charles stopped performing and checked into a drug rehabilitation hospital to break his long addiction to heroin. By the late sixties, he was putting his own style to jazz and rock standards. He had hit singles with covers of the Beatles' "Yesterday" (1967) and "Eleanor Rigby" (1968). Charles continued touring and did some recording during the seventies, and he had an important part in the movie *The Blues Brothers* in 1980. His 1982 album *Wish You Were Here Tonight* was a return to country-style music.

Sam Cooke (Sam Cook, 1935–1964) began his professional singing career in 1951, when he took the lead vocal role in the established and successful gospel group the Soul Stirrers. He decided to branch out into secular music in 1956, but wanted to avoid the criticism that had been leveled at other gospel singers who "sold out" by leaving pure gospel music. To that end, he used the name Dale Cooke when he recorded "Lovable" (1956). He left the Soul Stirrers, dropped the pseudonym, changed record companies, and in 1957 released "You Send Me." Its success was the beginning of his pop career, as well as the beginning of the influence his light, high, pop and gospel vocal style would have on future singers. Although Cooke was in his middle-to-late twenties when his biggest hits were on the charts, he became a teen idol for young African Americans in much the same sense Dion, Fabian, and Frankie Avalon were for white teens. Cooke's sweet, naive, teen idol image was shattered when he was shot to death in a motel room in 1964 by a woman who claimed he had attacked her.

Another musical innovator who started performing simply to make enough money to survive was **James Brown** (born in 1933). By the time he was five years old his mother had left him to be raised by her sister. His father was around from time to time, but did not live with him. Brown earned his own money and helped support his aunt by dancing on street corners for tips; the more elaborate his dance steps, the more money he made. The experience could not have been pleasant at the time, but it certainly had an effect on the wild stage antics that later became part of his act. As a youth he

Listening Guide

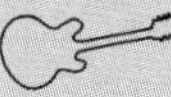

	"What'd I Say" by Ray Charles (1959)	**"What'd I Say (Part Two)" by Ray Charles (1959)**
Tempo:	The tempo is approximately 180 beats per minute, with four beats in each bar.	The tempo is about 180 beats per minute, with four beats in each bar.
Form:	The recording has eleven choruses of the twelve-bar blues form.	The recording begins with eight bars of call-and-response nonsense syllables between Charles and a vocal group. The twelve-bar blues form is used in sections where Charles sings lyrics.
	The first, second, and seventh blues choruses are instrumental. The first is piano alone, the second has piano with percussion, and the seventh has bass, piano, and percussion.	There are no instruments and no particular melody or chords during the eight-bar sections of nonsense syllables, imitative of Cab Calloway's use of call-and-response in the late twenties.
Features:	A polyrhythm is formed by Charles' uneven beat subdivisions in his vocals and piano and the even beat subdivisions maintained by the percussionist.	The polyrhythmic effect is less obvious than in the other recording because the piano and percussion are softer.
	Charles is the only singer, but a horn section responds in a gospel style in the last few choruses.	A vocal group responds to Charles' vocals, taking the place of the horn section in the first recording.
	Vocal choruses begin with an instrumental stop time, with instruments punctuating the beginnings of bars.	The piano accompanies the voice through the vocal choruses.
	The recording ends with a group of people talking as if they are at a party where the recording is being made.	The recording begins with what appears to be a continuation of the earlier recording.
Lyrics:	The lyrics warn Charles' woman that he will send her away if she does not start loving him right. The fifth and ninth choruses' lyrics quote "Pine Top's Boogie Woogie" (1928) by pianist Pine Top Smith.	The lyrics concentrate on dancing and feeling good, without references to a problem relationship. The text of the fourth chorus quotes from "Pine Top's Boogie Woogie" (1928).

Source: Both versions on Time-Life Music, *The Rock 'N' Roll Era, 1959;* Time-Life Music, *Solid Gold Soul, Ray Charles 1954–1966;* and *Ray Charles—Anthology,* RHI 75759.

sang gospel in the Augusta Baptist Church in Augusta, Georgia, and by his early twenties (in the mid-fifties) he was accepted into the gospel group the Swanees. Not content to stay in the background, Brown became the lead singer. The Swanees changed their name to the Famous Flames when they began to sing nonreligious music.

The first hit song recorded by James Brown and the Famous Flames was the gospel-styled, but thematically secular, "Please, Please, Please" (1956). The recording used the triplet pattern in the piano that was common in gospel, doo-wop, and some rhythm and blues, along with Brown's pleading and emotional vocals. A listening guide to "Please, Please, Please" can be found on page 74.

Brown's dramatic and energetic vocal embellishments fit well into his wild stage act, which involved rhythmic dance steps, leg splits, and drops to his knees. Brown became deeply involved with his music onstage; he would show the audience that he was giving his all by collapsing on the floor as if from a heart attack during a song, something he had often seen African American preachers do during worship services. In Brown's act, the Famous Flames would then cover his body with a cape and carry him to the side of the stage before he would miraculously recover and finish the song. In some performances, that rejuvenation was sufficient to carry him through encores of attacks and music. For very good reason, James Brown has been called Mr. Dynamite, the

James Brown on the Dick Cavett Show in 1970
UPI/Bettmann

Hardest Working Man in Show Business, Soul Brother Number One, the Godfather of Soul, and the Man with All the Names.

With his recording of "Out of Sight" (1964) and "Papa's Got a Brand New Bag" (1965), Brown developed a new style that was more dependent on African-influenced polyrhythms than melody. That style was the beginning of what became known as funk.

■ James Brown's funk style and funk music by later performers will be discussed in Chapter 15, Funk and Disco.

James Brown delivered sermon-like messages in "Cold Sweat" (1967), "Say It Loud—I'm Black and I'm Proud" (1968), and "King Heroin" (1972). "Say It Loud—I'm Black and I'm Proud" spoke to the very roots of African American pride, encouraging hard work leading to positive achievements for his people. He was publicly praised by Hubert Humphrey (vice president under Lyndon Johnson) for his effective efforts at directing African Americans toward a peaceful movement for equal rights. His music and his messages were meaningful to many white rock fans too, and he traveled to entertain troops in Vietnam and Korea. In "King Heroin," Brown preached to his audience about the dangers of drug abuse. The song was reminiscent of an anti-alcohol song called "King Alcohol," by Oliver Ditson (published in 1843). Because James Brown had grown up poor, with little supervision and direction in a world permeated by drugs, prostitution, and street crime, his songs delivered a musical message that displayed a deep understanding of the problems faced by many of his fans.

Though he always maintained a following with rhythm and blues fans, Brown's pop audience diminished somewhat through the seventies. He was featured in the movie *The Blues Brothers* (1980), and he revived his following with the album *Bring It On* in 1983. In 1985 he performed "Living in America" in the movie *Rocky IV.* Three years later, soul's Godfather was back in the news for some non-musical activities that landed him in a South Carolina prison for two-and-a-half years. Many rumors were reported, but officially he was found guilty of aggravated assault and resisting arrest. After his release from prison, he was right back on stage to tape a special concert for cable television which was aired in June of 1991. James Brown has been an influence on both the soul and funk movements, as heard in the music of Sly and the Family Stone and George Clinton's Parliament and Funkadelic.

Jackie Wilson (1934–1984) began his career in 1953 when he took Clyde McPhatter's lead vocal spot with the

Listening Guide

"Please, Please, Please" as recorded by James Brown and the Famous Flames (1956)

Tempo: The tempo is approximately 74 beats per minute, with four beats in each bar.

Form: The recording is introduced by Brown's rhythmically free singing of "please" three times. Once the instruments enter and establish a steady beat, the song is composed of six eight-bar periods, all of which follow the same basic chord progression and melodic outline.

Features: Uneven beat subdivisions are maintained throughout the recording.

The drums accent a strong backbeat.

Brown's vocals are full of dramatic melismas and a sense of rhythmic freedom.

Doo-wop influences include the style of the backup vocal group, the triplet patterns played on the piano, and the use of the standard doo-wop chord progression in the fifth and sixth bars of each eight-bar period.

The instruments break at the last two beats of the sixth bar and all of the eighth bar of each period to allow for Brown's solo voice to be heard without accompaniment.

Lyrics: A man is proclaiming his love and begging his lover not to leave him.

Source: *James Brown: 20 All-Time Greatest Hits!* Polydor 314-511326.

The Impressions (lef to right): Sam Gooden, Curtis Mayfield, and Fred Cash
Michael Ochs Archives/Venice, CA

Dominoes. From Detroit, Michigan, Wilson had been a singer of gospel music with a versatile voice that was equally at home in pop music. He had many hit records and an energetic stage presence that enabled him to captivate an audience much as James Brown had, even using the fake heart attack and recovery as part of his act. Wilson continued to perform into the seventies, but he suffered a real heart attack on stage in 1975 and lapsed into a coma. Wilson remained comatose until his death in 1984.

Jackie Wilson was an important influence on the development of Motown and other soul styles that became popular during the sixties. His successful hits of the fifties were sung in gospel style, but the instruments (sometimes even including large string sections) and vocal groups that accompanied him came as much from a white-pop tradition as from the black gospel and blues traditions. Whereas James Brown had developed a style and message that exemplified African American pride, Sam Cooke and Jackie Wilson sang music that was as much intended for white audiences as it was for African American audiences.

Chicago Soul

The blues center of Chicago developed its own smooth style of soul music. With doo-wop-style vocals backed

Listening Guide

"Amen"
as recorded by the Impressions (1963)

Tempo: After the rhythmically free introduction, a tempo of about 126 beats per minute with four beats in each bar is clearly established by the bass and drums.

Form: The instrumental introduction stresses no clear metric pattern, but once the brass establishes the beat, the instruments play a five-bar introduction. After the introduction, the form is based on eight-bar phrases. An A section is played eleven times with no contrasting sections inserted between the repetitions.

Features: Beat subdivisions are uneven throughout the recording.

The drums put a slight stress on the backbeat, particularly toward the end of the recording.

The bass plays a very distinctive and repetitious one-bar descending riff with one note on each beat.

The drums are played in a militaristic march style that includes many snare-drum rolls.

Horns hold chords in the introduction and then provide responses to the vocals beginning at the end of the second A section. The responses often repeat the melody of the vocals on the word "amen," reminding the listener of that word.

Each complete sentence of lyrics begins at the end of one A section, pauses, and then continues in the next A section.

The recording builds in intensity by getting louder and raising the key one-half step in the fifth and ninth A sections.

A gradual **ritard** brings the recording to an end.

A vocal melisma at the end adds a gospel touch.

Lyrics: The lyrics make references to Jesus, who is unnamed, and repeat the word "amen" as an expression of the singers' faith in Him as the savior.

Source: Time-Life Music, *Classic Rock, 1964: The Beat Goes On;* and *The Impressions' Greatest Hits,* MCA 1500.

by dance bands similar to the one used in the Crew-Cuts' recording of "Sh-Boom," **The Impressions** defined the Chicago soul style. Formed by teenagers Jerry Butler and Curtis Mayfield, who had sung with the Northern Jubilee Gospel Singers, the Impressions sang pop ballads with a more controlled emotionalism than was typical of gospel music. On their recording of "For Your Precious Love" (1958), the **baritone** Butler sang lead and the rest of the group harmonized above and below him. Butler left for a solo career in 1959 and Mayfield, a tenor, took over the lead vocals. He sang lead on the Impressions' recording of "Gypsy Woman" (1961), which features flamenco-style guitar rhythms and the clicking of castanets in the background. Mayfield also produced the recording, "Amen," which was a featured song in the movie *Lilies of the Field* (1963) and a hit single for the Impressions. The listening guide on page 75 discusses that recording as an example of the smoothness of the Chicago soul sound.

As the Civil Rights Movement pushed forward through the sixties, Curtis Mayfield's songs gave support and encouragement to African Americans. Such songs include "It's All Right" (1963), "I'm So Proud" (1964), "Keep On Pushing" (1964), "People Get Ready" (1965), and "We're a Winner" (1968). Mayfield left the Impressions in 1970 and created the greatest success of his career with his soundtrack for the film *Superfly* (1972). He provided music for other films and continued to tour and record. Mayfield suffered severe injuries when a light fixture fell on him during a rehearsal in 1990. At first he was paralyzed from the neck down, but later showed improvement, giving fans hope that he might someday recover and resume his career.

Listening Guide

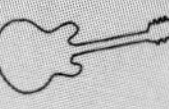

"In the Midnight Hour" as recorded by Wilson Pickett (1965)

Tempo: The tempo is approximately 112 beats per minute, with four beats in each bar.

Form: The song is comprised of one six-bar instrumental introduction, two seventeen-bar choruses, one eight-bar instrumental section, and two more seventeen-bar choruses.

Features: Booker T. and the MGs provide a guitar, organ, bass, and drums rhythm section to which a horn section with trumpet and three saxophones (alto, tenor, and baritone) has been added.

The bass is played at a higher dynamic level than the rest of the rhythm section, and its constant motion provides a contrast to the sustained notes played by the horns.

The characteristic horn section sound is based on the playing of **major chords** in parallel motion.

Even beat subdivisions are maintained throughout.

The drums keep a strong backbeat.

Pickett's black gospel background is evident in his lead vocal.

Lyrics: The lyrics are about the singer's desire to wait until the quiet of midnight to be with his lover.

Source: Time-Life Music, *Solid Gold Soul, 1965;* Time-Life Music, *Classic Rock, 1965;* and *Atlantic Rhythm & Blues, 1947–1974, Volume 5, 1962–1966,* Atlantic 14-81620.

Memphis Soul

Memphis, Tennessee, had been an important center for developments in rock musical styles since the early fifties when Sam Phillips moved there to record blues singers and, eventually, Elvis Presley and other early rockabilly singers. In the sixties, musicians in Memphis took the gospel-based vocal styles of singers like James Brown and Jackie Wilson and combined them with the energetic rhythm-and-blues style of Little Richard to create their own brand of soul music. Most of the Memphis soul artists began their careers recording for the Memphis-based record company Stax or its companion label, Volt. Many of the Stax and Volt recordings were later distributed nationally by the Atlantic label.

Memphis soul recordings had a fairly consistent instrumental sound backing the singers, because the instrumental group **Booker T. and the MGs** played on many of the recording sessions, in addition to having instrumental hits of their own. The group was named after their organist/arranger, Booker T. Jones, but the name also served as a tribute to the African American educator Booker T. Washington. "MG" stood for "Memphis Group." The group's guitarist, Steve Cropper, was an important songwriter in the Memphis soul style, often collaborating with others to write several of the biggest hits of the soul movement. Cropper's guitar style added a country flavor to the soul style. The MGs' emphasis on the bass was influential on music to follow (including reggae). Members of Booker T. and the MGs provided the backup band for the Blues Brothers both on tour and in the movie *The Blues Brothers* (1980). Individual members pursued their own careers until the early nineties, when they reunited with a series of new drummers to replace Al Jackson, who died in 1975. In 1994 they released a new album, *That's the Way It Should Be.*

In addition to the guitar, organ, bass, and drums instrumentation of Booker T. and the MGs, the Memphis recording sessions often included a horn section, such as that heard in Wilson Pickett's recording of "In the Midnight Hour."

Wilson Pickett (born in 1941) was born in Alabama but moved to Detroit, where he sang gospel music with the Violinaires. In 1959, at age nineteen, he abandoned his gospel-style grunts and shouts to sing rhythm and blues ballads with the Falcons. His old gospel vocal style returned when Jerry Wexler, his producer on the Atlantic label, sent him to record in Memphis. A listening guide for "In the Midnight Hour" can be found on page 76. The song was co-written at the recording session by Pickett and Steve Cropper, guitarist in Booker T. and the MGs.

The parallel movement of the trumpet and saxophones in the recording of "In the Midnight Hour" was so commonly used in Memphis recordings that it became known as the "Memphis horn sound." The even beat subdivisions separate the style of the song from most rhythm and blues, but the gospel-influenced vocals make it a good example of Memphis soul. The recording's very active bass line was also characteristic of Memphis soul.

Atlantic Records' producers took Pickett to the Fame Studio in Muscle Shoals, Alabama, to record in the late sixties. In the early seventies, he was recorded by producers Gamble and Huff in Philadelphia. After several label changes, Pickett was still recreating the rough and soulful style he established with his early Memphis recordings in the early nineties.

Otis Redding (1941–1967) became the biggest-selling singer at Stax Records. His vocal style was reminiscent of both the aggressiveness of Little Richard and the crooning sound of Sam Cooke, to which he added a tremendous amount of emotional energy. In "Try a Little Tenderness" (1966), for example, he built up tension with his long gospel melismas, gradually increasing the intensity of the song as he moved from one verse to the next. Redding wrote many of his own hit songs, including "Respect," which he recorded in 1965 and Aretha Franklin covered two years later.

Redding's impassioned singing won him a tremendous following in African American communities in the mid-sixties, and his performance at the Monterey Pop Festival in 1967 added white fans to that following. The biggest hit of his career, "(Sittin' on) The Dock of the Bay" (1967), co-written with Booker T. and the MGs' guitarist Steve Cropper, was recorded only three days before Redding and several members of his band, the Bar-Kays, died in an airplane crash in 1967.

After Redding's death, **Johnnie Taylor** (born in 1938) moved into the position of top-selling artist for Stax Records. Taylor's early singing career included some time with the Soul Stirrers, with whom Sam Cooke had also sung. Other singers in the Memphis soul style included **Rufus Thomas** (born in 1917), who had been performing as a dancer and singer since the thirties. He recorded as a rhythm and blues singer for Sun Records in the early fifties, then moved to the Stax label and adopted a soul style during the sixties and seventies. His daughter, **Carla Thomas** (born in 1942), recorded in Memphis and was given the title "The Queen of Soul" after she recorded the album *King and Queen* with Otis Redding in 1967. Stax Records went bankrupt in the mid-seventies, leaving many artists to find new record labels or continue performing without recording. Both Rufus and Carla Thomas continued to play club dates and tour. Johnnie Taylor was signed to record for Malaco Records and released a new album, *Real Love,* in 1994.

Atlantic Records

Co-producers and writers Ahmet Ertegun and Jerry Wexler at the Atlantic Record Company in New York were responsible for much of the success of soul singers Ray Charles, Wilson Pickett, Otis Redding, Aretha Franklin, and many others. Ertegun and Herb Abramson formed Atlantic Records in 1947, sometime before the birth of rock-influenced soul music. Some of the early artists represented by Atlantic included blues singer Joe Turner (whose recording of "Shake, Rattle and Roll" was discussed in Chapter 3) and the doo-wop group the Drifters. Eventually the company distributed recordings by a diverse group of bands including Crosby, Stills, Nash and Young; the Velvet Underground; and Led Zeppelin, but from the late fifties through the sixties, Atlantic was one of the primary distributors of soul music in the United States.

Of course the sound of any recording will vary greatly depending on the studio and studio musicians used to record it. Atlantic's producers moved their artists from one studio to another depending on what kind of soul sound Ertegun and Wexler had in mind for a particular session. Their own studio was in New York, but when they went down to the Stax Record Studio in Memphis and used the Stax backup bands—Booker T. and the MGs or the Bar-Kays—their productions had much similarity to the tight, Memphis sound of Stax's own artists. That sound stressed the electric guitar, an active bass line, and the parallel motion of the Memphis horn sound. Ertegun and Wexler also used the Fame Studios in Muscle Shoals, Alabama, to create a similar southern rock style.

Aretha Franklin was born in Memphis, Tennessee, in 1942, the daughter of a Baptist minister. When she was six, her father moved the family to Detroit, and by the time she was a teenager, Franklin had already spent most of her life singing gospel in her father's church. She was soon traveling to sing at other churches and concert halls, where she met many of the great gospel

Aretha Franklin
Bettmann

singers of her time, including Clara Ward, Mahalia Jackson, and Sam Cooke. At age eighteen she moved to New York and began to record secular songs, including a blues in the classic blues style of Ma Rainey and Bessie Smith titled "Today I Sing the Blues" (1960). Franklin sang her early secular songs with a more restrained approach than she had used for gospel music, because her producer from Columbia Records was trying to build her career around a style like that of jazz singer Nancy Wilson. It was not until 1966 that Aretha signed with Atlantic Records. Jerry Wexler took her to Muscle Shoals, Alabama, for a recording session in which he encouraged her to put the energy, dramatic delivery, and emotion she had used in gospel performances back into her vocals. After returning to her more passionate gospel style, she had one hit after another, winning her the title "Lady Soul." A listening guide to "Respect," one of Franklin's first Atlantic singles is on page 79.

From 1969 through the early seventies, Franklin experimented with a variety of different performance styles and images. Duane Allman of the Allman Brothers Band played guitar on her recordings of "The Weight" and "Eleanor Rigby" in 1969. She was even accompanied by a pop-styled string section on "Call Me" (1970). In 1972 she recorded a collection of her own songs on the album *Young, Gifted and Black.* She continued to

Listening Guide

"Respect"
as recorded by Aretha Franklin
(recorded in 1966, released in 1967)

Tempo: The tempo is approximately 112 beats a minute, with four beats in each bar.

Form: The recording begins with a four-bar instrumental introduction followed by three ten-bar A sections with vocals, an eight-bar instrumental B section, another A with vocals, and a C section comprised of four four-bar phrases.

The A sections each have three phrases of lyrics. The first two are two bars long and the third is six bars long.

The first phrase of the C section has an instrumental stop time with Franklin beginning her vocal by spelling out the word "respect."

Features: Even beat subdivisions are maintained by the instruments, but Franklin's vocals sometimes go into uneven subdivisions.

The introduction has the Memphis horn sound of horns playing parallel sustained chords, a guitar playing short riff patterns, and a very active bass line.

The active bass continues through most of the recording.

The drummer maintains a strong backbeat on the snare drum; a tambourine keeps a steady beat.

The backup vocals repeat words out of Franklin's vocal lines, serving to support her message.

The instrumental B section features an improvised tenor saxophone solo.

Lyrics: Franklin uses most of Otis Redding's lyrics that demand respect for the African American community as well as respect from a lover. Franklin's version added the section in which R-E-S-P-E-C-T is spelled out and she asks her man to T.C.B. (slang for "take care of business").

Source: Time-Life Music, *Classic Rock, 1967;* and *Aretha's Greatest Hits*, Atlantic 8295.

perform and record through the eighties, and appeared as a singing waitress in the movie *The Blues Brothers*. Franklin's personal life was haunted with tragedy during the eighties. Her father, sister Carolyn, and brother/manager Cecil died from a variety of causes and she divorced her husband. She continued to record and perform, and was awarded her fifteenth Grammy for her album *One Lord, One Faith, One Baptism* (1987). Aretha Franklin was the first woman to be inducted into the Rock and Roll Hall of Fame.

Motown

Berry Gordy, Jr. (born in 1929), was an African American songwriter from Detroit who saw that the white audience of the fifties had matured to the point that it was ready to accept music by African American performers, but he also recognized that African Americans needed to achieve more than simple acceptance. They needed respect. After the success of the songs "Reet Petite" (1957) and "Lonely Teardrops" (1959), which he had written for Jackie Wilson, Gordy decided to form his own record company. He called his recording studio and record company **Motown** in recognition of Detroit's nickname, the "Motor town." Through the period of racial unrest and riots of the sixties, Motown artists sang of love and other human concerns with which people of all races, religions, and political beliefs could identify. Gordy cultivated in his performers a sophisticated image, helping to bring respect and self-esteem to the African Americans who saw them as role models.

In addition to Motown, the company's record labels included Tamla, Gordy, and, after the mid-sixties, Soul, VIP, Mowest, and Melody. Their music publishing company was called Jobete (for Gordy's daughters, Joy, Betty, and Terry). Most of the performers at Motown during the early sixties lived in the Detroit area and had little or no previous professional experience in music when they auditioned to record for the company. Gordy molded them into a sound and image that he, with his team of writers, producers, and choreographers, created. To that end, he opened a finishing school he called International Talent Management Incorporated (ITM). Gordy hired Maxine Powell, an African American woman who owned the Maxine Powell Finishing and Modeling School, to train Motown's performers to drop the African American modes of walking, speaking, and dancing with which they had grown up and to adopt the sense of grace and style that would be expected of members of the white upper class. Powell told one performer after another that no matter where they performed they were to act as if they were at the White House or Buckingham Palace. Choreographer for the Motown acts was Cholly Atkins. He had been a dancer in a night club act called the Rhythm Pals, and then became primary choreographer for groups hired to perform at New York's Apollo Theater before moving on to Motown.

Maxine Powell and others at ITM also oversaw the style of dress Motown artists wore on stage. The sixties were a time when most rock or pop groups dressed in matching outfits, but those outfits were not necessarily very sophisticated. Groups from New York, even African American groups like the Dixie Cups, would perform in simple skirts or pants and sweaters. Such casual dress would not be found on a Motown artist, at least not during the sixties. Motown's female acts wore sparkling gowns or other glamorous clothing, while male performers wore tuxedos. Of course, a male singer might take off his coat and loosen his tie during his act, but the effect was still one in which the performer would look appropriate performing at a posh venue. Even the Motown performers' names were chosen to promote the sparkling image. After being hired at Motown, the Matadors became the Miracles, the Primes the Temptations, the Primettes the Supremes, the Marvels the Marvelettes, the Four Aims the Four Tops, and Steveland Morris became Stevie Wonder.

Motown's producers used sophisticated background arrangements that often included orchestral string sections along with jazz instrumentation, such as saxophones and/or brass instruments. Gospel influences were evident through the use of tambourines, staple instruments in African American churches, and call-and-response vocals. A few songs, such as "Money," the early hit by Barrett Strong (1960), were based on the traditional blues progression, but other blues and gospel colorations such as blue notes were rare. Motown arrangements often featured infectious rhythms played to continuously repeating bass lines (ostinatos). Latin rhythms were used in some recordings, such as Smokey Robinson and the Miracles' "Mickey's Monkey" (1963), which was based on a Cuban Son **claves beat** (played by wooden sticks tapped together). That rhythm is notated as follows:

Son claves rhythm

The Temptations' "Cloud Nine" (1968) used the polyrhythmic patterns of the Brazilian samba. White musical traditions such as even beat subdivisions and orchestral instrumentation were used as often as African American traditions, assuring that the Motown sound would appeal to the musical tastes of as broad an audience as possible.

In addition to the importance of Motown's singers, writers, and producers, credit for the Motown Sound must also be given to Motown's regular backup band, the Funk Brothers. Made up of musicians with backgrounds in both bebop jazz and rhythm and blues, they were so essential in the recording studio that Berry Gordy, Jr. would not allow them to leave Detroit without special permission, and even then for a very limited period of time. Under their contract they were allowed to play non-Motown gigs locally, but Gordy wanted them on call for recording sessions whenever he needed them. The core members of the Funk Brothers were leader and keyboard player, Earl Van Dyke; guitarists, Robert White, Eddie Willis, and Joe Messina; bass player, James Jamerson; and drummer, Benny Benjamin. When Benjamin was not available, Uriel Jones was his usual standby. Some of Motown's producers also called on Pistol Allen to play drums when they wanted his particular shuffle beat pattern. Of course other musicians, usually with jazz backgrounds, or, in some cases orchestral string players, were added to the group for particular sessions, but the Funk Brothers were the basis of the Motown Sound.

The jazz background of the Funk Brothers made the Motown Sound different from previous doo-wop or soul recordings because jazz experience pushed them to be more active in their individual parts while not covering the singers. James Jamerson, for example, had no desire to play the two-beat or repetitious cliché bass lines common in previous popular styles of music. He played walking bass lines with **chromatic passing tones** and syncopated eighth-note patterns played by bebop jazz musicians. What separated his work from that of the bebop jazz school was his use of a Fender electric bass for most of his Motown recordings (jazz musicians were still using the string [upright] bass). Jamerson actually preferred to use the string bass, but recognized that the volume and clarity of an electric instrument was needed, so he would record the bass line first on the string bass and then overdub the same part on the electric bass. Jazz influences are also clear with the addition of vibes, which were sometimes played along with other instruments in unison to add timbre without standing out on their own.

The three guitarists in the Funk Brothers each played their own special role in many of the recordings. Robert White generally filled out the rhythm section with smooth strums of chords on the beats. He used a large hollow-body electric guitar (a Gibson L-5) that provided a mellow, but still well-amplified **timbre.** White also became known for his solo tone quality when he used his thumbnail to pluck out melody lines. Eddie Willis added blues-style melodic fills on his Gibson Firebird (solid body) guitar. Joe Messina played a Fender Telecaster (solid body) guitar and would concentrate on stressing the backbeat (along with the drummer's snare drum) with fast, percussive strums of chords. In addition, Messina played whatever solo lines the producer requested of him, but stressing the backbeat was his primary function. The three guitarists worked together so much for so long that they could talk over a chart and produce an almost record-ready sound the first time they played it.

The Funk Brothers' leader, Earl Van Dyke, was not always the only keyboard player on a session because, while he often played on an acoustic Steinway (four-foot) piano, Johnny Griffith was sometimes called in to add parts on a Hammond organ and James Gittens on organ or vibes. Many Motown recordings also used out-of-the-ordinary percussion effects. The Supremes' hit "Baby Love" (1964), for example, begins with the sound of several people stomping out the beat on plywood boards. Tambourine and conga drums were also used from time to time for their own special effects.

Because Motown productions were musically complex and most of the performers were untrained in music until they began to sing for the company, writers and producers were needed. William **Smokey Robinson** (born in 1940) was a singer who had written songs for his group, the Matadors, in 1957. Berry Gordy, Jr., heard them just as he was beginning to look for talent to start his record company, and with a new name, **The Miracles**, they became one of Motown's first important groups. Robinson sang lead with the Miracles and also wrote and produced for many of Motown's other acts, including the Marvelettes, Marvin Gaye, Mary Wells, and the Temptations. He eventually became vice president of Motown Records.

The songwriting and production team **Holland-Dozier-Holland** was responsible for many of Motown's biggest successes. Brian Holland and Lamont Dozier first worked together on "Please Mr. Postman," sung by the Marvelettes in 1961. At that time Brian's brother, Eddie Holland, was under contract with Motown as a singer. He had some success with the single "Jamie" in 1962, but decided that he did not like performing and joined with Brian Holland and Lamont Dozier as co-writer. The Holland-Dozier-Holland team wrote and produced all of the Supremes' hits between 1964 and the beginning of 1968. They also wrote a lot of the material recorded by the Four Tops, the Isley Brothers (while they were with Motown, 1965–1968), and Martha and the Vandellas. The writing trio remained with Motown until 1968, when they left to start their own company, Invictus/Hot Wax.

Another Motown singer who gave up his performing career to concentrate on songwriting was **Barrett Strong**, whose songs became hits when performed by Marvin Gaye, Gladys Knight and the Pips, Rare Earth, Jimmy Ruffin, Edwin Starr, and the Temptations. Strong often co-wrote with writer/producer **Norman Whitfield**. Motown's biggest seller of the sixties, "I Heard It Through the Grapevine" (Marvin Gaye's hit from 1968), was co-written by Whitfield and Strong and produced by Whitfield.

The jazz and soul style of Ray Charles was a great influence on soul singer **Marvin Gaye** (Marvin Gay, 1939–1984). A preacher's son from Washington, D.C., Gaye had been singing gospel music and playing the organ since his youth. Berry Gordy, Jr., heard Gaye with the Moonglows while they were on tour in Detroit and invited him to record as a soloist for Motown. Soon after joining the Motown family, Gaye also joined the Gordy family by marrying Anna Gordy, Berry's sister. Gaye was a tenor, but he had a wide vocal range and the stylistic range to sing such gospel-styled songs as "Can I Get a Witness" (1963), as well as smooth love songs, like his duet with Tammi Terrell, "You're All I Need to Get By" (1967). After a long career with Motown, Gaye left the label in 1982. He was in the middle of a comeback when he was shot and killed by his father in 1984 after an argument.

Female groups were very popular during the early sixties. Most of the groups produced in New York sang very light, pop-styled songs designed for a teenage, or even pre-teen, audience. Motown's girl groups included **The Marvelettes**, who recorded primarily to please a young age group, but also **The Supremes**, who generally sang about love and lost relationships to a slightly more mature audience. Another girl group at Motown, **Martha and the Vandellas**, had a more aggressive and gospel-oriented style than was typical for the company's female vocalists. Each of these groups had many successes, but the Supremes, with their very refined sound and image, outpaced the others in number of pop chart hits.

The prolific team Holland-Dozier-Holland, who wrote almost every hit the Supremes recorded, maintained a certain consistency from one song to another. Their compositions used almost no backbeat, but instead maintained a constant and steady pulse played by bass and tambourines. The baritone saxophone was a favored instrument for solo spots. The instruments usually maintained even beat subdivisions, but lead singer Diana Ross' solos added a gospel touch through the use of uneven beat subdivisions and embellishments at phrase endings. Holland-Dozier-Holland used a variety of song forms besides the standard AABA, and they copied arrangers' tricks dating back to dance band styles of the 1940s. One such trick was the use of a portion of the song's refrain as an introduction, as in "Stop! In the Name of Love" (1965). "Baby Love" (1964) even changes key, something quite rare in pop-rock music. The Supremes' songs often repeated the introductory melody (the **hook**) over and over at the end, bringing a feeling of completeness to the composition.

The Motown company and its productions changed somewhat through the years. The rather regimented soul and pop hits from the early to middle sixties gave way to pre-funk influences and the increasing use of electronic instruments in the late sixties and through the seventies. In 1971, Berry Gordy, Jr., moved his entire operation to Hollywood in order to add films to Motown's list of productions. The Supremes' former lead singer, Diana Ross, became a very successful film star with *Lady Sings the Blues* (1972), in which she portrayed jazz singer Billie Holiday, and *Mahogany* (1975).

The Temptations were one of Motown's most popular male groups. Gordy gave them their seductive name; they had previously called themselves the Elgins and then the Primes. They signed in 1962, but it took two years before their recordings achieved any commercial success. As was often the case, Gordy experimented quite a bit before he found just the right combination of writers and producers for their performing act. Smokey Robinson proved to be the Temptations' most successful writer and producer on their early hit recordings, and Norman Whitfield after the mid-sixties. On page 83 is a

The Supremes (left to right): Florence Ballard, Mary Wilson, and Diana Ross
Michael Ochs Archives/Venice, CA

listening guide for their hit song "My Girl" (1965), the structure of which was based on the eight-bar phrase lengths commonly used at Motown. The song had a polished, thick background that included the large number of instruments heard in other pop-oriented productions of the early to middle sixties.

The Temptations' musical style changed in several ways throughout their career. Their lead vocalist was tenor Eddie Kendricks until baritone David Ruffin took over the solos, beginning with "My Girl" in 1965. The depth and resonance of the baritone voice changed the group's overall sound. Ruffin left the group for a solo career in 1968 and was replaced by another baritone, Dennis Edwards. Up to that point, the group's music had followed the Motown tradition of pop universality, but the most dramatic change occurred when Ruffin departed. Norman Whitfield, who became their sole producer in 1967, had been listening to the polyrhythmic funk styles of James Brown and Sly and the Family Stone and decided to try to emulate it for the Temptations' recording of "Cloud Nine" (1968).

Although the song "Cloud Nine" made clear references to drugs on one level, its message reached beyond that. It described the very poor economic conditions under which many youths in African American ghettos were raised, in an attempt to show why some turned to drugs for escape. Lyrics of that type would never have been allowed at Motown during the early sixties, when the entire organization was centered on themes that reflected respectable universality, but Gordy let the company change with the times.

Most of the time, Gordy maintained complete control over the careers of his musicians, and few were able to gain control of their own work. One of the first to earn the freedom to write and produce his recordings was **Stevie Wonder** (born in 1950). Blind from birth, Steveland Morris (his father's last name was Judkins) spent his childhood playing a number of musical instruments, including harmonica, bongo drums, and piano. He began to record as "Little Stevie Wonder" for Motown's Tamla label at age twelve. Wonder recorded some studio-produced songs, but his first hit was his live-performance recording of "Fingertips (Part II)" (1963). Wonder's blindness and gospel-style voice earned him a reputation as a young Ray Charles.

When he turned twenty-one years old in 1971, Wonder renegotiated his contract with Motown so that he would have complete control of his recordings. He got married, moved to New York, and made some significant changes in his writing and production styles. The changes were influenced by many of the same funk stylings that Norman Whitfield used in his productions for the Temptations in the late sixties. With the album *Music of My Mind* (1972), Wonder began to incorporate more gospel, jazz, and rhythms with origins in Africa and Latin America into his compositions. He overdubbed his own singing and playing of most of the instruments on his recordings and grew fond of the tonal capabilities of the **synthesizer.**

On his own, Wonder began to write songs that expressed his personal concerns and paid tribute to people he admired. He commented on the problems surrounding racism in "Living for the City" (1973); "Sir Duke" (1977), a tribute to Duke Ellington and other jazz legends, included jazz-band-style horns reminiscent of Ellington's band. "Master Blaster (Jammin')" (1980) was a tribute to the Jamaican reggae singer, Bob Marley, and it appropriately used a reggae beat and bass line. Wonder was among those who led a march on Washington, D.C. in 1978 to encourage Congress to honor Martin Luther

Listening Guide

"My Girl"
as recorded by the Temptations (1965)

Tempo: The tempo is about 112 beats per minute, with four beats in each bar.

Form: The song has seven eight-bar sections, with a four-bar introduction repeated as an extension after the third section.

The fourth section is instrumental, but includes vocal responses.

Features: The instrumental introduction begins with two bars of a rhythmic bass pattern using even beat subdivisions, followed by two bars of an ostinato pattern repeated throughout the recording.

The guitar line in the introduction (and later in the recording) serves as an example of Robert White's distinctive thumbnail-plucked solo sound.

The backbeat is introduced with finger snaps and then taken over by the drums.

The very polished production includes an orchestral string section and a brass section that plays fills.

The lead singer, David Ruffin, is responded to by the vocal group, but the vocal style is more pop than gospel.

Lyrics: The song is about how fulfilled the singer feels when he is with his girl. The song was a male expression of love that responded to an earlier Motown recording, Mary Wells' "My Guy" (1964).

Source: Time-Life Music, *Solid Gold Soul, 1965;* Time-Life Music, *AM Gold, 1965;* Time-Life Music, *Classic Rock, 1965;* and *The Temptations Sing Smokey,* Motown 37463-5205.

King's birthday with a national holiday, and his song "Happy Birthday" (1980) was written in King's memory.

Through the eighties and into the nineties, Stevie Wonder continued to make hit records and receive well-deserved rewards such as his Best Original Song Oscar for "I Just Called to Say I Love You" from the movie *The Woman in Red* (1984) and a Grammy for his album *In Square Circle* (1985). Wonder wrote and recorded the soundtrack to Spike Lee's movie *Jungle Fever* (1991), and followed that with a new album that updated his style with hip hop influences, *Conversation Peace* (1995).

Berry Gordy, Jr., liked having a child star like Little Stevie Wonder at Motown, but, as was bound to happen, Wonder soon outgrew that image. Wonder was nineteen years old when **Michael Jackson** (born in 1958) and his four older brothers signed with Motown, and the young Jackson quickly became the company's new child star. Gordy teamed himself with others to write and produce songs for the Jackson Five, and, as befit their child-star image, their music was very pop-oriented and geared to teen and pre-teen fans. The Jacksons' father had managed their career before they came to Motown, and he continued as their manager after they signed with Gordy's company. He was aware that Stevie Wonder had been allowed to produce his own music, and when he was refused control of his sons' productions, he decided the group should leave Motown. They signed with the Epic label in 1976 and, after a lawsuit filed by Motown, changed their name to **The Jacksons**. The group's membership had changed slightly, because Jermaine Jackson stayed at Motown, having married Gordy's daughter, Hazel. The Jacksons remained a group of five, however, because the family's next-youngest male member, Steven Randall (Randy) Jackson, joined to take his brother's place. In later years, their little sister Janet also entered the music business.

Michael Jackson was singing very pop-oriented songs that included a throbbing disco beat, which was popular when he became a solo star during the late seventies. In 1979 he teamed up with producer/arranger Quincy Jones for the very successful album *Off the Wall.* Feeling pressure to at least match its success with a follow-up album, the two accomplished more than just a musical smash with *Thriller* in 1982. The album sold close to forty million copies and broke through the racial barriers of MTV. African American artists had previously not been given much airplay on the music-video television channel. The record-breaking album had the most hit singles ever on one album, one of which was "Beat It," featuring a guitar solo by heavy metal star Eddie Van Halen. Jackson's next album, *Bad* (1987), broke yet another record, achieving more top ten hits than any other album. *Bad* included Jackson's departure from his disco-influenced pop style with the still very electronic, but more gospel-oriented style of the message song "Man in the Mirror." The recording included a vocal group whose increasing prominence as the song progressed had the effect of many people agreeing with Jackson's "changes-start-with-the-individual" message, and was an effective use of backup vocals. After battling a number of problems in his personal life, Jackson returned to the studio for a new solo album in 1995, *HIStory: Past, Present and Future, Book One.* In 1996 it was reported that he was entering a large-scale agreement to form a new entertainment company.

The Commodores signed a contract with Motown in 1971. Their early recordings were in a funk-influenced rhythm and blues style much influenced by James Brown and Sly and the Family Stone. The group members had been sharing songwriting duties until the

The O'Jays (left to right): Walter Williams, Sammy Strain, and Eddie Levert
Michael Ochs Archives/Venice, CA

success of ballads written and sung by **Lionel Richie** (born in 1949) began to overshadow the popularity of their other recordings, and he became the group's principal songwriter. After some hits outside the Commodores, such as his duet with Diana Ross on the theme for the movie *Endless Love* (1981), Richie left the group in 1982 to concentrate on solo projects.

While the Commodores went from funk to a ballad style, Motown Records signed another funk singer, **Rick James** (born in 1952). The first time James was signed at Motown he was with the Mynah Birds, an unusual Motown group because it included white members Neil Young and Bruce Palmer. The Mynah Birds' recordings were never released and the group broke up, with Young and Palmer later joining the folk-rock group Buffalo Springfield. James came back to Motown as a singer, writer, and producer in 1978. He called his late-seventies style "punk-funk," and although the music itself was more funk than punk, he drew from both styles an emphasis on street life and drugs. In addition to performing, he worked as a writer and producer for Teena Marie, the Temptations, and Carl Carlton.

The Motown Company was sold to MCA Records in 1988. Stevie Wonder, the Commodores, Lionel Richie, and Rick James continued to record on the Motown label into the nineties. Jermaine Jackson switched labels to Arista for his recordings released in the late eighties and nineties.

Philadelphia Soul

Philadelphia was well known for its contributions to pop music of the fifties and early sixties through the nationwide popularity of its television program "American Bandstand." By the middle sixties, the production team of Kenny Gamble and Leon Huff moved their concentration away from pop music to create a soul style that remained popular well into the eighties. The success of their male vocal group, the Intruders, caused them to form the Philadelphia International Record Company and, under that label, they proceeded to produce hit after hit for the **O'Jays**, the Spinners, and Harold Melvin and the Blue Notes. In the late seventies, they signed former Chicago soul singer Jerry Butler to continue his solo career on their label. The Philadelphia soul sound was backed by sophisticated arrangements played by the Philadelphia International house band, MFSB (which stood for Mother, Father, Sister, Brother—although the members were not really related at all), that was made up of several keyboard players, guitarists, horn players, and percussionists. A listening guide to one of the biggest hits produced by the Philadelphia International Record Company during the seventies on page 85. The O'Jays followed "Love Train" with a number of other hit records and successful live performances. They had membership changes but three of the original members (Walter Williams, Eddie Levert, and Bill Isles) were still with the group in the nineties. They welcomed the nineties with two hit albums, *Emotionally Yours* (1991) and *Heartbreaker* (1993).

One of the Philadelphia International Record Company's most important stars of the late seventies and early eighties was former Harold Melvin and the Blue Notes lead singer **Teddy Pendergrass** (born in 1950). An enormously talented writer and singer, Pendergrass' career with Philadelphia International was cut short when he suffered partial paralysis from injuries received

Listening Guide

"Love Train"
as recorded by the O'Jays (1973)

Tempo: The tempo is approximately 126 beats per minute, with four beats in each bar.

Form: After a four-bar instrumental introduction, the form is based on a series of eight-bar phrases with vocals ordered as follows: A B B^1 A B B^1 A C A A A (1/2 with a fade out). (B^1 is based upon, but not exactly like, the melody of B.)

The eight-bar A sections (made up of two four-bar phrases) stress the need for the world to get on the "Love Train," and serve as a refrain, having the same lyrics each time they repeat.

The eight-bar B and B^1 sections are paired, but use different lyrics each time. In each pair, the lyrics to the first B section mention parts of the world that the "Love Train" will visit, and the B^1 section lyrics stress the fact that the train can solve the world's problems.

Each eight-bar B and B^1 is also constructed of two similar four-bar phrases.

The C section has vocal "ahs" over the thick instrumental texture.

Features: The beat subdivisions are even in the instrumental parts, but the vocals sometimes relax into uneven subdivisions.

The drums maintain a fairly strong backbeat.

The instrumental texture is very thickly mixed and includes a large (or overdubbed) orchestral string section, electric organ, and bass. The drums stand out from the thick texture and can be heard very clearly.

The vocals include almost conversational interjections from the backup singers.

Lyrics: The "Love Train" is traveling around the world and the singers promise that it will solve problems for all who get on it.

Source: Time-Life Music, *Sounds of the Seventies, 1973;* and *The O'Jays' Greatest Hits,* CBS 39251.

in a car accident in 1982. The paralysis did not affect his voice, so he was able to continue his recording career. He reappeared on the Electra label and had several hits on the rhythm and blues charts, including "Hold Me" (1984). He recorded with Whitney Houston on "Love 4/2" (1986) and "Joy" (1988).

Influences of Soul on Later Styles

The soul style James Brown developed in 1964 included a horn section used for rhythmic, even polyrhythmic, pulsations behind moving lines on the guitar and bass. That horn section sound was incorporated into some of the later sixties and seventies recordings by such Memphis soul musicians as Johnnie Taylor in "Who's Makin' Love" (1968) and Rufus Thomas in "Do the Funky Chicken" (1970). The sound also became the root of funk styles of the seventies, which will be discussed in Chapter 15. The horn sound of Memphis soul also became the basis for much big-band jazz rock, by groups like Bill Watrous' Manhattan Wildlife Refuge Band, Maynard Ferguson's band, and a number of other rock-influenced big bands of the eighties.

Summary

Soul was a tremendously popular style of music that had its roots in the gospel and rhythm and blues styles of the fifties. It spread out into several styles in different parts of the country during the sixties and continued to be popular and influential in later decades. Most soul singers began their careers by singing black gospel music, and they carried their emotional intensity from gospel into the secular themes of soul songs. While most of the singers maintained their gospel stylings, the basic style of soul recordings varied depending on the producers' choices of instrumentation and instrumental arrangements. The most important record companies to promote soul were Chess and Vee Jay in Chicago, Stax and Volt in Memphis, Atlantic Records in New York, Motown in Detroit, and Philadelphia International in Philadelphia. The producers of each of those companies provided their own characteristic style, adding to the soul index.

Terms to Remember

Baritone (voice)
Chromatic passing tones
Claves beat
Hook
Major chords
Ritard
Synthesizer
Timbre

CHAPTER 8

The British Invasion

By 1964, most American rock fans had all but forgotten the raw backbeat of rockabilly and blues-based rock styles of the fifties. Songs about puppy love sung by teen idols and girl groups accompanied by thickly arranged studio orchestras had dominated the sound of rock music for several years. Even rockabilly's originator, Elvis Presley, had long since dropped his rebellious James Dean image and had become a movie star who sang more pop ballads than rock. In November 1963, the American spirit of optimism was crushed by the shocking assassination of President John F. Kennedy. All these factors created a void that made the country's young music fans ready for something new. The sound that captured their attention came from Britain.

Like America, Britain had different musical styles centered in various parts of the country. London was the hub for groups whose music and image were identified with youth subcultures such as the **Mods** and **Rockers** (musically, Mods liked "modern" music; Rockers preferred rockabilly and older rock styles), but the city's music fans also supported groups that played American blues and rhythm and blues. Rock groups from the northern industrial city of Manchester and its seaport neighbor, Liverpool, had a less serious connection with these subcultures and were generally not interested in the blues, instead tending toward a simple, folk-based music called **skiffle,** and later rock music by Buddy Holly. The sound of groups from Liverpool and Manchester was referred to as "Mersey beat," after the name of the river that flows through Liverpool and near Manchester. The first British group to invade the American charts in 1964 was a Mersey beat group, the Beatles.

Skiffle

Skiffle was a very simple style of British folk music that developed out of a combination of American folk music and early New Orleans jazz. Some of the first skiffle singers to record in Britain had previously been members of jazz bands in the early fifties. One such singer/banjoist/guitarist was **Lonnie Donegan** (Anthony Donegan, born in 1931), who became known as Britain's "Skiffle King." Donegan even made skiffle records that charted in the U.S. top ten—"Rock Island Line" (1956, a cover of a song by Leadbelly) and "Does Your Chewing Gum Lose Its Flavor (On the Bedpost Over Night)?" (released in Britain in 1958 and in the U.S. in 1961). Skiffle used simple chords that young guitarists could master with little practice and it required little more than the guitar, or sometimes a homemade bass and strumming on a washboard. The simplicity and rhythmic fun of skiffle made it popular among young people throughout Britain.

The Quarry Men (left to right): Colin Hanton, Paul McCartney, Len Garry, John Lennon, and Eric Griffiths

Michael Ochs Archives/Venice, CA

The Beatles

In Liverpool in March 1957, **John Lennon** (1940–1980) acquired his first guitar and soon formed a skiffle group called the Quarry Men, named for his school, Quarry Bank High School. In July of that year, while performing with the group at a local church picnic, he met **Paul McCartney** (born in 1942), who was soon asked to join the group; he and Lennon also began to work occasionally as a duo called the Nerk Twins (sometimes spelled "Nurk"). The Quarry Men changed their name to Johnny and the Moondogs and invited **George Harrison** (born in 1943) to join them. All three played guitar and sang, which was sufficient for skiffle, but a drummer and a bass player were needed to play the rock music that most interested them. Stu Sutcliffe, a friend Lennon had met at art college, was not a musician, but Lennon persuaded him to use the money he received after selling some artwork to buy a bass guitar. Owning a bass qualified him to join the Moondogs. Drummer Tommy Moore was also enlisted, and the group's name was again changed, this time to the Silver Beatles; by 1960 it became simply the Beatles, partly to echo the insect name of Buddy Holly's Crickets. The deliberate misspelling gave them an eye-catching name, and "beat" suggested not just the musical term but the social rebellion of the American Beat movement.

By late 1960 the Beatles had a new drummer, Pete Best, and the group had become good enough that they were hired to perform in clubs in Hamburg, Germany. Their repertoire consisted mostly of covers of songs by American artists Chuck Berry, Little Richard, Buddy Holly, Gene Vincent, and others. After several trips and many long hours playing in Hamburg, they returned to Liverpool and played at the Cavern Club, a popular spot for teenagers. The group lost Sutcliffe during a trip to Hamburg in 1961 when he decided to stay there with his German girlfriend and work as an artist; he died of a brain hemorrhage not long afterwards. The Beatles chose not to replace him, so McCartney switched from guitar to bass, giving the group the same basic instrumentation as the Crickets, with Harrison on lead guitar, Lennon on rhythm guitar, McCartney on bass, and Best on drums.

The Beatles had gotten to know singer Tony Sheridan, who had also been performing in Hamburg, and Sheridan asked the group to accompany him on his German recording of "My Bonnie" (1961). They were billed as the Beat Boys on the recording, but when it was sold in Liverpool, their fans knew it was the Beatles. When the recording of "My Bonnie" was requested at a Liverpool record store, the manager of the store, Brian Epstein, was impressed enough to go to the Cavern Club to hear the Beatles. Epstein was wealthy, interested in the music business, and looking for a new creative job, so he offered to manage the group's career, and the Beatles soon agreed. One of the first demands Epstein made was that the group clean up its leather-jacketed Rocker image and wear neat, matching suits and shorter hair.

After several record companies rejected the group's recordings, Epstein finally got the Beatles a contract with EMI, where they were assigned to the Parlophone subsidiary and producer **George Martin** (born in 1926). Martin had no previous experience with rock music, but had produced light classical music and comedy records by Beyond the Fringe, Spike Milligan, and Peter Sellers. Martin's background in the classics led to the use of string quartets and other classical instrumentation on some of the Beatles' recordings, and his comedy work had involved considerable experimentation with **musique concrète** sound effects, which he used later on the Beatles' *Sgt. Pepper's Lonely Hearts Club Band* album (1967). Musique concrète was a French term for the electronic manipulation of natural sounds on tape, a technique used at the time by many avant-garde classical composers to create new sounds.

Before the Beatles' first session, George Martin told Lennon, McCartney, and Harrison that, while Best might be satisfactory for their Cavern Club bookings, he wanted to use someone else for recording. The Beatles decided that Best had to go, and to replace him, they hired **Ringo Starr** (Richard Starkey, born in 1940, nicknamed for his habit of wearing rings), the drummer for another Liverpool group, Rory Storm and the Hurricanes, whom the Beatles knew from bookings in which the groups had shared the billing. In September 1962, the Beatles reentered the studio to record their first single, "Love Me Do," backed with "P.S. I Love You." George Martin did not know Ringo's abilities, so he hired studio drummer Andy White for the session. As it turned out, they recorded a version of "Love Me Do" with White on drums (and Ringo on tambourine), and a version with Ringo on drums. Both versions were used: the one with White drumming was released on their first album, *Please Please Me* (1963), and the other, with Ringo drumming, was released as the single.

Throughout 1963, the Beatles' popularity escalated in Britain, but EMI's American label, Capitol, had no interest in releasing the group's recordings because they felt their sound would not suit American tastes. Certainly, the 1963 release of *Introducing the Beatles* on the Vee Jay label had not sold enough to indicate the group's potential in the U.S. Finally, in January 1964, a large publicity campaign accompanied Capitol's reluctant release of the album *Meet the Beatles,* a slightly different version of the group's second British album, *With the Beatles.* The single taken from the album, "I Want to Hold Your Hand," was an immediate hit on the American charts. By February 1964, when the Beatles arrived for their first visit to America, thousands of fans followed them everywhere they went. Their televised performances on "The Ed Sullivan Show" brought them into the homes of teenagers across the country. Beatlemania had begun, opening the American pop charts to a great number of British groups and bringing about what became known as the British Invasion. A listening guide to the Beatles' first American hit is on the right side of this page.

The Beatles were special among rock groups of the sixties because their music progressed from one album to the next as their experience and musicianship grew. They started out playing covers of songs by Chuck Berry, Little Richard, Carl Perkins, and others, and their early compositions showed these influences as well as those of American pop and soul styles. Lennon and McCartney wrote most of the group's hits, more often separately than in collaboration, though they frequently asked each other for advice on particular sections of songs. Their most popular early efforts were lighthearted love songs like "She Loves You" and "I Want to Hold Your Hand," but by 1965 they had begun to write more poetic lyrics and to use acoustic guitar more often, evidence of the influence of Bob Dylan's introspective, folk-oriented compositions. They did their share of studio experimentation in the early days, too, using feedback in the introduction to "I Feel Fine" in 1964.

The soundtrack for the movie *Help!* (1965) and the album *Rubber Soul* (1965) both showed further advancements in the Beatles' writing and playing styles. Harrison's increasing interest in Indian culture and music led him to learn to play the sitar, which added a new color to their arrangements. The lyrics of many of the songs on these albums contained deeper meanings than their

Listening Guide

"I Want to Hold Your Hand" by the Beatles (1964)

Tempo: The tempo is about 132 beats per minute, with four beats per bar.

Form: After three eighth-note pickups and a four-bar introduction, the song follows an A A B A B A form. Each A section is composed of eight bars and a four-bar refrain. The B sections are eight bars with a three-bar extension. The final A is extended by another repeat of the refrain.

Features: The beat pattern in the introduction creates an interesting effect by placing a stress on the third eighth-note pickup, making that half-beat sound like a **downbeat** (first beat of a bar). It is not until the vocals enter that the actual downbeat becomes clear.

Beat subdivisions are even throughout the recording.

The drums maintain a traditional, danceable rock backbeat.

The instrumentation is based on that of the Crickets: electric lead and rhythm guitars, electric bass guitar, and drums.

The instruments all function as accompaniment to the vocals, with no instrumental solo sections.

In several places, a hand-clapped rhythmic pattern creates an interesting polyrhythmic effect.

Lyrics: The lyrics simply and directly express the wish stated in the title.

Source: *Meet the Beatles!*, Capitol 90441; and *Past Masters, Volume 1*, Capitol 90043.

earlier works had. Lennon's "Norwegian Wood (This Bird Has Flown)" was a cryptic story about an affair he had fallen into, and in "Run for Your Life" he spoke of the commitment he expected from a lover. McCartney wrote about the need for depth in a relationship in "I'm Looking Through You." The group had not stopped performing love songs, but they wrote of love in broader terms than they had previously. The use of "love" in "The Word" (1965), for example, was much more complex than the simple statement made in "She Loves You" (1964). As an example of the tremendous changes the Beatles' music underwent after their recording of "I Want to Hold Your Hand," compare that listening guide with the listening guide to "Norwegian Wood" on page 90.

The 1966 American albums *Yesterday . . . and Today* and *Revolver* contained songs such as "Nowhere Man" and "Eleanor Rigby," which searched for meaning in life, and "Taxman," which criticized government control over peoples' pocketbooks. The Beatles had progressed far beyond their formative, imitative early style and had put themselves at the forefront of creativity in rock music. They had also become tired of touring, and their compositions had become too complex to perform effectively onstage. So, in August of 1966, the Beatles performed their last concert together, in San Francisco, and began to concentrate even more on their efforts in the recording studio.

With the help of their producer, George Martin, the group recorded an album that became one of the masterpieces of rock music, *Sgt. Pepper's Lonely Hearts Club Band* (1967). All of the music on the album was planned around a single theme—an idea influenced by the Beach Boys' *Pet Sounds* album from the previous year—but *Sgt. Pepper* went a step further. Rather than simply grouping songs with lyrical relationships, they made them part of a musical whole, a concert in a circus-like atmosphere complete with audience noises and whirling circus organ sounds. The lyrics for "Being for the Benefit of Mr. Kite!," in fact, came directly from a Victorian poster advertising a circus performance. Despite the lightness of McCartney's "Lovely Rita," many of the songs expressed the loneliness mentioned in the album's title. The Beatles had been influenced by the psychedelia of their time, and references to the illusions created by psychedelic drugs were evident in "Lucy in the Sky with Diamonds," (which fans took to represent the drug LSD) "Within You Without You," and "A Day in the Life." The album used musique concrète techniques on "Being for the Benefit of Mr. Kite!," for which Martin cut up a tape recording of a steam calliope and spliced the pieces of tape together (some were spliced in backwards), for a background that sounded like what might be heard at a circus. Along with using other nontraditional sounds on the album, the Beatles put some animal noises at the end of "Good Morning, Good Morning," recalling the sound of the barking dog at the end of the Beach Boys' *Pet Sounds* a year earlier.

The Sitar

As is the case in many large countries, musical traditions vary in different areas of the land. Such is the case in India where instruments and practices common in the north are different from those in the south. Musicians in both the north and the south use plucked-string instruments with fretted fingerboards. The instrument used in southern Indian classical music is called the vina, and its northern counterpart, the sitar. It was the sitar that first came to the attention of rock musicians in the middle sixties, primarily due to the commercial success of concerts given by sitarist Ravi Shankar. It was Shankar who taught Beatle George Harrison to play the instrument.

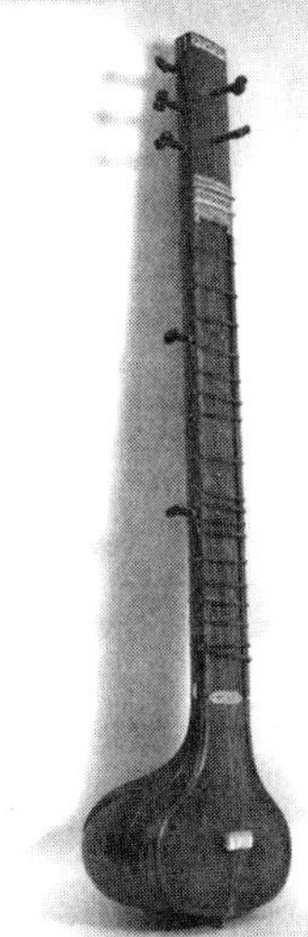

An Indian Sitar
Bettmann Archive

The sitar has a very distinctive sound when compared with any instrument of European origin because its frets are metal bars positioned almost an inch above the wooden fingerboard. That amount of space allows the player to bend the strings much further away from the pitch than would be possible on a guitar. The **microtones** created by that type of string bending contribute to the sitar's unusual timbre. Another sound that is characteristic of the sitar is the constant humming of a set of **sympathetic strings** set under the plucked strings. They are called sympathetic strings because they are not plucked, but instead vibrate in sympathy with the strings above them that are played. The sound created by the sympathetic strings is called a **drone,** or sustained tone. Most modern sitars have four or five melody strings and two or three additional drone strings. The frets are movable in order to be made to fit whatever key is required by a particular **raga,** or Indian melody. The body of the sitar is a pear-shaped gourd and on some sitars (not the one pictured here) the instrument's sound is enhanced by a resonator gourd at the top of the instrument's neck.

By the time the Beatles recorded *Sgt. Pepper,* their music, lyrics, and production techniques had developed far beyond what they had done only three years earlier. The listening guide to "A Day in the Life," on page 91, will point out the complexity of their later work.

Listening Guide

"Norwegian Wood"
as recorded by the Beatles (1965)

Tempo: The tempo is based on a waltz rhythm of three beats in each bar, with the primary accent only on the first of those three beats, or the downbeat. The approximate tempo of the waltz measures is 60 beats per minute.

Form: The form is based on eight-bar phrases ordered as A A A A B B^1 A A A A B B^1 A A A. (B^1 is like B except that it ends differently.) The first two A phrases are instrumental, the first featuring solo acoustic guitar and the second with that guitar joined by the sitar. The seventh, eighth, and last (eleventh) A phrases also feature the sitar with the guitar.

Features: The vocals are sung gently, creating an almost dreamy effect.

The primary accompaniment instruments are acoustic rhythm guitar and the sitar, which is featured in the second A of the introduction, in the other instrumental sections, and at the ends of vocal phrases. The bass and tambourine add subtle support to that accompaniment.

The sitar stands out from the other instruments because of its ability to bend notes much more than can be done on a guitar.

Lyrics: The song tells a story through suggestion, leaving much to the listener's imagination. The obvious points of the story are that the singer was invited into a girl's room where the two sat on the floor, drank wine, talked, and presumably went to bed together (although the singer claims to have slept in the bathtub). The girl had gone to work in the morning so the singer sat alone and enjoyed watching a fire. The relatively long and dreamy sitar solo after the suggestion of going to bed and the similarity between the words "Norwegian wood" and "knowing she would" caused much speculation and excitement for young listeners.

Source: *Rubber Soul,* Capitol 90453 or 46440.

As the Beatles attempted to expand their awareness of the world and human relationships through transcendental meditation and experiments with drugs, the four individuals were growing apart both personally and artistically. Their manager, Brian Epstein, who had been instrumental in keeping them on a single path for many years, died of a drug overdose in 1967. The group continued to record, but the unity of their earlier days was gone. Their short television film, *Magical Mystery Tour* (1967), and its subsequent album had some thought-provoking moments, but did not come up to the standard set by the *Sgt. Pepper* album. Their next effort, *The Beatles* (1968, often called the "White Album" because of its unadorned white cover), exemplified the individuality of the group members. Lennon had Japanese-American artist Yoko Ono add vocal sound effects on "Birthday" and "The Continuing Story of Bungalow Bill," and Harrison had Eric Clapton play lead guitar on "While My Guitar Gently Weeps." A variety of musical styles were also evident on the album. McCartney parodied the Beach Boys' vocal group sound on "Back in the U.S.S.R." and borrowed Dylan's acoustic folk style for "Blackbird." Ringo contributed "Don't Pass Me By," a country-styled composition. Lennon also experimented with **tape loops** on "Revolution 9," and wrote sentimental ballads such as "Julia," in memory of his late mother, and "Good Night," to his five-year-old son, Julian. Lennon divorced Julian's mother, Cynthia in 1968 and began his personal and musical relationship with Yoko Ono. The pair released their own album, *Two Virgins,* about the same time the group released *The Beatles.*

The last album the Beatles recorded was *Abbey Road* (1969). Side one of the album had a variety of unrelated, individual songs, but side two centered on the theme of the group's impending breakup, and some rather subtle musical devices were used to help express that theme. "She Came in Through the Bathroom Window" related one of the many problems that had beset the group on tours—crazed female fans attempting anything and everything in order to get at them. "You Never Give Me Your Money" was a reference to the lawsuits group members had filed against each other over the business problems of their Apple Corporation. From the time Brian Epstein died, Paul McCartney felt that the burden of holding the group together had fallen on him, and his song "Carry That Weight" hinted at those feelings. During "Carry That Weight," the musical theme from "You Never Give Me Your Money" was reprised, reminding the listener of the groups' legal battles and suggesting that the weight had become too much and that McCartney had given up his efforts to keep the group together. This idea of using a melody to remind the listener of a theme expressed earlier in a musical work has often been used in classical music, particularly in operas, in which a melody or melodic fragment (called a *leitmotif* in opera and an *idée fixe* in

Listening Guide

"A Day in the Life" by the Beatles (1967)

Tempo: A tempo of about 76 beats per minute, with four beats per bar, is maintained throughout the recording. The B sections, however, stress a double note beat to the point that the tempo can be heard as 152 beats per minute.

Form: The recording flows out of the previous album cut. An eight-bar introduction is made up of four bars of solo acoustic guitar and then four bars with the guitar joined by bass and piano. The basic formal structure is A A A B A, with sections of unequal lengths and long extensions and sound effects before and after the B section (which is sung by McCartney). The A sections are nine and ten bars long, and the B section is ten (or twenty, if counted at 152 beats per minute) bars long.

Features: Even beat subdivisions are maintained throughout the recording.

The drums add support and rhythmic color to the various sections of the recording, but do not maintain a steady, traditional beat or backbeat.

The instruments include strummed acoustic guitar, electric bass, piano, drums, and, in a few places, a forty-piece orchestra. The create the sound mass between the third A and the B section, four recordings of the orchestra were mixed to have the effect of a 160-piece orchestra.

The recording ends with a long extension of an echo of the final piano chord.

Lyrics: The lyrics (Lennon's for the A sections, McCartney's for the B section) attempt to depict everyday life. Lennon's lyrics refer to reading newspaper articles (one serious, one absurd) and seeing a movie. McCartney's lyrics convey what it feels like to get up and face the world each day. In contrast to those of "I Want to Hold Your Hand," the lyrics of "A Day in the Life" are not so easily understood and are open to interpretation. The experiences depicted are common, but the descriptive ways they are depicted give the song a depth the Beatles' earlier songs do not have.

Source: *Sgt. Pepper's Lonely Hearts Club Band,* Capitol 46442.

The Beatles and their producer during the "All You Need Is Love" session (left to right): Paul McCartney, John Lennon, Ringo Starr, George Martin, and George Harrison
Michael Ochs Archives/Venice, CA

symphonic music) represented a particular character or mood. *Abbey Road* closed with "The End," in which McCartney, Harrison, and Lennon each took turns playing guitar solos and Ringo played a drum solo. "The End" was followed by silence and then a short song about the Queen of England. The Beatles were finished as a group.

Each of the Beatles pursued his own career during and after the group's breakup. John Lennon married Yoko Ono, and the two worked in tandem on various projects, including a number of efforts to support the cause of peace. They moved to New York and made recordings separately and together, Lennon often using Phil Spector as his producer. (Spector was the producer brought in to sift through the Beatles' *Let It Be* tapes.) In 1975, Lennon gave in to a long-time desire to return to the roots of his own musical style and recorded an album he called simply *Rock 'n' Roll.* All the songs on the album were covers of fifties hits by American artists, including Gene Vincent, Chuck Berry, Fats Domino,

Buddy Holly, Larry Williams, Lloyd Price, Sam Cooke, and Little Richard. After that project Lennon stopped recording and settled into a relaxed home life with Yoko Ono and their son, Sean. It was not until five years later that he and Ono reentered the studio to record the album *Double Fantasy* (1980). In December 1980, one of the most tragic ironies in rock history occurred when Lennon, who had always stood for peace, was shot to death by a "fan" outside his New York apartment.

Paul McCartney also married an American, Linda Eastman, but they made their home in Britain. He recorded the solo album *McCartney* (1970), and he and his wife recorded *Ram* (1971) before they formed the group Wings, which was enormously successful in the seventies. In addition to recording and touring with Wings, McCartney wrote songs and produced albums for friends. He also organized *The Concerts for the People of Kampuchea* in 1979 to raise money for food and medical aid for the poor in Kampuchea (formerly Cambodia). Wings broke up in 1981, after McCartney became reluctant to tour as the result of threats he had received following the murder of John Lennon. The McCartneys continued to record and appear in some live concerts in the eighties, but they took a break from touring until 1990 when they performed new music along with many Beatle songs that the Beatles had never performed live. In 1993, McCartney launched his band on a world tour following the release of his new album, *Off the Ground.* He also confirmed that he would join George and Ringo to provide music for a new Beatles documentary.

George Harrison wrote and recorded albums of his own and also became very involved in movie production for Handmade Films, where he often worked with members of the British comedy troupe Monty Python. Ringo Starr pursued his own career as a singer and actor and occasionally played drums on recordings made by the other ex-Beatles. Harrison and Starr played together on several of Harrison's albums, including the successful *Cloud Nine* (1987). In 1989 Ringo put together what he called his All-Starr Band for a tour. The band included Nils Lofgren, Billy Preston, Joe Walsh, Dr. John, Jim Keltner, Rick Danko, Levon Helm, and Clarence Clemons. Of those members, only Lofgren and Walsh were in the 1992 "All Starrs" accompanied by Dave Edmunds, Todd Rundgren, and others.

The three living Beatles finally dropped their various feuds and regrouped to record two new Beatle songs, "Free As a Bird" (1995) and "Real Love" (1996), which were released along with many rare tracks and outtakes from the past on two double-CD volumes entitled *The Beatles Anthology 1* (1995) and *The Beatles Anthology 2* (1996). The new songs were indeed recorded by all four Beatles because tapes made by John Lennon were used as the basis of the recordings, with the other Beatles adding new vocals and instrumental tracks. *The Beatles Anthology 3* was released later in 1996.

Other Mersey Groups

Like the Beatles, most of the groups from Liverpool and Manchester used a lead guitar, rhythm guitar, bass guitar, and drums. The origin of that instrumental combination lay in American rockabilly of the fifties, except that in most rockabilly the lead guitarist played a hollow-body electric instrument, the rhythm guitar was a steel-strung acoustic, and the bass was an acoustic (string) bass. Buddy Holly had been among the first to use a solid-body electric guitar for his lead playing, and his rhythm guitarist used an electric, though hollow-bodied, rhythm guitar. His bassist played a standard string bass much like that used by other rockabilly groups. Many British groups whose music was influenced by Holly and by rockabilly updated the instrumentation by using amplified bass guitar instead of the large acoustic instrument. Although some Mersey groups occasionally added piano—or, as in the case of Gerry and the Pacemakers, orchestral string sections—to their recordings, the Mersey sound depended heavily on guitars.

The Searchers formed in 1961 and became performers at Liverpool's Iron Door club, the Cavern's primary competition. The historical importance of the Searchers did not lie in their original music, as most of their important recordings were covers. Rather, it was the way their guitarists focused on across-the-strings picking patterns commonly used in folk music (but played on the electric guitar) that influenced American folk-rock groups like the Byrds just a few years later. Another of their influences on folk rock was their use of group vocals instead of just one regular lead singer.

From Liverpool's neighboring city of Manchester, Freddie Garrity of **Freddie and the Dreamers** wore Buddy Holly-style horn-rimmed glasses as he danced and sang in front of his group. Even Freddie's unique dancing did not make his band a match for the Beatles in popularity, but Manchester's other groups, the Hollies and Herman's Hermits, certainly challenged the American success of the Beatles, if only for a couple of years. **The Hollies**, formed in 1962 by singer Allan Clarke and singer/guitarist Graham Nash, chose their name to identify themselves with Buddy Holly. Although their music did not reach America until the release of the single "Bus Stop" in 1966, their popularity allowed them to stay together through much of the seventies and attract attention when they regrouped in the eighties. Graham Nash left in 1968 because he wanted the group to record his "Marrakesh Express" instead of Dylan covers for the album *Words and Music by Bob Dylan* (1969). Nash's song ended up being an early hit (1969) for his new group Crosby, Stills and Nash. Perhaps in an effort to compete with the new American country/folk style of their departed member, the Hollies recorded "Long Cool Woman (in a Black Dress)" (1972), which sounded as if they had been listening to quite a bit of California's country-rock music, particularly that of Creedence

The Kinks (left to right): Peter Quaife, Dave Davies, Mick Avory, and Ray Davies

UPI/Bettmann

Clearwater Revival. As a tribute to the performer who had inspired them to play music, the Hollies recorded the EP *Buddy Holly* (1980) to commemorate what would have been Holly's forty-second birthday.

The most commercially successful group from Manchester was **Herman's Hermits**, started by singer/guitarist/actor Peter Noone. They were first known as the Heartbeats, but changed the name to make use of Noone's nickname, Herman. Between 1965 and 1967, Herman's Hermits had many American hit singles, most of which were directed at a younger audience than that of the Beatles. Like the Searchers, the Hollies, and other Mersey groups, the Hermits played guitars, bass, and drums. Herman's boy-next-door image was not unlike that of Buddy Holly, except that Herman's music had a less serious tone than Holly's.

Rock in London

London is such a large city that it had room for many different trends in rock music. The blues- and rhythm-and-blues-styled rock groups like the Rolling Stones, the Yardbirds, and the Animals had the following of one group of fans, while others preferred the clean-cut sound and image of the Dave Clark Five, Peter and Gordon, and Petula Clark. The Kinks had formed as part of the blues revival, but their experimentation with distorted sound effects led them away from their traditional blues orientation. The youth subculture known as the Mods (or Modernists) had short hair, wore trendy suits, rode motor scooters (rather than "real" motorcycles), and used amphetamines. Groups from London during the mid-sixties with Mod followings included the Small Faces, the Who, and, to some degree, the Kinks.

The Kinks

The British group that cared the least about invading America was the Kinks. When they toured the United States, they expressed their disdain for the customs and lifestyle they saw, and returned to Britain to write songs about their experiences. They later recorded an entire album full of their complaints about America, *Everybody's in Showbiz* (1972). While putting down America, the Kinks also wrote songs that drew attention to the British customs and traditions they preferred, as in the song "Afternoon Tea" (1968), and the album *The Kinks Are the Village Green Preservation Society* (1968).

The Kinks were formed as the Ravens in 1962 by singer/guitarist Dave Davies and his bassist friend Peter Quaife. The group had not been together long when Davies' older brother, **Ray Davies** (born in 1944), began to sit in as a guitarist on his breaks from art college. At the beginning of 1964, Ray finally decided to quit school and remain with the band. He renamed them the Kinks, because he saw them as a bunch of kinky misfits, and became their writer and leader. From Muswell Hill, just north of London, the group played in the same London blues clubs that gave the Rolling Stones their start. The Kinks' drummer, Mick Avory, joined after playing with other blues revival groups, including the Rolling Stones.

As was the case with most other bands of the British Invasion, the Kinks started out by playing covers of fifties rock hits. Their first recording was a cover of Little Richard's "Long Tall Sally" (Little Richard in 1956, Kinks in 1964). Ray Davies realized that to establish and maintain a career they should concentrate on writing their own material and develop their own distinctive sound, which began by slitting their amplifier speaker to

Listening Guide

"You Really Got Me" as recorded by the Kinks (1964)

Tempo: The tempo is approximately 138 beats per minute, with four beats in each bar.

Form: The recording begins with a four-bar introduction that consists of four statements of the one-bar guitar riff that continues to repeat throughout the recording. The drums enter in the third bar.

The introduction is followed by three twenty-bar sections, with a ten-bar instrumental section between the second and third sections. Each of the twenty-bar sections follows the form A A B C. The A and B phrases are each four bars long and the C phrases are eight bars long. The instrumental section is based on two-and-one-half repetitions of A.

Features: Even beat subdivisions are used throughout the recording.

The drums maintain a strong backbeat, and a tambourine supports the tempo by playing on each beat.

The guitar uses fuzztone created by a cut speaker cone.

The riff pattern begins with a half-beat pickup and then plays three beats ending with a half-beat rest.

Abrupt key changes occur between sections. Section B is one whole-step higher than A, and C is another fourth higher than B (a fifth higher than A). The pitch of the riff changes along with the key changes. Each new section begins in the original key and then changes key in the same places as did the first section.

An interesting effect is created by shifting the vocal accents from the way the lyrics would normally be spoken (even in England). Instead of accenting "you" and "got" in "you really got me," Davies accents "really" and "me."

Lyrics: The singer is so completely captured by a girl that he can't sleep and wants to be with her forever.

Source: Time-Life Music, *Classic Rock, 1964;* and *The Kinks Greatest Hits*, Rhino 70086.

get the distorted **fuzztone** for their powerful hit "You Really Got Me" (1964). At a time when most rock singers were using their music to express feelings of love, or in many cases lust, Davies sang about being "Tired of Waiting for You," wanting a girlfriend to "Set Me Free" (1965), and coldly asking women "Who'll Be the Next in Line" (1965).

The popularity of the Kinks' hit "You Really Got Me" caused a widespread interest in the fullness and roughness of fuzztone. Eventually, fuzz boxes were sold, allowing musicians to use the sound whenever they wanted to without having to cut their speakers. On the left is a listening guide to the song that stirred up the interest in fuzztone.

By late 1965, Davies began to expand his lyrical range to comment cynically on other peoples' values and lifestyles in his lyrics, losing his pop following in the process but gaining a faithful entourage of "Kink kultists." "A Well Respected Man" (1966) was the first of many songs he wrote about people he saw as lacking the creative energy needed to rise above society's dictates, people who were content to live boring existences simply by fitting into a socially acceptable mold. Davies made effective use of repetition in his music to express the monotony of the life his lyrics depicted. In some ways, "A Well Respected Man" took a dig at the London Mods, many of whom were among the Kinks' most ardent fans. He further insulted the subculture for its penchant for trendy fashions in "Dedicated Follower of Fashion" (1966). The song "Sunny Afternoon" (1966) appeared on the surface to express an enjoyment of a lazy summer day, but, as was typical of Ray Davies' compositions, it had a deeper meaning. A more careful listening revealed that their old, "well-respected man" had been accused of being not so respectable after all, having been victimized by taxes and women and having nothing left except time to laze in the sun.

By the late sixties, theme albums consumed Davies' interest. In 1970, the group's *Lola Versus Powerman and the Moneygoround, Part One,* addressed problems rock stars face in their careers. It contained the hit single "Lola," which put the Kinks back on the American charts. In the song, a young man is surprised to find that the beautiful Lola is in fact a transvestite. The theme may have been shocking to some listeners, but the subject of sexual ambiguity was not new to rock audiences who remembered Little Richard's image in the fifties or David Bowie's in the late sixties.

The Kinks had several personnel changes over the years, and by the time they recorded *Give the People What They Want* (1981), only three of their original members, Ray and Dave Davies and Mick Avory, remained, joined by bassist Jim Rodford and keyboardist Ian Gibbons. Adding synthesizers to the group's instrumental makeup for their highly electronic, energetic album *State of Confusion* (1983), Ray Davies' compositions contained comments on "Young Conservatives"

The Who (left to right): John Entwistle, Roger Daltrey, Keith Moon, and Pete Townshend
Michael Ochs Archives/Venice, CA

and "Clichés of the World (B Movie)." Still looking cynically at the world, this time at the modern-day preoccupation with videos, he discussed dishonest business practices in "Video Shop" and the youthful pastime of renting a movie and viewing it over and over in "Repetition," both from the 1986 album *Think Visual.* The Kinks went back on the road for a U.S. tour in 1993 to promote their new album, *Phobia,* but neither the tour nor the album achieved the success they had known in the past. Their 1995 album, *To the Bone,* was released only in Britain.

The Who

The Who came to rock music from a background in early jazz styles. Teenage banjo player **Pete Townshend** (born in 1945) and trumpeter **John Entwistle** (born in 1946) formed a **trad jazz** band (traditional jazz, meaning New Orleans- or Chicago-styled Dixieland) called the Scorpions in 1959. Townshend's parents were musicians and taught him some of the basics of music and its notation. Townshend taught himself to play a number of instruments, including guitar, accordion, piano, and drums, in addition to the banjo. Entwistle had picked up the guitar when he heard the twangy guitar sound of Duane Eddy but decided to set it aside to play bass when Townshend starting playing guitar.

Entwistle met **Roger Daltrey** (born in 1944) in 1962. Daltrey had played some skiffle guitar and then graduated to lead guitar with his own band, the Detours. Entwistle joined the Detours as bass player and soon brought in Townshend to play rhythm guitar. Daltrey fired the group's singer, Colin Dawson, to become both lead guitarist and lead vocalist. Along with drummer Doug Sanden, the Detours began to play at various clubs in London. Their repertoire consisted of covers of instrumentals by the Ventures and their British counterparts, the Shadows, traditional Dixieland jazz tunes (with Daltrey on trombone, Entwistle on trumpet, and Townshend on banjo), some blues songs by John Lee Hooker, and later some then-current hits by the Beatles. Gradually they added some Motown and other soul-styled American music.

Although all of the members maintained other jobs, the group practiced regularly and their musicianship developed quickly. In 1963, at the suggestion of a friend, they changed their name to the Who, and decided to look for another drummer because Sanden was not experimental enough for them. **Keith Moon** (1947–1978), who had been playing drums for a British surf group called the Beachcombers, asked for a chance to sit in with the Who. On that occasion Moon played with such energy that he broke the bass drum pedal; and though the destruction of instruments had not yet become a part of the Who's act, they were impressed by Moon's aggressive playing and made him their new drummer.

In 1964, the Who signed with manager Pete Meaden, who had some ideas about molding a group image from having worked for Andrew Oldham, the Rolling Stones' manager. Meaden was a Mod and set about to change the Who's style to appeal to mods. He had them rename themselves the High Numbers, get their hair cut, and dress themselves in trendy suits. The Motown Sound was very popular with Mods, so he had them increase that part of their repertoire and eliminate the older Dixieland and surf styles. He rewrote the lyrics to two American rhythm and blues songs to include Mod references, and had the High Numbers record them for release as a single. Although the group had been well received in Mod clubs, their record "I'm the Face" backed with "Zoot Suit" (1964) received bad reviews and sold few copies. The High Numbers' stage performances were improving, with Townshend, Daltrey, and Moon each competing for the audience's attention. Townshend strummed powerful guitar chords, his arm revolving in complete circles, Daltrey twirled his microphone around, and Moon thrashed at his drums as violently as possible.

The attention of film directors Kit Lambert and Chris Stamp was drawn to the High Numbers because they were looking for a band to use in a film on rock music. Only a short television film was made, but Lambert and Stamp became the group's managers. Out of fear that the name the High Numbers would soon become dated, the group returned to calling themselves the Who. With some inspiration from the choppy guitar rhythms of the Kinks, and with session player Jimmy Page on rhythm guitar, the Who recorded their first hit, an original song by Townshend called "I Can't Explain" (1965). This was soon followed by the single "My Generation," and the Who were on their way to international stardom. On the right is a listening guide to "My Generation."

Although Daltrey's stuttering of the lyrics to "My Generation" was connected with the fact that the amphetamine-taking Mods had a reputation for being inarticulate, the Who was slowly in the process of dropping their Mod image. After "My Generation" was a hit in Britain, the Who recorded a short version of the song called "My Favorite Station" to advertise a new program for BBC's Radio One. The Who followed that advertisement with others for such things as Coca-Cola. Their experience with the recording of rock-based radio ads was the basis for choosing advertising as the theme in their first theme album, *The Who Sell Out* (1967).

The Who were not known to many rock fans in the United States until after their 1967 performance at the Monterey Pop Festival, by which time their attention-drawing antics had grown into the complete destruction of guitars, amplifiers, microphones, and drums on stage. During their chaotic stage performances, John Entwistle kept the music going as long as possible, standing beside the wreckage. He never seemed to care to draw audience attention to himself, but concentrated on his playing while the rest of the group put on the visual show. Because the band had only one guitarist, and Townshend was more a rhythm guitarist than a lead player, Entwistle developed his bass technique to enable him to play lines that often functioned as both lead and bass.

The Who's first American hits were "Happy Jack" and "I Can See For Miles" (both 1967). Townshend began to consider the possibility of expanding beyond the standard pop format of two- to three-minute songs and writing a rock **opera,** beginning with the ten-minute "mini-opera" he had written for the album *Happy Jack* (1967). "Rael" had been planned as a mini-opera on *The Who Sell Out,* but too much was cut from the original by the time the album was pressed. Finally, in 1969, the Who produced a

Listening Guide

"My Generation"
as recorded by the Who (1965)

Tempo: The tempo begins at approximately 192 beats per minute, but it varies somewhat through the recording and slows down gradually at the end. There are four beats in each bar.

Form: After a four-bar introduction, the form is based on twenty-bar periods, most of which are made up of five four-bar phrases that end with the words "my generation" (or an instrumental version of the melody previously sung with the words). The last two times those periods are played they are extended to be longer than the earlier ones. The first period begins with the words "people try" and the second period begins with "why don't."

Features: Uneven beat subdivisions are used through most of the recording.

A strong backbeat is maintained by the drums throughout most of the recording.

The first four four-bar phrases of each period have a solo vocal line in the first two bars and then a group vocal response in the next two ending with the words "my generation."

The third period is instrumental, with electric bass improvising around the solo vocal melody and guitar taking the place of the group vocal responses.

Daltrey stutters and stammers on the solo vocal lines, often causing slight variations in the tempo of the music accompanying him.

The music abruptly changes key by moving up one whole-step three times during the recording, making the ending a tritone (three whole-steps) higher than the beginning. The key changes happen just after the third (the instrumental) period, in the fifth bar of an instrumental extension of the fourth period, and during the long final extension.

Lyrics: The song is an outcry for rebellious youths who want to be free to do as they please and don't ever want to be like "old" people.

Source: *The Who Sings My Generation,* MCA Records 31330; and *Greatest Hits,* MCA Records 1496.

double-album-length opera about a boy who turned deaf, dumb, and blind after being traumatized by his violent home life, but whose talent for playing pinball eventually brings about a miraculous healing and return to the world of sight and sound. *Tommy* proved to be an artistic and commercial breakthrough and was hailed as a powerful stage piece, although the group rarely performed it in its entirety. The entire opera became known worldwide through the 1975 film *Tommy,* directed by Ken Russell. A new, live version of *Tommy* hit Broadway in 1993.

Townshend intended to follow *Tommy* with a science-fiction theme album for which he had experimented with sounds produced by a synthesizer and sequencer. He abandoned the theme idea, but his innovative and distinctive synthesizer effects were featured on the album *Who's Next* (1971) and its hit single, "Won't Get Fooled Again." In that song Townshend expressed disillusionment about the effectiveness of protest movements at a time when many movements were ending and were being reevaluated by those who had participated in them. The Who's Mod association returned for their next rock opera, *Quadrophenia* (1973), based on the long-standing controversy between the Mods and the Rockers. Six years later the opera became a film directed by Franc Roddam. *The Who by Numbers* (1975) was not planned as a theme album in the sense of having a storyline, but a theme expressing uncertainty about a future as aging rock stars was present in such songs as "However Much I Booze" and "Success Story." Townshend picked up an accordion for the album's only hit, "Squeeze Box."

The members of the Who had never gotten along well socially, and they worked together best when they had plenty of time away from each other between recording projects and tours. The one who had the most problem handling life on his own was Keith Moon. Nothing could control his drinking or his extreme mood and personality changes. His wife and daughter left him in 1974. His new girlfriend managed to get him into hospitals to clean the alcohol out of his system, but he returned to his old habits when he was back on his own. The last Who album he lived to record was *Who Are You* (1978). In September 1978, Moon died of an overdose of Heminevrin, an anti-alcoholism sedative, combined with an excess of alcohol in his system. A movie tribute to the Who's career with Moon, called *The Kids Are Alright,* was released in 1979.

Needing a new drummer, the Who chose **Kenney Jones** (born in 1948), a friend of theirs from another London-based Mod band, the Small Faces (later called the Faces). There was no point in Jones' trying to imitate the wild playing of Keith Moon. Moon had such an individualistic style that he was virtually impossible to imitate. Instead Jones, a competent and powerful drummer in his own right, brought his own musical personality to the group. Along with a change of drummer, the group added keyboard player John "Rabbit" Bundrick to their new sound. Bundrick was from Texas, but had been a studio musician in England, playing on albums by Free and other bands since the early seventies.

Having overcome the loss of Moon, the group lost its enthusiasm for touring when eleven concertgoers were trampled to death in a rush of thousands of fans at Cincinnati's Riverfront Coliseum in 1979. Concert promoters had sold tickets at a single price, with no reserved seats (called festival seating), causing a desperate stampede for the best view of the stage. The group went onstage not knowing about the tragedy. After they were informed about it, they did not want to continue their tour, but they feared that if they canceled they might never want to tour again. Two and a half years after Moon's death, the Who came out with another album, *Face Dances* (1981), which featured the hit "You Better You Bet." In that same year they contributed to Paul McCartney's *Concerts for the People of Kampuchea.*

By the early eighties, the frustration of advancing age and the pressure to make his group appeal to fans who wanted to hear the old Who classics was taking its toll on Townshend. In 1982, the group recorded *It's Hard* and went on what was advertised as their last tour, which ended in December of that year. Individual members continued to work on their own projects, but in 1990 the Who returned with a reunion tour of America, including performances of *Tommy* in New York and Los Angeles.

Summary

The year 1964 was the beginning of a British Invasion that never really came to an end. The music played by British groups was based on American music, to which the British added their own themes and styles. Mersey beat groups such as the Beatles, Gerry and the Pacemakers, the Searchers, the Hollies, and Herman's Hermits were much influenced by Buddy Holly and the Crickets. The Beatles expanded their Holly-influenced style by adding elements of Bob Dylan's folk style and poetic lyrics, psychedelic music, Indian music, and new techniques of studio production.

The rock music of London was influenced less by Buddy Holly and more by the blues and the tastes of the Mods and the Rockers, the young subcultures prevalent at the time. The Who, and to a lesser degree the Kinks, started out as Mod bands. While most American teens did not relate to British subculture connections, they could appreciate the Kinks' criticisms of modern society and the Who's rough display of energy on stage.

Terms to Remember

Downbeat
Drone
Fuzztone
Mods
Microtones
Musique concrète
Opera
Raga
Rockers
Skiffle
Sympathetic strings
Tape loops
Trad jazz

CHAPTER 9

The Blues Revival

American jazz and jazz-related popular music had intrigued the British since the nineteenth century, when the blackface minstrel show with its songs, dances, and characteristic type of humor found its way across the Atlantic. The classic ragtime of James Scott, Joseph Lamb, and, of course, Scott Joplin reached England through published sheet music, and thousands of amateur pianists struggled to master the intricacies of the music's syncopated rhythms. During the early decades of the twentieth century, a number of American jazz soloists and groups toured Britain, as well as the rest of Europe, creating quite a furor over the new music, which, in some ways, gained greater acceptance in Britain and Europe than in America, where it too often was considered the primitive product of an inferior people. The development of the recording industry, too, helped to bring American music to the attention of the rest of the world. Groups imitating those on the American recordings sprang up all over Europe, and jazz became an international music with its roots in African American culture.

American rock and roll became popular in England during the late fifties. Although some American performers did tour in Britain, the English soon produced their own soloists and groups who patterned themselves after various American originals. On the heels of Elvis Presley, Gene Vincent, and Eddie Cochran came their British imitators, Tommy Steele, Billy Fury, and Joe Brown. When American rhythm and blues and rockabilly styles were superseded by the blander, dance-oriented style popularized on "American Bandstand," some British fans turned to the pop rock of Cliff Richard and Marty Wilde. Those who could not relate to that pop style became disillusioned with rock and abandoned it for the older, gutsier type of music in which fifties rock was rooted—the blues.

British musician Chris Barber started a band in 1954 that played trad jazz, skiffle, and country blues at clubs in London. As Barber's following grew, musicians who had played with him left to form their own groups. By the early sixties, blues clubs had sprung up all over the city. Among the more successful bands were Cyril Davies' Rhythm and Blues All-Stars (formed in the late fifties), Alexis Korner and Cyril Davies' Blues Incorporated (formed in 1961), the Rolling Stones (formed in 1962), John Mayall's Bluesbreakers (formed in 1963), The Spencer Davis Rhythm and Blues Quartet (formed in 1963, later renamed the Spencer Davis Group), the Yardbirds (formed in 1963), and the Graham Bond Organisation (formed in 1963). In addition to making many cover recordings of American blues songs, these British groups wrote original material based on the blues style.

Most of the British blues covers were not sanitized and countrified versions of the blues originals, as were those made by white artists in America during the fifties. The British covers of the early sixties, although often not exact copies, were as close to the style and feel of the originals as they could get, including the use of bottlenecks and string-bending techniques on the guitar and

The Rolling Stones in 1964 (left to right): Bill Wyman, Brian Jones, Mick Jagger, Charlie Watts, and Keith Richards
Michael Ochs Archives/Venice, CA

cross-key relationships on the harp. Some of the covers added more interesting and active bass or lead guitar lines than were heard in the original recordings; the tempos varied, with some covers slightly faster than the originals and some slower; and at times some modifications were made in melodies. But the important point was that these covers did not involve changes in the basic character of the music. The British were not covering the blues in order to make commercial hits. They were playing the blues out of a real love, respect, and enthusiasm for the music. Some of the groups did indeed go on to commercial success through more pop-oriented music, but even then their styles retained the influence of their earlier experience with the blues.

In the early fifties, Cyril Davies played banjo in a trad jazz band, but as he became more attracted to pure blues he concentrated on singing and playing the harp. With guitarist Alexis Korner, Davies formed the amplified blues group **Blues Incorporated,** which became the training ground for many blues-styled rock artists, including drummers Charlie Watts and Ginger Baker, singer Mick Jagger, and bassist Jack Bruce.

The Rolling Stones

The Rolling Stones of the nineties was not a blues band, but the Rolling Stones of the early sixties was one of Britain's best. Their bohemian lifestyle was shocking to most conventional Britons, but then they never cared to appeal to the conventional. They played an expressive, like-it-or-go-to-hell brand of the blues, and because both the music and their rebellious image appealed especially to young audiences, they attracted untold numbers of blues fans. They became one of the longest-lived groups in the history of rock music. In the course of their career they veered away from the blues in most of their original compositions, but their concerts continually revived their blues roots.

Two members of the Rolling Stones, **Mick Jagger** (born in 1943) and **Keith Richard** (born in 1943), had attended the same primary school. (Keith's name had been mistakenly spelled "Richards" enough times that he eventually adopted the final "s" himself.) Although they lost contact with each other for ten years, they had both become blues fans after hearing Muddy Waters perform in England in 1958. When they ran into each other again in 1960 they began to work together, joining various blues groups in London. In 1962 they formed the Rolling Stones, naming their group after the "rolling stone" that represented a tough and independent man in blues songs like "Rollin' Stone" and "Mannish Boy" (both recorded by Muddy Waters).

The original Rolling Stones included singer/harpist Mick Jagger, guitarist Keith Richards, guitarist **Brian Jones** (1942–1969), pianist Ian Stewart and other musicians who played with them off and on during their first year. In December 1962, **Bill Wyman** (William Perks, born in 1936) was added on bass, and in January 1963, **Charlie Watts** (born in 1941) joined as drummer. When Andrew Oldham was signed as their manager, he chose to remove Stewart from the official group roster, although Stewart did continue to do occasional work with the band throughout their career until his death in 1985.

Although they started out playing the blues, most of the Stones' more popular early recordings were covers of songs by other rock artists. Their first hit in England (1963) was a cover of Chuck Berry's "Come On"; their second was "I Wanna Be Your Man" (1963), by Lennon and McCartney; and their third was a 1964 cover of Buddy Holly's "Not Fade Away." As the following listening guide shows, the Stones' recording did not follow Holly's style at all. They turned the pop-rockabilly

Listening Guide

	"Not Fade Away" by Buddy Holly (1957)	**"Not Fade Away" by the Rolling Stones (1964)**
Tempo:	The tempo is about 184 beats per minute, with four beats in each bar.	The tempo is about 208 beats per minute, with four beats in each bar.
Form:	Each stanza has eight bars, with one line of lyrics in two bars, a guitar response to the line lasting two bars, followed by two more bars of lyrics and another two bars of guitar response.	The basic form of the original is followed, except that the stanzas are kept at eight bars each, where Holly used occasional extra bars in instrumental sections.
Features:	The drums keep a soft Bo Diddley beat (notated in Chapter 2).	The "feel" of the Bo Diddley beat is present, especially with the use of maracas, which were common in Bo Diddley's own recordings. The tambourine adds a black gospel feel.
	The backbeat is present, but not prominent. Instrumental stop time is used (only the drums continue) during Holly's lead vocal lines.	The backbeat is not prominent. There is no stop time; all the instruments keep the rhythm going behind Jagger's vocal lines.
	A vocal group (probably not the Crickets) imitates some of the Bo Diddley beat kept by the drums with punctuations on beats two and four, and then beats two and three of the two-bar instrumental responses.	The beat pattern sung by the vocal group in Holly's recording is kept by the harmonica, but the use of blue notes changes the style from one of clean, crisp pop to include some blues color.
Lyrics:	Holly sings the lyrics as if he were politely informing a girl that she was eventually going to be his lover.	Jagger's vocal tone, singing Holly's same lyrics, sounds much more demanding—even arrogant—in his pronouncement that the girl will soon be his.

Source: Holly's recording: *Buddy Holly/The Crickets: 20 Golden Greats,* MCA 1484.

The Rolling Stones' recording: *The Rolling Stones,* AKO 7375; and *Big Hits, Volume 1 (High Tide & Green Grass),* AKO 8001

song into rhythm and blues. At the top of this page is a comparison of the two recordings.

By 1964, the Beatles had become well known internationally, and the Stones followed along, gaining a reputation as the Beatles' nasty opposites. While the Beatles wore matching suits, had neatly trimmed hair (though too long by American standards), and maintained a respectable image, the Stones wore anything they wanted, looked scraggly, and did their best to repulse adult society. American teens preferred the Beatles at first, but the Stones soon won a large following. After all, rebellion had long been part of the history of rock and roll music.

The music that most closely influenced the style of the group's first three American-released albums was that of blues and blues-rock artists Chuck Berry, Bo Diddley, Willie Dixon, and Muddy Waters, some of whose songs they covered. The Stones also covered "Route 66," which had been a hit for Nat "King" Cole in the forties and was recorded by Chuck Berry in 1961, but instead of imitating Cole's or Berry's vocal style they roughened the sound to be closer to that of their old favorite, Muddy Waters.

Of the blues revival groups, the Rolling Stones became the most popular in America. In addition to blues recordings by Muddy Waters and others, the Rolling Stones covered American soul and Motown songs on their early albums. When they appeared in the concert movie *The T.A.M.I. Show* (1964), they followed soul artist James Brown; watching the movie, it becomes clear that the types of dance routines that later became a regular part of Mick Jagger's stage performances can be traced to Brown's influence. The influences of soul music were apparent in Jagger's and Keith Richards' own songs, an early example of which was "Satisfaction" (1965).

Andrew Oldham knew that groups who depended on outside songwriters would not remain popular as long as those who wrote their own songs, so he pushed the group to improve their songwriting skills. Their earliest efforts included ideas contributed by all group members, and rather than credit all of them, they made up the

The Rolling Stones in 1989 (left to right): Bill Wyman, Mick Jagger, Keith Richards, and Ron Wood. Charlie Watts is in the background
AP/Wide World Photos

name "Nanker-Phelge" to use for that purpose. Jagger and Richards developed writing skills as a team, and their songs gained much more commercial success than the group's cover records had.

An obvious change in the Rolling Stones' musical style came about when Jagger and Richards began to write more of their own songs. *Aftermath* (1966) was the group's first all-original album. Blues and soul roots were still evident, but cultures other than those of African Americans were also being explored. The Indian sitar, played by the group's most versatile musician, Brian Jones, added a new timbre on "Paint It Black." The sitar, also used by the Beatles during the same time period, was in vogue for many rock groups, both American and British. In addition to the sitar, other nonstandard (for the Stones) instruments used on *Aftermath* were the dulcimer (played by Jones on "Lady Jane"), harpsichord, and marimba (played by Jones on "Under My Thumb"). Reflecting the macho image they had maintained since early in their career, both "Stupid Girl" and "Under My Thumb" enraged anyone sensitive to women's issues.

The album *Their Satanic Majesties Request* (1967) was musically experimental, particularly on the part of Brian Jones, who had become intrigued with the possibilities afforded by the use of electronic instruments. He played a **mellotron** (*mel*ody + elec*tron*ics) on "2000 Light Years from Home." The influence of drugs can be heard in some of the Stones' wandering, unfocused instrumentals, which conveyed a feeling of time expanding. The psychedelic artwork on the cover of *Their Satanic Majesties Request* was reminiscent of other drug-influenced albums that were being put out in San Francisco during the same period. The Stones had experienced problems with the authorities because of their use of drugs. In England the group's fans believed the title of the album was inspired by the fact that the drug arrests of various group members had kept them from touring freely—British passports contained a line which began "Her Britannic Majesties . . . Request . . ."

The Stones' *Beggars Banquet* album (1968) was released five months later than planned because of controversy over the cover the group wanted to use. Once again, they demonstrated they would do anything to challenge society's standards of acceptability, on their album covers and in their songs. "Street Fighting Man" sang of fighting in the streets in much the same way that the American Motown group Martha and the Vandellas had sung of dancing in the streets. Motown's goal was to encourage a peaceful movement toward racial integration and equality, but the Stones cultivated the image of macho fighters. Again experimenting, Brian Jones provided distorted sounds on the recording of "Street Fighting Man," playing an Indian tamboura.

Beggars Banquet proved to be the end of Brian Jones' participation with the Rolling Stones. Although by some accounts he had been asked to leave because his drug use had gotten out of hand, he announced he was quitting the band to explore other musical directions. He

Listening Guide

"Miss You" as recorded by the Rolling Stones (1978)

Tempo: The tempo is approximately 112 beats per minute, with four beats in each bar.

Form: The form is based on an almost hypnotic repetition of a four-bar phrase with pickups. The repetition of that phrase is broken only once by two four-bar contrasting phrases. The contrast occurs in the phrases with lyrics that ask why the singer's "baby" is waiting so long.

There are four instrumental sections: 1) the instrumental introduction is three phrases long; 2) a one-phrase (four-bar) instrumental with soft vocal responses follows the pair of contrasting phrases; 3) a two-phrase (eight-bar) instrumental occurs five phrases later and features a tenor saxophone solo; 4) the recording concludes with three phrases that feature a harmonica solo and then fade out.

Features: Beat subdivisions are generally uneven, except for the drums, which maintain even subdivisions.

The drums maintain a very steady pulse on each beat, sometimes evenly accenting each beat and other times alternating the accents with a strong emphasis on the backbeat. The regular pounding of the beat is very much part of the dance-oriented disco style.

The vocals are the primary attraction of the recording. Jagger changes his voice in many ways—from soft, subtle begging to an effective imitation of African American "jive talk" as he mimics a friend's voice on the phone.

Lyrics: The singer is so obsessed by how much he misses the person to whom the song is directed that he cannot do anything but think about that person.

Source: *Some Girls,* Rolling Stones Records 40449.

never had an opportunity to do any experimenting on his own, however: He went to sleep while sitting alone in his swimming pool and drowned in July 1969. **Mick Taylor** (born in 1948), from John Mayall's Bluesbreakers, replaced Jones as the group's second guitarist.

Another tragedy hit the Rolling Stones that same year. While on a very successful American tour, they decided to give a free concert at the Altamont Speedway in California. Woodstock had been such a successful rock extravaganza that the time seemed right for another large outdoor gathering of rock fans. To avoid calling in uniformed guards their fans would resent, the Stones followed the advice offered by San Francisco's Grateful Dead and hired members of a motorcycle gang, the Hell's Angels, to handle security for the event. A young African American man, Meredith Hunter, was stabbed to death in front of the stage by "security officers"; the stabbing was recorded during the taping of *Gimme Shelter,* a documentary about the Stones' tour. This much-publicized incident at Altamont certainly lessened the positive attitude toward rock festivals that the success of Woodstock had engendered.

Although the Rolling Stones started their musical life as a blues band, by the early to mid-seventies they had become one of the most eclectic groups in rock and roll. By that time, almost all of their recordings were original compositions by Jagger and Richards, and the team had learned to assimilate many of the existing styles of popular music. On their *Sticky Fingers* (1971) and *Exile on Main Street* (1972) albums, "Sister Morphine" was styled after American folk ballads; gospel-style call-and-response vocals were used on "I Got the Blues" and "Tumblin' Dice"; and "Dead Flowers," "Moonlight Mile," and "Loving Cup" could have been mistaken for American country, even hillbilly music. The blues style of the group's past was evident in "Shake Your Hips," which used blues harmonica, and the guitar in "Casino Boogie" played the old single-chord rhythm and blues style. Both British and American folk and country styles were evident on the *Goat's Head Soup* (1973) and *It's Only Rock 'n' Roll* (1974) albums, and the title cut of the latter used a rhythm and blues beat. Motown's influence was not forgotten with the cover of "Ain't Too Proud to Beg," The Temptations' hit from 1966.

In 1975, Mick Taylor left the group and was replaced by **Ron Wood** (born in 1947), who had previously worked with the Faces and the Jeff Beck Group. As varied as the Rolling Stones' musical styles had become, the album *Black and Blue* contained a new surprise in the form of African and Jamaican element. "Hot Stuff" was based on rhythms and vocal devices that could be heard in modern-day Kenya and Tanzania and "Cherry Oh Baby" was a cover of a reggae song by Eric Donaldson. The giant-selling album *Some Girls* (1978) and its hit, "Miss You," showed that the group did not remain untouched by the disco dance craze of the time. A listening guide to that recording is on this page. *Emotional Rescue* (1980) continued with disco influences, but also included a Jamaican ska rhythm in "Send It to Me" and a country style in "Indian Girl." The albums *Tattoo You* (1980) and *Undercover of the Night* (1983) contained a combination of both funk and country-styled tunes. On *Dirty Work* (1986), "Too Rude" used a reggae rhythm and bass line.

The band took a short break while both Jagger and Richards recorded solo albums during the late eighties, but the Rolling Stones were back on the road for a massive tour to promote their *Steel Wheels* (1989) album. That tour was followed by other band members recording solo albums and the long-expected announcement that Bill Wyman was leaving the band. It took almost two years for a replacement to be found. The new member was **Darryl Jones,** a young African American bassist who had previously worked with jazz trumpeter Miles Davis and also played on Sting's album *The Dream of the Blue Turtles* (1985). The album that followed, *Voodoo Lounge* (1994), won a Grammy award for 1994's Best Rock Album.

The recorded output of the Rolling Stones from 1962 through the nineties gave their fans quite an aural-cultural tour through a number of international musical styles, as well as several different period styles, ranging from early British folk to early American country blues to current styles. Borrowing the music of other peoples and other times served to broaden the group's own style. But no matter what style of music they played, or whose recording they covered, they always remained, unmistakably, the Rolling Stones.

Other Important British Blues Revival Bands

The Rolling Stones were exceptional in having stayed together for so long with so few membership changes. It was more typical for musicians of blues revival groups of the sixties to move from one band to another quite often. The blues was such a distinct musical style, with its own musical language and such well-established formal traditions, that it was very easy for musicians to walk on stage and perform with others with whom they had never worked before. Blues musicians improvised much of what they played, and as long as the improvisations followed the traditional twelve-bar harmonic progression, or some variant of it, and as long as the musicians listened and were responsive to each other, whatever they played would fit together. Clearly, some combinations of players worked better than others, but part of the joy of playing an improvised music such as the blues, lay in the musical give-and-take among the musicians.

It was already mentioned that Blues Incorporated had frequent personnel changes, but an even more important group that functioned as a training ground for many a blues-rock musician was **John Mayall's Bluesbreakers.** The group was formed in 1963, and throughout its existence Mayall's singing and harp, guitar, and keyboard playing remained faithful to the blues tradition. Many of his Bluesbreakers left to form commercial rock groups, but their experience in playing the blues continued to influence their rock styles. Among the rock musicians who worked with the Bluesbreakers early in their careers were guitarists Eric Clapton, Mick Taylor, and Peter Green; bassists John McVie, Jack Bruce, and Andy Fraser; and drummers Keef Hartley, Aynsley Dunbar, and Mick Fleetwood. John Mayall was sometimes called the Father of the British Blues because of the Bluesbreakers' importance to the blues revival.

Spencer Davis had sung and played both guitar and harp only as a hobby when he formed the Spencer Davis Rhythm and Blues Quartet, renamed **The Spencer Davis Group,** in 1963. Singer/guitarist/keyboardist **Steve Winwood** (born in 1948) and his brother Muff, a bassist, had played in trad jazz bands until they joined with Davis to form his blues band. The group's hit recordings "Gimme Some Lovin' " and "I'm a Man" (both written by Steve Winwood) were made in 1967 and featured Steve Winwood as the singer. After the Spencer Davis Group broke up, Steven Winwood formed and recorded with Traffic, worked with Eric Clapton in Blind Faith, and later had a solo career in which he blended his blues background with jazz, folk, and even classical music.

One of the best examples of a blues musician moving from one group to another was singer **Rod Stewart** (born in 1945). After a bit of experience singing folk music on street corners, Stewart sang and played blues harp with several groups in the London clubs. With his rough-edged vocal sound, he was able to capture the vocal quality of the African American bluesmen. Blues groups with which he performed and recorded during the mid-sixties included the Hoochie Coochie Men (with Long John Baldry), the Aynsley Dunbar Retaliation (with Jack Bruce of Cream and Peter Green of Fleetwood Mac), and Shotgun Express (with Peter Green and Mick Fleetwood of Fleetwood Mac). By 1967, Stewart was becoming less of a blues purist, and he began singing non-blues rock music in his bluesy style. He joined the Jeff Beck Group, after which he went on to the Faces (formerly the Small Faces) and then established a successful solo career.

Another British singer who patterned his vocal style after the sound of African American blues and rhythm and blues singers was **Eric Burdon** (born in 1941). He had been an art student in Newcastle upon Tyne until he became involved with the blues, the popularity of which had spread from London to his hometown in the north of England. He joined the Alan Price Combo as lead singer in 1962. Keyboard player Price and his group had been playing blues and rhythm and blues since 1958. With Burdon, the group became a popular club attraction with such a wild stage act that their fans began calling them **The Animals,** a name that stuck with them.

The Animals covered many American blues and rhythm and blues songs by Bo Diddley, John Lee Hooker, Fats Domino, and Chuck Berry. Not only was Burdon very good at imitating the tonal quality of the African American bluesmen, but Alan Price did an

Cream (left to right): Jack Bruce, Ginger Baker, and Eric Clapton, in a reunion performance of "Crossroads" at the 1993 Rock and Roll Hall of Fame induction ceremonies in Los Angeles
AP/Wide World Photos

impressive imitation of Bo Diddley's distinctive guitar style on his electric organ. The Animals also did non-blues songs, such as the American folk song "House of the Rising Sun" (1964), and with that and their original songs they became less a blues group and more a rock group with a style that was rooted in the blues.

Another in the lineup of British blues bands was **The Yardbirds,** formed in London in 1963. Their lead guitarist, Anthony "Top" Topham, was replaced by **Eric Clapton** (born in 1945) after the group had been together for only four months. The Yardbirds started out playing covers of American blues recordings and gained a following at some of London's blues clubs. When blues singer/harpist Sonny Boy Williamson No. 2 (Rice Miller) visited London in December 1963, he chose the Yardbirds to be his backup group. Only two months after those performances with Williamson, the Yardbirds were in a studio making a professional recording that led to a contract.

For the next year or so the Yardbirds covered tunes by John Lee Hooker, Bo Diddley, Howlin' Wolf, Sonny Boy Williamson, Willie Dixon, and Chuck Berry. But with the success of the Beatles and other British groups in America in 1964, most members of the group decided to stop playing the blues and try a more commercial style of music. The idea worked, and they achieved pop stardom in 1965 with "For Your Love," but they paid a price. Eric Clapton, the most blues-loving of the Yardbirds, refused to play guitar on any more pop recordings and left the group. To replace him, they first approached **Jimmy Page** (born in 1944). Page had earned a great deal of respect as a blues guitarist who could play almost any form of popular music, including the Yardbirds' new commercial style, but he was so successful as a studio musician that he was not looking to join a group as a regular member. Tours would have caused him to lose studio jobs. Page recommended **Jeff Beck** (born in 1944), who had been playing with a rhythm and blues band called the Tridents, and shortly thereafter Beck joined the Yardbirds.

Musically, Beck turned out to be a good choice. The Yardbirds were developing a very commercial, psychedelic stage act, and Beck eagerly joined in by playing his guitar behind his head and experimenting with amplifier **feedback.** He also made frequent use of string bending, a technique that was not exclusively a part of the blues tradition; it was often employed on the sitar and other Indian stringed instruments. Beck even used his technique to imitate the sound of the sitar in the Yardbirds' recording of "Heart Full of Soul" (1965).

Although Beck was a fine musical addition to the group, he turned out to be undependable in other ways. His performances were inconsistent, sometimes requiring the other group members to fill in for him when he was not paying attention to what he was supposed to be playing. He would even miss concerts, choosing instead to be with his girlfriend. In need of a new player to stimulate himself and mollify the group, Beck asked Jimmy Page to join so the two of them could play lead guitar together. Page finally did join the Yardbirds, playing lead guitar alone in Beck's absence and sharing the spot when Beck was there. Beck finally quit the group in 1966 to form his own band, leaving Jimmy Page as the sole lead guitarist. When the other members left, Page put together a new group called the New Yardbirds. That group stayed together for a long and successful career as Led Zeppelin.

■ Musically, Led Zeppelin was an important link between the blues and heavy metal. Their music will be discussed in Chapter 18, Hard Rock and Heavy Metal.

Clapton remained closely tied to the blues for most of his career. Before joining the Yardbirds in 1963, he had played with two rhythm and blues groups, the Roosters and Casey Jones and the Engineers. Upon leaving the Yardbirds, he joined John Mayall's Bluesbreakers

Listening Guide

"Crossroads"
as recorded by Cream (1968)

Tempo: The tempo is about 138 beats per minute, with four beats in each bar. It is quite a bit faster than Robert Johnson's recording, which was about 88 beats per minute.

Form: The instrumental introduction is a full twelve-bar chorus; Johnson's introduction was less than four bars.

Cream maintains the traditional twelve-bar blues form throughout and does not employ Johnson's addition of beats and bars.

The entire recording has eleven choruses of the blues. The first, fifth, sixth, eighth, ninth, and tenth are all instrumental. The instrumental solos are improvised with a sense of freedom, while still remaining connected to the blues harmonic form.

Features: The drums accent the backbeat through most of the recording.

Clapton uses a solid-body electric guitar with fuzztone and low tension strings to allow for more sliding and bending of notes than Robert Johnson did on his guitar.

Bruce plays riff patterns and also jazz-influenced long walking lines on the bass.

Lyrics: The lyrics are basically taken from Robert Johnson's song "Cross Road Blues," with the addition of one chorus (the third that has lyrics in Cream's recording) from another song by Robert Johnson, "Traveling Riverside Blues." That new chorus is repeated after two instrumental choruses. The additional lyrics outline the singer's plans to take his rider to Rosedale to a **barrelhouse** (a bar or honky-tonk), indicating that he is secure, free, and has his own transportation, in sharp contrast to the subject of Johnson's "Cross Road Blues" who is poor and is ignored by people who pass him on the road.

Source: Time-Life Music, *Classic Rock, 1969: Shakin' All Over; Wheels of Fire*, Polydor 827578; and *Strange Brew—Very Best of Cream*, Polydor 816639.

and played with them fairly regularly for just over a year, from April 1965 to July 1966. The Bluesbreakers' frequent personnel changes gave Clapton an opportunity to work with a variety of blues musicians. He particularly liked **Jack Bruce**'s (born in 1943) bass playing, and when **Ginger Baker** (born in 1939) sat in on the drums one night, Clapton asked the two of them to join him to work as a trio. At that time, they intended to play the blues in small clubs and did not foresee the tremendous success they would have as **Cream.** The group made its debut in 1966 at the Windsor Festival in England, where they brought their blues-styled songs and improvisations with super speed and high volume to a rock audience that was ripe for the experience.

Cream's 1968 recording of Robert Johnson's "Cross Road Blues" (1936) was a successful link between the old country blues and the new blues-based rock. Although the members of Cream obviously loved the rough quality of Johnson's style, they did not copy it in their recording, which they retitled "Crossroads." Johnson had played with the rhythmic freedom out of which the blues form had developed (as was pointed out in the discussion and listening guide to Johnson's recording in Chapter 2). Cream's more modern audience, however, required the sort of polish and formalism to which they had become accustomed. Cream was also made up of three very technically proficient instrumentalists and, where Johnson used his guitar primarily to accompany his singing, Cream displayed their talents through six all-instrumental choruses of the twelve-bar form. On the left is a listening guide to Cream's recording of "Crossroads":

Other British covers of the late sixties included the Jeff Beck Group's recordings of Willie Dixon's "I Ain't Superstitious" and "You Shook Me"; Cream's recordings of Dixon's "Spoonful," Robert Johnson's "Four Until Late," and Howlin' Wolf's "Sittin' on Top of the World"; and Led Zeppelin's recordings of Dixon's "I Can't Quit You Baby" and "You Shook Me." A comparison of any of these recordings with the original versions reveals that the late-sixties British blues groups remained less faithful to the old styles than their early-sixties predecessors had.

After just over two years together, Cream disbanded. They felt they had made the musical statement they had gotten together to make, and all three wanted to move on to other experiences. Clapton and Baker formed a new group with Traffic's keyboardist/singer Steve Winwood and Family's bassist, Rich Grech. The new group, Blind Faith, was short-lived, putting out only one album, *Blind Faith* (1969).

After Blind Faith broke up, Clapton worked with a variety of groups for short periods of time, including Derek and the Dominos, a group that included American southern-rock guitarist Duane Allman. The name "Derek" was a combination of the names Duane and Eric, and the two guitarists shared lead guitar lines in much the same way that Allman and Dickey Betts had in Allman's own group, the Allman Brothers Band. Derek and the Dominos recorded "Layla" (1970), one of Clapton's greatest musical and personal statements, inspired by his infatuation with Beatle George Harrison's wife, Pattie (whom Clapton later married and divorced). The lyrics to "Layla" included a quote from Robert Johnson's "Love in Vain."

Personal depression led to a heroin habit that kept Eric Clapton from being an active performer during much of 1971 and 1972. He managed to kick the habit with the help of the Who's Pete Townshend, who organized and played with Clapton in *The Rainbow Concert* (January 13, 1973). The concert, which also featured guitarist Ron Wood, Steve Winwood, and Rick Grech, turned out to be Clapton's much-needed comeback. From that point on, Clapton worked as a soloist, with a variety of musicians serving as his backup band. In many ways his later style became more commercial than he would ever have allowed back in his Yardbird days, but the influence of the blues continued to color his music. His career hit a new peak when he was awarded six Grammys in 1993. An additional Grammy was awarded to Clapton, this time for Best Traditional Blues Album, for *From the Cradle,* released in 1994.

Listeners who know seventies music better than that of the sixties might think of Fleetwood Mac as a pop group. In their early years, however, **Fleetwood Mac** included several veterans of other blues revival groups in England. Mick Fleetwood had played drums for various blues groups from the early to the mid-sixties, and he and guitarist Peter Green met bassist John McVie while they were all members of John Mayall's Bluesbreakers. Fleetwood, Green, and McVie were joined by guitarist/singer Jeremy Spencer to form Peter Green's Fleetwood Mac in 1967. The name "Fleetwood Mac" combined the names of Fleetwood and McVie. They recorded covers of songs by Robert Johnson, Elmore James, and Howlin' Wolf, as well as blues-styled originals by Peter Green and Jeremy Spencer.

While Fleetwood Mac was beginning its career, Christine Perfect was developing a career of her own. Between 1967 and 1969, she was the pianist/singer for the blues group Chicken Shack. While with that group, Perfect married John McVie of Fleetwood Mac. Although she claimed to have been tempted to settle down and make a career as a housewife, she changed her mind when she won the *Melody Maker* poll as "Female Vocalist of the Year" in 1969. She organized her own band, called Christine Perfect, but by 1970 the inevitable happened—Christine McVie joined her husband's group.

During the early seventies Fleetwood Mac left the blues behind to experiment with more commercial music. The McVies and Fleetwood stayed with the band through various personnel changes and in 1974 moved to California, where they were joined by Americans Lindsey Buckingham and Stevie Nicks. In that form, and after Buckingham's departure, Fleetwood Mac had great success playing country-rock-influenced pop music.

The success of the British blues revival rejuvenated American interest in the blues. For American musicians and rock music fans, the British blues revival had a meaning beyond just the popularity of the music played by British groups. American blues musicians in cities like Chicago had managed to maintain their careers by playing the blues through the late fifties and early sixties, but the rock industry as a whole had not considered their music to be suitable competition for the pop style being marketed to teenagers at the time. Music by blues groups was not given the distribution or airplay it would have needed to gain national popularity, but that soon changed after the British blues hit the American charts.

The American Blues Revival

The blues had been essential to rock music through most of the fifties, but it gave way to the sounds of teenage pop singers and dance music between 1959 and 1964. The smooth rhythm and blues style of Fats Domino and some doo-wop groups managed to stay on the pop charts through the early sixties, and some dance music such as "The Twist" (1960) followed the blues form (without its style, in the case of Chubby Checker's hit recording), but many blues-based rock musicians from the fifties either stopped performing at the end of the decade or continued with less commercial success.

American rock promoters were not interested in the blues until after the mid-sixties, when British covers of American blues recordings became popular in the United States. The British versions captured much of the vitality of the original recordings and sparked an American blues revival as young American blues groups were finally offered recording contracts. New blues groups formed, and not only recorded in such blues centers as Chicago, but also made the blues an important part of the psychedelic sound of San Francisco during the late sixties, the jazz-rock sound in many different parts of the country, and the southern-rock movement of the seventies.

One young American singer/harpist who was attracted to the blues during the early sixties was **Paul Butterfield** (1942–1987). Living in Chicago, he had the opportunity to hear such blues legends as Muddy Waters and Howlin' Wolf, and in 1963 he formed the Paul Butterfield Blues Band with guitarists Elvin Bishop and Mike Bloomfield. The band found success in blues clubs in the Chicago area and, by 1965, had a record contract. After their second album, *East-West* (1966), failed to gain the attention the group had sought, Bloomfield left to pursue a solo career; he died of an accidental drug overdose in 1981. Bishop went solo in 1968. The Butterfield band experimented with soul and other styles, finally breaking up in 1972. Butterfield continued to perform and record until his drug-related death in 1987.

Janis Joplin
Michael Ochs Archives/Venice, CA

Jimi Hendrix in concert
Michael Ochs Archives/Venice, CA

In New York, keyboard and guitar player Al Kooper abandoned his role as a songwriter and studio musician to form his own blues group, **The Blues Project,** in 1965. Among his many involvements with other people's music, Kooper played the organ on several of Bob Dylan's albums, including *Highway 61 Revisited* (1965) and *Blonde on Blonde* (1966). Kooper's album *Super Session* (1968) featured guitarist Mike Bloomfield from Paul Butterfield's band.

- Al Kooper and guitarist/singer Steve Katz disbanded the Blues Project in order to form the jazz-rock band Blood, Sweat and Tears in 1968. Their music will be discussed in Chapter 13, Jazz Rock and Fusion.

From Los Angeles came the blues revival group **Canned Heat.** The group had originally formed as a jug band to play a rural form of the blues, with someone blowing and humming into a whiskey jug in place of a brass instrument. Jug bands had a style related to country blues, but with the renewed popularity of urban blues, Canned Heat decided to replace the jug with amplified instruments playing in a rhythmic, boogie-woogie-based style. Their performance at the Monterey Pop Festival in 1967 put them in the spotlight as an important new rock band. Some of their songs, such as "On the Road Again" (1968), did not follow a blues form but instead were based on a single chord with the blues feel implied through the use of string bending and blue notes. "Going Up the Country" (1969) was a traditional twelve-bar blues, and its commercial success earned them a place at the Woodstock Festival in New York in the summer of 1969. The group's success continued in 1970, but late that year guitarist/harpist Alan Wilson, who had written and sung the lead vocal on "On the Road Again," died of a drug overdose. Canned Heat remained together during the seventies, but failed to recapture their earlier success. They later lost their primary lead singer, Bob Hite, who died in 1981.

Women were generally the most important of the early classic blues singers, and the rock singer whose interest in the blues was most clearly stimulated by women's blues recordings was **Janis Joplin** (1943–1970). Joplin's favorite singers were Bessie Smith and Willie Mae "Big Mama" Thornton, and although Joplin eventually sang music other than the blues, she never lost the dramatic delivery she had learned from listening to Smith and the gutsy, throaty Thornton. After moving to San Francisco from her home in Port Arthur, Texas, Joplin joined the newly formed folk/blues group Big Brother and the Holding Company, and, with them, stole the show at the Monterey Pop Festival in 1967. Some of the songs she recorded with Big Brother and the Holding Company included "Down on Me" and "Piece of My Heart."

- Joplin's recording of "Ball and Chain" is compared to that of Willie Mae Thornton in Chapter 2, The Blues Roots of Rock Music.

Listening Guide

"Red House" as recorded by the Jimi Hendrix Experience (1967)

Tempo: The tempo is approximately 66 beats per minute, with four beats in each bar.

Form: The recording has five choruses of the twelve-bar blues. The introductory first chorus and the fourth chorus are instrumental.

Features: Uneven beat subdivisions are used throughout the recording.

The drums maintain a very strong backbeat.

The sound of bass on the recording is played on a hollow-body electric guitar with the bass turned up.

Hendrix's guitar plays the fills and is featured during the instrumental choruses. He bends single and double strings, adds vibrato by shaking his finger that holds down the string, slides from one note to another, and varies his tone by using the wah-wah pedal in different ways.

Lyrics: The singer has returned to his girlfriend after a long absence to find she has moved away, so he decides to love her sister instead.

Source: *Jimi Hendrix Experience: Smash Hits,* Reprise 2276.

By 1968 Joplin decided she was tired of singing with a group that used only guitars, bass, and drums, and left Big Brother and the Holding Company to form the Kozmic Blues Band. The group, which included organ, bass, and drums, plus the jazz-band sound of a **horn section** (brass instruments and saxophones), recorded "Try (Just a Little Bit Harder)" in 1969, then broke up in 1970. Joplin's last recordings, including "Cry Baby" and "Me and Bobby McGee" (the latter written by Joplin's friend, Kris Kristofferson), were made with another band she had formed, the Full-Tilt Boogie Band, which included organ, electric piano, guitar, bass, and drums. Joplin was planning to get married and make other major changes in her life when she died of a heroin overdose in October 1970.

Many other blues-based rock guitarists of the sixties experimented with the use of feedback between the guitar and amplifier, but none used it with as much control and psychedelic flash as **Jimi Hendrix** (1942–1970). Like Janis Joplin, Hendrix made the blues one of the most important ingredients of late-sixties American rock but did not live to carry that style into the seventies. Hendrix taught himself to play the guitar by copying the recordings of Muddy Waters, Chuck Berry, and B. B. King.

Raised in Seattle, Jimmy Hendrix (the "Jimi" spelling came later) served in the army for two years, but was discharged because of a back injury he sustained in a parachute jump in 1961. His release from the army left him free to pursue his love of music. At times using the stage name Jimmy James and at others calling himself Maurice James, Hendrix began working with various groups in nightclubs and bars. By 1964 he had moved to New York City and quickly gained a reputation that enabled him to work behind some of the most popular performers of the day, including Sam Cooke, Ike and Tina Turner, Wilson Pickett, Little Richard, and even B. B. King. He formed his own band, Jimmy James and the Blue Flames, in 1965. Chas Chandler of the Animals heard the group in 1966 and was so impressed that he talked Hendrix into leaving the group and moving to London to form a new band. **The Jimi Hendrix Experience** was formed as a trio, with Hendrix playing a fiery lead guitar, and two English musicians, bassist Noel Redding and drummer Mitch Mitchell, ably backing him. Their recordings of "Hey Joe," "Purple Haze," and "The Wind Cries Mary" were successful in England before the group ever appeared in front of an American audience.

Hendrix's reintroduction to his homeland came when the Jimi Hendrix Experience played the Monterey Pop Festival in 1967. Hendrix brought the group's performance to a memorable conclusion when he "sacrificed" his guitar by setting it on fire. The flaming guitar act did not become a regular part of Hendrix's performances, however, because it was too distracting (and expensive). He preferred to concentrate on playing the blues, or blues-styled rock music. He influenced many of the guitarists who followed him, and occasionally those guitarists would pay tribute by including lines from Hendrix's recordings in their own performances. The opening to "Foxey Lady" (1967), for example, was quoted by Blue Cheer in "Summertime Blues" (1968), and Hendrix's guitar solo at the beginning of "Purple Haze" was used in the Huey Lewis and the News recording "I Want a New Drug" (1983). Hendrix drew upon his traditional blues background when he wrote and recorded "Red House," for which a listening guide is included here.

After dissolving the Experience in 1968 Hendrix moved to New York, where he built the Electric Ladyland Studio to make experimental recordings with various musicians, including guitarist John McLaughlin. Hendrix organized various groups to back him at such concerts as the Woodstock Festival in 1969. He toured a little in early 1970, but in September of that same year he choked to death in an unconscious state after taking an overdose of barbiturates.

The original home of the blues was not Chicago but the South, and the American blues revival's greatest success of the seventies were recorded by southern bands and musicians like the Allman Brothers Band, ZZ Top,

Listening Guide

	"Hoochie Coochie Man" as recorded by Muddy Waters (1954)	"Hoochie Coochie Man" as recorded by the Allman Brothers Band (1970)
Tempo:	The tempo is about 76 beats per minute, with four beats in each bar.	The tempo is about 108 beats per minute, with four beats in each bar.
Form:	The form is based on a twelve-bar blues with the first. A second being eight bars long, resulting in a sixteen-bar chorus.	The form is the same sixteen-bar blues used by Waters.
	The introduction is two bars long.	The introduction is twenty bars long—a four-bar introduction plus a full sixteen-bar instrumental chorus.
	The introduction is followed by three sixteen-bar choruses.	The introduction is followed by six sixteen-bar choruses.
Features:	Each A section has a two-beat instrumental stop time segment.	Each A section has a two-beat instrumental stop time segment.
	The drums maintain an uneven beat subdivision with little or no backbeat.	The drums slightly accent the backbeat and keep a constant uneven beat subdivision that creates a feeling of twelve subbeats to each bar (triplets).
	The piano usually plays triple-beat subdivisions, but at times lapses into a duple subdivision, creating a polyrhythm with the drums.	All musicians maintain the same uneven beat subdivisions.
	The recording has no instrumental choruses.	The introduction, the third, and the fifth choruses are instrumental.
Lyrics:	The lyrics refer to many popular forms of voodoo and other occult practices whose observers believe that charms hold real power. A "mojo" is a good-luck charm, which the singer asserts will keep him very good at satisfying women.	The first chorus with lyrics is a reworded version of Waters' first chorus, the second is a reworded version of Waters' third chorus, the fourth is a version of Waters' second chorus, and the sixth is basically a repetition of he first. The song's meaning is not changed, but is amplified by the changes.

Source: Muddy Waters' recording: Time-Life Music, *The Rock 'N' Roll Era, Roots of Rock, 1945–1956;* and *Best of Muddy Waters,* Chess Records 9255.

The Allman Brothers' recording: *Beginnings,* Polydor 827588.

guitarist Johnny Winter, and his brother, keyboardist/saxophonist Edgar Winter. The music played by these and other southern-rock musicians was not exclusively a blues-rock style; it combined the blues with other southern music styles, including country, jazz, and gospel. **The Allman Brothers Band**'s first two albums included covers of Muddy Waters' "Trouble No More" and Willie Dixon's song (that Waters made famous) "Hoochie Coochie Man." Above is a comparison of the two recordings of "Hoochie Coochie Man."

As has been the case with other rock covers of the blues, the Allman Brothers Band played faster, added more and longer instrumental sections, and stressed the backbeat more than Muddy Waters. The sexual references in the original recording, however, have been amplified (rather than removed, as many fifties country singers did in their blues covers) in the Allman Brothers' version. "Hoochie Coochie Man" was also covered by some British blues revival groups of the sixties, including the Bluesbreakers (with John Mayall, Eric Clapton, and Jack Bruce) and Manfred Mann.

ZZ Top was formed in Texas in 1970. Two of the group's members, bassist Dusty Hill and drummer Frank Beard, had played the blues in a sixties group called

American Blues before putting together ZZ Top with guitarist/singer Billy Gibbons. Sometimes referred to as a "power trio" because of the way all three members pushed their instruments to a very high volume level, ZZ Top played music that was not exclusively the blues, though much of it was, including their twelve-bar blues hit, "Tush" (1975).

- Both the Allman Brothers Band and ZZ Top were important bands of the southern-rock movement and will also be discussed in Chapter 12, Revivals of Country-Styled Rock.

The mid-sixties revival of interest in the blues also aided the careers of many of the blues artists who had first recorded during the fifties. The success of B. B. King's live performances enabled him to move from a string of small record companies to the ABC label, giving his recordings greater distribution that ever before. By 1965 his album *Live at the Regal* had established him as a major blues artist, and his fans included as many whites as African Americans. He even began to put records on the pop charts as early as 1964.

Two pairs of brothers contributed much to the cause of advancing the blues in the seventies and beyond: Johnny and Edgar Winter, and Jimmie and Stevie Ray Vaughan. **Johnny and Edgar Winter** (born in 1944 and 1946 respectively) were raised in a musical family in Texas. They first performed together as an Everly Brothers-influenced duo during the fifties, but then moved on to concentrate on the blues. As a guitarist, Johnny Winter had moderate success during the late sixties, attracting more attention from other musicians than from the general public. Among the musicians who respected his work were Mick Jagger and Keith Richards, who wrote the song "Silver Train" for Winter to record on his *Still Alive and Well* (1973) album. Winter's most popular recordings were made during the seventies, but he continued to perform and record for blues lovers into the nineties. His *Guitar Slinger* (1984) album was nominated for a Grammy award.

Singer, saxophonist, and keyboard player Edgar Winter played in his brother's band for a while and then left to form the rhythm and blues band White Trash. After the breakup of that band, he formed the hard rock band the Edgar Winter Group. Their greatest commercial successes occurred at the beginning of their recording career with the single "Frankenstein" hitting number one on the pop charts and the album *They Only Come Out at Night* (1972) charting in the top ten. In later years Edgar Winter's career continued on through live performances, recordings, and some work on movie soundtracks. He and his brother have occasionally worked together. Both brothers are easily recognizable because they are albinos and as such have distinctively light skin and very white (and very long) hair.

Also from Texas, **Jimmie and Stevie Ray Vaughan** (born in 1951, and 1954–1990, respectively) grew up listening to and copying guitar solos by B. B. King and others, eventually forming bands and developing guitar styles of their own. Jimmie was a member of the Fabulous Thunderbirds from 1974 to 1990, until he quit the band to play with his brother. The Thunderbirds recorded and toured through the eighties, having their greatest commercial success with their *Tuff Enuff* album in 1986. At the same time that the Fabulous Thunderbirds were experiencing the high point of their career, Jimmie's younger brother Stevie Ray and his band Double Trouble placed several albums in the top forty. Stevie Ray Vaughan was known for his gutsy, Hendrix-inspired guitar style. His career quite likely had not yet reached its peak when he was killed in a helicopter crash in 1990, right after playing a concert with his brother, Eric Clapton, Robert Cray, and several other blues stars of the eighties.

From the northern state of Delaware, guitarist/singer **George Thorogood** (born in 1951), and his group, **The Destroyers,** helped to revitalize Elmore James' bottleneck style and Bo Diddley's rhythms by updating them for seventies and eighties audiences. Thorogood formed the Destroyers in 1973, but he temporarily postponed their career to give himself a chance to pursue one of his other interests—semi-pro baseball. After his return to music, the Destroyers played at a few concerts on the Rolling Stones' 1981 tour and continued their career playing the blues and blues-based rock music. Thorogood's original hit "I Drink Alone" (1985) was the blues both in style and in twelve-bar form. Despite slow album sales, George Thorogood and the Destroyers were still touring and recording in the mid-nineties.

Robert Cray (born in 1954) learned to play the guitar after hearing the Beatles in 1964. By the late sixties, he had formed a band that played psychedelic rock inspired by the Grateful Dead, and also some Memphis soul music including instrumentals by Booker T. and the MGs and songs by the duo Sam and Dave. With his own band, Cray spent the seventies developing a distinctive blues vocal style that was very clean and modern-sounding compared to the thick, throaty quality of earlier blues singers. Cray used a solid-body guitar to play clean, fluid lines punctuated by chords and bent notes, filling out the more modern rock orientation of his sound. The Robert Cray Band played at the San Francisco Blues Festivals of 1977 and 1978. Their albums of the early eighties were successful, but as many blues performers have done in the past, they veered away from the blues into more of a soul style for later albums, including *Strong Persuader* (1987). Later albums such as *Midnight Stroll* (1990) and *I Was Warned* (1992) included the Memphis horn sound that had been popularized on many of the middle-sixties soul records released on the Stax and Volt labels.

Summary

The blues was the basis for most rock music of the early and mid-fifties, but while it was not being marketed to teens in America, the British were in the process of discovering it. By 1963 blues clubs had become very popular in London, and the young blues groups that played in them carefully copied the styles of such performers as Muddy Waters, John Lee Hooker, and Howlin' Wolf. Some of the most important British blues performers whose music became popular in America during the mid-sixties included John Mayall's Bluesbreakers, the Rolling Stones, the Animals, the Yardbirds, and Fleetwood Mac.

The success of British blues bands proved the blues had new appeal for young American audiences, opening the doors to recording careers for the Paul Butterfield Blues Band, Canned Heat, and Janis Joplin, as well as other American blues musicians. American blues guitarist/singer Jimi Hendrix had moved to England to make his first blues-based rock recordings, but returned to the U.S. to continue his career. By the seventies the blues became a significant element in the South with the music of such bands as the Allman Brothers Band and ZZ Top. In other parts of the country, George Thorogood and Robert Cray formed blues bands whose careers escalated during the eighties and continued in the nineties.

Terms to Remember

Barrelhouse
Feedback
Horn section
Mellotron

CHAPTER 10

Garage Bands, Bubblegum, and Power Pop

The British groups that came to America during the mid-sixties had not created any new sounds; they started their own careers by playing music that had originated in the United States. For the most part, however, it was not the music of the sixties that they played, but the blues and rockabilly of the fifties. The British copied Little Richard's vocals, Chuck Berry's lead guitar lines, and Bo Diddley's rhythms. They played the blues, imitating the vocal style of Muddy Waters and the slide guitar style of Elmore James. Their groups played guitars, bass, and drums with the energetic backbeat they had heard in Buddy Holly's recordings. The mere fact that the groups were self-contained, playing their own instruments, made them sound different from the studio-blended, wall of sound slickness that had become typical of early-sixties American rock.

In very general terms, the British Invasion groups blew the New York-based pop sound off the American charts, but in so doing, they paved the way for American blues groups, garage bands, and folk-rock performers playing non-pop rock to move from regional to national success. The young Paul Butterfield started his blues band in Chicago a year before any British groups had been heard in America, but he did not initially find commercial success; record company executives did not push for national advertising for the blues until after British groups started scoring blues hits. Following the British successes, raucous garage bands like the Standells copied the Rolling Stones; the Count Five used the distorted sound effects of the Yardbirds and the Kinks; and the Sir Douglas Quintet, formed in Texas, first publicized itself as if it were English.

Garage Bands

Garage bands were so named because most of the bands were made up of untrained musicians who practiced in their garages, producing a raw, unrefined sound. As most of the bands were made up of young people with under-developed musical skills, they often covered songs by other groups, but occasionally came up with something original. The idea that anybody who could afford an instrument could be in a band was so appealing that by 1965 garage bands were entertaining (or disturbing) neighborhoods all over the country. The most successful songs were ones that were easy for other bands to cover when they played for junior high or high school dances. Lyrics tended to be very simple, sometimes bordering on raunchy, with stories about girls, partying, and fast cars. A few of the songs dealt with meaningful statements such as the antidrug message in Paul Revere and the Raiders' "Kicks," but those were exceptions rather than the rule. Generally any hint of sophistication in the music or the message would remove a song from the garage band category. Eventually, particularly in Detroit, messages of angry rebellion became part of the sound,

Listening Guide

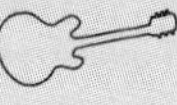

"Louie Louie"
as recorded by the Kingsmen (1963)

Tempo: The tempo is approximately 126 beats per minute, with four beats in each bar.

Form: The recording begins with a four-bar introduction with a one-beat pickup.

The song is structured around a two-bar chordal ostinato that repeats throughout.

The vocal phrases are four bars long (two repetitions of the ostinato).

The instrumental section is sixteen bars long (eight repetitions of the ostinato).

Features: The drums keep even beat subdivisions, but uneven subdivisions are used in the vocals, the guitar solo, and occasionally the electric piano.

The drums maintain a strong backbeat.

Lyrics: The Kingsmen's recording of this song is famous for its inaudible vocals, but the little that can be understood sounds very much like a sloppy version of the lyrics in Richard Berry's original recording. Using Berry's recording as a guide, the singer has been sailing on a ship for three nights and days thinking constantly about the girl that is waiting for him. He is haunted by the smell of the rose in her hair and plans never to leave her again once she is back in his arms.

Source: Time-Life Music, *Classic Rock, 1964: The Beat Goes On; The Best of the Kingsmen,* Rhino 70745; and *Best of "Louie Louie,"* Rhino 70605.

and it was that combination of simple, crude, and energetic music with aggressive vocals that eventually became punk in the seventies.

One of the most simple and, at the same time, influential of the early garage band songs was "Louie Louie." "Louie Louie" was written and first recorded by Richard Berry in 1956, but it was the Kingsmen's recording that hit and made it one of the most often-covered songs of the era. It had all the necessary elements for garage band music: it was simple, repetitious, and the way **The Kingsmen**'s singer, Jack Ely, slopped through the lyrics lent an air of promiscuity. The belief that the song was too risque was so prevalent that the recording was banned in some places. A listening guide to "Louie Louie" can be found above.

Paul Revere and the Raiders
Michael Ochs Archives/Venice, CA

The two-bar ostinato that serves as the basis of "Louie Louie" has much in common with that of "La Bamba." This is not surprising in that the song's writer, Richard Berry, was playing in a Mexican band (Ricky Rivera and the Rhythm Rockers) in Los Angeles when he wrote "Louie Louie" in 1955. Richard Berry was African American, but the primary musical influence on this particular song and his own recording of it seems more to be from his work with Mexican music than with African American styles.

The Kingsmen had a couple of other hit records, including one of the sillier songs of the garage band style, "The Jolly Green Giant" (1965). The band broke up in 1967, but guitarist Mike Mitchell formed another group with the same name and continued to perform with them on oldies shows into the nineties.

Because so many garage band musicians were untrained in music and inexperienced as writers, it was very common for garage bands to have one lucky hit but be unable to follow it with anything that equaled its success. Some of the garage bands who made their names on a single hit record included the Premiers, Cannibal and the Headhunters, the Castaways, the Standells, the Leaves, the Syndicate of Sound, Count Five, the Music Machine, the Seeds, and ? and the Mysterians. One band that did not fall into that category was **Paul Revere and the Raiders,** who cashed in on the idea of fighting British bands for the attention of fans by wearing pseudo Revolutionary War costumes. Paul Revere was the name of the

Listening Guide

***"Kicks"* as recorded by Paul Revere and the Raiders (1966)**

Tempo: The tempo is approximately 132 beats per minute, with four beats in each bar.

Form: After a four-bar introduction, the form is structured as A B C D A B C D C C, with C having the same lyrics each time and serving as a refrain.

The A, B, and C sections each have eight bars.

The first D section has four bars. The second D has eight bars.

Features: Even beat subdivisions are maintained throughout the recording.

The backbeat is not stressed.

The two-bar guitar riff that begins the recording and repeats through each A section is played on a twelve-string electric guitar and is reminiscent of earlier recordings by the folk-rock group the Byrds. Another, lighter textured guitar riff appears in each D section.

The bass enters in the third bar of the introduction playing a short ascending and then descending riff that is repeated through each A section. The bass adds an insistent feel as it pulsates the basic beats during the first six bars of the C sections and then pounds out an eighth-note pulse on the last two bars of each C section.

Lyrics: The singer warns a girl the "kicks" she gets from drugs will not solve any of her problems and will create more problems as she takes stronger drugs.

Source: Time-Life Music, *Classic Rock, 1966: Midnight Ride*, Columbia 9308; and *Paul Revere and the Raiders' Greatest Hits*, Columbia 35593.

band's keyboard player, but the group's leader was their singer and saxophonist, Mark Lindsay. Paul Revere and the Raiders had many top forty hits even into the seventies. Above is a listening guide to one of their early hits. Paul Revere and the Raiders changed membership a number of times through their career. Mark Lindsay finally left in 1976 and later had some success singing for commercials. Paul Revere continued on with a new version of the band and was still performing in the early nineties. Despite the fact that some garage bands lasted into the seventies, the garage band sound was beginning to die out by the late sixties as other styles such as bubblegum became popular with rock's youngest fans.

Bubblegum

The Beatles had become idols to American teenagers and, as those teens got older, the Beatles music also progressed to express more mature themes, leaving younger fans behind. American record producers were not about to let the young audience go unsatisfied, so they attracted them by forming **The Monkees.** The Monkees were featured in a television program containing skits imitative of the Beatles' playful antics in the movie *A Hard Day's Night.* The members were chosen from a group of musicians and actors who answered an advertisement announcing the intended formation of the group. Michael Nesmith and Peter Tork were musicians before joining the Monkees; Davy Jones and Mickey Dolenz were actors who had to learn to sing and play instruments while with the group. Jones was British, and his accent aided their connection with the Beatles. At first the group's producers would not allow any of the Monkees to play on their recordings, but eventually the need for live performances became evident and they worked together as musicians in addition to acting on the TV show.

The Monkees reached a new audience during the late eighties when MTV reran their old television series. Jones, Dolenz, and Tork decided to capitalize on the revival of interest in their band by making a few new recordings and touring. Nesmith, who went on to become a successful video producer after the Monkees disbanded, chose not to rejoin the group, but he did join the trio on stage at least once in 1987. The original quartet regrouped in 1996.

The commercial success of the Monkees made it clear to the music industry that even preteens had money to spend on records and were a large body of listeners who were worth patronizing. The style called "bubblegum" resulted. Early examples of bubblegum were recorded under the names the Ohio Express, the 1910 Fruitgum Co., and others, but none of those groups actually existed outside of the recording studio. That didn't matter when fans were not old enough to drive themselves to live concerts or to stay out late for them anyway. The records by the Ohio Express and the 1910 Fruitgum Co. were written and produced by Jerry Kasenetz and Jeff Katz in Ohio and recorded by singer Joey Levine backed by studio musicians. Songs like "Yummy Yummy Yummy" and "Chewy Chewy" (both 1968) gave the style its name.

Of the many bubblegum records that made the charts during the late sixties and early seventies, the one that may best represent the style was "Sugar, Sugar" by

Listening Guide

"Sugar, Sugar" as recorded by the Archies (1969)

Tempo: The tempo is approximately 123 beats per minute, with four beats in each bar.

Form: After a four-bar introduction, the form is based on eight-bar periods that follow the pattern A A B A A B A A A A.

Features: Beats are subdivided both evenly and unevenly, with the tambourine generally playing even subdivisions and the voice and other instruments maintaining uneven subdivisions.

Hand claps are heard on the backbeats.

A distinctive two-bar riff is played on the first and second bars and repeated on the third and fourth bars of each A section.

The recording ends by fading out at the end of the final A section.

Lyrics: The singer's girl is so sweet that her kisses taste like sugar and honey.

Source: Time-Life Music, *Classic Rock, 1969: The Beat Goes On;* and *Best of the Bubblegum Years,* Special Music Co. 4914.

another group made up of studio musicians, **The Archies.** The Archies were created by Jeff Barry, a songwriter/producer from New York's Brill Building, and were named for the old comic strip character, Archie. A television cartoon series called "The Archies" was backed by a soundtrack recorded by the Archies "group." Above is a listening guide to "Sugar, Sugar." As have many rock styles marketed to a very limited group, bubblegum died out after a short life, giving way to other youthful styles.

Power Pop

The Beatles' influence on American rock music of course extended far beyond the formation of the Monkees; in fact, it might not be an exaggeration to say that their influence was incalculable. There were a number of American bands whose styles were quite obviously Beatles-influenced and who bear mentioning here. Along with the Searchers, the Beatles influenced the distinctive twelve-string guitar sound and group vocals used by the folk-rock band the Byrds. The Beatles were also imitated by the San Francisco-based Beau Brummels, who started out in 1964 playing covers of Beatle songs. Another band formed in 1964 to copy the Beatles was the Knickerbockers, from New Jersey. By the early seventies, a new style emerged from the music played by the vast number of Beatle-influenced bands—power

Listening Guide

"Go All The Way" as recorded by the Raspberries (1972)

Tempo: The tempo is approximately 134 beats per minute, with four beats in each bar.

Form: The form is constructed of sections of varying lengths and a returning sixteen-bar period that functions as a **refrain.** The refrain has two vocal phrases, each of which stresses the title text "go all the way."

The recording begins with four repetitions of a two-bar riff followed by another two-bar riff that is also played four times. The total length of the introduction is sixteen bars. A four-bar vocal phrase then introduces the sixteen-bar refrain. Another four-bar phrase is sung and followed by another repeat of the refrain. That is followed by a twenty-one-bar section that begins with the opening riff and then is extended with vocal interpolations. The refrain returns to be followed by a contrasting eight-bar instrumental section and then a seven-bar section that concludes with a long holding of the final chord.

Features: Uneven beat subdivisions are used throughout the recording.

The drums accent a strong backbeat.

Influences of the Who's and the Kinks' use of fuzztone can be heard in the guitar and bass.

Beginning in the fourteenth bar of the twenty-one-bar middle section, the vocals imitate the Beatles' layering of the words "come on" from their song "Please Please Me" (recorded in 1962).

Lyrics: The singer is rhapsodizing about his girlfriend, who said that she feels so good with him that she wants them to "go all the way."

Source. Time-Life Music, *Sounds of the Seventies—1972;* and *Raspberries ("Capitol Collector's" Series),* Capitol, 92126.

The Raspberries (left to right): Dave Smalley, Jim Bonfanti, Eric Carmen, and Wally Bryson
AP/Wide World Photos

pop. Power pop was given the "pop" part of its name because the songs were based on well-crafted, memorable melodies with clever lyrics, as were some of the early songs by the Beatles. Power pop songs also often included catchy-sounding group harmonies like those sung by the Beach Boys in the early sixties. The "power" part of the name was tacked on because the music was often backed by the kinds of distorted guitar riffs employed by British Invasion bands such as the Kinks and the Who.

The Memphis-based group **Big Star** made records that greatly influenced the development of the style, but they never managed to reach the large-scale commercial success of some other power pop bands. Big Star was formed by singer/songwriter Chris Bell (1951–1978) in 1971, but he left the group to pursue a solo career in 1973 and died in a car accident five years later. Their singer, Alex Chilton (born in 1950) had previously sung with the Box Tops but left them to join Bell in Big Star. Chilton eventually became the group's primary singer, guitarist, and songwriter. One of Big Star's best-remembered songs was "September Gurls" (1974). The song's lyrics expressed love, insecurity, and sensitivity, and were backed by Beatles/Byrds-like electric twelve-string guitar. That along with a catchy melody in the bridge made "September Gurls" an influential example of power pop despite its relative lack of pop-chart success. A cover of the song done by the Bangles on their *Different Light* album in 1985 drew more attention and sold more copies than did Big Star's original. Big Star broke up in 1978, and since then Alex Chilton has recorded and toured with several other bands, as a soloist, and with a revised version of Big Star. Paul Westerberg of the Replacements gave Chilton credit for the influence Big Star's music had on his own by having Chilton play guitar on the Replacements' *Tim* (1985) album and recording the song "Alex Chilton" on the Replacements' *Pleased to Meet Me* (1987) album.

The Raspberries were a seventies power pop group that achieved large commercial success with their early Beatles-influenced style and a singer who both looked and sang much like Paul McCartney, Eric Carmen (born in 1949). Clearly aimed at a youthful audience, their self-titled first album had a raspberry-scented scratch-and-sniff sticker on the cover. The album contained the biggest hit of the Raspberries' career, the enticing "Go All The Way." The listening guide on page 115 points out many of the characteristics that were common among power pop records. The Raspberries broke up in 1974, and Carmen turned to a pop ballad style for a successful solo career that continued into the eighties.

Power pop continued on as a style beyond the demise of Big Star and the Raspberries, but few power pop bands achieved much commercial success. The Knack, who had a big hit with "My Sharona" in 1979, had a power pop-influenced new wave sound and style. More recent bands such as R.E.M., the dB's, and Belly have clear connections with the style.

Summary

With their "Invasion" in 1964, the British had taken hold of the American rock audience so quickly and completely that American record companies, promoters, and musicians responded in a variety of ways. Many young American musicians formed bands that imitated some of the most popular British groups. The result of those efforts to compete with the popularity of British music was the development of a new American sound played by garage bands. One of the most successful and long lasting of the garage bands was Paul Revere and the Raiders, who were still performing in the early nineties.

The American group, the Monkees, was formed for a television show patterned after the Beatles' movie, *A Hard Day's Night* (1964). The tremendous success of the Monkees proved that preteens would buy records and the result was a style aimed at that market, bubblegum. Following the heyday of bubblegum, power pop, an early-seventies style that began with groups imitating the well-crafted pop style of early Beatles songs, emerged. Power pop has had lasting influence on music into the nineties.

Terms to Remember

Refrain

CHAPTER 11

Psychedelic Rock

The late sixties was an era of experimentation and innovation in rock music and the cultural values it expressed. Many of those values had been influenced by the work of such writers and poets as Allen Ginsberg (born in 1926), Jack Kerouac (1922–1969), and Gregory Corso (born in 1930). Known as the **Beats** (and their followers as "beatniks"), from the word "beatific" (meaning blissfully happy), Ginsberg, Kerouac, Corso, and others decided that inner peace could only be achieved by one who was completely free from the artificial constraints of society. In the case of Ginsberg, personal freedom required that, among other issues, society accept homosexuality. He maintained that America's claim of being "the Land of the Free" was simply not valid. He saw America as a hypocritical, oppressive society in which some citizens were despised and legislated against because of their rejection of conventional morality and their choice of nontraditional lifestyles. In order to force his point, he wrote in crass and exhibitionistic language, drawing attention to his point of view. Ginsberg influenced the thinking of many of his generation, as well as numerous members of the psychedelic counterculture of the late sixties and the androgynous leaders of the glitter movement that followed. Drugs, particularly marijuana, and Eastern meditation were often used by the Beats and their followers to increase awareness.

The desire for freedom expressed through the Beats' writings was an attempt to duplicate the sort of creativity and individuality they heard in improvisations by jazz musicians. The bebop jazz played by Charlie "Bird" Parker, Dizzy Gillespie, and Thelonious Monk during the forties, as well as the bebop-influenced **cool jazz** styles of Miles Davis, Gerry Mulligan, and Chico Hamilton in the fifties, were all an integral part of the movement. Bebop and cool jazz were both generally played by small groups of musicians that included from one to three lead instruments and a rhythm section of guitar or piano, bass, and drums. At times, particularly in some of Gerry Mulligan's groups, the rhythm section would include only bass and drums. With so few musicians, written arrangements were not necessary. A song title or even just a chord progression along with a key center and someone counting to establish a tempo was all that the musicians needed to begin an improvisation that could continue as long as the musicians and/or the audience wanted. Individual solos would become almost conversational, as one player would take off on a line that would respond to—and perhaps imitate and then move beyond—what another soloist had played. In this and other ways the music was both very free and very personal. Beat writers tried to capture that same expressive intimacy and uninhibited sense of free rhythmic flow in their works.

At times the Beats and their followers gathered in coffeehouses to perform and listen to readings of their works, and the interrelationship of the writing style with music led to readings that were accompanied by live jazz. In such situations the music would accompany the reading or enter responsively at the ends of lyric phrases. Either way, the arts of music and poetry were melded for personal and free expression. Many of the Beats' works were written in an almost casual style to capture that sense of improvisation experienced in the live performances.

The Beat movement started in New York, but after Lawrence Ferlinghetti (born in 1919) moved to San Francisco and established the City Lights Bookshop, City Lights Press publishing company, and *The City Lights Journal,* all of which featured works by Ferlinghetti and many of his like-minded friends, he convinced Ginsberg, Kerouac, and Corso to join him there. San Francisco was attractive because it had (at the time) fairly lax enforcement of drug laws, good cheap wine, and a number of citizens who were ripe for new experiences. The Beat movement suffered criticism from literary societies in both New York and San Francisco, and the Beat writers' works did not even gain acceptance as literature until the seventies. Conservative critics believed the poets to be dangerous to the basic fabric of society, and in reviewing their works generally blasted them unmercifully. Some of the writers were still in San Francisco, or had left and returned, to be part of the psychedelic counterculture centered there during the sixties.

The San Francisco Sound

Political and social issues of the middle to late sixties, such as the Vietnam War and the Civil Rights Movement, brought attention back to many of the criticisms of American culture that had earlier been expressed by the Beat writers. Even to young people who had never read the Beat writers, it seemed that concepts of love, freedom, and individual worth did not hold the importance they should, and that their parents and society in general had become money-grubbing and materialistic. A wish to return to basic human values led to the development of a new culture, or counterculture, in such cities as San Francisco. Referred to as "hippies" or "flower children," this new group stood for peace, free love, and nonmaterialism. They often stood out from the rest of the community by wearing loose, casual clothing decorated with beads and other ornaments, sporting long hair, and maintaining a lifestyle that often centered on communal sharing of possessions.

The use of mind-altering **psychedelic drugs** such as LSD (lysergic acid diethylamide, also called acid) had also become common within the subculture, giving the name psychedelic rock (or acid rock) to the music favored by San Francisco's hippies. LSD was not declared illegal until late 1966, so it was often readily available at parties and concerts. The effects of the drug included a feeling of timelessness, increased physical and visual sensitivity, unreal and rather dreamlike connections between thoughts, and vivid hallucinations. Musicians tried to recreate these effects in their music, generally through long instrumental improvisations on one or two repeating chords, often involving one musician responding to what another had just played.

The Indian **sitar** became a popular psychedelic instrument in part because of an interest in Eastern thought (another manifestation of the Beats' influence) but also because of the hypnotic effect of the drone of the instrument's sympathetic strings against the swelling sound of other strings being bent (tightened and therefore raised in pitch) by the player. The sympathetic strings were not plucked by the sitarist, but they would vibrate when corresponding notes were played on other strings. That vibrating, or humming, of a group of strings created the drone, a long, sustained tone. In Indian music, the drone was supported by the **tamboura.**

Drug-induced, dreamlike visions were recreated in psychedelic artwork on posters and album covers, as well as in light shows at concerts and in films. Many of the psychedelic artists took their imagery from works of art created in the early to middle twentieth-century artistic style called **surrealism.** The surrealist style had developed as a visual expression of psychoanalyst Sigmund Freud's (1856–1939) studies of the unconscious mind and visions in dreams. Surrealist artists Giorgio de Chirico (1888–1978) and Salvador Dali (1904–1989) painted scenes containing recognizable objects from the real world put into shapes and settings in which they could not actually function or exist. One of the best-known surrealistic paintings was Dali's *The Persistence of Memory* (1931), in which clock faces melted over a wall and a tree branch. No clock could do that in the real world, of course, but in a dream or a drug-induced state any vision could exist. Surrealist art took things outside of or beyond reality and thus was the perfect visual correlative of psychedelic music.

The philosophy of **existentialism,** developed originally by Soren Kierkegaard (1813–1855) and further expanded by Jean-Paul Sartre (1905–1980), influenced the alienation from society embraced by the Beats and the hippie counterculture. Existentialism itself has been interpreted in a variety of ways, but for the hippies it became an attitude that stressed the importance of freeing the individual from the hostility of the outside, tradition-bound world. Once individuals were free, they had no need to be restrained by the expectations of others, and so could act as their own mood or personal beliefs dictated. They were required, however, to take responsibility for their actions, according to the tenets of existentialism. The young hippies who adopted an existential philosophy felt free, even obligated, to drop out of the world of their parents and to refuse to fight in Vietnam. Those who did not sign up for the draft, or who did sign up but refused military service, had to choose whether to be jailed or to leave the country—not knowing if they would ever be allowed to return. Those decisions were faced by many who had made the existential choice of refusing to follow the dictates of society.

The freedom felt by the hippie generation was celebrated at the "First Human Be-In" in San Francisco's Golden Gate Park in January 1967. Beat poets Allen Ginsberg and Gary Snyder read to the crowd, and the music for the program was played by Quicksilver Messenger Service, the Grateful Dead (or, as they were known, the Quick and the Dead), and Jefferson Airplane. The national exposure the event received attracted many like-minded people to San Francisco, and the summer of 1967 was dubbed the "summer of love" by those who attended the many other outdoor concerts and "love-ins." The First Human Be-In also paved the way for other large rock festivals during the next two years, many of which featured San Francisco bands, in Monterey and Newport (California) and in other parts of the country as well, including Miami, Atlanta, Atlantic City, and Lewisville (Texas), and also for the well-publicized Woodstock Festival in New York.

No group of musicians mastered the techniques of extended improvisations better than **The Grateful Dead,** a name founder Jerry Garcia (1942–1995) claimed to have discovered in an ancient Egyptian prayer. Garcia was a guitarist and bluegrass banjo player who earlier had led a group called Mother McCree's Uptown Jug Champions, with guitarist Bob Weir and keyboard/harmonica player Ron "Pigpen" McKernan. They changed their name to the Warlocks when they switched to electric instruments in 1965 and were joined by bassist Phil Lesh and drummer Bill Kreutzmann. In the same year, they became known as the Grateful Dead and joined other San Francisco-based bands for free concerts and acid parties, as well as more formal gatherings in clubs and auditoriums. Eventually they moved to Ashbury Street, which bordered Golden Gate Park and which became the base of operations for most members of the hippie counterculture in San Francisco.

Musically, the Grateful Dead's commercial recordings displayed the group's ability to blend country, folk, blues, and Latin influences with rock, but they generally failed to capture on vinyl the excitement of their live performances. When the band decided to give their fans an album recorded live, they could not resist calling it *Live Dead* (1970). The double album contained several of the long improvisations for which the group had become famous. The entire first side was one composition, "Dark Star," a continuous improvisation.

Long instrumental improvisations like "Dark Star" were not commercial because they had little appeal for the rock listeners who wanted short, catchy songs they could sing along with. Such recordings could never fit on a 45 r.p.m. record and were not suitable for AM radio. The same could be said for much of the music played by the Grateful Dead and other psychedelic groups. The radio, however, was still the essential medium that allowed music to reach large audiences. The changes in the music and demands of its fans finally brought about changes in rock radio itself.

AM vs. FM Radio

Before the late sixties, rock music had been played mainly on commercial AM stations, stations that maintained their financial support from advertisers who required they play only songs from the top ten or top forty in order to appeal to the largest possible number of listeners. **AM** (amplitude modulation) **radio** was a system that could carry sound far beyond a line-of-sight distance, but was often full of static and, at that time, could not be transmitted in stereo. The **FM** (frequency modulation) **radio** system had been invented during the thirties, but did not come into regular commercial use until the sixties when the advantages of static-free, high-fidelity stereo sound became more important than the drawbacks of FM's limited range, line-of-sight transmission. At first, FM stations received funding to broadcast classical music because of listeners' demands for improved sound quality, and soon a number of subscriber-supported stations appeared. Finally, FM stations airing rock music went into operation and became the primary vehicles for the dissemination of psychedelic rock and other "underground" music that AM radio stations ignored.

In San Francisco, it was former top forty AM disc jockey Tom Donahue who decided to reject the pop-station format and start an FM psychedelic radio station that aired extended album cuts and featured new and noncommercial bands. Eventually, the superior sound quality of FM led to its adoption by an increasing number of commercial stations.

Several members of the Grateful Dead were as much at home in country music as they were in rock, and this background was evident on their *Workingman's Dead* and *American Beauty* albums (both 1970). The music on these albums departed from the psychedelic freedom of *Live Dead* by basing the songs on more organized arrangements. A listening guide to "Uncle John's Band," from *Workingman's Dead* is on page 121.

By 1970 the Grateful Dead's psychedelic mixture of country, blues, and whatever else they were in the mood to play attracted a following of "dead heads," whose way of life was to go from one Dead concert to another, selling food, posters, jewelry, and other wares. During the seventies, the band experienced several personnel changes, and even disbanded from 1974 to 1976, but their popularity remained constant with their hard-core fans. Even through the yuppie era of the eighties, with its electronically sophisticated new wave and new age sounds, fans experienced a time warp at Grateful Dead

Listening Guide

"Uncle John's Band" by the Grateful Dead (1970)

Tempo: The tempo is approximately 132 beats per minute, with four beats per bar for most of the recording. Rhythmic interest is added when the fourth and eighth bars of each A section are shortened to only three beats. The instrumental D section also varies the beat pattern by alternating four- and three-beat bars.

Form: The recording begins with an eight-bar introduction comprised of two bars of a single strummed acoustic guitar, two bars of two strummed acoustic guitars with bass, and then four bars of those instruments with another acoustic guitar playing a lead line.

After the introduction, the recording continues in sections of varying lengths as follows: A A B C C A A C B D C B.

Each A section is sixteen bars (the fourth and eighth of which have only three beats) with lyrics followed by a two-bar extension.

Each B and C section is made up of eight four-beat bars. The second C and D are both instrumental. The C section functions as a refrain with repeated lyrics.

The instrumental D section is based on a rhythmic pattern that plays a seven-beat pattern (one four-beat bar followed by one three-beat bar) seven times before going back into the four-beat pattern of most of the rest of the recording.

The last C section is preceded by silence and sung *a cappella* (without instrumental accompaniment).

The second and final B sections have the same lyrics as the C refrain.

The recording ends with an extension of the last B, which fades out.

Features: Even beat subdivisions are followed throughout the recording.

A backbeat is played softly on a wood block in parts of the recording, but not stressed in most places.

Strummed acoustic guitars and electric bass provide the main instrumental accompaniment with additional color added by such Latin percussion instruments as **guiro,** maracas, claves, and conga drums.

The harmonized group vocals include two voices above the main melody.

Lyrics: The lyrics stress virtuous living and ask the listener to go with the singers to visit "Uncle John's Band" by the riverside so that Uncle John can take them home. If one sees a Christian baptism as going home, then Uncle John can be seen as John the Baptist.

Source: Time-Life Music, *Sounds of the Seventies—1970; Workingman's Dead,* Warner Brothers 1869; and *Skeletons from the Closet,* Warner Brothers 2764.

concerts which offered them a nostalgic return to the psychedelic sixties. Their music continued to embody the attitudes and spirit of the psychedelic rock era three decades after its heyday.

For many, that era came to an abrupt end with the death of Jerry Garcia in August of 1995. Surviving Grateful Dead members did not deny that they might decide to play together again, but said that they did not feel right about continuing under the same name without Garcia. Solo projects included drummer Mickey Hart's album *Mystery Box* (1996) with song lyrics by Dead lyricist Robert Hunter, bassist Phil Lesh's plans to compose a piece commissioned by the Berkeley Symphony Orchestra, and guitarist Bob Weir's work with his new band, Ratdog. Cuts from an unfinished studio album by the Grateful Dead might be included in a future box set.

Quicksilver Messenger Service, a group that frequently shared billing with the Grateful Dead, was also known for its long jam sessions consisting of instrumental improvisations better appreciated in a live concert situation than on record. Their twelve-minute improvisation on "The Fool" (recorded in 1967) served as an example of their live performance style, which was similar to the Grateful Dead's. Like the Dead's "Dark Star," most of "The Fool" was an extended improvisation on two alternating chords, but it had a subtle bolero rhythm pattern repeated throughout. (The Latin bolero used a duple subdivision and was quite different from the triplet pattern used in *Boléro* by Ravel.) Latin percussion instruments were not used in "The Fool," but Quicksilver Messenger Service added conga drums in recordings such as "What About Me" (1970).

One of the most commercially popular psychedelic bands was **Jefferson Airplane.** Formed by singer Marty Balin and guitarist/singer Paul Kantner in 1965, the group first played folk rock, but soon changed their

The Grateful Dead in 1993
AP/Wide World Photos

sound to one with a harder edge. Balin sang in harmony and alternated leads with Signe Anderson (formerly Signe Toly), until she left and was replaced by Grace Slick (formerly Grace Wing). After Slick joined, Balin continued to share the vocal roles, but it was Slick's dramatic voice and stage appearance that became the hallmark of the sound and style of Jefferson Airplane. Two songs she had previously recorded with her earlier group, the Great Society, "Somebody to Love" and "White Rabbit" (both 1967), emerged as statements of the hippie counterculture's beliefs in free love and drugs when Jefferson Airplane recorded hit versions. "Somebody to Love" served as a suitable theme song for 1967's "summer of love" in San Francisco.

"White Rabbit" was based on Lewis Carroll's protosurrealistic story "Alice's Adventures in Wonderland" (1865). The strange, dreamlike manipulation of the physical world Alice experienced in Wonderland was recalled in the song, which was banned in some cities for its drug implications; it made reference to a world that changed after Alice took pills and ate mushrooms. Musically, the song was interesting because it did not follow a standard pop-song form with repeated verses. It started with a soft beat and quiet mood that gradually intensified, without obvious seams, to a high-energy ending. An exotic touch was added by the use of the **phrygian mode** (a sixteenth-century mode composed of the natural notes from E to E, often used in flamenco music) and bolero-influenced rhythm patterns.

Much of Jefferson Airplane's music was commercial because it consisted of short, single-length songs with vocals and a rock backbeat, but they also employed the long improvisations favored by other groups of the era. Although their roots were in folk rock, the Airplane made recordings in many other styles, the most experimental of which involved the avant-garde (for the time) use of electronic sound effects in "Chushingura" (1968). They also made general statements about the hippie culture through songs like "Crown of Creation" (1968), which stressed the need for loyalty among the members of the counterculture, calling outsiders "obstructionists." "Volunteers" (1969) identified the counterculture as a social revolution.

Kantner had used the name *Jefferson Starship* on an album he recorded in 1970, and after Jefferson Airplane disbanded, he and Slick formed a new group under that name. The group's style had changed, however, tending more toward pop ballads than statement-making psychedelia. For recordings in the mid-eighties, the group cut their name to Starship because Kantner had left and had taken with him the legal right to use the name Jefferson. The original members of Jefferson Airplane regrouped with a new drummer and two keyboard players for their reunion album *Jefferson Airplane* in 1989. Members of Jefferson Airplane, Jefferson Starship, and others formed Jefferson Starship—The Next Generation during the early nineties. They recorded a live album, *Deep Space/ Virgin Sky* (1995) that included new songs and some rerecordings of the groups' old hits.

The blues was well represented in the psychedelic rock movement through the noncommercial songs and instrumentals by the Quicksilver Messenger Service, as well as by the attention-riveting vocals of **Janis Joplin** with her bands Big Brother and the Holding Company (1967–1969), the Kozmic Blues Band (1969), and the

Carlos Santana in 1969
Robert Altman/Michael Ochs Archives/Venice, CA

Full-Tilt Boogie Band (1970). Steve Miller had been a guitarist/singer in blues revival groups in Chicago during the mid-sixties, and he moved to San Francisco in 1966 to form the Steve Miller Blues Band. After their 1967 performance at the Monterey Pop Festival, they removed the word "blues" from their name, and as **The Steve Miller Band** expanded their style in more commercial directions.

Mexican-born guitarist Carlos Santana formed the Santana Blues Band in San Francisco in 1967. Like the Steve Miller Band, they soon dropped the "blues" out of their name and called themselves simply **Santana**. They developed a distinctive sound by adding two Latin conga drummers to the band. Exotic polyrhythms created by the congas in conjunction with their regular drummer gave a new coloration to the group's otherwise blues-based style. Santana's popularity moved beyond the confines of San Francisco when they brought the Woodstock audience to its feet after an impassioned performance of "Soul Sacrifice." Santana applied their colorful Latin rhythms to "Black Magic Woman" (1970), a blues-styled song written by Fleetwood Mac's original guitarist, Peter Green. A listening guide to Santana's biggest hit record is on the right. Santana's next hit, "Oye Como Va" (the Spanish title translates as "How's it going?" or "What's happening?"), was a cover of a recording by Tito Puente's Latin band.

Listening Guide

"Black Magic Woman" as recorded by Santana (1970)

Tempo: The tempo is approximately 120 beats per minutes, with four beats in each bar.

Form: The form is based on a series of twelve-bar periods that do not follow a blues progression. The introduction begins with organ and the guitar enters on the fifth bar. The instrumental introduction is a total of thirty-four bars long, the last twelve bars of which feature Carlos Santana's guitar solo following the basic melody of the twelve-bar periods to follow. That main melody begins with three beats of pickups, with the first vocal twelve-bar period actually beginning on the word "woman." A final instrumental section fades out by the end of the seventh bar.

Features: Beat subdivisions are generally uneven.

Backbeats are not stressed.

Subtle Latin rhythms are played by percussion instruments in the background.

Carlos Santana's guitar solos beautifully surround and then move away from the core melody that is the basis of his improvisation. His effective use of string bending enhances his guitar style.

Lyrics: The singer is so bound to a woman that he feels as if he were under a spell caused by black magic.

Source: Time-Life Music, *Sounds of the Seventies—1970; Abraxas*, Columbia 30130; and *Santana's Greatest Hits*, Columbia 33050.

■ In the early seventies, Carlos Santana collaborated on special projects with jazz musicians, including John McLaughlin and Stanley Clarke. This will be discussed in Chapter 13, Jazz Rock and Fusion.

Psychedelic Rock Beyond San Francisco

Venice Beach in Los Angeles became a gathering place for southern California hippies. Allen Ginsberg and other Beats often appeared for poetry readings in its several coffeehouses. Of the psychedelic bands formed in Los Angeles, **The Doors** were the most important. The group chose their name as a shortened version of *The*

The Doors (left to right): Ray Manzarek, Jim Morrison, John Densmore, and Robby Krieger in 1968
UPI/Bettmann

Doors of Perception, a book by Aldous Huxley (1894–1963) about the influences of drugs. The phrase was previously used by William Blake (1757–1827), although in his case it did not refer to drugs. The Doors were formed by keyboard player Ray Manzarek (born in 1935) and poet/singer Jim Morrison (1943–1971), both of whom had studied filmmaking and saw their dramatic stage performances as the door through which they would bring new awareness to their fans. Other members were guitarist Robby Krieger (born in 1946) and drummer John Densmore (born in 1944), who had both belonged to the Psychedelic Rangers.

For most of the Doors' songs, Morrison wrote poetry that Krieger set to music. Their favorite song themes were influenced by Beat poetry. The Beats' interest in both sex and drugs, for example, could be heard in "Light My Fire" (1967), which was based on almost hypnotic repetition of the organ theme along with sexually suggestive and drug-related lyrics. When the Doors were invited to perform on "The Ed Sullivan Show," they were allowed to perform "Light My Fire," but Morrison had to promise to take the word "higher" out of the lyrics and change it to something that would not be taken as a reference to drugs. He broke his promise and sang the word loudly and clearly, and because the show was aired live, it could not be cut by the producers. A listening guide to "Light My Fire" is on page 125.

The Doors gained a great number of fans across the country between 1967 and 1969, but they were unable to go on the long concert tours those fans craved because of Morrison's chronic abuse of drugs and alcohol. He had become completely undependable on stage, being so careless about his language and actions that he was eventually arrested for public obscenity and indecency. His arrest for lewd behavior in Miami in 1969 caused a break in the group's professional activities because Morrison had to attend the court proceedings on the matter. Although the judge dropped the charges for lack of evidence that Morrison had actually exposed himself on stage, the negative publicity surrounding the case hurt the band's commercial image and promoters were hesitant to hire them.

After the Miami incident, Morrison changed his stage persona. He threw out his leather pants in exchange for more conservative dress, gained weight, and grew a beard. He also became more introverted and detached from the rock star image he had previously affected. The Doors continued to record and to perform occasionally in concerts, but Morrison began to look for solace more in his poetry and film experiments than in music. Finally, after the completion of the *L.A. Woman* album (1971), he took a break and moved to Paris to rest. He died of a heart attack while he was there.

With Morrison's death, the Doors were reduced to an instrumental trio. They tried to continue as such, but disbanded to pursue solo projects. In 1978 they released the album *An American Prayer,* which contained their music dubbed over Morrison's recitation of his poetry. The mystique of Jim Morrison continued well after his death. The Doors' music enjoyed a resurgence in popularity in the late seventies and early eighties, to the point that their albums sold better during this revival than when they were first released. Oliver Stone revived their memory again with his movie *The Doors* (1991).

Despite the importance of San Francisco and Los Angeles for their counterculture enclaves, California had no monopoly on the psychedelic movement. Similar events were happening in many parts of the U.S. and in

Listening Guide

"Light My Fire"
as recorded by the Doors (1967)

Tempo: The tempo is approximately 126 beats per minute, with four beats in each bar.

Form: After a five-bar introduction the form is structured as: A B A B and an improvised instrumental section 145 bars in length, then A B A B and an extension.

The A sections are eight bars long and the B sections are seven bars long.

The long instrumental section features the organ for the first seventy bars, the guitar with organ accompaniment for the next seventy bars, and then a repeat of the five-bar introduction. The musical basis of the improvisation is a one-bar, two-chord ostinato (repeating pattern).

The B sections function as a refrain and have the same lyrics each time.

The lyrics to the third A section are a repetition of the second A, and the lyrics to the fourth A are a repetition of the first A.

The recording ends with an extension based on the B section followed by a repeat of the instrumental introduction.

Features: Even beat subdivisions are maintained throughout the recording.

The drums keep a strong backbeat in the B and the instrumental sections, but accent the backbeat more softly in the A sections.

The bass lines are played on the organ.

Lyrics: The singer asks a girl to help him get as high as possible. Both sex and drugs are hinted at as part of the trip.

Source: *The Doors,* Elektra 74007; and *The Doors Greatest Hits,* Elektra 515.

England. Jimi Hendrix had moved to London to start his band **The Jimi Hendrix Experience,** and Hendrix's blues-based but psychedelic-influenced guitar style became the model for other guitarists for years to come. The Jimi Hendrix Experience debuted in the U.S. at California's Monterey Pop Festival in 1967 and many U.S. tours followed. Hendrix had always admired Bob Dylan's music and his psychedelic version of Dylan's "All Along the Watchtower" became Hendrix's first top twenty hit in the U.S. The listening guide on page 126 compares Hendrix's recording to the original by Dylan. Dylan has said he liked what Hendrix did with the song, and he even made some changes in his own live performances because of Hendrix's influence.

The Jimi Hendrix Experience broke up in 1969. Hendrix moved back to the U.S. and worked with a variety of musicians, often including Experience drummer Mitch Mitchell. Hendrix's performance of the "Star Spangled Banner" was a highlight of the Woodstock Festival in 1969. Just through his playing of the national anthem, Hendrix managed to make statements that supported the feelings and attitudes of the hippie counterculture. Between bits of melody Hendrix broke off to make his guitar sound like bombs were going off, a reminder of the fact that the Vietnam War still raged on, and after the melody where the words "land of the free" would be sung, his guitar line took a dive from a very high to a very low note as if to say those words did not ring true. Hendrix died the following year, but the influence he had on other rock guitarists and the psychedelic movement in general continued on.

Other blues revival groups like Cream and even the Beatles were greatly influenced by the psychedelic movement. Pink Floyd was a psychedelic group in the beginning of their career, but after 1967, when their writer/guitarist/singer Syd Barrett left, they became much more important as an art rock group than as a psychedelic one. The music of Pink Floyd will be discussed in Chapter 16, Art Rock.

Many influences of psychedelic music could be seen in rock music of the seventies and eighties, and the entire counterculture experience remained present at any concert given by the Grateful Dead. Even Prince adopted some aspects of the psychedelic style for his *Around the World in a Day* (1985) album. A serious return of interest in psychedelic music played by new bands, however, began in the early nineties when psychedelic drugs came back into common use. **Phish,** a newer band that captured some of the sense of musical diversity, free-form spontaneity, and surrealism appealed to psychedelic audiences of the nineties. Like the Grateful Dead, Phish performed better live than in the studio because they liked to play long, wandering improvisations and to be able to interact with their audiences. Their 1995 album, *A Live One,* captured that modern psychedelic style well.

Summary

Psychedelic rock was not a single style of music, but rather the music of the peace-and-love-minded counterculturists grouped in San Francisco as well as in other parts of the U.S. and England. Psychedelic rock music expressed an "in-group" identity inspired by the Beat writers and attempted to provide a drug-influenced mood and atmosphere to aid escape from the outside

Listening Guide

	"All Along the Watchtower" as recorded by Bob Dylan (1968)	***"All Along the Watchtower" as recorded by Jimi Hendrix (1968)***
Tempo:	The tempo is about 126 beats per minute, with four beats in each bar.	The tempo is about 116 beats per minute, with four beats in each bar.
Form:	The lyrics and instrumentals fall into eight-bar sections, but the basis of the musical form is a two-bar chord progression with a descending bass line. Both the chord progression and the bass line repeat throughout the recording. (This form is called a **passacaglia** in classical music.)	The form of Dylan's recording has been followed, except Hendrix extends one of the instrumental sections from eight to thirty-two bars, and he adds an extension with vocal comments to the ending.
Features:	Even beat subdivisions are maintained throughout the recording.	Even beat subdivisions are maintained by the instruments, but the vocals occasionally relax into uneven subdivisions.
	The eight-bar instrumental introduction includes two bars of strummed acoustic guitar, two bars of that pattern with harmonica, and then four bars with electric bass and drums. Those instruments are the only ones used in the recording.	From the beginning to the end the instrumental background is a thick texture created by rhythm guitar, keyboard instruments, electric bass, two drums, and congas.
	No backbeat is accented.	The drums and tambourine play a very strong backbeat.
	Dylan plays the harmonica during the instrumental sections.	The instrumental sections are used to feature Jimi Hendrix's distinctive and colorful guitar style.
	Dylan plays his harmonica to fill between his vocal phrases. His guitar supplies only accompaniment.	Hendrix plays his guitar to fill between his vocal phrases. Other instruments play the accompaniment.
Lyrics:	The lyrics portray a conversation between two people in which they express their desire to escape to a world where simplicity and truth are valued.	Dylan's lyrics are kept the same and even amplified through the repetitions of bits of phrases at the end of the recording.

Source: Dylan's recording: *John Wesley Harding,* Columbia 9604; and *Bob Dylan's Greatest Hits, Volume II,* Columbia 31120.

Hendrix's recording: Time-Life Music, *Classic Rock, 1968: Shakin' All Over; Electric Ladyland,* Reprise 6307; *Jimi Hendrix Experience: Smash Hits,* Reprise 2276; and *The Essential Jimi Hendrix,* Reprise 2245.

world. Whether the music had the country and folk roots of jug band music; the commercial flair of Jefferson Airplane; the blues roots of the Steve Miller Band, Janis Joplin, or Jimi Hendrix; the Indian influences of Quicksilver Messenger Service; the Latin rhythms of Santana; the dramatic stage performances of the Doors; or the combination of styles played by the Grateful Dead, psychedelic rock shared the favorite themes of its fans and was musically influenced by their fascination with the effects of psychedelic drugs.

Terms to Remember

AM radio
Beats
Cool jazz
Existentialism
FM radio
Guiro
Passacaglia
Phrygian mode
Psychedelic drugs
Sitar
Surrealism
Tamboura

CHAPTER 12

Revivals of Country-Styled Rock

After the decline of fifties rockabilly, it was not until the late sixties that a non-pop country-rock style regained popularity. Many fifties rock fans could not relate to the pop music of the late fifties, and they began to listen to more folk-oriented music by such performers as the Chad Mitchell Trio; the Kingston Trio; the Limelighters; Peter, Paul and Mary; and Bob Dylan. Many of the songs those groups sang were old, having counterparts in the traditional British folk songs from which they had evolved, but others were new compositions written in the old style. The late-sixties country-rock sound grew out of the revival of interest in folk music.

As in most country styles, the vocals were very important in folk music. The instruments played by folk groups varied, but acoustic guitar and string bass were usually included and drums seldom were. In 1965, **Bob Dylan** horrified his folk-loving fans by adding drums, amplified instruments, and a rock beat to his recordings. He lost much of his folk audience, but created a new style of music called folk rock. Dylan later added elements of country music to his compositions, in particular those on the albums *John Wesley Harding* (1968) and *Nashville Skyline* (1969). In some ways, these albums were a return to his folk roots because the music on them (at least on *John Wesley Harding*) was as much like folk as it was like country. Dylan had always been a fan of country artists like Hank Williams and Hank Snow, and his interest in playing country music may have been renewed by his performances with the Hawks (formerly the backup band for rockabilly singer Ronnie Hawkins) during the mid-sixties. To record *Nashville Skyline,* Dylan went to Nashville (where he had recorded *Blonde on Blonde* in 1966 and *John Wesley Harding* in 1968) and hired country musicians Charlie Daniels and Johnny Cash for the sessions. Much of the music on *Nashville Skyline* exhibited a fairly standard country instrumentation—strummed acoustic guitars, electric lead guitars, electric bass, honky-tonk piano, and drums, with the occasional use of pedal-steel guitar, which added more country flavor.

These two Dylan albums, along with Gram Parsons and the International Submarine Band's album *Safe at Home* (1967), the Byrds' *Sweetheart of the Rodeo* (1968), and the Flying Burrito Brothers' *The Gilded Palace of Sin* (1969) helped forge the style known as country rock, the latter three albums sharing a common element: Gram Parsons.

Country Rock

Gram Parsons (Cecil Conner, 1946–1973) wrote songs and played the guitar with the International Submarine Band until 1968, when he joined **The Byrds,** a folk-rock group from Los Angeles, and convinced them to do a country album. Parsons' goal was to combine country music with rock, but in many ways the album that resulted, *Sweetheart of the Rodeo* (1968), was more of a country album with occasional rock influences than a real melding of country and rock styles. The most rock-oriented cut on the album was "One Hundred Years from Now" (written by Parsons). It was rock-oriented because it followed a four-beat metric pattern, used a strong backbeat, and it had background instrumentals that, at times, almost obscured the lead vocals, something country musicians generally avoided. Other songs, like "Pretty Boy Floyd" and "You're Still on My Mind," had a rock beat, but the strong bluegrass influences in the former and the honky-tonk style of the latter made it difficult to call them rock. "Blue Canadian Rockies," "Hickory Wind," and "Christian Life" were all in triple meters, common for country, but very unusual for rock. Although the album was not the synthesis of country and rock styles that later groups would perfect, it was an important influence on many of those groups.

Parsons left the Byrds after refusing to tour in South Africa because of his opposition to apartheid. In 1968 he and former Byrd Chris Hillman formed **The Flying Burrito Brothers,** a group that included the country timbre of pedal-steel guitar, a strong rock backbeat, and Everly Brothers-influenced vocal harmonies. Parsons quit the Burrito Brothers in 1970 and was joined by singer **Emmylou Harris** (born in 1947) on his solo albums, *GP* (1972) and *Grievous Angel* (1973). The exposure Harris gained through her appearances on Parsons' albums and concert tour helped her establish a career in country and country-rock music. An important pioneer of the country-rock sound, Parsons died in 1973; though the cause of death was never established, a combination of drugs and alcohol was evident in the autopsy. Groups and individuals who followed his lead in developing country-rock music remembered Parsons through newly written song tributes and covers of his compositions.

The Buffalo Springfield was a folk-rock group that originally included musicians who became important in the development of country rock, including guitarist/singer/writer Neil Young, guitarist/singer/writer Stephen Stills, guitarist/singer Richie Furay, bass player Bruce Palmer, and drummer Dewey Martin. Jim Messina joined the group to play bass when needed and to work as their recording engineer. Two of the country-influenced songs recorded by the group, "Go and Say Goodbye" and "Hot Dusty Roads," were written by Stills. After the breakup of the group, he went on to work with David Crosby from the Byrds, Graham Nash from the Hollies, and Neil Young in the folk-rock groups Crosby, Stills and Nash, and Crosby, Stills, Nash and Young.

When Buffalo Springfield disbanded in 1968, Jim Messina and Richie Furay formed the country-rock group **Poco.** Although it took them a long time to gain commercial success, Poco was among the earliest to include such country instruments as pedal-steel guitar and dobro in their regular instrumentation. The group survived many personnel changes, including the loss of Messina (who formed a duo with Kenny Loggins), and eventually changed their style to include as much rhythm and blues as country. Poco's greatest commercial successes were "Crazy Love" and "Heart of the Night," from the album *Legend* (1978).

Listening Guide

"Lyin' Eyes" by the Eagles (1975)

Tempo: The tempo is approximately 132 beats per minute, with four beats in each bar.

Form: The song is basically made up of eight-bar verses with a repeating chord progression, except the sections that include the words "lyin' eyes" serve as a refrain made up of two eight-bar phrases followed by one six-bar instrumental phrase.

An eight-bar instrumental introduction is followed by six eight-bar verses with lyrics, the twenty-two-bar refrain, four eight-bar verses, another refrain, six eight-bar verses, and the refrain again with repetitions to extend the ending.

Features: Steel and twelve-string guitars play fills between the singers' phrases.

The drums maintain an even beat subdivision with a subtle accent on the backbeat.

Honky-tonk piano can be heard in the background.

The electric bass guitar plays on beats one and three, as was standard in two-beat country bass rhythms, but the bass player in this recording places the notes on beats one and three into a pattern that gives his line a Latin feel, with notes on the second half of beat two and sometimes also after beat four, notated as follows:

Lyrics: The song tells a story about a young woman who married for money, is cheating on her husband, and is thinking about the current state of her life. The lyrics repeat during the refrains, accusing the woman of having eyes that expose her lies.

Sources: *One of These Nights*, Elektra 1039; and *Eagles—Their Greatest Hits, 1971–1975*, Asylum 105.

The Eagles (left to right): Bernie Leadon, Glenn Frey, Don Henley, Randy Meisner, and Don Felder

Michael Ochs Archives/Venice, CA

Some country-rock groups first played as jug bands which, in addition to the jug bass, used guitar and harp (harmonica). **The Nitty Gritty Dirt Band** started out in 1966 as the Illegitimate Jug Band, a group that had played bluegrass and country swing, but they changed their name and switched to country rock after hearing Gram Parsons with the Byrds. The band was close to breaking up when their version of "Mr. Bojangles," originally written and recorded by Jerry Jeff Walker, became a hit single. In the country tradition of using songs to tell stories, the song was about an old man who traveled around the country dancing on street corners for tips.

In 1972, the Nitty Gritty Dirt Band went to Nashville to record a three-record set, *Will the Circle Be Unbroken,* for which they brought in the best country musicians available. The album provided a stimulus for the country-rock style because it introduced fans of the Nitty Gritty Dirt Band to great country musicians. Shortening their name to the Dirt Band in 1976, they received some notoriety by becoming the first American rock group to tour the Soviet Union in 1977. In later years they put the "Nitty Gritty" back in their name, continuing to play country and country-rock music to new audiences.

When **Linda Ronstadt** (born in 1946) moved from Arizona to Los Angeles in 1964, she began her recording career with a group called the Stone Poneys. Ronstadt had grown up listening to country singers—Hank Williams was among her favorites—and their influences were evident in her vocal performance on the Stone Poneys' recording of "Different Drum" (1967). The recording was as much country as rock and Ronstadt was soon featured on the *Grand Ole Opry* and on "The Johnny Cash Show." Her first solo albums were not great commercial successes, but they brought her to the attention of manager/producer Peter Asher, formerly of the British folk-pop duo Peter and Gordon. Under Asher's production, Ronstadt recorded hits that consistently topped both the pop and country charts, a combination of styles known as crossover country music.

After establishing a career for herself as a crossover singer, Ronstadt went on to record music in other styles, including Motown and reggae songs, Broadway show tunes, jazz-influenced standards by George Gershwin and Cole Porter (arranged and conducted by Nelson Riddle), and eventually, traditional Mexican songs with a mariachi band. Ronstadt's first of three albums of songs in Spanish was called *Canciones de Mi Padre (My Father's Songs,* 1987) as a tribute to her Mexican father. The album was enormously popular with many Mexican Americans, but sparked criticism among others who resented her not having used her father's name throughout her career (Ronstadt was her mother's maiden name). Ronstadt's later albums in Spanish were less successful than the first one, and in 1993 she returned to a pop style with songs in English.

Linda Ronstadt's backup band for her country album *Linda Ronstadt* (recorded in 1971, released in 1972) included guitarist/singer Glenn Frey, guitar/banjo/mandolin player and singer Bernie Leadon, bass player/singer Randy Meisner, and drummer/singer Don Henley. After working together on Ronstadt's album they decided to form their own band, **The Eagles**, and soon became one of the most important and successful country-rock bands to come out of southern California in the seventies. The Eagles played a more complete fusion of country and rock musical styles than most previous country-rock groups. Their recording of "Take It Easy" (1972) used a rock beat, but the sound of a five-string banjo playing continuously in the background gave it a definite country flavor. The strummed acoustic guitar on their recording of "Best of My Love" (1974) made it sound like folk rock, but the electric guitar fills were country-styled. "Lyin' Eyes" (1975) was rock music with the country timbres of electric bass, electric guitar fills, honky-tonk piano, and mandolin, as well as storyline lyrics. It did not use a traditional two-beat bass, however; the bass established a Latin-influenced beat. A listening guide for "Lyin' Eyes" is on page 128.

"Lyin' Eyes" was only one of many international hits for the Eagles. The country direction of their music

Listening Guide

"The Weight"
as recorded by the Band (1968)

Tempo: The tempo is roughly 72 beats per minute, with four beats in each bar.

Form: A two-bar introduction is followed by a one-bar **vamp** (a simple accompaniment pattern). The vamp sets up the instrumental pattern that accompanies the voice when it enters on the next bar.

The song is basically structured in eight-bar periods, each containing new lyrics and followed by a refrain. The refrain has four bars of four beats each, a three-beat bar, another four-beat bar, and a four-beat vamp leading into the next period.

The last two refrains are extended by vamps and repeated sections.

The recording ends with a four-bag tag.

Features: The beats are subdivided evenly throughout the recording.

The drums keep a steady backbeat through most of the recording, but occasionally vary it by slipping into even accents on all four beats.

The piano plays fills in a honky-tonk style.

During group vocals a high voice sings above the main melody, as was common in hillbilly style and was characteristic of country music in the sixties.

Lyrics: The lyrics are religious, about Jesus (who is not named) carrying the weight of people's sins.

Source: *Music from Big Pink*, Capitol 46069.

changed somewhat in 1976 when guitar/banjo/mandolin player Bernie Leadon quit and was replaced by rock guitarist Joe Walsh. The change did not harm their commercial appeal, and they continued to place songs such as "Hotel California" (1976) and "Life in the Fast Lane" (1977) at the top of the pop charts. In the early eighties, the group broke up to allow Frey and Henley to pursue solo careers.

Drummer/singer/writer Don Henley was joined by guitarist Danny Kortchmar for the album *I Can't Stand Still* (1982) with the hit single "Dirty Laundry." Assured that he was on the right track, Henley continued his solo career as more of a singer/songwriter than as a drummer. Glenn Frey was equally successful in his solo work. He had a number of hit songs, but decided to try his hand at writing music for television and films. His hit single "The Heat Is On" (1984) was on the soundtrack to Eddie Murphy's film *Beverly Hills Cop,* and a later hit single, "You Belong to the City" (1985), was featured in the television program "Miami Vice." Frey also wrote the theme song for the 1991 movie *Thelma and Louise.* He even ventured into acting and appeared in a few "Miami Vice" episodes. In 1994, the Eagles reformed for a mammoth tour, a live appearance on *MTV Unplugged,* and a new album, *Hell Freezes Over.*

In northern California, **Creedence Clearwater Revival,** led by brothers John and Tom Fogerty, took rock music and flavored it with country or rockabilly guitar fills and country-influenced lyrics to create their own brand of country rock. Without the stand-up bass and acoustic rhythm guitar sound of country music, they still managed to capture the energy of rockabilly. Except for occasional covers, such as "Suzie Q" (1968) by rockabilly singer Dale Hawkins, most of their songs were written by **John Fogerty** (born in 1945). Country lyrical themes that stressed love for the southern landscape and personal pride in the face of hard economic conditions were evident in "Born on the Bayou," "Green River," "Fortunate Son," and "Down on the Corner" (all 1969). Country stylings could also be heard in their live concert repertoire, including "Tombstone Shadow," with its country guitar fills, and "Don't Look Now," with country guitar and two-beat bass lines.

Creedence Clearwater Revival broke up in 1972, but John Fogerty began to experiment with overdubbing techniques and made a number of recordings on which he played all of the parts—guitar, bass, keyboards and drums. He used his own name for rock recordings made by that method, but used **The Blue Ridge Rangers** for his recordings of traditional country songs. As the Blue Ridge Rangers he had hit singles beginning with Hank Williams' "Jambalaya (On the Bayou)" in 1973, but it was not until his *Centerfield* album in 1985 that he returned to the attention of his old rock fans and created a new following for his music.

Rockabilly singer Ronnie Hawkins had moved his group, the Hawks, from Arkansas to Toronto, Canada, and during their stay there all of the members except drummer Levon Helm left the group and were replaced by Canadian musicians. This new group went on to back up Bob Dylan during the mid-sixties and eventually began working on their own material, calling themselves **The Band.** Their first two albums established their reputation as a country-rock group, but they were also very much influenced by the blues, white gospel, and brass bands, as well as other musical styles. Their first album, 1968's *Music from Big Pink* (named for a house owned

The Band (left to right): Levon Helm, Garth Hudson, Robbie Robertson, Rick Danko, and Richard Manuel
Michael Ochs Archives/Venice, CA

by two members), was not any more a country album than a rock album, though it included many examples of the influences of country vocal and instrumental styles. As most members of the Band were singers, they developed a distinctive group sound with interweaving independent vocal lines. A listening guide showing the general form and country characteristics of "The Weight," from the Band's *Music from Big Pink* is on page 130.

The Band continued their career for a number of years, adding soul and other styles to their country-based sound. Eventually they decided they were tired of life on the road, and thought it best to announce the end of the group with a big party and concert they called "The Last Waltz" (1976). A string orchestra was hired to play waltzes through the dinner hour, and musician friends including Muddy Waters, Ronnie Hawkins, Bob Dylan, Paul Butterfield, Eric Clapton, Ringo Starr, Joni Mitchell, Emmylou Harris, Neil Young, Neil Diamond, and Van Morrison joined them on stage for the concert. Director Martin Scorsese filmed the concert, and it was released as a movie, *The Last Waltz,* in 1978. The Band performed in 1983, but without Robbie Robertson, who was concentrating on his own solo career. Robertson was replaced by guitarist Jimmy Weider, and then three years later keyboard player Richard Manuel committed suicide, requiring further personnel changes. In 1993 the Band released a new album, *Jericho.*

Just as the Band was eclectic, drawing from numerous styles, **The Grateful Dead**'s music included blues, jazz, and folk music as much as it did country. Members Jerry Garcia and Phil Lesh wanted to play country music without the rock influences of the Grateful Dead's music and thus formed the country band **New Riders of the Purple Sage.** However they could not maintain membership in two groups, and quit their country group. Of importance to the development of country rock were the Grateful Dead's two albums in 1970, *Workingman's Dead* and *American Beauty.* Both contained newly composed country-styled music utilizing country instruments such as the banjo and steel guitar and containing the lyrical themes often found in country songs.

Once the combination of country and rock music was popularized by rock musicians, country musicians themselves began to use rock rhythms and instrumentation in their performances. Some of the country performers who have recorded in a country-rock style include Johnny Cash, Kris Kristofferson, Nicolette Larson, Dolly Parton, Kenny Rogers, Leon Russell (who recorded country music under his real name, Hank Wilson), Wanda Jackson, Waylon Jennings, and Loretta Lynn. From Springfield, Missouri, the Ozark Mountain Daredevils recorded old-style hillbilly string-band dance music and country-pop-rock albums through the middle and late seventies. The Amazing Rhythm Aces in Knoxville, Tennessee, played a combination of blues, bluegrass, country, and rock music that could best be characterized as country rock. Country rock was not a classification in which performers necessarily remained throughout their careers. It was often a style many country and rock musicians played from time to time before moving on to other styles.

The West Coast was the home of many country-rock musicians, but the nationwide popularity of the style led to the formation of bands in other parts of the U.S. as well. One such group, **Pure Prairie League,** formed in Ohio in 1971. Their personnel changed often, and by 1977 not a single original member was left. Multiple guitars playing rhythmic picking patterns common in country and folk music traditions supported by electric bass and a strong rock backbeat in the drums

The Allman Brothers Band (left to right): Jaimoe Johanny Johanson, Berry Oakley, Duane Allman, Butch Trucks, Gregg Allman, and Dickey Betts
Michael Ochs Archives/Venice, CA

was the basis of their instrumental sound, but through their many incarnations the group sometimes included members who played keyboard, banjo, fiddle, dobro, mandolin, and, in the late seventies, saxophone and flute. They often used group vocals or Everly Brothers-influenced vocal duos. Pure Prairie League had several hit singles and albums including the top ten hit "Let Me Love You Tonight" (1980) from *Firin' Up.* Founding member and lead singer Craig Fuller left Pure Prairie League in 1973 and ended up out on the West Coast singing lead and playing guitar in the regrouping of Little Feat in 1988.

Little Feat was formed in California in 1969 by Lowell George and Roy Estrada, former members of Frank Zappa's Mothers of Invention, and they became enormously popular in the eastern and southern parts of the country. George was a singer and writer who played blues harp, guitar, and slide guitar; Estrada played bass guitar. The original Little Feat also included classical pianist/composer Bill Payne and drummer Richard Hayward. They combined country rock with the blues and Memphis soul to perform songs that often revealed George's sense of humor. Their *Dixie Chicken* album (1973) introduced very strong influences of funk, gospel, and jazz, along with the twin lead guitar timbre of the Allman Brothers Band, and those additions led them away from country rock into southern rock.

George died of a heart attack before Little Feat had finished recording its *Down on the Farm* album in 1979. The remaining band members completed the album, but released it with the announcement that it would be their last. It seemed that was the case for the next nine years, but in 1988, Hayward and Payne put together the old band with the addition of a new guitarist/trumpet player, Fred Tackett, and Pure Prairie League's former singer/guitarist Craig Fuller to revive their lively music making. Their 1991 album, *Shake Me Up,* had eleven new songs that recaptured the sense of humor that they had become famous for when George was writing most of their songs. Still combining styles, the album featured the blues, boogie-woogie piano, and female singers providing gospel-influenced backup vocals, along with a solid rock backbeat. Little Feat's music has so many elements of southern rock it is hard to believe it was recorded in Hollywood and not in New Orleans. Little Feat continued to tour and record, but with much less commercial success than they had known in the seventies.

Folk-rock musicians often infused their musical sound with country timbres by adding instruments like the steel guitar, but **Neil Young** (born in 1945) turned away from his folk-music past and recorded the album *Old Ways* in 1985. Although he used a rock beat on a couple of tracks, it was basically a country album. Eight of the ten cuts were recorded in Tennessee, where Young was joined by guitarist/singer Waylon Jennings, guitarist/singer Willie Nelson, fiddler Rufus Thibodeaux, and many other well-established country musicians. The album was preceded by the hard rock album *Re*act*or* (1981), the experimental computer-generated album *Trans* (1983), and the rockabilly-styled *Everybody's Rockin'* (1983), none of which represented the folk-based style for which Young was famous. Young's record company, Geffen Records, had gone along with those experimental styles, but felt that *Old Ways* had drifted too far from the type of music fans expected from Young to generate sufficient sales and did not want him to release it. The album was indeed too country-styled for rock radio, and Young's reputation as a rock musician would most likely have caused country fans to avoid it. Young was ultimately allowed to release the album, provided that he promised to return to his more familiar style in the future. For fans of country rock, the album was an important addition to the sound of the eighties. Young's later work did indeed receive more critical and popular appeal. By the nineties he was considered by many to be the Godfather of Grunge, thanks to bands such as Pearl Jam claiming his influence. Young recorded the album *Mirror Ball* (1995) with Pearl Jam.

Many consider country rock a seventies style that has stayed alive only through the continued work of the original artists, but the Illinois group **Uncle Tupelo** (formed in 1987 and disbanded in 1994) and its offshoots **Wilco** and **Son Volt** (both formed in 1994) were drawing crowds of new, young fans to their lively interpretations of country rock in the nineties. The new bands play music influenced by Hank Williams, Neil Young, and others while also updating their sounds with punk influences. For fans of country rock the popularity of these bands offers hope for a continuing revival of the style in the future.

Southern Rock

Many southerners have long considered their region to be almost a separate country, set apart from the rest of the United States. One expression of that philosophy came through southern rock, which was generally an aggressive music played by musicians who projected a very macho, stubbornly independent, outlaw image. The movement began around 1968, at about the same time as country rock, when **The Allman Brothers Band** started playing music that combined elements of blues, soul, and country.

The Allman Brothers Band moved from their home in Florida to Macon, Georgia, to record at the Capricorn Records studio. The two lead guitarists, Duane Allman and Richard "Dickey" Betts, as well as the two drummers, Jaimoe Johanny Johanson (John Lee Johnson) and Butch Trucks, gave the group a distinctive sound. The twin lead guitars created a sound that was thick and full compared to the usual single lead guitar in most rock. In the song "Trouble No More" (written by M. Morganfield, a.k.a. Muddy Waters) from the group's first album, the introduction and some guitar fills in the instrumental choruses featured the two lead guitars playing in octaves. In other instrumental sections of the recording, the two lead guitars used a technique often employed in jazz when two musicians improvised together, **trading twos,** meaning that the soloists alternate, each playing two-bar phrases ("twos") that give the effect of a musical conversation between them. The lines played by the lead guitarists in the Allman Brothers Band were not typical country lines, but were closer to the long, expressive guitar lines common in the blues tradition.

In October 1971, when the group was right at the beginning of a successful and influential career, Duane Allman died in a motorcycle accident. *Eat a Peach* (1972) contained three tracks that had been recorded before Duane's death, but for the remainder of the album the twin lead sound was changed to that of a single lead guitar. Missing their trademark guitar style, Gregg Allman, originally the group's keyboard player, hired Chuck Leavell to play keyboards so that Allman could join Dickey Betts on lead guitar and revitalize the band's unique guitar style. Above is a listening guide to "Ramblin' Man" from the album *Brothers and Sisters.*

Legal and personal problems caused the Allman Brothers Band to break up in 1976, and individual members pursued solo careers. In 1978 members of the

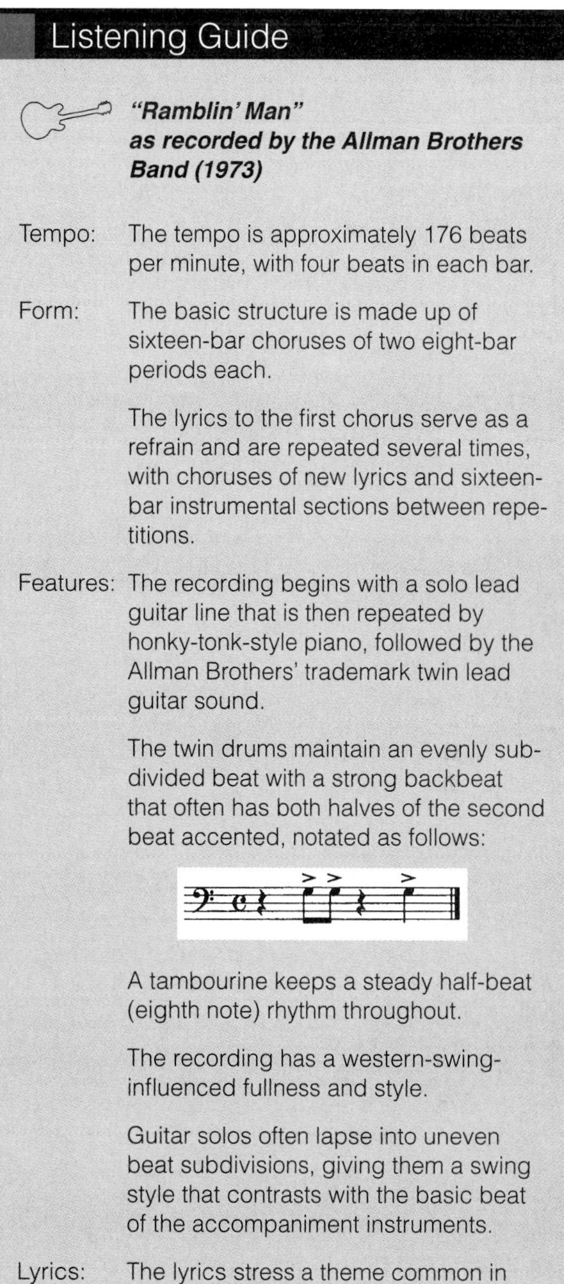

Listening Guide

"Ramblin' Man" as recorded by the Allman Brothers Band (1973)

Tempo: The tempo is approximately 176 beats per minute, with four beats in each bar.

Form: The basic structure is made up of sixteen-bar choruses of two eight-bar periods each.

The lyrics to the first chorus serve as a refrain and are repeated several times, with choruses of new lyrics and sixteen-bar instrumental sections between repetitions.

Features: The recording begins with a solo lead guitar line that is then repeated by honky-tonk-style piano, followed by the Allman Brothers' trademark twin lead guitar sound.

The twin drums maintain an evenly subdivided beat with a strong backbeat that often has both halves of the second beat accented, notated as follows:

A tambourine keeps a steady half-beat (eighth note) rhythm throughout.

The recording has a western-swing-influenced fullness and style.

Guitar solos often lapse into uneven beat subdivisions, giving them a swing style that contrasts with the basic beat of the accompaniment instruments.

Lyrics: The lyrics stress a theme common in southern rock, in which the male singer makes it clear that he must be free and avoid being "tied down" to one woman.

Source: Time-Life Music, *Sounds of the Seventies—1973;* and *Brothers and Sisters,* Polydor 825092.

Listening Guide

"The South's Gonna Do It" as recorded by the Charlie Daniels Band (1975)

Tempo: The tempo is approximately 176 beats per minute, with four beats per bar.

Form: An instrumental introduction made up of two eight-bar periods is followed by twelve choruses of twelve-bar blues, the third, fourth, fifth, sixth, ninth, tenth, eleventh, and twelfth of which are instrumental.

Features: The hillbilly-style fiddle introduction uses stop time with drum accents. The fiddle is joined by a steel guitar, then by bass and drums.

The bass plays a shuffle rhythm pattern (uneven beat subdivisions).

The drums strongly accent the backbeat.

The first chorus is played in a honky-tonk style.

Some of the instrumental sections contain multiple fiddle parts.

A boogie-woogie bass pattern is played by both the bassist and the pianist.

The recording ends with a jump blues riff pattern, reminiscent of Louis Jordan's style of the forties.

Lyrics: The theme exudes pride in the South and in music from the South. Various popular southern rock musicians and bands are named along with their home city or state.

Source: *Nightrider,* Epic 34402; and *The Charlie Daniels Band—A Decade of Hits,* Epic 38795.

original band, including Gregg Allman, appeared in concert with Dickey Betts' band Great Southern and a new album, *Enlightened Rogues,* (1979) followed. The reunion was not to last, however, but fans in the eighties and nineties have had opportunities to hear offshoot bands such as the Dickey Betts Band or the Gregg Allman Band as well as occasional regroupings of the Allman Brothers Band.

The twin lead guitar and twin drum sound of the Allman Brothers Band was imitated by many groups in the South, including **The Charlie Daniels Band.** Charlie Daniels was an eclectic country musician who played hillbilly fiddle, electric guitar, and slide guitar. His song "The South's Gonna Do It" exemplified the southern pride of the entire southern-rock movement as well as any single piece of music could, even to the point of including in the lyrics names of many well-known performers of the style (also mentioning the state or city where each originated). In addition, in the music itself Daniels managed to incorporate several southern musical styles, both black and white in origin, including hillbilly, honky-tonk, boogie-woogie, and the blues. The different styles were brought out in various sections of the recording. The listening guide points out those styles.

A genuine love for the South and its music led Daniels to organize an annual concert in Nashville called *The Volunteer Jam Concert.* Starting in 1974, the concerts have continued with enormous success and goodwill among the country, rock, and country-soul musicians invited to perform. Live albums and television programs have been recorded at these concerts.

Daniels' most popular recording was "The Devil Went Down to Georgia" (1979), a novelty song based on the old myth of the devil as a musician with whom great players competed in musical duels. Daniels also tended toward political statements in his songs from time to time (common in rock, but rare in country), and while it was generally more common for rock musicians to take liberal stands, his were often rather conservative. Daniels continued to record and tour during the eighties and nineties, often using his music to express his opinions about America's treatment of Vietnam veterans, bringing drug dealers and other criminals to justice, and various other subjects. His 1994 album, *The Door,* was his first gospel album.

In 1970, the Texas-based power trio **ZZ Top** began building a career that lasted well beyond that of many southern bands. Guitarist/singer Billy Gibbons had played with the psychedelic band Moving Sidewalks when that band's single, "99th Floor," was popular in the South. They once opened for the Jimi Hendrix Experience, and Gibbons took advantage of the opportunity by watching the way Hendrix controlled distortion and fuzztone in his solos. After Moving Sidewalks broke up, Gibbons enlisted bassist Dusty Hill and drummer Frank Beard, both of whom had previously played in the Dallas band American Blues. ZZ Top's first album, *The First Album* (1970), was not an immediate hit, but it did set them up for a successful tour and later recordings. Their career was built on the following gained through their tours and album sales more than on hit singles.

ZZ Top's hit single "Tush" (1975) followed the twelve-bar blues form and had bottleneck guitar solos during the instrumental sections. The band frequently used images of the Southwest during their concerts in the seventies, not only in their music, but also in the cactus, snakes, and cattle with which they often shared their stage. The band took a three-year break during the beginning of the eighties and finally entered the new decade with the hit singles "Gimme All Your Lovin" and "Sharp

Lynyrd Skynyrd (left to right, back row): Leon Wilkeson, Artimus Pyle, Allen Collins, Leslie Hawkins, Gary Rossington, Ronnie Van Zant, Steve Gaines, Jo Billingsley; (front): Billy Powell, Cassie Gaines

Michael Ochs Archives/Venice, CA

Dressed Man" from their album *Eliminator* (1983). The album title referred to a 1933 Ford automobile, and their rustic cowboy image had been exchanged for one built around fast modern cars and mock designer jumpsuits.

The original trio was still hitting the pop charts with hit records and videos in the nineties. Their 1994 album, *Antenna,* so named as a tribute to early rock radio stations in Mexico that were heard all over Texas, was a top twenty hit on the album charts. Members of ZZ Top acknowledged the importance of country and blues influences on their music by raising funds for the Delta Blues Museum in Clarksdale, Mississippi.

The Marshall Tucker Band interpolated both honky-tonk and jazz styles into the southern-rock sound. The group was formed by brothers Toy and Tommy Caldwell and was named for the man who owned the rehearsal hall they used. All its members were from South Carolina, but they went to Capricorn Records in Macon, Georgia, to record (the Allman Brothers Band also recorded there). Choosing not to copy the Allman Brothers Band's instrumentation, they used a single lead guitar, rhythm guitar, steel guitar, bass, drums, and their own unique contribution—improvised jazz-style solos on alto saxophone, flute, or keyboards. For their *Long Hard Ride* album (1976), they hired guest artists Charlie Daniels on fiddle and John McEuen (from the Nitty Gritty Dirt Band) on banjo and mandolin. Like other southern-rock groups, the Marshall Tucker Band celebrated their southern heritage, singing about their home state of South Carolina and their attachment to the land. Tommy Caldwell died after a car accident in 1980 and was replaced by Franklin Wilkie, an old friend of the band. In 1981, the album *Dedicated* was made in Caldwell's memory. After several other personnel changes, a version of the Marshall Tucker Band was still together and recording in the nineties, but more as a country band than a country-rock one. Toy Caldwell recorded a self-titled solo album in 1992, and died in 1993.

Hank Williams, Jr. (born in 1949), the son of famous country singer and songwriter Hank Williams (1923–1953), was a country musician who appreciated the way southern rock synthesized the styles of country and rock music. He had always disliked the stereotyped characterizations that often separated musicians and fans of the two styles, so he decided to record an album with members of some of the bands he liked. The result was *Hank Williams, Jr., and Friends* (1976), which included Charlie Daniels, Chuck Leavell (from the Allman Brothers Band), and Toy Caldwell (from the Marshall Tucker Band). In later years Hank Williams, Jr. returned exclusively to his career in country music, making no further efforts to reach out to a rock audience.

Of all southern-rock bands, **Lynyrd Skynyrd** most completely captured the national rock audience. The name was a respelling of Leonard Skinner, a high school teacher who had criticized the members of the group for having long hair. From Jacksonville, Florida, the group played hard rock music with the Allman Brothers Band's characteristic twin lead guitar sound, which Lynyrd Skynyrd turned into a triple lead. Not denying the influences the Allman Brothers had on them, the group's first album, *Pronounced Leh-Nerd Skin-Nerd* (1973), included "Freebird," written and recorded to honor the late Duane Allman.

Though none of the group members were from Alabama, Lynyrd Skynyrd wrote "Sweet Home Alabama" as a retort to Neil Young's songs "Alabama" and "Southern Man," in which Young (a Canadian) had dared to depict southern stereotypes. The listening guide on page 136 outlines characteristics of country, gospel,

Listening Guide

"Sweet Home Alabama" as recorded by Lynyrd Skynyrd (1974)

Tempo: The tempo is approximately 100 beats per minute, with four beats in each bar.

Form: The structure is based on repeating eight-bar periods, with occasional four-bar instrumental sections between some of the periods.

A simple three-chord progression is followed in each four-bar phrase.

Features: The drummer maintains a strong backbeat with even beat subdivisions.

A female vocal group sings responses to the lead singer, Ronnie Van Zant, in a black-gospel-influenced style.

The single lead guitar is often joined by two other lead guitars, creating the sense of fullness of the Allman Brothers' twin lead guitar sound.

The piano plays in a honky-tonk style.

Lyrics: The lyrics convey a strong feeling of southern pride, both in the response to Young's references to the South, and also through the way the South is affectionately personified as "she."

Source: Time-Life Music, *Sounds of the Seventies—1974;* and *Lynyrd Skynyrd Band—Gold & Platinum,* MCA 6898.

and rock music in Lynyrd Skynyrd's recording of "Sweet Home Alabama."

In October 1977, en route from a show in South Carolina to one in Louisiana, their chartered plane crashed, killing lead singer Ronnie Van Zant, guitarist Steve Gaines and his sister, backup vocalist Cassie Gaines, and badly injuring other band members. Back performing in 1980, two of Lynyrd Skynyrd's guitarists formed the Rossington-Collins Band and rerecorded "Freebird" without vocals as a tribute to Ronnie Van Zant. The popularity of Lynyrd Skynyrd's music lasted through the ten years after their crash, and the surviving members, including guitarists Gary Rossington and Ed King, keyboardist Billy Powell, bass player Leon Wilkeson, and drummer Artimus Pyle, formed a new version of Lynyrd Skynyrd with Ronnie's brother Johnny Van Zant as lead singer, and new members Randall Hall on guitar and female backup singers Dale Rossington (Gary Rossington's wife) and Carol Bristow. Another original member, guitarist Allen Collins, would have joined the group and did make an appearance at some concerts, but was unable to play because of injuries he suffered in an automobile accident in 1986. The new band released the album *Legend* (1987), which included several B sides of old singles and recordings that had been left unfinished by the original band. Although Allen Collins died in 1990, the rest of the revival band continued to work together into the middle nineties, and Johnny Van Zant also had some success as a solo artist.

Molly Hatchet and .38 Special were two other southern bands (from Jacksonville, Florida, like Lynyrd Skynyrd) that followed the multiple lead guitar sound of the Allman Brothers Band and Lynyrd Skynyrd. **Molly Hatchet** named themselves after a legendary southern prostitute known as Hatchet Molly, who reputedly castrated her clients. They played highly amplified, guitar-heavy music that was as tough as the image their name gave them. With a sound almost closer to heavy metal than to country, they remained popular as a touring band through the late seventies and into the eighties. **.38 Special** had connections with Lynyrd Skynyrd that were more than just musical. Donnie Van Zant, the brother of Ronnie and Johnny Van Zant of Lynyrd Skynyrd, was their singer. In true Allman Brothers fashion, they had two lead guitarists and two drummers.

Rockabilly Revival

The history of rock music has been a continuous cycle of revivals of earlier styles, and, indeed, a natural part of the search for something new in any art involves a reappraisal of the past, on which the new can be founded. The early eighties saw many new-wave groups look back to the fifties and sixties for stylistic revitalization. Brian Setzer was a leader of the Bloodless Pharaohs when he decided to give up new-wave music and form a rockabilly trio. The group included Setzer on guitar and lead vocals, Lee Rocker (Lee Drucker) on string bass and backup vocals, and Slim Jim Phantom (Jim McDonell) on drums. In remembrance of the many rockabilly songs from the fifties, in which "cats" were free-spirited young people, they called themselves **The Stray Cats.** Patrons of Long Island clubs heard them first, but it was only a short time before they moved to England to begin their recording career. Although their style was based on fifties rockabilly, the Stray Cats did not spend much of their time covering old songs. They made a few covers—Johnny Burnette's "Baby Blue Eyes," for example—but most of their music was new and original. Their first two albums, *Stray Cats* and *Gonna Ball* (both 1981), were released only in England, but in 1982 a compilation of songs from those albums, *Built for Speed,* was released in the U.S. *Rant n' Rave* (1983) was a follow-up album for the group in both Britain and America. The Stray Cats disbanded in 1984 and regrouped in 1986, but had less success with their later recordings. Brian Setzer moved in a completely new direction with his album *The Brian Setzer Orchestra* (1994), which featured arrangements of pop and rockabilly songs performed in a swing style.

Other eighties bands played with rockabilly's uptempo beat and slapping bass, but with a less traditional approach than the Stray Cats. In Los Angeles the punk band **X,** particularly when guitarist Billy Zoom was with them between 1977 and 1985, played many songs with a rockabilly beat and rockabilly guitar lines. Zoom had played with rockabilly star Gene Vincent during his comeback attempt of the early seventies. After leaving X, Billy Zoom moved on to work with **The Blasters,** another eighties L.A. band that played rockabilly and other traditional rock styles from the fifties.

Rockabilly did not remain popular for more than half a decade in its first stage of existence during the fifties, and lasted for even less time in its eighties revival. The reason for that probably lies in the fact that rockabilly is quite limited in form, style, and instrumentation. The influence rockabilly has had on rock music as a whole, however, is limitless. Without the rockabilly sound that Sam Phillips and Elvis Presley recorded in 1954, it is possible that Carl Perkins, Jerry Lee Lewis, Roy Orbison, Eddie Cochran, Gene Vincent, Buddy Holly, the Everly Brothers, Ronnie Hawkins, and the Band would never have played rock and roll. Without all of those performers, the many groups that were influenced by them would not have played rock as they did. Sam Phillips and Elvis Presley did not invent rock and roll in the Sun Records studio, but they most certainly influenced it for decades to come.

Summary

Country influences on rock music of the early sixties were limited to pop songs recorded by singers whose background experience and style were rooted in country music traditions. Non-pop country styles returned to rock music during the late sixties. Some characteristics of country music that influenced that style included lyrical themes that told stories or expressed love of a rural lifestyle; two-beat bass patterns; even beat subdivisions; occasional waltz (triple meter) rhythm patterns; using lead instruments to fill space between singers' phrases instead of playing through them; and the use of country instruments such as the steel guitar.

Solo performers such as Bob Dylan and groups such as the Byrds and the Buffalo Springfield had established careers in folk rock during the mid-sixties and effectively combined their folk styles with characteristics of country music to create an early form of country rock. With the exception of some recordings by the Band, which was made up of musicians from Arkansas and Canada, country rock was generally a western style popularized by such singers and groups as Linda Ronstadt, the Eagles, Creedence Clearwater Revival, and Little Feat.

While country rock was becoming established as an important and popular style in the West, musicians in the southern states had begun to combine country music and rock to create an often aggressive, always proud style known as southern rock. The Allman Brothers Band were among the first of the bands to define the style with their twin lead guitars and twin drums instrumentation, which influenced the instrumental makeup of the Charlie Daniels Band, Lynyrd Skynyrd, Molly Hatchet, and .38 Special. Southern rock generally included other southern styles such as blues, gospel, and jazz, in addition to country and rock music.

Both country rock and southern rock were very popular during the seventies, and many of the bands playing those styles survived into the eighties. Even rockabilly, a style that had lasted only a short time during the fifties, returned to rock charts in the eighties. Country music was a basic ingredient in the development of rock music during the fifties, and country music is bound to remain of importance to rock as long as rock remains a viable musical style.

Terms to Remember

Trading twos

Vamp

CHAPTER 13

Jazz Rock and Fusion

In a variety of ways, jazz has always been a part of rock. The blues was important to the development of both jazz and rock, but because jazz started very early in the twentieth century it had already evolved into a number of different styles before rock came on the scene. Various jazz styles influenced rock in different ways at different times. Early rock music by Bill Haley and the Comets, for example, was influenced by both big-band jazz and the blues. Haley's western swing style combined country music and jazz, and many of his rock recordings were western-swing and hillbilly-boogie-styled blues covers. The blues became rockabilly when performed by country musicians such as Elvis Presley, Carl Perkins, and Jerry Lee Lewis, who sped up the tempos, changed lyrics, and added country-style instrumental sections. Jazz instruments such as the saxophone were used to play jazz-style improvisations in the bands that backed early rock performances by many African American artists, from Little Richard in the fifties through the many soul, Motown, and funk musicians of the sixties and later.

Most rock music has some characteristics that came from jazz, but the terms "jazz rock" and "fusion" did not refer to just any combination of jazz and rock music. They were very particular styles that developed during the late sixties. Jazz rock combined the horn section sound of swing dance music, as played by most of the big bands of the forties and fifties, with a rock rhythm section and rock beat. It almost always used vocals, an element more essential to rock than to jazz. Fusion was a somewhat experimental jazz style that made use of rock instrumentation and took some rhythmic and melodic patterns from rock. Fusion was primarily an instrumental music; when vocals were included they were usually not given any more prominence than the instrumental solos. Jazz rock tended to be more closely related to rock, whereas fusion maintained clear connections with its jazz roots.

While small-group jazz styles, including most performances of the blues, centered on the practice of improvisation, the large swing bands could not have so many instrumentalists improvising at the same time and, therefore, played from written arrangements. Individual instrumentalists were allowed to improvise solo choruses accompanied by part or all of the band, but most of the music played by swing bands was predetermined by an arranger who, in effect, established a band's style. Typical instrumental groupings commonly employed in jazz-style big bands included a rhythm section consisting of piano, acoustic or amplified guitar, string bass, and drums; a brass section (trumpets and trombones); and a woodwind section (saxophones, whose players often doubled on related instruments such as clarinets and flutes). These combinations of instruments grew to be so commonly associated with jazz that when rock styles such as soul and funk used horn sections of brass instruments or saxophones, they automatically created a link with jazz.

Defining exactly what constitutes jazz music or jazz style is not an easy task. Improvisation is, of course, an important element, but even without it jazz can exist. Jazz style is a "feel," as a jazz musician would term it—an approach to the melodic and harmonic material that is unique to the idiom. And, as Duke Ellington maintained, "It don't mean a thing if it ain't got that swing." Jazz arrangements, no matter how carefully notated, cannot be effective without the infusion of musical instincts that jazz musicians bring to a performance. Jazz players sense how long to dwell on a note, when to bend it, what notes to accentuate and which ones merely to suggest, what liberties to take with the beat, and any number of other, often subtle techniques of jazz interpretation. A well-written arrangement in jazz style, if put in front of musicians whose background is only in, say, symphonic music, would not "swing," but would sound stilted and stiff. The players would certainly be proficient enough as instrumentalists, but they would not have the necessary background and experience to convincingly produce stylistic jazz.

Rock music likewise developed its own instrumentation, phrasing practices, and "feel" that, when mixed with elements of jazz to create jazz rock or fusion, were emphasized or de-emphasized depending on the backgrounds and interests of the musicians. Even the standard types of improvised solos are different in rock than in jazz. Rock solos tend to stay within a single scale or **mode,** whereas jazz solos more often include nonchordal tones and move from one mode to another creating harmonic complexities with the chords played by the rhythm section. Rock guitarists will even stay within notes of a particular finger pattern rather than move to avoid repeated patterns. Rock solos also tend to be less rhythmically complex than jazz ones. Jazz soloists often set up rhythmic patterns that contrast with that of the accompaniment. Even the number of notes and the speed at which they are played is often different between rock and jazz. Rock solos are often very fast, flashy, and continuous, where silence is as important as the playing of notes in jazz. Certainly, Miles Davis' trumpet style serves as a perfect example of the use of silence as a musical element.

Jazz rock often took fairly conventional rock forms and simply enhanced them with a horn section playing jazz-inflected arrangements. Fusion often included rock-styled solos played on amplified instruments using distortion and feedback, as well as various types of synthesizers that had become standard rock equipment by the late sixties. Jazz rock was pretty easily understood as rock music, and because the horn sections had been used in rock styles like Memphis soul and James Brown's rhythm and blues, they did not sound foreign. Fusion, on the other hand, was often barely recognizable as rock, and much of it seemed further from standard rock styles than jazz rock was from swing band styles.

Jazz Rock

Much jazz rock of the late sixties was played by former blues revivalists who added sections of brass and/or woodwind instruments to their rock instrumentation. One of the earliest of the jazz-rock bands was **The Electric Flag,** formed in 1967 in San Francisco by guitarist Michael Bloomfield, who had played with the Paul Butterfield Blues Band in Chicago the year before, and singer Nick Gravenites. The Electric Flag consisted of a rhythm section that included keyboards, bass, and drums, and a horn section including trumpet and two saxophones, a tenor and a baritone. The group had several personnel changes and disbanded after only a year and a half together, but their commercial success sparked other musicians to create their own jazz-rock bands.

In Chicago in 1967, guitarist/singer Terry Kath and clarinetist/saxophonist Walter Parazaider decided to form a jazz-rock band, calling it the Big Thing. The group consisted of a horn section—trumpet, trombone, and saxophone—backed by a rock rhythm section of guitar, keyboards, bass, and drums. Most of the members of the group were also singers and group vocals were often featured in their recordings. They changed their name to Chicago Transit Authority before recording their first self-titled album in 1969, but because of objections from city officials shortened their name to **Chicago** for future work. Chicago's early recordings captured the energy and spontaneity of a jazz band and included jazz-style improvisations by individual group members, but they eventually attracted a larger audience by recording in more of a pop style.

Chicago added Brazilian percussionist Laudir de Oliveira to their lineup in 1974, and had to replace guitarist/singer Terry Kath after his accidental death in 1978. The first two replacements did not stay with the band very long, but finally singer/guitarist Bill Champlin (who also played keyboards) joined to fill Kath's spot. Bassist/singer Peter Cetera left to concentrate on his solo career in 1984, but, again, the band continued on, replacing him with Jason Scheff. Their 1992 tour featured a string of their old hits. They rerecorded jazz tunes on their *Night & Day: Big Band* (1995) album, including old classics such as Duke Ellington's "Caravan," first recorded by Ellington in 1937, and Glenn Miller's "Moonlight Serenade," recorded in 1939.

Singer/keyboard player Al Kooper had recorded with the Royal Teens during the late fifties, had played sessions with Bob Dylan in 1965 (for Dylan's *Highway 61 Revisited* album), and had been a member of the Blues Project. Kooper liked the idea of combining rock and jazz instruments and styles and, in 1968, formed his own jazz-rock band, **Blood, Sweat and Tears.** Although the group's personnel changed often through their career, Blood, Sweat and Tears always maintained a strongly brass-oriented sound. The first version of the band included two

Blood, Sweat and Tears in concert
Michael Ochs Archives/Venice, CA

trumpeters, both of whom doubled on fluegelhorn (a trumpet-like instrument with a larger, conical bore that gives the instrument a fuller and mellower tone), and a trombonist who doubled on recorder. Other instrumentalists included an alto saxophonist, and a keyboardist who doubled on both flute and trombone, as well as a guitarist, a bassist, and a drummer. Based in New York, the band played music by many of the city's best-known writers, including Harry Nilsson, Gerry Goffin and Carole King, and Laura Nyro, as well as arrangements of classic songs, like Billie Holiday's ballad "God Bless the Child" (Holiday in 1941, Blood, Sweat and Tears in 1968).

Kooper left soon after the first album and was replaced by a very distinctive, bluesy-voiced singer from Surrey, England, David Clayton-Thomas. The listening guide on page 141 points out some of the main jazz influences in Blood, Sweat and Tears' popular recording of "Spinning Wheel," from the first album Clayton-Thomas recorded with the band, *Blood, Sweat and Tears* (1968).

Some of the rhythmic complexities of well-arranged jazz-band music are represented in "Spinning Wheel," particularly in the way tempo and metric shifts are used. As is generally true of big-band jazz, some solo instruments are given time to improvise—most notably the bebop-style trumpet solo in the instrumental passage after the third A section—but the overall organization of the music was carefully planned in advance. The use of even beat subdivisions through most of the song is a characteristic of rock music, not jazz.

In addition to jazz and rock styles, the album *Blood, Sweat and Tears* also included a piece of classical music played with jazz-rock instrumentation, "Variations on a Theme by Erik Satie," an arrangement of French composer Erik Satie's (1866–1925) piano composition "Trois Gymnopédies." Classical influence was also obvious in the organization of songs and pieces on the album because it opened and closed with the same Satie piece, producing what is called a **closed form.**

Blood, Sweat and Tears' dynamic singer, David Clayton-Thomas left the group for a couple of years in the early seventies, but found that he had had more success with the group than in his attempt as a soloist. His return was stressed by the renaming of the band to Blood, Sweat and Tears Featuring David Clayton-Thomas. One version or other of the group stayed together through the eighties and into the nineties, but with so many personnel changes that no original members (Clayton-Thomas not having been part of the original band) remained.

Fusion

The jazz-rock style of the Electric Flag, Chicago, and Blood, Sweat and Tears was more rock or, in the case of Chicago's later work, pop music influenced by jazz than it was any sort of equal combination of jazz and rock. A more jazz-styled music with rock influences was created by jazz trumpeter **Miles Davis** (1926–1991) in the mid- to late sixties. Called "fusion" (though not by Davis), the style was further developed by musicians who worked with Davis and later formed their own bands.

From as early as the mid-forties, Davis had been playing bebop with such performers as alto saxophonist Charlie Parker, bassist Charles Mingus, and drummer Max Roach. With some help from arranger Gil Evans, Davis recorded the innovative album *Birth of the Cool* (1949), which sparked the development of the cool-jazz style that was popular with the Beat writers of the fifties. Through the late fifties and mid-sixties, Miles Davis led a number of ensembles, in which the personnel often changed, and experimented with the music, replacing traditional scales and progressions of chords with different, often startling, melodic and harmonic structures.

Listening Guide

"Spinning Wheel" as recorded by Blood, Sweat and Tears (1968)

Tempo: The tempo is about 96 beats per minute with four beats in each bar, but the speed doubles during the instrumental section that precedes the last A section. The last A section returns to the beginning tempo.

Form: The form of the song has a returning A section that is eight bars long. The first A section begins when the singer enters and gradually introduces new instruments one by one, with a cowbell added in the third bar, drums in the fourth, and a tambourine in the fifth.

The second A section is followed by an eight-bar refrain with a ten-bar extension.

The refrain, or B section, is followed by another A.

Features: The recording begins with a **crescendo** (increase in volume, or loudness level) of the horn section followed by the horns playing a single bar (four beats) of a **sixteenth-note** (four notes in each beat) rhythmic pattern.

Even beat subdivisions are maintained throughout the recording, except during the improvised trumpet solo.

Each A section has an instrumental stop time in the seventh bar; the last A has the stop time in both the seventh and the eighth bars.

During the repetitions of the A sections, the horns punctuate the rhythm by playing chords where the drums are accenting the beat, sometimes (but not always) the backbeat.

After the third A, there is an extended instrumental section with a trumpet solo in a bebop jazz style.

The last A (after the instrumental section) repeats the lyrics of the third A, and it is followed by a metric shift in which the half beats of the basic tempo become accented in patterns of threes, creating a temporary change to a $\frac{9}{8}$ meter.

The new meter breaks into a playful improvisation by a recorder, a flute, and an alto saxophone, with a muted trumpet accentuating the second and third notes of the triple patterns.

The recording ends with the sound of maracas shaking and band members making casual comments about the quality of the recording.

Lyrics: The "spinning wheel" represents fate, and the song stresses that one need not worry about the future, because it is already planned.

Source: *Blood, Sweat and Tears,* Columbia 9720.

In 1968, Davis began to add rock elements to his music. Among these rock elements were the use of: (1) an evenly subdivided rock beat in the drums; (2) bass patterns involving short repeated lines (ostinatos) that functioned to give the music a simpler sense of organization; and (3) instruments commonly associated with rock such as electric piano, electric guitar, and electric bass guitar (Davis had rarely used guitar in his previous recordings). Most jazz styles that Davis had played in the past maintained a rhythmic flow of uneven beat subdivisions—the swing feel—that jazz inherited from its roots in the blues. Jazz bass lines were rarely as repetitious as those in rock, but tended more toward long walking bass patterns, and jazz groups were still using acoustic basses long after rock groups had switched to electric bass guitars. By the time Davis recorded the albums *In a Silent Way* and *Bitches Brew* (both 1969), he had begun to use heavy rock-styled drum patterns. The listening guide to "Miles Runs the Voodoo Down" from the *Bitches Brew* album serves as an example of Davis' innovative fusion style.

Miles Davis continued to incorporate elements of rock music into his recordings in the seventies, even to the point of altering the tone quality of his horn. He added electronic devices like those used by Jimi Hendrix and other rock guitarists to reproduce tonal variations in his trumpet sound similar to what was heard in hard rock and heavy metal guitar styles. A number of musicians who played on *Bitches Brew* and other fusion albums with Davis put together fusion bands of their own. Guitarist John McLaughlin assembled **The Mahavishnu Orchestra,** keyboardist Josef Zawinul formed **Weather Report** (with saxophonist Wayne Shorter), keyboardist Chick Corea (who played on "Miles Runs the Voodoo Down") started **Return to Forever,** and keyboardist Herbie Hancock formed the jazz-funk **Headhunters.**

Another musician who developed an interest in fusion was rock guitarist **Carlos Santana** (born in 1947), who branched out from the Latin-based rock style of his own band to record the album *Love, Devotion, Surrender* (1973), on which he collaborated with fusion

Miles Davis
Michael Ochs Archives/Venice, CA

Listening Guide

"Miles Runs the Voodoo Down" as recorded by Miles Davis (1969)

Tempo: The tempo at the beginning and end of the recording is about 116 beats per minute, with four beats per bar. The beat is intentionally sped up and slowed down again very gradually as the intensity builds and relaxes. The tempo of much of the middle section is about 126 beats per minute.

Form: No standard form with repeated sections is followed throughout the recording, although Davis' use of a returning **motive** (short bit of melody) gives the effect of formal unity.

Features: Even beat subdivisions are maintained throughout the recording.

Jazz instruments used include trumpet, soprano saxophone, bass clarinet (though not typical in jazz), acoustic bass, and drums (three set drummers and one auxiliary percussionist).

Rock elements include two electric pianos, electric bass guitar, electric lead guitar, and the use of distortion.

John McLaughlin's electric guitar playing includes rhythmic punctuations similar to those used by guitarists in funk bands led by James Brown or Sly Stone, as well as a rock-style solo about one-third of the way through the recording.

No standard type of chord progression is followed; the track is based on a single chord to which individual soloists add **chord extensions** and **non-chordal tones.** The bass players play repeated riff-like (ostinato) lines.

Many of the solos used the **dorian mode** (natural notes from D to D), which differs from a major scale because it has lowered third and seventh degrees.

Distortion in the guitar and keyboard increases as the intensity builds and the tempo quickens.

The texture is thickened by dense polyrhythms behind the soloists. Polyrhythms over a single chord are perhaps influenced by James Brown's or Sly Stone's funk style, but Davis' rhythms are less repetitious than theirs because more instruments are involved.

The thick texture creates a full, almost hypnotic, effect.

Lyrics: The instrumental recording has no vocals.

Source: *Bitches Brew*, Columbia 40577; and *Columbia Years, 1955–1985*, Columbia 45000.

musicians, including McLaughlin, keyboardist Jan Hammer, and drummer Billy Cobham, all members of the Mahavishnu Orchestra.

Santana returned to his own band and continued to play fusion, often hiring musicians who had earlier worked with Miles Davis, including keyboardist Herbie Hancock, drummer Tony Williams, and saxophonist Wayne Shorter (the soprano saxophone soloist on "Miles Runs the Voodoo Down") to record with the band.

Virtuoso bass guitarist **Jaco Pastorius** (1951–1987) joined Weather Report in 1976 and was featured on the group's most successful album, *Heavy Weather* (1977). From that album, Josef Zawinul's composition "Birdland," named for the famous New York nightclub where he had once heard Count Basie's band, became a fusion classic, and was covered by Maynard Ferguson's big band and the vocal group Manhattan Transfer. Despite the use of rock instrumental timbres, including Pastorius' bass guitar solos in the recording, its smooth, danceable rhythm showed the inspiration of Basie.

One of the more rock-oriented of the fusion bands was formed as the Dixie Grits by southern-rock guitarist **Steve Morse** and bassist Andy West while the two were in high school. Attending college was not important to Morse until he heard a performance by classical guitarist Juan Mercadel. Mercadel demonstrated so much technical facility and control of his instrument that Morse decided to study with him at the University of Miami at Coral Gables, Florida, where Mercadel was on the faculty. The Dixie Grits remained together, but after the other members left, Morse joked that he and West were the "dregs" of the Grits, and they chose to name their next band **The Dixie Dregs.**

The University of Miami had a leading jazz program, with such fusion musicians as guitarist Pat Metheny and bass guitarist Jaco Pastorius teaching workshops. Having studied composition there in a curriculum that included both classical and jazz, and combining this with his rock experience, Morse wrote arrangements for the Dixie Dregs that had them playing a variety of musical styles, from Allman Brothers-style blues rock to fusion. In addition to a keyboardist, a bassist, and a drummer, their lineup included Allen Sloan, who played electric violin and doubled on other instruments, and Morse, who played guitar, guitar synthesizer, and banjo. Their all-instrumental debut album, *Free Fall* (1977), displayed a fusion style reminiscent of some work by Weather Report and the Mahavishnu Orchestra, with funk rhythms and a rock drumbeat, while also showing their southern roots in one cut that was a hoedown featuring Morse playing banjo. The band shortened its name to the Dregs in the early eighties and broke up shortly thereafter. Morse later formed a trio called the Steve Morse Band, in which he played organ and synthesizers in addition to fast, heavy-metal-style guitar.

Other Jazz Influences on Rock

Singer/songwriter **Joni Mitchell** added jazz stylings to her music when she recorded the *Miles of Aisles* album (1974) with the fusion band L.A. Express. The album included live versions of several of her earlier, folk-styled compositions like "You Turn Me On, I'm a Radio," "Big Yellow Taxi," "Woodstock," and "Both Sides Now," with Mitchell playing acoustic guitar, mountain dulcimer, and piano, and with the L.A. Express adding their full fusion band sound, including woodwind instruments, electric guitar, piano, bass, and drums. Mitchell continued to work with L.A. Express bassist Max Bennett, drummer John Guerin, and woodwind player Tom Scott on *Hejira* (1976), but without the full band sound; most of the songs on the album had no more than two musicians playing with her at any one time, often a bass player and a drummer or a bass player and a guitarist. Fusion guitarist Larry Carlton and Jaco Pastorius were also featured on the album.

Pastorius' virtuoso technique and vibrant personality stimulated Mitchell's interest in jazz experimentation, and the two collaborated often during the late seventies, Pastorius taking time out from his regular duties with Weather Report. He was particularly important on her *Mingus* album (1979), for which Mitchell put lyrics to some of the last music written by legendary jazz bassist Charles Mingus. Mingus had Lou Gehrig's disease and died before the album was completed; it became a tribute to him upon his release. Pastorius played bass on and arranged the horn section for "The Dry Cleaner from Des Moines" on the *Mingus* album. Other important fusion musicians on the recording included John McLaughlin, Wayne Shorter, and Herbie Hancock. A listening guide is on page 144.

The vocal techniques used by Joni Mitchell in this recording have a long and respected history in jazz. Louis Armstrong first recorded **scat** vocals on "Heebie Jeebies" in 1926. He and other singers such as Ella Fitzgerald, Eddie Jefferson, and Jon Hendricks sang scat solos that were as complex as many of the solos by bebop instrumentalists. At times, Jefferson and Hendricks took the lines of famous instrumental solos and put texts to them, creating the same type of effect used by Mitchell. Mitchell's jazz-styled albums were not commercially successful, and she returned to a more pop-oriented style for subsequent recordings.

Pastorius continued to record and tour with Weather Report until he formed his own group, Word of Mouth, in 1982. One of the most technically proficient and musically sensitive bassists in either jazz or rock, he unfortunately also became known for his insobriety and violent behavior. In 1987, he died from head wounds after being beaten by a club manager who would not allow him to enter an establishment from which he had been banned.

Listening Guide

"The Dry Cleaner from Des Moines" as recorded by Joni Mitchell (1979)

Tempo: The tempo is approximately 184 beats per minute, with four beats in each bar.

Form: After a short, out of tempo instrumental build up, the recording consists of fourteen choruses of a twelve-bar blues followed by a six-bar coda. The fourth, eighth, ninth, tenth, eleventh, and thirteenth bars are instrumental or mostly instrumental.

Features: Uneven beat subdivisions are maintained throughout the recording.

A subtle backbeat is accented by the drums and tambourine.

Vocal choruses do not repeat a single melody, but rather sound as if Mitchell's voice were singing lines that an instrumentalist would improvise.

Mitchell uses scat vocals in the sixth chorus.

Vocals are double/multiple tracked in the twelfth chorus.

A horn section is featured in the fourth and fourteenth choruses, and individual instruments take turns soloing in those and other choruses (guitar in the fourth, and alto saxophone in the ninth, tenth, and eleventh).

Lyrics: The song is about luck as it applies to gambling. It is sung from the perspective of a gambler who loses everything while watching a dry cleaner from Des Moines win.

Source: *Mingus,* Asylum 505.

Pianist Donald Fagen met guitarist/bassist Walter Becker while they were students together at Bard College in Annandale-on-Hudson, New York. Both jazz lovers, they experimented with jazz, pop, and rock styles in various bands they organized with friends while at college. Fagen, a self-proclaimed beatnik, had a penchant for the inventive types of chords and chord progressions used in jazz, some of which he incorporated into his own compositions. After doing some writing for other performers, Fagen and Becker decided to form their own band, **Steely Dan,** to have more control over their compositions.

Steely Dan started out as a foursome, and later grew to six members, but by 1974 all the regulars except Fagen and Becker had left the group, partly because of their leaders' reluctance to tour. Fagen and Becker disliked life on the road, and basically, had lost interest in merely recreating their recorded performances for concert audiences. As songwriters they were perfectly happy to be rid of the pressures of touring, and for recording they enjoyed the new freedom to use whatever musicians they wanted for any given session. Guitarist Jeff "Skunk" Baxter and singer/keyboardist Michael McDonald, for example, were brought in for the *Pretzel Logic* album (1974); they later joined the Doobie Brothers.

Some influences of jazz could be heard in Steely Dan's earliest albums, which included compositions ranging from pop rock to country rock to amalgams of several styles, but jazz inflections became more important as time went on.

Two tracks on *Pretzel Logic* served as tributes to jazz greats. Alto saxophonist Charlie Parker was the inspiration for "Parker's Band." And Fagen and Becker did more than simply pay tribute to Duke Ellington and his jazz orchestra in "East St. Louis Toodle-oo"; they covered Ellington's own 1927 recording very closely, copying the notes and phrasing of the original, though at the same time updating the sound by using electric guitar (with effects) and pedal-steel guitar as solo instruments where Ellington had used muted trumpet and saxophone.

Fagen and Becker continued to call on well-established jazz and fusion musicians for their later albums, some of whom included alto saxophonist Phil Woods (for "Doctor Wu" on 1975's *Katy Lied*), tenor saxophonist John Klemmer (for "The Caves of Altamira" on *The Royal Scam* in 1976), and tenor saxophonist Wayne Shorter (for the title cut on *Aja* in 1977). In 1978, jazz bandleader Woody Herman paid Fagen and Becker a tribute when he asked them to supervise recordings his own Thundering Herd big band was going to make of several Steely Dan compositions. Herman, a reed player, singer, and bandleader since the thirties, had become interested in jazz-rock styles and had added a number of jazz-rock arrangements to his band's repertoire. Becker and Fagen spent most of the eighties apart, each pursuing solo careers. Then in 1993 they regrouped an eleven-member version of Steely Dan to play their hits on a very successful U.S. tour. They continued to tour in the later nineties.

In 1985, British songwriter/musician Gordon Sumner (born in 1951), better known as **Sting** (because of a black-and-yellow shirt he wore early in his career), left his new-wave band, the Police, to start a solo career. He used jazz and fusion musicians on his first album, *The Dream of the Blue Turtles* (1985), giving him a new reputation in jazz, although Sting's own guitar playing and vocals were more reminiscent of the reggae-influenced rock for which the Police were known. The musicians in Sting's new band included jazz saxophonist Branford

Joni Mitchell
UPI/Bettmann

Marsalis, Weather Report drummer Omar Hakim, ex-Miles Davis bassist Darryl Jones, and jazz keyboardist Kenny Kirkland. Marsalis was the older brother of Wynton Marsalis, the trumpeter famed for winning Grammy awards in both jazz and classical music. Unlike his classically trained brother, Branford Marsalis concentrated exclusively on jazz, which he studied as a serious art form. His solos on Sting's *The Dream of the Blue Turtles* became the album's closest links to jazz. Overall the album achieved an effective blending of rock, reggae, and jazz in what was basically a pop style.

Branford Marsalis and Kenny Kirkland returned for the recording of Sting's second jazz-influenced album, *Nothing Like the Sun* (1987). Veteran jazz arranger and pianist Gil Evans joined Sting to work on several arrangements for the album, including the Jimi Hendrix composition "Little Wing." As a jazz arranger, Evans had worked with Miles Davis on several albums, including *Birth of the Cool* in 1949, and had also recorded many jazz albums of his own. Evans' arrangements and Marsalis' solos were the only true jazz stylings on the album, which Sting never claimed to be more than a pop-rock album enriched by jazz. The use of jazz phrasing and jazz harmonies produced a richness and expressiveness rare in rock. In interviews, Sting claimed to have learned much from working with Gil Evans, but unfortunately, any possibility of subsequent jazz-related collaborations ended when Evans died in 1988.

Jazz, rock, and a large dose of rhythm and blues combined in an all-new way in the music of Boston's **Morphine.** Formed in 1992, Morphine had an unusual instrumentation in that it lacked guitar, keyboards, or any middle or high register melodic instruments. In a few instances tenor saxophone, guitar, or piano were used to enhance individual album cuts, but those instruments were not part of the band's standard lineup. Singer/bass player Mark Sandman played a two-string electric slide bass and sang in a voice imitative of the low pitches and dark timbres of his instrument. Dana Colley usually played the baritone saxophone, at times double tracked with tenor. Morphine's original drummer, Jerome Deupree left the group after recording their first album, *Good* (1992), and was replaced by drummer Billy Conway. The band's third album, *Yes* (1995), was considered by many to be their best to date.

Other innovative combinations of rock and jazz appeared during the nineties. British keyboard player/producer Mel Simpson and sampler/programmer Geoff Wilkinson assembled a group of jazz musicians, samples from classic jazz records collected from the Blue Note records catalog, and rap vocals to create the jazz/rock/rap sound of Us3.

Summary

Of the many ways jazz has influenced rock music, only those styles specifically called jazz rock and fusion were discussed in any detail in this chapter. Blues, blues revival, soul, and funk-rock styles also used jazz instruments played with jazz phrasing and style. The jazz rock of the late sixties was, for the most part, brought about simply by combining jazz band horn sections with a rock band instrumentation of electric guitar, electric keyboards, electric bass guitar, and drums.

When Miles Davis' groups added rock elements to their jazz styles (in some cases avant-garde jazz), they united jazz's harmonic richness with the driving power of rock instrumentation and amplification. The result was not pure jazz and not pure rock, but fusion. Davis' late sixties album *Bitches Brew* included several musicians who went on to form their own fusion bands. Depending on the backgrounds and inclinations of the musicians in the group, some of these fusion groups attracted a large rock following while others appealed primarily to jazz audiences.

The jazz influences on such rock musicians as Joni Mitchell, Donald Fagen and Walter Becker, Sting, and others were primarily demonstrated in their decision to use jazz musicians for their backup bands and for their recordings. The result was not jazz, but then it was not intended to be jazz. It was rock with the sensitivity and harmonic complexity of jazz, and a style that gained the attention of many appreciative fans who did not care about labels or categories, but who simply wanted to listen to expressive and interesting music.

Terms to Remember

Chord extensions
Closed form
Crescendo
Dorian mode
Mode
Motive
Non-chordal tones
Scat
Sixteenth notes

CHAPTER 14

Singer/ Songwriters

The seventies was an era that expected personal statements from many of its singers. Many causes addressed by sixties folk and folk-rock singers had lost much of their earlier relevance by the seventies. American involvement in Vietnam was lessening after a cease-fire agreement was signed in 1970, and by that time the Civil Rights Movement had made some progress toward the equality African Americans and other minorities had struggled to attain. The murder at the Rolling Stones' concert at Altamont, California (1969), and the drug-related deaths of Jimi Hendrix (1970), Janis Joplin (1970), and Jim Morrison (1971) took much of the glamour away from the psychedelic movement. While rock music of the seventies was not all soft and mellow (hard rock and heavy metal styles developed through the decade), many people preferred intimate songs simply accompanied by acoustic guitar, piano, or a small backup group.

Before discussing individual singer/songwriters and their songs it is necessary to define exactly who fits into this category. As the chapter title indicates, the subject is people who sing songs that they have written themselves. They may also choose to write for other performers, but it is their singing of their own songs under their own names (rather than that of a specific band) that is of importance in this style. Elton John, for example, might be considered a singer/songwriter except that he has not written his own lyrics. His commercially successful songs have all been co-written with lyricists such as Bernie Taupin and a few others. He did write wonderfully memorable melodies for those songs and he is a great performer, but the personal communication between the writer singing directly to the listener is not present in such situations. Singer/songwriters have been very popular for decades, and of the many great ones in the history of rock music, only a few can be represented here. Some others will be covered in chapters that specifically discuss the singers' styles of music or that place them in a newer category such as "alternative rock."

James Taylor (born in 1948) was a singer from Boston, Massachusetts, who, like so many others, moved to New York to play in folk coffeehouses. He went to London, where he worked with producer Peter Asher, a singer from the British duo Peter and Gordon. After one unsuccessful album there, Asher and Taylor both moved to Los Angeles, where Asher produced Taylor's introspective *Sweet Baby James* album (1970). Many of the songs on the album were written by Taylor while he was institutionalized to recover from heroin addiction. "Fire and Rain" described Taylor's feelings about lost relationships and served as an example of his sensitive, almost confessional style.

Taylor was married to singer/songwriter **Carly Simon** (born in 1945) from 1972 to 1981. Simon had grown up in a musical environment; her father, who co-owned the Simon and Schuster Publishing Company in

Van Morrison
Michael Ochs Archives/Venice, CA

New York, was a classical pianist, and her older sister, Joanne, was an opera singer. Carly Simon played both the piano and the guitar, and recorded some songs with piano accompaniment and others with guitar accompaniment. The expression of personal feelings and experiences was an important part of her singer/songwriter style, and her song "You're So Vain" (1971) was her attack on a conceited star she had dated. Mick Jagger sang backup vocals on the recording. After Simon married James Taylor the two continued to concentrate on their own solo careers, though they made occasional recordings together, such as "Mockingbird" (1974) and "Devoted to You" (1978). Simon did not often perform in concert because of her stage fright. However, she did sing a duet with Taylor at the *No Nukes* benefit concert in 1979. On her *Torch* album in 1981, Simon attempted a new—or rather, old—style by singing pop standards by Hoagy Carmichael, Rodgers and Hart, and others, accompanied by a lush studio orchestra. Later in the eighties Simon had a number of successes with songs she wrote and sang for movie soundtracks, including "Coming Around Again" from *Heartburn* (1987) and "Let the River Run" from *Working Girl* (1989). She also branched out into writing children's books and has said that she might write a novel.

A singer/songwriter whose music was enhanced by jazz as well as folk and rock music was **Van Morrison** (George Ivan Morrison, born in 1945). As a teenager in Belfast, Northern Ireland, Morrison learned to play the guitar, harmonica, and saxophone. He played with a rhythm and blues band during the early sixties and its influences could be heard in his work with his rock band, **Them.** Them's most successful American singles were "Here Comes the Night" and "Mystic Eyes" (both 1965), although they are also remembered for their song "Gloria," which was an American success when covered in 1966 by a Chicago garage band called the Shadows of Knight.

Morrison left Them in 1966 and moved to Boston to begin a solo career as a singer/songwriter. His song themes often dealt with relationships and events the listener would assume to be taken from Morrison's own life experiences. "Brown Eyed Girl" (1967), for example, was a song to a girl who left him alone and lonely. Through the song he sings about the good times of their relationship in an effort to convince her to return to him. In some of his recordings Morrison strummed an acoustic guitar in a folk style, and for other recordings, such as "Moondance" (1970), he hired jazz musicians to accompany him. Rhythm and blues and a jazz horn

Listening Guide

"Domino"
as recorded by Van Morrison (1970)

Tempo: The tempo is approximately 132 beats per minute, with four beats in each bar.

Form: The recording begins with a four-bar introduction played by the guitar, with drums entering on the third bar. The first vocal section is sixteen bars long with four four-bar phrases, and is followed by a twenty-bar refrain with vocals that include the song title, "Domino." A riff-based eight-bar instrumental interlude is next, with four bars of a horn riff and then four bars of the rhythm section featuring bass on the riff. Another sixteen-bar vocal section and twenty-bar refrain is followed by a ten-bar extension and then a coda using the riff from the interlude played earlier.

Features: Uneven beat subdivisions are used throughout the recording.

There is a subtle stress on the backbeat through most of the recording.

Lyrics: The lyrics are obscure and may be interpreted a number of ways, one of which is that the singer would rather die than allow his actions or feelings to be analyzed by anyone else.

Source: Time-Life Music, *Sounds of the Seventies—1970; His Band & Street Choir,* Warner Brothers 1884; and *Best of Van Morrison,* Mercury 841970.

section were used on "Domino" (1970), Morrison's highest charting single release. A listening guide to that recording is on page 148.

Morrison's greatest commercial successes came in the early seventies, and although he suffered from stage fright, he continued to record and perform long after his commercial success had waned. He ventured back to traditional blues and recorded with John Lee Hooker and Charlie Musselwhite on their album *Never Get Out of These Blues Alive* (1972). After returning to Ireland in the mid-seventies, he took a break from recording and went back to America, this time to California, and added some of Ray Charles' soul sound to his music. In later years he also recorded Celtic folk music from his homeland with the traditional Irish band the Chieftains. Morrison and John Lee Hooker recorded and performed together again in the early nineties, as can be heard on the live album *A Night in San Francisco* (1994).

A singer/songwriter from a more strictly folk background, **Joni Mitchell** (Roberta Joan Anderson, born in 1943) performed with her husband, folksinger Chuck Mitchell, before divorcing him and establishing her own solo career. Raised in Saskatoon, Canada, she developed a distinctive rural-folk vocal style in which she changed her tone quality at different pitch levels. She learned to play the piano, which was helpful to her as a songwriter, but usually accompanied herself with folk-style acoustic guitar or mountain dulcimer. Some of her songs, including "Both Sides Now" (Judy Collins in 1968) and "Woodstock" (Crosby, Stills, Nash and Young in 1970 and Matthews' Southern Comfort in 1971), became hits for others. In addition to being a successful songwriter and performer, Mitchell was an artist, and many of her own albums, as well as those recorded by friends, featured her paintings on the covers.

Mitchell's debut album was released in 1967, but it sold slowly. It was a difficult time to begin a career as a folksinger because so many folk protest singers already had well-established careers. The seventies were ready for Mitchell's personal style, however, and "Big Yellow Taxi" (1970) gave her the start she needed. Through that song, Mitchell expressed ideas many listeners could relate to. In general, she sang about the human tendency to recognize the value of the things and people around them only after they are no longer there. The song included examples from nature and the ways in which urban development removed it from people's lives, and the loss of her husband, who drove away in a "big yellow taxi." Mitchell's feelings about her divorce and ex-husband resurfaced in other songs, including "The Last Time I Saw Richard" (1971). Trying a more commercial style on her next album, *Court and Spark* (1974), provided Mitchell with the biggest hit single of her career, "Help Me," for which a listening guide follows.

Mitchell followed that success with some experimental use of unusual (for rock or American folk music) instruments. For example, on *The Hissing of Summer Lawns* (1975), she used stick-beaten drums from Burundi, Africa. She had worked with a jazz group, the L.A Express, for some concerts and recordings in 1974, and went back to a jazz-influenced style for a live album with jazz bass virtuoso Jaco Pastorius and guitarist Pat Metheny in 1976. Mitchell returned to a pop style in her work in the eighties.

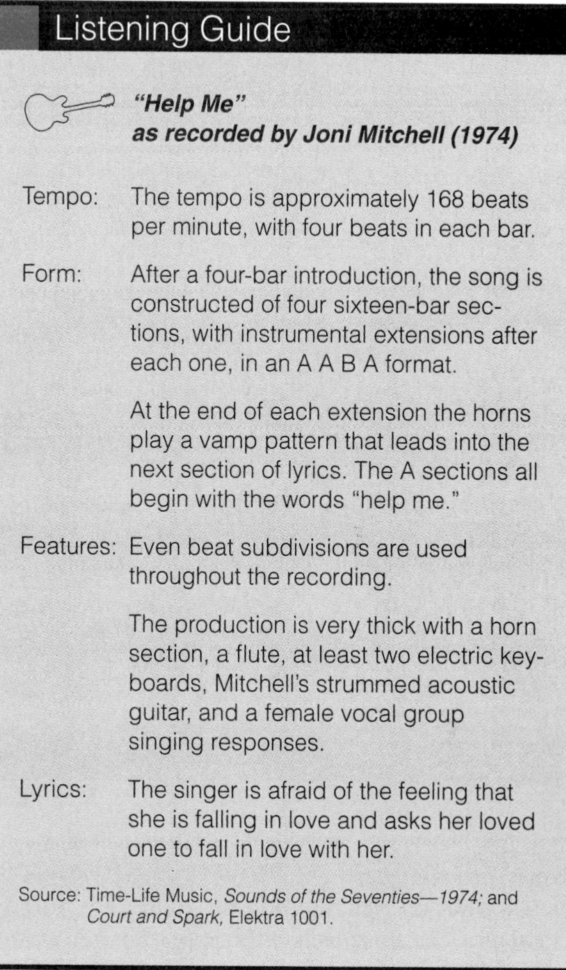
Listening Guide

"Help Me"
as recorded by Joni Mitchell (1974)

Tempo: The tempo is approximately 168 beats per minute, with four beats in each bar.

Form: After a four-bar introduction, the song is constructed of four sixteen-bar sections, with instrumental extensions after each one, in an A A B A format.

At the end of each extension the horns play a vamp pattern that leads into the next section of lyrics. The A sections all begin with the words "help me."

Features: Even beat subdivisions are used throughout the recording.

The production is very thick with a horn section, a flute, at least two electric keyboards, Mitchell's strummed acoustic guitar, and a female vocal group singing responses.

Lyrics: The singer is afraid of the feeling that she is falling in love and asks her loved one to fall in love with her.

Source: Time-Life Music, *Sounds of the Seventies—1974;* and *Court and Spark*, Elektra 1001.

■ Mitchell's recordings with jazz musicians are discussed further in Chapter 13, Jazz Rock and Fusion.

Mitchell performed on stage very few times during the eighties and nineties, but continued to write and record. Her songs on such albums as *Dog Eat Dog* (1985) concentrated less on her personal life and relationships and more on social and political issues. She also continued her work as an artist, and her paintings and photographs have been displayed in galleries around the world.

Another important singer/songwriter of the seventies was the former Brill Building writer **Carole King** (Carole Klein, born in 1942), who divorced her writing partner/husband, Gerry Goffin, and moved to Los Angeles in the mid-sixties. She finished the decade working and recording with various musicians from both Los Angeles and New York, and writing songs for others as well as herself. Blood, Sweat and Tears recorded her song "Hi-De-Ho." She gave "You've Got a Friend" to

Billy Joel
Michael Ochs Archives/Venice, CA

James Taylor to record and also put it on her own album, *Tapestry* (1971). *Tapestry* not only earned King a Grammy award for Album of the Year, but it sold so well over such a long period of time that it charted in the top forty for sixty-eight weeks, making it one of the best-selling albums of all time.

Jazz-rock fusion began to creep into her pop-oriented style with the *Wrap Around Joy* album (1974) and its single, "Jazzman." She began in the eighties by returning to her sixties writing style and recording *Pearls: Songs of Goffin and King* (1980). For that album she recorded a new version of "One Fine Day," which she and Goffin had written for the Chiffons in 1963. King continued to write and record in the nineties while also branching out into acting. She starred in Willy Russell's musical *Blood Brothers* on Broadway in 1994.

Jackson Browne was born in Heidelberg, West Germany, in 1948, but spent his youth in southern California just outside Los Angeles. Though primarily a keyboardist, he played the guitar with the Nitty Gritty Dirt Band when they were first formed as the Illegitimate Jug Band (1966). After he left them, he moved to New York and played his folk-style songs in the coffeehouses where so many folk singers started their careers. Browne's songs were recorded by other performers before he moved back to California and recorded his own first hit, "Doctor My Eyes" (1972). On the strength of that hit single and its album, *Jackson Browne,* he toured with other folk-rock and country-rock performers, including Joni Mitchell and the Eagles. His following grew and his albums sold reasonably well through the next five years, but he most effectively captured the hearts of singer/songwriter fans with his emotionally charged "Here Come Those Tears Again" (1977), written at a time when he was trying to accept his wife's suicide.

Browne's semi-autobiographical hit "Running on Empty" (1978) was the title cut from an album recorded during a tour. To capture every aspect of life on the road, some cuts were recorded backstage and in hotel rooms. Paralleling Bob Dylan's antiwar stands of the early sixties, Browne organized and performed at many rallies opposing nuclear weapons and nuclear energy. He exchanged his acoustic guitar for synthesizers on his 1986 album *Lives in the Balance,* but Browne's folk-rooted use of music to express political and social concerns was still at the forefront of his creative efforts. The album included songs that voiced concerns about the danger posed by nuclear weapons and American involvement in foreign countries, particularly Nicaragua. Introspective themes relating to problems in Browne's personal life reemerged in songs on his 1993 album *I'm Alive,* which was released soon after his breakup with actress Daryl Hannah.

Billy Joel (born in 1949) was a singer/songwriter of the seventies whose career extended into the eighties and nineties. He played keyboards in various rock bands in the late sixties in New York, including the Echoes, the Hassles, and Attila, before establishing a solo career. Personal statements about the singer's own life experiences and those of people close to them are central to the

Listening Guide

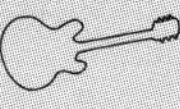

"We Didn't Start the Fire" as recorded by Billy Joel (1989)

Tempo: The tempo is approximately 148 beats per minute, with four beats in each bar.

Form: The form is based on eight-bar sections with a few short instrumental interludes and one vocal extension. The sixteen-bar instrumental introduction is based on the melody and rhythm pattern of the B section played twice through. Conga drums are used from the beginning, but the set drums and the strong backbeat enter at bar nine of the introduction.

After the introduction, the form can be diagrammed as follows: A, interlude, A B A A B C, interlude, A B A with extension, B A A B with extension, B B B B. The first interlude is four bars of instrumental similar to the introduction. The second interlude is two bars of electronic sounds and conga drums. The first extension adds four more bars to the A section. The second extension adds electronic sounds.

The B section is made up of one four-bar phrase that is repeated. It functions as a refrain.

The C section is based on the A section, but on a different chord and at a different vocal pitch.

Features: Even beat subdivisions are maintained throughout the recording.

A very strong backbeat is kept by the drums.

The performance opens with electronic effects and audience noise.

The instrumental background is very thick and includes electronic effects.

The vocals are more spoken than sung and often stay on one pitch for an entire phrase.

A vocal group sings the B sections.

An instrumental stop time is used to emphasize the vocal in the fifth B section.

Loudness level and intensity builds during the last few B sections, then it drops in the final B.

The recording ends with a fade-out.

Lyrics: The lyrics to the A sections consist of names of famous people, songs, movies, places, and other things, all of which are connected with memories of world events that happened during Billy Joel's lifetime (since 1949). The B sections begin with the words "we didn't start the fire," reminding the listener that we are all born into a world that we cannot control.

Source: *Storm Front,* Columbia 44366.

singer/songwriter style. So although his writing and performance style was very pop-oriented at times, Joel also stepped outside that mold to make more serious statements in songs like "Goodnight Saigon," about a war veteran, and "Allentown," about the problems of unemployment. Billy Joel flitted through memories of events that influenced his generation in his hit recording of "We Didn't Start the Fire" (1989). A listening guide to that recording can be found above.

Four years after the release of *Storm Front* Joel released another enormously successful album, *River of Dreams* (1993). *River of Dreams* included songs that covered a variety of musical styles from fifties-oriented doo-wop to sixties-styled pop and his own ever-popular style of ballad writing. The album cover featured a painting by Joel's wife, model Christie Brinkley. Brinkley and Joel shocked many fans who had thought them to be one of the happiest couples in the entertainment business when they divorced in 1994.

Bruce Springsteen's (born in 1949) music developed out of youthful experimentation with almost every rock style imaginable, from the rockabilly and rhythm and blues styles of Elvis Presley and Chuck Berry to Dylanesque folk rock, from the wall of sound pop style of Phil Spector to the raunchy proto-punk sound of garage bands. Out of these styles he fashioned an energetic, tradition-based rock and roll style that, especially through its song texts, spoke to the American working class on its own level.

Having worked solo and in groups for years, and having achieved some local popularity in his native New Jersey, Springsteen was signed to Columbia Records in 1972 by John Hammond, Sr., who had discovered Bob Dylan a decade earlier. His first album, *Greetings from Asbury Park, N.J.* (1973), included folk-rock-style

Bruce Springsteen playing "Born in the U.S.A." to a sellout crowd in Washington, D.C. in 1985
UPI/Bettmann

Listening Guide

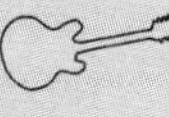

"Born in the U.S.A." as recorded by Bruce Springsteen (1984)

Tempo: The tempo is approximately 122 beats per minute, with four beats in each bar.

Form: The entire recording is based on almost hypnotic repetition of a two-bar riff. The eight-bar instrumental introduction and the phrases of lyrics are organized around eight-bar sections, each section being comprised of four statements of the riff. The sections that repeat the title lyrics and slight variations of them give them the impression of being refrains, but they are lyric refrains that are not based on contrasting music.

Features: Uneven beat subdivisions are maintained through most of the recording.

The constantly repeating riff and a very strong backbeat in the drums are the most outstanding features of the instrumental portion of the recording.

Springsteen's powerful vocals support the sense of anger in the lyrics.

Lyrics: The song is sung from the point of view of a Vietnam veteran who returned to the U.S. after having lost his brother in the war and was turned down for a job, given no assistance from the Veterans Admission Office, and ended up in prison.

Source: *Born in the U.S.A.*, Columbia 38653.

productions comparable to those of singer/songwriters like James Taylor. The album received favorable reviews from critics but sold poorly. His next effort, *The Wild, the Innocent, and the E Street Shuffle,* released later the same year, was more rock-oriented and featured many of the musicians who would make up Springsteen's E Street Band. It was at this time that Springsteen began to attract attention for his dramatic stage performances and emerged as a headline act. In 1975, the group found the national spotlight with the critically acclaimed album *Born to Run,* recorded using Spector-influenced wall of sound production, and followed it up with a national tour. Shortly thereafter, Springsteen appeared on the covers of *Time* and *Newsweek,* and the magazine stories depicted him as the new rock phenomenon.

Lawsuits between Springsteen and his manager kept Springsteen from recording for two years, but he continued to tour and to write new material. Some of his songs were saved for his gloomy 1978 album *Darkness on the Edge of Town,* and others were given to other artists to record first. His song "Fire" was recorded by Robert Gordon in 1978 and a year later by the Pointer Sisters. Springsteen collaborated with New York-based punk rock singer/poet Patti Smith on "Because the Night."

Springsteen experimented with a more commercial sound for the double album *The River* (1980), which contained the hit single "Hungry Heart." The album's title track served as a particularly good example of Springsteen's compassion for the underprivileged. In the song, Springsteen uses the river to represent a young man's passion for life and love. Early in the song he and his girlfriend dive into the river, but once family responsibilities and difficulties finding enough work overtake them, the young man goes back to find that the river is dry. Some of that feeling of hopelessness carried over to the lyrics of many of the songs on the album *Born in the U.S.A.* (1984), but the driving beat of the music gave it a more commercial appeal. Through the album's title song, Springsteen attacked the lack of support, both from the government and in the job market, given to veterans of the Vietnam War. Many people did not bother to listen to the song to find out what Springsteen was really saying and made grandiose statements about its being a great patriotic statement. A listening guide to that recording is on this page.

Springsteen separated himself from his hard-rocking E Street Band in 1989 and released two albums, *Human Touch* and *Lucky Town* (1992), both of which contained songs about changes in his personal life, namely the breakup of one marriage and the raising of a family with his second wife, singer Patti Scialfa. Springsteen won an Academy Award and four Grammys for the song "Streets of Philadelphia" that was featured on the soundtrack of the movie *Philadelphia* (1994).

Throughout his career, Springsteen's music ranged from tender, personal statements in a folk style to hard-driving rock and roll. His work supported many of the causes expressed in his songs, including efforts to raise money for Vietnam veterans and to support union workers on strike. His concerts swept his fans through over three hours of music, through songs that reflected the concerns of much of the American middle class. Springsteen's level of performance energy brings him as close as anyone to a real competition with James Brown for the title of the Hardest Working Man in Show Business.

Through the works of Bruce Springsteen and others, the soft singer/songwriter style of the seventies gradually changed from an acoustic folk style into an amplified sound with a strong rock beat in the eighties. That style was well displayed by **John Cougar Mellencamp** (born in 1951). In the early days of his career Mellencamp had allowed producers to control his sound and image; his first manager dropped his real name, billed him as Johnny Cougar, and marketed him as the tough teen from the great Midwest (he was from Indiana).

Tracy Chapman in 1991
Corbis/Bettmann

Listening Guide

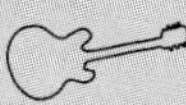

"Give Me One Reason" as recorded by Tracy Chapman (1995)

Tempo: The tempo is approximately 94 beats per minute, with four beats in each bar.

Form: Both the music and the text follow the classic twelve-bar blues form. Each chorus begins with three eighth-note pickups. There are nine choruses, the first and sixth of which are instrumental.

Features: Uneven beat subdivisions are used throughout the recording.

A backbeat is maintained by the drums and a tambourine through most of the recording.

The first chorus is played by solo amplified acoustic guitar. The solo vocals enter for the second chorus; lead guitar, bass, and drums are added for the third; and backup vocals are added for the fourth and eighth choruses. The sixth chorus is instrumental featuring a guitar solo.

Lyrics: The singer is going to leave unless the person to whom the song is directed will convince her to stay. It is strongly hinted that a declaration of love is what she would like to hear.

Source: *New Beginnings,* Elektra 61850.

Eventually Mellencamp, who was more interested in expressing honesty than fitting a preset image, switched producers and began to use his real name along with the stage name.

The album *Nothing Matters and What If It Did* (1980) was produced using synthesizers and many overdubbed tracks. Mellencamp decided that he was tired of synthesizers and recordings that were difficult to recreate on stage, and vowed to do away with such techniques in the future. The producer of Mellencamp's next album, *American Fool* (1982), wanted to overdub a horn section like that used in many of the Memphis soul recordings of the sixties, but Mellencamp refused. Mellencamp had cut his band to the basic two guitars, bass, and drums instrumentation, and wanted the album to be recorded only by that band, with no overdubbing. After a lot of resistance, he got his way, and the result was the hit single "Hurt So Good," with its return to the basic simplicity of rock music. Mellencamp showed a new maturity on *The Lonesome Jubilee* (1987), an album that expressed concerns about such universal themes as the awareness of the shortness of life and the need to care about others. His next album, *Big Daddy* (1989), also dealt with universal issues, particularly those relating to his personal life, including the breakup of his marriage. That sober mood was broken, at least to a degree, in his 1991 album, *Whenever We Wanted.* He also made his first attempt at acting and directing in a movie, *Falling From Grace,* in the same year.

Mellencamp has often said that his songs all start out as folk songs—it is when he decides what instruments to use on the production of each album that his style becomes varied. By the time he released the album *Dance Naked* (1994), he had remarried and he and his wife had a baby boy. The old-time rock and roll energy of that album reflected Mellencamp's attitude about his life at that time. Despite the title of *Mr. Happy Go Lucky* (1996), the carefully produced album revealed a more serious John Mellencamp who had recently been confronted by his own mortality after having a heart attack and being told he had the potential for continuing heart problems.

In 1988, the rock audience was introduced to a new singer/songwriter, **Tracy Chapman** (born in 1964). With a strong, deep, almost velvety voice, she sang with the personal commitment and compassion of many of the singer/songwriters of the seventies while also matching the communicative strength of the social protesters of the sixties. Her acoustic guitar accompaniment gave her recordings some of the flavor of folk music, but the addition of a thick background to such sensitive love songs as "Baby Can I Hold You" placed her sound unmistakably in the eighties. While representing a strong, self-sufficient modern woman, Chapman also sang about the hardships of America's poor. In her hit single "Fast Car," for example, she sang of a young girl who dreams of escaping from the drudgery of life with her parents and who ends up telling her partner, who has treated her badly, to use the "fast car" to leave her so she can take care of herself.

Chapman's next two albums did not match the commercial success of her debut, and some critics began to describe her career as a "flash in the pan." Their remarks were made too soon, however, as she revived her career with *New Beginning* in 1995. A listening guide to the hit single "Give Me One Reason" from that album can be found on page 154. "Give Me One Reason" was the only blues on *New Beginning.* In fact, it was not a new song, but one that Chapman had written back in 1986. The other songs on the album dated from 1994 and expressed a variety of thoughtful and introspective themes about Chapman's life and her concerns about problems in the world. Optimism, the beauty of nature, and faith in humanity were central themes of several of the songs. Chapman's voice, song themes, and acoustic guitar maintained a clear connection with folk traditions, while the background production sound updated the music to what might be called nineties folk rock.

Summary

Singer/songwriters of the seventies tended less toward political issues and more toward the expression of personal thoughts and interests than had most folk-rock singers of the sixties. The messages they communicated were sometimes quite individual and introspective and at other times more universal. Whatever the message, the singers effectively reflected the sentiments of large numbers of people, and the style remained popular into the nineties. The style of the music played by singer/songwriters was as diverse as the song themes. Some put away their acoustic guitars and used synthesizers, while others rejected the sound of modern electronic instruments. The communication of thoughts and ideas between the musician and the listener has always been part of folk music, and this was stressed by the singer/songwriters who came from the folk tradition.

CHAPTER 15

Funk and Disco

Funk

Funk was a very distinctive style that used polyrhythms, syncopated bass lines, and short vocal phrases with a considerable amount of repetition of those rhythm patterns and phrases. Funk vocals were often sung in a work-song style with a conversational delivery. The first examples of funk were recorded by the Godfather of Soul himself, James Brown. As was discussed in Chapter 7, Brown's soul style was deeply rooted in black gospel music. His funk style, however, was influenced by polyrhythmic music straight from Africa.

Brown's backup musicians maintained a constant rhythmic accompaniment using polyrhythms among the bass, drums, and horn section while still having a clear accent on the downbeat. Horns were used to punctuate the rhythm but not to play melodic lines. Both the bass and guitar parts involved either repeated riffs or rhythmic pulsations. Chord changes were generally minimal. The recording that introduced this style, "Out of Sight" (1964), was followed by a more successful recording in a similar style, "Papa's Got a Brand New Bag" (1965), for which a listening guide follows on page 157.

Although the blues chord progression was used in "Papa's Got a Brand New Bag," other recordings in Brown's new "proto-funk" style maintained a single chord for long sections of the music, drawing attention to the rhythms instead of the chords or melody. As an example of the types of polyrhythms used in Brown's recordings, the following notation shows how the four-way polyrhythms were used in "Papa's Got a Brand New Bag." Only the rhythms are notated—not the pitches for the horns and bass.

This new style of James Brown's had such an appealing, hypnotic sound that it was copied by other groups. One of these groups was **Sly and the Family Stone. Sly Stone** (Sylvester Stewart, born in 1944) and his brother, Freddie Stewart, grew up singing gospel music in their San Francisco church. Sylvester took classes in music theory at Vallejo Junior College and learned to play a number of instruments, in addition to working as a singer and songwriter. He produced a number of recordings by San Francisco bands, including the Beau Brummels, the Mojo Men, the Vejtables, and the Great Society (with Grace Slick, who later sang for Jefferson Airplane).

The Stewart brothers started a group called the Stoners in 1966, but it lasted only a year. They added more musicians and formed Sly and the Family Stone. The

Listening Guide

"Papa's Got a Brand New Bag" as recorded by James Brown (1965)

Tempo: The tempo of the beat is about 126 beats per minute, with four beats per bar.

Form: The twelve-bar blues form is followed throughout, with an introduction and six full choruses.

Features: The basic beat subdivision is even, but Brown's vocals sometimes relax into uneven subdivisions.

The backbeat is accented by the guitar.

Even sixteenth-note subdivisions strummed on the guitar add energy at the end of each chorus (except the last).

Polyrhythms are created among the horns, the bass, and the drums. Each maintains its own rhythmic pattern that is simple and repetitious but different from that of the other instruments.

Lyrics: The lyrics tell us that Papa's "bag" is dancing.

Source: Time-Life Music, *Classic Rock, 1965: Shakin' All Over;* and *Papa's Got a Brand New Bag,* Polygram 847-982.

word "family" referred both to the fact that Sly had his siblings in the group and to the group's inclusion of black and white members. The interracial, family-of-human-beings image made an important statement in support of the Civil Rights Movement that was under way at the time. The group also included female members playing instruments, such as trumpeter Cynthia Robinson and pianist Rose "Stone" Stewart, at a time when women instrumentalists were not common in rock groups. By the time they recorded "Dance to the Music" in 1968, the group had taken James Brown's polyrhythmic vamps using minimal chord changes, added electronic fuzztone, and imitated Motown's stress on all four beats, avoiding the strong backbeat common in most styles of rock music.

Bigotry was a concern to Sly Stone, and the group's song "Everyday People" (1969) made fun of hangups about skin color as well as other forms of bigotry. Other songs, like "Don't Call Me Nigger Whitey" (1969), made an even stronger statement about the same subject. "Everyday People" was more rock-styled than the group's other recordings, with a heavy backbeat, gospel-style call-and-response vocals, and the even beat subdivisions common in early Motown recordings.

The recording by Sly and the Family Stone that had the greatest influence on the development of funk music was "Thank You (Falettinme Be Mice Elf Agin)" (1970). The recording was reminiscent of the Memphis soul sound of Booker T. and the MGs, updated with fuzztone guitar and polyrhythms set over minimal chord changes. A listening guide can be found on page 158.

The polyrhythmic funk style of Sly Stone influenced other funk musicians who followed him, and his

Sly and the Family Stone (left to right): Rose Stone, Larry Graham, Sly Stone, Freddie Stone, Gregg Errico, Jerry Martini, and Cynthia Robinson

Michael Ochs Archives/Venice, CA

Listening Guide

"Thank You (Falettinme Be Mice Elf Agin)" as recorded by Sly and the Family Stone (1970)

Tempo: The tempo is approximately 108 beats per minute, with four beats in each bar.

Form: The form is comprised primarily of eight-bar sections, most of which have new lyrics on each repetition; other sections serve as a refrain by repeating the title of the song.

An eight-bar instrumental introduction is followed by two eight-bar sections, the eight-bar refrain, and then a four-bar instrumental section. The major part of the song has two more eight-bar sections with new lyrics and the refrain, one more new eight-bar section, and then four repetitions of the refrain with a fade-out on the last one.

Features: Each instrument repeats its own rhythmic patterns, but polyrhythms are created between the separate patterns of the electric guitar, bass, and drums as is notated below (only the rhythms are notated—not the pitches):

The beats are subdivided evenly throughout the recording.

Lyrics: The lyrics refer to street fights and violence, and efforts on the part of the singer to avoid those problems and "be himself" through family unity and music.

Source: Time-Life Music, *Sounds of the Seventies—1970;* and *Sly & the Family Stone—Greatest Hits,* Epic 30325.

use of bizarre spelling as seen in the song title "Thank You (Falettinme Be Mice Elf Agin)" was also used by other funk musicians as a play on jive talk.

Plagued by rumors of drug problems and a growing reputation for missed performances, Sly Stone recorded the album *There's a Riot Goin' On* (1971), which spoke of his disillusionment with the world around him. Despite castigation by critics and by much of the group's white audience, the album was a commercial success. Stone's problems continued and later successes were followed by periods of depression and drug abuse. He toured with George Clinton's P-Funk All-Stars and with Bobby Womack during the early eighties and occasionally worked as a studio musician in later years, but nothing he did could match the importance of his early work. Whatever the future holds, Stone deserves to be remembered for his effective antiracism statements and his influence on the development of funk.

During the seventies, a funk style called **street funk** developed. Street funk was generally dominated by strong bass guitar lines, harmonies filled in by guitars and/or keyboards, complex rhythms played by a variety of drums (including Latin bongo and conga drums), a **flat-four beat** (all four beats accented evenly), and often included a party atmosphere complete with whistles, tambourines, and conversational vocals. Kool and the Gang, the Ohio Players, and George Clinton and his groups Parliament and Funkadelic were popular street funk groups.

Kool and the Gang began their career in 1964 as a jazz group influenced by Thelonious Monk, Miles Davis, and John Coltrane, using the name the Jazziacs. They commercialized their sound and renamed themselves the Soul Town Review for a short time, before their leader, Robert Bell, gave himself the nickname "Kool" and renamed the group in 1968. Their style of street funk was very lighthearted and danceable. A listening guide to their recording of "Funky Stuff" (1973) follows on page 159.

Funk style, as represented by "Funky Stuff," had changed greatly in the eight years since James Brown recorded "Papa's Got a Brand New Bag," because the form had become loose and constantly changing, whereas Brown's recordings had been rather traditional, often using the twelve-bar blues. The polyrhythmic texture created by the overlapping instrumental parts playing different repeating patterns, however, was still very much based on Brown's mid-sixties style. Kool and the Gang left much of their street funk style behind to play disco-influenced dance music during the late seventies, and in the next decade they concentrated on a smoother ballad style. They were still placing hits on the rhythm and blues charts in the late eighties, but had less success in the nineties.

Funk has been an African American style of music from its very beginnings, but its appeal spread beyond American soil to Scotland where the **Average White Band** (a.k.a. **AWB**) formed in 1972. The use of the word "average" in the group's name was intended as a joke, and the truth was that they were anything but average. They were introduced to a rock audience in 1973 when they opened for Eric Clapton at London's Rainbow Theatre. The all-star band that backed Clapton in that concert included the Who's Pete Townshend, Traffic's Steve Winwood, former member of the Jeff Beck Group and later the Rolling Stones, Ron Wood, and other performers.

The Average White Band's music was based on a steady flow of even beat subdivisions and stress on the

Listening Guide

"Funky Stuff"
as recorded by Kool and the Gang (1973)

Tempo: The tempo is about 104 beats per minute, with four beats in each bar.

Form: There is no formal structure that can be described in terms of repeated sections of music. The form changes as the recording progresses and yet enough elements are repeated that the work has the feeling of continuity usually defined by form. The classical term for this approach is the **through-composed form.**

Features: The entire recording is based on a single chord (G7) and changing variants on that chord, including a flatted fifth (D♭), the removal of the seventh (F), and a sharped ninth (A♯ or, **enharmonically,** B♭).

The guitar occasionally colors the single-chord feel by playing notes in the chord on which the recording is based, and then slipping down to **neighboring tones** and back to the basic chord.

The recording begins with a police whistle, and that sound recurs as if it were one of the regular instruments in the group.

The jazz background of the musicians is evident in the musical lines and the phrasing of the horn section.

The horns usually play in **unison** or octaves, but in some places they play in **fourths.**

Infectious polyrhythms keep the recording in constant motion. The rhythms played by each instrument or instrumental section change as the recording progresses. Some instruments play single-bar patterns, while others play patterns of two or more bars, creating a very complex texture that is constantly in development.

Lyrics: The melody and the lyrics are repetitious and function to create a "party-like" atmosphere; they are of the same importance to the texture as the instruments are.

Source: *Kool & the Gang Spin Their Top Hits,* De-Lite Records 822536.

backbeat in the drums countered by syncopated bass lines, as was the funk style of James Brown and others. Their saxophone section, however, played repeating melodic patterns that used less rhythmic punch than did the horn sections in many other funk bands. The result was a very solid and danceable beat with an interesting polyrhythmic background that was as much disco in style as it was funk. Their most successful album was their second one, *AWB* (1974), which won a Grammy for the single "Pick Up the Pieces." They lost their drummer, Robbie McIntosh, to a heroin overdose in 1974. Later recordings did not match the popularity of the *AWB* album and members spent most of the eighties recording with other groups. Most of the original members were back performing together in the middle nineties.

Another funk group that created a style with great commercial appeal was **Earth Wind & Fire.** They formed in Chicago in 1969, but recorded their most successful albums in the middle seventies. Earth Wind & Fire varied their funk style by sometimes adding Latin rhythms, but it was their gentle group vocal sound that set them apart from other bands. At times their group vocal sound was much like that of Motown's Temptations or Four Tops, and, like those groups, different soloists would share lead lines. The singers in Earth Wind & Fire, however, often sang at a higher pitch level than most other groups. The high pitches were sung using a gentle tone quality, giving them an almost ethereal effect. Their soundtrack for the movie *That's the Way of the World* (1975) won them a Grammy for the single "Shining Star." Despite several personnel changes, the group was still together and recording in the nineties.

The Ohio Players developed out of a rhythm and blues group called the Ohio Untouchables that formed in Dayton, Ohio, in 1959. They switched to a funk style in the early seventies and placed hits on the pop as well as the rhythm and blues charts in the middle of the decade. Two of their biggest hits were "Fire" (1974) and "Love Rollercoaster" (1975). By the late seventies their sound had lost some of its energy and their sales slowed. They changed from one record company to another during the eighties and were no longer together in the nineties.

Singer, songwriter, and producer **George Clinton** (born in 1941) formed **Parliament** (originally the Parliaments) as a vocal group styled after Motown's Temptations. Clinton had moved to Detroit and was hired by Motown as a staff writer, but none of his groups recorded for Motown. It is quite possible that he was not asked to perform at Motown because Clinton's bizarre stage persona was too much for Berry Gordy's tightly controlled production company. Clinton and Parliament were signed by the Westbound Record Company, and recorded using Jimi Hendrix-like distorted guitar lines and the funky polyrhythms of Sly and the Family Stone,

George Clinton
Michael Ochs Archives/Venice, CA

along with the conversational vocals the Temptations had used in "Cloud Nine." Clinton created science-fiction characters and stage sets for Parliament that sometimes made reference to social conditions.

In 1968, Clinton formed a new group he called **Funkadelic.** Both Parliament and Funkadelic had flexible membership, and some musicians were common to both, but he had them record on separate labels and maintain their separate identities in performances. In contrast with Parliament's science-fiction characters and stories, Funkadelic's music was built around images and sounds from horror movies. Clinton later combined both groups' members and images and called them the Mothership Connection, Parliafunkadelicment Thang or P-Funk All-Stars. Clinton himself had several colorful names including Dr. Funkenstein, Maggot Overload, and Uncle Jam.

Clinton worked with such constantly changing groups of musicians that his style varied quite a bit over the years. One change that became an important influence on later funk music was the replacement of electric bass guitar with synthesized bass lines. That sound was introduced on Parliament's hit recording "Flash Light" (1978). A listening guide to that recording follows on page 161.

Clinton took a break from performing from 1983 through 1989, but portions of his music became popular with new, young listeners when used as backup samples by rap vocalists. He produced the album *Freaky Styley* (1985) for the Red Hot Chili Peppers. Merging his own style with one he had influenced, his 1989 album, *The Cinderella Theory,* included vocals by Public Enemy's Chuck D and Flavor Flav. With the tremendous popularity of rap during the nineties, Clinton has been featured as an old master of funk in recordings and videos by many rappers. He performed on the *Lollapalooza* tour of 1994.

Disco

The term "disco" was first used in post-World War II France when clubs began playing recorded dance music rather than using live bands. During the sixties such clubs were called discothèques. Disco music of the seventies began with the soul styles of Detroit (Motown Records) and Philadelphia (Philadelphia International Records) that became popular in homosexual and African American clubs in New York before the dance craze spread to the rest of the country. The musicians and singers of disco

Listening Guide

***"Flash Light"* as recorded by Parliament (1978)**

Tempo: The tempo is approximately 108 beats per minute, with four beats in each bar.

Form: After a four-bar introduction with pick-ups, the recording is based upon a continuous repetition of four-bar sections, some of which are paired with vocal phrases.

Features: Even beat subdivisions are used by most of the instruments, but the vocals often follow uneven subdivisions.

The backbeat is stressed through hand claps.

The rhythm played by the drums at the very beginning of the recording is imitated in the initial bass riff.

The bass lines are played by a synthesizer.

Polyrhythms are created between the separate patterns of the synthesized guitar, bass, and drums.

The recording includes long, extended repetitions of the four-bar sections that include dubbing of prerecorded fragments of music, rhythmically random lines played on a synthesizer, and vocal interpolations all held together with the rhythmic playing of the drum beat, hand claps, and bass line.

Lyrics: The vocals are repetitious, casual, and conversational. One singer expresses the need to sleep, but various lights beckon her to keep dancing instead.

Source: *Classic Funk, Volume One,* React Entertainment Corp. 50003.

music did concertize, as have most other rock musicians, but the essence of disco lay in the clubs themselves, where the dancers were the performers.

Because the music was intended to be played from records by disc jockeys, many disco records had "bpm" (beats per minute) indications on the labels so that recordings could be chosen to easily **segue** from one to another without changing the speed of the beat. Many disco records began with a rhythmically free introduction to allow the tempo to change from that of the previous record played and to give dancers time to get out on the dance floor. Other recordings such as Donna Summer's "Love to Love You Baby" (1975) were longer than singles normally were, again, to allow dancers a continuous flow of music.

Musically, disco was somewhat related to seventies street funk in that each beat was strongly accented, although not always at an even dynamic level. Many disco recordings also featured group backup vocals that created a party-like atmosphere or used whistles and other sounds to invite listeners to join into the festivities and dance. In fact, Kool and the Gang followed their street funk recording of "Funky Stuff" with disco hits such as "Ladies' Night" (1979).

One of the earliest important disco singers, songwriters, arrangers, and producers was **Barry White** (born in 1944), whose disco records were made with a forty-member orchestra he called the Love Unlimited Orchestra. White was born in Texas, where he sang and played the organ for his church. In Los Angeles as a teenager, White became a singer and pianist with a rhythm and blues group. He spent time working as an A&R (artist and repertory) man at a record company before 20th Century records contracted him as a singer. After the top ten success of his single "I'm Gonna Love You Just a Little More Baby" (1973) he formed his Love Unlimited Orchestra and made one hit disco record after another through the seventies. As the popularity of disco waned in the eighties, White had fewer records making the pop charts, but he did continue to record. His deep, lush voice made it back onto the pop charts in 1994 with the album *The Icon Is Love* and its hit single "Practice What You Preach."

The movie *Saturday Night Fever* (1977) helped spread the popularity of disco dancing to a massive mainstream audience. **The Bee Gees** had already had considerable success on the American pop charts with such hits as "I've Gotta Get a Message to You" (1968) and many others, but with the popularity of *Saturday Night Fever* and its hit soundtrack album they had three number one hits, "How Deep Is Your Love," "Stayin' Alive," and "Night Fever," and enjoyed continuing success after that. Other top forty hits from the *Saturday Night Fever* soundtrack were the Trammps' "Disco Inferno" and Tavares' "More Than a Woman." Kool and the Gang, and KC and the Sunshine Band, also contributed to the movie soundtrack.

Donna Summer (Donna Gaines Summer, born in 1948) was generally considered to be the Queen of Disco. Her disco hit "Love to Love You Baby" (1975) provided a full seventeen minutes of dreamy music for dancing. After a series of Grammy awards and disco hits that included "Last Dance" from the soundtrack for the movie *Thank God It's Friday* (1978), "Hot Stuff," and "Bad Girls" (both number one hits in 1979), she continued to place records in the top forty and was still recording in the early nineties. Another important female disco star was Gloria Gaynor (born in 1949), whose biggest hit was "I Will Survive" (1979). "King of

Chic (from left): Luci Martin, Nile Rodgers, Bernard Edwards, Alfa Anderson, and Tony Thompson (hidden from view)

Pop" Michael Jackson's singing style was far broader than disco, but his *Off the Wall* (1979) album added dance tracks such as "Don't Stop 'Til You Get Enough" to the disco repertoire. The Village People capitalized on stereotypical homosexual images and themes with their disco hits "Y.M.C.A." (1978) and "In the Navy" (1979).

One of the most successful and influential of the disco groups of the late seventies and early eighties was **Chic.** Formed by bassist/writer/producer Bernard Edwards and guitarist/writer/producer Nile Rodgers in New York, Chic also included two female singers and a drummer. Beginning with "Dance, Dance, Dance (Yowsah, Yowsah, Yowsah)" in 1977, their top ten hits also included "Le Freak (Freak Out)" (1978), "I Want Your Love" (1979), and "Good Times" (1979). Their style was characterized by the pounding beat found in most disco, interesting and very active bass lines, and Cuban-influenced rhythms. The following is a listening guide to their most influential recording, "Good Times":

Listening Guide

"Good Times"
as recorded by Chic (1979)

Tempo: The tempo is approximately 108 beats per minute, with four beats in each bar.

Form: The recording is based on the constant repetition of a four-bar pattern, with the lyrics often pairing with that repeated pattern to make up eight-bar phrases.

Features: Even beat subdivisions are used throughout the recording.

Each beat is solidly accented by the bass.

Drums and hand claps accent the backbeat.

The harmonies avoid any sense of cadence at a tonic chord, creating a feeling that the music could play on forever.

A synthesized string section is used to play fills at the ends of vocal lines.

The bass plays a riff pattern that uses a Cuban-influenced rhythm.

Lyrics: The lyrics are sung by a group that is dancing and wants to continue to dance even though the hour is getting late.

Source: Time-Life Music, *Sounds of the Seventies—1979;* and *1975 Only Dance 1979,* Warner Special Products JCD-3148.

Later records that bore the influence of Chic's "Good Times" included the Sugar Hill Gang's "Rapper's Delight" (1980) and Queen's "Another One Bites the Dust" (1980). Chic broke up in 1983, but both Edwards and Rodgers continued to be successful as producers. Bernard Edwards produced Robert Palmer's album *Riptide* (1985), which included the hit single "Addicted to Love." Nile Rodgers produced *Let's Dance* (1983) for David Bowie, *Like a Virgin* (1984) for Madonna, and *She's the Boss* (1984) for Mick Jagger. The pair reformed Chic in 1992, but the group has not been able to recapture their past success.

Disco's steady, pounding beat was an important influence on music during the eighties and nineties, particularly on American new-wave bands such as Blondie. It was also an influence on the synthesized dance music called techno, which was still popular in the early nineties. Much of the music sampled or imitated to provide background for early rap recordings also came from funk and disco recordings. The widespread use of video screens throughout former disco clubs has made the visual images of performers more important than they were in the disco era. Whether disco dancing returns to the popularity it experienced in the late seventies or not, disco music continues to make its mark on the popular culture of the nineties.

Summary

James Brown created an early funk style in 1964, when he put conversational vocals over a repetitious, polyrhythmic accompaniment. Just four years later Sly Stone further developed funk by adding a distorted guitar sound and an even four-beat pattern to Brown's basic formula. Other writers and performers, such as George Clinton, created elaborate science-fiction characters and bizarre stage shows, and made funk into a party music. Called street funk, recordings by such groups as Kool and the Gang featured party sounds, whistles, and conversational vocals.

Disco was party music with an emphasis on dancing. The steady, throbbing beat of disco music was intended for one thing and one thing only: to encourage every listener to get up and dance. Both funk and disco have continued to be important influences on later music styles including techno and rap.

Terms to Remember

Enharmonic
Flat-four beat
Fourths
Neighboring tones
Segue
Street funk
Through-composed form
Unison

CHAPTER 16

Art Rock

The growth of interest in theme albums and the establishment of FM radio stations that played longer works influenced some musicians in the late sixties to expand rock music in more artistic directions. Several new rock styles grew out of the music by these artistic rockers, most of whom were British, and the name given to this group of styles was art rock (the term "progressive rock" might be used, except that much jazz rock is also progressive rock). The simplest form of art rock used instruments normally associated with symphony orchestras, such as violins, violas, and cellos, or wind instruments such as the flute, in addition to the usual rock instrumentation; this was an extension of what had been done earlier by producers Phil Spector and George Martin. A more complex style was created by musicians who wrote multi-movement works, such as those common in classical music, in addition to recording their own versions of classical works themselves. A third, even more experimental art-rock style was based on ideas from the works of modern composers of **avant-garde** and electronic music.

Art Rock Combining Rock and Classical Instrumentation

The Moody Blues were formed in 1964 by musicians who had previously played in blues and rhythm and blues bands in Birmingham, England. They did write original songs, but their most popular early recording, "Go Now!" (1965), was a cover of a ballad by American rhythm and blues singer Bessie Banks. By the end of 1967, the Moody Blues had changed some of their personnel and had also modified their sound by incorporating a classical **orchestra,** the London Festival Orchestra conducted by Peter Knight, into their rock arrangements. "Nights in White Satin" (1967, rereleased in America in 1972) was among their most popular recordings made with the orchestra. The listening guide on page 165 is intended to point out musical complexities in the **meter** and form of the piece, as well as the ways orchestral instruments have been combined with the rock guitar, bass, and drums.

It was very difficult to work with a large orchestra on a regular basis. Rehearsals had to be organized well in advance, and touring with so many musicians was prohibitively expensive. In order to keep the orchestral sound, the Moody Blues found that they could use an electronic instrument, the mellotron, to imitate the orchestra. The mellotron supplied them with a variety of electronic effects, such as the wavering of tone on the word "strange" in the recording "Isn't Life Strange?" (1972), in addition to various orchestral timbres. The Moody Blues did from time to time work with orchestral musicians, but they never again added any of those instrumentalists to their regular personnel.

Some form of the Moody Blues has continued on into the nineties. The group took a few breaks in order for

Listening Guide

"Nights in White Satin" as recorded by the Moody Blues (1967)

Tempo: The basic tempo is 52 beats per minute, with four beats in each bar and each beat subdivided into three equal parts. Technically, the time signature is twelve-eight ($\frac{12}{8}$) and is notated with each of the four slow beats (at 52 per minute) made up of three **eighth notes,** putting twelve of those eighth notes into each bar.

Form: A solo singer sings a four-bar melody (the A section) two times through. The melody is based on an **aeolian mode** (natural notes from A to A), accompanied by the orchestra backing the rock instruments.

The orchestra grows louder for a four-bar B section.

Another two A sections and one B section with a one-bar extension are followed by a twelve-bar instrumental section that features flute, plucked acoustic guitar, and strings with a rock drummer accenting the backbeat.

The instrumental interlude is followed by two more A sections and one B section with an extension.

The recording continues with a dramatic orchestral statement based on the A and B themes (melodies).

Features: The recording begins with a swirl of sound played by the strings, flute, harp, and chimes before the drums enter to establish a beat pattern for a two-bar introduction.

The drums maintain a fairly strong backbeat through most of the recording, but drop out for the orchestral finale.

The recording concludes with the recitation of a poem that conveys the same mood as the rest of the lyrics. (The poem is not included in some shortened versions of the recording.)

Lyrics: The lyrics express a feeling of alienation from people other than the loved one to whom the song is addressed.

Source: *Days of Future Passed,* Threshold 820006; and *This Is the Moody Blues,* Threshold 820007.

members to concentrate on solo projects, and they also had several membership changes. The group that recorded the hit single "Your Wildest Dreams" (1986) and the 1993 PBS special *A Night at Red Rocks with the Colorado Symphony Orchestra* included flutist/singer Ray Thomas, guitarist/singer Justin Hayward, bassist John Lodge, and drummer Graeme Edge—all of whom were also on the recording of "Nights in White Satin" in 1967.

The mellotron was soon used by many groups wanting to add orchestral effects to their rock sound. Among those was **Genesis,** formed in 1966 by singer/flutist Peter Gabriel, keyboard player Tony Banks, bassist/guitarist Mike Rutherford, and guitarist Anthony Phillips. They went through three drummers until Phil Collins joined late in 1970. Phillips left in 1970 and was replaced by Steve Hackett.

During the early seventies, Genesis created multimovement works with classical overtones for their albums. Elaborate stage acts were also becoming very popular by that time, and Genesis used their music to create a surrealistic, at times even grotesque, fantasy world which they portrayed on stage, with Gabriel as the central actor making many outrageous costume and character changes. David Bowie, Queen, Roxy Music, and other glitter performers were concentrating on theatrical stage performances around the same time and were also using classical instruments and musical forms. As far as the music was concerned, little separated some of the British glitter groups from the art-rock groups. It was the glorification and celebration of androgynous sexuality that was central to glitter, but not to art rock, that separated the two styles more than any specific musical characteristic.

Glitter rock will be discussed in Chapter 17, Glitter and Glam.

For one of Genesis' most dramatic productions, *The Lamb Lies Down on Broadway* (1974), Gabriel played Rael, a New York City street punk who goes through a process of self-discovery when he finds himself transported to a surrealistic netherworld. Although Genesis started out as a group of four equally productive writers, Gabriel wrote the majority of the lyrics for *The Lamb,* and his stage performances had become the focal point of the band for much of the audience. When Gabriel decided to leave Genesis in 1975, they were faced with more than the need for a singer. They emerged with a somewhat altered style and image when Phil Collins assumed the double role of lead vocalist and drummer. Collins had a singing voice that was strikingly similar to Peter Gabriel's, and he had a dramatic flair that enabled him to portray some of the characters Gabriel had, though he never attempted to play these roles quite as elaborately as Gabriel. On tours, Genesis added another drummer so Collins could concentrate on singing. The group gravitated toward a more commercial pop sound from the late seventies and into the eighties with several top ten hits, including the title track to their *Invisible Touch* (1986) album. More successes followed with their 1991 album, *We Can't Dance,* which was followed by live albums during the next two years.

After leaving Genesis, **Peter Gabriel** (born in 1950) recorded a series of albums, all entitled *Peter Gabriel,* followed by *So* in 1986, which strayed from his interest in science-fiction-styled futurism and classical timbres and instead incorporated musical internationalism through the addition of instruments and vocal sounds from Asia and Africa. Gabriel's inclusion of Senegalese singer Youssou N'Dour helped introduce N'Dour to Gabriel's fans, resulting in N'Dour's inclusion on the 1988 Amnesty International tour with Gabriel, Sting, Bruce Springsteen, and Tracy Chapman. Gabriel won a Grammy for Best New Age Performance for his music on the soundtrack for the movie *The Last Temptation of Christ* (1989). His personal life and broken love relationships were the subject of his 1992 album, *Us,* which he followed with the live double album *Secret World Live* (1994).

Another rock group to perform with orchestral instruments was **Procol Harum.** They formed in 1966 and gained international success with "A Whiter Shade of Pale." For their studio albums, group members who normally played piano, organ, guitar, bass guitar, and drums added to the studio orchestra by overdubbing such instruments as celeste, marimba, recorder, conga drums, tabla, tambourine. The group's singer/pianist, Gary Brooker, did most of their orchestral arrangements. After recording five albums with studio orchestras the group decided that orchestral musicians played their best in live situations, and to capture the brilliance of live performance they recorded *Procol Harum Live: In Concert with the Edmonton Symphony Orchestra* (1971). This project was a success because "Conquistador," which had been ignored when released in 1967, became an international hit when revamped and recorded on the live album. Procol Harum changed membership often, but Brooker, organist Matthew Fisher, guitarist Robin Trower, and lyricist Keith Reid lasted through most of their time together. They disbanded in 1977 and reformed in 1991.

A blues revival band from Blackpool, England, in the late sixties, the John Evan Band included singer/flutist/guitarist/saxophonist **Ian Anderson** (born in 1947 in Scotland, but raised in Blackpool). When the John Evan Band broke up, Anderson decided to form a group of his own, calling it **Jethro Tull** (after the author of an eighteenth-century book on agriculture). At first the group played more blues and jazz than anything resembling what was soon to be called art rock; in fact, one of their earliest successful concert performances took place at the British National Jazz and Blues Festival in 1968.

Although jazz continued to be an important part of Jethro Tull's style, their first connection with art rock appeared on the group's second album, *Stand Up* (1969), which featured Anderson's flute playing on their recording of the "Bourrée" from the Suite in E Minor for lute by German composer J. S. Bach (1685–1750). Anderson used a distinctive flute technique that included humming and/or fluttering his tongue while blowing into the flute. While his tone was far from being a traditional classical sound, it had an energetic drive that worked well for Jethro Tull's music. The idea of **flutter-tonguing** and singing into wind instruments had been used by avant-garde classical instrumentalists and composers who were searching for new sounds on traditional instruments. Jethro Tull's recording of the Bach "Bourrée" started out with the original two-part composition, varied rhythmically using uneven beat subdivisions. After the original music was played, the group played variations that exemplified the continuing influence of jazz and blues on their style. In addition to using the flute, which was heard more in classical and jazz music than in rock, many of Jethro Tull's recordings used a synthesizer to add orchestral timbres.

As a lyricist, Ian Anderson used his music to make statements about society and politics. The album *Aqualung* (1971), for example, though not sacrilegious in general terms, contained songs that were clearly critical of organized religion. In later years he spoke out against, among other things, nuclear power and drug abuse. After taking some time off from recording for a period in the mid-eighties to fish for salmon in Scotland, he regrouped Jethro Tull with a modernized approach to blues-styled rock, adding distorted guitar timbres on his album *Crest of a Knave* (1987), for which the band won a Grammy for Best Hard Rock/Metal Performance. Many of the group's long-faithful fans were happy that they won a Grammy, but questioned their inclusion in that particular category. Jethro Tull continued to record and tour in the nineties, but with less commercial success than they had known in the past.

One of the most popular of the British art-rock groups of the seventies was **The Electric Light Orchestra.** Much more of a "rock orchestra" than the Moody Blues had been, the group consisted of traditional rock instruments—electric guitars, bass, and drums—along with a scaled-down version of an orchestral string section. Guitarist/singer/writer Roy Wood and guitarist/keyboardist/writer/singer Jeff Lynne formed the Electric Light Orchestra in 1971. At that time they were still members of the Move, a rock band that had dabbled in many styles from folk to psychedelic rock, but they ended up concentrating more on an orchestral sound and the Move soon disbanded. For the first recording by their new orchestra, *Move Enterprises Ltd. Presents the Services of the Electric Light Orchestra* (1972, released in America as *No Answer*), they used the Move's drummer, Bev Bevan, and two temporary members, one playing several wind instruments, and the other, violin.

An inevitable split occurred between the two writers, Wood and Lynne, because each had different ideas about the musical direction of their new orchestral sound. Wood wanted the rock orchestra to be styled after Phil Spector's wall of sound productions of the early sixties, while Lynne wanted to work toward the more classically oriented productions the Beatles had made with George Martin. Wood finally left the Electric Light Orchestra to form another group, Wizzard, and Lynne gradually molded the Electric Light Orchestra to fit his own plans. His rock orchestra included Lynne on guitar, keyboards, and vocals; a keyboard player who often used synthesizer; a drummer, a violinist, two cellists, and a string bass player. The four members from the string section of an orchestra, a synthesizer to add wind or percussive effects, and heavily overdubbed vocals enabled them to create a thick orchestral and choral sound, played with a rock backbeat. The Electric Light Orchestra developed their stage show into an elaborate space-age extravaganza with a giant space ship and a laser display as part of the act.

Major changes had to be made in the Electric Light Orchestra after their violinist and two cellists left in 1978. Lynne's solution was to use a full orchestra with forty-two musicians and a large male choir for the *Discovery* album (1979). The use of a real orchestra did not result in a classical sound, however; the album ended up more disco- and pop-styled than classical. After working on record production for other performers as well as several movie soundtracks, Lynne, the old Beatle fan, was chosen by George Harrison to co-produce Harrison's 1987 comeback album, *Cloud Nine.* They also recorded together in the Traveling Wilburys. By the nineties Lynne stopped working with the Electric Light Orchestra to concentrate on production work. The new group, Electric Light Orchestra, Part II, has only one member from the original group, drummer Bev Bevan.

Art Rock by Classically Trained Performers

Groups that added orchestral instrumentation to what was basically a rock-band setup created an extremely popular form of art rock, but not one requiring a great deal of classical training on the part of the rock musician. Another style of art rock was played by musicians with more extensive classical backgrounds. These musicians composed original works in classical structures, but they also recorded their own versions of well-known classical pieces. This is not to say they were writing "classical" music. They were rock musicians playing for a rock audience, but adding a rock rhythm section to what was based on a classical work or their own work set in a classically influenced form.

Yes, one of the first and longest lasting of the art-rock supergroups, was formed in 1968 by singer/percussionist Jon Anderson, guitarist/singer Peter Banks, keyboardist Tony Kaye, bassist Chris Squire, and drummer Bill Bruford. The members of Yes were interested in creating classically structured music that included full-group vocal harmonies. The group's personnel changed during their career, including at various times guitarist Steve Howe, drummer Alan White, and keyboard players Rick Wakeman, Geoff Downes, and Patrick Moraz. Early in their career, Yes used the synthesizer to add new instrumental timbres and to fill out their sound without the use of an orchestra. However, eventually their music developed around the virtuosic technical skills of its instrumentalists instead of concentrating on synthesized orchestral sounds.

All of the members of Yes were competent soloists, and their album *Fragile* (1971), recorded when the group included Anderson, Howe, Wakeman, Squire, and Bruford, had each musician taking a turn as the featured performer on a track, with ensemble playing on other tracks. One of *Fragile*'s full-group tracks, "Roundabout," is discussed in the listening guide on page 168.

The high level of musicianship of each member of Yes is obvious in their recording of "Roundabout," both in the way the individual instruments are played and in the careful way they play as a group without getting in each other's way. The arrangement is quite complex and is played with the sensitivity one would expect of classical musicians.

Yes followed *Fragile* with other albums using the classical multi-movement form called a **suite.** In the eighteenth century, suites, such as the suite for lute whose theme Ian Anderson borrowed for Jethro Tull's recording of "Bourrée," were collections of instrumental pieces based on dance rhythms and forms. Dances themselves were not important to art-rock performers or to their general audience, and Yes freely used the title "suite" to identify classically influenced multi-movement compositions such as those on their *Close to the Edge* (1972) and *Relayer* (1974) albums.

Yes had essentially broken up by the early eighties, but was then reformed by Anderson, Kaye, Squire, White, and a new guitarist from Johannesburg, South Africa, Trevor Rabin. That version of Yes charted a number one hit single with "Owner of a Lonely Heart" (1983). Group members and former members argued over the ownership of the name *Yes,* under which various members recorded and toured. The eight members who had been fighting over the name finally reunited in a large version of the group for the recording of *Union* (1991) along with a very successful world tour. In 1993 Anderson, Bruford, and Howe recorded with the London Philharmonic Orchestra. The members who had recorded "Owner of a Lonely Heart" in 1983 regrouped to record *Talk* in 1994.

Another group with constantly changing membership, but no questions about who owned the name, was **King Crimson. Robert Fripp** (born in 1946), a guitarist with a background in both classical music and jazz, was the central and only constant figure in King

Listening Guide

"Roundabout"
as recorded by Yes (1971)

Tempo: The basic tempo is about 135 beats per minute with four beats in each bar, although each A section varies the beat pattern by including one two-beat bar.

Form and Features: The recording opens with a crescendo of sound probably produced by playing a tape-recorded sound backwards.

The taped sound dissolves into an acoustic guitar playing **harmonics** and a classically influenced melodic pattern in a free tempo.

At the end of this introduction, the guitar plays a progression establishing the tempo of the song, and a very active bass and the drums enter playing an eight-bar vamp. The vamp pattern continues under the beginning of the vocal line.

The first verse of lyrics is sung to the A section of music, which is ten four-beat bars long, but the regular beat pattern is broken by two-beat bars both at the beginning and at the ending of the verse.

The music to the A section is repeated to the lyrics of the second verse.

The B section follows the two A sections, and it also changes from two-beat to four-beat bars, giving a feeling of complex irregularity to the beat pattern.

The drums maintain a strong backbeat, which remains steady through each two- and four-beat pattern.

After another A and B section, an instrumental section features a bass riff, a synthesizer, and many percussion effects.

When the A theme and vocal line return, a synthesizer plays a repetitious pattern very similar to the minimalistic themes used by modern composer Philip Glass.

The synthesizer pattern continues behind the acoustic guitar, which returns to the theme played in the introduction.

A section of improvisation on the organ is backed by guitar and bass with the drums maintaining a strong backbeat.

The A and B sections repeat and are followed by group vocals, with one group of three singers overdubbed on top of another group of three singers.

The recording ends with a repetition of part of the guitar solo that was played at the beginning. Classical composers also often closed their works with a repetition of a musical idea from the beginning to balance the form.

Lyrics: The lyrics can be interpreted many different ways, but it is helpful to know that roundabouts are English traffic circles, where drivers can change their course of direction if they wish.

Source: Time-Life Music, *Sounds of the Seventies—1972 Take Two;* and *Fragile,* Atlantic 19132.

Crimson, which he formed in 1969. For King Crimson's music, Fripp melded together avant-garde electronics, jazz, and psychedelic effects.

In addition to his work with King Crimson, Fripp experimented with avant-garde electronic sound effects with British composer/producer Brian Eno during the early to middle seventies. They used two tape recorders to develop a sound-delay box that Fripp could use with his guitar, a sound system they called Frippertronics. Fripp had become increasingly interested in experimental electronic work, and disbanded King Crimson to have more time to spend on projects of that variety during the late seventies.

Fripp reformed King Crimson in 1981, this time with drummer Bill Bruford, formerly of Yes. Their new work drew on some of the musical variety and richness of their past work, as well as incorporating touches of African polyrhythms. One of Fripp's greatest concerns was to avoid the tendency of reverting to older styles and creating, in his words, a "dinosaur" sound. In hopes of maintaining a fresh approach, Fripp outlined rules for the group to follow, based on such ideas as the importance of each musician maintaining musical independence from other band members while still listening carefully and allowing the others' ideas to be heard. Fripp wanted freedom and spontaneity for each of the musicians while still keeping unity within the group sound.

Fripp formed a new version of King Crimson in 1994 with former members guitarist/singer Adrian Belew, bassist Tony Levin, and drummer Bill Bruford, along with new members drummer Pat Mastelotto and Trey Gunn, who played the Chapman stick, a twelve-string instrument that functions as both a bass and a guitar. Contracted by Virgin Records, they recorded *Thrak* in 1995.

Many British art-rock groups made recordings based on works from standard classical repertoire, but few recorded as many extended classically-based works as **Emerson, Lake and Palmer.** Keyboardist Keith Emerson had played with another British art-rock group, the Nice, between 1967 and 1970, during which time they arranged and recorded an "Intermezzo" from the *Karelia Suite* by Jean Sibelius (1893), and "America," a medley of themes from Leonard Bernstein's musical *West Side Story* (1957). Guitarist and bass player Greg Lake came to the group from King Crimson, and drummer Carl Palmer had previously played in a number of British rhythm and blues groups, including the Crazy World of Arthur Brown.

In addition to rearranging classical works, Emerson wrote his own compositions in the multi-movement format followed by classical composers. "The Three Fates," from the album *Emerson, Lake and Palmer* (1970), drew on mythological themes of ancient Greece. Each movement was named for one of the goddesses who the ancients believed had control of the spinning (Clotho), the measuring (Lachesis), and cutting (Atropos) of the threads of human lives. Another multi-section work was the album *Tarkus* (1971), the first side of which portrayed a world inhabited by partially mechanical animals engaging in battles for life.

For their world tour following the *Brain Salad Surgery* (1973) album, the trio amassed one of the most elaborate stage sets of the era. Their thirty-six tons of equipment included a quadraphonic sound system, and Carl Palmer's revolving percussion setup required an elevator platform to enable him to reach it all. The musical effects were highlighted with lights, lasers, and explosions. This sort of extravaganza was instrumental in sparking a renewed interest in the small, simple, intimate rock of the pub-rock revival later in the seventies. Interestingly enough, even though Emerson, Lake and Palmer were known for their long, elaborate works, their most popular recordings tended to be such intimate ballads by Greg Lake as "Lucky Man" (1971), "From the Beginning" (1972), and "C'est la Vie" (1977).

Emerson, Lake and Palmer broke up for a time and Carl Palmer became the percussionist for **Asia,** an art-rock group featuring guitarist Steve Howe and keyboard player Geoff Downes from Yes and singer/bassist John Wetton from King Crimson. Drummer Cozy Powell, formerly with the Jeff Beck Group and Rainbow, joined Emerson and Lake to form Emerson, Lake and Powell, but he gave the percussion position back to Palmer in 1987, and the original trio was back together after nearly eight years apart. In the early nineties Emerson, Lake and Palmer's very successful tour of Europe and both North and South America assured them that they still had faithful fans, but their new albums did not sell well. In 1994 they returned to the studio to record *In the Hot Seat.*

Art Rock Influenced by Avant-Garde Trends

While the Electric Light Orchestra and others went from live orchestras to mellotrons to enhance their sound, and Emerson, Lake and Palmer and others played elaborate arrangements of classical compositions, other rock musicians explored more avant-garde compositional styles. Two of the most important twentieth-century styles to influence rock music were **minimalism** and the organization of sound effects not traditionally used in music, both natural and electronic, into musical compositions. Minimalism is also called **systematic music,** and both terms describe the characteristics of the sounds they represent, as the music involves systematically organized repetition of a minimal amount of musical material. The musical material is most often one or more motives (short bits of melody) and the systematic organization usually involves some sort of variation, such as gradual changes in length, melody notes, or rhythms through many repetitions. This style became popular through the works of composers like Terry Riley, Steve Reich, and Philip Glass during the sixties, having originated in part through influences of music from parts of Asia and Africa.

Composer Edgard Varèse (1883–1965) pioneered another important avant-garde style by incorporating nonmusical sounds into musical compositions as early as the thirties. He created music he described as "organized sound," including such effects as hammered anvils, sleigh bells, and sirens, along with traditional percussion instruments such as bells and drums of various kinds, in his work *Ionisation* (1931). He later manipulated and organized natural and electronic sounds for his *Poème électronique,* composed for the Brussels World's Fair of 1958.

Among those rock groups who used both minimalism and nonmusical sounds effectively was **Pink Floyd.** A blues-loving art student who played the guitar and sang, Syd Barrett (Roger Keith Barrett) joined with friends from a London architectural school to form the Pink Floyd Sound in 1965. The name was a tribute to two blues musicians from the Carolinas, Pink Anderson and Floyd Council. The group's early repertoire of traditional blues and Rolling Stones-style rhythm and blues was expanded to include wandering, psychedelic improvisations and light shows as Barrett became increasingly involved with the use of psychedelic drugs. However, it was the shorter compositions "Arnold Layne" and "See Emily Play" that were their most popular early recordings.

The Pink Floyd Sound shortened their name to Pink Floyd and released their first album, *The Piper at the Gates of Dawn,* in 1967. The album included some of Barrett's most creative experiments in special effects, such as sounds that jumped from the left speaker to the right speaker in "Interstellar Overdrive." On the tour following the album, Barrett's desire to be completely original and, probably more important, his excessive use of LSD, were the source of many problems. He became

Pink Floyd (left to right): David Gilmour, Nick Mason, Roger Waters, and Richard Wright
Michael Ochs Archives/Venice, CA

undependable at concerts, and he refused to lip sync to songs for television appearances. When Pink Floyd returned to Britain they decided it was necessary to add another guitarist, David Gilmour, even before they had the nerve to fire Barrett. Barrett managed to stay with the group to contribute to "Jugband Blues" and "Remember a Day" on their *A Saucerful of Secrets* album (1968), but he soon drifted away, leaving the group to continue without him. Roger Waters and Richard Wright shared the bulk of the songwriting duties in Barrett's place.

Pink Floyd continued to include extended psychedelic improvisations with repeated electronic sound effects in their music, and they soon attracted the attention of British movie producers and classical composers who were interested in electronics. The spatial music on some of their albums was recorded for movie soundtracks. Electronics expert Ron Geesin worked with them on the recording of their experimental *Atom Heart Mother* album (1970) and, after the album's release, they became the first rock group to be invited to perform at the Montreux Classical Music Festival.

Many experimental classical composers had become interested in the idea of using randomly gathered material as the basis for a sound collage. The Beatles' producer, George Martin, had used the idea when he spliced together pieces of prerecorded tapes as sound effects on the Beatles' *Sgt. Pepper's Lonely Hearts Club Band* album (1967). For their *Meddle* album (1971), Pink Floyd decided to experiment further with the organization of new, but randomly produced sounds. "Echoes," which took up one entire side of the album, was made up of bits of material taped by band members who had gone into the recording studio individually and recorded whatever ideas came to them at the moment, without concern for any general scheme, key, chord progression, or other kind of unifying device. The segmentation and organization of the tapes came later when the pieces of tape were put together for the recording. Also from the *Meddle* album, "One of These Days" used Varèse's idea of including nontraditional sounds in a piece of music; it also included some of the repetitious, but slowly changing electronic patterns that were being used by minimalist composers.

Roger Waters (born in 1944), who had become the group's principal writer, wanted to create a theme album out of an idea he had used for the cycle of songs titled "Eclipse," which the band had performed in concert in 1972. The theme came from his own past and his feelings of alienation, depression, and even paranoia over the fact that he had grown up without a father (his father died when his plane was shot down during World War II). After many months of work on the song cycle, it grew into an album that was the longest-lasting success of Pink Floyd's career, *The Dark Side of the Moon* (1973). Beginning and ending with a heartbeat, the album cuts were joined by the insane muttering, screaming, and demonic laughter of the depressed protagonist.

"Money," a popular track from the album, included the nontraditional musical sounds of rhythmically organized ringing cash registers, but more interesting musically was its rhythmic organization using seven-beat bars. To a nonmusician, who most likely would not think to count the beats but would still be very used to the feel of the standard rock four-beat bar, the effect of seven-beat sections was slightly, inexplicably discomforting. The seven-beat pattern did break and revert to a standard four-beat pattern during the last part of the instrumental improvisation section, but the seven-beat pattern

Listening Guide

"Money"
as recorded by Pink Floyd (1973)

Tempo: The tempo is about 120 beats per minute, with seven (or four followed by three) beats in each bar through most of the recording, but in one part of the instrumental section there are four beats per bar.

Form: The form and chord progression are based on the twelve-bar blues in a minor key.

Two twelve-bar A verses are followed by a twelve-bar instrumental section that features a funk-style tenor saxophone solo along with keyboard, bass, and drums.

After the instrumental chorus featuring the saxophone, the beat pattern changes from seven to four per bar, and three twenty-four-bar instrumental sections feature the guitar as a solo instrument. The twenty-four bars continue to follow the blues progression, with each bar of the progression doubled in length.

The seven-beat pattern returns just before the singer returns to repeat the A section.

The four-beat-per-bar pattern returns at the end of the song.

Features: The recording begins with the sounds of old-fashioned cash registers ringing and their change drawers opening. Those sounds fall into the seven-beat pattern that is then picked up by the bass when it enters.

After the bass establishes its pattern, the drums enter, accenting the second, fourth, and sixth beats of the seven-beat pattern. The effect is quite different from a standard rock backbeat that accents beats two and four of a four-beat pattern, because the four-beat pattern allows for exactly every other beat to be accented as one pattern leads into another. With the seven beats in this recording, the accents are placed on every other beat until the final beat number seven (which is not accented) goes to beat one (which is also not accented), resulting in two unaccented beats in a row. Two bars of a standard rock four-beat pattern and two of the seven-beat pattern used in "Money" are notated as follows:

The bass line, which repeats a seven-beat pattern throughout most of the recording, changes to a four-beat pattern during the instrumental section that uses four-beat patterns.

The recording ends with casual conversation that continues into the next album cut.

Lyrics: The lyrics depict the self-centered, money-grubbing attitudes of people who want more than they need for themselves and do not care about anyone else.

Source: *The Dark Side of the Moon,* Capitol 46001; and *A Collection of Great Dance Songs,* Columbia 37680.

returned just before the voice reentered. Also important to the overall effect of the recording of "Money" was the constant repetition of a bass line with changing melodic lines above it. Above is a listening guide to the recording.

The Dark Side of the Moon was enormously successful, and planning a follow-up album was difficult. Pink Floyd reminisced about their early relationship with Syd Barrett, who had dropped out of their lives, and the *Wish You Were Here* album (1975) was a tribute to him. Their long-lost member actually appeared in the studio while the group was finishing the recording of the song "Shine on You Crazy Diamond," but he left as quietly as he had entered, unrecognized by his former colleagues. He had been hospitalized for LSD-related mental and emotional problems and was not able to care for himself or work effectively. Roger Waters had not gotten over his own depressed emotional state and used his songs to express his feelings about having lost his father in addition to having lost Barrett. An inflatable airplane that was made to crash in front of the stage during the tour for the albums *Wish You Were Here* and *The Dark Side of the Moon* served as a physical reminder of his father's death.

Waters portrayed human beings as animals when he wrote songs for the album *Animals* (1977). His view of humanity was reminiscent of George Orwell's in his book *Animal Farm* (1945). *Animals* included such songs as "Pigs (Three Different Ones)," "Sheep," and "Dogs." A gigantic inflated pink pig floated in the air above the band during concerts on the *Animals* tour and became a symbol that the group used again in later years.

It was two years before Pink Floyd produced another album, and when *The Wall* (1979) was released, it served as a very personal view into the psyche of Roger Waters. He was pessimistic about every aspect of life in modern society. He found no solace in his relationships with his mother and wife, and he viewed formal education as

Frank Zappa on stage in 1988
UPI/Bettmann

confining and as inhibiting freedom of thought. That view of education was clearly expressed in the song "Another Brick in the Wall (Part 2)," the music of which was repetitious and (as performed in the movie version) featured a large group of expressionless children singing along. In general, *The Wall* was about a young man who acted out his feelings of alienation by building a wall around himself, only to find that he was susceptible to decay from within and that no meaningful hope for the future existed. On stage, Pink Floyd had a wall constructed between them and their audience during the show. After the wall crashed into a smoky mess, band members wandered through the debris in childlike confusion. The wall set was too elaborate to carry throughout a normal tour and was only used in London, New York, and Los Angeles. A movie called *The Wall* was made in 1982 featuring Bob Geldof (lead singer for the Boomtown Rats) as the lost and unhappy protagonist. Many of the characters' illusions were portrayed through wildly psychedelic animated sequences.

The Final Cut (1983) was Pink Floyd's last album with Roger Waters. The album was dedicated to his father, and on it he explored the reasons for society's warlike tendencies. Waters separated himself from Pink Floyd as he delved into the theme of broken relationships for his first solo album, *The Pros and Cons of Hitchhiking* (1984), which he wrote after having just gone through a divorce. Again, his music fully expressed his depressed emotional state. The threat of nuclear war became the subject of a subsequent solo effort, *Radio K.A.O.S.* (1987). Waters revived his music from Pink Floyd's album *The Wall* at the Berlin Wall in Germany, replacing Pink Floyd with a large group of rock stars including Van Morrison, Joni Mitchell, Sinéad O'Connor, the Scorpions, and others. Guitarist Jeff Beck joined Waters for his next album, *Amused to Death* (1992), on which his depressed view of mankind returned.

Waters' separation from Pink Floyd created a legal war, because Waters felt he was the most essential person in the band and the other members had no business continuing to use the name Pink Floyd or the symbol of the floating pig in his absence. The group's album *A Momentary Lapse of Reason* (1987) was very successful, and Waters' old bandmates had become his unwanted competition. Pink Floyd continued on, seemingly not missing Waters at all. Their 1994 album *Division Bell* hit number one on the U.S. album charts and its instrumental cut, "Marooned," won a Grammy.

For the most part, art rock was a British phenomenon. Some American groups, such as the Tubes, performed a very theatrical version of art rock, but most of their albums were more appreciated by critics than by large numbers of fans. The one American whose work paralleled many of the avant-garde characteristics and experimentation of the British artists was **Frank Zappa** (1940–1993). Zappa played rhythm and blues and rock guitar, but became interested in contemporary experimental art music by the composers Edgard Varèse, Igor Stravinsky (1882–1971), and Karlheinz Stockhausen (born in 1928). Varèse was among the first composers to gain acceptance for musical works that included sounds played by nontraditional musical instruments. Stravinsky became known for his dynamic use of complex rhythmic patterns, and Stockhausen had gained much attention for his work with electronics and spatial effects in performance. Although Zappa's music was influenced by many rock and jazz styles as well, the rhythms and timbres of modern art composers often flavored his style.

Zappa gained a reputation for more than just the sound of his music, however; he became, for many, a spokesperson for freedom of expression in a world where people claimed to be free but blindly followed pop trends. Many of Zappa's views about the importance of individual freedom were similar to those of the Beats. With his band of constantly changing members, **The Mothers of Invention,** Zappa aimed attacks at American notions about "respectability" in such songs as "Plastic People" and "America Drinks and Goes Home." He followed that by taking a stab at the tastes of some of his own fans by mocking the Beatles with an album called *We're Only in It for the Money* (1967). Roles and attitudes he found to lack substance were among his targets for criticism, such as phony conformity among those involved in the hippie counterculture in San Francisco and the gutlessness of the punk movement in Hollywood.

Because Zappa often spoke out for freedom of expression, he opposed any form of censorship. His album *Joe's Garage, Acts 1, 2, and 3* (1979) was an effort to create a rock opera that expressed his hatred of censorship by describing a mythical time when music was declared to be illegal. In 1986, the album *Frank Zappa Meets the Mothers of Prevention* had a "Warning/Guarantee" label suggesting anyone who would curtail freedom of speech was dangerous to society. The label was an obvious dig at parents who had organized a group to require warnings on rock album covers to prevent their children's exposure to objectionable material.

The language Zappa used kept many of his recordings off the radio, but his albums continued to sell well. When he went further than his record company would allow, he formed his own recording company. Even with his own recording studio and record label, however, Zappa still depended on Mercury Records to distribute his albums to record stores. His arrangement with his distribution company was working well until he wrote and recorded the song "I Don't Wanna Get Drafted," which criticized President Carter's reinstatement of the military draft, and Mercury Records refused to distribute it. The only way Zappa could think of to get out from under the control of distribution companies was to bypass both the distributors and the record retailers and to accept mail orders directly from his fans. He did just that, calling his new mail-order company Barking Pumpkin. (Many of the Barking Pumpkin albums eventually became available in stores through CBS International.)

Zappa occasionally recorded albums based on older rock styles, particularly doo-wop or rhythm and blues, but he also tended toward very progressive jazz, such as that pioneered by Miles Davis during the late sixties. Davis' influence was clear in the long, odd-numbered beat patterns on Zappa's *Uncle Meat* album (1969). Contemporary jazz also influenced the album *Hot Rats* (1970), which featured fusion violinist Jean-Luc Ponty. He played with Ponty and other fusion musicians off and on throughout the ensuing years and often added jazz stylings to recordings of his own.

Listening Guide

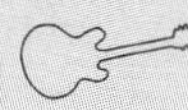

"Valley Girl"
as recorded by Frank Zappa (1982)

Tempo: The tempo is approximately 144 beats per minute, with four beats in each bar.

Form: The lengths of sections in the recording vary, particularly the lengths of Moon's monologues. The opening section is ten bars long and leads directly into a monologue. This opening section functions as a refrain, and it returns two other times. An eight-bar contrasting section begins with the words "on Ventura" the first time and "less ideas" the second. The ending is a very long extension of the monologue.

Features: Both even and uneven beat subdivisions are used.

The drums accent the backbeat.

A driving bass line repeats riff patterns and then extends and improvises around them.

Lyrics: Moon Unit Zappa utters many trite slang phrases as she delivers several monologues about trivial things of concern to her as a self-centered, spoiled little girl. Frank Zappa's overdubbed responses comment on the lack of meaningful thought in what Moon has to say and call her a "valley girl."

Source: *Ship Arriving Too Late to Save a Drowning Witch,* Barking Pumpkin/Capitol 74235; and *Strictly Commercial: The Best of Frank Zappa,* Rykodisc 40500.

Zappa wrote for traditional orchestras for some recordings, particularly movie soundtracks, but the more experimental sounds could be heard in his use of nonmusical sounds (sometimes provided by the Mothers of Invention playing along with a classical orchestra) and free rhythmic organization. Zappa worked with Edgard Varèse's widow to organize and host a concert of music by Varèse in New York in 1981. Zappa's complex rhythms, which often avoided the regularity of a steady beat, showed strong influences of Stravinsky's music, and he credited Stockhausen's work with electronic sounds as an influence on his own experiments in that field.

The styles of music among Zappa's recorded output were so varied that representing him with a single recording is impossible. For that matter, half-a-dozen examples could not adequately cover his career. "Valley Girl" was chosen to use here because it was his only top forty hit single, and it well represents his (and his daughter, Moon Unit's) sense of humor in making a social comment.

Despite his reputation as a rock guitarist and social critic, Zappa's abilities as a composer were taken seriously by others in the classical field, and composer/conductor Pierre Boulez commissioned Zappa to compose a suite of seven dances which was called *The Perfect Stranger* (1984). The recording was conducted by Boulez and played by musicians from his Ensemble InterContemporain. In 1988, Zappa's *Jazz from Hell* won a Grammy for Best Rock Instrumental in 1987. Zappa spent much of the late eighties and early nineties remastering his earlier works for release on CD, and recording new ones. He died of prostate cancer in 1993. Both as a musician and as a social critic, Zappa became successful in many different areas of contemporary music, and never failed to make his beliefs and observations clearly understood.

The German duo of Ralf Hutter (born in 1948) and Florian Schneider (born in the late forties) set aside their piano and flute to play all electronic instruments under the name **Kraftwerk.** Utilizing preprogrammed tapes, synthesizers, oscillators, sequencers, and drum machines with occasional computer-produced vocals, as well as natural vocals, Kraftwerk set the stage for many of the synthesizer and techno-rock bands of the eighties and nineties. Their recordings were very successful in Europe, especially in England, and their fourth album, *Autobahn* (1974), hit the top forty on the American charts. For the recording of that album the band had expanded to four members and included electronic percussion instruments that were much more complex than the drum machines they had used in the past. Autobahns are the major highways in Germany, and one side of the album was based on the sounds one might hear during a trip on an autobahn. On stage, the members of Kraftwerk stressed the technological sources of their music through their robotic appearance and movements. Kraftwerk's *Computer World* (1981) sold in the U.S., but not enough to match their earlier works. Their 1991 album *The Mix* was a collection of earlier works.

In New York, **Laurie Anderson** (born in 1947) produced art films, videos, and music that appealed to rock fans whose tastes and interests went beyond commercial art rock. Her greatest commercial success in music was "O Superman," from her *Big Science* album (1982). The "O Superman" single and the album were appreciated by many for their own merits, but to Anderson they were just a section of a major work (seven hours in performance) called *United States.* Like Kraftwerk and other avant-garde groups of the time, Anderson used electronic instruments and electronically treated vocals, but she also added acoustic instruments to her compositions. Despite the success of the single "O Superman," most of her music was supplemental to her art and could not be properly appreciated without being connected to that art. Unlike many art-rock groups that performed only in large concert halls or stadiums, Laurie Anderson's performances could often be heard in art museums and at art festivals, thus demonstrating the attraction she had within the art, rather than just the art-rock, world. Anderson continues to record and tour in the nineties.

Summary

Art rock was so named because it was influenced by styles and characteristics of "art," or "classical," music. It developed out of experimentation during the late sixties in which rock musicians attempted to expand rock from a popular art into one they saw as more elite. Groups such as the Moody Blues, Genesis, Jethro Tull, and the Electric Light Orchestra added orchestral instruments, or synthesized sounds of those instruments, to create a style that was a logical extension of earlier efforts by producers Phil Spector and George Martin. Other groups, such as Yes, King Crimson, and Emerson, Lake and Palmer, were led by classically trained rock musicians who wrote music in the multi-movement forms often used in classical music. They also used their groups' rock instrumentation to rearrange and record well-known classical works.

Electronics and sound effects had been used by twentieth-century classical composers, and Roger Waters made use of that idea by incorporating effects such as wind, cash registers, or voices and television laugh tracks into recordings by Pink Floyd. The almost hypnotic effect of constant repetition with subtle variation, developed by minimalist composers Steve Reich and Philip Glass, was also used effectively by Pink Floyd. An American exception in a British-dominated style, Frank Zappa wrote works based on a very free organization of rhythms and polyrhythms much like those used by classical composers.

Whether an art-rock group used traditional classical orchestral instruments or electronic or other nontraditional sounds introduced to music by contemporary classical composers, the result was a synthesis of art music and rock music. Critics of the style claimed that the melding of those two dissimilar styles was pretentious, that rock music had its own values without holding itself up against the historical importance of classical traditions. Music listeners disagreed, however, and many forms of art rock remained popular with millions of faithful fans all over the globe for more than two decades and will probably continue to do so into the future.

Terms to Remember

Aeolian mode	Meter
Avant-garde	Minimalism
Eighth notes	Orchestra
Flutter-tonguing	Suite
Harmonics	Systematic music

CHAPTER 17

Glitter and Glam

In some ways the glitter movement was a reaction against sixties rock and its counterculture, but, in other ways, it was an extension of that culture. Where rock of the sixties stressed folk and psychedelic singers' pleas for humanitarian causes, glitter performers of the seventies portrayed themselves as self-indulgent stars who reveled in being at the center of big, theatrical showplaces. Where many bands of the sixties had four or five members on stage playing and singing with only their amplifiers in the background, glitter shows were giant extravaganzas with more attention placed on the glittery sets than the musicians. Sexual freedom had been part of the sixties counterculture, but glitter performers stressed a new view of that freedom as the stars flaunted androgynous images. These images can be seen as another manifestation of rock's rebellious nature; the image of a man wearing makeup and feminine clothing, for example, was used to provoke outrage among members of polite society, and thereby satisfied the fans. Glitter was more show than social statement, but the images shocked the same people the Beat writers had attacked in their works.

Glitter Rock

The Beat movement spread to England when the Beat writers' works reached British bookstores. The teenaged David Robert Jones read Jack Kerouac's novel *On the Road* (1957) and was impressed by the book's characters who were able to express their feelings of alienation from the conformist middle-class society that surrounded them. Jones himself felt penned in by a family that included an older half-brother who had a number of emotional and psychological problems. Thus, the sense of personal freedom demanded by the Beats had great appeal for Jones. Having played saxophone since the age of twelve, Jones began his escape from his family by spending his spare time playing jazz with a band called George and the Dragons. His love of jazz gradually gave way to an interest in rhythm and blues, and by 1963, he was singing with the Hooker Brothers. The Hooker Brothers changed their name to the King Bees, and then to David Jones and the King Bees.

Jones began to frequent London's Mod clubs and left the King Bees to sing with such Mod bands as the Manish Boys and the Lower Third. Allen Ginsberg's demands for acceptance of homosexuality had, along with other antiestablishment movements of the time, sparked a trend of performers wearing androgynous dress in both New York and London. As part of his act Jones developed such an image, one to which he returned many times during his career. He needed a new stage name after 1966 when the Monkees emerged with their British singer, Davy Jones, and because he wanted his musical art to "cut like a knife through lies," he picked the name Bowie, after the knife. **David Bowie**

Listening Guide

"Space Oddity" as recorded by David Bowie (1968)

Tempo: The tempo is approximately 69 beats per minute, with four beats in each bar.

Form: The form is rather complex, with less repetition than in most standard song forms. The introduction is followed by two six-bar A sections, two seven-bar B sections, one six-bar C section, an instrumental section, another B, a five-bar D, another C, and an instrumental ending.

Features: Strummed acoustic guitar gradually increasing in volume is used as an introduction; a snare drum enters, playing a military march beat.

The recording is heavily produced, with a large (or overdubbed) group of string instruments and other orchestral instruments blended into the background. A rhythmically strummed acoustic guitar precedes the instrumental sections.

Electronics and strings playing glissandos give the recording "spacy" sound effects (the string glissandos are the most obvious at the very end of the recording).

The recording does not follow traditional chord progressions in a single key for any length of time; **modulations** (changes of key center) to remote keys add to the effect of instability and the feeling of floating away from home base.

Bowie sings alone but has also overdubbed his voice, producing a duo effect.

Lyrics: The vocals are used to play a little drama in which Bowie sometimes sings the role of ground control on earth and other times the role of Major Tom out in space.

Source: *Space Oddity,* Ryko 10131; and *Changesbowie,* Ryko 0171.

(born in 1947) was to become one of the first and most influential stars of the glitter movement.

Because of his interest in theater and art (he had also been a commercial artist) Bowie would not simply walk out on stage and sing songs backed by a band. He wanted to create a character for himself and make his

David Bowie
Michael Ochs Archives/Venice, CA

performances theatrical experiences. Stanley Kubrick's movie *2001: A Space Odyssey* (1968) and the popular interest in space that was brought on by the American moon landing in 1969 provided the image he was searching for—an astronaut named Major Tom who in Bowie's "Space Oddity" (1969), chose to live in alienation from humanity in space over returning to earth. A listening guide to this recording is included here.

Bowie's use of simple strummed acoustic guitar was in contrast with the spacy sound effects of electronic instruments and string glissandos, providing a reminder that the song included characters speaking from both earth and space. His space-age image and sound was one to which he returned during the early seventies with his Ziggy Stardust character, at which time he called his band the Spiders from Mars. In 1980, the astronaut from "Space Oddity" returned in the song "Ashes to Ashes (The Continuing Story of Major Tom)."

Bowie respected the work of Bob Dylan and adopted a Dylan-influenced persona for himself during the early seventies, playing an acoustic guitar with a harmonica strapped around his neck and singing folk-styled songs, but that image did not last long, because by that time it was too late for the folksinger image to attract much attention.

In 1971, Bowie went beyond androgyny on the cover of the British version of the album *The Man Who Sold the World,* which pictured Bowie relaxing on a day bed with the same sort of hairdo worn by Hollywood movie actresses of the forties, wearing an elegant dress, and holding the queen of diamonds playing card in his limp-wristed hand. The glitz and glamour of glitter rock to follow was shaped by that image. The album cover, not surprisingly, was banned in the United States, but the music on the album was very much influenced by the dark, repetitious drone of Lou Reed's New York proto-punk group of the late sixties, the Velvet Underground.

Bowie's earlier interest in rhythm and blues returned for "The Jean Genie" (1972), a song he wrote about his musician friend Iggy Pop (James Jewel Osterberg). During the same time period, Bowie experimented with a great variety of musical influences ranging from Rolling Stones-style rock to pop songs that Frank Sinatra might have sung in Las Vegas. He tried disco and funk on the *Young Americans* album (1975) and the song "Fame," which he wrote with John Lennon and Carlos Alomar. The next year he collaborated with electronic composer Brian Eno on one of Eno's albums, and that experience influenced his own experimental album *Low* (1976). Eno also worked with Bowie on Bowie's later albums, including *"Heroes"* (1977), the theme of which was inspired by Bowie's visions of the German people's efforts to lead normal lives in the face of the dehumanizing Berlin Wall that divided their city.

Bowie concentrated on theatrical and movie roles in the early eighties. He played the lead role (John Merrick) in *The Elephant Man* (1980) on Broadway and was featured in the movies *The Hunger* (1983) and *Merry Christmas, Mr. Lawrence* (1983). Grandiose glitter effects returned to his rock performances in his 1987 "Glass Spider" tour that followed the release of his *Never Let Me Down* album. He had fourteen performers on stage, with a 64-foot wide translucent spider hanging above. Only five of the performers were musicians—the rest were dancers, acrobats, and fire eaters. In 1990, David Bowie attempted to put a nostalgic end to many of his past stage personae by doing a "greatest hits" tour during which he said he was singing the Major Tom role and many other images from his past for the last time. By that time, Tin Machine was planning its second album, *Tin Machine '91,* and Bowie was enjoying the role of band member as a change from his solo star status. His next solo album, *Black Tie White Noise* (1993) revealed his more soulful and serious self. As full of changes as his past has been, David Bowie is ripe with possibilities for the future.

In general, defining Bowie's musical style is difficult because he did not adhere to a single style and did not work with a regular band. His music and musicians were always chosen to fit the character he was portraying at the moment. The idea of music being almost secondary to the act itself was something that was at the heart of most glitter rock. The most important component of the genre was the grandiose production that turned rock into theater. Of course, Bowie sometimes did scale down his act to a more conventional musical performance, but it was not then a glitter performance. Whether it was Elton John, Marc Bolan, or Gary Glitter prancing around in sparkling costumes and taunting the audience with whatever sexual images they were displaying at the moment; the art-influenced music of Queen and Roxy Music; the heavy metal-influenced music of Kiss and Alice Cooper; or in later years, a pop show by Boy George or glam-metal by Bon Jovi, glitter meant one thing—theater.

Like Bowie early in his career, **Elton John** (Reginald Kenneth Dwight, born in 1947) first played rock music with a blues revival group in London. Dwight was trained as a classical pianist, and even won a scholarship to attend London's Royal Academy of Music, but he gave that up to join the group, Bluesology. When he started his solo career he created his stage name out of the names of Bluesology's singer, Long John Baldry, and saxophonist Elton Dean. Not the actor Bowie was (although he did play the part of a boy who sang "Pinball Wizard" in the movie version of the Who's *Tommy*), John fell into the glitter category with his flamboyant dress and elaborate stage performances. With high platform shoes and sparkly eyeglasses of every imaginable shape, he made the piano rock as few had since the days of Little Richard and Jerry Lee Lewis.

Elton John's musicianship and wide-ranging influences gave him complete control of a number of styles ranging from the sensitive ballad "Your Song" (1970) to the pop rock of "Bennie and the Jets" (1974). Some fans also consider Elton John to be a singer/songwriter, but that is really not true given the fact that the lyrics to almost all of his songs were written by Bernie Taupin although John wrote the melodies. Tribute was paid to the successful writing team in 1991 when performers such as Eric Clapton, Phil Collins, Tina Turner, and Sting recorded their songs on the album *Two Rooms.*

One of the top-selling artists of the seventies, John's career and personal life experienced many highs and lows during the eighties. His most successful single of the decade was "That's What Friends Are For" (1985), recorded with Dionne Warwick, Gladys Knight, and Stevie Wonder. During that time he experienced a failed marriage, suffered a vocal loss that required throat surgery, and battled addictions to cocaine and alcohol. Vowing to recover from his problems and also to use his talent to help others, he hospitalized himself in 1990 to remove the drugs from his system and established the Elton John AIDS Foundation, to which he donated support money. His career revived in the nineties with the 1992 album *The One,* which sold as well as his hit albums of the seventies, and the music he composed for the soundtrack of Disney's movie *The Lion King* (1994), which won both a Grammy and an Oscar.

Elton John's glitter image remains with those who saw him perform during the seventies. Audiences of the eighties and nineties tended to prefer less glamour on stage and many of the former glitter stars continued their careers without the theatrical displays. Elton John sold

Queen at London's Wembley Stadium in 1989 (left to right): John Deacon, Freddie Mercury, and Brian May
Reuters/Bettmann

items that contributed to his early image at a Sotheby's auction in London in 1988, further distancing himself from his glitter style.

The Mod clubs in London served as the musical training ground for another glitter star, **Marc Bolan** (Marc Feld, 1948–1977). Bolan's glitter image often included the same androgynous sexuality that his friend David Bowie had adopted in the late sixties. Bolan led several different versions of the group Tyrannosaurus Rex (known later as **T. Rex**), the first of which was a duo with Steve Peregrine Took (Steve Porter). They added unusual percussion effects, such as African talking drums and Asian gongs, to what was basically an acoustic, folk-oriented sound. The next version of T. Rex was Bolan and artist/percussionist Micky Finn, and that pair broadened their acoustic guitar sound with the addition of four violins. They finally decided that rock and roll required a rhythm section and added a bass player and a drummer for their hit recording "Bang a Gong (Get It On)" (1971).

The British group **Queen** placed itself in the glitter category by virtue of the androgynous implications of its name. Singer Freddie Mercury (Frederick Bulsara), guitarist Brian May, bassist John Deacon, and drummer Roger Meadows-Taylor were all completing college degrees in fields other than music when they decided to

Listening Guide

"Bohemian Rhapsody" as recorded by Queen (1975)

Tempo: The tempo is about 72 beats per minute, with four beats per bar in the introduction, but the tempo varies from one section of the recording to another.

Form and Features: The elaborate group vocals were created by overdubbing the voices of group members Freddie Mercury, Roger Taylor, and Brian May. The soloist, who sings the role of the murderer, is Freddie Mercury.

The mini-opera begins with *a cappella* group vocals introducing the story and setting the mood in much the way a recitative (sung recitation or dialogue that tells the story) might in a classical opera. The protagonist (Mercury) begins his aria with the second verse of lyrics. He is accompanied by a strong backbeat in the drums that drops out and then reenters. The tempo is slightly faster than the introduction.

Percussion instruments are used to add color to the meanings of the lyrics. Soon after the word "shivers" in the second verse, for example, chimes are used to convey the feeling of shivering.

Although the third verse repeats the melody of the second verse, the rest of the verses change with the dramatic events in the story, rather than have the form dictated by standard "song form" types of repetitions.

The fourth verse, or section, is faster than the previous verses (about 144 beats per minute) and uses **antiphonal choruses** (vocal groups that call out and answer one another) to express their positions for and against the release of the murderer. The dramatic way in which one chorus repeats lines just sung by the protagonist is reminiscent of the operetta style of Gilbert and Sullivan.

Heavy bass and distorted guitar sounds add power to the fourth section, in which the murderer begs for his freedom.

The mini-opera ends at a fairly slow tempo (about 80 beats per minute) with a softly sung epilogue about the fact that the drama did not matter that much to the murderer after all. The lyrics and melody heard at the end were used earlier, helping to give a balanced musical form to the piece. The last sound is that of a gong.

Lyrics: The recording is a mini-opera, sung from the perspective of a man who has just committed a murder and confesses it to his mother. One chorus represents a society that begs for leniency and the other a society that wants to get rid of the murderer. Beelzebub (the Devil's sidekick) is ready for him, but the man wants to be free. An epilogue, however, states that ultimately the murderer believes nothing really makes any difference.

Source: *A Night at the Opera,* Hollywood 61065; and *Classic Queen,* Hollywood Records 61311.

try for rock stardom. They had all done some playing in other groups, but did not want Queen to spend years playing in small clubs. Instead, they worked on a demo tape and an elaborate stage act before approaching a record company. When they finally did sell their tape, they were ready for superstardom.

Queen's music was hard rock with heavy-metal-flavored guitar lines, but it also approached art rock in its well-crafted arrangements and production techniques. With overdubbed guitar parts and four-part close harmony vocals, they achieved dramatic effects that were unsurpassed in most of the rock music of their time. Their stage show eventually included a touch of the most elaborate genre within classical music with *A Night at the Opera* (1975). From that album, "Bohemian Rhapsody" was a mock operetta ("little opera"), the components of which are discussed in the listening guide above.

Queen's music ceased to be so "glittery" and dramatic during the eighties, and both their hard rock and classical influences gave way to fifties rockabilly (using Chuck Berry-style guitar lines) with "Crazy Little Thing Called Love" (1980) and the funky "Another One Bites the Dust" (1980). Queen joined forces with glitter star David Bowie for "Under Pressure" in 1981.

As had been the case for many other glitter acts of the seventies, Queen's recordings of the eighties met with reduced success. Their 1991 album, *Innuendo,* was their last due to the AIDS-related death of their dynamic singer, Freddie Mercury. Remaining group members were joined by stars such as Elton John, David Bowie, and Def Leppard for a memorial concert in 1992. The attention given to "Bohemian Rhapsody" in the movie *Wayne's World* (1992) as well as the release of *Greatest Hits, Classic Queen,* and *Live at*

Wembley '86 (all 1992) exposed Queen's music to a new, younger audience.

Another English group, **Roxy Music,** combined colorful pop-art-influenced clothing with thick and glittery makeup for their image, and put a fifties pop-song style together with avant-garde synthesizer effects for their music. Their synthesizer experimentalist, Brian Eno, left in 1973, but the group continued its use of electronics by replacing him with a classically trained violinist and synthesizer player, Eddie Jobson. Most of their music was written by their singer, Bryan Ferry, whose glittery stage images ranged from androgynous outfits of all kinds to a white tuxedo and even a Nazi-like uniform. Ferry had a solo act for a while in which he pranced around on stage singing Leslie Gore's "It's My Party," keeping the original gender of the lyrics. Much of the music he wrote and performed with Roxy Music had a similarly bizarre sense of humor, as in the song "In Every Dream Home a Heartache" (1973), about sex with an inflatable doll, and the parody on early-sixties dance trends, "Do the Strand" (1973). Roxy Music continued on through the early eighties, but with many personnel changes and a lessened commercial success in the U.S. They attempted to revive their career with the release of *Heart Still Beating* in 1990, which was recorded at a live concert in 1982. Individual members attempted solo careers, including Bryan Ferry, who was still recording in the nineties.

Although glitter rock was primarily a British style because it originated in England and was more popular there than in the United States, by the early seventies there were several glitter groups in New York. Following in the footsteps of the Beats (and also pop artist Andy Warhol), Lou Reed's band, **The Velvet Underground,** taunted the conservative element of society by performing songs about things such as bisexuality and homosexuality. **The New York Dolls** took up where Reed left off, donning stacked-heeled shoes and heavy makeup to create an androgynous glitter image.

■ The Velvet Underground's and the New York Dolls' musical influences on punk rock will be discussed in Chapter 19, Punk Rock and New Wave.

American heavy metal acts such as Kiss (from New York) and Alice Cooper (from Detroit) performed their music with such theatrics that they were as much glitter as heavy metal. Despite their name, **Kiss** had an act that was based more closely on images from horror movies than on sexual themes. The group members wore heavy facial makeup, playing roles of a lover, a cat, a spaceman, and a devil, but it was more theatrical than androgynous. They spit fake blood, breathed fire, and filled the stage with smoke and a light show, in addition to doing what rock musicians used to do exclusively, play music. **Alice Cooper** (Vincent Furnier, born in 1945) sometimes wore androgynous dress and at other times provided competition for Kiss' displays of horror with mock murders and executions by guillotine or electric chair on stage. As if the deaths themselves were not enough, they were often followed by grotesque exhibitions of the mutilated body parts left after the executions. Alice Cooper played music, but like the music of other glitter rockers, it shared the spotlight with the theatrics.

■ The music of Kiss, Alice Cooper, and the eighties metal bands will be discussed in Chapter 18, Hard Rock and Heavy Metal.

Listening Guide

"Nothin' But a Good Time"
as recorded by Poison (1988)

Tempo: The tempo is approximately 130 beats per minute, with four beats in each bar.

Form: The instrumental introduction is composed of a four-bar riff played four times and then extended two more bars. The form is based on eight-bar phrases, although the two phrases that begin with the song title have an additional one-bar extension. Each phrase begins with two eighth-note pickups.

Features: Uneven beat subdivisions are used throughout the recording.

The drums maintain a strong backbeat.

A twenty-four-bar instrumental section ends with the opening riff played twice.

The instrumental section features solo guitar.

Lyrics: The song is sung from the point of view of someone who resents having to work so hard to get enough money to have a good time.

Source: *Open Up and Say . . . Ahh!,* Capitol 48493.

Glam Bands of the Eighties and Early Nineties

Androgynous glitter-influenced hairdos and makeup made a new appearance on heavy metal stages with such eighties performers as Bon Jovi (from New Jersey), Mötley Crüe (from Los Angeles), and Twisted Sister (from New Jersey). The long, full hairdos and makeup were added to black leather, chains, and tattoos, giving these newer bands a much tougher image than was common for the glitter performers of the past. Song themes by the glam bands tended to be less oriented toward mini-dramas than those of the glitter groups, leaving the theatrics to the stage sets and "glamorous" looks and costumes worn by glam band members.

Poison in 1987 (left to right): CC. Deville, Brett Michaels, Bobby Dall, and Rikki Rocket
AP Wide World Photos

Poison had their own hairdresser in their drummer, Rikki Rockett (Richard Ream, born in 1961). The band formed in Pennsylvania, but relocated to Los Angeles where they became one of the most successful L.A. glam bands during the style's heyday in the late eighties. On page 180 is a listening guide to one of their top ten hits.

Poison's commercial success was partially due to their versatility. Another hit from the same album (*Open Up and Say . . . Ahh!*), "Every Rose Has Its Thorn," was a ballad. Poison's next two albums also sold well and the band was still together in the mid-nineties, but by that time the elaborate costumes and stage theatrics of both glitter and glam had begun to give way to the growing popularity of alternative groups whose looks and staging generally avoided such glitz.

Summary

Sexual ambiguity had been present in rock music before the glitter stars of the early seventies took to the stage with makeup, dresses, and high heels, but it had never before been so blatant. For the purposes of understanding and enjoying the music and the stage shows of the androgynous glitter artists, it did not matter whether the artists were gay, bisexual, or just very convincing actors; the purpose of the music was to enhance the all-important glamorous show. The music of most glitter acts, particularly that of David Bowie, Roxy Music, and Queen, reached beyond the standard rock styles, incorporating other forms of art music that became popular as art (or progressive) rock. In a sense, many of the glitter artists' performances themselves became theatrical works of art.

Eighties glam bands added heavy-metal-influenced power to their glittery looks of long hair and makeup. The music and images of glam bands were generally less tough than those of heavy metal groups, and glam bands often sang songs with positive messages.

Terms to Remember

Antiphonal choruses

Modulations

CHAPTER 18

Hard Rock and Heavy Metal

Hard rock and heavy metal are loud, powerful, and aggressive styles that developed out of the sounds of such blues revival bands as the Rolling Stones, Cream, and the Yardbirds, with further influences from the Who and the Jimi Hendrix Experience. Although a certain amount of overlap existed between the styles of hard rock and heavy metal, they remained fairy separate, with hard rock maintaining closer connections with its blues and folk-rock roots. Hard rock singers were generally as capable of singing ballads as they were of singing loud, heavy rock songs, while heavy metal singers concentrated on screaming often-obscured lyrics to audiences caught up more in the power of the sound than with any meaning in the words. Hard rock bands often included acoustic guitars played in the strummed or plucked patterns used in folk music, sometimes updating their sounds with the addition of synthesizers, while heavy metal bands generally used the electric guitar, bass, and drums instrumentation used by the Jimi Hendrix Experience, Cream, and Led Zeppelin. (Heavy metal bands did sometimes vary their sound by using acoustic instruments, but that was the exception, not the rule.) Heavy metal also often included highly amplified and seemingly uncontrolled sound. It was aggressive and macho, frequently stressing rebellious attitudes of young men who felt caught between boyhood freedoms and society's expectations of manhood, to the point of employing symbols of death and destruction to appeal to their aggressions as well as to upset their parents and other authority figures. Hard rock bands, on the other hand, usually sang songs that more often expressed themes about love and human relationships. Perhaps for that reason, female performers were successful in hard rock while heavy metal remained male dominated.

Distortion and feedback were characteristic of both hard rock and heavy metal. Distorted amplification was probably first recorded by Link Wray in "Rumble" (1958), for which Wray poked a pencil through the speaker of his amplifier to achieve the effect. The Kinks copied that sound by cutting into a speaker cone with a razor blade for their recording of "You Really Got Me" (1964). Not long after that, various electronic distortion devices were developed to enable musicians to produce and control these effects by the use of foot pedals. Feedback between the guitar and amplifier—not an artificial effect, but achieved simply by striking a guitar note or chord and then holding the instrument in front of the amplifier—was used by several British groups during the mid-sixties, including the Beatles in "I Feel Fine" (1964), the Who in "My Generation" (1965), and the Yardbirds in "Shapes of Things" (1966). It soon came into common use in hard rock and heavy metal.

The effects of distortion and feedback used in some hard rock and most heavy metal music were enhanced through the guitarists' use of **power chords.** Power chords are not traditional chord structures such as those used in most rock music. Instead they are just two bass

Listening Guide

"Sunshine of Your Love"
as recorded by Cream (1967)

Tempo: The tempo is about 116 beats per minute, with four beats in each bar.

Form: The formal structure is four repetitions of a twenty-four-bar blues form. The form is simply a twelve-bar blues in which each section is twice the normal length. (Instead of four bars of the initial chord in the first A section, there are eight; instead of two bars of the next chord as the first half of the next A section, there are four; and so on, except that some single-bar chords are added to the eight-bar B section.)

Features: A bass riff is the most important bit of melody in the recording; it not only repeats throughout most of the recording, but it is also paralleled by the guitar and the beginning of the vocal melody. The riff is played four times as an introduction to the first chorus. (The chorus begins when the voice enters.) The riff is notated as follows:

The guitar and bass are in octaves using even note subdivisions. (The arrow over the F note indicates that the players bend their strings while playing it, producing a blue note about halfway between F and F♯.)

The riff is two bars long and is based on a single chord, requiring it to be played through four times on the single chord during the first A section of each chorus (eight bars). The riff changes pitch to fit the next chord for two repetitions of the riff (four bars). It returns to the first pitch level for two more repetitions on the last four bars of the second A section.

The beginning of the B section varies the normal blues progression, playing single bars of chords not usually part of the blues structure before ending the chorus. Because the riff is two bars long, it would not fit that new-chord-in-each-bar progression and is omitted during the endings of the B sections.

The third twenty-four-bar chorus is instrumental, with the riff continuing on the bass, and with the guitar as the solo instrument. The guitarist, Eric Clapton, quotes from the song "Blue Moon" at the beginning of his guitar solo. (Quoting from standards or well-known melodies while improvising is a sort of game for musicians, and a way to keep listeners on their toes.)

Baker uses two bass drums to produce a heavy, throbbing pulse, uncharacteristically accenting beats one and three of each four-beat bar and playing softly on the backbeats.

The recording ends with a long extension of the last musical idea at the end of the fourth chorus and then fades out.

Lyrics: The lyrics begin by expressing the anticipation of spending the night with a lover. Later, the singer rhapsodizes about the experience and says he wants it to continue.

Source: Time-Life Music, *Classic Rock, 1968; Disraeli Gears,* Polydor 823636; and *Strange Brew—Very Best of Cream,* Polydor 811639.

notes that are the interval of a perfect fourth or a perfect fifth apart, for example "G" on the sixth string played with "C" or "D" on the fifth. When those notes are played and distorted, the sound of another note that is much lower than the guitar can normally play is created as a **resultant tone.** Power chords can be rhythmically pounded or sustained—either way they add much to the heavy depth and weight of the metal sound.

Early Influences on Hard Rock and Heavy Metal

The powerful British blues revival trio **Cream** formed to play Chicago blues classics like Willie Dixon's "Spoonful" (1966) and Muddy Waters' "Rollin' and Tumblin'" (1966), but changed their style to include distortion and extended improvisations like those by the Jimi Hendrix Experience. On Cream's *Disraeli Gears* album (1967), the song "Sunshine of Your Love" was organized around a blues-derived element called a **bass riff** (a relatively short, low, repeated melody), a device that became a basic characteristic in hard rock and heavy metal to follow. As played by Cream's bassist, Jack Bruce, the repeated riff gave the recording an almost hypnotic effect that provided a footing from which the voice, lead guitar, and drums could freely improvise without causing the music to lose its unity. The importance of the riff was stressed by the voice that often paralleled it. Another characteristic of Cream that influenced a lot of hard rock and heavy metal was the bottom-heavy sound created by Ginger Baker's use of two bass drums, a sound clearly represented in "Sunshine of Your Love." A listening guide to the recording is on page 183.

Cream and other psychedelic-influenced blues revival bands of the late sixties became essential links between the blues and the hard rock and heavy metal styles of the seventies. The paralleling of the lead and bass guitar lines Cream used in "Sunshine of Your Love" was something the Jimi Hendrix Experience often used to create a very thick, full, powerful reinforcement of the riff. It was later copied by heavy metal bands.

Hard Rock

The pubs in London were the birthplace of the hard rock sound in Britain, beginning with **Free,** which was formed in 1968. The members of Free had come from the blues revival groups Brown Sugar, John Mayall's Bluesbreakers, and Black Cat Bones. In one of their most popular recordings, "All Right Now" (1970), Free's blues roots were evident through their use of a riff in the introduction, but they did not maintain it as the central theme of the song as most heavy metal bands of the time would have done. The guitar used heavy distortion effects and the drums maintained a very strong backbeat, characteristic of most hard rock.

Singer Paul Rodgers and drummer Simon Kirke continued their careers with another hard rock band, **Bad Company,** which used Free's riffs, distortion, and strong backbeat, but not the loud, rebellious themes or uncontrolled sounds of heavy metal. By the late seventies, the group had begun to experiment with synthesizers and updated their sound with new-wave influences, such as the throbbing, repeated-note pulse on each half beat played by the bass in "Rock and Roll Fantasy" (1979). Bad Company took a four-year break from 1982 to 1986 and then regrouped with a new singer, Brian Howe. They were still recording in the nineties, with only drummer Simon Kirke and guitarist Mick Ralphs remaining from their original lineup. Paul Rodgers recorded a solo album after leaving Bad Company and then sang in Jimmy Page's group, the Firm, in the middle eighties. Rodgers returned to his blues roots by recording songs by Muddy Waters and Jimi Hendrix in the early nineties.

Many American hard rock groups formed during the late sixties and early seventies as the style became popular with fans who wanted to hear stronger rock than the music by singer/songwriters of the period, but who found heavy metal too hostile and theatrical. **Steppenwolf** was formed in 1967 by musicians with backgrounds in blues, country, and folk rock—all styles that influenced most hard rock music. Steppenwolf's recording of "Born to Be Wild" (1968) contained the words "heavy metal" (in reference to a motorcycle), and although Steppenwolf's music did not fit completely into the heavy metal mold that was in the process of taking shape, the song gave the style a name. Steppenwolf followed "Born to Be Wild" with many other recordings, but that song title stayed with them on later albums *Reborn to Be Wild* (1977) and *Born to Be Wild—A Retrospective* (1991). Their membership changed many times with guitarist/singer John Kay (Joachim Krauledat, born in 1944) as the only original member who lasted into the nineties.

Heart evolved out of a group called the Army that was formed in Seattle in 1963. The Army passed through many style and personnel changes before turning to hard rock in 1972. Sisters Ann and Nancy Wilson had both been folk and folk-rock singer/guitarists before joining Heart, and that background was evident in their early Heart recordings such as "Crazy on You" and "Magic Man" (both 1976). Heart's membership changed often, and the Wilson sisters' folk roots gradually disappeared. Eventually, their sound in the late eighties was almost as aggressive as many heavy metal bands on some recordings, although still without the wild theatrics of the genre. Ballads such as "Alone" (1987) were also part of their late-eighties style. Just as many other hard rock bands had done during the late seventies and through the eighties, Heart added the new-wave characteristic of a half-beat pulse played by repeated notes on the bass for songs like "If Looks Could Kill," from *Heart* (1985). Heart continued to tour and record in the nineties, but the Wilson sisters had other projects as well. Ann and Nancy Wilson were joined by longtime friend guitarist/keyboard player Sue Ennis and singer/multi-instrumentalist Frank Cox in the acoustic group, Lovemongers. With that group they recorded a version of Led Zeppelin's Celtic folk-influenced "Battle of Evermore." The Wilson sisters own the Bad Animals studio at which several Seattle bands such as Pearl Jam, Alice in Chains, and Soundgarden have recorded. In 1994 Heart released a CD-ROM multimedia package, *Heart: 20 Years of Rock & Roll.*

A hard rock group from Boston, Massachusetts, **Boston** was formed by musician and engineering whiz **Tom Scholz** (born in 1947), who had a master's degree in mechanical engineering and had experimented with multiple-tracked overdubbing techniques. With his friend Brad Delp doing the vocals, Scholz recorded instrumental parts in his home studio and produced a tape for a hard rock album that was eventually released as *Boston* (1976). Scholz and Delp put together a band to do live performances of their music. As was often the case with American hard rock music, folk influences were heard in Boston's music, right alongside the distorted lead guitar sound and the heavy backbeat of blues-influenced hard rock. Following is a listening guide to "More Than a Feeling," from the *Boston* album.

Scholz released a second Boston album two years after the first, but felt that he really needed more time to

Listening Guide

"More Than a Feeling" by Boston (1976)

Tempo: The tempo is about 108 beats per minute, with four beats in each bar.

Form: The seven-bar instrumental introduction begins with an acoustic twelve-string guitar playing a picking pattern in a folk guitar style, which is then joined by electric lead guitar using distortion.

The form has two main sections that alternate with each other. The A section has nine bars with lyrics that change with each repetition and an instrumental section with the guitar playing lead at the end. The instrumental sections at the end of the first two A sections are six bars long; the third A is much longer and moves gradually into the B section.

The B sections begin with the lyrics of the song title and each one is longer than the one before it. The first B section is thirteen bars long, followed by a three-bar repetition of the introductory twelve-string guitar pattern.

Features: Lead guitar with distortion and a strong backbeat in the drums are both present throughout most of the recording, as is true of most hard rock.

The first and second B sections (the ones beginning with the words in the song title) have a surprise **cadence** (a resolution to a chord; a **surprise cadence** is a resolution to an unexpected chord) on the word "away."

The recording is heavily produced, with many layers of sound supporting the timbre of the twelve-string acoustic guitar.

Lyrics: The lyrics are often obscured by the instruments, but they generally question the depth of relationships.

Source: *Boston,* Epic 34188.

do the things he wanted for the next one. He spent six years preparing the tapes for *Third Stage* (1986). On that album, he chose not to use synthesizers and stacks of large amplifiers as he had in the past; instead, he replaced them with a variety of organs, including a theater organ with its many sound effects, and the small guitar amplifier he had invented called the Rockman. The result was a thick, but modern production sound that continued to use the twelve-string guitar timbre of his earlier works. By the time Scholz was ready to record a fourth Boston album, *Walk On* (1994), his former band members had gone on to solo careers and he was the only original member left.

Pat Benatar (Patricia Andrzejewski, born in 1953) was an important female hard rock singer of the eighties although her background would not seem to be one that would lead her into such a tough style of singing. The daughter of an opera singer, she studied opera herself at the Juilliard School of Music until she quit to marry a GI, Dennis Benatar. She worked as a singing waitress and then a lounge singer in various Manhattan night clubs, but when she tried to get a record contract she was repeatedly rejected because her image and style were "too feminine." After she adopted an aggressive, hard rock style she attracted the interest of Chrysalis Records and was given a record contract. Her image was never as angry and hateful as women in the punk movement; instead, Benatar screamed about pained love relationships in such songs as "Heartbreaker" (1979), "Treat Me Right" (1981), and "Love is a Battlefield" (1983). Benatar divorced her first husband and married the guitarist in her band, Neil Giraldo. By the middle eighties Benatar's style was moving away from the hard-edged sound of her past. Her 1991 album *True Love* was primarily a collection of blues songs that received a lukewarm reception by her fans.

Hard rock was still very much alive during the eighties and nineties, if only as an aggressive style that had more commercial appeal than the power-laden heavy metal bands of the era. When **Bon Jovi,** a respelling of singer John Bongiovi's (born in 1962) name, first toured as an opening band for the Scorpions and for Judas Priest, the members of Bon Jovi commented that they could not identify with the tough attitude of those or most other heavy metal bands. Their songs were intended to be positive messages for their fans and they wanted to promote their own much espoused philosophy of "be all you can be" (not unlike the motto of the U.S. Army). This theme is certainly evident in the song "Livin' on a Prayer," for which a listening guide follows on page 187.

John Bongiovi, Jr., used the name Jon Bon Jovi when he acted in and recorded the soundtrack for the movie *Young Guns II* (1990). He returned to his band in the early nineties for further success with top ten hit singles such as "Always" from the album *Cross Road* (1994).

British Heavy Metal

Most British heavy metal tended to use riffs as the basic structural element of the music. The riffs were usually played by the bass, and often started on high notes and ended on low notes, giving a very heavy, powerful effect. Just as in Cream's "Sunshine of Your Love," the

Pat Benatar in 1988
Michael Ochs Archives/Venice, CA

Jon Bon Jovi performing in Vancouver, Canada in 1988
Reuters/Bettmann

Listening Guide

"Livin' on a Prayer"
as recorded by Bon Jovi (1986)

Tempo: The tempo is approximately 126 beats per minute, with four beats in each bar.

Form: The form is based on four-bar phrases that are usually paired into eight-bar periods.

The sections are organized according to the format: Introduction A B A B Instrumental B.

The recording begins with a gradual build up of synthesized sounds. The bass enters to establish the beat pattern for four bars, after which the drums and sounds from a **voice box** play an eight-bar introduction. A four-bar spoken line enters as if to tell a story.

Each A section is sixteen bars long (two eight-bar periods).

Each B section is sixteen bars (two eight-bar periods), followed by a two-bar vamp (first time) or extension (later B sections).

The instrumental section is eight bars long.

The recording ends by fading out during a final extension of the last B section.

Features: Even beat subdivisions are maintained throughout the recording.

The drums maintain a strong backbeat through most of the recording.

The voice box creates an interesting and rhythmic sound effect that had not been in common use in rock recordings for a decade or more (since *Frampton Comes Alive!* in 1976).

The bass line is very active through most of the recording, and the guitarist plays solos between sections of vocals and during the instrumental section. The keyboard maintains a full background.

The key changes during the final B section (up one-half step), accenting the theme of "getting better" in the future.

Lyrics: Tommy and Gina love one another, but are having financial problems. They survive by encouraging one another that they can live on their prayers for a better future.

Source: *Slippery When Wet*, Mercury 830264.

riffs would drop off during instrumental improvisations that took place somewhere near the middle of the recording and then would return to reintroduce the vocals. British heavy metal was generally less concerned with interesting vocal lines or complicated chord progressions, both characteristics being more common in American heavy metal. The central concern of the British groups was power.

Since most British heavy metal fans were young and aggressive teenagers who lived in a country studded with medieval castles with dark, foreboding chambers of torture and execution, their favorite fantasies of power were often related to those types of images. The torture chambers still had "iron maidens" and other instruments of death left from the time when they were actually used. British schoolchildren would visit these places, perhaps later imagining the horrible deaths that took place so long ago, often near their own homes. While the images portrayed by American heavy metal groups tended more toward scenes from horror movies—something more in line with the experience of American youths—British heavy metal music and stage sets stressed demonic images and medieval rituals.

Group names, such as Black Sabbath and Judas Priest, and album covers and posters with symbols of witchcraft and death shocked some parents into believing the music was satanic and would be the end of anything positive in their children's lives. The young fans, of course, reveled in their parents' aversion to the music, just as Elvis Presley fans had in 1954 and Rolling Stones fans had in 1964; but these fans also realized that the songs were more often about the fear, not the worship, of evil. The fans could enjoy the power of the music, horrify their parents, who they felt did not understand them anyway, and indulge themselves in fantasies that represented an aggressive confrontation of things people fear most—evil and death.

Led Zeppelin was of great importance to the development of heavy metal. The group was formed by musicians who had been part of the British blues revival, and they continued to play covers of songs by blues artists like Howlin' Wolf and Willie Dixon. In their early music, they often used bass riffs not unlike those in Cream's "Sunshine of Your Love." As one example, "Dazed and Confused," from their first album, *Led Zeppelin* (1969), used a long, slow, descending bass riff. Although Jimmy Page gave himself writer's credit for the song, it was a cover of "Dazed and Confused" (1967) by American folk-rock musician Jake Holmes. Page had heard Holmes perform it when Page was in New York on tour with the

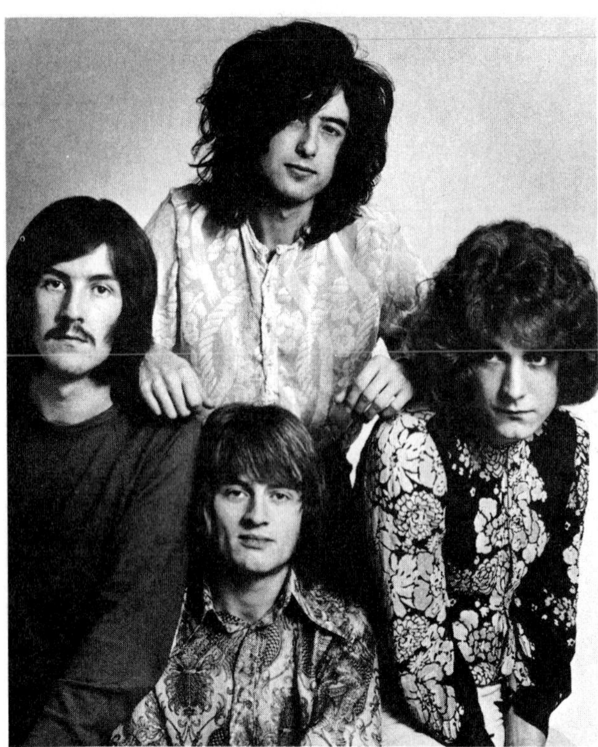

Led Zeppelin (clockwise from left): John Bonham, Jimmy Page, Robert Plant, and John Paul Jones

Michael Ochs Archives/Venice, CA

Yardbirds in 1967. He wrote new lyrics, called it "I'm Confused," and performed it with the Yardbirds, not recording it until they broke up and he formed Led Zeppelin. Holmes' song title was used for Led Zeppelin's version. Leaving questions about authorship aside, both versions had a slowly descending bass riff repeating continuously through all but the improvised break sections. The effect was much the same as that of the bass riffs used by Jimi Hendrix and Cream—they served as the musical foundation of the piece. A comparison of the two recordings follows on page 189.

The long instrumental improvisation in both versions of the song, but particularly in Led Zeppelin's, was a direct outgrowth of psychedelic music's efforts to give the listener the feeling that he or she was experiencing eerie connections of thoughts and images, as if in a drug-induced state, stretched out without a perceptible measure of the passage of time. The return of the bass riff was intended to bring the listener back to the real world.

Led Zeppelin continued to use bass riffs as the foundation of many of their later recordings, but it did not remain the prominent characteristic of their style that it had been in 1969. The riff they used in "The Immigrant Song" (1970), for example, was short and more rhythmic than melodic. Led Zeppelin's music of the late sixties also helped to define other characteristics of heavy metal, with Robert Plant's screeches and moans as part of his dramatic vocal delivery, and also with new guitar sounds, such as that created by Jimmy Page's drawing a violin bow across the strings of his guitar.

By the early seventies, the group had expanded their early heavy metal sound by incorporating music based on Celtic folk traditions, as in their song "The Battle of Evermore" (1971). Their most popular recording, "Stairway to Heaven," was never released as a single but was included on the group's untitled 1971 album (often referred to as *Led Zeppelin IV* or *Zoso*). It began with a melody reminiscent of English Renaissance music played by a guitar and a group of recorders (woodwind instruments of the flute family popular in England during the sixteenth century), but later the song developed the power and form of blues-based heavy metal.

In addition to introducing stylistic developments that influenced other heavy metal bands, Led Zeppelin was interested in occult phenomena and used cryptic symbols on their album covers. The lyrics to "Stairway to Heaven" were inspired by Plant's reading of *Magic Arts in Celtic Britain,* by Lewis Spence, and the group encouraged the spread of rumors that they had included messages to Satan in their records that could be heard if the records were spun backwards. After all, the people who destroyed their records out of fear of what they thought they contained had already paid for them in the first place, and the publicity only drew more fans who wanted to identify with something their parents would hate. Page bought and lived in the home of Aleister Crowley (1875–1947), the legendary British occultist who was believed to be a satanist. Page left fans to fantasize about the band's use of his castle of evil and magic. It was the setting in which their drummer, John Bonham, died in 1980, but the doctor who signed the death certificate did not suspect that any forces other than a very large amount of alcohol and an upset stomach were to blame. After Bonham's death, Led Zeppelin chose to disband rather than find a new drummer.

Jimmy Page worked on a number of projects after the breakup of Led Zeppelin. The former singer for Free and Bad Company, Paul Rodgers, joined him to record two albums with the Firm, and seven years later Page was joined by the former singer for Deep Purple and Whitesnake, David Coverdale, for the album *Coverdale/Page* (1993). Robert Plant spent that same time recording solo albums with a variety of backup musicians. Plant and Page worked together as the Honeydrippers in 1984, and Page contributed a guitar solo to "Tall Cool One" for Plant's album *Now and Zen* (1988). Some of Led Zeppelin's old favorite songs were included on the album *No Quarter: Jimmy Page and Robert Plant Unledded* (1994), which was recorded with the London Metropolitan Orchestra. They also recorded with an Egyptian ensemble, musicians from Marrakech, as well as other musicians playing folk and rock instruments. John Paul Jones was working with Diamanda Galás at that time and recorded the album *The Sporting Life* (1994).

Black Sabbath took the hypnotically repetitious bass riff idea of Cream and Led Zeppelin, mixed it with Zeppelin's occult mystique, and led British heavy metal

Listening Guide

	"Dazed and Confused" as recorded by Jake Holmes (1967)	***"Dazed and Confused" as recorded by Led Zeppelin (1969)***
Tempo:	The tempo is about 54 beats per minute, with four beats per bar.	The tempo is roughly 54 beats per minute, with four beats per bar.
Form:	After a seven-bar introduction, the singer has three five-bar A sections with lyrics. An instrumental improvisation is placed between the second and third A sections.	The introduction and the three A sections have been shortened to four bars each. An extension has been added after the second and third A sections and a long improvisation, based on Holmes' instrumental is inserted between the second and third A sections.
Features:	Uneven beat subdivisions are maintained throughout the recording.	Uneven beat subdivisions are maintained throughout the recording.
	The backbeat is not stressed.	A soft backbeat is kept in the A sections.
	The recording begins with harmonics played on an acoustic guitar, followed by the soft entrance of a two-bar descending quarter-note bass-riff pattern.	The introduction begins with a bass riff very similar to Holmes' recording, answered by harmonic-like sounds played on the electric guitar.
	The bass riff stops during a subtle rhythmic call-and-response-style improvisation between muffled guitar strums and rhythmic taps on the soundboard of the guitar. Eventually a short bass riff enters and repeats under a guitar imitating the sound of an Indian sitar.	The bass riff stops for a short instrumental interlude in which the instruments stress a **triplet** beat pattern (emphasizing three subdivisions of each beat) at the end of all but the first A sections. The bass riff also stops for an extended call-and-response-style improvisation in which rhythm patterns of short bass riffs are answered by the drums, and the distorted guitar exchanges responses with the vocal screeches and moans. The improvisation goes into a section that is triple the speed of the rest of the recording.
	An abrupt ending follows a short section of intense strumming on the guitar.	Another extended improvisation brings the recording to an end after the fading away of a distorted guitar line.
	The original bass riff returns with the voice.	The original bass riff returns with the voice.
	The recording is three minutes and forty-five seconds long.	The recording is six minutes and twenty seconds long.
Lyrics:	The singer is confused about where he stands in his relationship with a lover.	The lyrics are different from those in Holmes' recording. The singer is upset about having been treated badly by his lover, but he still wants her.

Source: Holmes' recording: *Nuggets, Volume 10, Folk Rock,* Rhino Records 70034.

Led Zeppelin's recording: *Led Zeppelin,* Atlantic 82144.

Black Sabbath (left to right): Terry "Geezer" Butler, Bill Ward (on drums), Toni Iommi, Ozzy Osbourne
© Brian D. McLaughlin/Michael Ochs Archives/Venice, CA

into the seventies. Like the Who, Cream, and Led Zeppelin, Black Sabbath had one lead guitarist, a bassist, and a drummer to back their central attraction, vocalist **Ozzy Osbourne** (John Michael Osbourne, born in 1948). The listening guide on page 191 to "Paranoid," Black Sabbath's only top ten hit in Britain, outlines some important characteristics of seventies heavy metal.

Black Sabbath began to soften their dark-power-centered image and record occasional ballads, such as "Changes" from the *Volume 4* album (1972), a song based on a waltz pattern which featured piano and mellotron in place of heavy guitar, bass, and drums. They also used acoustic guitars on "Laguna Sunrise" (1972). Despite the title and witchcraft-like symbolism on the cover of the *Sabbath, Bloody Sabbath* album (1973), the group began to drift away from their earlier demonic image. As often happens when a group changes a very strong, well-established style or image, their popularity began to decline, particularly in Britain. Osbourne quit Black Sabbath in 1978, and they became a group that other singers used as a springboard into solo careers. Ronnie James Dio, formerly with Elf and Rainbow, sang with Black Sabbath before forming **Dio;** and ex-Deep Purple singer Ian Gillan joined Black Sabbath before forming **The Ian Gillan Band.** Only guitarist Tony Iommi remained with Black Sabbath throughout their career. The other two original members, bassist Terry "Geezer" Butler and drummer Bill Ward, left and returned several times. The original band members reunited to perform at the 1985 *Live-Aid* concert in Philadelphia, and they joined Ozzy Osbourne at the end of what was billed as his last tour in 1992. The recording of "I Don't Wanna Change the World" that was made during that tour won Osbourne his first Grammy.

After Ozzy Osbourne left Black Sabbath he organized his own group, **The Blizzard of Ozz.** For that group he imported the talented young guitarist and songwriter Randy Rhoads from the California-based band Quiet Riot. While on tour after two successful albums in 1982, Rhoads and members of the band's road crew were in a plane crash, and Rhoads was killed. Rhoads was soon replaced and the tour went on, but Osbourne sorely missed Rhoads' writing partnership.

Osbourne's "wild madman" image was an important ingredient of the appeal he had for his young, rebellious fans. He disgusted many parents with such acts as biting the head off a live dove and urinating on the Alamo while on tour in Texas, but the publicity he received from those activities just increased his appeal to his fans. Eventually, he paid for his perverse antics when he bit the head off a bat a fan had thrown onstage in 1982 and had to undergo a series of painful rabies shots after the show. Osbourne was greatly criticized for his song "Suicide Solution," and was sued by parents who blamed the song for their own son's death, though Osbourne claimed it was actually an antialcoholism song written after the alcohol-related death of AC/DC's singer, Bon Scott, in 1980. Osbourne won the lawsuit.

Listening Guide

"Paranoid"* *as recorded by Black Sabbath (1970, released in 1971)

Tempo: The tempo is approximately 164 beats per minute, with four beats in each bar.

Form: The form is based on four-bar phrases that are paired into eight-bar periods. After an eight-bar introduction, the periods follow the pattern A B A C B A B B B A B A A. All of the A periods have two phrases of vocals except the final one, which is instrumental. The B periods are instrumental and often function as vamps in that they do not feature a contrasting melody, but rather maintain the basic beat and bass riff in preparation for the next entry of another vocal A period. The third and fourth B sections feature guitar solos. The C period has a new melody and vocals in which the singer asks for help.

Features: Even beat subdivisions are kept by the drums and bass, but the voice and guitar subdivide the beat unevenly.

The most prominent feature is the pounding of the bass drum and electric bass guitar on each beat.

The drums accent a strong backbeat.

Bass riff patterns repeat through much of the recording.

Fuzztone is used in the guitar solo instrumental.

Lyrics: The singer cannot find happiness and feels that it is too late to think he ever will.

Source: *Paranoid,* Warner Bros. 3104.

Deep Purple was a heavy metal band that almost turned in the direction of progressive rock, or art rock. During their first few years the group's progressive elements were emphasized by the keyboard playing of classically trained Jon Lord. The band's guitarist, Ritchie Blackmore, added his psychedelic-influenced blues riffs, creating a successful combination of the styles. By 1969, Ian Gillan's vocals and Ritchie Blackmore's guitar style led the band toward the newly developing heavy metal style, while Lord pulled in the art-rock direction by writing a concerto for the band to perform with the Royal Philharmonic Orchestra at London's Royal Albert Hall. (**Concertos** are compositions in which an orchestra plays with a featured soloist or small group.) Despite the critical acclaim they received after performing the concerto in 1969, the band's next efforts moved away from art rock and further in the direction of heavy metal. Like most British heavy metal, their music was blues-influenced and riff-based. Often, as in "Smoke on the Water" (1972), the riff involved a low guitar line with the bass paralleling it an octave below.

In 1975, Ritchie Blackmore left Deep Purple and was joined by American musicians from the upstate New York band Elf to form **Rainbow.** Most of Rainbow's music was co-written by Blackmore and other band members, and while former Elf member Ronnie James Dio was with them, the band explored exotic cultures of the past in such works as "16th Century Greensleeves" (1975) and "Gates of Babylon" (1978). Their "16th Century Greensleeves" was quite different from the traditional song "Greensleeves," dating from the Renaissance. Though a sixteenth-century castle was the setting described in the lyrics, and the musical style of that earlier time was suggested by the use of modal harmonies, the melody was not the original "Greensleeves." The music of "Gates of Babylon" was based on melodic themes styled after modern Middle-Eastern scales which, at least to Western ears, had an ancient and foreign sound. The devil was mentioned in the song, as was common for British heavy metal, but with the warning of death to anyone who would dare to "sleep" with him.

After many personnel changes the members who were in Deep Purple during the early seventies regrouped in 1984 and recorded *Perfect Strangers,* which was well received by their long-faithful fans. Disagreements among band members kept them from recording and touring regularly, although they did manage to get together long enough to record *The Battle Rages On* in 1994.

Judas Priest, a band that came to symbolize British heavy metal during the eighties, did not tour the United States until the late seventies, even though they had been together, slowly building a following in England, since 1971. For the first three years they were together, they used the most common early-seventies heavy metal instrumentation—a singer, a single guitarist, a bass player, and a drummer. In 1974 they added a second lead guitarist, expanding their powerful sound with their two lead guitarists playing parallel lines, in much the same way the Allman Brothers and other American southern-rock bands of the late sixties and early seventies had. This very full lead sound made Judas Priest's debut album, *Rocka Rolla* (1974), noticeably different from the music played by a trio of instruments, which had become standard for early heavy metal bands. A listening guide to "Victim of Changes" from their second album, *Sad Wings of Destiny* is on page 193.

The power of this and other recordings by Judas Priest suited their image, which favored the black-leather-jacketed biker look; Halford sometimes even roared out on stage on a Harley-Davidson motorcycle.

Three members of Judas Priest (left to right): K. K. Downing, Rob Halford, and Glenn Tipton

Michael Ochs Archives/Venice, CA

Marlon Brando popularized leather jackets with his "tough guy" image in the fifties, but Judas Priest added chains and metal to the leather to give a "metallic" twist to their rebellious image. The later album *Screaming for Vengeance* (1982) and its single "You've Got Another Thing Comin'" brought Judas Priest a very large following in the United States.

In 1986 the American press had nonmusical events to report on about Judas Priest when the parents of two teenagers who attempted suicide after listening to the album *Stained Class* (1978) filed suit against the band. One of the teens died in the attempt and the other was badly injured and died from a drug overdose three years later. The parents alleged that members of Judas Priest put the words "do it" and some backmasked references to suicide in the album cut "Better By You, Better Than Me." The court heard no evidence to support the claims of subliminal messages, but did hear evidence about other problems in the lives of the teenagers and the case was dismissed. After the trial, band members said that if they believed that subliminal messages could affect their listeners, the messages they would choose to put on albums would be ones that would encourage album sales and concert attendance, and certainly not ones that could possibly destroy their fans. Judas Priest followed the trial decision with another album, *Painkiller* (1991), after which Halford left the band to form Fight.

British rock bands had visited Germany regularly during the sixties, and German rock groups often styled themselves after their English counterparts. Two brothers from Hannover, Germany, Rudolf and Michel Schenker, formed **Scorpions** in 1970. They recorded an album, *Lonesome Crow* (1972), with the sibling guitarists following the blues revival tradition of one (Michel) playing lead and the other (Rudolf) playing rhythm. While most of Scorpions' music followed the riff-based style of British heavy metal, they also wrote interesting melodic lines similar to those common in American heavy metal. Of the British groups that influenced them, **UFO,** which Michel Schenker eventually joined (changing the spelling of his name to "Michael"), was the most important. UFO had become very popular in continental Europe during the early and middle seventies, although English audiences had mostly ignored them. Schenker left UFO in 1979 to form the Michael Schenker Group. He returned to Scorpions to record *Lovedrive* (1979), but left again to work with other bands. Schenker rejoined the newly reformed UFO to tour during the middle nineties.

The powerful drive of heavy metal required singers to force their voices, sometimes to the point of damage to the vocal cords. After Scorpions' *Animal Magnetism* album (1980), their lead singer, Klaus Meine, could no longer sing and was forced to have surgery to have nodes scraped off his vocal cords. After the surgery, Meine went to Vienna for voice lessons to learn to sing without straining. The training involved techniques similar to those learned by classical singers, but Meine did not turn away from heavy metal, as his vocals on Scorpions' *Blackout* album (1982) clearly demonstrate.

In 1988 Scorpions became the first heavy metal band to tour in the Soviet Union, and the following year they were invited back to perform in the Moscow Music Peace Festival, this time joined by Ozzy Osbourne and Bon Jovi. The song "Wind of Change" (1991) was about their Russian visits. Again giving tribute to social and political changes, this time in their own country, the album *Face the Heat* (1993) included songs about the reunification of Germany.

Blues- and riff-based British heavy metal had spread all over the world and, by the early seventies, was copied by bands as far away as Australia. One such band, **AC/DC,** formed in 1973. Brothers Malcolm and Angus Young had moved to Australia from Glasgow, Scotland, in 1963. Their older brother, George Young,

Listening Guide

"Victim of Changes"
as recorded by Judas Priest (1976)

Tempo: The tempo is about 84 beats per minute, with four beats per bar. The bars are subdivided in halves to the point that a double-time feel is created and the beat sounds twice as fast.

Form: A twelve-bar A section (made up of three phrases of lyrics and two repetitions of the riff) is followed by an eight-bar B (two phrases with riffs), a six-bar instrumental, another A, another B, a C with a new riff, and finally a long, riff-based instrumental.

The beginning riff returns to end the recording, balancing the form.

Features: The drums accent the backbeat very heavily.

The recording begins with electronic sounds, which then give way to the bass riff that continues through much of the song.

More than one riff is used throughout the recording, but each is short (a single bar in length) and repeats over and over before changing.

The vocalist, Rob Halford, often intones on a single note; melody is not lacking in British metal, but it is not the most important element.

Stop-time, an effect commonly used in the blues, is used in sections where the instruments fall silent between words Halford sings; they return to support him on certain words.

Lyrics: The singer expresses his frustration about a woman's drinking and infidelity.

Source: *Sad Wings of Destiny*, RCA 4747; and *The Best of Judas Priest*, RCA 4933.

was a member of the Easybeats, a pop-rock group that had one international hit, "Friday on My Mind" (1967); Malcolm and Angus wanted to surpass his success. High-voltage heavy metal was the style of music the brothers chose to play, as the name AC/DC (alternating current/direct current) indicates.

AC/DC's style developed in the British riff-based tradition; they varied it, however, by using repeated riffs only as introductions and endings, not continuing them during the central part of the song. Sex and violence were their favorite themes, and the group's graphic lyrics kept many radio stations from playing their music. Bleaker, more depressing themes followed the death of the band's heavy-drinking vocalist, Bon Scott, who died early in 1980. Scott was replaced by Brian Johnson, whose powerful vocals gave tribute to his predecessor on the album *Back in Black* (1980).

A rapport between band members and fans was an important element at most heavy metal concerts, and AC/DC's paid tribute to that relationship on their album *For Those About to Rock, We Salute You* (1981). (The title was a paraphrasing of the call the gladiators of ancient Rome gave to the Emperor when they entered the arena to engage in battle to the death: "We who are about to die salute you!") Still recording in the early nineties, AC/DC's album *Razors Edge* (1990) gave them a top forty single, "Moneytalks."

Following the dual lead guitar idea brought to heavy metal by Judas Priest, and also adding punk influences, the English band **Iron Maiden** built its image around the theme of death and destruction favored by so many British groups. They named themselves after a medieval torture and execution device that surrounded and then stabbed its victim with multiple spikes, reinforcing this image by using as their symbol a rotting corpse spitting blood. Many of Iron Maiden's song lyrics portrayed medieval and even earlier mythical stories of torture and death, but some also stressed such current issues as the atrocities of war in the twentieth century and the horrors of potential nuclear war. Horrifying their fans' parents, Iron Maiden included a section of the biblical Book of Revelation and its image of "the beast," or the Antichrist, on the album *The Number of the Beast* (1982). Although the main theme projected fear of the beast, the band was still strongly criticized by concerned groups who did not understand this message and feared the influence it might have on young fans. Iron Maiden's first British hit, "Run to the Hills," from *The Number of the Beast* album, was sung from the perspective of Native Americans being slaughtered by European settlers in the United States. Iron Maiden was still recording and touring in the early nineties. They had many personnel changes over the years, with only bassist Steve Harris and guitarist Dave Murray remaining from the original band.

The British band **Def Leppard** formed just one year after Iron Maiden and followed the double lead guitar style of Judas Priest. The band members were teenagers when they began working together and signed a recording contract in 1979. They started out touring with well-established, older groups, and their youth helped them win the adulation of young fans. Although they occasionally donned medieval attire, Def Leppard's song texts were generally closer to traditional rock themes about human relationships and the attractions of alcohol rather than the demonic themes projected by other British heavy metal acts. Musically, they used riffs as introduction themes, but broke away from them through the course of their songs.

Def Leppard's career climaxed with the release of their third album, *Pyromania* (1983), and a long tour followed it. Their career and immediate future were interrupted by a car accident on New Year's Eve that same year when their drummer, Rick Allen, lost his left arm. Allen was determined to continue playing the drums, and the band decided to let him try because they felt Allen was as important to the band as any other member. In 1987, he resumed recording and touring with Def Leppard, aided by an elaborate arrangement of pedals rigged to his drums that allowed him to use his feet to play the beats his left arm would have played. The band was hit with another tragedy when guitarist Steve Clark died in 1991. They chose not to replace him for the recording of their next album, *Adrenalize* (1992), but Def Leppard retained their double lead guitar style by having Phil Collen double track the guitar parts. Clark was later replaced by Vivian Campbell. Def Leppard's next album, *Retro Active* (1993), was a collection of old "B" sides and covers, but that did not mean that it lacked the hard-edged appeal for which the band was known. It made the top ten album charts in the U.S.

American Heavy Metal

Heavy metal was not solely a British invention. It developed out of the playing styles of many late-sixties groups, both British and American. One of the first American groups to use heavy metal's distorted guitar sound was **Iron Butterfly,** from San Diego, California. Their recording of "In-A-Godda-Da-Vida" (1968), which fans took to mean "In a Garden of Eden," was based on a strong, descending bass riff similar to those in British heavy metal recordings. Unlike those recordings, however, they used an electric organ as their main instrument and added distorted guitar sounds. The seventeen-minute-long original recording of "In-A-Gadda-Da-Vida" broke away from the riff for more than two minutes of drum solo, after which the guitar and the organ played back and forth in an instrumental call-and-response pattern that served as a break before the bass riff returned. Iron Butterfly recorded several other albums, and their single "Easy Rider" was included on the soundtrack of the film *Easy Rider* (1969). They broke up in the late seventies, but have gotten back together from time to time for concert appearances.

Jimi Hendrix certainly had considerable influence on the playing style of the "Motor City Madman," **Ted Nugent** (born in 1948). Like Hendrix, Nugent played loud, passionate psychedelic music during the late sixties. In fact, Nugent's act with the Amboy Dukes included many of Hendrix's tricks of controlled, screeching feedback sound effects and plucking the guitar strings (or pretending to) with his teeth. When he first started playing, Nugent took guitar lessons where he learned to use all four fingers on his fingerboard hand instead of avoiding the little finger when playing lead, like many self-taught guitarists tended to do. The additional finger allowed for more speed and melodic extensions that would be harder to reach without it, and he did his best to prove his technical superiority by challenging other guitarists to competitions. Nugent also insisted on using hollow-body electric guitars because he claimed their resonance allowed him to enhance his feedback. Ideologically, he differed with many rock musicians and fans of the time because he spoke out against the use of drugs and for private possession of guns. He also became famous for bow-hunting for food and taunting animal rights activists. From the middle seventies through the early nineties Nugent recorded under his own name with various different musicians singing and playing backup for him. He also recorded with Damn Yankees in the early nineties.

From the northeastern part of the United States, **Aerosmith** formed in 1970 and spent several years imitating the post-blues-revival styles of the Rolling Stones and the Yardbirds. The group did not copy their British predecessors by covering their recordings; Aerosmith's singer Steven Tyler and guitarist Joe Perry co-wrote their own songs. However, Tyler styled his vocals and stage personality after Mick Jagger, and the basic hard and assertive rhythm and blues beat adopted by Aerosmith came from their British counterparts. Like the Rolling Stones, Aerosmith also added folk and country characteristics to their rhythm and blues style. The introduction to "Dream On" (1973), for example, was played on electric instruments, but modeled after the types of picking patterns used by folk musicians on acoustic guitar. Later in the recording, hard-rock-style guitar distortion joined the folk-based sound, but the result was still more like a folk ballad played on amplified instruments than a heavy metal sound. In "Walk This Way," Aerosmith used blues-based riffs and country influences of a very steady, evenly subdivided beat, with strong accents on the first and third beats of each bar. To that they added drums accenting the backbeat. "Walk This Way" introduced Aerosmith's music to younger fans when the group performed it with rappers Run-D.M.C. in 1986. Band members had a number of private disputes that caused their two guitarists, Joe Perry and Brad Whitford, to leave the group for solo careers, but the original group reunited to record *Pump* (1989). Aerosmith signed a new four-album contract in 1991 and continued to top the charts with hit singles and videos in the nineties.

In the occult tradition that was central to Led Zeppelin's act, Vincent Furnier reportedly used an Ouija board to find the name he used for himself and for his band; the board chose **Alice Cooper.** Furnier was from Detroit, but moved to Phoenix and then to Los Angeles to find audiences who would accept the group's unconventional

Alice Cooper in 1972
UPI/Bettmann

Listening Guide

"School's Out"
as recorded by Alice Cooper (1972)

Tempo: The tempo is approximately 132 beats per minute, with four beats in each bar.

Form: After a twelve-bar introduction the form is structured: A Interlude B Interlude C Instrumental (based on A) A B C C B with sections of unequal lengths.

Each A section is eight bars long. The first A is followed by a four-bar interlude with no guitar riff and a very strong pounding on each beat.

Each B section is twelve bars long and includes a four-bar vocal phrase that begins with the words "school's out" sung three times through. The B section functions as a refrain. The first B section is followed by a four-bar instrumental interlude.

Each C section is eight bars long and has a lighter instrumental and vocal timbre with children singing the old "No more pencils, no more books, . . ." school song.

The first C section is followed by an eight-bar instrumental section based on the A section.

The recording ends with an extension of the last B section, a school bell ringing, and then a descending electronic sound.

Features: Uneven beat subdivisions are maintained throughout the recording.

The backbeat is not stressed.

The two-bar opening guitar riff pattern is played six times in the introduction and then also repeated through each A section. The riff is not heard in the rest of the recording.

After leaving the riff pattern, the lead guitar, using fuzztone, continues playing in the background or plays fills after vocal phrases.

Lyrics: The singer is both forceful and exuberant about the ending of the school term.

Source: Time-Life Music, *Sounds of the Seventies—1972; School's Out,* Warner Bros. 2623; and *Alice Cooper's Greatest Hits,* Warner Bros. 3107.

routines, which included live snakes and staged executions. Back in Detroit in 1971, Alice Cooper became one of the first American heavy metal groups to score hit singles. Their music was as loud, aggressive, and distorted as that of British groups, and they used riffs, but the riffs did not serve as the basis of the main melodies as they had in British heavy metal, and their music was often quite melodic and contained more understandable lyrics than British heavy metal. Songs such as "Eighteen" (1971), "School's Out" (1972), and "No More Mr. Nice Guy" (1973) were not full of death-and-destruction themes, but were based on subjects close to their young fans' actual experiences. The listening guide to Alice Cooper's "School's Out" provides an example of American heavy metal of the seventies.

Cooper borrowed many of his stage effects from horror movies and was even featured on a 1975 television special called *Alice Cooper—The Nightmare.* After some time playing slightly less aggressive music, Cooper returned to his former strength with the album *Raise Your Fist and Yell* (1987), from which the song "Freedom" made a strong statement against censorship. Alice Cooper ended the eighties by recording his first top twenty single, "Poison" from the album *Trash* (1989). His theatrical stage antics finally made it into the movies with his appearances in *Prince of Darkness* (1988), *The Decline of Western Civilization, Part II—The Metal Years* (1988), *Freddy's Dead: The Final Nightmare* (1991), and *Wayne's World* (1992).

Another American heavy metal band that formed during the late sixties, this time in New York, used the names Soft White Underbelly, Oaxaca, and then the Stalk-Forrest Group before settling on **Blue Öyster Cult.** They spent the early seventies touring with Alice Cooper and created an appropriately hair-raising stage act centered on mythological characters, such as the ancient Greek god Cronos, who devoured his own children. While not completely abandoning the riff-oriented style common to heavy metal, "(Don't Fear) the Reaper" (1976) and other recordings showed a degree of musical refinement with harmonized vocals and interesting melodies that were sometimes accompanied by folk-rock-style twelve-string electric guitar. While the musical complexities of "(Don't Fear) the Reaper" did not characterize most American heavy metal, they did represent an extreme in the American interest in melody over the constant-riff orientation of British metal.

Blue Öyster Cult went on large-scale tours while still managing what few groups have been able to do after having national hits—they played small clubs under their first name, Soft White Underbelly. For years only the select group of fans aware of the name camouflage were rewarded by hearing Blue Öyster Cult in close quarters. Blue Öyster Cult maintained their dark, mythological image through the eighties, but their albums released after *Fire of Unknown Origin* (1981) saw declining sales. In 1994 they rerecorded some of

Van Halen in 1983 (left to right): Alex Van Halen, David Lee Roth, Eddie Van Halen, Michael Anthony
AP/Wide World Photos

their best-known songs for the album *Cult Classic.* Music from that album was included in the score for Stephen King's TV mini-series *The Stand* (1994).

The American trend toward melodic and theatrical heavy metal was maintained through the late seventies and into the eighties by another New York-based band, **Kiss.** The heavily costumed, horrific images the members portrayed on stage were laughed at by critics, but eventually became popular with the youngest of heavy metal fans and remained so with those fans into the mid-eighties. Kiss' image was enhanced by the fact that none of the members allowed themselves to be photographed without their character makeup for the first twelve years of their career. The powerful, distorted guitar sound on "Rock and Roll All Nite" was commercialized by heavy studio production. Because Kiss played to a younger audience than most heavy metal bands, they continued to produce a lighter version of the heavy metal genre; "Beth" (1976), for example, was a ballad. Evidence of the band's youthful following could be seen in the large number of Kiss comic books that Marvel Comics sold. Band members were even featured in a movie called *Kiss Meets the Phantom of the Park* (1978) that was televised on NBC. As Kiss' fans grew up, the group changed their image by taking off their makeup, and producing loud, potent heavy metal.

Despite several personnel changes, Kiss was still recording in the nineties. Some of their early fans who later became successful musicians got together to tell critics who continued to denounce Kiss just what they thought of the criticism by recording old Kiss songs on the *Kiss My Ass* (1994) album. Musicians on the album included Garth Brooks, Lenny Kravitz, and Anthrax. The original members of Kiss reapplied their trademark makeup and went back on the road in 1996.

Not all American heavy metal revolved around ghoulish, horror-movie stage acts. Brothers Edward and Alex Van Halen formed the band **Van Halen** in 1974. Their father was a musician who saw to it that they had early classical training in piano. The family moved from Nijmegen in the Netherlands to Pasadena, California, in 1968, and the two teenagers formed a rock band called Mammoth. The band played a repertoire of early heavy metal by Cream and Black Sabbath, as well as soul and funk music by James Brown, at every school dance or backyard party they could. They attracted singer David Lee Roth from the Redball Jets and bassist Michael Anthony from Snake when they regrouped under the name Van Halen. With the production assistance of Gene Simmons from Kiss, they recorded an album that was eventually bought and released by Warner Brothers Records of Los Angeles.

Musically, Van Halen took full advantage of guitarist Eddie Van Halen's extensive musical training. Although most of that training was as a pianist, as a guitarist he made use of classical techniques such as natural and **artificial harmonics** (which can be used to play entire melodies) utilized by classical guitarists. He worked out innovative methods to combine slurring and hammering patterns (pulling and hitting the strings instead of plucking or strumming) with both hands on his guitar neck, creating sound effects that were new to rock guitar. At the same time, singer David Lee Roth worked up a stage routine to rival such classic performers as James Brown.

Van Halen's first top forty hit was a cover of the Kinks' "You Really Got Me." Read the listening guide to Van Halen's recording on page 198 and compare it with the guide to the Kinks' original recording that was presented in Chapter 8, The British Invasion.

By the end of the seventies, Van Halen was touring with Black Sabbath, a band they had copied just a few years earlier, and constantly upstaged the longer-established group. Although Black Sabbath's career managed to survive the inevitable comparisons, it was newer groups like Van Halen that led heavy metal to a revival in the eighties.

Eddie Van Halen puts his keyboard background to use on a synthesizer for "Jump" and the somber-toned "I'll Wait," both from the band's *1984* album. He had used a synthesizer in the background of such earlier recordings as "Dancing in the Street" (1982), but feared that his heavy metal fans would not appreciate its use as a primary instrument. Van Halen's fans stood by them for the style change, however, and "Jump" became a hit single.

Listening Guide

"You Really Got Me" as recorded by Van Halen (1978)

Tempo: The tempo is approximately 138 beats per minute, with four beats in each bar.

Form: The recording begins with an eight-bar introduction consisting of eight repetitions of the one-bar guitar riff that continues to repeat throughout most of the recording. The drums enter in the fifth bar.

The introduction is followed by three twenty-bar sections with vocals, and a sixteen-bar instrumental section between the second and third sections. Each of the twenty-bar sections follows the form A A B C. The A and B phrases are each four bars long and the C phrases are eight bars long. The instrumental section is based on four repetitions of the A section.

Features: Even beat subdivisions are used throughout the recording.

The drums maintain a strong backbeat.

The guitar uses elaborate sound effects including much fuzztone.

The riff pattern begins with a half-beat pickup and then plays three beats, ending with a half-beat rest. It is strongly supported by the bass.

The riff breaks into guitar and/or bass solo lines at the ends of phrases and at the final phrase of the instrumental section.

Abrupt key changes occur between sections. Section B is one whole-step higher than A, and C is another fourth higher than B (a fifth higher than A). The pitch of the riff changes along with the key changes.

An interesting effect is created by shifting the vocal accents from the way the lyrics would normally be spoken. Instead of accenting "you" and "got" in "you really got me," Roth accents "really" and "me." This accenting and most of the lyrics imitate the original recording by the Kinks in 1964.

Lyrics: The singer is so completely captured by a girl that he can't sleep and wants to be with her forever.

Source: *Van Halen*, Warner Bros. 3075.

The growing competition for stage dominance between Eddie Van Halen and David Lee Roth finally culminated in Roth's leaving the group in 1985 to pursue a solo career. His replacement, Sammy Hagar, had been the singer in Montrose, a southern California band that had shared bills with Van Halen back in their days as Mammoth. Van Halen's career with Hagar proved to be more successful than did Roth's solo career. Eddie Van Halen quit drinking and changed his image in the nineties, calling himself "Edward" and sporting a new short hair cut, and the band played on with the album *Balance* (1995). Fans of the original Van Halen band received a surprise in 1996 when David Lee Roth returned, displacing Hagar as the band's singer. The reunion was not to last, however, and Roth was again removed from the band. Former Extreme singer Gary Cherone took his place.

Yngwie J. Malmsteen was not an American, but he did his recording in Los Angeles and his musical style fit into the American heavy metal of the eighties. From a musical family in Stockholm, Sweden, Malmsteen studied classical guitar before applying its techniques to electric guitar. Having played technically advanced pieces by such composers as J. S. Bach and Nicolo Paganini, both of whom he credited on his early albums, he was able to play very complex, **contrapuntal guitar parts.** Because he had a highly developed finger-picking technique, he was not limited to the use of a pick in his playing. His album covers paid tribute to Jimi Hendrix, whose influence inspired Malmsteen to dedicate his life to rock music.

Malmsteen moved to California and played with the groups Steeler and Alcatrazz during the early eighties; he left Alcatrazz to form **Rising Force.** Clearly no satanist in any sense of the word, Malmsteen took his "disciple of hell" image from traditional stories about the violinist Nicolo Paganini (1782–1840), who used his brilliant performances to make women fall at his feet. In his time it was rumored that Paganini had made a pact with the devil to grant him prodigious technical facility in exchange for his soul. For song themes, Malmsteen also drew from ancient Greek mythological characters such as Icarus, who attached feathers to his arms with wax in an attempt to fly. Like Eddie Van Halen, Yngwie Malmsteen successfully combined classical and rock guitar techniques, and both guitarists pushed rock guitar styles beyond their earlier simplistic linear patterns into more technically oriented and creative sorts of musical statements. Unfortunately, Malmsteen paid a price for pushing his hands so hard to play very fast, because he overworked them to the point that he developed tendinitis in the middle eighties. His right hand was further injured in a racecar accident in 1987. Despite some rumors that he might even have suffered some brain damage as a result of that accident, he was still recording and touring in the nineties.

Heavy metal fans often wanted to hear their bands "say it like it is" with no holding back for the sake of

Rush (left to right): Alex Lifeson, Neil Peart, Geddy Lee
Michael Ochs Archives/Venice, CA

other people's feelings. Los Angeles-based **Guns N' Roses** certainly fit that bill. Whether or not lead singer Axl Rose said it "like it really is" was much disputed, but the sense of completely carefree personal freedom he portrayed was a major part of his and his band's appeal. Musically, Guns N' Roses fit the old hard rock category as much as they did heavy metal because it was not uncommon for lead guitarist Slash to use an acoustic guitar for a folk-influenced effect or for the band to add horns, vocal choirs, or synthesized sounds to their recordings. This musical diversity was well displayed on the band's first studio album, *Appetite for Destruction* (1987), which some fans saw as their best. Guns N' Roses disgusted many of their fans by including a song by Charles Manson on their *Spaghetti Incident?* (1993) album. Axl Rose kept the band's name alive through news broadcasts covering his many fits of foul language and violence, but by 1994 rumors that the band was breaking up began to spread.

Expansions of the Heavy Metal Style

As the eighties progressed, the terms hard rock and heavy metal became almost interchangeable and even somewhat outdated. Many bands and promoters chose to use glam, thrash, speed metal, or any number of other names to identify the newer versions of what began as heavy metal. Countering the violent and alienated themes of some of those styles, bands playing heavy metal music with a Christian lyric message became increasingly popular during the early nineties. Among those were **King's X** and **Stryper.**

Within the genre of heavy metal, **Rush** was one group that spent much of its lengthy career exploring sounds outside of its Led Zeppelin-based roots. Yet Rush's music remained sufficiently powerful and distortion-oriented to still be considered on the outskirts of heavy metal. The Canadian power trio's beginnings lay in the youthful friendship between classical-turned-rock guitarist Alex Lifeson and bass player Geddy Lee. They formed a guitar, bass, and drums trio to play Led Zeppelin and Cream covers at various high school dances and clubs. Neil Peart replaced their first drummer in 1974 and also became their lyricist.

Rush began to separate from their heavy metal roots with their album *Fly by Night* (1975). The music was still loud and heavy, and song themes about the power of evil still connected them with British heavy metal, but they began to use extended classical forms in multi-movement works. Such art-rock bands as Yes had used classical forms before, but the idea was rare in heavy metal. The most successful example of that structure was "By-Tor & the Snow Dog," for which Canada recognized Rush with a Juno award, the equivalent of an American Grammy, as best group.

Early in their career, Rush played out science-fiction stories through some of their songs and albums.

The album *2112* (1976), for example, was built around the theme of one human being battling the forces of a very depersonalized society in the year 2112. They also occasionally used their songs to make social or political statements. "The Trees" (1978) was based on Quebec's efforts to secede from Canada, "Distant Early Warning" (1984) expressed fear about the potential dangers associated with both peaceful and wartime use of nuclear power, and "Nobody's Hero" (1993) was about the AIDS crisis. They began to broaden their sound by adding synthesizer to some of their recordings in the early to middle eighties, but left that techno style behind in 1989. Although Rush was best known for theme albums, they did end up with one top forty hit single on the U.S. charts, "New World Man" (1983). A listening guide to that recording is included here. Rush was still recording and touring during the early nineties.

Like Rush, Seattle's **Queensrÿche** began with a power-oriented heavy metal style, but then moved in a more progressive direction concentrating on theme albums rather than hard and heavy individual songs. Queensrÿche's stage persona was quite different, almost diametrically opposite, from that of most heavy metal bands because they tended to avoid stressing the personality of any one particular band member and, instead, united as a quintet with a message. Musically, they owed their style to the British band Judas Priest, from whom they copied the powerful effect of using twin lead guitars. Thematically, however, Queensrÿche was quite unique, presenting dramatic theme albums about futuristic characters losing their battle against the evils of society. A sense of alienation and lack of control is clear in many of their dramas. Their 1988 album, *Operation: Mindcrime,* for example, tells of a government plot involving efforts to control the mind of a political assassin. The next two albums of new material brought Queensrÿche more commercial success than they had known in the past, particularly the single "Silent Lucidity" (1990). Fans had to wait four long years for the release of *Promised Land* (1994).

Hard rock, heavy metal, and all of the subsequent related styles clearly developed out of African American blues music because the earliest groups that played in those styles were formed by musicians who had been part of the sixties blues revival. However, the commercially popular hard rock and heavy metal groups were all made up of white musicians. This changed with the introduction of New York's **Living Colour** and their combination of metal and soul styles. Living Colour was formed by guitarist/writer Vernon Reid, who was involved in the foundation of an organization to aid communication among African American bands, the Black Rock Coalition. A strong spokesperson for the position of African Americans in American society, Reid's socially conscious lyrics commented on the unrealistic images of the lifestyles of many African

Listening Guide

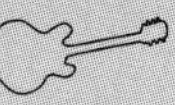

"New World Man"
as recorded by Rush (1982)

Tempo: The tempo is approximately 160 beats per minute, with four beats in each bar.

Form: A sixteen-bar instrumental introduction is followed by seven sections of unequal lengths. Frequent changes of key keep the sections with similar melodies from forming actual A or B sections, but each section ends with a four-bar instrumental extension or with repetitions of the title text, "New World Man." The first section with vocals includes two lyric lines that begin with "he's a" and "he's got a problem" and is twenty bars long including the instrumental extension with which it ends. That music returns later with vocal lines that begin with those same lyrics, but then continue with new lyrics. The next section is twelve bars long, including an instrumental extension. It begins with the words "learning to" the first and third times it is played and the words "trying to" the second time. A third section is sixteen bars long and begins with "he's got to make." Later in the recording a section similar to that begins with "he's not concerned." The recording ends with repetitions of the title text.

Features: Both even and uneven beat subdivisions are used.

The backbeat is accented by the drums.

A single-bar riff pattern played by a synthesizer begins the introduction and continues to repeat through most of the recording.

Other riff patterns one or two bars in length are repeated by the bass at various sections of the recording.

Key changes are frequent, including changes within individual sections.

Lyrics: The song is about the various temptations and pressures the modern world presents to a man and his efforts to find ways to resist and/or deal with them.

Source: *Signals,* Mercury 810-112.

Metallica in 1988 (left to right): James Hetfield, Lars Ulrich, and Jason Newsted
Michael Ochs Archives/Venice, CA

Americans portrayed in television programs. They were also critical of political leaders and of the ways poor people were victimized by others. "Open Letter (to a Landlord)," for example (from *Vivid,* 1988) described the plight of many such people who, though not necessarily African American, were poor and deserving of consideration for their need for security. Reid was very open in his dealings with stereotypes, as was heard clearly in the song "No, I'm Not Gonna Rob/Beat/Rape You, So Why You Want to Give Me That Funny Vibe?" (1988). With an instrumental style rooted in heavy metal and vocals (by Corey Glover) greatly influenced by any number of soul singers from the sixties, Living Colour made its mark as an important band that expanded the style of heavy metal. Living Colour broke up in 1995.

Speed Metal and Thrash

Speed metal combined heavy metal vocals and fuzztone guitar timbres with the intense, throbbing beat of punk. Just as the term "speed" indicates, the music often included instrumental solos played at breakneck speed. Thrash metal shared many of the characteristics of speed metal, but was angrier and stressed the demonic themes of earlier British heavy metal. With the development of these new styles, the former distinctions between British and American styles, for the most part, dissolved.

One of the earliest bands to synthesize punk's energy with the power of heavy metal was the British band **Motörhead** (formed in 1975). "Motorhead" is slang for someone addicted to methedrine or speed. Presumably the umlaut was included in the name to make it look exotic or foreign. Motörhead first performed as the opening act for the Damned, causing them to be pegged as a punk band. Their music was certainly derived from punk, but not simply the British punk style played by the Damned and the Sex Pistols. The flashy guitar solos of the American "Madman of Motor City," Ted Nugent, and the early punk style played by the MC5 and the Ramones also influenced their style. Motörhead's image was the leather-jacketed biker, and their sound was fast, tight, and loud. They soon gained a large British following and served as inspiration for later bands, including Iron Maiden, Guns N' Roses, and many of the American speed metal bands. After many personnel changes, the only original member left in the nineties was bassist/singer Ian "Lemmy" Kilminster. None of the changes marked a reduction of power, however, and the band was still bursting eardrums at concerts and on recordings in the middle nineties.

Some of the best-known bands to follow Motörhead's fast and loud lead included three California-based bands—**Metallica,** Megadeth, and Slayer. While raw power was an important element in the music played by these bands, their lyrics sometimes portrayed death and destruction as the evils of drug use and war, not unlike the music of folk singers or singer/songwriters of the sixties and seventies. For example, the title track from Metallica's *Master of Puppets* (1986) album served as a powerful statement about the dangers of drug use. A listening guide to that recording follows on page 202.

Listening Guide

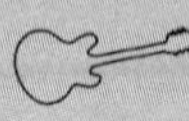

"Master of Puppets" as recorded by Metallica (1986)

Tempo: The tempo is approximately 208 beats per minute through most of the recording, but the center C section is half that speed, or about 104 beats per minute. Most bars have four quarter-note beats ($\frac{4}{4}$ meter), but bars with five eighth-note beats ($\frac{5}{8}$ meter) are placed at the ends of phrases in the A section. The B section includes some two-beat bars ($\frac{2}{4}$ meter).

Form: After an extended instrumental introduction, the form follows the following pattern: A B A B C D Instrumental Extension A B Instrumental Extension.

The A sections are each made up of five phrases of vocals and one instrumental phrase. Each phrase is made up of three four-beat bars followed by one bar of five half beats ($\frac{5}{8}$ meter). The B sections function as refrains, always beginning with the words "come crawling faster." They begin with four-beat bars, but then change to phrases constructed of four-beat and occasional two-beat bars at the section that begins "master of puppets." The meter is further complicated by the use of quarter-note triplets in that same section.

The instrumental C section is played at half the speed of the rest of the recording and is constructed of asymmetrical bar and phrase lengths that avoid the repetition of a regular metric pattern.

The D section is based on four-bar phrase lengths with four beats in each bar.

Features: Even beat subdivisions are used throughout the recording.

The drums sometimes punctuate individual beats of the bass riff and guitar pattern, but at other times, fall into a regular rock backbeat.

The guitars and bass generally play together in short, repeated riff patterns.

The intensity of the very fast beat is accentuated by the use of phrases that end with shortened bars because the listener's ear expects to hear the beat-and-a-half that is missing, but instead hears the next phrase enter.

Power chords add depth to the sound.

The instrumental C section provides a break from the intensity of the rest of the recording.

The beat is slower and the rhythm guitar plays smooth **arpeggio** patterns around which synthesized lead guitar weaves melodic lines.

The recording ends with band members laughing at their puppet victim.

Lyrics: The singer plays the role of a drug that has gained control of the person to whom the song is directed. He demands to be called "master" and promises to kill his puppet victim.

Source: *Master of Puppets,* Elektra 60439.

Metallica's bassist, Clifford Lee Burton, was killed in a bus crash while the band was touring in Sweden in 1986. He was replaced by Jason Newsted. Political themes were added to Metallica's next album, . . . *And Justice for All* (1988), and despite very little airplay on radio or video stations it charted in the top ten. Powerful speed metal bands seldom had the pop-chart success that Metallica experienced. The album *Metallica* (1991) shot to number one the week it was released and contained several top forty hit singles.

Thrash metal, another style rooted in both punk and earlier heavy metal, was played by bands like New York's **Anthrax.** Those roots became particularly clear when a speed or thrash metal band covered an old song by a punk or metal band. Sex Pistols songs such as "Anarchy in the U.K." and "God Save the Queen" as well as songs by Black Sabbath were favorites that newer bands often covered. Audiences often slam-danced their way through the concerts, just as the Sex Pistols' own fans did a decade or more earlier. The lyrics of original songs by speed metal or thrash metal bands were generally directed at an audience of very angry and aggressive young people who felt a great sense of alienation from society. This kind of theme was certainly not uncommon for rock music in general, but the anger was more intense in this music than it was in pre-punk times.

With the EP *I'm the Man* (1987), Anthrax became the first metal band to add rap vocals to their sound. They continued to develop that style, eventually touring with Public Enemy and then rerecording Public Enemy's

"Don't Believe the Hype" with the rappers themselves. Anthrax was still recording in the middle nineties.

Death Metal

Black Sabbath, Iron Maiden, and other heavy metal bands from the past painted images of death and the power of the devil or other demons, but to some metal fans in the eighties and nineties those bands stopped short of creating an image that could really horrify. Modern audiences did not want images that were merely reminiscent of death and evil; some youths became obsessed to the point that they wanted lyrics about real-life murderers and a sense of a "real" presence of Satan. Beginning as an underground movement, albums by death metal bands such as Death, Obituary, Cancer, and many others first circulated among small circles of teens who had met at concerts or through underground newspapers. By the middle eighties the death metal following had grown to the point that albums began to be distributed nationally and some appeared in music stores that were willing to handle them.

One of the most important and influential of the death metal bands was **Slayer,** formed in Huntington Beach, California, in 1982. They recorded their *Reign in Blood* (1986) album while under contract with Def Jam Records, but the company's distributor, Columbia, refused to allow the album's release. It was finally distributed by Geffen Records, and the fact that it sold enough to make the top 100 on the pop charts indicated that death metal had indeed been pulled out of the underground. The song "Angel of Death" from the *Reign in Blood* album is sometimes cited as an important example of death metal because of its horrible and graphic portrayal of death at Auschwitz during the holocaust. The song's expression of Nazi brutality is one that many non-death metal fans could understand and perhaps even appreciate, but many listeners would likely object to other lyrics on the album. Never allowing themselves to "sell out" to commercialism, Slayer was still pounding out aggressive depression in the mid-nineties.

> Death metal was an important influence on the development of grindcore, a style of metal that developed from a combination of thrash metal, hardcore punk, and industrial music. Grindcore will be discussed in Chapter 23, Underground and Alternative Rock Styles.

Summary

Hard rock developed out of the blues revival during the late sixties and shared some of the characteristics of heavy metal, such as loud, distorted guitar timbres and a strong backbeat, but it generally had more commercial appeal than heavy metal. Hard rock bands often played slow ballads in addition to the hard, driving backbeat of other music in the style, and they also used instruments such as acoustic piano, acoustic guitar, and synthesizers. The punk-related fast pulse of new wave became common in hard rock of the eighties, although other characteristics of new wave were not usually present. Hard rock was music that appealed to the many fans who craved loud, danceable rock music, but did not identify with the macho heavy metal bands, androgynous glitter groups, or punk and new-wave bands of the seventies and eighties.

Heavy metal music developed out of riff-based blues revival music in which extreme, distorted sound effects were used. The hypnotic repetition of the riffs along with the loud, screeching guitars, power chords, and pounding drums laid down a powerful foundation for songs that stressed fear of death, destruction, or evil. Whether the songs were about mythological beasts or images from horror stories, the music was aggressive and emotionally satisfying to its young, mostly male fans. Even heavy metal bands whose songs centered on antiwar themes created such rebellious and angry music that people who did not listen closely to the lyrics assumed that the bands were trying to cause violence rather than warn against it.

While British heavy metal styles continued to use blues-influenced riffs as the basis for their music, many American bands concentrated more on melodies with less reliance on repeated riffs. Americans also tended to write songs with themes that were closer to the life experiences of their fans than those by their British counterparts, who favored medieval death-and-destruction themes. Because horror movies were more a part of the American fans' experience than ancient castles, American heavy metal bands tended to draw on the make-believe horrors of monster movies for their stage images.

Heavy metal had undergone many changes by the late eighties. The music played by classically trained musicians in Van Halen, Yngwie Malmsteen's Rising Force, Rush, and Queensrÿche developed into a highly technical and progressive style of music. Going in another direction completely were the thrash and death metal bands that combined punk's anger and violence with heavy metal riffs and screeching, distorted guitars. Although heavy metal has suffered the criticisms of many who fear the effects the music may have on young and impressionable fans, it has continued to appeal to its followers for a number of years and is certain to spark disagreement among critics and fans for many years to come.

Terms to Remember

Arpeggio
Artificial harmonics
Bass riff
Cadence
Concerto
Contrapuntal guitar parts
Power chords
Resultant tone
Surprise cadence
Triplet
Voice box

CHAPTER 19

Punk Rock and New Wave

The musical style called punk rock developed in the United States out of the raw and energetic music played by the garage bands of the mid-sixties. Most of these bands were formed by teenagers who learned to finger basic guitar chords and flail away at drums and cymbals in their own garages, while playing at as high a decibel level as their neighbors would tolerate. The resulting sounds were rough, raw, and musically undisciplined, but expressed the interests of teenagers and brought rock music back to their level.

At the same time recordings by teenaged garage bands were hitting the pop charts, a slightly older, artistically trained but jaded group of musicians in New York were writing poetry and singing about urban decay. That sort of idea for artistic expression had been at the root of several literary, artistic, and musical styles in the twentieth century, including the dadaist movement and the Beat movement. The dadaists were a group of artists in Zurich, Switzerland, after World War I, who saw no intrinsic value in a civilization that was capable of the sort of devastation brought by war and developed a style that turned its back on the artistic traditions of the past. Because, in their view, madness and chaos had prevailed over human reason, as exemplified by the war, they named their art using the nonsense syllables **dada,** and fashioned their works out of trash.

The same fear of the potential the human animal had for violence, along with the awesome power of modern-day weapons, influenced many later artists to share the concerns and emulate the work of the dadaists. The Beat poets and writers of the fifties—Allen Ginsberg, Jack Kerouac, William Burroughs, and others—directed their feelings of anger at what they considered a fat, self-centered, and self-righteous society that gave lip service to freedom for mankind but still excluded anyone who was not white, male, heterosexual, and economically stable. The manner in which the Beats openly confronted the problems that most people ignored—as well as the dada-influenced desire to produce an anti-art to express the belief that society had lost all sense of value—was at the philosophical root of the punk movement, which eventually spawned a style of music.

Early Influences on the Development of Punk

Lou Reed (born in 1943) wrote poetry about street life, prostitution, and drugs in New York. He had been trained as a classical pianist, but no Mozart or Beethoven sonata could express what he had to say about, or to, society. While a student at Syracuse University, Reed played the guitar in rock bands with bass player Sterling Morrison. The pair met avant-garde composer and multi-instrumentalist John Cale in 1964. Cale's principal instruments were the piano and viola, and Reed, Morrison, and Cale decided to work together, leaving

The Velvet Underground (left to right): Doug Yule, Lou Reed, Sterling Morrison, and Maureen Tucker

Michael Ochs Archives/Venice, CA

traditional rock and roll styles aside to experiment with new forms of expression. They added a drummer and called their group the Primitives, the Warlocks, and the Falling Spikes before they settled on **The Velvet Underground.** Reed recited his poems to simple and repetitious melodies while Cale played a continuous, pulsating drone on his electric viola. Their first drummer quit and was replaced by Maureen Tucker. True to the style of the dada artists of the past, Tucker sometimes added trash-can lids to her drum set.

The Velvet Underground met pop artist Andy Warhol in 1965. Warhol was already well known for his transformation of soup cans and other mundane images into art. Interested in mixing media, Warhol had the Velvet Underground play for his traveling artwork, the Exploding Plastic Inevitable. He painted a banana for the cover of their first album and had them add a singer/actress friend, Nico (Christa Päffgen), to sing on some cuts. *The Velvet Underground & Nico* was recorded in 1966 but was not released until a year later. Reed's songs concentrated on harsh themes such as drug addiction and sadomasochism. He sang as if he were intimately aware of all aspects of urban street life, but coolly above it and alienated from any concerns about the people involved. The music was repetitious, unemotional, and only vaguely related to most commercial rock. A listening guide to "Heroin" from that album follows on page 206.

The Velvet Underground's next album, *White Light/White Heat* (1968), expressed themes similar to those of its predecessor. Drugs were an important element of street life, and the album's title track was Reed's anthem to amphetamines. Traditional song and musical forms were ignored and repetitious drones, occasionally interrupted by screeching feedback, were established to accompany his monologues. The work was not commercial, but it functioned to express the coldness and gloom Reed saw in the world. Cale eventually left the group to do his own recording and to produce albums for other non-mainstream musicians. The Velvet Underground continued with Doug Yule replacing Cale, and they maintained the group name with other musicians after Reed's departure in 1970. Reed went on to enjoy a successful, often controversial solo career. In 1989 he and Cale reunited to perform a piece called *Songs for 'Drella,* their tribute to Andy Warhol, who had died in 1987. Original members of the Velvet Underground regrouped under the name of their drummer, Moe Tucker, for her 1991 album, *I Spent a Week There the Other Night.* They toured Europe in 1993. After the tour Reed, Cale, and Tucker continued their solo careers. Sterling Morrison died of non-Hodgkin's lymphoma in 1995.

The Velvet Underground's first efforts influenced the development of punk as a musical style. Their emotionless portrayal of themes centering on alienation from human concerns and their use of repetitious musical ideas became characteristic of both punk and new wave. The highly emotional expression of anger at the heart of most punk music came from the garage band sound. Musically, this anger was expressed through a constantly pounding eighth-note beat (often strummed on the guitar or plucked on the bass) and shouted vocals. Behind the fast throbbing pulse of the guitar and/or bass, the drums usually played a traditional rock backbeat.

A high school rock band called **The MC5** (the Motor City Five) from Lincoln Park, Michigan (just outside Detroit), developed a loud and angry style. Formed in 1965, they moved to Detroit after graduation and by 1967 had connected themselves with a radical political group called the White Panthers. The MC5 drew attention to themselves by playing for those who rioted at the 1968 Democratic Convention in Chicago. Their first

Listening Guide

"Heroin"
as recorded by the Velvet Underground (1966)

Tempo: The tempo varies greatly throughout the recording. The introduction opens with a pulse on the half beats (eighth notes) establishing a tempo of 72 beats per minute, with four beats in each bar. In bar ten, another guitar enters with a lead pattern at which point all of the instruments speed up gradually to about 96 beats per minute. Each A section speeds up more to about 144 beats per minute, and then slows back down to about 96 beats again. The tempo returns to about 72 beats per minute at the very end.

Form: After the introduction, the form is based on three A sections of thirty bars each and then a final A that is extended to over double that length. A new set of lyrics begins each section, but the beginning and ending of each section is established as much by the tempo changes (back to 96 beats per minute) as by the vocals. The longer final section extends the middle, which is played at the fast tempo of about 144 beats per minute and includes many chaotic sound effects created by electric guitars and electric viola.

Features: Even beat subdivisions are maintained throughout the recording.

No backbeat is present. The bass drum is hit on beat four of each bar of the introduction and then at irregular intervals in the slow parts of the recording. The drum is used to support the intensity of the faster parts by playing on each half beat.

Once the rhythm guitar enters at the first beat of the second bar of the introduction, it plays on the first beat of every bar through the rest of the recording, alternating between just two chords.

Lyrics: The song portrays the effect heroin has on the addict. Sung from the addict's point of view, the exhilaration as the drug enters his body is expressed in the lyrics and in the increasing tempo of the music. The addict says he knows the drug has caused his alienation from the rest of society, and he knows it will kill him, but he still cannot and will not do without it.

Source: *The Velvet Underground & Nico,* Verve/Polydor 823290; *The Best of the Velvet Underground,* Verve 841164.

album, *Kick Out the Jams* (1969), was criticized and refused airplay because of its obscene lyrics, which their record company, Elektra, replaced on a reissued version of the album. With two guitars and plenty of distortion, the MC5 combined the power of heavy metal with the raw garage band sound, all infused with their own belligerent, indignant attitude.

While a student at the University of Michigan, James Jewel Osterberg sang and played drums with a rock group called the Iguanas (from which he took the name Iggy). In 1967 he formed his own band, **Iggy Pop and the Stooges,** and played repetitious, angry, and pessimistic music. On stage, Iggy Pop acted out his disgust with society by hitting himself with his microphone and by cutting his skin with pieces of glass and then smearing the bloody mess with peanut butter. John Cale, who had recently left the Velvet Underground, was hired to produce the group's first proto-punk album, *The Stooges* (1969). Iggy Pop developed an addiction to heroin and his career might have ended after that album had he not been befriended by David Bowie, who produced albums and wrote songs for him. Pop's career continued into the nineties, but his importance to the punk movement lay in his early self-destructive image.

New York Punk

The loud, raw, rebellious sound of the MC5 and the Stooges and the alienated attitude of the Velvet Underground was picked up in the early seventies by **The New York Dolls,** who added some glitter to punk and then passed it on to other New York groups and to the angry youth of London. Formed in 1971, the New York Dolls were five men who donned lipstick, heavy eye makeup, and stacked heels to perform songs about "bad" girls, drugs, and New York street life. The themes were similar to those of the Velvet Underground, but the attitude was less serious. From the MC5 and the Stooges, the Dolls took heavily distorted guitar lines and a powerful pounding beat, which they combined with Rolling Stones-like rhythm and blues. On page 207 is a listening guide to "Personality Crisis," from the group's debut album, *The New York Dolls* (1973).

The New York Dolls established a large following in late-night clubs in New York, but despite their attempts, failed to gain commercial success in other parts of the country. By 1975 most of the group members had left the band, although singer David Johansen and guitarist Sylvain Sylvain continued performing as the New York

The New York Dolls (left to right): Arthur Kane, Jerry Nolan, David Johansen, Sylvain Sylvain, and Johnny Thunders
Michael Ochs Archives/Venice, CA

Listening Guide

"Personality Crisis" as recorded by the New York Dolls (1973)

Tempo: The tempo is about 155 beats per minute, with four beats in each bar.

Form: The recording begins with a sixteen-bar instrumental introduction.

The piano enters, in a honky-tonk style, at bar four.

The basic structure is composed of eight-bar periods organized according to an AABA song form. The B sections repeat lyrics about the frustrations of having a "personality crisis."

A short break (of silence) occurs between the second and third AABA sections.

Features: Each beat is evenly subdivided into two parts, creating a constantly throbbing pulse twice the speed of the basic beat. The fast pulse is created by the guitarist, the chords played by the pianist's right hand, and the drummer on the cymbals.

The drummer maintains the backbeat on the bass drum (in rock, the backbeat is usually kept with the snare drum).

The vocals are shouted almost in a **monotone** (a single, unvaried tone), although there are occasional pitch changes when the chords change or to emphasize a particular word.

Heavy distortion is used by the guitarist.

Lyrics: The lyrics are about a person who plays a role dictated by society during the day but then goes wild at night in an effort to shake off the day's frustrations.

Source: *The New York Dolls,* Mercury 832752.

Dolls for another two years. After the demise of the Dolls, David Johansen recorded several solo albums, and then reemerged in the late eighties with a new persona, calling himself Buster Poindexter and singing songs in a variety of older rhythm and blues styles. Several albums by the New York Dolls were released during the eighties, but they were all old recordings that were made back in the seventies. Johnny Thunders and Jerry Nolan both died in the early nineties.

A nightclub in the Bowery district of New York City, called CBGB & OMFUG (Country, Blue Grass, Blues & Other Music For Urban Gourmets, usually shortened to CBGB's), was the starting place for many New York punk bands, including Television, the Patti Smith Group, and the Ramones. **Television** was formed in 1973 by poet/singer/guitarist Thomas Miller, who gave himself the stage name Tom Verlaine, after the French symbolist poet Paul Verlaine (1844–1896). The original Verlaine was known for his use of symbolism, metaphor, and lyricism, all of which Miller tried to emulate in the lyrics he wrote for Television. The group's first bass player, Richard Hell (Richard Myers), spiked his hair and wore torn clothing, creating an image that later became standard for British punks. Television's music combined a Velvet Underground-influenced punk sensibility with melodic lead guitar lines and psychedelic-style wandering improvisations. Members of Television went their separate ways for just over thirteen years and then reunited in 1991 to record the album *Television* (1992) and to perform at the Glastonbury Summer Festival in England.

Patti Smith (born in 1946) was an artist and writer from Chicago who established herself professionally in New York. She wrote poetry, plays, and articles, many of which were published. Rock journalist and guitarist Lenny Kaye provided simple guitar accompaniments for Smith's reading, and later singing, of her poetry. Ex-Velvet Underground member John Cale produced the Patti Smith Group's debut album, *Horses* (1975), which combined the musical simplicity of the Velvet Underground with Smith's gutsy and energetic vocals and a pounding punk beat. The album included a new version of the song "Gloria" [recorded by Them and the Shadows of Knight (both 1966)]. Smith's singing of a male text was intended to shock the average listener in much the same way that Beat poetry had years before. The next year she covered the Who's "My Generation" (the Who in 1965, Patti Smith in 1976), in which she shouted obscenities making it clear that hers was a new and angrier generation. Smith eventually married Fred "Sonic" Smith, ex-guitarist for the MC5, and moved to his home in Detroit, where she continued to write while also raising their children. A more philosophical, even guardedly optimistic Patti Smith released the album *Dream of Life* in 1988. A book of Smith's poetry entitled *Early Work: 1970–1979* was published in 1994, and later that same year her husband died. She continued on, however, and made occasional concert appearances. She recorded *Gone Again* in 1996.

Another New York-based band, **The Ramones,** formed in 1974 and named themselves after Paul Ramon, a pseudonym Paul McCartney had used for a time early in his career with the Beatles. Each group member adopted Ramone as a last name. Only their drummer, Tommy Ramone (Tom Erdelyi), had worked as a professional musician; consequently he became both manager and producer of the group, continuing in these roles even after he stopped playing with the group in 1977. The Ramones' very simple, fast, high-energy music and monotone vocals became the prototype for much punk rock to follow. Most of their songs lasted two minutes or less and were written by the group members as a team. The Ramones did not release their first album, *Ramones,* until 1976, but their performances in England helped influence the beginnings of the punk movement there in 1975.

The Ramones remained a high-energy punk band until the early eighties, when they began branching out from punk to experiment with new styles. Early-sixties wall of sound producer Phil Spector was brought in for the *End of the Century* album (1980), but the result was a disaster in the minds of the Ramones' punk fans. The album included a hilarious rendition of "Baby I Love You," the 1964 Ronettes hit that Spector had written and produced. After other experiments with non-punk styles of music, the Ramones returned to their punk energy for *Too Tough to Die* (1984), produced by their original producer and drummer, Tommy Erdelyi. The Ramones played on for another eleven years and then left their fans with their final album, *Adios Amigos* (1994).

British Punk

Groups of British lower- and middle-class teenagers in the mid-seventies had grown to detest the lifestyles and traditional values of their parents, and had come to believe they were caught up in an economic and class-ridden social system over which they had no control—one they viewed as relegating them to a life of near poverty with no hope of securing jobs that would pay them enough to better themselves. Entertainment, even movies or dances, was too expensive for them. Rock music played by wealthy stars surrounded by grandiose stage sets and light shows meant nothing to them. Stylish clothes were out of their reach. The attitude of those teens was one of anger, frustration, and violence. They were antigovernment, antisociety, and antifashion. They adopted a way of dressing in torn second-hand clothing with large safety pins holding the pieces together. The look reflected their rejection of the standard image of respectability and became a symbol of their feelings of alienation.

The raw, pounding music of the New York Dolls and the Ramones was transported to London by **Malcolm McLaren** (born in 1946), the owner of an antifashion clothing store in London called Sex. He was sympathetic to the feelings of the angry youth to whom he sold torn clothing, some of which was even made out of plastic trash bags, and wanted to produce a sound that would express their attitudes. He was impressed with the New York Dolls, whom he saw in London and eventually contracted to manage, but their breakup left McLaren to form his own group in London. McLaren knew that one of his employees at Sex, Glen Matlock, played bass with his friends, guitarist Steve Jones and drummer Paul Cook, in a group called Swankers. He had an angry young customer, John Lydon, who did more hanging around than buying. Lydon had no experience as a singer, but the sound McLaren was after required no more polish than the rebellious youth already had. McLaren put the quartet together, changing Lydon's name to Johnny Rotten, and used his store's name as the basis of their group name, **The Sex Pistols.**

Just as McLaren wanted, the Sex Pistols evoked disgust everywhere they went. Their music had the constant pounding and loud distorted guitar that had been part of the punk sound in Detroit and New York, but unlike the New York Dolls this group was not just toying with rebellion. They were completely caught up in highly emotional anger. They wanted to repulse the establishment and provoke authorities into retaliating against them, and that attracted more fans than their music by itself did. Performances were stopped in mid-song, concerts were canceled, and radio programmers pulled their music off the air. Their first single, "Anarchy in the U.K.," was recorded in 1976 under the EMI label and sold well in Britain in early 1977, but was removed from record stores by EMI because of the vulgar language the group used on a British television program, "The Today Show." Matlock left the Sex Pistols, and Rotten brought in a friend, John Ritchie, to play bass. The group renamed Ritchie, Sid Vicious.

The Sex Pistols had gained such a reputation that other bands began forming, copying their distorted guitar, bass, and drums instrumentation with monotone-shouted vocals even before the Sex Pistols had an album out. The energy level of the music was high, and violence at their performances became common. A punk dance—or a sort of non-dance—called the **pogo,** in

Sid Vicious and Johnny Rotten during a Sex Pistols concert in Atlanta, Georgia, in 1978
UPI/Bettmann

which people simply jumped straight up and down, was started at the Sex Pistols' concerts. The Pistols lost record contracts as fast as they signed them, and they finally ended up on the Virgin label.

One sure way to anger a respectable English citizen is to show disrespect for the Queen. Queen Elizabeth II was celebrating her Silver Jubilee (the twenty-fifth anniversary of her coronation) in 1977, and in her "honor," the Sex Pistols released a single whose title was the same as that of the English national anthem—"God Save the Queen." The Sex Pistols' lyrics were so foul and insulting that the song was banned from British radio and television; the title was not even allowed to be printed on chart listings, so it made its way up the charts as a black line. A listening guide to the recording follows on page 210. The commercial success of "God Save the Queen" and the album that followed, *Never Mind the Bollocks, Here's the Sex Pistols* (1977), made it clear that the punks spoke for many young people in Britain.

The Sex Pistols toured Europe and the United States—they had to tour if they wanted to continue to perform, because no promoters in England would hire them. They tried to stir up American youth by changing the "U.K." to "U.S.A." in performances of their British hit "Anarchy of the U.K.," but in most places they were received more as oddities than as a musical group. With nowhere left to go, but having made their statement and begun a movement, the Sex Pistols disbanded in early 1978. Vicious moved to New York with his girlfriend, Nancy Spungen, whom he was later accused of killing [this event was brought to movie audiences in *Sid and Nancy* (1986)]. Vicious died of a drug overdose before the investigation was completed. Johnny Rotten took back his real name, Lydon, and formed an alternative rock band called Public Image, Ltd., that only toyed with punk. Paul Cook and Steve Jones spent some time playing backup for ex-New York Dolls and Heartbreakers guitarist Johnny Thunders on his album *So Alone* (1978) before they formed another British punk band, the Professionals.

Listening Guide

"God Save the Queen" as recorded by the Sex Pistols (1977)

Tempo: The tempo is about 145 beats per minute, with four beats in each bar. Each beat is evenly subdivided into two parts, creating a constant, throbbing pulse.

Form: The recording begins with a four-bar instrumental vamp followed by an eight-bar instrumental introduction.

The form is based on eight-bar periods, organized according to an AABA song form with added C sections.

Most A sections begin with the words of the song's title.

Two full AABA sections are followed by another A section with vocals, an instrumental period, another A with vocals, and then three new C periods based on repetitions of words from earlier B periods.

Features: Although the guitar and drums both keep the fast pulse of the beat subdivisions from time to time, it is most clearly maintained by loud, repeated bass notes.

The drums maintain a backbeat.

The guitar is very heavily distorted, creating a background mood of anarchy and disorder.

Most of the vocals are shouted in a monotone by Johnny Rotten alone, with the group joining him in the C section.

Lyrics: The lyrics express a very depressed view of Britain's economy, social system, and government, emphasizing that there is no hope for anything positive in the future and anyone who is hopeful is only dreaming.

Source: *Never Mind the Bollocks, Here's the Sex Pistols*, Warner Bros. 3147.

The raw energy of punk was maintained through the music of bands that fashioned themselves after the Sex Pistols, and, surprisingly to many, the original members reformed the Sex Pistols with Glen Matlock back on bass in 1996. It was rumored that they even offered to perform a benefit concert for the newly divorced Princess Diana. Given their disdain for the monarchy in the past, their offer added an ironic sense of humor to their nasty past reputation.

The MC5 and Iggy Pop and the Stooges were the musical influences on another Malcolm McLaren-managed British punk band, **The Damned.** In addition to playing fast, angry music, the Damned engaged in such punk stage activities as taunting and spitting at the audience while accepting the same in return. The first British punk band to release a single, "New Rose" (1976), and an album, *Damned, Damned, Damned* (1977), the Damned traveled to New York and played at CBGB's. Not a commercial success, the Damned were denied their request to tour with the Sex Pistols. For the most part, the Damned played fast, hard punk music that stressed anger for anger's sake. They toured the United States in 1977, and, along with the Sex Pistols, served as a major influence on the development of the punk movement in California. The Damned remained together until their breakup in 1989, having placed hits on the British pop charts through almost every year of their career.

One of the most important and longest-lasting groups of the British punk movement was **The Clash.** Except for their bass player, Paul Simonon, who picked up his first bass when he joined the group, the members were experienced musicians. Singer/guitarist Joe Strummer (John Mellor) had been with a rock band called the 101'ers, and both guitarist Mick Jones and drummer Tory Crimes (Terry Chimes) came to the Clash from the London S.S. Crimes was replaced by Nicky "Topper" Headon after the group recorded their first album. Instead of just expressing the multidirectional anger the Sex Pistols had, the Clash's songs zeroed in on some of the central causes of punk rebellion: youth unemployment, racism, and police brutality. In addition to using punk's familiar rhythmic throb, they took Jamaica's music of rebellion and added a reggae beat to some of their music. They signed with CBS records, a move criticized by some fans who believed that all punk belonged underground. British punk fans had learned to use the music as background for their own expressions of anger, and violence flared at concerts. At one concert auditorium, seats were actually torn up from the floor during a Clash performance. The Clash had two top forty U.S. hits with "Train in Vain (Stand by Me)" (1980) and "Rock the Casbah" (1982).

Through several membership changes, Simonon and Strummer were still with the Clash to record *Cut the Crap* in 1985, but the band folded within the next year. Old material was rereleased on several collections during the early nineties, and the Clash had its only number one British hit with the 1991 rerelease of "Should I Stay or Should I Go" (originally released in 1982) after the song was used in a commercial for Levi's jeans.

The Sex Pistols, the Damned, and the Clash were only three of many British punk bands that formed and recorded in 1976 and 1977. Among those other bands,

The Dead Kennedys (Jello Biafra, second from left)

Chelsea expressed the anger of the unemployed in their single, "Right to Work" (1977); Billy Idol, singing with **Generation X,** released "Your Generation" (1977); and **X-Ray Spex** and their female singer, Poly Styrene (Marion Elliot), brought a violent feminist message to punk with the single "Oh Bondage Up Yours!" (1977). London did not have a monopoly on British punk. **The Buzzcocks** formed in Manchester and expressed rebellious, youthful attitudes in their singles "Breakdown" and "Boredom" (both 1977). Many bands stayed with the short songs, fast pulse, and shouted vocals of the Sex Pistols and the Damned, while the Clash's inclusion of reggae added some variation to the punk style. The energy level and simplicity of punk soon spread beyond its original antigovernment and antisociety causes and themes.

Guitarist/singer Paul Weller had played folk and rock music with friends in casual jam sessions after school. Eventually drummer/singer Rick Buckler and bassist/singer Bruce Foxton joined him, and by 1974 the trio had begun to work seriously on their performance repertoire. They decided to call themselves **The Jam** as a reminder of their early playing sessions. Hammering away at a fast pulse similar to other British punk groups, the Jam was introduced to London audiences in 1976. While the Sex Pistols were wearing punk clothing and shouting obscenities about the Queen and her government, the Jam appeared in conservative suits and ties with a British flag behind them and openly supported the monarchy and the government (though they agreed with other punks on the issue of anti-immigrant racism in Britain). The Jam was, in effect, a group of latter-day Mods who mixed a punk beat with music by earlier Mod groups, such as the Who and the Kinks, and other music popular with the Mods, particularly Motown-style soul. After the Jam's breakup in 1982, Weller continued to be influenced by American soul music in his work with Style Council. Style Council even performed with Curtis Mayfield during the early eighties. Weller's band of the early nineties was called the Paul Weller Movement.

Hardcore Punk on the West Coast

When British punk bands like the Sex Pistols and the Damned toured the United States, their music, while not commercially successful, struck a nerve in both San Francisco and Los Angeles and sparked a punk movement there. Punk groups from California used the same rock instrumentation as the British punks, but their attitude was much different from their British counterparts. Whereas the Sex Pistols and other British punks spoke for angry youth who were experiencing a desperate economic situation, the American punks had jobs, food, and clothing readily available to them. That did not keep anger and violence out of their music, however; the groups had plenty to say about their ex-hippie parents' worn-out (or worse yet, sold-out) values, and the U.S. government's involvement in the politics of Asian and South American countries as well as its support of an oppressive regime in South Africa.

The Dead Kennedys formed in San Francisco in 1978 and played fast, heavily distorted music with shouted monotone vocals that condemned the U.S. government and other institutions for a multitude of offenses, and yet also displayed a sense of humor. The Dead Kennedys' lyricist/singer, Jello Biafra (Eric Boucher), adopted his stage name when he heard that the government had sent a shipment of Jell-O to the starving people of Biafra in Africa, calling it foreign aid. Their debut album, *Fresh Fruit for Rotting Vegetables*

Listening Guide

"Kill the Poor" as recorded by the Dead Kennedys (1980)

Tempo: The recording has a slow introduction sung in a tempo of roughly 96 beats per minute, with four beats in each bar. After the introduction the tempo suddenly jumps to about 208 beats per minute with four beats per bar. The fast pulse that earlier punk superimposed on top of a slower beat becomes the main beat through the placement of the drummer's backbeat at the faster speed.

Form: The recording begins with one eight-bar vocal introduction intoned by Biafra, accompanied by guitar distortion and occasional drum rolls; the drums begin a regular backbeat in the seventh bar.

The vocal introduction continues with another period, this time of seven bars, followed by a fast drum roll that serves to introduce the fast beat pulse of the rest of the recording.

A four-bar instrumental vamp establishes the faster tempo.

A series of repeating A and B periods separated by two four-bar instrumental vamps and two eight-bar instrumental periods follows. The A periods feature Biafra intoning lyrics at such a fast pace that they are barely understandable, and the B periods feature the constant repetition of the title lyrics, "kill the poor."

Features: Even beat subdivisions are maintained throughout the recording.

In the fast section, the bass keeps the pulse by playing repeated notes.

The harmonies are more complex than those of most other punk rock.

Lyrics: The lyrics satirically praise the U.S. government for developing a bomb that can kill people while leaving property undamaged, and suggest that, in order to save money otherwise wasted on welfare, the bomb be used to kill poor people.

Source: *Fresh Fruit for Rotting Vegetables,* Cherry Red Records, B Red 10.

(1980), included "Holiday in Cambodia," inspired by the Sex Pistols' "Holidays in the Sun." Also on the album was "Kill the Poor," which made a very strong satirical statement against those who put money into the development of the neutron bomb (a device that killed people, but left structures intact) but resisted governmental aid to America's poor. The satirical position was reminiscent of *A Modest Proposal* by Irish satirist Jonathan Swift (1667–1745), in which Swift proposed the English solve the problem of starvation in Ireland by eating Irish children. A listening guide to "Kill the Poor" is included here.

The Dead Kennedys attacked the Moral Majority on the EP *In God We Trust, Inc.* (1981). Their album *Plastic Surgery Disasters* (1982) left the government alone for a while, instead of criticizing average American lifestyles in "Winnebago Warrior" and "Terminal Preppie." After a break of several years, during which its members produced and supervised recordings by other punk bands for their Alternative Tentacles label, the Dead Kennedys were back with their usual political and social satire in *Bedtime for Democracy* (1986), which even attacked the punk community itself in "Chickenshit Conformist" and "Macho Insecurity."

By 1988, the Dead Kennedys had broken up and Biafra became known for his solo "spoken word" performances. In 1989, he recorded *The Power of Lard* with members of Ministry. Since then Biafra has worked with several other bands and aided many others by promoting their music on the Alternative Tentacles label. Other former members of the Dead Kennedys also continued their careers—guitarist East Bay Ray joined Skrapyard, and bassist Klaus Flouride formed an acoustic band, Five Year Plan, in the nineties.

A large hardcore punk culture developed in Los Angeles during the late seventies and early eighties and includes such bands as Black Flag, the Germs, X, and Catholic Discipline, all of whom were featured in the movie *The Decline of Western Civilization* (1980), directed by Penelope Spheeris. One of the first and longest-lasting of the L.A. bands was **Black Flag,** a name chosen because a black flag is a symbol for anarchy. The group's music shared the fast beat, distorted guitars, and monotone vocal style of British punk bands like the Sex Pistols, and their short songs decried the meaninglessness of their lives and the anger they felt toward the establishment and all authority figures. So much violence erupted at their concerts that most Hollywood clubs banned them. Their personnel changed fairly often, with only guitarist Greg Ginn remaining through their career. The group remained true to violent punk-styled music until 1984, when they broke away from hardcore punk and included some very long songs with heavy metal characteristics such as elaborate distorted guitar solos and repeating bass riffs. Black Flag broke up in 1986 and Ginn worked with a group called Gone before continuing on with a solo career, under both his own name and under the stage name Poindexter Stewart.

Devo (left to right): Bob Mothersbaugh, Bob Casale, Mark Mothersbaugh, Alan Meyers, and Jerry Casale
Michael Ochs Archives/Venice, CA

Black Flag's singer, Henry Rollins had considerable success with Rollins Band and with a band he called Henrietta Collins and the Wifebeating Childhaters. Like Jello Biafra, Rollins has performed as a spoken-word artist.

Another L.A.-based punk band, **X,** was welcomed at the clubs that had banned Black Flag. X played both high-energy punk and Velvet Underground-influenced pulsating drones, but they also added occasional touches of country music, rockabilly, and heavy metal styles. Their producer was Ray Manzarek, the Doors' organist, and their first album, *Los Angeles* (1980), featured him performing on their cover of the Doors' "Soul Kitchen." X was formed in 1977 by singer/bassist John Doe, singer Exene Cervenka, guitarist Billy Zoom, and drummer Don J. Bonebrake. Zoom admired fifties rock styles such as rockabilly and the music and guitar style of Chuck Berry, and often played solos showing those influences. Doe and Cervenka, husband and wife, were both modern-day Beat poets, and their duo vocals, sung in a monotone unison or at the interval of a fifth, became X's trademark. Zoom left the group in the mid-eighties and was replaced by Tony Gilkyson, with whom X continued their career as the most popular punk band in Los Angeles. X was still doing occasional live concerts and recording during the mid-nineties, having lasted through Cervenka and Doe's divorce and their continuing solo careers.

American New Wave

During the late seventies many rock fans felt that rock music had gotten old, fat, and complacent and was in need of an infusion of new energy. Punk certainly had the necessary energy, but it was far too violent and anti-establishment to appeal to the mass audience. Punk's half-beat pulse, monotone vocals, and emotional alienation were adopted by groups that played within more mainstream popular rock styles, and the term "new wave" began to be used to categorize the music of some of those bands. In actuality, almost any new sound from the sixties onward was temporarily dubbed new wave until it became mainstream and a newer wave took over, but the label finally stuck for the post-punk music of the mid- to late seventies.

Whereas punk was almost always played only by guitar, bass, and drums, new-wave bands often added electronic keyboards, saxophones, or other instruments. Punk guitarists and bass players used distortion to cloud melodies or chord changes; new-wave musicians produced a clean, slick sound. The throbbing pulse that punk bands created by angrily strumming their electric guitars was transformed by new-wave bands into a fast, clear playing of repeated notes on the electric bass.

One of the best examples of a new-wave band that stressed a very slick version of the fast pulse of punk along with chant-like monotone vocals was **Devo.** Devo was formed by singer/keyboardist Mark Mothersbaugh and bass player Jerry Casale, who were both art students at Kent State University in Ohio. Their main purpose in putting together a band was to produce *The Truth about De-Evolution* (1975), a film that took a humorous and sardonic look at the dehumanization of modern society. Their group was named as a play on "de-evolution." After completing the film, Devo recorded the single "Jocko Homo" (1976), which was so unemotional it sounded as if it were being performed by robots. Devo used their dehumanized image on stage and in videos, often appearing with a little robot mascot they called Booji. Devo put their early singles on their first album, the title of which, *Q: Are We Not Men? A: We Are Devo!* (1978), came from lyrics in "Jocko Homo." A listening guide to "Jocko Homo" follows on the next page.

Listening Guide

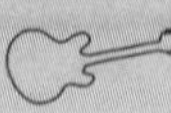

"Jocko Homo"
as recorded by Devo (1976)

Tempo: The tempo is about 240 beats per minute with seven beats in each bar of the first section ($\frac{7}{4}$ meter), and about 120 beats per minute with four beats ($\frac{4}{4}$ meter) in each bar of the second section.

Form and Features: An instrumental (electronic) introduction begins with four bars of a seven-beat pattern in which each bar is subdivided into a four-plus-three accentuation. The next four bars of the seven-beat pattern are then subdivided into a three-plus-four configuration. The effect of the unusual and uneven seven-beat patterns, and the effect of the shift in the accenting of the subdivisions, is one of instability, as if one is lost in an electronic web.

Even beat subdivisions are maintained throughout the recording.

No backbeat is used, even in the four-beat section of the recording.

The seven-beat patterns continue through three periods on monotone vocals, including a section involving a call-and-response exchange maintaining that the members of Devo are not human.

Between the second and third vocal periods, an instrumental section repeats parts of the introduction.

After the three vocal periods in a seven-beat pattern, an instrumental section repeats parts of the instrumental introduction sequentially; that is, the same music is repeated at different pitch levels. In this case, the pitch of each repetition is higher than that of the previous one.

The fast pulse of the beats in the seven-beat section is maintained with pulsating repeated notes in the bass as the tempo turns to a slower four-beat pattern.

A new melody is used at the beginning of the four-beat sections, but later in the section a variation of the earlier melody is sung.

At the very end, the fast seven-beat pattern returns for a short instrumental section.

Lyrics: The lyrics express the belief that the coldness of the modern world has had a dehumanizing effect on mankind.

Source: *Q: Are We Not Men? A: We Are Devo!*, Warner Bros. 3239.

Devo's clean electronic sound, and their songs about a modern world in which human beings are dehumanized by the increasing dependence on robots and computers, were entertaining and accessible to a mass audience. Their second album, *Duty Now for the Future* (1979), rendered emotionless one of the most common rock song themes, human attraction and love, with the songs "Strange Pursuit" and "Triumph of the Will." Devo's later work continued to use humorous, dehumanized electronic music, but much of it had also evolved (devolved?) into commercialism, and Devo began to stress a dance beat and older rock styles instead of continuing to make statements about modern society. They even commercialized to the point of recording "elevator music" for **Muzak** during the eighties. Devo did some touring in the early nineties.

Another new-wave band whose early recordings employed punk-influenced musical characteristics in much the same way that Devo had was **Talking Heads,** formed in New York in 1975. Like Devo, Talking Heads was formed by art students. Singer/guitarist David Byrne and drummer Chris Frantz had attended the Rhode Island School of Design and had played in a group called the Artistics. After leaving that group, they formed a trio with a classmate of theirs, Tina Weymouth, who played bass and synthesizer (Frantz and Weymouth later married). The three moved to New York and were hired to play at CBGB's. The name Talking Heads came from their observation that television often avoided full body shots and showed only people's heads, talking. The trio recorded the single "Love Goes to Building on Fire" (1977), but by the time they recorded their first album, *'77* (1977), they had added another member, guitarist/keyboardist Jerry Harrison. Harrison had played with Jonathan Richman and the Modern Lovers, an early seventies group that concentrated on keeping the style of the Velvet Underground alive. Talking Heads' simple, pounding rhythmic pulse with Byrne's forced, near-monotone vocals on bizarre songs like "Psycho Killer" placed the band well within the new-wave category.

Minimalist composer and producer Brian Eno joined Talking Heads for their second album, *More Songs About Buildings and Food* (1978). Eno worked with electronic sound effects and added a new and, for the time, modern character to the group's music. They fused their very angular, electronic sound with the rhythms of soul music in their cover of Al Green's song

"Take Me to the River" (1978). Talking Heads' interest in soul music inspired them to explore other styles of African American music, and they used polyrhythms common in the music of some African cultures on such tracks as "I Zimbra" from their *Fear of Music* album (1979). African rhythms returned on *Remain in Light* (1980), and Byrne added gospel singers and soul and funk musicians to perform with the group on tour. Sides three and four of the live greatest-hits album *The Name of This Band Is Talking Heads* (1982) featured the group with their temporarily expanded membership.

Talking Heads took a break from recording during the early eighties and then regrouped as a quartet (without Eno) to record later albums. *Speaking in Tongues* (1983) combined lyrics expressing the new-wave alienation from emotion with complex funk rhythms and avant-garde electronic sounds. The 1984 concert film *Stop Making Sense* brought many of the group's earlier songs to a wider audience. *True Stories* (1987) was the soundtrack for a movie by Byrne. Talking Heads remained together until the end of 1991, but by that time Weymouth and Frantz were well established with their own band, Tom Tom Club, and Byrne had a successful solo career.

Many of the bands formed during the mid- to late seventies played with enough of the musical characteristics of punk or new wave to gain a reputation within those styles, even though much of their music did not really fit into the new-music genre. **Blondie,** for example, formed in 1975 and debuted at New York's CBGB's. Their first album, *Blondie* (1976), put them on the commercial outskirts of new wave, but their later music was even less characteristic of the style. Deborah Harry, their blond lead singer after whom the band was named, seldom sang in a new-wave monotone and tended more toward pop-style melodies. Blondie toyed with disco in "Heart of Glass" and "Call Me" (both 1980), reggae in "The Tide Is High" (a 1980 cover of a reggae song by the Jamaican, John Holt), and a commercial brand of rap in "Rapture" (1981). Blondie broke up in 1982 and individual members pursued solo careers, but none matched the success they had known as Blondie.

Part of the attraction of new wave was its simplicity when compared to the grandiose scale of the performances by many glitter and art-rock groups of the seventies. That simplicity, in many ways, was not only a reaction against the excesses of the other styles, but was also a return to what rock music had been during the fifties. New-wave groups such as **The Cars,** from Boston, combined the unemotional (almost monotone) vocals and the pounding beat of punk music with Chuck Berry-influenced guitar and an angular version of a rhythm and blues beat to form a tradition-rooted new-wave style. Singer/guitarist/writer Ric Ocasek formed the Cars in 1976 and remained their central figure. His songs were not as cold and unemotional as those of the New York groups, but the Velvet Underground-style sense of alienation from emotional attachments was well represented in "My Best Friend's Girl" (1978), in which Ocasek coolly reported that his friend's girl had once been his own girlfriend. Feelings like jealousy were considered old-fashioned to new-wave modernists. *Door to Door* (1987) was the last album the Cars recorded together, but several of the members continued to do solo work under their own names. In addition to recording for himself, Ocasek produced albums for other bands.

Just after Talking Heads had stretched their new-wave style to include soul, and Blondie had expanded theirs to include disco, **The B-52's** from Athens, Georgia, produced a self-titled album that took a lighthearted look at new wave. They played simple music with monotone but chatty and conversational vocals, and combined it with early-sixties teen dress and slang expressions. Their name was a slang term for the heavily ratted and smoothed-over bouffant hair style that had been popular during the early sixties and was worn by the group's two female members, Cindy Wilson and Kate Pierson. Most members had had little musical training when the group formed, but its music was simple and they learned to play well enough to meet the demands of their style. Many of their songs and stage acts poked fun at the pop dance steps of the early sixties.

An interesting combination of completely different new-wave styles resulted when David Byrne of Talking Heads was brought in to produce the B-52's *Mesopotamia* album (1982). Byrne's brilliant control of percussion and clean electronic sound effects gave the group an entirely new sound that pleased Byrne's fans, but took away much of the playful style for which the B-52's were known. The group stopped working with Byrne and returned to their old style for later recordings. The B-52's lost their guitarist, Ricky Wilson, who died of AIDS in 1985. Their drummer, Keith Strickland, replaced Wilson on guitar. Cindy Wilson left in 1990, but returned for occasional performances. The group's light-hearted style was well suited to their version of "Meet the Flintstones" which was used in the movie *The Flintstones* (1994).

British New Wave

Punk and new wave's emphasis on simplicity put rock music back into intimate settings. In New York, those settings were nightclubs like CBGB's; in most parts of England they were pubs. **Pub rock** was an English back-to-the-roots movement that began during the early seventies but did not become commercially successful until later in the decade when many fans finally grew tired of large-scale rock. Many of the pub-rock bands, such as Brinsley Schwarz, Ducks Deluxe, Rockpile, and the Rumour, were popular alternatives to punk, and musicians in those groups became important as British new-wave artists.

Elvis Costello
Michael Ochs Archives/Venice, CA

Few performers from the pub-rock scene attracted as much attention or were as influential as **Elvis Costello** (Declan MacManus, born in 1955). MacManus was raised in Liverpool, where the American sound of Buddy Holly and the Crickets was popular and being updated by such groups as the Beatles and the Hollies (from the neighboring city of Manchester). MacManus wrote songs throughout his teenage years, and then joined a British bluegrass band called Flip City, moving to London to perform with them and record demos of his songs.

MacManus signed with Stiff Records in 1975, but he, his producer, Nick Lowe (a pub-rock musician originally in Brinsley Schwarz and later with Rockpile), and one of Stiff's owners, Jake Riviera, left the company so Riviera could manage MacManus' career at Radar Records. With the new stage name Elvis Costello, MacManus took Buddy Holly's boy-next-door image and changed it from naive to neurotic. As befit that image, many of Costello's songs centered on relationships, and in particular on insecurity about relationships with women. Another favorite subject was politics, as was heard in his first single, "Less Than Zero" (1977), which attacked fascism. Costello teamed with a California-based country-rock band called Clover (without their usual singer, Huey Lewis) to record the album *My Aim Is True* (1977). In true pub-rock tradition, most of the music on the album followed a Buddy Holly-influenced pop-rockabilly style, but the angry and critical lyrics of "Less Than Zero" hinted at his future direction. Costello's second single, and his first hit in Britain, was the reggae-influenced "Watching the Detectives." (The song was included on the American version of his debut album, but not on the British version.)

For the album *This Year's Model* (1978), Costello formed a new backup band, the Attractions, and his music moved from pub rock to new wave. The Attractions provided a clean, strong accompaniment to Costello's punk-influenced, almost monotone vocals. He projected an arrogant, yet insecure image, in contrast to the angry confidence most punk singers displayed. The pounding half-beat pulse of punk was present on some cuts, but, as was also true of American new wave, its production made it clean-sounding, not wildly distorted. The beat and vocal style were exactly the modern sound new-wave fans wanted and Costello's career was launched. A listening guide to "Radio Radio," from *This Year's Model,* can be found on page 217.

Costello followed *This Year's Model* with an album that gained him more attention and commercial success in the U.S. than had any previous releases by British new wave artists, *Armed Forces* (1979). Not surprisingly, the song themes dealt with power struggles, but in this case they were on both a personal and an international level. The song "(What's So Funny 'Bout) Peace, Love and Understanding" suggested that tolerance be practiced. His next album, *Get Happy!!* (1980), followed just behind *Armed Forces* in terms of popular appeal. On that album Costello broadened his musical direction by adding American influences including the Memphis soul of Sam & Dave and Booker T. and the MGs, as well as Nashville-styled country music (in "Motel Matches"). The Attractions remained as Costello's regular backup band through most of his albums of the eighties, although he did break away from them to record with other musicians when he felt the need for a change.

For his *Spike* album in 1989, Costello used a different group of backup musicians on each track. In order to get exactly the people he wanted, he used recording studios in London, Dublin, New Orleans, and Los Angeles. The opening song, "This Town," included Roger McGuinn (formerly with the Byrds of L.A.) playing his famous electric twelve-string guitar, T-Bone Burnett on acoustic guitar, and England's own Paul McCartney on bass. McCartney also played bass on "Veronica," a song he co-wrote with Costello. From New Orleans, pianist Allen Toussaint and the Dirty Dozen Brass Band were added for "Deep Dark Truthful Mirror." Pretender Chrissie Hynde sang backup vocals on "Satellite." The song themes on *Spike* were as varied as the music. Costello often wrote songs about relationships, particularly problem ones, and "Baby Plays Around" was certainly in that vein, but knowing he co-wrote it with his wife makes it seem more like a general expression than a personal one.

Spike also contained some songs that made bold political statements. For example, no one could miss that "Tramp the Dirt Down" was about England's then Prime Minister, Margaret Thatcher. "Let Him Dangle," about an

Listening Guide

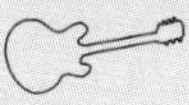

"Radio Radio"
as recorded by Elvis Costello and the Attractions (1978)

Tempo: The tempo is about 144 beats per minute, with four beats in each bar.

Form: The recording begins with an eight-bar instrumental introduction, made up of a two-bar pattern played four times.

The overall form is made up of two eight-bar A sections, a sixteen-bar B section, an eight-bar C section, two more A sections (with new lyrics), and a repetition of the B section and lyrics.

Features: The bass uses repeated notes to establish a fast (eighth-note) continuous pulse.

All of the A sections have a strong backbeat maintained by the drummer, but the B sections have no backbeat.

The C section contrasts with the music that precedes and follows it by modulating to a key a minor third higher than the rest of the song and having a lighter vocal tone quality, with organ in the background.

Costello sings in a monotone through most of the recording.

Lyrics: The lyrics stress the dependence some teens have on the radio for both entertainment and advice, and comments that the people he hears talking on the radio do not understand the young generation, so they try to use the power of radio communication to control young people's minds. Costello makes use of the old cliché "Never bite the hand that feeds you" in the lyrics to the C section, changing it to express his own bitterness toward the people who control radio.

Source: *This Year's Model,* Columbia 35331; and *Best of Elvis Costello and the Attractions, 1977–1984,* Columbia 35709.

actual incident from 1952 in which an innocent man was put to death, made more than a historical statement when the ending switched to the present tense and public demands for capital punishment. Although Elvis Costello was raised in England, his grandfather was from Ireland. Costello and his wife had moved from London to Dublin by the time Costello was making the album. His song "Any King's Shilling" was based on a story his Irish grandfather had told him, and he appropriately accompanied the song with Irish folk instruments such as the harp, bagpipes, and fiddles. On the cover of the *Spike* album, Costello billed himself as The Beloved Entertainer. Costello was back with the Attractions, to which he added Nick Lowe, to record *Brutal Youth* in 1994.

While Elvis Costello began his career by portraying an extreme example of male insecurity in modern culture, singer/writer/guitarist **Chrissie Hynde** (born in 1952) displayed a strong, tough, and yet somewhat vulnerable female image. Hynde was born and raised in Akron, Ohio, and played guitar with a rock band while an art student at Kent State University. A fan of British bands such as the Kinks and the Who, she moved to London in 1973 and got a job as a music reviewer for *The New Musical Express.* She decided to find a band to play with and worked with several musicians who later formed the Damned, as well as with Mick Jones, who later formed the Clash. In 1978, she recorded a demo tape which secured for her a contract with Real Records (Sire Records in the United States). Contract in hand, she hired British musicians to form **The Pretenders.**

In addition to Hynde as a singer, writer, and rhythm guitarist, the Pretenders included lead guitarist James Honeyman-Scott, bass player Pete Farndon, and a temporary drummer who was replaced by Martin Chambers after the recording of their first single, a cover of the Kinks' "Stop Your Sobbing." A strong backbeat and heavy-metal-influenced guitar lines gave the Pretenders a hard rock sound that was new wave because Hynde's vocals were generally void of any sort of tender emotion. The energy, and often the anger, of punk was present, but Hynde made the element of melody, whether it was her singing or Honeyman-Scott's guitar playing, more important than the fast, pounding punk beat.

The original membership of the Pretenders did not last long, because within a year after the release of their second album, *Pretenders II* (1981), Farndon left the band, Honeyman-Scott died of a drug overdose, and Hynde became pregnant. Determined to continue with her music, Hynde put together new musicians for the *Learning to Crawl* album (1983), and then another new group, which included American funk and fusion musicians, for *Get Close* (1987). Through the many personnel and musical changes in her band, however, Hynde maintained her tough new-wave image and stage personality. The 1994 album *Last of the Independents* provided a strong return for the Pretenders and included "I'll Stand by You," which charted in the top twenty.

Summary

The general label of "new music" may be applied to punk and new wave. Messages of song lyrics differed from one style to the other, with punk generally expressing multidirectional anger and new wave displaying a cool, modern, detached approach to life, unaffected by emotional concerns. Both styles were trimmed down from the grandiose rock styles of the seventies, which had created an unbridgeable distance between the performer and the audience. Punks resented music that was so complex most teens could never achieve the necessary technical proficiency to be able to play it—at least not without years of serious study. They were aware that rock had once been a young people's music and, armed with simple guitar, bass, and drums instrumentation, they performed music meaningful to them and their peers.

Although new wave used modern electronic instruments and made other concessions to commercialism, the style maintained punk's energetic pulse. Historically, nothing was really very new about any of the new-music styles, but to listeners who had grown accustomed to hearing art-rock groups use racks of synthesizers and dozens of instruments, or to heavy metal bands with stacks of screaming amplifiers behind them, the sound of new wave was refreshingly clean, clear, and modern.

Terms to Remember

Dada
Monotone
Muzak
Pogo
Pub rock

CHAPTER 20

Ska and Reggae

On his second trip to the New World in 1494, Columbus discovered Jamaica. An island in the Caribbean just south of Cuba, it was then settled by the Spanish, who killed most of the native tribes and brought in African slaves to work the land. The English took it over during the middle of the seventeenth century, and it became part of the British West Indies. The black population grew through several centuries to become the dominant race in a mixture of peoples including indigenous Indians and others originally from various parts of Europe and Asia. By the twentieth century, English had become the principal language of the country, but mixtures of other languages were commonly spoken in small towns outside the main population centers. Jamaica gained its independence from Britain in 1962. The rich mixture of cultures in Jamaica, its closeness to the southern United States—allowing access to AM radio broadcasts—and its historical relationship with Britain all contributed to the development of ska and reggae.

Jamaicans played a type of folk music called **mento,** a slow version of a Cuban-styled rumba combined with African rhythms. The name mento evolved from the Spanish word *mentar,* meaning "to mention," referring to the subtle ways their song lyrics, sometimes accompanied by symbolic dance steps, expressed personal complaints or social criticisms. Subtlety was necessary to avoid offending the person or group to whom the criticisms were directed while still getting the point across. One singer or one instrumentalist playing a melody instrument such as a flute or fiddle usually led the musical part of the performance. That leader was accompanied by percussionists as well as guitar or banjo players providing both rhythm and harmony.

Although European musical instruments were in use in Jamaica, mento and other folk music was often performed on homemade flutes and bowed string instruments made out of bamboo. Guitar-like instruments were made from wood with gut strings attached to a resonating gourd. Percussion instruments included drums and rattles of various kinds. Some drums had skins stretched over wooden, clay, or metal chambers, while others were made of bamboo or hollow tree trunks. A coconut shell scraped with a spoon was often part of the percussion section. Because so many languages were commonly spoken in Jamaica, no particular language was exclusively associated with mento. A dialect of English was the most common, and many mento melodies were variants of English folk songs.

During the late forties and early fifties, American rhythm and blues became quite popular in Jamaica, having reached the island by radio and through recordings. Much of the music played by American radio stations during the early sixties, however, had become too pop-styled to suit the Jamaican taste. With radio no longer a dependable source of entertainment, Jamaican disc jockeys set up large sound systems to play the music of performers such as Louis Jordan, Fats Domino, and various doo-wop groups. The disc jockeys played their records from the backs of trucks, creating discothèques out of vacant land in poorer areas of the island. A great deal of competition grew among the disc jockeys, each wanting to attract the largest crowds. In order to find rhythm and blues records that no other disc jockey had, they traveled to southern cities in the United States like Miami and New Orleans to buy records. The competition was so stiff, in fact, that to keep from revealing details about their new records, the disc jockeys usually even removed the labels.

Ska

As rhythm and blues styles became more familiar to the people of Jamaica, some began to play the music themselves. To the rhythm and blues beat they added characteristics of mento, along with elements of other styles that had reached them by radio, through traveling performers, or on records. A brass style of Cuban origin, reminiscent of that played by Mexican mariachi musicians (but without the exaggerated vibrato of the Mexican players), was sometimes mixed with other styles. Often the Jamaicans would include saxophone solos styled after those in rhythm and blues recordings, or forties jazz- or swing-style improvised solos played on trumpet or trombone. Modern musical instruments were mixed with traditional folk instruments, depending on what was available to a particular group. The style resulting from the combination of all of these musical and instrumental elements was called ska.

Ska combined so many different styles of music that the sound of different groups often varied considerably. The common element was a four-beat pattern based on rhythm and blues, but with some instruments playing a very strong accent on a subdivision (even or uneven) just after each of the four beats. That accent was strong enough to be heard as if it were the main beat, creating a feeling of a delayed beat. For this reason, the ska pattern is often called a "hesitation beat."

Harmonically and melodically, ska was related to rhythm and blues. Its melodies were often derived from rhythm and blues songs, and the ska versions usually employed the chord progressions used with the original melody. A blues progression was sometimes used, as was the common doo-wop progression of I–vi–ii–V. Newly composed ska melodies often emphasized certain melodic devices and contours that had a distinctively "ska" sound. One of these involved the use of the sixth note of the scale alternating in various rhythms with the upper key note (for example, an A going back and forth to a C in the key of C). The rhythmic pattern and the characteristic melodic skips used in ska defined it as a style. Most ska placed very little emphasis on the bass, and the result was a light and smooth music, unlike the more rock-styled, bass-heavy reggae that developed out of it.

Many of the people who enjoyed ska were poor. Traveling long distances and having to pay to attend live concerts was more than they could manage. Records, however, were snapped up by the disc jockeys to play out of their traveling concert trucks, where anyone could listen to them. Recording studios were built in Jamaica during the early sixties to record music by local groups. The first and most important of these studios, Studio One, was started and run by Clement "Coxsone" Dodd. Because singers were available even when instruments were not, many ska vocal groups formed and needed instrumental backing in order to make records.

One of the most often recorded instrumental groups was **The Skatalites,** a group that included a brass section made up of four trumpet/fluegelhorn players and two trombonists; a woodwind section of two alto and two tenor saxophonists; and a rhythm section of two guitarists, three keyboard players, one bass player, and three percussionists. The Skatalites recorded instrumental hits of their own, and backed such vocal groups as **The Maytals,** the Wailers, and the Heptones. The Skatalites had hits in Jamaica, and their recording of "Guns of Navarone" even made the British charts in 1967. The Skatalites accompanied the Maytals in "If You Act This Way" as outlined in the listening guide on page 221.

Records were important in spreading ska's popularity outside of Jamaica. England had communities of people who had immigrated from Jamaica, and ska became popular there. The British often called ska "blue beat" music. "My Boy Lollipop," a record made in Britain by a young Jamaican singer named Millie Small, combined a rock drumbeat with a ska hesitation beat, and became a hit single in both Britain and America in 1964. "My Boy Lollipop" was produced by Chris Blackwell, a Jamaican of British ancestry who moved to London and used the profit from his hit recording to establish the Island Record Company.

By 1966, ska began to undergo changes in Jamaica. Influences of Memphis soul music by such performers as Wilson Pickett and Booker T. and the MGs brought gospel-style call-and-response vocals and a heavy rhythmic bass line to ska performances. The tempo of the music also slowed down, and the result was a new ska-based style called **rock steady.** "Oh Ba-a-by" by the Techniques and "Rock Steady" by Alton Ellis were both rock steady recordings that became popular in Britain during the late sixties.

Jamaican disc jockeys continued to be the crucial element in disseminating the music to the poor people of Jamaica. Still in competition to outdo one another, and remembering hearing American radio disc jockeys make comments after records had begun playing, Jamaican disc jockeys built on that idea by talking in a rhythmic patter while ska and rock steady records were playing. The practice was called **toasting** when it was no more than rhythmic **patter-talk,** but eventually the talk involved manipulation of the recording during the disc

Listening Guide

"If You Act This Way"
as recorded by the Maytals (1964)

Tempo: The tempo is approximately 116 beats per minute, with four beats in each bar.

Form: After a four-bar introduction, the sections are all eight bars long and organized according to the following pattern: A A B A Instrumental B A Extension based on A. The same lyrics are used in the second, third, and fourth A sections, and the second B section repeats the lyrics of the first B section.

Features: The beat subdivisions are placed slightly before the even half-beat subdivision, but not early enough to be uneven.

There is no stress on the backbeats.

The solo singer is responded to by a vocal group in the A sections and by a horn section in the B sections.

The backing instruments include organ sustaining the chords and guitars strummed from the high strings to the low strings on the beat subdivisions.

The instrumental section features a tenor saxophone solo.

Lyrics: The singer is singing to a woman who told him she was true, and he is hurt to find that her crying indicates she was not.

Source: *Jamaica Ska,* Rhino Records 014.

jockey's performance. It then took the name **dubbing,** because changes were being made in the sound of the recording, and in some cases those changes involved dropping the sounds of some instruments or vocals out of the recording. Dubbing was soon performed in the recording studios as an essential element of spoken patter over a rock steady beat.

Reggae

In 1968, a fast form of rock steady was recorded by the ska group the Maytals in their recording "Do the Reggay." Eventually this new music that had evolved out of ska was called reggae. To Jamaicans, reggae meant "the king's music," and the king to whom it referred was Haile Selassie, the emperor of Ethiopia. Reggae groups used modern amplified instruments including lead and rhythm guitars, piano, organ, drums, and electric bass guitar, along with Jamaican percussion instruments. Bass players usually set up melodic patterns that they repeated throughout most of a piece of music. These patterns involved much syncopation, often avoiding important beats such as the first beat of the bar. In addition to being played loudly, the bass line was often emphasized by having the lead guitar parallel it in octaves. The typical reggae rhythm fell into a pattern of four beats with triple subdivisions, but unlike ska, it accented the first and third subdivisions, as had rhythm and blues. Another rhythm and blues element reggae employed was the accented backbeat, a characteristic that made it more easily accessible to rock music fans. The reggae beat differed from the rhythm and blues beat through the use of syncopated bass lines and the influence of other, Latin-styled rhythms.

Reggae was just as eclectic as ska, perhaps even more so, in terms of borrowing melodies and other musical characteristics from different styles. When they borrowed an American country melody, reggae musicians used a two-beat country bass along with typical reggae syncopations, and when they used a melody popularized by a jazz musician (even if the jazz musician was a guitarist who played in small groups), reggae groups tended to use a full jazz-band-style horn section for their recordings.

Reggae's infectious beat earned it more commercial success than the earlier musical styles from Jamaica. Reggae song lyrics usually centered on the concerns of the poor and socially downtrodden people who played it. Most reggae performers came from the west side of the capital city of Kingston, on the southeastern part of the island. The poverty and political subjugation of those people was the theme of the film *The Harder They Come* (1972), which starred the young ska and reggae singer **Jimmy Cliff** (born in 1948). Like the movie, the lyrics of many reggae songs dealt with threats of revolution, a call for people to stand up for their rights, and faith in their god, "Jah," to save them. The term **rudeboys** soon came into use to identify these poor Jamaicans who "rudely" sang or spoke out against their oppressors. Later ska bands and their followers also identified themselves as rudeboys.

The religion practiced by many reggae musicians was Rastafarianism, a name taken from Ras Tafari, the real name of Haile Selassie. Rastafarianism was based in Judeo-Christian theology, using the Christian Bible along with writings by the Jamaican-born African American minister Marcus Garvey (1887–1940) as its texts. One basic belief separating it from Christianity was that Ras Tafari was a Messiah-like prince sent by God. Selassie was the emperor of Ethiopia from 1930 until he was deposed in 1974, and many Rastafarians believed it was necessary for them to travel to Ethiopia. Also as part of their religion, Rastafarians were vegetarians, made sacramental use of marijuana, which they called ganja, and did not comb their hair, causing it to mat together in a style that became known as dreadlocks.

One of the most influential of the Rastafarian reggae groups was **The Wailers.** The Wailers originally formed

Bob Marley
Michael Ochs Archives/Venice, CA

in 1963 as a vocal group whose recordings were accompanied by the Skatalites. Both **Bob Marley** (1945–1981) and Peter Tosh belonged to the Wailers at that time. Members drifted away and the group broke up in 1966, but reunited a year later and began recording again in 1969. To avoid dependence on instrumental groups, some of the singers began to play instruments, and other instrumentalists were added as well. Their Jamaican-produced albums did moderately well in their homeland, but it was not until 1972 when a contract with Chris Blackwell's Island Records was signed that they had a chance at international success. The albums *Catch a Fire* and *Burnin'* were both released in England in 1973. British guitarist Eric Clapton covered the song "I Shot the Sheriff" from *Burnin'* and made Marley's song and its reggae beat an international hit. Clapton's cover drew attention to the Wailers, who began to tour on their own. A listening guide to the Wailers' recording of the song follows on page 223.

Peter Tosh left the Wailers in 1973 to pursue a solo career. Marley made changes in his group by adding more instrumentalists and a female vocal trio, one member of which was his wife, Rita Marley. Under the new name **Bob Marley and the Wailers,** their career took off and Marley became an international star. They toured all over the world and attracted large numbers of fans, particularly in Britain, Scandinavia, and Africa. Marley became enormously influential in Jamaica, but had enemies there as well, and an unsuccessful attempt was made to kill him and his wife just days before they were to give a free concert for the Jamaican people in 1976.

Marley died of cancer in May 1981. His mother, Cedella Booker, recorded a tribute to him called "Stay Alive" (1981), and his widow and their children continued to keep the Marley name alive with their own successful careers as reggae singers. Marley himself had given his children, Sharon, Cedella, David ("Ziggy"), and Stephen Marley, a start in the music business when he had them record his song "Children Playing in the Streets" in 1979. By the late eighties, **Ziggy Marley** (born in 1968) had established his own career as a writer and singer, with his siblings backing him as the Melody Makers.

Baritone singer **Peter Tosh** (Winston Hubert MacIntosh, 1944–1987) had done some solo work under various names, such as Peter MacIntosh and Peter Touch, while with the Wailers. On his own in 1973, Tosh wrote and recorded songs about his own life and problems as well as those of his people. His Rastafarian belief in the importance of ganja, which was illegal in Jamaica, was the source of many legal problems, and Tosh was arrested several times on drug charges. The songs on his album *Legalize It* (1976) demanded the drug's acceptance. His next album, *Equal Rights* (1977), urged Jamaica's poor to stand up to the government that had been ignoring their problems. Tosh recorded *Bush Doctor* (1978) with Rolling Stones Mick Jagger and Keith Richards, who released the album on their own label.

Tosh was a very influential spokesperson for his people and his religion, particularly after the death of Bob Marley. He had many battles with the police, and was involved in a number of lawsuits, both as defendant and as plaintiff, over various financial dealings. He expanded his political statements to include subjects of international concern with the music on his last album, *No Nuclear War* (1987). Tosh's life had been threatened many times, and he was aware that he lived in constant danger, but he identified with his homeland too much to move away. Gunmen entered his home in the fall of 1987 and shot him along with some visitors. Tosh died at a nearby hospital soon after the shooting.

The infectious beat of reggae attracted listeners in Africa, and after playing covers of Jamaican songs, many African musicians began to incorporate elements of reggae into their own styles. These styles varied from

Listening Guide

"I Shot the Sheriff" as recorded by Bob Marley and the Wailers (1973)

Tempo: The tempo is approximately 96 beats per minute, with four beats in each full bar.

Form: After a two-beat percussion flourish, the form is organized as follows: A B A B A B A B Instrumental.

The eight-bar A sections are composed of two four-bar phrases that begin with the words "I shot the sheriff" and serve as a refrain.

The B sections are composed of three four-bar phrases followed by a two-beat percussion flourish similar to the one introducing the song.

The final instrumental includes a few vocal statements and is based on a repeated A section.

A fade ending is used.

Features: The beat subdivisions in the A sections are basically even. Both even and uneven beat subdivisions are used in the B sections, often in different instruments at the same time.

A soft backbeat is maintained through most of the recording.

The backup vocalists sing in falsetto.

The B sections are polyrhythmic.

Lyrics: The singer shot a sheriff when the sheriff was trying to shoot him, but he did not kill the deputy he has been accused of killing. He says he will pay if found guilty, but wants it remembered that the only shooting he did was done in self defense.

Source: *Burnin'*, Tuff Gong 422-846200; *Legend—The Best of Bob Marley and the Wailers*, Tuff Gong 422-846210; and *This Is Reggae Music*, Island Records 9251.

one place to another, but in general the music became known as Afro-reggae.

Afro-Reggae

As an important part of the Rastafarian religion, Marcus Garvey taught that people of African descent needed to "return" to Africa in order to uplift themselves out of the position of subjugation they suffered in the New World. He founded the Universal Negro Improvement Association (UNIA) in Jamaica in 1911. He moved to the United States in 1916 and formed a related organization called Back to Africa. To make it possible for African Americans to reach Africa, Garvey established a steamship company called the Black Star Line. Although the steamship company was an economic failure, even while Garvey was still alive its name became a symbol for Garvey's efforts at communication among people of African descent across the Atlantic ocean.

The lyrics to Afro-reggae songs varied greatly, from angry and depressed themes to songs about love and positive attempts to improve the world. As one might expect, the more positive songs tended to come from the North rather than the South, where apartheid and its continuing residue negatively affected the lives of Africans. On page 225 is a listening guide for a typical Afro-reggae song, "Destiny" by Nigeria's Victor Uwaifo and his Titibitis.

In only nine years after it was first recorded in 1968, reggae had spread far beyond its origins to become a vehicle for political and social statements for many people of African descent worldwide.

Ska and Reggae Influences on Rock

Revolutionary song themes common to reggae drew the interest of British punk bands of the mid-seventies. Bands such as **The Clash** shared the poor Jamaican people's anger about police and government brutality and took stands against racism. The Clash covered Junior Murvin's song "Police and Thieves" (1977), and incorporated a reggae beat and reggae bass lines into some of their own songs, such as "White Man in Hammersmith Palais" (1978). A British punk band that became interested in the engaging pulse of reggae, though not the political messages behind the music, was **The Police,** who added a reggae beat and ska/reggae melodic contours to the song "Roxanne" (1978) and much of the music they recorded after that. No longer a punk band, the Police continued to write and record their winning mixture of pop, rock, and reggae, led by their singer/bassist/main songwriter, Sting (Gordon Sumner). Their *Reggatta de Blanc* album (1979) (the title literally meant "white reggae") gave them an international hit with the song "Message in a Bottle."

A late-seventies movement called Rock Against Racism or "RAR" was started by some reggae and similarly minded punk musicians in England. One of many people under attack by members of the movement was Eric Clapton because of a comment he made in support of Parliament member Enoch Powell at a Clapton concert in Birmingham in 1976. Powell had a reputation for making racist remarks against the many non-white immigrants living in England. Since Jamaicans were among those immigrants, and Clapton had used Jamaican music

Steel Pulse in concert in 1995

to his own advantage with his hit cover version of Bob Marley's "I Shot the Sheriff," RAR resented the remark.

Many concerts, tours, and other fund-raising events and recordings were organized to raise money to help RAR defend victims of racist attacks. Among the most outspoken bands in the movement was **Steel Pulse,** which formed in Birmingham, England, in 1975. As Rastafarians, they identified with Jamaican causes and looked toward Africa as the land of their roots. They eulogized Marcus Garvey in some songs and Haile Selassie in others. The concert at which their live album *Rastafari Centennial* (1992) was recorded was dedicated to Haile Selassie in celebration of what would have been his 100th birthday. The album was nominated for a Grammy award. Steel Pulse used their music to cry out against all racism, including that in the United States, as in their first Island Records release, "Ku Klux Klan" (1978). Other bands that supported the movement included the Mekons, X-ray Spex, Elvis Costello and the Attractions, Aswad, and the Clash.

Ska, reggae, or a combination of the two styles was used for individual singles or album cuts by many other groups of the seventies and eighties, even when no Jamaican influences were evident in the rest of their music. The ska hesitation beat or the syncopation of a reggae bass added welcome variety to the sounds of the period. Reggae's influences could be heard in Paul Simon's "Mother and Child Reunion" (1972), and Boston's J. Geils Band used a ska beat in "Give It to Me" (1973). Stevie Wonder paid tribute to Bob Marley, and to reggae in general, with his "Master Blaster (Jammin')" in 1980. The New York group Blondie covered "The Tide Is High" by Jamaican singer/writer John Holt in 1980, and returned the next year with their own version of Jamaican dub (known as rap in New York), "Rapture." Both Julian Lennon's "It's Too Late for Goodbyes" (1984) and Billy Joel's "You're Only Human (Second Wind)" (1985) were based on a ska beat.

Ska Revival and Oi!

Ska was revived in the late seventies in Coventry, England, by a former punk band, **The Specials.** In addition to fast-driving punk, the Specials had also played reggae. They tried to combine the two styles in a new way and found that reggae's ancestor, ska, had a much simpler rhythmic pattern than reggae and could be sped up to a punk tempo more easily. The new style merged the pulse and shouted vocals of punk with the hesitation beat of ska. The Specials took a strong stand against racism; the group itself was racially mixed, and that was an important

Listening Guide

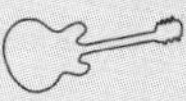

"Destiny"
as recorded by Victor Uwaifo and his Titibitis (1977)

Tempo: The tempo is approximately 160 beats per minute, with four beats in each bar.

Form: After a twenty-six-bar instrumental introduction, the recording is based on sections of varying lengths from eight to fourteen bars, with most sections ten bars long. The longer sections begin with the words "I," "we," or are instrumental. Two eight-bar sections begin with the word "our" and have a contrasting melody, but the chords remain the same as they were in the other sections.

Features: Beat subdivisions are uneven.

A subtle accent of the backbeat gives the feel of a hesitation beat.

Polyrhythms occur among the repetition of a bass riff, a section of three trumpets, and various African percussion instruments.

Trumpets respond to the voices in the way much African music uses call-and-response.

The entire recording is based on a regular alternation between two chords (tonic and dominant).

Lyrics: It takes hard work to achieve one's destiny, and the singers know not to depend on luck in place of work.

Source: *Black Star Liner: Reggae from Africa,* Heartbeat Records 16.

theme of much of their music. They formed their own record company, 2 Tone Records, and released the single "Gangsters" (1979), the commercial success of which established both their group and their company, at least for a few years. The Specials broke up by the end of 1981.

"Concrete Jungle" was recorded by the Specials for the movie *Dance Craze* (1979). A listening guide to that recording follows on page 226.

The 2 tone movement, as the racially mixed British ska revival was called, did not last any longer than the Specials' career, but it did effectively communicate the groups' antiracism message along with their new brand of ska beat. Guitarist Noel Davies wrote the song "The Selecter," which was recorded by the Specials with Davies playing guitar and was released as side two of the single "Gangsters." Fueled by the success of that single, Davies put together his own group, which he named **The Selecter,** and they recorded for 2 Tone Records. Like the Specials, the Selecter played a combination of punk and ska. The Selecter was a band that spoke for integration better than the other 2 Tone bands because it included black members with short hair, a black member wearing Rastafarian dreadlocks, a white member, and a female member. Like the Specials, the Selecter had some commercial success in Britain, but broke up in 1981.

The Specials (left to right): Jerry Dammers, Sir Horace Gentleman, Neville Staples, Terry Hall, Roddy Radiation, Lynval Golding, and John Bradbury.
Michael Ochs Archives/Venice, CA

Madness was another British punk group that added a ska hesitation beat to some of their music. They took their name from the song "Madness" by ska king Prince Buster, a disc jockey in Jamaica in the mid-sixties, to whom they dedicated their song "The Prince" (1979). Madness' sound was based on the fast ska beat and punk-like drive with shouted vocals that had been started by the Specials, but they also added a rough-toned saxophone playing the lead on most of their recordings, giving them a unique sound. Saxophone had often been used in early Jamaican ska recordings based on American rhythm and blues.

In the late seventies, Madness made strong statements against racism in much the same way that both the Specials and the Selecter had. After leaving 2 Tone Records for the larger Stiff Records, however, Madness found that skinheads and boneheads (people with very short-cropped, but unshaven heads) began to attend their concerts. Skinheads and other racist and nonracist extremist groups had been dancing to ska since it first

Listening Guide

"Concrete Jungle"
as recorded by the Specials (1979)

Tempo: The tempo is approximately 152 beats per minute, with four beats in each bar.

Form: After a fourteen-bar introduction, the recording has seven sixteen-bar sections ordered as follows: A B A B Instrumental A B.

The sixteen bars of each section are made up of four four-bar phrases.

The B sections all begin with the words "concrete jungle" and function as a refrain. The B sections end with the beat pattern used in the introduction.

Features: Beat subdivisions are slightly earlier than even half-beat subdivisions. An organ plays a chord on each subdivision.

The drums keep a strong backbeat.

The introduction is made up of group chanting and rhythmic pounding of a beat commonly used in cheers at sports events.

The vocals are sung in a punk-influenced monotone with occasional pitch changes at phrase endings.

Group vocals are used for emphasis and support the singer's statements that he needs to stay with his mates (friends).

Fuzztone lead guitar is featured in the instrumental section.

The electric bass plays reggae-influenced syncopations in some parts of the A sections, but plays on the beats during most of the B sections.

The bass plays melodic octaves during the instrumental section with the lower note on the beat and the upper octave note at the subdivision. This creates an interesting rhythmic pattern that stresses the slightly uneven subdivisions.

A loud sound of breaking glass is heard at the end of the second B section.

Lyrics: The singer has been threatened and carries a knife. He stays with his mates and walks on lighted streets out of fear for his life, and is ready to throw bottles in self defense.

Source: *The Specials*, Chrysalis 21265; and *Dance Craze*, Chrysalis 21783.

became popular in England during the sixties. Because Stiff Records did not have the antiracist reputation 2 Tone had, and Madness was an all-white group with very short-cropped hair, they were bound to attract such a following. After confrontations led to riots, the group began to write and perform fewer songs with political messages. By the beginning of the eighties, Madness had broken away from the ska movement and was playing British music-hall-style pop songs.

Ska had been a dance music in Jamaica, and the British punk-driven version became popular dance music as well. A movie called *Dance Craze* (1981) featured the music of the Specials, the Selecter, and Madness along with other British ska revivalist groups—the English Beat, Bad Manners, and the Bodysnatchers—and helped to establish the popularity of the style.

By the early eighties the music favored by skinheads, boneheads, and rudeboys (named after the Jamaican rebels of ten years earlier) was a more intense combination of punk and ska called Oi! Not all followers of Oi! were violently racist, although that was the case for some members of the movement. Racist or not, the basic statement behind Oi! was that punk had become mainstream to the point of being overly commercial. Oi! bands such as **Cockney Rejects** shouted anarchist statements and resisted any hint of commercialism. They made fun of the pop charts by naming their first two albums *Greatest Hits, Volume 1* and *Greatest Hits, Volume 2* (both 1980). As had happened to many punk bands of the past, a few of Cockney Rejects' records such as "The Greatest Cockney Ripoff" and "I'm Forever Blowing Bubbles" ended up on the British pop charts. Extremists in the Oi! movement were countered by the Scottish band **Oi Polloi,** which spoke out against racism, homophobia, and other hateful views.

While the 2 tone ska movement was at its peak of popularity in Coventry and Oi! was the brand of ska favored by skinheads, a group from Birmingham called **UB40** was combining ska, reggae, and dub-styled vocals with British pop styles. In many of their recordings, UB40 used both the ska hesitation beat and a reggae bass. They kept the Jamaican tempos and smoothness, not following the Specials' idea of incorporating a punk beat into their music. The most important difference between their music and Jamaican music was the lyrics. Their songs were about social issues of concern to the British working class rather than the problems of the Jamaican poor; even the name UB40 was taken from a code on the cards that were issued by the British government to apply for unemployment benefits.

UB40
©Anastasia Pantsios

Ska bands of the late eighties based their style on the post-punk styles of the British 2 tone movement a decade earlier, but this time the movement was not limited to one record label or, for that matter, even to one country. From 1985 through the nineties, ska bands were popular all over the U.S. and in various parts of Europe including West Germany, Italy, France, Holland, the Basque areas of Spain, and, of course, England. Perhaps the most well known of the American bands were **The Toasters,** from New York, and **Donkey Show,** from Los Angeles. As was also true of songs by the 2 tone bands, the later-day ska writers used their music to make political and social statements. Sections with dub-style vocal inserts were often included in their recordings.

Dub, Dancehall, and Ragga

By the early seventies the practice of stripping sampled sections of previously recorded music in new melodies or vocals developed into a style called dub. The term dub was derived from the "dubbing" of new vocals that had been done by disc jockeys back in the sixties. Early dub records were made specifically for disc jockeys to use as background for their vocal patter, and the "B" sides of many rock steady and reggae recordings were dub versions of the "A" sides. Generally, those dub versions either removed the original vocals completely or allowed them to float in and out of the recording. Sometimes everything was removed from the recording except the bass and drums. Echo effects were often added and eventually slide faders and echo delays were used.

One of the early creators of this style was **King Tubby** (Osbourne Ruddock, 1941–1989). Many Jamaican producers learned their craft by working with King Tubby, who continued to develop new effects to add to his recordings. Examples of King Tubby's seventies dub styles are collected on several albums, including *King Tubby Meets the Upsetter at the Grass Roots of Dub* (1974). By 1988 Tubby was using computers to digitalize his work. He was at the high point of his career and planning to build his own new studio when he was shot and killed during a robbery near his home in 1989.

The primary purpose of Jamaican music was dancing and the dub-influenced dance music that developed during the early eighties was called dancehall for exactly that reason. Much dancehall music featured the trimmed down, uncluttered simplicity and strong emphasis on the bass line that was common in dub music. Dancehall also used electronic echo effects and was often an accompaniment for disc jockey patter. Disc jockeys Yellowman (Winston Foster) and General Echo (a.k.a. Ranking Slackness) and the session band Roots Radics were important in the development of dancehall.

An electronic form of dancehall was more aggressive—and sometimes angry or even violent—lyrics called ragga (or sometimes raggamuffin) developed in the middle eighties. The first recording in this style was "Under Me Sleng Teng" (1985) by Wayne Smith. Aggressive attitudes about sex entered ragga music with such records as "Wicked in Bed" by Shabba Ranks, and female singers and dancers responded by wearing very suggestive outfits and outrageous blond wigs. Ranks' tour of South Africa sparked an interest in ragga there.

Jamaicans, particularly Rastafarians, always looked to Africa for inspiration, and ska, reggae, and the many other musics stemming from those styles were based on characteristics of African music. It is natural, then, that Africans themselves would adopt and create their own versions of Jamaican music.

Summary

The development of both ska and reggae in Jamaica served as an example of an interesting musical synthesis that resulted from the mixing of people of different cultures. Blues, jazz, and rock all came out of similar intercultural mixes in the United States. Ska developed out of mento, rhythm and blues, and other music heard in Jamaica. It shared characteristics of those styles, but also developed a distinctive sound and rhythm of its own. During the mid-sixties, ska musicians slowed down their music and added a heavy bass line after hearing American soul music, particularly Memphis soul. That new sound was called rock steady, and when it was played faster it became reggae. Reggae was the music of the Rastafarian religious movement, and it became a vehicle for both religious and political statements.

It was the political rebelliousness as much as the musical style of reggae that made it attractive to British punk bands during the late seventies. Reggae's backbeat and its emphasis on the bass made it attractive to many other rock musicians who left politics out of their performances. Ska was updated when rock musicians combined it with punk. Both ska and reggae became internationally important musical styles, although more so in Britain, Europe, and Africa than in the United States.

Since the sixties, Jamaican disc jockeys had been sampling sections of previously recorded music, and then dubbing new patter-spoken lyrics. By the seventies, new techniques were developed and a new style of reggae called dub became popular. Electronic echo and other types of effects were added to dub to create the dance music called dancehall. The angry and aggressive music called ragga developed out of dancehall in the middle eighties.

Terms to Remember

Dubbing
Mento
Patter-talk
Rock steady
Rudeboys
Toasting

CHAPTER 21

Hip Hop and Rap

The hip hop culture and rap music originated in New York during the mid-seventies and grew to nationwide popularity in the eighties. Rap involved spoken lyrics performed in a rhythmic patter over complex, funk-styled rhythms. Spoken poetry has long been important in African and African American culture as a form of communication. Griot singers in Africa kept track of and commented on their peoples' history through their spoken and sung poetry. During the days of slavery, the poetic lyrics of spirituals included at least two levels of meaning, allowing slaves to tell one another about pathways to freedom while sounding like simple religious songs to white listeners.

A group of writers in Harlem during the twenties wrote honest and insightful works that portrayed ghetto life. At times they even used common street dialect and speech patterns that were not considered to be "correct" English. Langston Hughes (1902–1967) was one such poet who was criticized by his own people for exposing that underground language. Hughes added to the African American flavor of his poetry by using phrases that imitated the rhythmic flow of jazz melodic lines and he often mentioned the music in his works. Despite the initial criticism aimed at the writers, the movement, which became known as the Harlem Renaissance, soon came to be credited for the open-minded honesty of the works, and "ghetto language" became more openly recognized as an important expression of life in Harlem and other African American communities.

Singers of country blues and other rural styles of the twenties and thirties such as Blind Willie Johnson, Pine Top Smith, and Memphis Minnie sometimes used patter speech in sections of their songs. American rhythm and blues singer Louis Jordan had used rhythmic speech patterns in songs such as "Saturday Night Fish Fry" during the forties, and James Brown used a similar style in message songs of the sixties such as "King Heroin" and "Say It Loud—I'm Black and I'm Proud." These types of patter-spoken vocals were not exclusive to African or African American traditions. Nineteenth-century English operettas such as Gilbert and Sullivan's *H.M.S. Pinafore* (1878) and *The Pirates of Penzance* (1879) included patter songs such as "The Major General Song." Disc jockeys in Jamaica during the late sixties developed a style of patter-talk called toasting or dubbing that may have been influenced by Louis Jordan's and/or James Brown's speech patterns. Funk disc jockeys in New York imitated those Jamaican disc jockeys to create their vocal style.

East Coast Rap

One of the first disc jockeys to "rap" in the Bronx was Jamaican **DJ Kool Herc** (born in 1957). Herc moved to New York when he was twelve years old and he was already very familiar with the sounds of Jamaican toasters Big Yough, I-Roy, and others. Like the Jamaicans

Sugar Hill Gang
Corbis-Bettmann

before them, New York rappers wanted the message of their lyrics to be clearly understood by their listeners and the patter-spoken format served their purposes quite well.

From the sixties through into the nineties, racial tensions of the Civil Rights Movement and strong statements by Malcolm X and others sparked a new generation of African American poets who held nothing back in their protest of the way their people had been treated by white America. One of the most outspoken of these groups—and one that managed to get their messages recorded and widely released—called themselves **The Last Poets.** As had been true of the earlier writers from Harlem, jazz, as well as the more contemporary styles of rhythm and blues and soul music, was heard along with their poetry. The graphic and controversial language the Last Poets used to express their sentiments served as an important influence on the angry rap music later recorded by Public Enemy and other rap groups from Harlem.

Not all rap from Harlem or New York's South Bronx was necessarily angry, however. Some of it was designed to be fun for listening, for break dancing, and for personal expression. The first rap record was **The Sugar Hill Gang**'s "Rapper's Delight" (1979). "Rapper's Delight" immediately appealed to dancers because it was based on the rhythm track of the disco record "Good Times" by Chic. The three rappers on "Rapper's Delight" ("Master Gee" Guy O'Brien, born in 1963; "Wonder Mike" Michael Wright, born in 1958; and "Big Bank Hank" Henry Jackson, born in 1958) were asked to make the record after they had been heard rapping at a party. The original version of the record was fifteen minutes long and represented casual conversation during which each rapper boasted about himself and his image within the hip hop culture. Its success proved that rap vocals combined with dance music had appeal outside of Harlem when it made the top forty on the pop charts. Lyrics on early rap records varied from the serious view of ghetto life in Grandmaster Flash's "The Message" (1982) to the comic routines played out by the Fat Boys and practically everything in between.

After the success of "Rapper's Delight" indicated that there was commercial appeal for what many disc jockeys had been doing in their live shows for some time, **Grandmaster Flash** (Joseph Saddler, born in 1957) and others such as Kurtis Blow (Kurt Walker, born in 1959) and Afrika Bambaataa (Kevin Donovan, born in 1960) stepped into recording studios to make their own statements to the new, large audience. To accompany their rhythmically spoken vocals, the disc jockeys played recordings by **scratching,** which involved quickly changing the direction of a record's rotation, over and over, to create a rhythmic pulse over which they could "rap." Another copy of the same record would sometimes be played continuously on another turntable during the scratching. Multiple turntables were also used to insert sections from one recording into another (a technique known as **cutting**) and to segue from one recording to another using a **vari-speed control** to maintain a constant beat pattern when the two were not recorded at the same speed.

Because rap was primarily a vocal style with roots in certain disc jockeys' use of prerecorded records as background, many rappers took to the practice of **sampling** background music for their records. Sampling involved taking selected sections from other recordings and repeating and mixing those sections to create a background sound. Of course, many of the artists whose music was "sampled" saw the practice as stealing, and the ensuing lawsuits caused rap vocalists to credit the sources of their samples. This eventually included the sharing of royalties. Without using samples, the vocalists had to come up with their own newly recorded accompaniments, and synthesizers and drum machines became common replacements for samples.

Salt-N-Pepa was the first successful female rap group. Often called the Queens from Queens, Salt-N-Pepa was a trio that included Salt (Cheryl James, born in 1964), Pepa (Sandy Denton, born in 1961) and DJ Spinderella (Dee Dee Roper). They sometimes sang in a sixties girl-group style along with their patter-spoken vocals. The sixties influence on Salt-N-Pepa's style did not end with the vocals when they covered songs such as

Salt-N-Pepa (left to right): DJ Spinderella, Salt, Pepa
Corbis-Bettmann

"Twist and Shout" and added guitar solos that were not part of the funk or rap tradition. Salt-N-Pepa's recording of "Expression (Half-Step)" serves as an example of their style and is outlined in the listening guide on page 232.

Salt-N-Pepa made social statements through songs such as "Negro Wit' an Ego" (1990), in which they sang about their pride in their African American heritage. However, their songs were more often personal statements about their needs as women and the ways they want men to treat them. The trio won a Grammy for "None of Your Business" in 1994.

The Native Tongues Posse was a general title used by several rap artists or groups from Manhattan who used their very funky and danceable music to support song themes that displayed pride in their African roots. Often dressing in African clothing, these vocalists stressed optimism and unity in their portrayal of street life in Harlem and other African American neighborhoods. The older rap disc jockey Afrika Bambaataa and his group the Zulu Nation was the model for the late-eighties group **The Jungle Brothers,** led by Nathaniel Hall who called himself Afrika Baby Bambaataa. The "jungle" referred to in the group's name was indeed Harlem, and songs such as "Tribe Vibes" from *Straight Out the Jungle* (1988) celebrated the brotherhood the singers shared with their neighbors. The violent sexism for which some rap had become known was nowhere to be seen in the music of the Native Tongues Posse. The Jungle Brothers' song "Behind the Bush" expressed the desire to share love and mutual respect with their women.

Another member of the Native Tongues Posse, **Queen Latifah** (Dana Owens, born in 1970) chose her name because "latifah" represents delicate sensitivity in the Muslim culture. She was joined by the British singer **Monie Love** (Simone Johnson, born in 1970) for a song that could be called a hip hop anthem to feminism, "Ladies First" (included on *Yo! MTV Raps, Volume 2*). In addition to representing sisterhood among women, the song also displayed the Afrocentric orientation of the Native Tongues Posse in the call-and-response style vocals performed by Queen Latifah and Monie Love. Queen Latifah won a Grammy for her recording "U.N.I.T.Y." (1994), which she dedicated to her brother, who died in a motorcycle accident. She also gained quite a bit of fame for her role on the television show "Living Single" and appearances in several movies.

The goal of many of the political and social statements in East Coast rap was to encourage more unity among African Americans and urge them to make stronger demands for equality. Some band members and their fans wore "X" on their shirts or caps to represent their support of the teachings of Malcolm X. Grandmaster Flash and the Furious Five described some of the problems related to life in a ghetto in their recording of "The Message" (1982), but that song did nothing to support African American pride or, for that matter, to encourage any changes to aid their situation. However, it may have awakened white listeners to the realities of inner-city life. The Temptations (in "Cloud Nine" from 1968 and other songs) had done that to a degree, but rap made more clear demands for change.

Stronger and more clearly directed social and political messages came from rap groups recorded by the **Def Jam Record Company,** which was formed by Russell Simmons and Rick Rubin in 1984. At that point rap was still primarily a "black" style, but Rubin, who was white,

Listening Guide

"Expression (Half-Step)" as recorded by Salt-N-Pepa (1989)

Tempo: The tempo is approximately 108 beats per minute, with four beats in each bar.

Form: The introduction is polyrhythmic and the primary beat pattern is not established until the first A section begins with the words "express yourself." The form follows the pattern: A B A Interlude B A Interlude B A A A Interlude.

The eight-bar A sections serve as refrains.

The twelve-bar B sections have continuous patter-spoken vocals that alternate single-bar antecedent and consequent phrases. (The consequent phrase provides a sense of resolution to the incomplete-sounding end of the antecedent phrase.)

The first interlude section is four bars long, and the second is eight bars. Both feature the polyrhythms used in the introduction and include barely understandable comments spoken by men.

The final nine-bar section alternates bars from the A and interludes.

Features: Even beat subdivisions are maintained throughout the recording.

Once the first A section begins, a very strong backbeat is kept by the drums.

The bass line is very active and often polyrhythmic against the rest of the instruments.

The group vocals of the A sections are sung in a two-part, girl-group pop style.

All three singers share the patter-spoken vocals of the B sections, at times alternating phrases in a conversational manner and at other times finishing one another's thoughts.

Lyrics: It is established from the beginning that self-expression is necessary to experience life to the fullest. Part of the self-expression comes through group criticism of others about who they are with or where they got their money. Another part of the expression is in the singers' pride in being women who have control of their world. The very danceable rhythm of the A sections and the vocals about working their bodies leaves room for expression of physical needs and desires.

Source: *Yo! MTV Raps, Volume 2,* Jive Records 1420.

was out to sell a new, bold sound that would revolutionize popular music. Two of Def Jam's earliest groups were the African American rappers **Run-D.M.C.** and the white, more rock-oriented group, **The Beastie Boys.** Run-D.M.C. accomplished some breakthroughs for rap when they became the first rap group to have albums that went gold, platinum, and double platinum; the first rappers on "American Bandstand"; and the only rappers on the widely-viewed Live Aid show. The signing of the Beastie Boys was seen by some as Rick Rubin's exploitation of rap to make it more palatable to white listeners, but he made up for that, in some ways, by also signing Public Enemy to Def Jam Records. By the late eighties the Beastie Boys had moved to Capitol Records and they had a top forty hit with "Hey Ladies" (1989). They broadened their style to include more funk and toured with Dr. Funkenstein himself, George Clinton, as well as Smashing Pumpkins and others, in Lollapalooza '94. Run-D.M.C. rappers Darryl McDaniels and Joseph Simmons spent some time during the early nineties recovering from drug and alcohol addictions, and added Christian themes to the group's 1993 album *Down with the King.*

Sometimes called the Black Panthers of rap, **Public Enemy** spoke out from New York to let the world know what they thought about the low-class status of many African Americans. Their primary rapper, **Chuck D** (Carlton Ridenhour, born in 1960), began his career as a disc jockey on a college radio station. He had grown up seeing police brutality and a growing drug problem in his own community as well as the ways in which African American artists were often ignored by commercial radio and video stations, and he decided it was time to make his own statements to the world—and to make them as strong as possible. He referred to his rap lyrics as the CNN (Cable News Network) for African Americans. His goal was to let people know what the lives of real African Americans were like and to say he and his people were not going to put up with "ghetto life" any longer.

Chuck D's fellow rapper and "minister of information," Professor Griff, laid the groundwork for others to attack Public Enemy for racism when he made anti-Semitic remarks to an interviewer for the *Washington Times.* When one's reputation is built on an antiracist stand and one attacks another race (or culture), humanism ceases to be the issue and self-centered supremacy rears its ugly head. Well aware of this, Chuck D made it clear that Griff's remarks did not represent the beliefs of other members of Public Enemy by firing Griff. Chuck D

Flavor Flav (left) and Chuck D (right) of Public Enemy
AP/Wide World Photos

used the recording "911 Is a Joke" (from the album *Fear of a Black Planet*) to point out his thoughts about ineffective public assistance programs in his neighborhood. A listening guide follows on page 234.

Where Chuck D had gained a reputation for his angry remarks between songs at concerts in the past, his performances in the nineties included serious talks about his personal commitments rather than a mere venting of rage. The state of Arizona was often a target of attack because (until the November, 1992, election) it did not recognize the national holiday for the late Dr. Martin Luther King, Jr.'s birthday. Chuck D released his feelings through his rap in "By the Time I Get to Arizona," and told members of the audience who were from Arizona to think about their state's affront to African Americans. If one can step back and look beyond the emotional charge of much of Public Enemy's raps to analyze the basic messages behind their lyrics, similarities can be drawn between their antiracist stance and that of what James Brown, Bob Marley, and even Bob Dylan had to say through their music. The title of Public Enemy's 1994 album, *Muse Sick N Hour Message* (Music and Our Message), played on the differences between the written and the spoken word.

Because many rappers tended to take the idea of self-expression to the point of using foul language and violent subject matter in direct and unpopular ways, rap has gained as much notoriety through the anti-rap press as it has through any traditional roads to success such as radio or television airplay. As had been the case in the music of some heavy metal and punk bands of the past, public banning or displays of record destruction sometimes created more sales than the records would likely have had to begin with. Such was the case when the **2 Live Crew** album *As Nasty as They Wanna Be* (1989) was banned in some states, including their home state of Florida. The group enjoyed their highly publicized position and even advertised the banning by calling their next album *Banned in the U.S.A.* (1990). **Sister Souljah** (Lisa Williamson) was not well known outside of New York when President Bill Clinton (then a presidential candidate) attacked what he saw as racism in her lyrics, turning her into an instant cause célèbre.

West Coast Rap

While East Coast rappers spoke out for African Americans on more general political subjects, rappers on the

Listening Guide

"911 Is a Joke"
as recorded by Public Enemy (1990)

Tempo: The tempo is approximately 104 beats per minute, with four beats in each bar.

Form: The form is based on eight- and sixteen-bar phrases ordered as follows: A B C Extension B C Extension C A.

The eight-bar A sections are basically instrumental, but include verbal comments in the background.

Each B section contains sixteen bars of rap vocals. The rhythmic patterns of the rap vocals are made up of four-bar antecedent and consequent phrases paired into eight-bar periods.

The eight-bar C sections function as a refrain, beginning with the words "get up" and then including the song title, "911 Is a Joke." The first C is followed by a four-bar extension that begins with a laugh and the second is followed by an eight-bar extension similar to the first extension.

Features: Even beat subdivisions are maintained throughout the recording.

The drums play a strong backbeat through most of the recording.

Funk polyrhythms are played by the bass, guitar, and horn (or synthesized horn sound) sections.

The production includes much mixing and overdubbing, creating a very full background. That background includes indistinguishable vocal chatter that sounds as if the recording was done at a party.

Call-and-response vocals are used in the extensions to the refrains.

The recording ends by fading out.

Lyrics: The singer claims he had called the emergency number 911 a long time ago, and no one has responded. He believes the whole idea of the emergency squads' availability to help people is a cruel joke because they will get paid whether they do their job or not, so the squads don't really care about people, particularly those in African American neighborhoods.

Source: *Fear of a Black Planet*, Columbia 45413; and *Yo! MTV Raps, Volume 2*, Jive Records 1420.

country's West Coast had more of a tendency to take stands on gang-related issues, particularly the way in which the police handled (or, they would say, contributed to) street violence. They insisted that the kids they spoke for didn't have the slightest idea about political figures or the government because the kids had daily problems dealing with violence on the streets—a violence politicians knew existed, but ignored. At times the rappers were accused of encouraging violent behavior when, from their point of view, they were merely reporting about it from an inside perspective.

Among the most outspoken of the West Coast rap groups of the late eighties and early nineties was **N.W.A.** (Niggas with Attitude). "Gangsta Gangsta," from their *Straight Outta Compton* (1988) album, even begins with gunshots. From that same album, "Express Yourself" makes it clear that N.W.A. planned to continue to "say it like it is" in their Los Angeles neighborhood. Charles Wright & the Watts 103rd Street Rhythm Band, whose recording was used for the sampling in N.W.A.'s recording were not a rap band, but a soul-oriented funk band from the Watts area of Los Angeles.

N.W.A.'s lead rapper, **Ice Cube** (O'Shey Jackson, born ca. 1969) left the group for a solo career and was replaced by former solo rapper, **Eazy-E** (Eric Wright, 1973–1995). In spite of the way N.W.A. felt about pop chart success in "Express Yourself," their albums *100 Miles and Runnin'* (1990) did well on the pop charts and their *Efil4zaggin* (a backwards spelling of "niggaz 4 life," 1991) broke commercial records for rap by entering the pop charts at number one. Of course that may not have happened had *Billboard* not just changed its chart research system to the new SoundScan computer system so that the charts were based on actual sales figures instead of interviews with record store managers. Nevertheless, N.W.A.'s sales did make it appear that they had come to express attitudes shared by many others. N.W.A. broke up after the *Efil4zaggin* album. Eazy-E died of complications from AIDS in 1995, and other members Ice Cube, Dr. Dre (Andre Young, born in 1965), and M. C. Ren (Lorenzo Patterson) continued to record and perform as soloists. Dr. Dre produced Snoop Doggy Dogg's successful album *Doggystyle* (1993).

N.W.A. and other L.A.-based rappers had been talking about violence and police brutality for years when the 1992 L.A. riots occurred following not guilty verdicts for police officers who had beaten motorist Rodney King. In response to over 100 requests for interviews, Ice Cube would only say, "No justice, no peace." When he finally was willing to discuss the subject with newspaper columnists, he said his songs had already outlined the problems in Watts. Another rap/heavy metal singer from L.A., **Ice-T** (Tracy Morrow), also stressed the subject of police brutality in his lyrics. He followed the L.A. riots with even more anger than ever in his song "Cop Killer" (1992), in which he said he would go out and "dust off" some cops. The song "Cop Killer" upset many

Ice Cube
© B. Little/Sygma

people who feared the reaction it may have sparked, but Ice-T responded that there was a very big difference between his fans sitting back and listening to him talk about what he might do to vent his anger and their actually going out and doing it themselves. The word was not the deed, in other words. After death threats were aimed at his record company, Ice-T pulled the song from future copies of his *Body Count* (1992) album. Time-Warner, parent company of Ice-T's record company, Sire, decided to take more control of future lyrics or art work that might be objectionable to the general public, and Ice-T chose to cancel his contract with Sire rather than change the art work he had planned for the cover of his *Home Invasion* (1993) album. The independent label Priority issued that album and Ice-T followed its release by signing with Virgin records, which released *Born Dead* (1994).

The violent world from which many of L.A.'s rappers came was clear in 1996 when Death Row Records star Tupac Shakur was shot to death while riding in a car with the owner of his record company, Marion "Suge" Knight. At the time of his murder, Shakur was waiting for an appeal of his conviction for sexually abusing a nineteen-year-old girl. Knight had also been in and out of jail for various charges including assault and probation violations. Death Row Record's other star rapper, Snoop Doggy Dogg, had recently been acquitted of murder charges at the time of Shakur's death.

The reputation of anger and violence associated with rap from L.A. was somewhat mitigated by the

Listening Guide

"Express Yourself" as recorded by N.W.A. (1988)

Tempo: The tempo is approximately 96 beats per minute, with four beats in each bar.

Form: The recording begins with a short conversation, after which instruments and rap vocals enter for the A section. The form follows the pattern: A B A B A B.

The A sections are long, continuous periods of rap vocals made up of alternating single-bar antecedent and consequent phrases. The first A is twenty bars in length and the second and third are each twenty-four bars.

The eight-bar B sections serve as refrains and are mostly instrumental except for the addition of the title words, "Express Yourself."

Features: Even beat subdivisions are maintained throughout most of the recording, but the vocals and some individual instruments sometimes fall into uneven subdivisions.

The first beat of each bar is accented by the bass and the drums maintain a backbeat.

Funk-influenced polyrhythms are played by the drums, bass, and rhythm guitar.

The bass plays a reggae-influenced two-bar riff pattern through most of the recording. The instrumental parts and the vocal phrasing of the title words have been sampled from the introduction and instrumental background in the recording of "Express Yourself" (1970) by Charles Wright & the Watts 103rd Street Rhythm Band.

The instrumental sampling drops out for a two-bar instrumental break in bars fifteen and sixteen of the first A section.

The recording ends by fading out.

Lyrics: The lead singer says he is in a "correctional facility," but is proud of his past and ready to put down anything that would cause a person to become a system follower instead of expressing his or her own opinions and beliefs. Among the things he puts down are drugs and rappers who try for commercial success, forgetting the violence of their lives in the ghetto.

Source: *Straight Outta Compton,* Ruthless-Priority Records 57102; and *Yo! MTV Raps, Volume 2,* Jive Records 1420.

light-hearted, nonviolent work by **Coolio** (Artis Ivey, born ca. 1972). It is not that Coolio's music was untouched by problems in his community. "County Line," from his first album, *It Takes a Thief* (1994), pointed out problems experienced by people on welfare, but the album cut "Fantastic Voyage" expressed the fun of a dream trip to the beach. The title cut from his *Gangsta's Paradise* (1995) took a thoughtful look at the world of gang rivalry and the people who are more hurt than helped by it. This view was certainly a change from earlier statements that tended to portray street violence as unpreventable.

Latino Rap

Many Spanish-speaking Puerto Ricans, Cubans, or other Latinos in New York and Mexicans/Chicanos, Cubans, or other Latins in Los Angeles identified with break dancing and other aspects of hip hop culture from its very beginnings. The result was the development of a rap style that used a combination of Spanish and English and slang from the Latin American barrio. Latino rap became particularly important in Los Angeles because of the competitive desire to match the ethnic orientation of gang raps by African American rappers. One of the leaders of the Latino rappers was **Kid Frost** (Arturo Molina, Jr., born in 1962). Like N.W.A. had for African Americans in L.A., Kid Frost used his raps to point out instances of street violence and police brutality in his own neighborhood with songs such as "Homicide" and the title cut from his *Hispanic Causing Panic* (1990) album. "La Raza (La Raza Mix)," from that same album, became an anthem representing Latin rap. A listening guide to that recording follows on page 237.

As can be heard in "La Raza," background music used by Kid Frost and other Latin rappers varied from much African American rap because it often used Latin rhythms and samples from sixties recordings by Santana and others. Incorporating samples from such artists helped to emphasize their ethnic identity. By the middle nineties, Kid Frost changed his name to "Frost." Other important Latin rappers from L.A. included Cypress Hill and the more politically outspoken Proper Dos.

Kid Frost
© Greg Allen/Retna, Ltd.

Rap Combined with Other Styles

West Coast rap was linked to the gang-related themes of anger and violence, but, just as Manhattan had groups that spoke out for peace and brotherhood, rappers like **Hammer,** from Oakland, California, shared concerns about racism, prejudice, and homelessness in nonviolent language with a very soulful, funk-styled background sound. His music appealed to large, multiracial audiences. The result was music that critics attacked as banal and "sold out" to commercialism, but that reached out to listeners resistant to hard core rap. Commercial or not, there was a sense of sincerity behind most hip hop and rap music.

Arrested Development formed in Atlanta, Georgia, in 1988. They took the funky lightness and pride in African American culture of New York's Native Tongues' rappers and backed their vocals with drums and sometimes even folk-related instruments such as banjo and harmonica. A writer for the newspaper *20th Century African,* Arrested Development's leader, Speech (Todd Thomas, born in 1968), was very outspoken about the need for young people to recognize that not all rappers tell them the truth. He further pointed out that the "f" word young fans should be hearing in the music with which they identify is "freedom." Arrested Development's positive message reached many rap fans with their two top ten hits, "People Everyday" and "Mr. Wendal" (both 1992). The title of their 1994 album,

Listening Guide

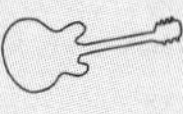

"La Raza (La Raza Mix)" as recorded by Kid Frost (1990)

Tempo: The tempo is approximately 108 beats per minute, with four beats in each bar.

Form: The from is based on the repetition of a one-bar bass riff. After a four-bar instrumental introduction, the vocals and instrumental sections that feature saxophones form eight-bar sections, but the riff and the two chords it uses remain constant, allowing for no real contrasting sections.

Features: The backbeat is stressed by the drums.

Both even and uneven beat subdivisions are used. Even subdivisions are maintained by the drummer using a stick on a closed high-hat, and uneven subdivisions are used in the vocals and by the saxophones.

The most distinctive instrumental part is the riff played on an electric bass guitar.

A guitar plays a two-bar pattern that reaches across the repetitions of the one-bar riff.

Two saxophones play the same melody a single beat apart, creating an interesting reverberation or echo effect.

A xylophone improvises in the background of the last part of the recording.

The instrumental background is based on a sample from "Viva Tirado—Part 1" (1970) by El Chicano.

Lyrics: The lyrics are made up of phrases in Spanish, English (together called "Spanglish"), and Gypsy patois used in parts of Spain and Mexico. The lyrics include phrases that express pride in "La Raza" (the race), and various "in-group" comments about people known to Kid Frost and his group.

Source: *Hispanic Causing Panic,* Virgin 86169; and *Latin Lingo: Hip-Hop from the Raza,* Rhino 71923.

Zingalamaduni, refers to a beehive of culture in the African language of Swahili.

An effective combination of rap vocals and jazz music was created by New York's **Digable Planets,** formed in 1989. Noting the ways that insects seem to work together with each individual acting for the good of the community instead of looking out only for themselves, members of Digable Planets each adopted insect names: Butterfly (Ishmael Butler), Ladybug (Katrina Lust), and Squibble the Termite (Michael Gabredikan), and later additions Doodlebug (Craig Irving) and a new Ladybug (Mary Ann Vieira). Jazz musicians whose works greatly influenced the music of Digable Planets included saxophonists Eddie Harris and Sonny Rollins and the group Jazz Crusaders.

By the late nineties, rap had been around long enough that it had been combined with any number of other styles of music, and each different combination helped the patter-spoken vocal sound of rap poetry reach new groups of fans. Regardless of the style of the music backing rap vocals, and regardless of the message of the vocals, rap singers always expressed a sense of sincerity. Like singer/songwriters, rappers usually wrote their own lyrics and performed them in a way that made their messages seem to speak what they perceived as truth.

Summary

Rap is a patter-spoken vocal style that developed out of a variety of vocal styles, mostly of African or African American origin. Jamaican disc jockeys popularized the rhythmic speech patterns with their "toasting" and "dubbing" styles. Funk disc jockeys in New York picked up the Jamaican sound and popularized it through live and radio performances before it was recorded for commercial sales.

Rap lyrics varied greatly, from some East Coast groups that spoke out about racism experienced by African Americans in Harlem or other ghettos to a number of West Coast groups that decried messages about gangs and street violence. Rap vocals did not always carry angry or violent messages, however, as many rap groups represented positive images and themes. Whatever the message behind the lyrics, rap singers wrote of common experiences from a very personal level, lending a sense of sincerity to their music.

Terms to Remember

Cutting
Sampling
Scratching
Vari-speed control

CHAPTER 22

Mainstream Rock of the Eighties and Nineties

In a period of just over forty years, rock music matured and expanded into a great diversity of styles, some of which had their heyday and then died out and others which have undergone continuous evolution since they began. As was described in the early chapters of this book, rock music became a distinctively recognizable type of music during the fifties and on through the sixties. Many important newer styles, such as country and southern rock, funk, jazz rock, fusion, art and glitter rock, hard rock, heavy metal, punk, and reggae all began during the late sixties and greatly broadened the meaning of the term "rock music" as they developed through the seventies and, in some cases, beyond. By the eighties, much rock music drew from a combination of seventies styles. The term "mainstream" can be used to identify that music because it developed out of the main stream of the rock music that preceded it.

As has been the case with every style of music discussed in this book, many musicians and groups deserve to be covered in this chapter, but space allows for only a few. It is hoped that enough can be gained from the discussion of music that is covered here for readers to see for themselves how music by others might also fit into this broad category of rock music.

Mainstream Artists

Both soul and funk are important elements in the music of **Prince** Rogers Nelson (born in 1959) from Minneapolis, Minnesota. Prince wrote and produced his own first album of erotic dance music when he was only eighteen years old. His father, John Nelson, was a jazz musician whose stage name was Prince Rogers, and his mother was a singer. Although the young Prince never had formal music lessons, music and instruments were readily available to him and he eventually learned to play many instruments, including piano, guitar, and drums. Prince wrote his own music and played his own instrumental parts on almost all of the tracks on his first five albums, although he kept some of his old friends such as bass player André Cymone (André Anderson, who later had his own solo career) for occasional support in the studio and to back him on tour.

Prince's style basically combined funk with rock, but it also showed the influences of new wave, disco, and rap. His songs merely toyed with eroticism until 1980's *Dirty Mind* album, which was too explicit to get any airplay. Its mixture of funk and pop music with fuzztone guitar still attracted a large audience, despite the lack of radio publicity.

A listening guide to Prince's first top ten hit single, "Little Red Corvette" from his first top ten hit album, *1999* (1982) is on page 239.

Prince decided to add a backup band he called the Revolution for his next project, *Purple Rain* (1984), which included an album, film, and concert tour. That project clearly established Prince as a major star. Five top

Prince
© David Corio/Michael Ochs Archives/Venice, CA

forty hit singles were released from the album, and it won three Grammys and an Oscar for Best Original Song Score. The movie (directed by Albert Magnoli) was Prince's acting debut and gave fans an insightful look at a very human celebrity who, in the film, lets his stardom ruin him. Prince added Sheila E. to sing backup vocals on the *Purple Rain* soundtrack and gave her career a boost by contributing to her first solo album, *The Glamorous Life* (1984), and having her open his *Purple Rain* concerts. In 1985, Prince established his own record label, Paisley Park (distributed by his former record company, Warner Brothers) and continued to produce movie soundtracks and other albums with much success. Later soundtracks included music for the films *Under the Cherry Moon* (1986) and *Batman* (1989).

Prince's career experienced many ups and downs during the nineties. His new band, the New Power Generation, worked well with him on *Diamonds and Pearls* (1991) and *The Symbol Album* (1992), both of which included hit singles. The New Power Generation also included rapper Tony M (Anthony Mosely), adding a hip hop connection to Prince's widely diverse style. Prince followed these successes by changing his name to an unpronounceable symbol, baffling all but his most dedicated fans. "Since then he has been called "Formerly" or "The Artist," both names being shortened versions of the "the artist formerly known as Prince." His recordings of the mid-nineties showed that his career was on a down swing. He was married in 1996. His three-disc album *Emancipation* (1996) represented his freedom from his contract with Warner Bros. and the start of his own label, NPG Records. The album was also about the much anticipated birth of his first child.

Listening Guide

"Little Red Corvette" as recorded by Prince (1982)

Tempo: The tempo is approximately 126 beats per minute, with four beats in each bar.

Form: After about nine bars of introduction, the form is based on eight-bar sections. The sections are ordered as follows: A A B A A B Instrumental C B B B D B B B B.

The B sections are made up of a four-bar phrase that is repeated. The repeated phrases function as refrains. They usually repeat the same lyrics, but the lyrics are varied and drop out at times during some of the repeated B sections at the end of the recording.

The instrumental section is based on the B section and features a guitar solo.

The C section is eight bars long; the D section is sixteen bars long.

Features: Even beat subdivisions are used through most of the recording, but the vocals sometimes relax into uneven subdivisions.

A strong backbeat is played in the drums through much, but not all, of the recording.

The instrumental background is rather full and features an electronic organ.

Prince plays all of the instrumental parts and sings the lead vocal except for the addition of a guitar soloist and two backup singers.

The recording begins by slowly building up volume out of silence and ends by fading out very slowly.

Lyrics: The girl who drives the "Little Red Corvette" is moving from one man to another too quickly for the singer to feel comfortable with her. The references to cars and horses are subtle, but obvious, sexual metaphors.

Source: *1999*, Warner Bros. 23720.

Roles played by female performers changed by the middle seventies and continued to evolve in the eighties. In the fifties and early sixties, female singers generally portrayed very meek and sweet personalities as had female pop singers before them. By 1964, Mary Weiss of the Shangri-Las had a bit of a "tough" image, but that was more a reflection of her relationship with the "leader of the pack" than it was a reflection of her own personality. In the late sixties, Janis Joplin and Grace Slick displayed some independence, but they both showed vulnerability at times. The feminist revolution and the sense of individual freedom of the punk movement came together to change these perceptions in the stage personality of Patti Smith, who went so far as to invite a woman to visit her room when she sang the male lyrics to "Gloria." Several punk and new wave groups had women as instrumentalists, including the Velvet Underground with Maureen Tucker as drummer, Talking Heads with Tina Weymouth as bassist, and the Pretenders with Chrissie Hynde as guitarist, writer, and singer. On the West Coast in the middle seventies, Ann and Nancy Wilson assumed the leadership of Heart, and the Runaways formed as a quintet of tough and independent young women who were out for a good time and didn't care how they got it. From the Runaways, guitarist/singer Joan Jett continued this sense of independence with the Blackhearts, lead guitarist Lita Ford went on to a solo career, and bassist/singer Micki Steele joined the female quartet, the Bangles.

Madonna
AP/Wide World Photos

Other female singers of the late seventies and beyond played less tough, but still more realistic roles than had most of their counterparts twenty years earlier. Blondie's Deborah Harry was cold and detached, and Madonna made it clear that she was an individual who did not care what other people thought, as long as she got what she wanted. Singer/songwriter Tracy Chapman, on the other hand, managed to express a great deal of independence while being anything but tough or cold. Her music and image made a new statement for women in general, and, perhaps more important, for African American women.

Of all of those female performers, **Madonna** (Madonna Louise Ciccone, born in 1958) gained the most commercial appeal and success. Her debut album, *Madonna* (1983), hit the charts in both Britain and the U.S., and many successful albums and singles followed. The dance orientation of her music was influenced by her long-time involvement with dance. She studied ballet and earned a scholarship to study dance with New York's Alvin Ailey and also worked under choreographer Pearl Lang. In 1979, she went to France and performed in a disco revue in Paris. Her acting career began in 1980 when she played a small role in a low budget film called *A Certain Sacrifice,* directed by Stephen Jon Lewicki. Madonna's lead role in *Desperately Seeking Susan* (1985) launched her career as a movie star and led to other movies and a live theater debut in *Speed the Plow* (1988) on Broadway in New York. Many of Madonna's video and movie roles play up her sex symbol image, but in her hit recording "Papa Don't Preach" she portrayed a young woman in need of her father's approval. A listening guide to that recording follows on page 241.

Madonna allowed her fans to see much of her offstage personality in her film *Truth or Dare* (1991). The movie was made on tour and, according to Madonna, the stage show was originally going to be the focus of the movie. It was not until the tour was progressing and the cameras were rolling that she decided to take them backstage. Whatever the future might hold for her acting career, Madonna has certainly been an important singer and performer representing a dance-oriented rock style of the nineties. Madonna's career hit a new high when she signed a multimillion-dollar contract with Time Warner in 1992. The tremendous success of her next two albums, *Erotica* (1992) and *Bedtime Stories* (1994), and the hit singles they contained showed her to be living up to Time Warner's expectations. Madonna played Eva Peron in the film version of *Evita* (1996), a musical by Andrew Lloyd Webber and Tim Rice.

While punk and new wave were still being played by a number of bands during the mid- to late eighties, their influences had also spread to new bands that used punk's pounding beat in a pulsating bass but did not otherwise show characteristics typical of the style. One such band, **R.E.M.,** came from Athens, Georgia and redefined southern rock for the eighties. Not only did R.E.M. not stress

Listening Guide

"Papa Don't Preach" as recorded by Madonna (1986)

Tempo: The tempo is approximately 126 beats per minute, with four beats in each bar.

Form: After a sixteen-bar introduction, the form is structured as follows: A A B C A B C Instrumental B C C_1 Instrumental.

The A and B sections are eight bars each, except for the third B section that is extended with two extra bars of lyrics that add emphasis to the last vocal phrase about the singer's being in love.

The ten-bar C sections are eight-bar phrases followed by two bars of extension stressing the singer's decision to keep her baby. The C section begins with the words of the title, "Papa Don't Preach" and functions as a refrain.

The first instrumental section (within the text of the song) is based on the A section.

The sixteen-bar C_1 section is made up of the first four bars of the C section sung through four times.

The final instrumental is sixteen bars based on the C section. It fades out by the final bar.

Features: Even beat subdivisions are maintained throughout the recording.

A synthesized string orchestra plays the first eight bars of the introduction and then adds to the background in the remainder of the recording.

The drums enter at the ninth bar of the introduction, playing a very strong backbeat through the rest of the performance.

In addition to the drums, rock instruments used include electric bass, keyboards, both acoustic and electric guitars, and percussion.

Backup vocalists support the lead vocal in the final C_1 section.

Lyrics: The singer is telling her father that she is pregnant, in love with the baby's father, and planning to marry him and keep her baby. She knows that her father does not like her boyfriend, and begs him to not preach to her, but just give them his blessing. She also asks for advice, but nothing in the song seems to indicate that she is prepared to accept it.

Source: *True Blue,* Warner Bros. 25442.

complicated or highly technical instrumental solos, but they did not even place Michael Stipe's vocals in the position of prime importance. Their drummer, Bill Berry, usually maintained a strong backbeat, and on top of that the sound of Peter Buck's guitar often overlapped the bass lines played by Mike Mills, so that no one part stood out clearly from another. Stipe had some of Bob Dylan's and Lou Reed's ability to maintain a low, drone-like vocal quality, but unlike them he allowed himself to blend in with the instruments. Especially in the early phase of the group's career, Stipe's lyrics were very difficult to understand, and the band's overall sound was almost a single layer of texture without the clear divisions between parts found in most rock music. On page 242 is a listening guide to "Radio Free Europe," from R.E.M.'s first album, *Murmur* (1983).

In R.E.M.'s later music, particularly their *Document* album (1987), Stipe separated his vocals from the texture of the band more than he had in the past. One reason may have been because *Document* contained many songs that made statements he wanted understood, such as the comment on the U.S. government's involvement in Nicaragua in "Welcome to the Occupation," and the anti-right-wing-extremist song, "Exhuming McCarthy."

R.E.M.'s *Out of Time* (1991) album included "Losing My Religion." The album, that single, and its video all won 1992 Grammy awards. For *Out of Time,* R.E.M. expanded its instrumentation to include mellotron, harpsichord, pedal-steel guitar, mandolin, bowed strings, horns, and even a female vocal group. On "Radio Song," the band created a funky background to which they added rap vocals by KRS-One from Boogie Down Productions. The B-52's singer Kate Pierson sang on "Shiny Happy People." Whereas R.E.M.'s previous album, *Green* (1988) had dealt with political issues, *Out of Time's* songs expressed the more personal themes of time, memories, and love. *Automatic for the People* (1992) made some dark and personal statements about life while also touching on politics with "Ignoreland"—a satire about the Reagan/Bush era.

After releasing their next album, *Monster* (1994), R.E.M. set off on their first world tour in five years. The tour had to break for a few months to allow Bill Berry to recover from surgery to remove a brain aneurysm, but they were able to reschedule the concerts and continue the tour. Peter Buck used heavily distorted and reverberated guitar timbres on the *Monster* album, and Sonic

Michael Stipe (left) and Peter Buck of R.E.M.

© Anastasia Pantsios

Youth's guitarist Thurston Moore joined in on one cut. On some songs, Michael Stipe's lyrics left much to the listener's imagination, as was not surprising to anyone who knows his cryptic writing style. That vagueness did not completely permeate the album, however. "Let Me In" clearly expressed Stipe's impassioned desire for contact with Kurt Cobain, whose suicide Stipe said he fearfully foresaw and wanted very much to prevent. R.E.M. released *New Adventures in Hi-Fi* in 1996.

The Dublin-based band **U2** emerged as a symbol of optimism and peace for the eighties and, like R.E.M., they did not stress the solo styles of individual instrumentalists but instead worked together to craft a thick instrumental timbre to which vocals were added. Drummer Larry Mullen, Jr., and singer/lyricist Bono Vox (Paul Hewson) were both born and raised in Ireland, but their guitarist/keyboardist, "The Edge" (David Evans), was originally from Wales, and bass player Adam Clayton was from England. The members of U2 grew up listening to such New York punk bands as Television, the Patti Smith Group, and the Ramones, but to create their own sound they took the rhythm and blues soulfulness of their countryman Van Morrison, the personal commitment of Bruce Springsteen, and the careful use of electronics to

Listening Guide

"Radio Free Europe" as recorded by R.E.M. (1983)

Tempo: The tempo is approximately 158 beats per minute, with four beats in each bar.

Form: The form is organized according to eight-bar periods ordered as follows: A A B A A B C A A B C A B C C. The C periods include repetitions of the lyrics in the title, "Radio Free Europe." The second C is followed by an extension consisting of electronic sound effects.

Features: Even beat subdivisions are maintained throughout the recording.

The recording begins with electronic sound effects.

The drums maintain a backbeat through much of the recording.

In the A and C periods, the bass plays the fast (eighth-note) pulse of repeated notes characteristic of punk and new wave.

The bass plays independent melody lines with syncopated rhythms in the B periods.

The picking patterns used in the guitar part use a repeating high note in a pattern reminiscent of the sound of a five-string banjo.

Lyrics: The lyrics are almost completely inaudible, being used more for Stipe to have something on which to vocalize along with the instruments than for the communication of any message.

Source: *Murmur*, I.R.S./A&M 44797-0014.

Bono of U2
© Anastasia Pantsios

fill out, but not overcomplicate, their basic guitar, bass, and drums instrumentation.

As has been the case with many other bands whose careers have lasted for any period of time, U2's song themes changed as the group members grew older and their interests and concerns changed. They were all nineteen or twenty years old when their debut album, *Boy* (1980), was released, and the songs on that album, at least in part, were a look into some of the confusion and even trepidation suffered by young people. Bono wrote the lyrics to "Out of Control" on his eighteenth birthday. Another song, "A Day Without Me," faced the general problem of suicide among young people, although it was specifically about the death of Joy Division's lyricist and singer, Ian Curtis. "The Electric Co." concerned itself with the horrible aftermath of an unsuccessful suicide attempt. Sound effects such as breaking bottles added to the sense of tragedy and confusion on the album.

Three of the four members of U2 were openly religious and, although they did not use their concerts as a platform from which to profess their own beliefs, they included religious themes in some of their songs. The song "Gloria," from their second album, *October* (1981), was inspired by Gregorian chant, a liturgical style of singing dating from the medieval period and still used in the Roman Catholic Church. Personal experiences were still the basis for other songs. Bono's mother died in an accident when he was a teenager and he had been haunted by his memories of her funeral; he wrote the song "Tomorrow" about his sense of loss. He went on to reevaluate the purpose of life, both for himself and, in general terms, for all humanity in the song "I Threw a Brick Through a Window." In all of their music U2 made a conscious effort not to be trendy, but instead attempted to make honest, meaningful statements, many of which became passionate cries for both personal and political peace.

In later years, U2 tended more toward the expression of political and international concerns rather than their earlier themes of personal introspection. They confronted the problem of war on their album *War* (1983), in which the song "Sunday Bloody Sunday" was an emotional appeal to end the violence in Northern Ireland. It also commented on immoral, unnecessary wars being fought even on Sunday, a day that most Christian religions consider holy. "Surrender" was an antiwar statement that also expressed concern about the deaths of individuals, including suicides. "New Year's Day" was a tribute to the Solidarity movement in Soviet-controlled Poland, for which they made an allusion to war by including militaristic snare-drum rolls. The Edge varied his guitar timbre by avoiding the guitar's bass strings in order to maintain a separation between the tone quality of his instrument and that of the bass. The overall group sound was filled out with echo effects. During concerts, Bono often waved a large white flag as a symbol of surrender and an end to war; the all-white flag had no nationalistic markings, making it a symbol of internationalism.

U2 continued the use of a thickened texture on *The Unforgettable Fire* (1984), but to that producer Brian Eno added a minimalistic style in the background timbres. The album's title came from an exhibition of Japanese artworks by artists who had lived through the World War II bombings of Hiroshima and Nagasaki. "MLK" was written as a tribute to Martin Luther King, and "Elvis Presley and America" honored rock music's beginnings. During 1986, U2 toured to support Amnesty International.

Listening Guide

"With or Without You" as recorded by U2 (1987)

Tempo: The tempo is about 108 beats per minute, with four beats in each bar.

Form: The recording begins with a twelve-bar instrumental introduction. The first four bars feature very soft arpeggio patterns on the synthesizer backed by drums. An eighth-note pulse played on the bass enters at the fifth bar.

The form is based on eight-bar periods in which the A periods each have new lyrics, the B's repeat the words in the song title, and the C's repeat lyrics about giving of oneself. The first B period is only four bars long, but the rest are eight bars. The form is organized as follows: A A B A B C A C B B B.

An instrumental section is placed between the second B period and the first C, but it does not include the fast, technical solos typical of other rock styles; instead, it serves as a break or an "interlude" between the vocal periods.

Features: Even beat subdivisions are maintained throughout the recording.

The bass plays repeated notes at each half beat, which was typical of much punk and new wave, except that the speed of the beat (and also the half beat) is much slower than in most punk or new wave.

The drums maintain a backbeat throughout the recording.

An ethereal or "otherworldly" background sound is played on a synthesizer.

The recording uses crescendos and **decrescendos** for a dramatic effect. It begins very softly, gradually builds in volume, then softens rather suddenly only to rebuild and then fade out.

Lyrics: The song is a statement of pained love, in which the singer expresses both the wish to be with his lover and the realization that their relationship does not work when they are together.

Source: *The Joshua Tree,* Island Records 422-842298.

U2's next effort, *The Joshua Tree* (1987), was a compassionate album that included songs of a personal nature, tributes to specific people and events, and songs that made general statements in support of the work done by Amnesty International. (The album insert even included addresses for those who might want to join the organization.) The song "One Tree Hill" was written for Greg Carroll, a member of the U2 support staff who died in a motorcycle accident, and "Red Hill Mining Town" was about a 1984 British miners strike that left many workers unemployed. "Mothers of the Disappeared" dealt with the pain felt by the families of political prisoners who were tortured or killed without trials. *The Joshua Tree* was also produced by Eno, whose style is obvious in the album's clean electronic background effects and the presence of a new-wave-influenced repeating pulse in the bass. This style is apparent in "With or Without You," and the listening guide above.

U2 followed *The Joshua Tree* with *Rattle and Hum* (1988), in which they paid tribute to many influential rock musicians, including Bob Dylan, the Beatles, Jimi Hendrix, and Bruce Springsteen. Despite the apparent flaunting of his rock star status with his new "Fly" image, Bono continued to make serious statements in his song lyrics. Much of 1992's *Achtung Baby* album expressed the pain the Edge endured during the breakup of his marriage. U2's video-heavy Zoo TV tour was inspired by the commercial appeal of MTV and Morning Zoo radio programs, but it was also comprised of songs regarding societal problems including racism. U2's 1993 album *Zooropa* sold less than earlier albums, but that did not discourage Island Records from signing the band to a multimillion-dollar renewal contract. The hit record "Hold Me, Thrill Me, Kiss Me, Kill Me" was on the soundtrack of the movie *Batman Forever* (1995). After a one-year break, U2 emerged with a whole new sound with the electronic dance record "Discotheque" (1996) and the album *Pop* (1997).

In the middle nineties, when angry or depressed alternative bands captured much of the attention of college-aged rock fans, **Hootie and the Blowfish** emerged with an entirely new image. They were absolutely normal, ordinary guys who liked sports and also played good music. Singer/guitarist Darius Rucker met guitarist Mark Bryan while they were both students at the University of South Carolina, in Columbia. The two performed as a duo called the Wolf Brothers. When they decided to expand their group they invited Mark's friend, bassist Dean Felber, to join. Their first drummer left after graduation and Jim "Soni" Sonefeld became his replacement. They named themselves after the "owl-eyed" and "big cheeked" looks of two of their friends and played covers of songs by the Eagles, R.E.M., U2, and others. Eventually they began writing their own songs and playing clubs around the southeastern United States. Their first EP, *Kootchypop* (1992) was self-produced and its sales figures were surprisingly high, attracting a contract with Atlantic Records in 1993. Their debut album, *Cracked Rear View* (1994) became the fastest-selling debut album in the history of Atlantic Records and was still on the top 200 of the pop charts two years later. The success of Hootie and the Blowfish's second album, *Fairweather Johnson* (1996), showed that the band had continuing appeal. As is true of "mainstream" music, their music combined elements of many rock styles: they used a combination of acoustic and electric instruments; Rucker's deep, expressive vocals featured characteristics of both blues and country singing styles; their song lyrics were generally straight forward expressions of the desire for a good time and positive relationships; and a strong backbeat in the drum adds the final rock touch to make for "good old rock and roll."

Summary

Mainstream rock music is music that has elements of any number of rock styles from the past combined in a way that is not directly imitative of any one group or performer, but not new and different enough to be considered a new style in itself. It is music that appeals to a large percentage of the rock audience. Many performers of the eighties and nineties fit this description, but Prince (now "The Artist"), Madonna, R.E.M., and U2 have stood out from others in terms of their tremendous and long-lasting popularity and influence on others who followed them. Hootie and the Blowfish are a nineties band whose widespread appeal might well be similarly long-lasting and influential on the rock of the future.

Terms to Remember

Decrescendo

CHAPTER 23

Underground and Alternative Rock Styles

After the shock of energy the punk movement gave to late sixties and seventies rock, many bands in the eighties and early nineties began searching for something new. Some concentrated on combining elements of older rock styles in new ways while others experimented with the possibilities afforded by the use of synthesizers and electronic sound effects. Out of all of this experimentation, a few styles emerged that captured the interest of college-age rock fans who desperately needed a sound they could identify with—music that provided an alternative to the Beatles, Rolling Stones, and Led Zeppelin songs their parents still enjoyed. They also wanted music far removed from the Tiffany and New Kids on the Block songs their younger siblings liked. Many different styles of music fit under the heading of alternative rock, but in general, it was geared for this audience of young adults with their own particular interests and attitudes. Some alternative rock songs dealt with traditional themes about love relationships, and some expressed concern about broader social, political, and economic issues. By the late eighties and early nineties, the economy in both Britain and the United States was especially bad for those just finishing school or entering the job market. The resultant social and economic strains were reflected in the negativity of some underground and alternative rock music, particularly industrial and, to a lesser degree, Gothic styles.

Underground and alternative rock fans did not want their groups to "sell out" to large record companies or change their styles to try to appeal to a mass market. Some bands, such as R.E.M., began as alternative, but once they hit pop chart success they became mass market. In their case, they had sufficient appeal that they were able to hold many of their original fans despite their shift from alternative status, but for bands that wanted to maintain their appeal to alternative fans, a hit on the *Billboard* charts was about the worst thing that could happen. Along the same lines, alternative bands generally avoided being dictated to by business executives at record companies or performance venues. The band Fugazi, for example, insisted that their CDs cost no more than eight dollars (when twelve to sixteen dollars was the standard in many CD stores) and their concert tickets be priced no higher than five dollars. They even had a mail-order address for their CDs in case a fan found them to be overpriced at a store. Changes in *Billboard's* rating system and the addition of "alternative" video television stations forced some alternative music up the pop charts, but in general, alternative and underground bands tried everything possible to avoid being "stars." The most important thing was to stay on the same economic level and continue to express the thinking and concerns of their fans.

Alternative Rock from Britain

Many British groups and solo artists who were considered alternative in the U.S. enjoyed pop chart success in

The Smiths in 1986
AP/Wide World Photos

Britain. One such band was **The Smiths.** During the four years they were together, from 1983 to 1987, they released seven albums (plus a greatest hits collection and a live album) and seventeen singles, many of which made at least the top twenty in England. In the United States, they maintained an alternative following with more airplay on college radio stations than on commercial ones and had no singles or albums that charted in the top forty. The Smiths' most noticeable member was singer/lyricist **Morrissey,** whose James Dean-like image and pensive, introverted songs often described loneliness and seclusion. Morrissey's choice of a fifties-style image was not surprising because the Smiths were from Manchester, where American fifties artists and images had been popular for decades. Earlier groups or solo artists from the Mersey area of England (which includes Liverpool) had been greatly influenced by Buddy Holly's fifties image, including the Beatles, the Hollies, and Elvis Costello.

The Smiths' musical direction was primarily controlled by guitarist/songwriter **Johnny Marr,** whose layered guitar tracks provided full, but catchy support for Morrissey's vocals. Marr left the Smiths to give himself the freedom to work on various projects with other singers including Bryan Ferry, Paul McCartney, David Byrne (with Talking Heads), the Pretenders, and Kirsty MacColl. In 1989, Marr was working as a regular band member in The The, but still allowed himself time for other projects, such as the album *Electronic* (1991) recorded with New Order's singer, Bernard Sumner.

Morrissey followed the breakup of the Smiths with a successful solo career, releasing one album a year beginning with *Viva Hate* (1988). His choices of backup musicians varied from album to album, at times including former members of the Smiths. As can be heard in "Everyday Is Like Sunday," he also had grown fond of the fullness provided by a synthesized orchestral background sound. During his solo career Morrissey's song themes expanded to include subjects of worldwide concern including problems in the economy and fear of nuclear war. A listening guide to "Everyday Is Like Sunday" follows on page 248. "Everyday is Like Sunday" was in the British top ten for six weeks, but did not enter the top forty in the U.S., where Morrissey remained an alternative rock artist.

Morrissey's album *Your Arsenal* (1992) introduced a new sound, or rather an old one, to Morrissey's style by using a rockabilly-influenced backup band. Songs on the album expressed Morrissey's concern about reports of an increase in Nazi-style racism among young people in Europe. *Vauxhall & I* (1994) returned to a style closer to that of the Smiths, and included a single that came close to reaching the U.S. top forty, "The More You Ignore Me, the Closer I Get." As has been the case with many other alternative artists, Morrissey's fan base has been steadily growing and pop chart hits are becoming more and more common.

Like the Buddy Holly image of the fifties, sixties psychedelic rock was another style that had remained popular in Manchester and Liverpool. Some of the alternative groups and soloists that toyed with it included the funk inspired **Stone Roses;** the sensitive but humorous **Julian Cope;** the Doors-influenced **Echo & the Bunnymen** (featuring Echo, the drum machine); the dark and tormented **Joy Division;** and the more lighthearted, post-Joy Division band **New Order.** Alternative bands from other parts of England included the neo-psychedelic singer/writer **Robyn Hitchcock;** the post-punk new-wave groups **XTC, Public Image LTD** (formed by former Sex Pistols vocalist John Lydon), and **Wire;** the neo-romantic synthesizer band **Depeche Mode;** and the dance band **Modern English.** Two distinctive Scottish groups that attracted many American fans of alternative music were the **Cocteau Twins,** a trio that featured Elizabeth Fraser's Yoko Ono-influenced airy vocals and lyrics in their own newly invented language,

Listening Guide

"Everyday Is Like Sunday" as recorded by Morrissey (1988)

Tempo: The tempo is approximately 116 beats per minute, with four beats in each bar.

Form: The form repeats and contrasts as follows: Introduction A B A A B A C A B Instrumental A A.

Each section is eight bars long except the C section, which has sixteen bars.

The second, fourth, and fifth A sections begin with the title words, "Everyday Is Like Sunday," and function as refrains.

The second instrumental A section fades out to end the recording.

Features: Even beat subdivisions are maintained by the instruments, but Morrissey's vocals sometimes lapse into uneven subdivisions.

A strong backbeat is maintained by the drums.

An eighth-note pulse is kept by the electric bass most of the time. The bass pulse often repeats a single note as was common in much new-wave music of the late seventies.

A guitar is sometimes featured, but a great deal of the instrumental background is played by a full-sounding synthesized orchestra.

Lyrics: The lyrics portray the end of the world written about in the Book of Revelations in the Bible. The singer welcomes the coming of Armageddon, the final battle between good and evil before the Day of Judgment. Also mentioned is the layer of nuclear dust that lands on the singer and his friend.

Source: *Viva Hate,* Sire/Reprise Records 25699; *Bona Drag,* Sire/Reprise Records 26221; and *never mind the mainstream . . . The Best of MTV's 120 Minutes, Volume 2,* Rhino Records 70546.

and the **Jesus and Mary Chain.** Although the name Jesus and Mary Chain might have been offensive to some, there was nothing sacrilegious about the group's music. They were formed by the brothers Jim and William Reid, near Glasgow, and used guitar noise and drones for their Velvet Underground-influenced style.

Just when it seemed that new groups from Britain were never going to make it big in the U.S. again, the release of *Definitely Maybe* (1994) by the Manchester band **Oasis** brought back memories of British bands from the past and gained favor with American listeners. Some even considered Oasis to have created a new British Invasion. The U.S. pop chart success of their second album, *(What's the Story) Morning Glory?* (1996), and its hit single "Wonderwall" made it seem that the group was, indeed, unstoppable. Problems between singer Liam Gallagher and his brother, guitarist Noel Gallagher, however, caused them to cancel several dates on their 1996 American tour and return to England early, leaving many questions about their future ability to work together effectively and further their success.

One of the most popular and longest-lasting alternative bands from England was **The Cure,** formed by Robert Smith, who grew up in the small town of Crawley, in Sussex, England. Smith was singer and guitarist for Easycure, which he started in 1976. They had shortened their name to the Cure by the time they released their first album, *Three Imaginary Boys* (1979, later reissued as *Boys Don't Cry*). Although influenced by the sense of freedom and nihilism inherent in the punk movement, the Cure's music was not centered around the anger of British punk. Instead the group played catchy guitar lines and a rhythmically pumping bass as a danceable accompaniment for songs that were often about loneliness and existentialism. The existential aspect of some of Smith's song themes was misunderstood by, what he called, "Philistine" critics. The song "Killing an Arab" (1979), for example, was dubbed as racist although, as Smith later explained, it was really a direct reference to the fatalistic indifference felt by the man who shot an Arab in the existential novel *The Stranger* (*L'Étranger,* 1942) by Albert Camus. As esoteric as the Cure's music and song themes may have seemed to some, their following continued to grow through the eighties and into the nineties, even having a top ten hit with "Love Song" from their most successful U.S. release *Disintegration* (1989). As far as image was concerned, Robert Smith's darkly lined eyes staring out from his pale, powdered face, as well as some of the depressing themes of his songs, approached the gloom of what became associated with the movement known as Gothic rock.

Gothic Rock

To latter-day followers of the punk movement in Britain, the word *Gothic* evoked images of gloomy medieval castles sitting atop isolated hills, still echoing screams from their torture chambers. Following that mood, some rock musicians abandoned the intensity of punk music to create a rock style known as Gothic rock, or death rock. The style gained many followers in England through the eighties and, by the early nineties, had become an important underground movement in the United States. Of course, different bands approached their music in different ways and the instruments they used varied greatly, but some basic characteristics remained fairly constant. Because the underlying theme of the music was portrayed by images of ancient powers that humans could not control, the music tended to stress low voices, bass instruments, and fairly slow tempos. Drones, common in secular music of the Middle Ages, were also common in Gothic rock. Electronic effects were applied to create almost hypnotic repetition of short melodic phrases that often approached, in style, the slower works by minimalist composers such as Philip Glass or Steve Reich. Perhaps because an active drummer would spoil the gloomy mood of the music, many of the bands used drum machines that did not always stress a rock backbeat. When organs, real or electronic, were used, they were made to sound like those in large, stone medieval cathedrals through the use of electronic reverberation.

However, the castles portrayed in Gothic novels and the secular music of the Middle Ages were only part of the sources for Gothic rock music. A development out of the negative view of society expressed in the punk movement, Gothic bands went back to the proto-punk music of the Velvet Underground, which also used drones and powerful thumps on a bass drum in place of standard rock drumbeats. David Bowie's very deep and dramatic vocal timbre was copied by many of the male singers in the Gothic movement, except the Gothic singers deepened the effect by singing at lower pitch levels.

Bauhaus' debut EP, *Bela Lugosi's Dead* (1979), introduced Gothic rock to Britain's underground market. Bela Lugosi was the Hungarian actor who played the title role in the 1931 movie, *Dracula.* Appropriate for that character, the nine-and-one-half minute song "Bela Lugosi's Dead" included song sections of haunting electronically produced sound effects that imitated the wind and was full of rattles and buzzes. A throbbing beat and backbeat pounded through most of the recording and a very low descending bass line repeated through much of it. Bauhaus' singer, **Peter Murphy,** maintained a repetitious monotone in his vocals, which were more spoken on pitch than sung. Adding to the gloomy mystery of the repetitions of the words "Bela Lugosi's dead" were the many repetitions of the words "Bela's undead," something horror stories often claim about vampires, including Dracula. The effect was connected to the sense of mystery created in many Gothic novels.

Bauhaus came to an end when Peter Murphy left the group to pursue a solo career. The three remaining members of Bauhaus survived Murphy's leaving by first splitting up and experimenting with other musicians and then by regrouping under the name **Love and Rockets.** As Love and Rockets, they reacted against the darkness of Bauhaus and even managed a top ten hit with one of their first singles "So Alive" (1989). As with a number of other groups who began in the alternative market, such success brought question to the band's previously earned underground rating.

Siouxsie and the Banshees were originally a punk band from Bromley, England. Sex Pistol Sid Vicious knew them and even played drums for their concert debut at a British punk festival in 1976. Soon after Bauhaus introduced their Gothic style to English audiences, Siouxsie (Susan Janet Ballion) and the Banshees added aspects of the Gothic style to their recordings for the next few years. "The Staircase (Mystery)" (1979), for example, used the low bass pulse, pounding drums, and electronic sound effects that were part of Bauhaus' style. Siouxsie's vocals, however, made no attempt at Peter Murphy's low pitch level and were based on her punk vocals of the past. Gothic mystery and sense of fear is clear in the lyrics to "The Staircase (Mystery)," in which Siouxsie sings about hearing footsteps of an unknown being approaching her. Those vocals are accompanied by the sound effects of swirling wind.

The city of Leeds gave the Gothic rock movement two important bands, **The Sisters of Mercy** and Mission (UK). Vocalist and principal song writer Andrew Eldritch was the central figure of the Sisters of Mercy. He stood on stage wearing very dark sunglasses, shrouded in black, singing in a hollow voice so deep and velvety that he sounded like David Bowie singing from the bottom of a well. Song themes often portrayed a depressing view of corruption among politicians and the media. Despite the fact that the band was English, they commented on American political figures as well as their own. The title of their album *Vision Thing* (1990) came out of a statement made by President Bush, who was quoted as having asked his speech writers to change their direction because he felt that his speeches lacked the "vision thing." Musically, the Sisters of Mercy avoided the use of acoustic drums and instead relied on a drum machine they named "Doktor Avalanche." Medieval touches included low drones (long-held notes) and an almost minimalistic use of short, repeated melodic fragments.

Several membership changes occurred through the ten-plus years the Sisters of Mercy were together; in fact, **Mission (UK)** was formed by former Sisters of Mercy guitarist Wayne Hussey and bassist Craig Adams. (The "UK" was added to the band's name for publication in the U.S. because a rhythm and blues band in Philadelphia held the copyright to the name the Mission.) The listening guide on page 250 analyzes the Gothic elements in a track from Mission (UK)'s debut album, *God's Own Medicine* (1986). "Wasteland" was written by members of Mission (UK) and was probably influenced by T. S. Eliot's (1888–1965) poem, "The Waste Land" (1922), which depicted the world as a place of spiritual drought. The poem also made reference to medieval imagery. On later recordings the band put their Gothic drones into other people's music with covers of such songs as the Beatles' "Tomorrow Never Knows," Neil Young's "Like a Hurricane,"

Listening Guide

"Wasteland"
as recorded by Mission (UK) (1986)

Tempo: The tempo is approximately 132 beats per minute, with four beats in each bar.

Form: The form is based on eight-bar periods and is structured as follows: Introduction Extension A A A A B Instrumental A A B Instrumental A_1 A_1 B B B.

The recording begins with a spoken sentence.

The instrumental introduction is made up of two eight-bar periods followed by an extension of three four-beat bars and one three-beat bar.

Each A and B section is eight bars in length. The B section functions as a refrain.

The first instrumental section (after the introduction) is made up of two eight-bar periods.

The second instrumental section has five eight-bar periods.

The vocal line is different in the A_1 sections than it is in earlier A sections, but the chords and instrumental riffs are too similar to the other A sections to call them C sections.

The end of the last B section devolves into electronic sound effects that end the recording.

Features: Even beat subdivisions are maintained throughout the recording.

A soft backbeat played in the introduction is replaced by a very strong backbeat played by the drums through the rest of the recording.

A four-bar chord progression is repeated through the entire recording, each eight-bar period having that progression played through two times. A bass riff also repeats during each four-bar pattern, creating what would be called a passacaglia in classical music.

The thick production sound includes layers of riff patterns played by the guitars and bass.

The patterns repeat in a minimalism-influenced way, not unlike some of the backgrounds that Brian Eno added to recordings by U2 and others he produced.

The deep, drone-like sound of the vocals is greatly influenced by some of David Bowie's vocals, except that Wayne Hussey (in this recording) sings in a lower register than Bowie generally used.

Lyrics: The song portrays the world as a wasteland where good and evil have been combined and pain is pleasure. As he laments at the beginning, the vocalist feels ignored and rejected by God.

Source: *God's Own Medicine,* Mercury Records, 830603; and *never mind the mainstream . . . The Best of MTV's 120 Minutes, Volume 1,* Rhino Records 70545.

and the Kinks' "Mr. Pleasant." One cannot help but wonder what the original songwriters would think of the covers.

Industrial Rock

The industrial rock movement began in England in the late seventies. The term industrial was used as a statement against what the movement's originators saw as the decay of urban life and its dependency on work in factory and industrial jobs. Thematically an extension of the punk movement, the industrial bands looked beyond the government and monarchy as reasons for rebellion and saw intrusive controls on every aspect of their lives. Even the art world was seen as lacking in freedom of expression because of too much concern for form and balanced structure. The industrialists' views on control were influenced by the sadistic desires to dominate all aspects of life and expression described by William Burrughs in his novel *Naked Lunch* (1959). Also inspired by that novel, various forms of sadomasochism became part of the stage performances of many industrial groups and group members and fans would pierce themselves with pins or other ornaments. Musically, very loud noise is the most important characteristic of many industrial recordings and performances.

Two of the most important early industrial bands were **Throbbing Gristle** and **Cabaret Voltaire.** Instruments used by these and other such bands were chosen primarily for the amount of noise they could produce and whether the instrument's noise would sound thick and muddy in the background or stand out

Listening Guide

"Stigmata"
as recorded by Ministry (1988)

Tempo: The tempo is approximately 152 beats per minute, with four beats in each bar.

Form: Most sections of the form are eight bars long, but many of those are extended into other lengths with no apparent pattern to the extensions. Since the vocals are all screams or shouts, it is impossible to analyze a form through melodic repetitions and contrasts. The two formal sections that do contrast with one another are each identified by their riff pattern. The first riff is one bar long, usually played eight times in succession (the A section). The second riff begins like the first riff, but cuts off early and is lengthened to two bars by drum accents. That two-bar riff is usually played through four times, making for another eight-bar section (the B section).

The introduction is made up of six bars of electronic sound effects; eight bars that include drum accentuations; eight bars of screams; sixteen bars of the first riff (A); eight bars of the second riff (B); and then screams that become electronically distorted. From there the vocals enter with barely audible lyrics and the A and B sections alternate (repeated and/or extended or not) through the rest of the recording.

Features: Even beat subdivisions are maintained throughout the recording.

A strong backbeat is kept through much of the recording, but the pattern is sometimes broken.

In addition to drums, the recording includes the use of electronic sound effects, distorted guitars, distorted bass (playing the riff patterns), distorted vocals, and other noises.

The vocals have been electronically altered by removing all high overtones and limiting the low pitches to create a robotic effect.

The repetitious riff and drum patterns along with the background noises create the feeling of being caught in a factory and doing and hearing the same things hour after hour.

Lyrics: "Stigmata" generally means that a person's flesh has been pierced or otherwise invaded by a foreign object, and the vocalist constantly screams about trying to get something out of his eyes (along with other references to such things as chewing on and being cut with glass and walking on splinters). The pain and anger are directed at someone who has lied to him.

Source: *The Land of Rape and Honey,* Sire Records 25799; and *never mind the mainstream . . . The Best of MTV's 120 Minutes, Volume 2,* Rhino Records 70546.

over the background. Instruments employed to stand out were horns, especially trumpet or cornet, and electric guitars played with a slide, a small electric fan, or even an electric drill. Synthesizers provided much of the background sound. Throbbing Gristle built their own keyboard instrument that had one octave of "notes," on which each note activated one or more cassette machines loaded with prerecorded tape loops containing electronic sounds and noises such as screaming voices. In some cases even the sound of an electric shoe polisher was pushed through amplifiers and distortion boxes. Throbbing Gristle subtitled their first U.S.-released album, *Throbbing Gristle's Greatest Hits* (1980), *"Entertainment Through Pain."* They broke up in 1986, but Cabaret Voltaire was still recording in the early nineties.

By the early eighties the industrial movement had made its way across the Atlantic and bands such as Chicago's **Ministry** formed to vent their anger at the modern world. The layers of noise for which industrial rock is known can be heard in Ministry's "Stigmata."

Industrial rock of the late eighties had spread to the U.S. and gained a new voice in Cleveland when vocalist Trent Reznor overdubbed his synthesizer-produced sounds and recorded his debut album, *Pretty Hate Machine* (1989), under the name **Nine Inch Nails.**

Grindcore, a style that combined the power of thrash/death metal with the pounding beat of hardcore punk and industrial noises, emerged in the late eighties. One of the most important bands to represent this style was the British band from Birmingham, **Napalm Death.** Their breakneck tempos and electronically altered vocals provided powerful support for angry lyrics about hypocrisy and injustice in the world. Before singing with Sony, which released their *Fear Emptiness Despair* (1994) album, Napalm Death's record company was Earache Records. Napalm Death's American

Bob Mould in 1989
AP/Wide World Photos

grindcore counterpart is the New York speed/thrash band Prong.

Post Punk in the United States

Minneapolis was an important center for post-punk bands of the eighties. The Replacements and Hüsker Dü stand out as Minneapolis bands that achieved a national following without "crossing over" into mainstream success. After hearing the Sex Pistols, guitarist/songwriter Paul Westerberg envisioned a whole new future for himself. He quit playing guitar in the band Neighborhood Threat because he was tired of playing covers of music by bands like Rush. Because Johnny Rotten's singing affected him as it did, he decided he needed to put together his own band. That band, **The Replacements,** never actually was a punk band in the sense that the Sex Pistols were, but they played loud and fast music that fit that general style. As Westerberg's songwriting matured, the band moved away from their angry punk roots voiced in such songs as "Shut-up" and "Kick Your Door Down" from their first album, *Sorry Ma, Forgot to Take Out the Trash* (1981), to some rather sensitive expressions of loneliness and insecurity as can be heard in "Answering Machine" (from *Let It Be,* 1984) and "Hold My Life" (from *Tim,* 1985). Hard-rocking songs such as "I.O.U." (from *Pleased to Meet Me,* 1987) and "Bent Out of Shape" (from *All Shook Down,* 1990) indicated that Westerberg is unlikely as ever to "sell out" to pop styles. The *All Shook Down* album represented further musical changes by adding studio musicians to the band's two guitars, bass, and drums lineup. Drummer Chris Mars quit the band after recording that album. Mars was replaced and the band continued on. Westerberg returned with a solo album, *14 Songs,* in 1993.

Hüsker Dü created a Sex Pistols-influenced sound of their own with very thick, high-volume buzzsaw guitar timbres that served to blur the distinctions between melody and rhythm. Their driving bass lines, pounding beat, and Bob Mould's sometimes-shouted monotone vocals were also derived from punk influences. On page 253 is a listening guide that serves as an example of their style. After Hüsker Dü disbanded in 1987, singer/songwriter **Bob Mould** experimented with a completely new direction for his *Workbook* album. It may have been his move from the noise and constant activity of the city of Minneapolis to the quiet of the Minnesota countryside that caused him to approach his music with a more relaxed acoustic sound. Some of Hüsker Dü's buzzsaw guitar style returned with Mould's middle-nineties band Sugar.

Washington, D.C. has had a very strong and political punk movement called straight edge since the early eighties, and the nineties band **Fugazi,** which formed in 1987, was born out of that movement. Fugazi's guitarist, vocalist, and primary song writer, Ian MacKaye, screamed out against drugs, alcohol, and people who were content merely being followers with his band **Minor Threat** back in 1981. After the breakup of that band, MacKaye moved on the short-lived band Embrace, with which he continued to attack drug usage and widened his social criticisms to condemn the uncontrollable greed for money and power he saw around him in the nation's capital. The late eighties saw a more mature, but still aggressively critical, MacKaye co-writing and sharing vocals and guitar solos with Guy Picciotto in Fugazi. The term fugazi meant "crisis situation" during the Vietnam War, and Fugazi's songs pointed at the money-grubbing values held by most Americans as being exactly that—a crisis situation. In support of their position that money should not run the world, Fugazi released its recordings on its own label, Dischord Records, at a cost far below the normal prices. As was mentioned earlier, Fugazi also kept ticket prices to their concerts at no more than five dollars. The band allowed no merchandise sales at their concerts—"This is not a FUGAZI T-shirt" shirts available at concerts were bootlegs the band had nothing to do with. Fugazi also allowed no age limit at concerts and requested no backstage catering, limousines, or other special treatment. Musically, Fugazi played hardcore punk updated with

Listening Guide

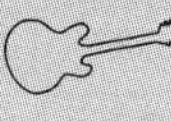

"Could You Be the One?" as recorded by Hüsker Dü (1987)

Tempo: The tempo is approximately 160 beats per minute, with four beats in each bar.

Form: After a two-bar introduction, the form is organized as follows: A B with Extension A B with Extension C Instrumental A B C C.

The A sections are eight bars long.

The B sections begin as eight-bar periods followed by extensions. The first extension adds six bars and the second adds two bars.

The C section is fourteen bars in length and uses melodic and lyric sections from the B section. The C section functions as a refrain.

The instrumental section is based on a full A section followed by a B section with a six-bar extension.

The recording ends by fading out.

Features: Even beat subdivisions are generally maintained through the recording.

A strong backbeat is kept by the drums.

The high intensity level created by the "buzzsaw" guitar timbre and active bass line are very much influenced by the instrumental effects in punk music.

As was also true of most punk rock, guitar, bass, and drums are the only instruments used.

Also in the punk tradition, the vocals are generally in a monotone.

Lyrics: The singer is searching for meaning in a relationship and asking if the person to whom the song is addressed might be the one for him. He must have been hurt before because he says that he is crying inside and wonders whether what he wants even matters at all.

Source: *Warehouse: Songs and Stories,* Warner Bros. 25544; and *never mind the mainstream . . . The Best of MTV's 120 Minutes, Volume 2,* Rhino Records 70546.

funk and reggae influences and maintained a large underground following into the nineties. Fugazi's appeal broadened beyond the underground in 1993 when *In On the Kill Taker* made it into the top 200 on the pop charts.

Prepared Instruments

Back in the twenties, composer Henry Cowell (1897–1965) had the idea of placing things on the strings of a piano to change the sound quality of the instrument. Cowell's student John Cage (1912–1992) became quite well known for his works that used the idea he called "prepared" piano. Since then a number of composers have "prepared" guitars and other instruments by hanging things such as paper clips or folded paper or foil wrap on or weaving things such as paper strips among the strings, so the idea of preparing instruments was quite old to the field of art music, but new to alternative rock.

An important and influential "no wave" band from New York, **Sonic Youth,** experimented with unusual guitar tunings and sound effects created by **prepared instruments.** "No wave" was art-influenced punk rock, and the idea of "preparing" musical instruments by placing screwdrivers, drum sticks, and other items between the strings did indeed come from art music. Feedback and dissonance were added with thick layers of sound created by the group's two guitarists, Lee Ranaldo (born in 1956) and Thurston Moore (born in 1958). Sonic Youth formed in 1981 and not only influenced the guitar-based sound of several of Seattle's grunge bands, but also helped to promote the Seattle sound by having these bands play opening performances at Sonic Youth concerts. Their female bass player and singer, Kim Gordon (born in 1953), has sometimes been dubbed the "Godmother of Alternative Rock." In addition to her work with Sonic Youth, Gordon earned that title through her many efforts to advance the careers of other women in alternative rock music. She co-produced Hole's debut album *Pretty on the Inside* (1991), co-directed videos for the Breeders, and worked with many other female bands. Married to Sonic Youth guitarist Thurston Moore, Gordon dressed their little daughter, Hayley Gordon Moore, in T-shirts with "Question Authority" written on them, and has often said in interviews that she hopes that her daughter can grow up in a world where she knows she can do anything she wants to with her life. Gordon does not even mind if Hayley decides not to be in a rock band.

One of the first Seattle bands to gain a strong following was **Soundgarden,** which recorded its first EP, *Screaming Life,* in 1987. The term "grunge" represented the loud crunch of their typical guitar sound. Many of the grunge bands (many of which do not like that title) recorded under the Sub Pop record label, although Soundgarden eventually moved to A&M. Soundgarden's singer, Chris Cornell, imitated the style of British heavy metal singers of fifteen or twenty years earlier. They also reached back to pre-metal sources for some of their music by playing covers of Led Zeppelin and even Howlin' Wolf songs. Guitar/bass riffs and distortion added to the heavy metal connection. Soundgarden released their most powerful album, *Superunknown,* in 1994. That album was not only a hit on the pop charts, but it won two Grammy awards for Best Hard Rock and Best Metal recordings for the album cuts "Black Hole Sun" and "Spoonman." Soundgarden was influential on other Seattle bands including Mudhoney and Nirvana.

Mudhoney put out their first EP, *Superfuzz Bigmuff,* in 1988. Like other grunge bands, they combined late sixties and early seventies metal guitar riffs and distortion effects with punk's intensity and noise level. **Nirvana** did not come from Seattle, but from Aberdeen, Washington, however they were influenced by the nearby Seattle bands, recorded for Sub Pop Records, and were very much a part of the grunge movement. Nirvana pulled itself out of the underground when it signed with a major label, Geffen Records, recorded the video "Smells Like Teen Spirit," and hit the pop charts with their *Nevermind* (1991) album. Later albums also sold well, but singer Kurt Cobain was torn between the responsibilities those in the limelight have to their fans and the fear that the band's antiestablishment messages were being overshadowed by popularity or missed completely by most of the band's followers. Both Cobain and his wife, Courtney Love, guitarist and singer with Hole, had a series of overdoses and other problems as a result of taking heroin, and even came very close to losing custody of their daughter, Frances Bean. Fans and musician friends alike feared that Cobain was losing his battle with drugs and the war within himself, but no one was able to keep him from shooting himself in April of 1994. Following Cobain's death, Nirvana broke up and their former drummer, Dave Grohl, started the Foo Fighters. Live performances of music recorded before and after the release of *Nevermind* were included on Nirvana's 1996 album *From the Muddy Banks of the Wish Kah.*

Of the Seattle-based bands that formed in the nineties, **Pearl Jam** took the grunge guitar-based style and antiestablishment message to the largest audiences yet. Pearl Jam's singer, Eddie Vedder (born in 1966), was in San Diego when a friend invited him to join the band, but other members had been in earlier Seattle bands such as Green River, Mother Love Bone, and Temple of the Dog. Pearl Jam became known for its refusal to allow Ticketmaster to control ticket costs, and unsuccessfully sued the agency for unfair business practices. They also refused to make videos or singles for songs on their second and later albums. Despite the popularity of those and other issues promoted by the band, the group's music was still the basis of its success. The influences of earlier musicians and bands such as Jimi Hendrix, the Doors, the Grateful Dead, the Beatles, and even the Stooges can be heard in Pearl Jam's guitar riffs and complex textures. Vedder's dramatic and passionate vocals effectively expressed the message behind the lyrics of Pearl Jam's songs, many of which deal with such issues as child abuse ("Jeremy" and "Alive" from *Ten,* 1991), loneliness ("Daughter" from *Vs.,* 1993), and problems the band had with the media ("Blood" from *Vs.*). In 1995 members of Pearl Jam performed and recorded an album with Neil Young. Pearl Jam continued to limit its live concert appearances, but each new album is awaited by thousands of fans. Without "selling out" their messages or their music, they have become one of the most important and popular bands within the alternative market.

Further down the West Coast, former punk musicians continued to churn out intense rock music. One of the best examples of post-punk in Los Angeles was led by former Black Flag singer Henry Rollins of **The Henry Rollins Band.** After the angry attitude of Black Flag's earliest recordings, a socially aware sense of humor emerged in songs such as "TV Party" (*Damaged,* 1981) in which the lyrics depicted the vapid banality of people who intentionally avoid any activity other than watching their favorite television shows and drinking beer. In his late eighties and early nineties recordings, Rollins continued to toy with serious social problems in an equally satirical manner. For example, in 1987 he temporarily renamed his band Henrietta Collins and the Wifebeating Childhaters and issued the EP *Drive by Shooting.* Post-punk musicians from both sides of the U.S. were well aware of what one another was doing and were known to work in support of each other. Rollins called on his longtime friend Ian MacKaye to produce some of his recordings. Rollins continued to record with his self-named band in the middle nineties. His former partner in Black Flag, Greg Ginn, also established himself as a solo artist and continued to record under his own name.

Riot Grrrls and Other Feminist Trends

Riot Grrrl was a name for a nationwide, networked group of young women who communicated their anger about sexual abuse, harassment, wife beating, and other issues through the in-your-face intensity of punk rock music. These forms of abuse have always been around, but Riot Grrrls pointed out that past generations of mothers dealt with them internally or denied their existence, thereby doing nothing to protect their daughters or even teach them to stand up for themselves. Songs sometimes quote the Grrrls' mothers saying such things as "Respect and be polite to your father and do anything he tells you to." Other times the songs contain repeated shouts about women's rights. The language in song lyrics and other statements by Riot Grrrls was direct and confrontational, but the goal of their message was the very positive one of making so much noise that others

Neil Young (R) jams with Eddie Vedder (L) and other members of Pearl Jam
Reuters–Bettmann

would notice and, hopefully, their own daughters would grow up in more positive environments.

The Riot Grrrl movement's **Bikini Kill** was led by singer/songwriter Kathleen Hanna (born in 1969). She was in Seattle when Nirvana and other grunge bands were forming, and was even credited with giving Kurt Cobain the song title "Smells Like Teen Spirit." In true alternative spirit, Bikini Kill would not sign with a major label and they worked with such producers as Fugazi's Ian MacKaye and former Runaways and Blackhearts singer Joan Jett. Hanna and Jett co-wrote some of the songs on Jett's 1994 album *Pure and Simple.* Bikini Kill and their British counterpart in the Riot Grrrl movement, **Huggy Bear,** toured together and both put songs on their shared album *Yeah Yeah Yeah Yeah* (1993).

Courtney Love was not directly associated with the Riot Grrrl movement, but did express many of the same concerns in her songs. Love's parents divorced when she was five and she spent the rest of her youth living in New Zealand with her mother. Once she was on her own she traveled in parts of Asia, the U.S., and England, supporting herself by working as a stripper. She spent some time in Liverpool, England, and then in Los Angeles, where she played a small role in the movie *Sid & Nancy* (1986). Before forming **Hole** in Seattle, she had sung in the female band Sugar Baby Doll, which also included Kat Bjelland (who later played guitar and sang in Babes in Toyland) and Jennifer Finch (who later played bass and sang in L7). Like some other alternative bands, Hole signed with a major label, in their case with Geffen, for the release of their second album, *Live Through This* (1994). The album was released just a week after Love's husband Kurt Cobain's suicide, adding more of a sense of agony to the pain expressed in some of the songs on the album. From that album the single "Doll Parts" gained critical recognition and placed in the top seventy on the pop charts. A listening guide follows on page 256. Love was featured in the 1997 movie *The People vs. Larry Flynt.*

The number of female bands and important women singers, writers, and musicians in alternative rock music of the nineties is so great that it would be impossible to credit them all in a general survey of rock history, and yet that is a major point in itself. It is fairly easy for most rock fans to name the major female musicians and writers from earlier decades when there were few women performers beyond those who merely sang songs others wrote for them to perform in front of a male band. That does not denigrate the importance of women performers of the past, but the time has finally come when women are striving to share equality with men in rock.

Courtney Love holding Frances Bean Cobain with Kurt Cobain (behind) in 1992
Corbis-Bettmann

Listening Guide

"Doll Parts"
as recorded by Hole (1994)

Tempo: The tempo is approximately 104 beats per minute, with four beats in each bar.

Form: The form is structured in four- and three-bar phrases. The first four phrases are four bars each, and they are followed by nine contrasting phrases (beginning with "I want to . . .") that are three bars each. Those are followed by another set of four four-bar phrases and then another set of three-bar phrases and repetitions of the final phrase of lyrics.

Features: Uneven beat subdivisions are used throughout the recording.

The drums accent the backbeat, although they and the bass drop out completely to add emphasis to the vocals on some phrases.

Love's very exhausted and world-weary vocals support the meaning of the lyrics.

Love adds emphasis to the repetitions of the final phrase by overdubbing her vocal line on the fourth through the seventh (out of eight) times she sings it.

Lyrics: The singer is abused and broken to the point that she does not really feel alive, and she warns that her listeners will also come to that point one day.

Source: *Live Through This,* Geffen Records 24631.

The songs women write and sing add an entire new range of points of view and emotion to rock music. Certainly women who deserve further attention for their contributions to alternative rock music include **Gina Birch** of Raincoats; **Kristin Hersh** (with and without Throwing Muses); **Tanya Donelly** of Throwing Muses, Breeders, and Belly; **Björk** (with and without the Sugarcubes); **Liz Phair; Nina Gordon** and **Louise Post** of Veruca Salt; **PJ Harvey; Sonya Aurora Madan** and **Debbie Smith** of Echobelly; and **Alanis Morissette.**

Summary

Alternative or underground rock was so named because it served as an alternative to rock music that was commercial or performed to please a broad audience. Most alternative bands avoided signing with major record labels or with promoters for fear that doing so might cause them to lose control of their music or their song lyrics. The bands did not want to be seen as rock stars, but rather as living on the same level as their fans. Their songs expressed the concerns of those fans, and in an economy that made it difficult for young adults to foresee dependable financial security for themselves, the attitudes in the songs were often depressed or angry.

The most depressed of the underground movements was Gothic rock (also called death rock), which portrayed the gloom and mystery of a Gothic novel with repetitious sounds influenced by music of the Middle Ages. The most angry movement was industrial rock, which portrayed the world as controlling and lacking any sense of freedom. There were elements of the antiestablishment push of the punk movement in most alternative and underground styles and many "post-punk" bands used the intense pounding beat, throbbing bass, and distorted guitars of punk bands like the Sex Pistols. Other alternative rock concentrated less on depression or anger, but still had lyrics, images, and/or music that was too individualistic or even bizarre for broad audience appeal. Female musicians, writers, and singers found much support and success within the field of alternative rock

Alanis Morissette in 1996
© AP/Wide World Photos

music, breaking some of the previous sexual barriers that held them behind men in rock music of past decades.

Rock has long since left its American roots in youthful hedonism to become an international medium for the communication of ideas. Granted, destructive youths still exist who use some kinds of rock music as part of their identity, just as they did in the fifties, and some critics still find it easier to blame the music instead of the perpetrators themselves for their actions. But so much rock music is full of positive and humanitarian statements that the music itself certainly has no intrinsic negativism. Political statements in rock music are often left-wing, and yet cries for universal understanding and peace are much more common than any other kind of extremist position. Music is not the only or necessarily the most efficient means to achieve peace, but more openness in communication among peoples could certainly aid the cause.

New sounds and styles of rock music are bound to develop in the future. If the past can provide any indication of what the future will bring, it is likely that old styles will be revived and reinterpreted to relate to the problems and concerns of new eras, and alongside those old styles new ones will develop. One of the most exciting things about rock music is that it directly expresses the feelings, aspirations, and dreams of its fans as often as it entertains them. Whether a particular rock style will last into the future or not does not really matter. The music changes with the times and people. Rock music is truly a music that is of, by, and for the people of its time and it is to be hoped, for the future as well.

Term to Remember

Prepared instruments

Glossary

A

a cappella
Describes group or choral singing without instrumental accompaniment.

acts
Self-contained sections of operas or musicals that end with a sense of completeness and are often separated by an intermission. A single act can be subdivided into shorter sections called scenes.

aeolian mode
See Modes

amateur
One who performs something such as music for the love of doing it as opposed to performing it professionally for money or other remuneration.

AM radio
An early (pre-FM) form of radio using an amplitude modulation (AM) system of broadcasting; the system can be used over great distances, but is subject to static and not capable of true high fidelity.

antecedent and consequent phrases
Melodic phrases that occur in pairs in which the first, the antecedent phrase, sounds incomplete and the second, the consequent phrase, brings the first to a final-sounding resolution.

antiphonal choruses
Groups of singers or instrumentalists that are separated by physical distance in performance and sing or play different material in response to one another.

aria
A dramatic song in an opera.

arpeggio
A chord that is broken, or played one or two notes at a time instead of all its notes being sounded together.

arrangement
Preplanned music involving written-out parts for instrumentalists in a band.

avant-garde
Very current, modern, and experimental.

B

backbeat
Beats two and four of a four-beat pattern, the accenting of which creates rock's basic rhythm.

ballad opera
Staged dramatic musicals in which spoken dialogue alternates with songs. Originally from Britain and popular in the American colonies during the eighteenth century.

baritone (voice)
The male singing voice in the vocal range that is between the higher tenor and the lower bass.

barrelhouse
A bar, or honky-tonk, originally with whisky barrels along the walls or used as tables; the boogie-woogie-based piano style often played in such places.

bass riff
A low, short, repeated bit of melody, often played by the bass guitar, or by bass and lead guitar together.

bass (voice)
The male singing voice with the lowest vocal range, lower than baritone.

beats
American writers and poets of the fifties and later whose works included social criticisms questioning the lack of individual freedom in American society, their followers were known as "beatniks."

beat subdivisions (even and uneven)
The subsections into which a single beat is divided. An even subdivision involves two equal notes; an uneven subdivision involves three equal notes, often with the first two notes tied together, making a long–short subdivision.

bebop
A modern jazz style pioneered in the early forties by alto saxophonist Charlie Parker, pianist Thelonious Monk, trumpeter Dizzy Gillespie, and others. Bebop was more harmonically, melodically, and rhythmically complex than earlier jazz and was usually played by small combos of musicians with a great amount of technical facility; also called bop.

bluegrass
A complex country style that developed from the early-twentieth-century string bands; it was first called bluegrass in the mid-forties. A variety of instruments may be used to play the music, but a five-string banjo and guitar are generally essential to authentic bluegrass.

blue notes
Notes that are lowered a half step or less. Early blues musicians lowered the third and seventh scale degrees, and bebop musicians lowered the fifth degree as well.

blues harp
A harmonica used to play blues; a technique called "cross harping" makes use of a harp played in a key one step or a fifth below that of the song, in order to have blue notes automatically available to the player.

boogie-woogie
A rhythmic piano style that uses repeating bass patterns.

bottleneck
A glass or metal tube that fits over a guitarist's ring finger or little finger and stops the strings of the guitar when it is slid up or down the instrument's fin-

gerboard. Originally, the glass tube was the neck of a bottle that had been broken off and sanded down for use by blues guitarists.

break
A technique in which instruments stop playing for a short period of time, allowing a singer or instrumental soloist to be heard alone.

bridge (of a guitar)
A piece of wood or metal attached to the body of the guitar to which the strings are attached or over which they pass.

bridge (of a song form)
The contrasting, or "B," section in a song form that has repeated "A" sections before and usually after the "B." Also called "release" or "channel."

cadence
An ending of a section of a piece of music consisting of harmonies that give a sense of finality.

call-and-response
The practice of singing in which a solo vocalist, the caller, is answered by a group of singers. The practice is also used with instruments, but its origins are vocal.

Chicago blues
A blues style that combined country and urban blues characteristics, recorded in Chicago during the late forties and the fifties.

chimes
A set of pitched, bell-like percussion instruments.

chord extensions
Notes that lie beyond the normal three or four notes of a chord. These additional notes are dissonant to the basic chord.

chromatic passing tones
A chromatic note that bridges between two notes of the diatonic scale and "passes through" as the melodic line moves from one of those notes to the other.

classic blues
A blues style of the twenties and thirties, in which female singers were featured as soloists with blues bands.

claves
(pronounced CLAH-vays) A pair of wooden sticks that are tapped together to produce a hollow-pitched sound; claves are used in certain Latin-based styles.

claves beat
The rhythm pattern played by the claves in a rumba.

closed form
A composition, or set of compositions, beginning and ending with the same musical material.

coda
An ending section to a musical work that functions to bring the work to a satisfying conclusion. Codas can be very short or extended with repetitions of earlier themes and occasionally some new material. The term "coda" comes from an Italian word for "tail."

comping
An accompaniment style used on either guitar or piano that does not require that the strong beats of the measure be articulated.

concerto
A multi-movement work for a soloist, or small group of soloists, and a large group of players, generally an orchestra, in which the soloist is accompanied by the orchestra.

conga drums
Large, long drums, usually in pairs, used in the conga and other Latin dances.

contralto (voice)
The lowest female vocal range. Also called alto.

contrapuntal guitar parts
Guitar parts that use counterpoint, or more than one melody at the same time.

cool jazz
A style of modern jazz developed by trumpeter Miles Davis, the Modern Jazz Quartet, baritone saxophonist Gerry Mulligan, and others. As the name implies, it is a style that is subdued, and it generally is played by a small group of instrumentalists.

copyright
The exclusive right to control the use of an artistic work for the amount of time allowed by law.

country blues
The earliest and simplest blues style, usually performed by a solo singer accompanied by simple guitar strumming with occasional melodic fills.

cover recording
A recording made subsequent to the original version; it may or may not follow the style or lyrics of the original.

crescendo
A gradual increase in loudness, or volume level.

crooning
The soft vocal style of Rudy Vallee, Bing Crosby, Perry Como, and others who tended to slide from one note to another giving the effect of warmth, intimacy, and sentimentality.

cross-harp playing
The practice of blues harmonica players using an instrument in a key other than that of the song to aid them in playing blue notes.

crossover
In country music, musicians who have expanded their styles to include pop music and playing techniques.

cutting
A technique used by disc jockeys to segue one recording into another using a vari-speed control on the phonograph to maintain a constant beat pattern through the change.

dada
A movement in art in which frustration over the destruction of human life that took place during World War I was expressed by fashioning artworks out of trash or other material put together in a chaotic form.

decrescendo
A gradual decrease in loudness, or volume level.

Delta blues
The country blues style of Robert Johnson and others who came from the Mississippi Delta region.

dobro
A steel-strung, guitar-like acoustic instrument with a raised metal section on the instrument's soundboard, played with a sliding bar, invented in the twenties.

dominant chord
A triad built on the fifth degree of a scale. In the key of C, the dominant chord is G-major, make up of the notes G, B, and D (also notated as V).

doo-wop progression
The chord progression of a tonic (I) chord, a sub-median seventh (vi^7) chord, a supertonic seventh (ii^7) chord, and a dominant seventh (V^7) chord, commonly used as the basis of fifties doo-wop songs.

dorian mode
See Modes

double time
A tempo that is twice as fast as the tempo that precedes it.

downbeat
The first beat of each bar.

drone
A sustained tone over or under which other music is played. For example, a bagpiper usually plays a continuous drone over which the melody is played.

dubbing (by disc jockeys)
Rhythmic patter-talk used by Jamaican disc jockeys while a recording was being played; also an engineering technique used to cut instruments or vocal parts out of a recording.

dubbing (in recordings)
Also called overdubbing; refers to the technique of adding instrumental, vocal, or other sounds to a recording that has already been put on tape. Dubbing requires a multiple-track tape machine (or two tape machines) to allow one track to be heard while the new one is being recorded.

dulcimer (plucked and strummed)
A stringed instrument with the fretted fingerboard along the full length of the hollow body of the instrument.

duple rhythm patterns
A meter that accents every other beat to create patterns of two or four beats.

E

eight-bar period
A section of melody make up of two four-bar phrases that create a sense of completion.

eighth notes
Notes that receive half the amount of time allotted to a quarter note.

embellishment
The addition of new notes to a melody that serve to decorate or vary it.

enharmonics
Notes that are actually at the same sounding pitch although they are given different pitch names. For instance, C♯ and D♭ sound the same but are notated differently and have different harmonic functions within chords.

existentialism
A twentieth-century philosophy that takes many forms, all of which stress the freedom and corresponding responsibility of the individual as he or she relates to society.

F

falsetto
A high male vocal range above the normal tenor voice.

feedback
A naturally produced, sustained, distorted squeal created when high-volume sound coming out of an amplifier is taken in by the pickup on the guitar (or a microphone) and then fed back into the amplifier.

fifths
Intervals that are five notes apart in the diatonic scale, with the first and fifth notes both counted. A fifth above the note C is the note G, counting as C, D, E, F, G.

fifth of a chord
The note that is the interval of a fifth above the root, or naming note, of the chord. In a C chord, the notes are C, E, and G and the fifth of the chord is G.

fills
Bits of melody or embellishment played between sections of the main solo melody.

five-string banjo
A banjo with a fifth string that is tuned higher than the fourth string and is plucked by the player's thumb. The fifth string is often used as a repeated drone or pedal.

flamenco
A very rhythmic and highly emotional dance music originated by the gypsies of southern Spain.

flat-four beat
A four-beat metric pattern in which all beats receive equal accenting.

flutter-tonguing
A technique that involves buzzing with the tongue while blowing into a woodwind or brass instrument.

FM radio
A form of radio invented in the early thirties, using a frequency modulation (FM) system of broadcasting. FM did not have the range of AM, and it was used almost exclusively by college and other noncommercial stations, until the late sixties, when demand for its clearer sound quality and stereo capabilities allowed FM stations to take the commercial market away from AM.

forte piano
The original name for the keyboard instrument later called the piano. The musical terms *forte* and *piano* mean "loud" and "soft." The combination of these two terms advertised the fact that the instrument could play at both loud and soft dynamic levels, allowing for greater expressiveness than earlier keyboard instruments such as the harpsichord.

four-bar phrase
A four-bar section of music ending with a partial or total feeling of completeness, most often paired with another four-bar phrase to make up a complete period ending with a cadence.

fourths
Intervals that are four notes apart in the diatonic scale, with the first and fourth notes both counted. A fourth above the note C is the note F, counting as C, D, E, F.

front line
The group of lead melodic instruments such as those used in early New Orleans jazz bands, usually including a cornet (or trumpet), a clarinet, and a trombone.

fuzztone
A distorted sound effect achieved by cutting through the speaker cone of an amplifier, playing a tube amplifier at a much higher volume than it was intended for, or using an electronic device that creates a controllable version of the sound.

G

glissando
A sliding effect created by playing a series of musical tones in rapid succession.

gong
A cymbal-like percussion instrument of Asian origin which has a very mellow, low-pitched ring that sustains for a long time.

gospel
A Christian religious music, especially a kind that evolved from spirituals sung in African American churches in the South.

griots
Oral poets in Africa who memorized and sang the story of their people's history.

guiro
A Latin American percussion instrument made of a hollow gourd with notches cut across the outside over which a stick is scraped.

H

harmonics (artificial)
The same as natural harmonics, except that the vibrating length of a string is changed by its being pressed against a fingerboard, allowing for a great number of harmonics beyond the few available on open strings. Full melodies can be played in artificial harmonics.

harmonics (natural)
High, clear tones produced by touching a vibrating string at a point exactly one-half, one-third, or one-fourth its full length, then plucking or bowing the string at another point to cause it to ring. When the string has been touched at its halfway point, the harmonic produced is an octave above the pitch of the open string; when it is touched at a point at one-third its length the harmonic is one octave and a fifth above the open string; and a touch at one-fourth the string length produces a harmonic two octaves above the open string.

harpsichord
A keyboard instrument in common use during the sixteenth through the

eighteenth centuries in which the strings are plucked rather than struck with hammers.

high hat
A piece of drum equipment operated by the left foot where two cymbals, facing each other on a rod mechanism, can be made to open and close; can also be played with sticks or brushes either open, for a ringing sound, or closed, for a tight, crisp sound.

hillbilly boogie
A proto-rock style of country music from the forties that used African American boogie-woogie rhythms and electric instruments.

honky-tonk
A bar or saloon; the boogie-woogie-styled piano often played in such places.

hook
A catchy melodic or rhythmic pattern that "hooks" or attracts the listener to want to listen to the rest of the song.

horn
(1) Generic term for any wind instrument, especially trumpet, trombone, or saxophone. (2) A brass instrument more correctly called the French horn.

horn section
(1) The section of a jazz band that includes brass and woodwind instruments. (2) A group of French horns.

hymns
Songs of praise, generally used to praise God in worship services.

I

improvisation
Spontaneous performance of music that has not been written or planned out in advance, based on a progression of harmonies and can involve a certain amount of interplay among several musicians.

J

jubilee
Fast and highly energetic types of spirituals.

jug band
A small blues, country, or folk group that uses a whiskey jug as a bass instrument, sounded by the player blowing into the mouth of the jug, which serves as a resonator for the deep tone produced.

K

kettledrums
Large, bowl-shaped drums made out of copper or brass with calfskin (or plastic) heads stretched across them and screws or pedals that the player uses to vary the pitch (also called timpani).

key
The name of the scale from which the melody and chords of a piece of music have been constructed.

L

lip syncing
Moving the lips to synchronize with a prerecorded song, giving the impression that the song is being performed live.

M

major chord
A chord based on a triad in which the bottom and next higher notes are a major third apart (four half steps) and the middle and highest notes are a minor third apart (three half steps). A C-major chord contains the notes C, E, and G.

major scale
A succession of eight notes in which the half and whole steps are ordered as follows: whole, whole, half, whole, whole, whole, half. The natural notes from C to the next highest C form a major scale.

maracas
A pair of rattles made of gourds or wood with small stones or beans inside.

mariachi band
A vocal-instrumental group of Mexican origin, consisting of strolling musicians who sing and play guitars and guitar-related instruments, violins, and trumpets.

marimba
A large, xylophone-like instrument with metal tubes as resonators under wooden bars of varying length (tuned to specific pitches) that are played with mallets.

melisma
An expressive and elaborate melodic improvisation sung on a single syllable.

mellotron
(From *Mel*ody + elec*tron*ic) An electronic keyboard instrument invented in England in the early sixties that uses taped recordings of acoustic (often orchestral) instruments to recreate the sounds of those instruments.

mento
A Jamaican folk music that combines a Cuban rumba with African rhythms. The name comes from the Spanish *mentar,* meaning "to mention," referring to the subtle way the music and dance express personal complaints or social criticisms.

meter
The basic repeating pattern of accented and unaccented beats followed through a composition or a section of a composition, usually indicated by the time signature.

microtones
Intervals smaller than a half-step often used in non-Western music.

minimalism
An avant-garde style of composition based on systematically organized repetition of a minimal amount of musical material; also called systematic music.

minor chord
A chord based on a triad in which the bottom and next higher notes are a minor third apart (three half steps) and the middle and highest notes are a major third apart (four half steps). A C-minor chord contains the notes C, E♭, and G.

minor key
A tonal center based on a minor scale.

minor scale
A succession of eight notes in which the half and whole steps are ordered as follows: whole, half, whole, whole, half, whole, whole. The natural notes from A to the next highest A form a natural minor scale. There are a number of other forms of minor scales in which some of the intervals are altered, such as harmonic minor and melodic minor.

modes
Scale-like patterns based on church music formulas dating from the Middle Ages. The natural notes (that is, notes produced by pressing only white keys on the piano) from C to C produce a Major mode, or major scale (also called the Ionian mode). The other modes are as follows: D to D, Dorian; E to E, Phrygian; F to F, Lydian; G to G, Mixolydian; A to A, Aeolian (the natural minor scale); B to B, Locrian.

mods
Short for "modernists"; the Mods were a sixties youth subculture in England who considered themselves the wave of the future; they usually had jobs, wore trendy clothes, rode around on motor scooters (rather than motorcycles) and took amphetamines. (*See also* Rockers)

modulation
A change of key or tonal center.

monotone
Nonmelodic, repetitive singing of a single pitch.

motive
A fragment, or short bit, of a melody.

movement
A complete piece of music written to be played with other movements to form a multi-sectional musical work.

musique concrète
An avant-garde type of musical composition in which natural, acoustic sounds have been prerecorded on a tape that is altered to change the sounds for use in performance.

muzak
A name for a commercial service that provides bland background music for use in public places or businesses.

N

neighboring tones
Notes that are not part of the chord with which they are played or sung, but that are one diatonic or chromatic step either above or below a chord tone.

non-chordal tones
Notes that are not part of the basic chord being played. The non-chordal tones may be dissonant with the chord, they may hint at another chord and create a bi-tonal effect, or they may merely add color to the basic chord. (*See also* Chord extensions)

octave
The distance between one note and the next note (higher or lower) of the same pitch name.

opera
A dramatic theatrical performance with orchestral accompaniment in which all or most of the roles are sung instead of spoken.

operetta
A short opera, usually of a lighter nature than opera.

orchestra
A large group of instruments (generally from thirty to a hundred or more players) that includes instruments from the string (bowed string), woodwind, brass, and percussion families, as well as piano, harp, and other instruments as required for a particular composition.

ostinato
A melody or melodic fragment, often but not necessarily in the bass, that repeats over and over through an entire piece or part of a piece of music. (From Italian, meaning "obstinate.")

overdubbing
The technique of adding more tracks of sound to a recording that has already been taped.

part singing
The singing of hymns or other songs using multi-voiced arrangements.

passacaglia
A form based on a continuously repeating chord progression and accompanying bass line.

patter-talk
Talking in rhythmic patterns; also called rap.

payola
The practice of bribing disc jockeys to induce them to play particular recordings on the air.

pedal-steel guitar
An electric version of the Hawaiian steel guitar that has a number of pedals that alter the pitches of the individual strings, is mounted on legs, and is played with a bar that slides along the strings; popular in country music.

pentatonic scale
A scale, or mode, that has five notes corresponding to the natural notes C, D, E, G, and A, any of which may be the first note of the series.

phrase
A complete-sounding section of melody or lyrics, usually from two to four bars long.

phrygian mode
A sixteenth-century mode composed of the natural notes from E to E, often used in Spanish flamenco music.

pickups
1) One or more notes that lead into a downbeat at the beginning of a musical phrase. 2) A contact microphone or other device that converts vibrations into electric impulses that allows the sound to be amplified.

pogo
A punk dance in which people jumped up and down as if they were on pogo sticks.

polyphonic texture
The sound pattern created by two or more independent melodies being played or sung at the same time.

polyrhythm
Music in which more than one rhythm pattern is played at the same time.

pop song form
The structure of repeated and contrasting sections of a song in which each section (represented as letters when the form is diagrammed) is usually similar in length and corresponds to an AABA pattern or some variant on that organization.

power chords
The full and deep sound created by two notes that are a perfect fourth or a perfect fifth apart played together on the bass strings of an electric guitar with added distortion. The depth of the sound is created by the resultant tone, or combination tone, that is lower than the notes that are actually played. Power chords are used in most hard rock and heavy metal music.

prepared instruments
Traditional musical instruments, usually ones with strings such as grand pianos or guitars, with items placed on, hung from, or woven between or among the strings to alter the instrument's sound. Items used can include bolts, sticks, cloth, paper, paper clips, folded pieces of foil wrap, or other things.

psalms
Texts from the Book of Psalms in the Old Testament of the Bible.

psychedelic drugs
Drugs such as LSD that generally produce a loss of sense of time and dreamlike distortions of the senses.

pub rock
An English "back to the roots of rock" movement of the seventies that reacted against large-scale, theatrical rock styles.

R

raga
A scale or melody used in Indian music.

ragtime
A type of music that used "ragged time," or syncopated rhythms; particularly popular between 1890 and 1915.

recitative
A type of singing used in opera that is much less melodic than arias, and which often imitates the way the lines would be spoken. Sung to fairly simple musical accompaniment, recitative is often used for dialogue in opera.

refrain
A phrase or period of text or music that is repeated several times within the course of a song or piece of music.

resultant tone
A low note that is created when two notes of a perfect interval are played above it. Also called a combination tone.

rhythm and blues
Called "race music" until the end of the forties, an originally African American popular music in which the backbeat was accented and beats were usually subdivided unevenly.

rhythm section
The group of musical instruments that maintain the beat pattern and the harmonic flow of a piece of music. Rhythm sections include bass, drums, and guitar and/or keyboard instruments.

riff (melodic and/or rhythmic)
A short melodic or rhythmic pattern repeated over and over while changes take place in the music played along with it.

ritard
A direction to slow down gradually.

rockabilly
Music that combined honky-tonk country music with blues and rhythm and blues. Rockabilly bands in the fifties generally used electric lead guitar, acoustic rhythm guitar, acoustic (standup) bass, and drums. (The name is a combination of *rock* and *hillbilly.*)

rockers
Members of an English youth subculture in the sixties who wore leather jackets, rode motorcycles (not motor scooters), and identified with American rockabilly music. (*See also* Mods)

rock steady
A Jamaican music that was basically a slowed-down version of ska, but included a syncopated bass line. When sped up, rock steady became reggae.

root note of a chord
The note on which a chord is built and after which the chord is named. In a C chord, the notes are C, E, and G and the root note is C.

rumba
An African-influenced Cuban dance that is quite energetic and uses a variety of complex rhythm patterns; popular during the thirties.

S

salsa rhythm
Popular music from Cuba based on rhythm patterns from Africa.

samba
An African-influenced Brazilian dance that stresses a duple rhythm pattern; popular in the forties.

sampling
The practice of taking selected sections from previously recorded records and repeating and mixing those sections to create a background sound to accompany new vocals.

saxophone
A woodwind instrument made of metal, but played with a single-reed mouthpiece similar to that of the clarinet. The saxophone family includes, (from the highest in pitch to the lowest) soprano, alto, tenor, baritone, and bass. In addition to those are several others that are either rarely used or obsolete.

scat (scatting)
A type of singing using nonsense syllables in a style that imitates instrumental improvisations commonly used in jazz.

scratching
A technique used by disc jockeys in which a record's rotation is rapidly changed from forward to backward repeatedly, to create a rhythmic pulse over which the disc jockey talks in a rhythmic patter or rap style.

secular
Nonreligious.

segue
The joining together, without pause, of two different pieces of music.

seventh chord
A chord that includes a note that is seven scale degrees above the root note of the chord; for example, a G^7 chord adds an F on top of the basic triad of G, B, and D.

shuffle beat
A rhythmic pattern based on uneven beat subdivisions in which a note is played on the beat and the next note is played on the last uneven subdivision of the beat, creating a "shuffling" rhythm.

sitar
A plucked string instrument from India that has frets, steel strings and gourds as resonating chambers. In addition to the strings plucked by the player, the sitar has a set of strings that vibrate sympathetically when notes to which they are tuned are played on other strings.

sixteenth notes
Note values of which there are four for every quarter note.

skiffle
A very simple British folk music that involved little more than melody and accompaniment by a strummed acoustic guitar, and rudimentary rhythm instruments such as washboard.

slapping bass
A name given to rockabilly bassists' practice of slapping the strings against the fingerboards of their instruments as they played.

snare drum
A drum that has skins stretched across both the top and bottom of its shell, with metal snares set to rattle against the bottom skin while the drum is played. The sound of a snare drum is often associated with military bands. The snare drum is the drum most often used for the backbeat in rock music.

sorrow songs
Slow, melancholy types of spirituals.

spirituals
American folk hymns and other religious songs that originated in the late eighteenth or early nineteenth centuries and developed into gospel music.

steel guitar
An American country instrument that developed from guitars brought by Mexican cattlemen to Hawaii in the late nineteenth century, but which were tuned to a major chord and placed across the player's lap; chords were changed by sliding a comb, a knife, or a steel bar up and down the strings.

stop-time
A technique in which instruments play only on, say, the first beat of each bar while a soloist continues performing. There are a number of stop time patterns: first and third beats, first and fourth beats, as well as patterns stretching over two or more measures (not to be confused with break).

street funk
A seventies funk style generally dominated by strong bass guitar lines, filled in harmonies by guitars and/or keyboards, complex rhythms from a variety of drums, a flat-four beat, and a party-like atmosphere.

string bending
A guitar technique used by many blues and rock guitarists in which the player pushes or pulls the string temporarily out of alignment, causing the string to tighten and the pitch to be raised.

string section
The bowed string instruments in an orchestra, consisting of violins, violas, cellos, and bass viols.

subdominant chord
A triad built on the fourth degree of a scale. In the key of C, the subdominant chord is F-major, made up of the notes F, A, and C (also notated as IV).

suite
In the eighteenth century, a multi-movement work that was generally a collection of dances preceded by a prelude. In the nineteenth and twentieth centuries, the term was also used for groupings of non-dance compositions.

surprise cadence
A resolution to an unexpected chord.

surrealism
An artistic style that developed out of Sigmund Freud's writings about the unconscious mind and visions in dreams. Surrealistic artists painted scenes containing recognizable objects from the real world put into shapes and situations in which they could not actually exist or function.

swing
A big-band jazz style of dance music popular during the thirties through the fifties.

sympathetic strings
Strings that vibrate and sound as the notes to which they are tuned are played on another string, causing them

to vibrate; sitars have a set of sympathetic strings.

syncopated rhythms
Rhythms that do not fit an expected pattern of accents. Syncopations include the accenting of weak beats and the absence of accents (or even silence) on strong beats.

synthesizers
Electronic sound generators (often keyboards) capable of modifying the sound generated.

systematic music
An avant-garde style of composition based on systematically organized repetition of a minimal amount of musical material; also called minimalism.

T

tag
A short section of music added to the end of a composition to emphasize that the piece is ending. The term "coda" is also used for a tag ending.

tamboura
An Indian drone instrument.

tango
A Cuban-influenced Argentinean dance popular during the twenties.

tape loop
A piece of magnetic tape recorded and then cut and spliced to form a loop that continues to repeat the recording, creating an echo effect.

tape splicing
The technique of cutting apart and putting together pieces of pre-recorded tape.

tempo
The speed of the beat of a piece of music.

tenor (voice)
The male singing voice with the highest vocal range.

texture
The relationship of melody to its accompaniment or to other melodies in a musical composition. The term is often used to refer to the relative thickness of the sound or to the type of compositional technique employed, e.g., homophonic or polyphonic.

theater organ
A large organ, designed to play background music in theaters, that is able to generate a variety of instrumental sound effects not usually found on an organ, such as drums, xylophone, and chimes.

theme (musical)
A melodic idea upon which a piece of music is based.

theremin
An electronic instrument that produces a tone that changes in pitch and dynamic level when the player moves his/her hands near its antenna and loop. The theremin was invented in the twenties by Leon Theremin.

through-composed form
A compositional structure that does not use the usual formal schemes of regular repetition and contrast, but rather employs a more extended spinning out of new musical material, although individual themes may reoccur.

timbre
(pronounced TAM-ber) Tone quality as it relates to the characteristic differences among musical instruments or singing voices.

timpani
See Kettledrums

toasting
A Jamaican name for the rhythmic patter-talk used by disc jockeys.

tonic chord
A triad built on the first degree of a scale or mode. In the key of C, the tonic chord is C-major, made up of the notes C, E, and G. (Also notated as I.)

trading twos (or fours)
A term for a type of improvisation used especially by jazz musicians in which two or more musicians take turns improvising on two- or four-bar sections of music.

trad jazz (traditional jazz)
Dixieland jazz in the style played in New Orleans and Chicago during the twenties.

tremolo
(1) Fast repetitions of a single note.
(2) Loud-soft undulations on a pitch; not to be confused with vibrato.

tremolo arm
A metal bar on an electric guitar attached to the bridge (to which the strings are fastened) that can be moved by the player to raise or lower the pitch of the strings to create an effect of vibrato; should more properly be called vibrato arm.

triad, or triadic harmonies
A chord that contains only three notes, each a major or a minor third apart from the next.

triple meter
A rhythmic pattern that accents the first of each of three equal beats.

triplet
A beat normally subdivided into two equal parts is subdivided into three equal parts.

twelve-bar blues
The classic blues form structured in three four-bar phrases that follows a particular chord progression based on four bars of a tonic chord, two bars of a subdominant chord, two bars of a tonic chord, one bar of a dominant chord, one bar of a subdominant chord, and two bars of a tonic chord. There are many variations of this basic progression of harmonies.

two-beat bass
A style of bass playing often used in country music in which the bass plays the root note of the chord on the first beat of each bar and the fifth of the chord on the third beat of each bar.

U

unison
The use of more than one instrument or voice playing or singing the same notes at the same time.

urban blues
A blues style that developed in the big cities and was generally more sophisticated and played by larger instrumental groups than the older country blues style.

vamp
A repeated pattern, usually without a melody, that serves to fill time before the main melody enters.

vari-speed control
A phonograph control that allows disc jockeys to vary the speed (and hence the pitch) at which a recording is played.

vaudeville
A type of live variety stage show that included songs, dances, comedy acts, and other types of general entertainment; popular from the middle nineteenth century into the twentieth century.

vibrato
The repeated raising and lowering of a pitch that produces an undulation in the tone.

voice box
Also known as a voice tube, the box plugs into the guitar and has a tube that attaches to the microphone stand for the guitarist to vocally affect the guitar timbre. The Electro-Harmonix Golden Throat and the Ibanex VOC Talking Machine were two voice boxes available during the seventies.

walking bass
The line played by a bass player that "walks" melodically between chord tones instead of jumping from one chord tone to another.

waltz
A dance in triple meter, or a piece of music that uses the rhythm pattern of the dance.

western swing
A type of country music that developed out of the string bands. It was influenced by certain characteristics of jazz such as uneven beat subdivisions, syncopations, and the use of wind instruments in addition to the usual country instrumentation.

Discography of Sources for Listening Guides

The recordings are listed in the order that they are used in the text.

Note: * indicates that the recording is new to the third edition of the text.

"Cross Road Blues" by Robert Johnson: *Robert Johnson/The Complete Recordings,* Columbia 46222

"Three O'Clock Blues" by B. B. King: *B. B. King Singin' the Blues/The Blues,* Flair Records/Virgin Records America 86296

"Ball and Chain" by Willie Mae Thornton: *Big Mama Thornton—Ball N' Chain,* Arhoolie 305

"Ball and Chain" by Janis Joplin: *Cheap Thrills,* Big Brother & the Holding Company, Columbia 9700

"Bo Diddley" by Bo Diddley: Time-Life Music, *The Rock 'N' Roll Era, 1954–1955;* or *Bo Diddley—His Greatest Sides, Volume 1,* Chess 9106

"I'm Walkin'" by Fats Domino: Time-Life Music, *The Rock 'N' Roll Era, 1957;* or *Fats Domino's Greatest Hits,* MCA 6170

"Long Tall Sally" by Little Richard: Time-Life Music, *The Rock 'N' Roll Era, 1956;* Time-Life Music, *Solid Gold Soul, 1956;* or *Little Richard's Grooviest 17 Original Hits,* Specialty 2113

"School Day" by Chuck Berry: Time-Life Music, *The Rock 'N' Roll Era, 1957;* or *Chuck Berry—The Great Twenty-Eight,* Chess 92500

*"I'll Never Get Out of This World Alive" by Hank Williams: *Hank Williams: Alone and Forsaken,* Mercury 697-124 057

"Shake, Rattle and Roll" by Joe Turner: Time-Life Music, *The Rock 'N' Roll Era, 1954–1955;* or *Atlantic Rhythm & Blues 1947–1974, Volume 2, 1952–1955,* Atlantic 14-81620

"Shake, Rattle and Roll" by Bill Haley and the Comets: *Vintage Music, Original Classic Oldies from the 1950's and 1960's, Volume 1,* MCA 31198 or MCA 1429

"Hound Dog" by Willie Mae Thornton: Time-Life Music, *The Rock 'N' Roll Era, Roots of Rock 1945–1955;* Time-Life Music, *Living the Blues, Blues Masters;* or *There's a Riot Goin' On: The Rock 'n' Roll Classics of Leiber and Stoller,* Rhino 70593

"Hound Dog" by Elvis Presley: Time-Life Music, *The Rock 'N' Roll Era, Elvis Presley 1954–1961;* or *Elvis' Golden Records, Volume 1,* RCA 5196

*"Burning Love" by Elvis Presley: *Elvis Burning Love and Hits from His Movies, Volume 2,* Camden CAD 1-2595

"Peggy Sue" by Buddy Holly: Time-Life Music, *The Rock 'N' Roll Era, 1957;* or *Buddy Holly/The Crickets: 20 Golden Greats,* MCA 1484

*"How Far Am I from Canaan?" by the Soul Stirrers with Sam Cooke: *Sam Cooke with the Soul Stirrers,* Specialty 7009

"Oh Happy Day" by the Edwin Hawkins Singers: Time-Life Music, *Classic Rock, 1969: The Beat Goes On; Super Hits, Volume 3,* Hollywood HT-167; or *Jubilation! Great Gospel Performances, Volume 1, Black Gospel,* Rhino 70288

"Crying in the Chapel" by Darrell Glenn: *The Best of Gospel, Volume 1,* Richmond N5-2260

"Crying in the Chapel" by the Orioles: Time-Life Music, *The Rock 'N' Roll Era, Roots of Rock 1945–1956;* or *Sonny Til and the Orioles—Greatest Hits,* COL 5014

"Sh-Boom" by the Chords: Time-Life Music, *The Rock 'N' Roll Era, 1954–1955;* or *Atlantic Rhythm & Blues 1947–1974, Volume 2, 1952–1955,* Atlantic 14-81620

"Sh-Boom" by the Crew-Cuts: *Partytime 50's,* PTY 9436

*"There Goes My Baby" by the Drifters: Time-Life Music, *The Rock 'N' Roll Era, 1959*

"Tutti-Frutti" by Little Richard: Time-Life Music, *The Rock 'N' Roll Era, 1954–1955;* or *Little Richard's Grooviest 17 Original Hits,* Specialty 2113

"Tutti-Frutti" by Pat Boone: *The Best of Pat Boone,* MCA 6020

*"La Bamba" by Ritchie Valens: *The Best of Ritchie Valens,* Rhino 70178; *Best of "La Bamba,"* Rhino 70617; or *La Bamba and Other Original Hits,* 3C-101

*"Will You Love Me Tomorrow?" by the Shirelles: Time-Life Music, *The Rock 'N' Roll Era, 1961*

"River Deep—Mountain High" by Ike and Tina Turner: *The Best of Ike & Tina Turner,* EMI 95846; or *Phil Spector: Back to Mono (1958–1969),* AKO 7118

*"Sweet Little Sixteen" by Chuck Berry: Time-Life Music, *The Rock 'N' Roll Era, 1958*

*"Surfin' U.S.A." by the Beach Boys: Time-Life Music, *The Rock 'N' Roll Era, 1963*

"Good Vibrations" by the Beach Boys: Time-Life Music, *The Rock 'N' Roll Era, The Beach Boys,*

1962–1967; Time-Life Music, *AM Gold, 1966;* Time-Life Music, *Classic Rock 1966;* or *Smiley Smile,* Capitol 93696

"Mr. Tambourine Man" by Bob Dylan: *Bringing It All Back Home,* Columbia 9128; or *Bob Dylan's Greatest Hits,* Columbia 9463

"Mr. Tambourine Man" by the Byrds: Time-Life Music, *Classic Rock, 1965;* or *The Byrds Greatest Hits,* Columbia 09516

"Ohio" by Crosby, Stills, Nash and Young: *Crosby, Stills, Nash & Young So Far,* Atlantic 19119

"What'd I Say" by Ray Charles: Time-Life Music, *The Rock 'N' Roll Era, 1959;* Time-Life Music, *Solid Gold Soul, Ray Charles, 1954–1966;* or *Ray Charles—Anthology,* Rhino 75759

*"Please, Please, Please" by James Brown and the Famous Flames: *James Brown: 20 All-Time Greatest Hits!* Polydor 314-511326

"Amen" by the Impressions: Time-Life Music, *Classic Rock, 1964: The Beat Goes On;* or *The Impressions' Greatest Hits,* MCA 1500

"In the Midnight Hour" by Wilson Pickett: Time-Life Music, *Solid Gold Soul, 1965;* Time-Life Music, *Classic Rock, 1965;* or *Atlantic Rhythm & Blues, 1947–1974, Volume 5, 1962–1966,* Atlantic 14-81620

"Respect" by Aretha Franklin: Time-Life Music, *Classic Rock, 1967;* or *Aretha's Greatest Hits,* Atlantic 8295

"My Girl" by the Temptations: Time-Life Music, *Solid Gold Soul, 1965;* Time-Life Music, *AM Gold, 1965;* Time-Life Music, *Classic Rock, 1965;* or *The Temptations Sing Smokey,* Motown 37463-5205

"Love Train" by the O'Jays: Time-Life Music, *Sounds of the Seventies—1973;* or *The O'Jays' Greatest Hits,* CBS 39251

"I Want to Hold Your Hand" by the Beatles: *Meet the Beatles!,* Capitol 90441; or *Past Masters, Volume 1,* Capitol 90043

*"Norwegian Wood" by the Beatles: *Rubber Soul,* Capitol 90453 or 46440

"A Day In the Life" by the Beatles: *Sgt. Pepper's Lonely Hearts Club Band,* Capitol 46442

*"You Really Got Me" by the Kinks: Time-Life Music, *Classic Rock, 1964;* or *The Kinks Greatest Hits,* Rhino 70086

*"My Generation" by the Who: *The Who Sings My Generation,* MCA 31330; or *Greatest Hits,* MCA 1496

"Not Fade Away" by Buddy Holly: *Buddy Holly/The Crickets: 20 Golden Greats,* MCA 1484

"Not Fade Away" by the Rolling Stones: *The Rolling Stones,* AKO 7375; or *Big Hits, Volume 1 (High Tide & Green Grass),* AKO 8001

*"Miss You" by the Rolling Stones: *Some Girls,* Rolling Stones 40449

"Crossroads" by Cream: Time-Life Music, *Classic Rock, 1969: Shakin' All Over;* Time-Life Music, *Guitar Rock—FM Classics; Wheels of Fire,* Polydor 827578; or *Strange Brew—Very Best of Cream,* Polydor 811639

"Red House" by the Jimi Hendrix Experience: *Jimi Hendrix Experience: Smash Hits,* Reprise 2276

"Hoochie Coochie Man" by Muddy Waters: Time-Life Music, *The Rock 'N' Roll Era, Roots of Rock, 1945–1955;* Time-Life Music, *Living the Blues, Blues Masters;* or *Best of Muddy Waters,* Chess 9255

"Hoochie Coochie Man" by the Allman Brothers Band: *Beginnings,* Polydor 827588

*"Louie Louie" by the Kingsmen: Time-Life Music, *Classic Rock, 1964: The Beat Goes On; The Best of the Kingsmen,* Rhino 70745; or *Best of "Louie, Louie,"* Rhino 70605

"Kicks" by Paul Revere and the Raiders: Time-Life Music, *Classic Rock, 1966;* Time-Life Music, *Guitar Rock—1966–1967; Midnight Ride,* Columbia 9308; or *Paul Revere and the Raiders' Greatest Hits,* Columbia 35593

*"Sugar, Sugar" by the Archies: Time-Life Music, *Classic Rock, 1969: The Beat Goes On;* or *The Best of the Bubblegum Years,* Special Music Co. 4914

*"Go All the Way" by the Raspberries: Time-Life Music, *Sounds of the Seventies—1972;* or *Raspberries ("Capitol Collector's" Series),* Capitol, 92126

"Uncle John's Band" by the Grateful Dead: Time-Life Music, *Sounds of the Seventies—1970; Skeletons from the Closet,* Warner Bros. 2764; or *Workingman's Dead,* Warner Bros. 1869

*"Black Magic Woman" by Santana: Time-Life Music, *Sounds of the Seventies—1970;* Time-Life Music, *Guitar Rock—1970–1971; Abraxas,* Columbia 30130; or *Santana's Greatest Hits,* Columbia 33050

"Light My Fire" by the Doors: *The Doors,* Elektra 74007; or *The Doors Greatest Hits,* Elektra 515

"All Along the Watchtower" by Bob Dylan: *John Wesley Harding,* Columbia 9604; or *Bob Dylan's Greatest Hits, Volume II,* Columbia 31120

"All Along the Watchtower" by Jimi Hendrix: Time-Life Music, *Classic Rock—1968: Shakin' All Over; Electric Ladyland,* Reprise 6307; *Jimi Hendrix Experience: Smash Hits,* Reprise 2276; or *The Essential Jimi Hendrix,* Reprise 2245

"Lyin' Eyes" by the Eagles: *One of These Nights,* Elektra 1039; or *Eagles—Their Greatest Hits, 1971–1975,* Asylum 105

"The Weight" by the Band: *Music from Big Pink,* Capitol 46069

"Ramblin' Man" by the Allman Brothers Band: Time-Life Music, *Sounds of the Seventies—1973;* Time-Life Music, *Guitar Rock—1972–1973;* or *Brothers and Sisters,* Polydor 825092

"The South's Gonna Do It" by the Charlie Daniels Band: *Nightrider,* Epic 34402; or *The Charlie Daniels Band—A Decade of Hits,* Epic 38795

"Sweet Home Alabama" by Lynyrd Skynyrd: Time-Life Music, *Sounds of the Seventies—1974;* or Time-Life Music, *Guitar Rock—1974–1975;* or *Lynyrd Skynyrd Band—Gold & Platinum,* MCA 6898

"Spinning Wheel" by Blood, Sweat and Tears: *Blood, Sweat and Tears,* Columbia 9720

"Miles Runs the Voodoo Down" by Miles Davis: *Bitches Brew,* Columbia 40577; or *Columbia Years, 1955–1985,* Columbia 45000

*"The Dry Cleaner from Des Moines" by Joni Mitchell: *Mingus,* Asylum 505

*"Domino" by Van Morrison: Time-Life Music, *Sounds of the Seventies—1970; His Band & Street Choir,* Warner Bros. 1884; or *Best of Van Morrison,* Mercury 841970

"Help Me" by Joni Mitchell: Time-Life Music, *Sounds of the Seventies—1974;* or *Court and Spark,* Elektra 1001

"We Didn't Start the Fire" by Billy Joel: *Storm Front,* Columbia 44366

*"Born in the U.S.A." by Bruce Springsteen: *Born in the U.S.A.,* Columbia 38653

*"Give Me One Reason" by Tracy Chapman: *New Beginning,* Elektra 61850

"Papa's Got a Brand New Bag" by James Brown: Time-Life Music, *Classic Rock, 1965: Shakin' All Over;* or *Papa's Got a Brand New Bag,* Polygram 847-982

"Thank You" by Sly and the Family Stone: Time-Life Music, *Sounds of the Seventies—1970;* or *Sly & the Family Stone—Greatest Hits,* Epic 30325

"Funky Stuff" by Kool and the Gang: *Kool & the Gang Spin Their Top Hits,* De-Lite 822536

*"Flash Light" by Parliament: *Classic Funk, Volume One,* React Entertainment Corp. 50003

*"Good Times" by Chic: Time-Life Music, *Sounds of the Seventies—1979;* or *1975 Only Dance 1979,* Warner Special Products JCD-3148

"Nights in White Satin" by the Moody Blues: *Days of Future Passed,* Threshold 820006; or *This Is the Moody Blues,* Threshold 820007
"Roundabout" by Yes: Time-Life Music, *Sounds of the Seventies—1972 Take Two;* Time-Life Music, *Guitar Rock—1972–1973;* or *Fragile,* Atlantic 19132
"Money" by Pink Floyd: *The Dark Side of the Moon,* Capitol 46001; or *A Collection of Great Dance Songs,* Columbia 37680
*"Valley Girl" by Frank Zappa: *Ship Arriving Too Late to Save a Drowning Witch,* Barking Pumpkin/Capitol 74235; or *Strictly Commercial: The Best of Frank Zappa,* Rykodisc 40500
"Space Oddity" by David Bowie: *Space Oddity,* Ryko 10131; or *Changesbowie,* Ryko 0171
"Bohemian Rhapsody" by Queen: *A Night at the Opera,* Hollywood 61065; or *Classic Queen,* Hollywood 61311
*"Nothin' But a Good Time" by Poison: *Open Up and Say . . . Ahh!,* Capitol 48493
"Sunshine of Your Love" by Cream: Time-Life Music, *Classic Rock, 1968; Disraeli Gears,* Polydor 823636; or *Strange Brew—Very Best of Cream,* Polydor 811639
"More Than a Feeling" by Boston: *Boston,* Epic 34188
"Livin' on a Prayer" by Bon Jovi: *Slippery When Wet,* Mercury 830264
"Dazed and Confused" by Jake Holmes: *Nuggets, Volume 10, Folk Rock,* Rhino 70034
"Dazed and Confused" by Led Zeppelin: *Led Zeppelin,* Atlantic 82144
*"Paranoid" by Black Sabbath: Time-Life Music, *Guitar Rock—1970–1971;* or *Paranoid,* Warner Bros. 3104
"Victim of Changes" by Judas Priest: *Sad Wings of Destiny,* RCA 4747; or *The Best of Judas Priest,* RCA 4933
"School's Out" by Alice Cooper: Time-Life Music, *Sounds of the Seventies—1972; School's Out,* Warner Bros. 2623; or *Alice Cooper's Greatest Hits,* Warner Bros. 3107
*"You Really Got Me" by Van Halen: *Van Halen,* Warner Bros. 3075
*"New World Man" by Rush: *Signals,* Mercury 810-112
"Master of Puppets" by Metallica: *Master of Puppets,* Elektra 60439
"Heroin" by the Velvet Underground: *The Best of The Velvet Underground,* Verve 841164; or *The Velvet Underground & Nico,* Verve/Polydor 823290
"Personality Crisis" by the New York Dolls: *The New York Dolls,* Mercury 832752
"God Save the Queen" by the Sex Pistols: *Never Mind the Bollocks, Here's the Sex Pistols,* Warner Bros. 3147
"Kill the Poor" by the Dead Kennedys: *Fresh Fruit for Rotting Vegetables,* Cherry Red, B Red 10
"Jocko Homo" by Devo: *Q: Are We Not Men? A: We are Devo!,* Warner Bros. 3239
"Radio Radio" by Elvis Costello and the Attractions: *This Year's Model,* Columbia 35331; or *Best of Elvis Costello and the Attractions, 1977–1984,* Columbia 35709
"If You Act This Way" by the Maytals: *Jamaica Ska,* Rhino 014
"I Shot the Sheriff" by Bob Marley and the Wailers: *Burnin',* Tuff Gong 422-846200; *Legend—The Best of Bob Marley and the Wailers,* Tuff Gong 422-846210; or *This Is Reggae Music,* Island 9251
*"Destiny" by Victor Uwaifo and his Titibitis: *Black Star Liner: Reggae from Africa,* Heartbeat 16
"Concrete Jungle" by the Specials: *The Specials,* Chrysalis 21265; or *Dance Craze,* Chrysalis 21783
"Expression" by Salt-N-Pepa: *Yo! MTV Raps, Volume 2,* Jive 1420
"911 Is a Joke" by Public Enemy: *Fear of a Black Planet,* Columbia 45413; or *Yo! MTV Raps, Volume 2,* Jive 1420
"Express Yourself" by N.W.A.: *Straight Outta Compton,* Ruthless-Priority 57102; or *Yo! MTV Raps, Volume 2,* Jive 1420
*"La Raza" by Kid Frost: *Hispanic Causing Panic,* Virgin 86169; or *Latin Lingo: Hip-Hop from the Raza,* Rhino 71923
"Little Red Corvette" by Prince: *1999,* Warner Bros. 23720
"Papa Don't Preach" by Madonna: *True Blue,* Warner Bros. 25442
"Radio Free Europe" by R.E.M.: *Murmur,* I.R.S./A&M 44797-0014
"With or Without You" by U2: *The Joshua Tree,* Island 422-842298
"Everyday Is Like Sunday" by Morrissey: *Viva Hate,* Sire/Reprise 25699; *Bona Drag,* Sire/Reprise 26221; or *never mind the mainstream . . . The Best of MTV's 120 Minutes, Volume 2,* Rhino 70546
"Wasteland" by Mission (UK): *God's Own Medicine,* Mercury 830603; or *never mind the mainstream . . . The Best of MTV's 120 Minutes, Volume 1,* Rhino 70545
"Stigmata" by Ministry: *The Land of Rape and Honey,* Sire 25799; or *never mind the mainstream . . . The Best of MTV's 120 Minutes, Volume 2,* Rhino 70546
"Could You Be the One?" by Hüsker Dü: *Warehouse: Songs and Stories,* Warner Bros. 25544; or *never mind the mainstream . . . The Best of MTV's 120 Minutes, Volume 2,* Rhino 70546
*"Doll Parts" by Hole: *Live Through This,* Geffen 24631

Selected Discography of Additional Recommended Recordings

AC/DC: *Who Made Who,* Atlantic 81650
Aerosmith: *Greatest Hits,* Columbia 36865
Almanac Singers, The: *Their Complete Original Recordings,* MCA 11499
Anthrax: *Among the Living,* Island 422-842447
Arrested Development: *3 Years, 5 Months & 2 Days in the Life of . . . ,* Chrysalis 21929
Avalon, Frankie: *The Greatest of Fabian & Frankie Avalon,* MCA 27097
Average White Band: *AWB,* Atlantic 19116
Bad Company: *Best of Bad Company,* Atlantic 81625
Beastie Boys: *Licensed to Ill,* Columbia 40238
Brown, James: *Live at the Apollo,* Polydor 823001
Buffalo Springfield: *Retrospective . . . Best of Buffalo Springfield,* Atco 38105
Clapton, Eric: *Time Pieces/Best of Eric Clapton,* Polydor 800014; and *From the Cradle,* Duck 45735
Clash: *The Story of the Clash: Volume 1,* Epic 44035
Cochran, Eddie: *Greatest Hits,* Curb/CEMA 77371
Cooke, Sam: *The Best of Sam Cooke,* RCA 3863
Creedence Clearwater Revival: *Chronicle, Volume 1,* Fantasy CCR-2
Deep Purple: *When We Rock We Rock and When We Roll We Roll,* Deep Purple 3223
Digable Planets: *Reachin' (A New Refutation of Time and Space),* Pendulum 61414
Eddy, Duane: *Twang Thang,* Rhino 71223
Electric Light Orchestra: *ELO's Greatest Hits,* Jet 36310
Emerson, Lake & Palmer: *Trilogy,* Cotillion 9903
Everly Brothers: *Cadence Classics: Their 20 Greatest Hits,* Rhino 5258
Francis, Connie: *Very Best of Connie Francis,* Polydor 827569
Franklin, Aretha: *Aretha Gospel,* Chess/MCA 91521
Genesis: *Three Sides Live,* Atlantic 2000
Guthrie, Woody: *Dust Bowl Ballads,* Rounder 1040
Heart: *Greatest Hits/Live,* Epic 36888
Hollies: *The Hollies' Greatest Hits,* Imperial 12350
Howlin' Wolf: *Howlin' Wolf/Moanin' in the Moonlight,* Chess 9195
Jackson, Michael: *Thriller,* Epic 38112
Jefferson Airplane: *The Worst of Jefferson Airplane,* RCA 4459
Jethro Tull: *M.U. Best of Jethro Tull,* Chrysalis 21078; and *Repeat: The Best of, Volume 2,* Chrysalis 21135

John, Elton: *Elton John—Greatest Hits*, MCA 2128
Jolly Boys, The: *Pop 'N' Mento*, Rykodisc 10187
Jolson, Al: *The Best of Jolson*, Decca 169
Jordan, Louis: *Best of Louis Jordan*, MCA 4079
King, Carole: *Tapestry*, Ode 34946
King Crimson: *In the Court of the Crimson King*, Editions EG-CAROL 1502
Kiss: *Double Platinum*, Casablanca 824155
Lewis, Jerry Lee: *Original Sun Greatest Hits*, Rhino 70255
Little Feat: *Waiting for Columbus*, Warner Bros. 3140
Living Colour: *Vivid*, Epic 44099
Lovin' Spoonful: *Anthology*, Rhino 70944
Lymon, Frankie, & the Teenagers: *Best of Frankie Lymon & the Teenagers*, Rhino 70918
Mamas and the Papas: *16 of Their Greatest Hits*, MCA 5701
MC5: *Kick Out the Jams*, Elektra 60894
Mellencamp, John Cougar: *American Fool*, Riva 7501
Memphis Minnie: *Anthologie*, Encyclopedia Records 520
Memphis Slim, Big Bill Broonzy, and Sonny Boy Williamson interviewed by Alan Lomax: *Blues in the Mississippi Night*, Rykodisc 90155
Miller, Glenn: *Marvelous Miller Moods: Radio Broadcasts During 1943–44*, RCA 1494
Monkees: *Then & Now . . . The Best of the Monkees*, Arista 8432
Nirvana: *Nevermind*, DGC 24425
Pearl Jam: *Ten*, Epic/Assc. 47857; and *Vs.*, Epic/Assc. 53136
Platters: *The Very Best of the Platters*, Mercury 314-510317
Police: *Every Breath You Take/The Singles*, A&M 75021-3902
Pop, Iggy, & the Stooges: *Raw Power*, Columbia 32111
Presley, Elvis: *The Complete Sun Sessions*, RCA 6414
Pretenders: *The Singles*, Sire 25664
Procol Harum: *Procol Harum Live in Concert with the Edmonton Symphony Orchestra*, Mobile Fidelity 10-00788
Queen Latifah: *All Hail the Queen*, Tommy Boy 1022
Queensrÿche: *Promised Land*, EMI 30711
Ramones: *Ramones Mania/Best of the Ramones*, Sire 25709
R.E.M.: *Out of Time*, Warner 26496; and *Monster*, Warner Bros. 45740
Ronstadt, Linda: *Greatest Hits*, Asylum 106
Run-D.M.C.: *Together Forever: Greatest Hits*, Profile 1419
Simon, Carly: *The Best of Carly Simon*, Elektra 109
Simon, Paul: *Graceland*, Warner Bros. 25447
Smith, Patti, Group: *Wave*, Arista 8546
Springsteen, Bruce: *The River*, Columbia 36854
Sting: *The Dream of the Blue Turtles*, A&M 75021-3750
Stray Cats: *The Greatest Hits*, Curb 77592
Summer, Donna: *On the Radio: Greatest Hits, Volumes 1 & 2*, Casablanca 822558
Talking Heads: *Popular Favorites 1976–1992*, Sire 26760
2 Live Crew: *Greatest Hits*, Luke 122
U2: *Achtung Baby*, Island 10347
Various artists: *American Songbook Series: Irving Berlin*, Smithsonian Collection of Recordings RD-048-1
Various artists: *Atlantic Rhythm & Blues 1947–1974, Volumes 1–7*, Atlantic 14-81620
Various artists: *The Beat Generation*, Rhino 70281
Various artists (including Ma Rainey and Bessie Smith): *The Blues 1923–1933*, ABC Music 836-046
Various artists: *D.I.Y.: Anarchy in The UK—UK Punk 1 (1976–1977)*, Rhino 71171
Various artists: *Hitsville USA: The Motown Singles Collection 1959–1971*, Motown 37463-6313
Various artists: *Rap Hall of Fame*, K-tel 3041
Various artists: *Roots of the Blues*, New World 80252
Various artists: *Roots of Rap: Classic Recordings from the 1920's and '30s*, Yazoo 2018
Various artists: *Songs by Stephen Foster*, Elektra/Nonesuch 9-79158
Various artists: *Top of the Stax, Volume 1*, Stax 88005
Various artists: *Top of the Stax, Volume 2*, Stax 88008
Various artists: *Towering Dub Inferno: The Roir Tapes*, Rykodisc 20152
Various artists: *The Trojan Story* (ska, rock steady, and reggae recordings), Trojan 100
Various artists: *Troubadours of the Folk Era, Volume 1*, Rhino 70262
Various artists: *Troubadours of the Folk Era, Volume 2*, Rhino 70263
Various artists: *Troubadours of the Folk Era, Volume 3*, Rhino 70264
Vaughan, Stevie Ray, & Double Trouble: *In Step*, Epic 45024
Ventures: *Walk, Don't Run*, EMI 93451
Vincent, Gene: *Capitol Collector's Series*, Capitol/EMI 94074
White, Barry: *Barry White's Greatest Hits*, 20th Century 493
Winter, Edgar & Johnny: *Together: Live*, Blue Sky 34033
ZZ Top: *Greatest Hits*, Warner Bros. 26846

Bibliography

This bibliography does not represent all of the sources consulted during the research on this book, and it cannot include the many magazine articles and interviews that were used in that research. It is a list of books that have been selected as most likely to provide additional general information for the interested student. Biographies or autobiographies of individual artists and books about individual groups might also be used for more concentrated study, but have not been included here in order to limit the list to general sources.

B

Bangs, Lester. 1987. *Psychotic Reactions and Carburetor Dung*. Edited by Greil Marcus. New York: Vintage Books.

Bashe, Philip. 1985. *Heavy Metal Thunder*. New York: Dolphin Books.

Betrock, Alan. 1982. *Girl Groups: The Story of a Sound*. New York: Delilah Books.

Broughton, Simon, Mark Ellingham, David Muddyman, and Richard Trillo, eds. 1994. *World Music: The Rough Guide*. London: The Rough Guides.

C

Charters, Samuel. 1981. *The Roots of the Blues: An African Search*. New York: Da Capo Press.

Charters, Samuel. 1991. *The Blues Makers*. New York: Da Capo Press.

Chernoff, John Miller. 1979. *African Rhythm and African Sensibility*. Chicago: The University of Chicago Press.

Christgau, Robert. 1981. *Rock Albums of the '70s: A Critical Guide*. New York: Da Capo Press.

Christgau, Robert. 1990. *Christgau's Record Guide: The '80s*. New York: Pantheon Books.

Costello, Mark, and David Foster Wallace. 1990. *Signifying Rappers*. New York: The Ecco Press.

D

Davis, Stephen. 1985. *Hammer of the Gods*. New York: William Morrow and Company, Inc.

DeCurtis, Anthony, James Henke, and Holly George-Warren, eds. 1992. *The Rolling Stone Illustrated History of Rock & Roll*. New York: Random House.

DeMartino, Dave. 1994. *Singer-Songwriters*. New York: Billboard Books.

E

Ennis, Philip H. 1992. *The Seventh Stream: The Emergence of Rock 'n Roll in American Popular Music*. Hanover, NH: Wesleyan University Press.

Erlewine, Michael, Vladimir Bogdanov, and Chris Woodstra, eds. 1995. *All Music Guide to Rock*. San Francisco: Miller Freeman Books.

F

Fernando, S. H., Jr. 1994. *The New Beats: Exploring the Music, Culture, and Attitudes of Hip-Hop*. New York: Anchor Books Doubleday.

Frame, Peter. 1980. *The Complete Rock Family Trees, Volumes 1 & 2*. New York: Omnibus Press.

Friedlander, Paul. 1996. *Rock and Roll: A Social History*. Boulder, CO: Westview Press.

Frith, Simon. 1982. *Sound Effects: Youth, Leisure, and the Politics of Rock 'n' Roll*. New York: Pantheon Books.

G

Gaar, Gillian G. 1992. *She's A Rebel: The History of Women in Rock & Roll*. Seattle: Seal Press.

Gambaccini, Paul, Tim Rice, and Jonathan Rice. 1991. *British Hit Singles*. 8th ed. London: Guinness Publishing.

Garofalo, Reebee, ed. 1992. *Rockin' the Boat: Mass Music and Mass Movements*. Boston: South End Press.

Garofalo, Reebee. 1997. *Rockin' Out: Popular Music in the USA*. Needham Heights, MA: Allyn & Bacon.

George, Nelson. 1985. *Where Did Our Love Go?* New York: St. Martin's Press.

Gerard, Charley, and Marty Sheller. 1989. *Salsa: The Rhythm of Latin Music*. Tempe, AZ: White Cliffs Media Company.

Gillett, Charlie. 1970. *The Sound of the City: The Rise of Rock and Roll*. New York: Outerbridge and Dienstfrey.

Gregory, Hugh. 1991. *Soul Music A–Z*. London: Blandford.

Grossman, Lloyd. 1976. *A Social History of Rock Music*. New York: David McKay Company.

Guralnick, Peter. 1986. *Sweet Soul Music: Rhythm and Blues and the Southern Dream of Freedom*. New York: Harper & Row.

H

Hamm, Charles. 1979. *Yesterdays: Popular Song in America*. New York: W. W. Norton & Company, Inc.

Hirshey, Gerri. 1985. *Nowhere to Run: The Story of Soul Music*. New York: Penguin Books.

Hitchcock, H. Wiley, and Stanley Sadie, eds. 1986. *The New Grove Dictionary of American Music*. London: Macmillan Press Limited.

J

Jones, K. Maurice. 1994. *Say It Loud! The Story of Rap Music*. Brookfield, CT: The Millbrook Press.

Juno, Andrea, ed. 1996. *Angry Women in Rock. Vol. 1*. New York: Juno Books.

K

Kernfeld, Barry, ed. 1988. *The New Grove Dictionary of Jazz*. London: Macmillan Press Limited.

L

Larkin, Colin, ed. 1995. *The Guinness Encyclopedia of Popular Music*. 2d ed. London: Guinness Publishing LTD.

Lazell, Barry. 1989. *Rock Movers & Shakers*. Edited by Dafydd Rees and Luke Crampton. New York: Billboard Publications, Inc.

Lewisohn, Mark. 1988. *The Beatles Recording Sessions*. New York: Harmony Books.

Lydon, Michael. 1990. *Rock Folk*. New York: Citadel Press.

M

Malone, Bill C. 1975. *Country Music, U.S.A.: A Fifty-Year History*. Austin, TX: University of Texas Press.

Marcus, Greil. 1982. *Mystery Train*. New York: E. P. Dutton & Co.

Marsh, Dave. 1985. *The First Rock & Roll Confidential Report*. New York: Pantheon Books.

Marsh, Dave. 1989. *The Heart of Rock & Soul: The 1001 Greatest Singles Ever Made*. New York: Plume Books.

Marsh, Dave, and Kevin Stein. 1994. *The New Book of Rock Lists*. New York: Simon & Schuster.

McDonough, Jack. 1985. *San Francisco Rock*. San Francisco: Chronicle Books.

N

Nelson, Havelock, and Michael A. Gonzales. 1991. *Bring the Noise: A Guide to Rap Music and Hip-Hop Culture*. New York: Harmony Books.

O

Obrecht, Jas. 1984. *Masters of Heavy Metal*. New York: Quill.

Orman, John. 1984. *The Politics of Rock Music*. Chicago: Nelson-Hall.

Otis, Johnny. 1993. *Upside Your Head!* Hanover, NH: Wesleyan University Press.

P

Palmer, Robert. 1981. *Deep Blues*. New York: Penguin Books.

Passman, Donald S. 1994. *All You Need to Know About the Music Business*. New York: Simon & Schuster.

Perry, Charles. 1985. *Haight-Ashbury: A History*. New York: Vintage Books.

Poe, Randy. 1990. *Music Publishing: A Songwriters Guide*. Cincinnati: Writer's Digest Books.

R

Raphael, Amy. 1995. *Grrrls: Viva Rock Divas*. New York: St. Martin's Press.

Robbins, Era A., ed. 1991. *The Trouser Press Record Guide: The Ultimate Guide to Alternative Music*. 4th ed. New York: Collier Books.

Roberts, John Storm. 1985. *The Latin Tinge*. Tivoli, NY: Original Music.

Romanowski, Patricia, and Holly George-Warren, eds. 1995. *The New Rolling Stone Encyclopedia of Rock & Roll*. New York: Rolling Stone Press.

Rose, Tricia. 1994. *Black Noise: Rap Music and Black Culture in Contemporary America*. Hanover, NH: Wesleyan University Press.

S

Savage, Jon. 1991. *England's Dreaming*. New York: St. Martin's Press.

Schaffner, Nicholas. 1982. *The British Invasion: From the First Wave to the New Wave*. New York: McGraw-Hill.

Shaw, Arnold. 1978. *Honkers and Shouters: The Golden Years of Rhythm & Blues*. New York: Collier Books.

Shemel, Sidney, and M. William Krasilovsky. 1985. *This Business of Music*. New York: Billboard Publications, Inc.

Stambler, Irwin, and Grelun Landon. 1984. *The Encyclopedia of Folk, Country & Western Music*. New York: St. Martin's Press.

Stanley, Lawrence A., ed. 1992. *Rap, the Lyrics*. New York: Penguin Books.

Street, John. 1986. *Rebel Rock: The Politics of Popular Music*. New York: Basil Blackwell Inc.

Sumrall, Harry. 1994. *Pioneers of Rock and Roll*. New York: Billboard Books.

T

Tosches, Nick. 1984. *Unsung Heroes of Rock 'n' Roll*. New York: Charles Scribner's Sons.

V

Vale, V., and Andrea, eds. 1991. *RE/SEARCH #6/7: Industrial Culture Handbook*. San Francisco: RE/SEARCH Publications.

W

Walser, Robert. 1993. *Running with the Devil: Power, Gender, and Madness in Heavy Metal Music*. Hanover, NH: Wesleyan University Press.

Weisbard, Eric, and Craig Marks. 1995. *Spin Alternative Record Guide*. New York: Vintage Books.

Whitburn, Joel. *The Billboard Book of Top 40 Hits*. New York: Billboard Books.

Whitburn, Joel. 1995. *The Billboard Book of Top 40 Albums*. New York: Billboard Books.

White, Timothy. 1990. *Rock Lives: Profiles and Interviews*. New York: Henry Holt.

Woliver, Robbie. 1986. *Bringing It All Back Home*. New York: Pantheon Books.

Index

A

C

E

F

Q

R

S

U

V

W

Chronology Chart

	Historical Events	Happenings in Rock Music
1970	National Guard kills four students at Kent State Univ., Ohio, at antiwar demonstration. Antiwar demonstrations cause the closing of U.S. colleges and universities. U.S. signs cease-fire agreement in Vietnam. SALT talks begin. First Earth Day celebration. Portable electronic calculators are marketed.	Nationwide, city councils and police fight to ban rock festivals. Folk rock popularity gives way to more introspective singer/songwriter style. Allman Brothers Band establishes southern-rock style. Santana records Latin rock style. Jimi Hendrix and Janis Joplin die.
1971	U.S. Mariner 9 orbits Mars. 18-yr.-olds given the right to vote. Pentagon papers on Vietnam War are publicized. Food and Drug Administration establishes the Bureau of Product Safety.	Glitter rock emerges, led by David Bowie and Marc Bolan. Proto-punk poet Patti Smith performs in New York. Philadelphia Int. Record Co. forms. Berry Gordy, Jr., moves Motown to L.A. Jim Morrison and Duane Allman die.
1972	Leakey, et al., find 2.5-million-yr.-old hominid skull. SALT I is signed. Nixon visits China. U.S. combat troops leave Vietnam. Strategic arms pact between U.S. and U.S.S.R. Watergate break-in. ERA is sent to states for ratification. Bombing resumes in Vietnam after impasse in peace negotiations.	"Underground" FM radio gains popularity over AM. "Oldies" radio stations play fifties hits. Country and Southern rock increase in popularity.
1973	Watergate hearings on national TV and radio. Airlines begin regular screening for weapons. Abortion is legalized nationwide. Vietnam peace pacts are signed, North Vietnam releases U.S. prisoners, last troops leave, military draft ends. Henry Kissinger is awarded Nobel Peace Prize. Vice President Agnew resigns.	Reggae becomes popular in U.S. The Everly Brothers break up. AM and FM radios standard in new U.S. autos. Pink Floyd releases *Dark Side of the Moon.* New York Dolls release debut LP. The group Television formed. Jim Croce and Bobby Darin die.
1974	Impeachment hearings open against Nixon; Supreme Court orders release of Nixon tapes; Nixon resigns presidency. Ford becomes president and pardons Nixon. Patty Hearst is kidnapped. National Guardsmen who shot students at Kent State are acquitted.	New York punk by Patti Smith, Television, the Ramones, and the New York Dolls popular at CBGB's. Cass Elliot dies.
1975	Attempt on life of President Ford. 140,000 refugees from South Vietnam are flown to U.S. U.S. and U.S.S.R. spacecrafts link in space. VCRs commercially available. Patty Hearst is arrested.	Government begins new probes into payola practices. Sex Pistols form in U.K. Blondie, Devo, and Talking Heads form in U.S. Disco becomes popular in gay and black clubs in New York. 12-inch singles are released to limited market.
1976	U.S. bicentennial celebrations. U.S. soft landing on Mars. Race riots in South Africa. Home computers are marketed. North and South Vietnam unite as a socialist republic. 29 die from mysterious "legionnaire's disease."	Liverpool's Cavern Club closes and sells pieces of stage to fans. Punk becomes stronger movement in U.K. than in U.S. Sid Vicious starts pogo dance craze. Lasers are used by the Who in concert. Highly synthesized disco gains wide popularity.
1977	Nobel Peace Prize is awarded to Amnesty International. U.S. is involved in Nicaragua. Carter becomes president. Panama Canal treaty is ratified. Conditional amnesty given to draft evaders. Energy Department is established.	NY disc jockeys use dubbing vocals. Some punk bands commercialize and develop new wave. Tape sales increase to 26% of recorded music on market. Elvis Presley, Marc Bolan, and members of Lynyrd Skynyrd die.
1978	First "test-tube" baby is born in U.K. U.S. and China establish a diplomatic relationship. Humphrey-Hawkins Bill passes Congress to help reduce unemployment.	Sex Pistols break up. Dead Kennedys form. Bee Gees' brand of disco is popularized through movie *Saturday Night Fever.* Blondie adds disco to punk style. 45 r.p.m. picture disks are sold. Keith Moon and Terry Kath die.
1979	Nuclear accident at Three Mile Island. 90 hostages (including 63 Americans) are taken at U.S. Embassy in Iran.	*No Nukes* concert and film. UNICEF concert at U.N. General Assembly. 11 fans die at Who concert in Cincinnati. Revival of old rock styles. Sid Vicious dies.
1980	U.S. boycotts Moscow Olympics. 8 Americans are killed in ill-fated attempt to free hostages in Iran. Mt. St. Helens erupts. Carter reinstates draft registration.	Frank Zappa starts his Barking Pumpkin company. *The Decline of Western Civilization* is filmed. John Lennon is murdered in New York. Bon Scott, Ian Curtis, John Bonham, and Steve P. Took die.
1981	Reagan becomes president. 53 American hostages are freed by Iran. AIDS (HIV) virus is discovered. Assassination attempt on life of Reagan. Air traffic controllers strike. Sandra Day O'Connor is appointed to U.S. Supreme Court.	Rap develops out of dubbing. Heavy metal splits into progressive, glam, and thrash in addition to older blues style. MTV airs. Popularity of Sony Walkman pocket tape players increase demand for cassette tapes. Bill Haley, Bob Marley, and Harry Chapin die.

Chronology Chart

	Historical Events	Happenings in Rock Music
1982	U.S. supports U.K. in Falklands. Peace Week demonstrations for disarmament. ERA is defeated in vote for ratification. Space Shuttle Columbia completes first operational flight. Dr. Barney B. Clark receives first permanent artificial heart.	The Who on "final" tour. Stray Cats revive rockabilly. John Belushi, Randy Rhoads, Murray "the K," Lester Bangs, and James Honeyman-Scott die.
1983	U.S. military is sent to Lebanon. U.S. Marine headquarters and French paratrooper barracks are bombed in Lebanon. Korean jet is shot down in Soviet airspace.	Duran Duran introduces British new romantic style. Muddy Waters, Dennis Wilson, and Karen Carpenter die.
1984	Famine in Ethiopia. First female vice presidential candidate. Vietnam vets settle with chemical companies over Agent Orange dispute. L.A. olympics. Vanessa Williams resigns as Miss America. Bishop D. Tutu is awarded Nobel Peace Prize.	Band Aid and USA for Africa raise money to help feed starving in Ethiopia. Everly Brothers reunite. Madonna releases debut LP. Jackie Wilson and Marvin Gaye die.
1985	Ethiopians starve while food rots on docks. U.S. sends aid to Contras in Nicaragua. U.S./U.S.S.R. disarmament talks begin. Government cuts student loan funds. *Achille Lauro* hijacking. New tax law passes. "Baby boomers" begin to turn 40.	Live Aid, Farm Aid, Artists United against Apartheid concerts. Organized efforts to censor rock lyrics with warning labels. Soul stars celebrate 50th anniversary of the Apollo Theatre in Harlem. Big Joe Turner and Rick Nelson die.
1986	First Martin Luther King Day is observed. Nuclear accident in Chernobyl, U.S.S.R. AIDS crisis escalates. U.S. astronauts die when Challenger explodes after takeoff. U.S. attacks Libya; Quaddafi threatens retaliation. U.S. imposes economic sanctions on South Africa. Hands Across America fund-raiser.	First annual Rock and Roll Hall of Fame bash in NY. Violent outbreaks plague Run-DMC concerts; deaths at Ozzy Osbourne and Judas Priest shows. "New age" music pacifies the yuppie generation. Amnesty International's Conspiracy of Hope tour. Richard Manuel, Ian Stewart, Sonny Terry, Cliff Burton, and Albert Grossman die.
1987	Marcos leaves the Philippines. Gay rights rally in Washington, D.C., displays AIDS quilt. Stock market crashes. Scandal causes Gary Hart to pull out of presidential race. Scandal causes Jim and Tammy Bakker to resign from P.T.L. leadership.	Paul Simon's *Graceland* features South African musicians. Metal bands dominate the charts. American and Soviet bands unite in Russia for The July Fourth Disarmament Festival. Farm Aid II. Lynyrd Skynyrd survivors reunite. Lee Dorsey, Buddy Rich, John Huston, John Hammond, Jaco Pastorius, Paul Butterfield, Peter Tosh, and Andy Warhol die.
1988	I.M.F. Treaty is signed. Glasnost becomes a distinct possibility. Launch of Discovery successful. U.S. Navy warship mistakenly shoots down a commercial Iranian airliner. Jimmy Swaggart scandal.	Atlantic Records celebrates 40th anniversary. Nelson Mandela Freedomfest in London honors imprisoned South African leader. Amnesty International's Human Rights Now! tour. Alternative rock bands combine old styles in search of new ones. Nico, Roy Buchanan, Andy Gibb, Dave Prater, Clifton Chenier, Gil Evans, Brook Benton, Memphis Slim, Chet Baker, Will Shatter, Eddie Vinson, Hillel Slovak, and Roy Orbison die.
1989	George Bush becomes president. Exxon oil spill in Alaska. Gorbachev visits Cuba and China. U.S. recognizes P.L.O. U.S. troops invade Panama. Students in Beijing demonstrate for Chinese political reforms. The Berlin Wall is removed.	Cat Stevens voices support of Iranian death threats against author of *The Satanic Verses*. Glam and metal bands are featured at Moscow Music Peace Festival. Yo! MTV Raps is added to MTV lineup. James Brown is jailed. Salvador Dalí, Abbie Hoffman, Nesuhi Ertegun, Gilda Radner, Graham Chapman, Keith Whitley, and John Cipollina die.
1990	East and West Germany reunite. Nelson Mandela is released from prison in South Africa. Iraq invades Kuwait. Operation Desert Shield troops leave for Saudi Arabia. Clean Air Act is signed to update the 1970 Clean Air Act.	"That's What Friends Are For" AIDS benefit concert. Judas Priest is exonerated on subliminal message charges. Allen Collins, Tom Fogerty, Stiv Bators, Brent Mydland, Cornell Gunter, Del Shannon, Stevie Ray Vaughan, Art Blakey, Jim Henson, Dexter Gordon, Johnny Ray, and Sarah Vaughan die.
1991	The Gulf War forces Saddam Hussein's troops out of Kuwait. Rodney King beating videotaped in L.A. Justice T. Marshall retires from the Supreme Court. Anita Hill testifies at Clarence Thomas confirmation hearing. Charges against Oliver North are dropped. Strategic Arms Reduction Agreement is signed. Magic Johnson announces his HIV infection. Middle East Peace talks begin. Soviet Union is replaced by Commonwealth of Independent States. UN expels Yugoslavia because of civil wars. Rajev Gandhi is assassinated.	James Brown is released from prison. Oliver Stone revives the sixties in the movie *The Doors*. Riot at Guns N' Roses concert in St. Louis. Debut of Paul McCartney's *Liverpool Oratorio*. Tenth anniversary of MTV. Post-punk bands join for Lollapalooza tour. "Record" stores stock only cassettes and CDs. Steve Clark, Steve Marriott, Johnny Thunders, Rob Tyner, Rick Griffin, Leo Fender, Doc Pomus, Freddie Mercury, Miles Davis, Stan Getz, Bill Graham, Gene Clark, David Ruffin, and James Cleveland die.